Lecture Notes in Computer Science　13512

More information about this series at https://www.springer.com/bookseries/558

Jung Hee Cheon · Thomas Johansson (Eds.)

Post-Quantum Cryptography

13th International Workshop, PQCrypto 2022
Virtual Event, September 28–30, 2022
Proceedings

Editors
Jung Hee Cheon 🆔
Seoul National University
Seoul, Korea (Republic of)

Thomas Johansson
Lund University
Lund, Sweden

ISSN 0302-9743   ISSN 1611-3349 (electronic)
Lecture Notes in Computer Science
ISBN 978-3-031-17233-5   ISBN 978-3-031-17234-2 (eBook)
https://doi.org/10.1007/978-3-031-17234-2

This Springer imprint is published by the registered company Springer Nature Switzerland AG
The registered company address is: Gewerbestrasse 11, 6330 Cham, Switzerland

Preface

PQCrypto 2022, the 13th International Conference on Post-Quantum Cryptography, was organized fully online, during September 28–30, 2022. The aim of the PQCrypto conference series is to serve as a forum for researchers to present results and exchange ideas on cryptography in an era with large-scale quantum computers. Following the same model as its predecessors, PQCrypto 2022 adopted a two-stage submission process in which authors registered their paper one week before the final submission deadline. The conference received 66 submissions. Each paper (that had not been withdrawn by the authors) was reviewed in private by at least three Program Committee members. The private review phase was followed by an intensive discussion phase, conducted online. At the end of this process, the Program Committee selected 23 papers for inclusion in the technical program and publication in these proceedings. The accepted papers cover a broad spectrum of research within the conference's scope, including code-, hash-, isogeny-, and lattice-based cryptography, multivariate cryptography, and quantum cryptanalysis.

Along with the 23 contributed technical presentations, the program featured three invited talks - by Peter Schwabe on "6 years of NIST PQC, looking back and ahead", by Andreas Hülsing on "Hash-Based Signatures: History and Challenges", and by Ward Beullens on "Breaking Rainbow takes a weekend on a laptop".

The Program Committee selected by voting a paper to receive the Best Paper Award: "Breaking Category 5 SPHINCS+ with SHA-256" by Ray Perlner, David Cooper, and John Kelsey.

Organizing and running this year's edition of the PQCrypto conference series was a team effort, and we are indebted to everyone who helped make PQCrypto 2022 a success. In particular, we would like thank all members of the Program Committee and the external reviewers who were vital for compiling the technical program. Evaluating and discussing the submissions was a labor-intense task, and we truly appreciate the work that went into this. On behalf of the community, we are indebted to Tanja Lange for organizing the meeting and managing all the technical challenges of an online event. We also thank the team at Springer for handling the publication of these conference proceedings.

August 2022

Jung Hee Cheon
Thomas Johansson

Organization

General Chair

Tanja Lange   Eindhoven University of Technology,
                                The Netherlands

Program Committee Chairs

Jung Hee Cheon   Seoul National University, South Korea
Thomas Johansson   Lund University, Sweden

Program Committee

Magali Bardet   University of Rouen Normandy, France
Daniel J. Bernstein   University of Illinois at Chicago, USA, Ruhr
                                University Bochum, Germany, and Academia
                                Sinica, Taiwan
Olivier Blazy   École Polytechnique, France
André Chailloux   Inria, France
Anupam Chattopadhyay   NTU Singapore, Singapore
Chen-Mou Cheng   Kanazawa University, Japan
Jan-Pieter D'Anvers   KU Leuven, Belgium
Leo Ducas   CWI, The Netherlands
Scott Fluhrer   Cisco Systems, USA
Philippe Gaborit   University of Limoges, France
Tommaso Gagliardoni   Kudelski Security, Switzerland
Steven Galbraith   University of Auckland, New Zealand
Qian Guo   Lund University, Sweden
Tim Güneysu   Ruhr-Universität Bochum and DFKI, Germany
Dong-Guk Han   Kookmin University, South Korea
David Jao   University of Waterloo, Canada
Howon Kim   Pusan National University, South Korea
Jon-Lark Kim   Sogang University, South Korea
Kwangjo Kim   Korea Advanced Institute of Science and
                                Technology, South Korea
Elena Kirshanova   Immanuel Kant Baltic Federal University, Russia,
                                and TII, UAE
Tanja Lange   Eindhoven University of Technology,
                                The Netherlands, and Academia Sinica, Taiwan

Changmin Lee	KIAS, South Korea
Christian Majenz	Technical University Denmark, Denmark
Alexander May	Ruhr-Universität Bochum, Germany
Rafael Misoczki	Google, USA
Michele Mosca	University of Waterloo and Perimeter Institute, Canada
Khoa Nguyen	Nanyang Technological University, Singapore
Ray Perlner	NIST, USA
Christophe Petit	Université libre de Bruxelles, Belgium
Rachel Player	Royal Holloway, University of London, UK
Thomas Prest	PQShield Ltd., UK
Thomas Pöppelmann	Infineon, Germany
Nicolas Sendrier	Inria, France
Jae Hong Seo	Hanyang University, South Korea
Benjamin Smith	Inria, France
Daniel Smith-Tone	University of Louisville and NIST, USA
Yongsoo Song	Seoul National University, South Korea
Damien Stehlé	ENS de Lyon, France
Rainer Steinwandt	University of Alabama in Huntsville, USA
Tsuyoshi Takagi	University of Tokyo, Japan
Keita Xagawa	NTT, Japan
Aaram Yun	Ewha Womans University, South Korea
Zhenfei Zhang	Etherium Foundation, USA

Additional Reviewers

Ward Beullens
Xavier Bonnetain
Cecilia Boschini
Pierre Briaud
Jan Richter-Brockmann
Maxime Bros
Benjamin Curtis
Thomas Debris-Alazard
Jelle Don
Yu-Hsuan Huang
Loïs Huguenin-Dumittan
Alexander Karenin

Markus Krausz
Mikhail Kudinov
Sabrina Kunzweiler
Georg Land
Matthieu Lequesne
Ekaterina Malygina
Charles Meyer-Hilfiger
Prasanna Ravi
Lars Schlieper
Tjerand Silde
Patrick Struck
Valentin Vasseur

Contents

Lattice-Based Cryptography

Cryptanalysis

Code-Based Cryptography

Hybrid Decoding – Classical-Quantum Trade-Offs for Information Set Decoding

Andre Esser[1]($\boxtimes$)(iD), Sergi Ramos-Calderer[1,2](iD), Emanuele Bellini[1](iD),
José I. Latorre[1,2,3](iD), and Marc Manzano[4]

[1] Technology Innovation Institute, Abu Dhabi, UAE
{andre.esser,sergi.ramos,emanuele.bellini,jose.ignacio.latorre}@tii.ae
[2] Departament de Física Quàntica i Astrofísica and Institut de Ciències del Cosmos,
Universitat de Barcelona, Barcelona, Spain
[3] Centre for Quantum Technologies, National University of Singapore,
Singapore, Singapore
[4] SandboxAQ, Palo Alto, CA, USA
marc@sandboxaq.com

Abstract. The security of code-based constructions is usually assessed by Information Set Decoding (ISD) algorithms. In the quantum setting, amplitude amplification yields an asymptotic square root gain over the classical analogue. However, already the most basic ISD algorithm by Prange suffers enormous width requirements caused by the quadratic description length of the underlying problem. Even if polynomial, this need for qubits is one of the biggest challenges considering the application of real quantum circuits in the near- to mid-term.

In this work we overcome this issue by presenting the first hybrid ISD algorithms that allow to tailor the required qubits to any available amount while still providing quantum speedups of the form T^δ, $0.5 < \delta < 1$, where T is the running time of the purely classical procedure. Interestingly, when constraining the width of the circuit instead of its depth we are able to overcome previous optimality results on constraint quantum search.

Further we give an implementation of the fully-fledged quantum ISD procedure and the classical co-processor using the quantum simulation library *Qibo* and *SageMath*.

Keywords: Decoding · Width reduction · Hybrid algorithms · Code-based cryptography

1 Introduction

The growing threat to modern widespread cryptography posed by the advancing development of quantum computers has led to a focus on other hardness assumptions. One of the leading and most promising proposals for post quantum

M. Manzano—This work was conducted while the author was affiliated with Technology Innovation Institute.

J. H. Cheon and T. Johansson (Eds.): PQCrypto 2022, LNCS 13512, pp. 3–23, 2022.
https://doi.org/10.1007/978-3-031-17234-2_1

cryptography is code-based cryptography. It has a long history of withstanding classical as well as quantum attacks and is considered to rely on one of the most well understood hardness assumptions. The list of the four KEM finalists of the ongoing NIST standardization process for post quantum cryptography [1] includes one code-based proposal (McEliece [10]) and two more can be found on the alternate candidate list (BIKE [2] and HQC [24]).

At the heart of all these code-based constructions lies the binary decoding or *syndrome decoding* problem. This problem asks to find a low Hamming weight solution $\mathbf{e} \in \mathbb{F}_2^n$ to the equation $H\mathbf{e} = \mathbf{s}$, where $H \in \mathbb{F}_2^{(n-k) \times n}$ is a random binary matrix and $\mathbf{s} \in \mathbb{F}_2^{n-k}$ a binary vector.

The best known strategy to solve this problem is based on Information Set Decoding (ISD) [27], a technique introduced by Prange in 1962. Since then, there has been a series of works improving on his original algorithm [4,8,11,22,23,28], mostly by leveraging additional memory. In the quantum setting Bernstein showed how to speed up Prange's algorithm by an amplitude amplification routine [5], which results in an asymptotic square root gain over the classical running time. The translation of advanced ISD algorithm to the quantum setting [19,20] yields only small asymptotic improvements. So far these improvements can not compensate for the introduced overhead in terms of width and quantum RAM if looking towards implementations. This is not surprising, since already Prange's algorithm with an only *polynomial* demand for qubits, is limited by its width requirements. This is because all code-based constructions usually involve parity-check matrices consisting of millions of bits.

To overcome this issue we develop hybrid classical-quantum ISD algorithms that enable us to reduce the required amount of qubits to any available amount while still providing quantum speedups. The idea of such classical co-processors has mostly been used to parallelize quantum circuits or instantiate circuits under depth constraints, e.g. when analyzing the quantum security of schemes under the MAXDEPTH constraint specified by NIST [2,6,7,14,18]. Under depth constraints, Zalka [30] showed that the optimal way to perform a quantum search is by partitioning the search space in small enough sets such that the resulting circuit only targeting one set at a time does not exceed the maximum depth. Then the search has to be applied for every set of the partition. However, this optimality result only holds under depth constraints, when instead imposing constraints on the width of the circuit, our trade-offs yield more efficient strategies.

A first attempt to formulate hybrid ISD algorithms were made by Perriello et al. in [26]. However, their construction splits into a classical ISD part and a quantum exhaustive search part allowing to speed up the classical procedure with exponential time T only by a polynomial factor. In comparison our trade-offs achieve speedups of order T^δ for $0.5 < \delta < 1$.

Our Contribution. As a first contribution we design the full circuit performing the quantum version of Prange's algorithm and provide a functional implementation using the quantum simulation library Qibo [12,13].[1] Further we describe an optimized circuit that only requires $(n-k)k$ bits to store and operate on the input matrix $H \in \mathbb{F}_2^{(n-k) \times n}$.

Our major contribution is the design of hybrid quantum-classical trade-offs that address the practical limitation on the amount of qubits. In particular, these trade-offs enable quantum speedups for any available amount of qubits. We study the behavior of our trade-offs for various different choices of code parameters. Besides the coding-theoretic motivated settings of full and half distance decoding, these include also the parameter choices made by the NIST PQC candidates McEliece, BIKE and HQC. Our trade-offs perform best on the BIKE and HQC schemes, which is a result of a combination of a very low error weight and a comparably low code rate used by these schemes.

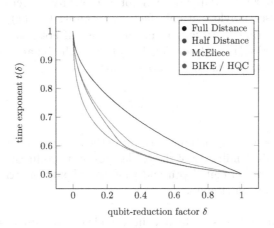

Fig. 1. Comparison of the achieved speedups of our trade-offs $t(\delta)$ (y-axis) plotted as a function of the qubit-reduction factor δ (x-axis).

Our trade-offs allow for a smooth interpolation between purely classical computations at a running time of T_C and a purely quantum based computation taking time $\sqrt{T_C}$. We interpolate between both complexities using a qubit reduction factor δ, where a fully classical computation corresponds to $\delta = 0$ and an entirely quantum based execution implies $\delta = 1$. For each trade-off we then state the running time for a given reduction factor δ as $t(\delta) \in [\![0.5, 1]\!]$, meaning that a reduction of the amount of qubits by a factor of δ implies a total running time of $(T_C)^{t(\delta)}$.

Figure 1 shows the behavior of our trade-off achieving the best results under limited width. For instance in the BIKE and HQC setting we can reduce the amount of qubits to only 1% ($\delta = 0.01$) of an entire quantum based computa-

---

[1] Our implementation (available at https://github.com/qiboteam/qISD) also includes an implementation of the Lee-Brickel [21] ISD improvement.

tion and still achieve a speedup of roughly $t(\delta) = 0.87$ compared to a classical computation.

2 Preliminaries

For two integers $a, b \in \mathbb{N}$ with $a \leq b$ let $[a, b] := \{a, a + 1, \ldots, b\}$. Further we write conveniently $[b] := [1, b]$. Let H be an $m \times n$ matrix and $I \subseteq [n]$, we write H_I to denote the projection of H onto the columns indexed by I. We use the same notation for vectors. For a binary vector $\mathbf{w} \in \mathbb{F}_2^n$ we define $\mathrm{wt}(\mathbf{w}) := |\{i \in [n] \mid w_i = 1\}|$ as the Hamming weight of $\mathbf{w}$. For two reals $c, d \in \mathbb{R}$ we let $[\![c, d]\!] := \{x \in \mathbb{R} \mid c \leq x \leq d\}$ be the (including) interval of all reals between c and d.

We use standard Landau notation for complexity statements, where $\tilde{\mathcal{O}}$-notation suppresses polylogarithmic factors, meaning $\tilde{\mathcal{O}}(f(x)) = \mathcal{O}(f(x) \log^i f(x))$ for any constant i. All logarithms are binary if not stated otherwise. We define $\mathrm{H}(x) := -x \log(x) - (1 - x) \log(1 - x)$ to be the binary entropy function and make use of the well-known approximation

$$\binom{n}{k} = \tilde{\Theta}\left(2^{n\mathrm{H}\left(\frac{k}{n}\right)}\right). \tag{1}$$

Quantum Circuits. Our algorithms are built in the quantum circuit model, where we assume a certain familiarity of the reader (for an introduction see [25]). Note that we use the term circuit depth and time complexity interchangeably when analyzing our quantum circuits.

Decoding and Linear Codes. A binary linear code $\mathcal{C}$ is a k dimensional subspace of $\mathbb{F}_2^n$ with minimum distance d, which is defined as the minimum Hamming weight of the elements of $\mathcal{C}$. We call n the code length and $R := \frac{k}{n}$ the code rate of $\mathcal{C}$. The code $\mathcal{C}$ can be defined via the kernel of a matrix $H \in \mathbb{F}_2^{(n-k) \times n}$, so that $\mathcal{C} := \{\mathbf{c} \in \mathbb{F}_2^n \mid H\mathbf{c}^T = \mathbf{0}\}$, where H is called a *parity-check matrix*. Note that for ease of exposition, we treat all vectors as column vectors so that we can omit vector transpositions.

A given point $\mathbf{x} = \mathbf{c} + \mathbf{e}$ that differs from a codeword by an error $\mathbf{e}$ can be uniquely decoded to $\mathbf{c}$ as long as $\mathrm{wt}(\mathbf{e}) \leq \lfloor \frac{d-1}{2} \rfloor$. This setting, in which the error weight is bounded by half of the minimum distance, is also known as *half distance* decoding, while the setting bounding it by d is known as *full distance* decoding. We study the performance of our algorithms in these settings for random codes, which are known to meet the Gilbert-Varshamov bound [17,29], i.e., $d \approx \mathrm{H}^{-1}(1 - R)n$.

The definition of the code via its parity-check matrix allows to treat the decoding procedure independently of the specific codeword by considering the *syndrome* $\mathbf{s}$ of a given faulty codeword $\mathbf{x}$, where $\mathbf{s} := H\mathbf{x} = H(\mathbf{c} + \mathbf{e}) = H\mathbf{e}$. Recovering $\mathbf{e}$ from given H and $\mathbf{s}$ is, hence, equivalent to decoding $\mathbf{x}$ to c. This leads to the definition of the *syndrome decoding problem*.

Algorithm 1. PRANGE

Require: parity-check matrix $H \in \mathbb{F}_2^{(n-k) \times n}$, syndrome $\mathbf{s} \in \mathbb{F}_2^{n-k}$, weight $\omega \in [n]$
Ensure: error vector $\mathbf{e}$ with $\text{wt}(\mathbf{e}) = \omega$ satisfying $H\mathbf{e} = \mathbf{s}$
1: **repeat**
2:     choose random permutation matrix $P \in \mathbb{F}_2^{n \times n}$ and set $H_I \leftarrow (HP)_{[n-k]}$
3:     solve linear system $H_I \mathbf{e}_1 = \mathbf{s}$ for $\mathbf{e}_1$
4: **until** $\text{wt}(\mathbf{e}_1) = \omega$
5: **return** $P(\mathbf{e}_1, 0^k)$

Definition 1 (Syndrome Decoding Problem). *Let $\mathcal{C}$ be a linear code with parity-check matrix $H \in \mathbb{F}_2^{(n-k) \times n}$ and constant rate $R := \frac{k}{n}$. For $\mathbf{s} \in \mathbb{F}_2^{n-k}$ and $\omega \in [n]$, the syndrome decoding problem $\mathcal{SD}_{n,k,\omega}$ asks to find a vector $\mathbf{e} \in \mathbb{F}_2^n$ of weight $\text{wt}(\mathbf{e}) = \omega$ satisfying $H\mathbf{e} = \mathbf{s}$. We call any such $\mathbf{e}$ a solution while we refer to $(H, \mathbf{s}, \omega)$ as an* instance *of the $\mathcal{SD}_{n,k,\omega}$.*

Prange's Information Set Decoding. Given an instance $(H, \mathbf{s}, \omega)$ of the $\mathcal{SD}_{n,k,\omega}$ Prange's algorithm [27] starts by choosing a random set $I \subseteq [n]$ of size $n - k$ and then solves the corresponding linear system

$$H_I \mathbf{e}_1 = \mathbf{s} \tag{2}$$

for $\mathbf{e}_1$.[2] Note that any solution $\mathbf{e}_1$ of weight $\omega' := \text{wt}(\mathbf{e}_1)$ can easily be extended to a vector $\tilde{\mathbf{e}} \in \mathbb{F}_2^n$ of same weight satisfying $H\tilde{\mathbf{e}} = \mathbf{s}$, by setting the corresponding coordinates to zero. Hence, if $\omega' = \omega$ the vector $\tilde{\mathbf{e}}$ forms a solution to the syndrome decoding problem. The algorithm now chooses random subsets I until $\omega' = \omega$ holds.

The algorithm is successful whenever $\mathbf{e}$ projected to the coordinates given by I is a solution to the linear system in Eq. (2), hence if $\mathbf{e}_1 = \mathbf{e}_I$. This happens whenever $\mathbf{e}_I$ covers the full weight of $\mathbf{e}$, in which case I or more precisely $[n] \setminus I$ is called an *information set*. Transferred to Algorithm 1 this applies whenever for the permutation chosen in line 2, it holds that $P^{-1}\mathbf{e} = (\mathbf{e}_1, 0^k)$ for $\mathbf{e}_1 \in \mathbb{F}_2^{n-k}$. The probability that the permutation distributes the weight in such a way is

$$q := \Pr\left[P^{-1}\mathbf{e} = (\mathbf{e}_1, 0^k)\right] = \frac{\binom{n-k}{\omega}}{\binom{n}{\omega}} . \tag{3}$$

Hence, the expected number of tries until we draw a suitable permutation P becomes q^{-1} and the expected time complexity is $T = q^{-1} \cdot T_G$, where T_G describes the cost for solving the linear system and performing the weight check.

Remark 1. Note that in the case of S existent solutions the time complexity to retrieve a single solution with Prange's algorithm becomes $\frac{T}{S}$.

---

[2] Note that in Algorithm 1 we model H_I as the first $n - k$ columns of HP, where P is a random permutation matrix.

3   A Quantum ISD Circuit Design

Let us briefly sketch how we realized the quantum design of Prange's algorithm, a detailed description of every part of the circuit can be found in the full version of this article [16]. Our design is composed of the following three main building blocks:

1) The creation of the uniform superposition over all size-$(n - k)$ subsets of $[n]$ (corresponding to the selection of information sets in line 2 of Algorithm 1).
2) The Gaussian elimination step to derive the error related to a given information set (line 3 of Algorithm 1).
3) A quantum search for an information set yielding an error of the desired weight (substituting the repeat loop in line 1 of Algorithm 1).

Superposition Circuit. We realize the creation of the superposition over all size-$(n - k)$ subsets in a bit-by-bit fashion, obtaining a depth of $(n - k) \cdot n$. This is possible since the number of sets including element i is independent of all subsequent elements $j > i$. More recent developments construct this superposition in depth linear in n [3]. However, since this part of the ISD circuit does not dominate the overall depth, we refrain from further optimizations.

Gaussian Elimination. Our Gaussian elimination circuit mostly resembles its classical analogue. The integration of the superposition and Gaussian elimination circuit works by first swapping all selected columns (determined by the superposition) to the back of the matrix and then implementing the Gaussian Elimination only on the last $n - k$ columns.

Quantum Search. The square root gain over the classical algorithm is achieved by employing an amplitude amplification procedure. Here the diffusion layer consists of our initial superposition circuit, while the sign flip is performed based on the Hamming weight of the error obtained by performing the Gaussian elimination circuit.

We find that our circuit has a depth of $\mathcal{O}\left(\frac{n^3 \log n}{\sqrt{q}}\right)$, where q is the probability detailed in Eq. (3). This corresponds to only a logarithmic overhead compared to a classical implementation. The width of the circuit is dominated by the space required for storing the parity-check matrix, which is $(n - k) \cdot n$. In the next section, we detail a procedure to reduce the width to about $(n - k) \cdot k = (1-R) \cdot R \cdot n^2$, relying on first transforming the parity check matrix into *systematic form* $H := (I_{n-k} \mid H')$, where $H' \in \mathbb{F}_2^{(n-k) \times k}$ via Gaussian elimination. We then show that the circuit can be adapted to work only with H' as input. However, the required amount of qubits is still quadratic in the code length n and, hence, one of the most limiting factors in terms of concrete implementations.

3.1   Reducing the Width for Free

In the following we assume the parity-check matrix H to be in systematic form, as shown in Fig. 2. We now describe how to adapt the quantum circuit to only require the matrix H' as well as the corresponding syndrome as an input, which saves $(n-k)^2$ qubits. Recall that the goal of the Gaussian elimination procedure is to obtain the identity matrix on the matrix projected to the columns of the currently selected subset by elementary row operations. Our previous quantum circuit achieved this by fist swapping all columns that belong to the selected subset (determined by the superposition) to the back of the matrix and then performing the Gaussian elimination always on the last $n-k$ columns. But since we now only obtain H' as input this is not possible anymore.

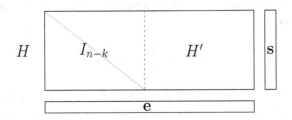

Fig. 2. Problem shape for input matrix in systematic form.

However, note that if any of the first $n-k$ columns, which are already unit vectors, belongs to the selected subset a single row swap is sufficient to obtain the desired unit vector in that column. Hence, we only implement a corresponding row swap on H' and **s**. Furthermore, the necessary swaps are fully determined by the index of the respective column and its position in the selected subset. Thus, we can embed them into the quantum circuit a priori. After the necessary row-swaps are performed, all columns of H' belonging to the corresponding subset are swapped to the back. Subsequently we perform the Gaussian elimination only on the last columns of H' that belong to the current selection. This procedure is depicted in Fig. 3, which shows the state of the matrix after all three operations have been performed for the chosen subset. Note that the first $n-k$ columns only serve an illustrative purpose and are not part of the input.

4   Classical-Time Quantum-Memory Trade-Offs

Next we introduce our trade-offs, allowing for an adaptive scaling of the algorithm to the available amount of qubits. Our trade-offs are divided in a classical and quantum computation part, where a decrease of the amount of qubits comes at the cost of an increased classical running time. Since the increase in running time is exponential we neglect polynomial factors by employing $\tilde{\mathcal{O}}$-notation. Our

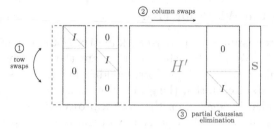

Fig. 3. Procedure to perform quantum version of Prange without first $n - k$ columns as input. Colored framed parts indicate columns belonging to the current selected subset. (Color figure online)

trade-offs allow for a smooth interpolation between purely classical computations at a running time of

$$T_C := \tilde{\mathcal{O}}\left(\frac{\binom{n}{\omega}}{\binom{n-k}{\omega}}\right), \tag{4}$$

(compare to Eq. (3)) and a purely quantum based computation taking time $\sqrt{T_C}$. Recall that we interpolate between both complexities using a qubit reduction factor δ and state the running time for a given reduction factor as $t(\delta) \in [\![0.5, 1]\!]$; meaning that a reduction of the amount of qubits by a factor of δ implies a total running time of $(T_C)^{t(\delta)}$.

We start with a trade-off based on shortening the underlying code, which already achieves a better than linear dependence between δ and $t(\delta)$. After that, we present a second trade-off based on puncturing the code which asymptotically outperforms the first one. However, for concrete parameters in medium scale both trade-offs remain superior to each other for certain values of δ. Finally, we obtain improvements by combining both methods.

4.1   Shortening the Code

Our first trade-off is based on shortening the underlying code before using it as input to the quantum circuit. In Prange's original algorithm k zero positions of **e** are guessed and then the linear system corresponding to the non-zero positions is solved in polynomial time. In our hybrid version the classical part consists in guessing $\alpha n \leq k$ zero coordinates of **e**, which allows to shorten the code and, hence, reduce the problem to a code of length $(1 - \alpha)n$ and dimension $k - \alpha n$, while the error weight remains unchanged (compare to Fig. 4). This reduced instance is then solved with our previously constructed quantum circuit. Should the quantum computation not result in an actual solution, the initial guess of zero coordinates was incorrect and we proceed with a new guess. Algorithm 2 gives a pseudocode description of our SHORTENED-HYBRID.

Theorem 1 (Shortened Hybrid). *Let $n \in \mathbb{N}$, $\omega = \tau n$ and $k = Rn$ for $\tau, R \in [\![0, 1]\!]$ and let T_C be as defined in Eq. (4). Then for any qubit reduction factor $\delta \in$*

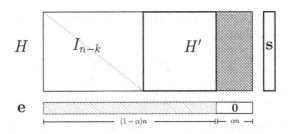

Fig. 4. Parity-check matrix in sysetmatic form where αn zero positions of **e** are guessed. Striped region of **e** indicates parts containing weight, crosshatched columns of H' do not affect **s**. Framed parts are used as input to the quantum algorithm.

Algorithm 2. SHORTENED-HYBRID

Require: parity-check matrix $H \in \mathbb{F}_2^{(n-k)\times n}$, syndrome $\mathbf{s} \in \mathbb{F}_2^{n-k}$, weight $\omega \in [n]$, qubit reduction factor $\delta \in [\![0, 1]\!]$

Ensure: error vector **e** with wt(**e**) $= \omega$ satisfying $H\mathbf{e} = \mathbf{s}$

1: $\alpha := (1 - \delta)\frac{k}{n}$
2: **repeat**
3:    choose random permutation matrix $P \in \mathbb{F}_2^{n\times n}$ and set $\tilde{H} \leftarrow HP$
4:    solve instance $(\tilde{H}_{[(1-\alpha)n]}, \mathbf{s}, \omega)$ via quantum algorithm returning $\mathbf{e}_1 \in \mathbb{F}_2^{(1-\alpha)n}$
5:    $\mathbf{e} \leftarrow P(\mathbf{e}_1, 0^{\alpha n})$
6: **until** $H\mathbf{e} = \mathbf{s}$
7: **return e**

$[\![0, 1]\!]$ *Algorithm 2 solves the $\mathcal{SD}_{n,k,\omega}$ problem in time $(T_C)^{t(\delta)}$ using $\delta(1-R)Rn^2$ qubits for the matrix representation, where*

$$t(\delta) = 1 - \frac{\frac{1}{2}\left((1-\alpha)\mathrm{H}\left(\frac{\tau}{1-\alpha}\right) - (1-R)\mathrm{H}\left(\frac{\tau}{1-R}\right)\right)}{\mathrm{H}(\tau) - (1-R)\mathrm{H}\left(\frac{\tau}{1-R}\right)},$$

for $\alpha = (1-\delta)R$.

Proof. Assume that the permutation P distributes the error such that

$$P^{-1}\mathbf{e} = (\mathbf{e}_1, 0^{\alpha n}), \tag{5}$$

for α as defined in Algorithm 2. Then it follows, that $\mathbf{e}_1$ is a solution to syndrome decoding instance $((HP)_{[(1-\alpha)n]}, \mathbf{s}, \omega)$. By the correctness of our quantum circuit the solution $\mathbf{e}_1$ is returned in line 4 and finally $\mathbf{e} = P(\mathbf{e}_1, 0^{\alpha n})$ is recovered.

Next let us analyze the running time of the algorithm. The probability of a random permutation distributing the error weight as given in Eq. (5) is

$$q_C := \Pr\left[P^{-1}\mathbf{e} = (\mathbf{e}_1, 0^{\alpha n})\right] = \frac{\binom{(1-\alpha)n}{\omega}}{\binom{n}{\omega}}.$$

Hence, we expect that after q_C^{-1} random permutations one of them induces the desired weight-distribution. The asymptotic time complexity for the execution of the quantum circuit to solve the corresponding $\mathcal{SD}_{(1-\alpha)n,(R-\alpha)n,\omega}$ problem is given as (compare to Sect. 3).

$$T_Q = \tilde{O}\left(\sqrt{\frac{\binom{(1-\alpha)n}{\omega}}{\binom{(1-R)n}{\omega}}}\right).$$

Since for each classically chosen permutation we need to execute our quantum circuit the total running time becomes

$$T = q_C^{-1} \cdot T_Q = \tilde{O}\left(\frac{\binom{n}{\omega}}{\sqrt{\binom{(1-\alpha)n}{\omega}\binom{(1-R)n}{\omega}}}\right).$$

Now let us determine $t(\delta) := \frac{\log T}{\log T_C}$. First observe that $T = \frac{T_C}{T_Q}$, which can be rewritten as

$$\log T_C - \log T_Q = \log T$$
$$\Leftrightarrow \qquad 1 - \frac{\log T_Q}{\log T_C} = \frac{\log T}{\log T_C} =: t(\delta).$$

An approximation of T_Q and T_C via the approximation for binomial coefficients given in Eq. (1) together with $\omega := \tau n$ and $k := Rn$ then yields

$$t(\delta) = 1 - \frac{\frac{1}{2}\left((1-\alpha)\mathrm{H}\left(\frac{\tau}{1-\alpha}\right) - (1-R)\mathrm{H}\left(\frac{\tau}{1-R}\right)\right)}{\mathrm{H}(\tau) - (1-R)\mathrm{H}\left(\frac{\tau}{1-R}\right)},$$

as claimed. Note that the input matrix of a code of length $(1-\alpha)n$ and dimension $(R-\alpha)n$ requires $(1-R)(R-\alpha)n^2$ qubits for the matrix representation (compare to Sect. 3). Hence, by setting $\alpha = (1-\delta)R$ we obtain a qubit reduction by

$$\frac{(1-R)(R-\alpha)n^2}{(1-R)Rn^2} = \frac{R-(1-\delta)R}{R} = \delta.$$

□

Next we simplify the statement of Theorem 1 for sublinear error-weight, which is, e.g., the case for McEliece, BIKE and HQC. Note that in the case of a sublinear error-weight, T_C can be expressed as

$$T_C := \tilde{O}\left(\frac{\binom{n}{\omega}}{\binom{(1-R)n}{\omega}}\right) = \tilde{O}\left((1-R)^{-\omega}\right), \tag{6}$$

see, e.g., [15, Remark A.1].

This allows us to give the following simplified corollary.

Corollary 1 (Shortened Hybrid for sublinear error weight). *Let all parameters be as in Theorem 1. For $\tau = o(1)$, we have*

$$t(\delta) = \frac{1}{2} \cdot \left(1 + \frac{\log(1 - (1 - \delta)R)}{\log(1 - R)} \right).$$

Proof. First we approximate T_Q similar to T_C in Eq. (6) as

$$T_Q = \tilde{\mathcal{O}} \left(\sqrt{ \frac{\binom{(1-\alpha)n}{\omega}}{\binom{(1-R)n}{\omega}} } \right) = \tilde{\mathcal{O}} \left(\left(\frac{1 - \alpha}{1 - R} \right)^{\frac{\omega}{2}} \right).$$

Now we can derive the statement of the corollary as

$$t(\delta) = 1 - \frac{\log T_Q}{\log T_C} = 1 - \frac{\frac{\omega}{2} \left(\log(1 - \alpha) - \log(1 - R) \right)}{-\omega \log(1 - R)}$$

$$= \frac{1}{2} \cdot \left(1 + \frac{\log(1 - (1 - \delta)R)}{\log(1 - R)} \right).$$ □

Figure 5 visualizes the relation between the qubit-reduction factor and the speedup for the full distance decoding setting with rate $R = 0.5$ and $\tau = H^{-1}(R) \approx 0.11$ and the parameters of the McEliece scheme, which are $R = 0.8$ and $\tau = o(1)$. We observed that the trade-off behavior is very insensitive to changes in the error-rate. Therefore the behavior for the settings of full and half distance as well as BIKE and HQC are almost identical, such that we only included the full distance case for the sake of clarity.

However, the trade-off is more sensitive to changes in the code-rate. We observe better performance the higher the code-rate, which lies in favour to mounting an attack against codes using McEliece parameters. To give a concrete example, our SHORTENED-HYBRID algorithm allows for a reduction of the necessary qubits by 80% (corresponding to $\delta = 0.2$), while still achieving a speedup of $t(\delta) \approx 0.82$ in the McEliece setting.

4.2 Puncturing the Code

While our SHORTENED-HYBRID decreases the amount of necessary qubits by shortening the code, our second trade-off instead aims at puncturing the code. In a nutshell, we consider only $(1 - \beta)n - k$ parity-check equations, rather than all $n - k$, i.e., we omit βn rows of the parity-check matrix. The subsequently applied quantum circuit, hence, needs fewer qubits to represent matrix and syndrome. The advantage over SHORTENED-HYBRID partly comes form the fact that each row saves n instead of only $n - k$ bits. Also the generated classical overhead is significantly smaller. This variant has similarities with the Canteaut-Chabaud improvement [9] in the classical setting. Here only a certain amount of columns (originally only one) of the identity part are exchanged in each iteration rather

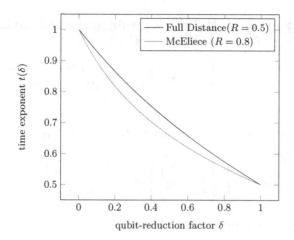

Fig. 5. Time exponent (y-axis) achieved by Theorem 1 for different code parameters plotted as a function of the qubit-reduction factor δ (x-axis).

than drawing a completely new permutation. In our case we fix βn columns of the permutation classically and then search for the remaining $n - k - \beta n$ quantumly. In addition we expect weight p on the fixed βn coordinates, where p has to be optimized.

We again start with a parity-check matrix H in systematic form. Now consider the projection of H onto its first $n - k - \beta n$ rows, we call the resulting matrix $\tilde{H}$. Clearly, a solution $\mathbf{e}$ to the instance $(H, \mathbf{s}, \omega)$ is still a solution to the instance $(\tilde{H}, \mathbf{s}_{[n-k-\beta n]}, \omega)$. Moreover, the matrix $\tilde{H}$ includes βn zero columns, which can safely be removed (compare to Fig. 6). This results in a matrix $\tilde{H}' = (I_{n-k-\beta n} \mid H') \in \mathbb{F}_2^{(n-k-\beta n) \times (1-\beta)n}$ corresponding to a code of length $(1 - \beta)n$ and dimension k. Still, by removing the corresponding coordinates from $\mathbf{e}$ we obtain a solution $\mathbf{e}'$ to the instance $(\tilde{H}', \mathbf{s}_{[n-k-\beta n]}, \omega - p)$, where $p := \mathrm{wt}(\mathbf{e}_{[n-k-\beta n+1, n-k]})$ is the weight of coordinates removed from $\mathbf{e}$. Eventually, once $\mathbf{e}'$ is recovered we can obtain $\mathbf{e}$ in polynomial time by solving the respective linear system.

A crucial observation is that disregarding βn parity-check equations could lead to the existence of multiple solutions to the reduced instance, i.e. multiple $\mathbf{e}'$ satisfying $\tilde{H}'\mathbf{e}' = \mathbf{s}_{[n-k-\beta n]}$ but yielding an $\mathbf{e}$ with $\mathrm{wt}(\mathbf{e}) > \omega$. Not that we can control this amount of solutions by increasing p. Also, our algorithm compensates for multiple solutions by recovering all solutions to the reduced instance by repeated executions of the quantum circuit. A pseudocode description of our PUNCTURED-HYBRID trade-off is given by Algorithm 3.

In the following theorem we first state the time complexity of our PUNCTURED-HYBRID in dependence on the qubit reduction factor δ. After this we derive the speedup $t(\delta)$ in a separate corollary.

Theorem 2 (Punctured Hybrid). *Let $n \in \mathbb{N}$, $\omega \in [n]$ and $k = Rn$ for $R \in [\![0, 1]\!]$. Then for any qubit reduction factor $\delta \in [\![0, 1]\!]$ Algorithm 3 solves the*

Algorithm 3. Punctured Hybrid

Require: parity-check matrix $H \in \mathbb{F}_2^{(n-k) \times n}$, syndrome $\mathbf{s} \in \mathbb{F}_2^{n-k}$, weight $\omega \in [n]$,
   qubit reduction factor $\delta \in [\![0,1]\!]$
Ensure: error vector $\mathbf{e}$ with wt$(\mathbf{e}) = \omega$ satisfying $H\mathbf{e} = \mathbf{s}$
1: choose p accordingly
2: $\beta := (1 - \delta)(1 - \frac{k}{n})$, $S := \frac{\binom{(1-\beta)n}{\omega-p}}{2^{(1-\beta)n-k}}$
3: **repeat**
4:    choose random permutation matrix $P \in \mathbb{F}_2^{n \times n}$ and set $\tilde{H} \leftarrow HP$
5:    transform $\tilde{H}$ to systematic form, $\tilde{H} = \begin{pmatrix} I_{n-k-\beta n} & 0 & H_1' \\ 0 & I_{\beta n} & H_2' \end{pmatrix}$ with syndrome $\tilde{\mathbf{s}}$
6:    $\tilde{H}' \leftarrow (I_{n-k-\beta n} \mid H_1')$, $\mathbf{s}' \leftarrow \tilde{\mathbf{s}}_{[(1-\beta)n-k]}$
7:    **for** $i = 1$ **to** poly$(n) \cdot S$ **do**
8:       solve instance $(\tilde{H}', \mathbf{s}', \omega - p)$ via quantum algorithm returning $\mathbf{e}' \in \mathbb{F}_2^{(1-\beta)n}$
9:       $\mathbf{e}'' \leftarrow H_2'\mathbf{e}'_{[n-k-\beta n+1,(1-\beta)n]} + \tilde{\mathbf{s}}_{[n-k-\beta n+1,n-k]}$
10:      **if** wt$(\mathbf{e}'') \leq p$ **then**
11:         $\mathbf{e} \leftarrow P(\mathbf{e}'_{[n-k-\beta n]}, \mathbf{e}'', \mathbf{e}'_{[n-k-\beta n+1,(1-\beta)n]})$
12:         **break**
13: **until** $H\mathbf{e} = \mathbf{s}$
14: **return** $\mathbf{e}$

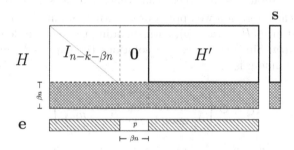

Fig. 6. Parity-check matrix where βn rows are omitted and $\mathbf{e}$ contains weight p on βn coordinates. Framed parts are used as input to the quantum algorithm.

$\mathcal{SD}_{n,k,\omega}$ *problem in expected time T_{PH} using $\delta(1 - R)Rn^2$ qubits for the matrix representation, where*

$$T_{\mathrm{PH}} = \tilde{\mathcal{O}} \left(\frac{\binom{n}{\omega}}{\sqrt{\binom{(1-\beta)n}{\omega-p}\binom{(1-\beta-R)n}{\omega-p}\binom{\beta n}{p}}} \cdot \max \left(1, \sqrt{\binom{(1-\beta)n}{\omega-p}} \cdot 2^{-(1-\beta-R)n} \right) \right)$$

with $\beta = (1 - \delta)(1 - R)$ and $p \in [\min(\omega, \beta n)]$.

Proof. Assume that the permutation distributes the error weight, such that for $P^{-1}\mathbf{e} = (\mathbf{e}_1, \mathbf{e}_2, \mathbf{e}_3) \in \mathbb{F}_2^{(1-\beta-R)n} \times \mathbb{F}_2^{\beta n} \times \mathbb{F}_2^{Rn}$ it holds wt$(\mathbf{e}_2) = p$. Now consider the permuted parity-check matrix in systematic form $\tilde{H}$ as given in line 5 of Algorithm 3 with corresponding syndrome $\tilde{\mathbf{s}}$. We obtain

$$\tilde{H}P^{-1}\mathbf{e} = (\mathbf{e}_1 + H_1'\mathbf{e}_3, \mathbf{e}_2 + H_2'\mathbf{e}_3) = \tilde{\mathbf{s}}.$$

This implies that $(\mathbf{e}_1, \mathbf{e}_3)$ is a solution to the syndrome decoding instance $(\tilde{H}', \mathbf{s}', \omega - p)$ with $\tilde{H}' = (I_{(1-\beta-R)n} \mid H_1')$ and $\mathbf{s}' = \tilde{\mathbf{s}}_{[(1-\beta-R)n]}$. The solution is then recovered by the application of our quantum circuit in line 8. Note that in expectation there exist

$$S := \binom{(1-\beta)n}{\omega - p} \cdot 2^{-(1-\beta-R)n}$$

solutions to our reduced instance. Since we apply our quantum circuit $\mathrm{poly}(n) \cdot S$ times and in each execution a random solution is returned, a standard coupon collector argument yields that we recover all S solutions with high probability. Now, when $\mathbf{e}' = (\mathbf{e}_1, \mathbf{e}_3)$ is returned by the quantum circuit, we recover $\mathbf{e}_2 = \tilde{\mathbf{s}}_{[(1-\beta-R)n+1,(1-R)n]} + H_2'\mathbf{e}_3$ and eventually return $\mathbf{e} = P(\mathbf{e}_1, \mathbf{e}_2, \mathbf{e}_3)$.

Next let us consider the time complexity of the algorithm. Observe that the probability, that $\mathrm{wt}(\mathbf{e}_2) = p$ for a random permutation holds is

$$q_C := \Pr\left[\mathrm{wt}(\mathbf{e}_2) = p\right] = \frac{\binom{(1-\beta)n}{\omega-p}\binom{\beta n}{p}}{\binom{n}{\omega}}.$$

Hence, after q_C^{-1} iterations we expect that there is at least one iteration where $\mathrm{wt}(\mathbf{e}_2) = p$. In each iteration we apply our quantum circuit $\tilde{O}(S)$ times to solve the reduced instance $(\tilde{H}', \mathbf{s}', \omega - p)$, corresponding to a code of length $(1 - \beta)n$ and dimension Rn. Since there exist S solutions the expected time to retrieve one of them at random is

$$T_Q = \tilde{O}\left(\sqrt{\frac{\binom{(1-\beta)n}{\omega-p}}{\max(1, S) \cdot \binom{(1-\beta-R)n}{\omega-p}}}\right),$$

according to Remark 1. The maximum follows since we know that there exists at least one solution. In summary the running time becomes $T_{PH} = q_C^{-1} \cdot T_Q \cdot \max(1, S)$, as stated in the theorem.

The required amount of qubits of the quantum circuit for solving the syndrome decoding problem related to the reduced code of length $(1 - \beta)n$ and dimension $(1 - R)n$ are roughly $R(1 - \beta - R)n^2$ (compare to Sect. 3). Thus, for $\beta := (1 - \delta)(1 - R)$ this corresponds to a qubit reduction of

$$\frac{R(1 - \beta - R)}{R(1 - R)} = \frac{1 - R - (1 - \delta)(1 - R)}{1 - R} = \delta.$$

$\square$

Theorem 2 allows to easily determine the corresponding speedup, whose exact formula we give in the following corollary.

Corollary 2 (Punctured Hybrid Speedup). *Let $n \in \mathbb{N}$, $\omega = \tau n$ and $k = Rn$, $p = \rho n$ for $\tau, R, \rho \in [\![0, 1]\!]$ and let T_C be as defined in Eq. (4). Then for any* *qubit reduction factor* $\delta \in [\![0,1]\!]$ *Algorithm 3 solves the* $\mathcal{SD}_{n,k,\omega}$ *problem in time* $(T_{\mathrm{C}})^{t(\delta)}$ *using* $\delta(1-R)Rn^2$ *qubits for the matrix representation, where*

$$t(\delta) = \frac{\mathrm{H}(\tau) - \beta\mathrm{H}\left(\frac{\rho}{\beta}\right) - \frac{1-\beta}{2} \cdot \mathrm{H}\left(\frac{\tau-\rho}{1-\beta}\right) - \frac{(1-\beta-R)}{2} \cdot \mathrm{H}\left(\frac{\tau-\rho}{1-\beta-R}\right) + \max(0,\sigma)}{\mathrm{H}(\tau) - (1-R)\mathrm{H}\left(\frac{\tau}{1-R}\right)}$$

for $\beta = (1-\delta)(1-R)$ *and* $\sigma = (1-\beta)\mathrm{H}\left(\frac{\tau-\rho}{1-\beta}\right) - (1-\beta-R)$.

Proof. Recall that $t(\delta) = \frac{\log T_{\mathrm{PH}}}{\log T_{\mathrm{C}}}$, where T_{PH} is the running time of Algorithm 3, given in Theorem 2. Now the statement of the corollary follows immediately by approximating the binomial coefficients in T_{PH} and T_{C} via Stirling's formula (see Eq. (1)). $\qquad\square$

In Fig. 7a we compare the behavior of our new trade-off to our previously obtained SHORTENED-HYBRID. Recall that the performance of SHORTENED-HYBRID is not very sensitive to changes in the error-rate. Thus, for settings with the same code-rate, i.e. full and half distance as well as BIKE/HQC, the solid lines are almost on top of each other. The dashed lines represent our new trade-off (Theorem 2) for which we optimized p numerically. It can be observed, that this trade-off outperforms the SHORTENED-HYBRID for all parameters. Here, we observe the best behaviour for low code-rates and small error-rates, which correspond to the case, where the solution is very unique. In these cases our PUNCTURED-HYBRID algorithm can disregard parity-check equations without introducing multiple solutions to the reduced instance. Hence, still a single execution of the quantum circuit suffices to recover the solution. The significance of the amount of solutions can be well observed by comparing the full and half distance settings. In the full distance setting there exists already one random solution in expectation, therefore any omitted parity equation leads to the existence of multiple solution and in turn leads to only a small improvement over SHORTENED-HYBRID. Contrary, the half distance setting allows for a significant improvement, which is due to the exponentially small probability of existing random solutions. Note that in the McEliece, BIKE and HQC setting the error weight is only sublinear, which lies in favour of our new trade-off, since the probability for existing random solutions is again exponentially small. BIKE and HQC furthermore use a very small error weight of only $\mathcal{O}(\sqrt{n})$ and specify a code-rate of $R = 0.5$, which results in a very unique solution. Consequently, in Fig. 7a it can be observed, that asymptotically for these settings the second trade-off improves drastically on SHORTENED-HYBRID.

Note that our formulation of the speedup for PUNCTURED-HYBRID in contrast to SHORTENED-HYBRID (see Corollary 1) still depends on the error-rate, not exactly allowing for $\omega = o(n)$. Thus, to obtain the asymptotic plot we compared the result of Corollary 1 to Theorem 2 for McEliece ($n = 6688, k = 5024, \omega = 128$), BIKE ($n = 81946, k = 40973, \omega = 264$) and HQC ($n = 115274, k = 57637, \omega = 262$), which are the suggested parameters for 256-bit security from the corresponding NIST submission documentations [2,10,24].

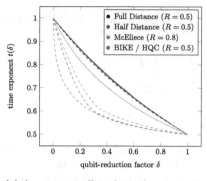 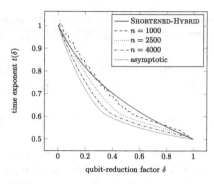

(a) Asymptotically achieved time exponents. New Theorem 2 (PUNCTURED-HYBRID) depicted as dashed lines, Theorem 1 (SHORTENED-HYBRID) as solid lines.

(b) Time exponents for concrete parameter sets. McEliece parameter sets satisfy $k = 0.8n$ and $\omega = \left\lfloor \frac{n}{5 \log n} \right\rfloor$. Non-solid lines correspond to PUNCTURED-HYBRID.

Fig. 7. Comparison of time exponents of SHORTENED-HYBRID and PUNCTURED-HYBRID (y-axis) plotted as a function of the qubit-reduction factor δ (x-axis).

To quantify the result of our new trade-off take e.g. the case of McEliece and a qubit reduction by 80% ($\delta = 0.2$), as before. Here we improve to a speedup of $t(\delta) \approx 0.74$, compared to 0.82 for SHORTENED-HYBRID.

However, for concrete medium sized parameters this asymptotic behaviour is not necessarily obtained. In Fig. 7b we show a comparison of both trade-offs for concrete McEliece parameter sets. Note that for all parameter sets the performance of SHORTENED-HYBRID is almost identical, which is why there is only a single solid line.

For these concrete computations we used the more accurate time complexity formula involving binomial coefficients rather than its asymptotic approximation to determine the speedup $t(\delta)$. Note that the discontinuity for our new trade-off is due to the restriction to discrete choices of p. We find that for parameters up to $n \approx 2500$ both trade-offs remain superior to each other for certain reduction factors δ. For larger values of n the PUNCTURED-HYBRID algorithm becomes favourable for all δ.

In the BIKE and HQC settings the PUNCTURED-HYBRID algorithm is favourable already for small parameters corresponding to $n \geq 1000$.

4.3   Combined Hybrid

Next let us outline how to combine both previous trade-offs to achieve an improved version. We first reduce the code length and dimension, again by guessing αn zero coordinates of $\mathbf{e}$ and removing the corresponding columns form H, i.e., we shorten the code. The remaining instance is then solved using our PUNCTURED-HYBRID algorithm, i.e., by first omitting βn parity-check equations (compare also to Fig. 8) and then using the reduced instance as input to the quantum circuit.

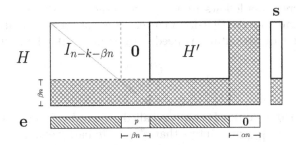

Fig. 8. Input matrix in systematic form where βn parity-check equations are omitted and αn zeros of **e** are known. The vector **e** is assumed to contain weight p on βn coordinates. Framed parts are used as input to the quantum algorithm.

Algorithm 4. COMBINED-HYBRID

Require: parity-check matrix $H \in \mathbb{F}_2^{(n-k) \times n}$, syndrome $\mathbf{s} \in \mathbb{F}_2^{n-k}$, weight $\omega \in [n]$, qubit reduction factor $\delta \in [\![0,1]\!]$

Ensure: error vector **e** with $\mathrm{wt}(\mathbf{e}) = \omega$ satisfying $H\mathbf{e} = \mathbf{s}$

1: choose α and p accordingly

2: $\beta := \left(1 - \frac{k}{n}\right)\left(\frac{\delta \frac{k}{n}}{\frac{k}{n} - \alpha}\right)$, $E := \frac{\binom{(1-\alpha)n}{\omega}}{\binom{(1-\alpha-\beta)n}{\omega-p}\binom{\beta n}{p}}$

3: **repeat**

4:     choose random permutation matrix $P \in \mathbb{F}_2^{n \times n}$ and set $\tilde{H} \leftarrow HP$

5:     $\mathbf{e}' \leftarrow$ PUNCTURED-HYBRID$(\tilde{H}_{[(1-\alpha)n]}, \mathbf{s}, \omega, \delta, \frac{\beta}{1-\alpha}, p)$ ▷ abort after E iterations of the outer loop

6:     $\mathbf{e} \leftarrow P(\mathbf{e}', 0^{\alpha n})$

7: **until** $H\mathbf{e} = \mathbf{s}$

8: **return e**

We give the pseudocode description of the procedure in Algorithm 4. Note that here we use β and p as input parameters to PUNCTURED-HYBRID, rather than to the choice made in Algorithm 3 (PUNCTURED-HYBRID). Further, since for an incorrect guess of αn zero positions the call to PUNCTURED-HYBRID will not finish, we introduce an abort after the expected amount of iterations on a correct guess.

Theorem 3 (Combined Hybrid). *Let $n \in \mathbb{N}$, $\omega \in [n]$ and $k = Rn$ for $R \in [\![0,1]\!]$. Then for any qubit reduction factor $\delta \in [\![0,1]\!]$ the $\mathcal{SD}_{n,k,\omega}$ problem can be solved in expected time T_{CH} using $\delta(1-R)Rn^2$ qubits for the matrix representation, where*

$$T_{\mathrm{CH}} = \tilde{\mathcal{O}}\left(\frac{\binom{n}{\omega}}{\sqrt{\binom{(1-\alpha-\beta)n}{\omega-p}\binom{(1-\beta-R)n}{\omega-p}\binom{\beta n}{p}}} \cdot \max\left(1, \sqrt{\binom{(1-\alpha-\beta)n}{\omega-p}} \cdot 2^{-(1-\beta-R)n}\right)\right)$$

with $\alpha \in [\![0,R]\!]$, $\beta = (1-R)\left(1 - \frac{\delta R}{R-\alpha}\right)$ and $p \in [\min(\omega, \beta n)]$.

Proof. The correctness follows from the correctness of Algorithm 2 and Algorithm 3. Therefore observe that for a correct guess of αn zero positions of $\mathbf{e}$, the expected amount of permutations needed by PUNCTURED-HYBRID to find the solution is

$$E := \frac{\binom{(1-\alpha)n}{\omega}}{\binom{(1-\alpha-\beta)n}{\omega-p}\binom{\beta n}{p}}.$$

Also note that PUNCTURED-HYBRID is called on a code of length $n' = (1 - \alpha)n$. Hence, setting $\beta' = \frac{\beta}{1-\alpha}$ guarantees that $\beta'n' = \beta n$ parity equations are omitted.

For the time complexity we have again with probability

$$q_C := \Pr\left[P^{-1}\mathbf{e} = (\mathbf{e}_1, 0^{\alpha n})\right] = \frac{\binom{(1-\alpha)n}{\omega}}{\binom{n}{\omega}},$$

a correct guess for αn zero positions (compare to the proof of Theorem 1). In each iteration of our combined algorithm we call the PUNCTURED-HYBRID algorithm. Inside this subroutine E iterations of the outer loop are executed, each performing

$$S = \tilde{\Theta}\left(\max\left(1, \frac{\binom{(1-\beta-\alpha)}{\omega-p}}{2^{-(1-R-\beta)n}}\right)\right)$$

calls to the quantum circuit. This quantum circuit is applied to solve the syndrome decoding problem defined on a code of length $(1 - \alpha - \beta)n$ and dimens $(R - \alpha)n$ with error-weight $\omega - p$ (compare to Fig. 8), which takes time

$$T_Q = \tilde{O}\left(\sqrt{\frac{\binom{(1-\alpha-\beta)n}{\omega-p}}{S \cdot \binom{(1-\beta-R)n}{\omega-p}}}\right).$$

Thus, eventually, the time complexity of the whole algorithm summarizes as $T_{CH} = q_C^{-1} \cdot E \cdot T_Q \cdot S$, as claimed. Finally, note that for given $\beta = (1 - R)\left(1 - \frac{\delta R}{R-\alpha}\right)$ we obtain a qubit reduction by

$$\frac{(R-\alpha)(1-R-\beta)}{R(1-R)} = \frac{(R-\alpha)(1-R)\left(1 - (1 - \frac{\delta R}{R-\alpha})\right)}{R(1-R)} = \frac{(R-\alpha) \cdot \frac{\delta R}{R-\alpha}}{R} = \delta.$$

$\square$

Our combination achieves the improved trade-off behavior depicted as dashed lines in Fig. 9. Here the values of p and α were optimized numerically. It shows that the combination of both trade-offs for most parameters improves on PUNCTURED-HYBRID (solid lines). Especially in the full distance decoding setting an improvement for nearly all δ is achieved. This is due to the fact, that the guessing of zero coordinates is an additional possibility to control the amount of solutions to the reduced instance and therefore to optimize the complexity of the PUNCTURED-HYBRID subroutine. This is also the reason why we achieve

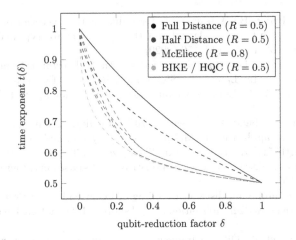

Fig. 9. Asymptotically achieved time exponents. The combined trade-off is depicted as dashed line, PUNCTURED-HYBRID is illustrated as a solid line.

no (asymptotic) improvement in the BIKE and HQC settings, here the solution is already so unique that the trade-off can not benefit from the new degree of freedom.

But also in the McEliece setting we achieve notable improvements. If we again consider a reduction-factor of $\delta = 0.2$ the combination improves the speedup to $t(\delta) \approx 0.69$ from 0.74 achieved by PUNCTURED-HYBRID. Furthermore, when focusing on near future realizations, i.e., the regime of small reduction factors, it is for example possible with just one percent of the qubits ($\delta = 0.01$) to achieve a speedup of $t(\delta) \approx 0.92$.

References

1. Alagic, G., et al.: Status report on the second round of the NIST post-quantum cryptography standardization process. US Department of Commerce, NIST (2020)
2. Aragon, N., et al.: BIKE: bit flipping key encapsulation (2020)
3. Bärtschi, A., Eidenbenz, S.: Deterministic preparation of Dicke states. In: Gąsieniec, L.A., Jansson, J., Levcopoulos, C. (eds.) FCT 2019. LNCS, vol. 11651, pp. 126–139. Springer, Cham (2019). https://doi.org/10.1007/978-3-030-25027-0_9
4. Becker, A., Joux, A., May, A., Meurer, A.: Decoding random binary linear codes in $2^{n/20}$: how $1 + 1 = 0$ improves information set decoding. In: Pointcheval, D., Johansson, T. (eds.) EUROCRYPT 2012. LNCS, vol. 7237, pp. 520–536. Springer, Heidelberg (2012). https://doi.org/10.1007/978-3-642-29011-4_31
5. Bernstein, D.J.: Grover vs. McEliece. In: Sendrier, N. (ed.) PQCrypto 2010. LNCS, vol. 6061, pp. 73–80. Springer, Heidelberg (2010). https://doi.org/10.1007/978-3-642-12929-2_6
6. Biasse, J.F., Bonnetain, X., Pring, B., Schrottenloher, A., Youmans, W.: A trade-off between classical and quantum circuit size for an attack against CSIDH. J. Math. Cryptol. **15**(1), 4–17 (2020)

7. Biasse, J.F., Pring, B.: A framework for reducing the overhead of the quantum oracle for use with Grover's algorithm with applications to cryptanalysis of SIKE. J. Math. Cryptol. **15**(1), 143–156 (2020)

8. Both, L., May, A.: Decoding linear codes with high error rate and its impact for LPN security. In: Lange, T., Steinwandt, R. (eds.) PQCrypto 2018. LNCS, vol. 10786, pp. 25–46. Springer, Cham (2018). https://doi.org/10.1007/978-3-319-79063-3_2

9. Canteaut, A., Chabaud, F.: A new algorithm for finding minimum-weight words in a linear code: application to McEliece's cryptosystem and to narrow-sense BCH codes of length 511. IEEE Trans. Inf. Theory **44**(1), 367–378 (1998)

10. Chou, T., et al.: Classic McEliece: conservative code-based cryptography, 10 October 2020 (2020)

11. Dumer, I.: On minimum distance decoding of linear codes. In: Proceedings of the 5th Joint Soviet-Swedish International Workshop on Information Theory, pp. 50–52 (1991)

12. Efthymiou, S., et al.: Qibo: a framework for quantum simulation with hardware acceleration. arXiv preprint arXiv:2009.01845 (2020)

13. Efthymiou, S., et al.: Quantum-TII/Qibo: Qibo (2020). https://doi.org/10.5281/zenodo.3997195

14. Esser, A., Bellini, E.: Syndrome decoding estimator. In: Hanaoka, G., Shikata, J., Watanabe, Y. (eds.) PKC 2022. LNCS, vol. 13177, pp. 112–141. Springer, Cham (2022). https://doi.org/10.1007/978-3-030-97121-2_5

15. Esser, A., May, A., Verbel, J., Wen, W.: Partial key exposure attacks on BIKE, Rainbow and NTRU. Cryptology ePrint Archive (2022)

16. Esser, A., Ramos-Calderer, S., Bellini, E., Latorre, J.I., Manzano, M.: An optimized quantum implementation of ISD on scalable quantum resources. arXiv preprint arXiv:2112.06157 (2021)

17. Gilbert, E.N.: A comparison of signalling alphabets. Bell Syst. Tech. J. **31**(3), 504–522 (1952)

18. Jaques, S., Naehrig, M., Roetteler, M., Virdia, F.: Implementing Grover oracles for quantum key search on AES and LowMC. In: Canteaut, A., Ishai, Y. (eds.) EUROCRYPT 2020. LNCS, vol. 12106, pp. 280–310. Springer, Cham (2020). https://doi.org/10.1007/978-3-030-45724-2_10

19. Kachigar, G., Tillich, J.-P.: Quantum information set decoding algorithms. In: Lange, T., Takagi, T. (eds.) PQCrypto 2017. LNCS, vol. 10346, pp. 69–89. Springer, Cham (2017). https://doi.org/10.1007/978-3-319-59879-6_5

20. Kirshanova, E.: Improved quantum information set decoding. In: Lange, T., Steinwandt, R. (eds.) PQCrypto 2018. LNCS, vol. 10786, pp. 507–527. Springer, Cham (2018). https://doi.org/10.1007/978-3-319-79063-3_24

21. Lee, P.J., Brickell, E.F.: An observation on the security of McEliece's public-key cryptosystem. In: Barstow, D., et al. (eds.) EUROCRYPT 1988. LNCS, vol. 330, pp. 275–280. Springer, Heidelberg (1988). https://doi.org/10.1007/3-540-45961-8_25

22. May, A., Meurer, A., Thomae, E.: Decoding random linear codes in $\tilde{\mathcal{O}}(2^{0.054n})$. In: Lee, D.H., Wang, X. (eds.) ASIACRYPT 2011. LNCS, vol. 7073, pp. 107–124. Springer, Heidelberg (2011). https://doi.org/10.1007/978-3-642-25385-0_6

23. May, A., Ozerov, I.: On computing nearest neighbors with applications to decoding of binary linear codes. In: Oswald, E., Fischlin, M. (eds.) EUROCRYPT 2015. LNCS, vol. 9056, pp. 203–228. Springer, Heidelberg (2015). https://doi.org/10.1007/978-3-662-46800-5_9

24. Melchor, C.A., et al.: Hamming quasi-cyclic (HQC) (2020)
25. Nielsen, M.A., Chuang, I.L.: Quantum Information and Quantum Computation, vol. 2, no. 8, p. 23. Cambridge University Press, Cambridge (2000)
26. Perriello, S., Barenghi, A., Pelosi, G.: A quantum circuit to speed-up the cryptanalysis of code-based cryptosystems. In: Garcia-Alfaro, J., Li, S., Poovendran, R., Debar, H., Yung, M. (eds.) SecureComm 2021. LNICST, vol. 399, pp. 458–474. Springer, Cham (2021). https://doi.org/10.1007/978-3-030-90022-9_25
27. Prange, E.: The use of information sets in decoding cyclic codes. IRE Trans. Inf. Theory 8(5), 5–9 (1962)
28. Stern, J.: A method for finding codewords of small weight. In: Cohen, G., Wolfmann, J. (eds.) Coding Theory 1988. LNCS, vol. 388, pp. 106–113. Springer, Heidelberg (1989). https://doi.org/10.1007/BFb0019850
29. Varshamov, R.R.: Estimate of the number of signals in error correcting codes. Docklady Akad. Nauk, SSSR **117**, 739–741 (1957)
30. Zalka, C.: Grover's quantum searching algorithm is optimal. Phys. Rev. A **60**(4), 2746 (1999)

How to Backdoor (Classic) McEliece and How to Guard Against Backdoors

Tobias Hemmert[1], Alexander May[2] , Johannes Mittmann[1] ,
and Carl Richard Theodor Schneider[2(✉)]

[1] Bundesamt für Sicherheit in der Informationstechnik (BSI), Bonn, Germany
{tobias.hemmert,johannes.mittmann}@bsi.bund.de
[2] Ruhr-University Bochum, Bochum, Germany
{alex.may,carl.schneider}@rub.de

Abstract. We show how to backdoor the McEliece cryptosystem such
that a backdoored public key is indistinguishable from a usual public
key, but allows to efficiently retrieve the underlying secret key.

For good cryptographic reasons, McEliece uses a small random seed
δ that generates via some pseudo random generator (PRG) the randomness that determines the secret key. Our backdoor mechanism works by
encoding an encryption of δ into the public key. Retrieving δ then allows
to efficiently recover the (backdoored) secret key. Interestingly, McEliece
can be used itself to encrypt δ, thereby protecting our backdoor mechanism with strong post-quantum security guarantees.

Our construction also works for the current *Classic McEliece* NIST
standard proposal for non-compressed secret keys, and therefore opens
the door for widespread maliciously backdoored implementations.

Fortunately, our backdoor mechanism can be detected by the owner
of the (backdoored) secret key if δ is stored after key generation as specified by the Classic McEliece proposal. Thus, our results provide strong
advice for implementers to store δ inside the secret key and use δ to
guard against backdoor mechanisms.

Keywords: Classic McEliece · Niederreiter · Backdoor · Public-key
cryptography · SETUP · Post-quantum cryptography

1 Introduction

Strong cryptography provides confidentiality to everyone. While this is in general
a highly desirable goal, it is a large obstacle for adversarial parties. Thus, there
exist strong interests to circumvent cryptographic mechanisms by e.g. installing
backdoors in cryptographic protocols. In a nutshell, a backdoored cryptographic
scheme is a scheme that provides strong cryptographic properties, unless one
possesses a key to a backdoor that allows for easy recovery of some secret value.

The process of establishing backdoors in cryptographic schemes is especially
promising during a standardization process. As an example, the Snowden revela-
tions showed that the Dual EC DRBG standard was maliciously backdoored [3].

Since we are now close to standardizing new cryptographic schemes for the
era of quantum computers, it is of crucial importance to understand whether

J. H. Cheon and T. Johansson (Eds.): PQCrypto 2022, LNCS 13512, pp. 24–44, 2022.
https://doi.org/10.1007/978-3-031-17234-2_2

the current candidate schemes allow for backdoor mechanisms. In this work, we address one of the candidates, the McEliece cryptosystem, for which we show how to install backdoors, as well as how to detect them.

Previous Work. The foundational works of Simmons [11,12] describe how digital signatures can be used to secretly communicate information over subliminal channels. Subliminal channels provide a way of adding hidden information to the plain communication by choosing values not at random, but depending on the hidden information. This core idea opened the pathway to a specific type of backdoors, where the hidden information simplifies attacking the backdoored scheme.

Young and Yung [14,15] initiated the area of *kleptography* which considers how an adversary $\mathcal{A}$ can subtly modify a cryptosystem such that it leaks some secret information that only $\mathcal{A}$ is able to recover, and whose output is indistinguishable from a legitimate system for anyone only having black-box access to it. An example for this is captured by their SETUP (Secretly Embedded Trapdoor with Universal Protection) notion. A SETUP mechanism encodes information into the public key of an asymmetric cryptosystem during the key generation process, allowing the adversary $\mathcal{A}$ to later retrieve the underlying secret key using $\mathcal{A}$'s secret backdoor key. A SETUP requires that given just the generated keys (i.e. without access to source code or to the secret backdoor key), it is impossible to tell whether the keys have been backdoored or not, and that nobody but the owner of the secret backdoor key can retrieve secret keys from public keys even if the implementation eventually gets revealed. This means in particular that a SETUP mechanism has to use asymmetric encryption to embed the secret information in its generated public keys.

RSA backdoors are described by Crépeau and Slakmon [5] who for example encoded half of the bits of the RSA prime p into the public RSA modulus N. However, their backdoor mechanisms do not satisfy all properties of a SETUP since they use a secret permutation that allows anyone with access to the source code to recover the backdoor information. Young and Yung describe a proper kleptographic mechanism for RSA in [16].

For post-quantum secure cryptosystems, very little is known about successful SETUP mechanisms. The work of Kwant, Lange and Thissen [7] describes a backdoor mechanism at the cost of increasing the probability of decryption failures, which might be used to leak information about the secret key. The work of Yang, Xie and Pan [13] however shows that [7] does not fulfill the SETUP notion since the backdoors can be detected efficiently. Moreover, Yang, Xie and Pan [13] introduce SETUP mechanisms for RLWE-based schemes that encode non-quantum secure ECC encryptions of the secret key into the generated public keys.

For code-based cryptosystems and especially McEliece, to the best of our knowledge no SETUP backdoor mechanism is known. Loidreau and Sendrier [8] show that there is a subset of weak Goppa polynomials that makes it feasible to enumerate them when attacking McEliece. This however does not fulfill the SETUP notion, because one can immediately identify from the secret keys that the resulting scheme has been backdoored. It also does not provide exclusive access. In the context of the NIST standardization process, [4] suggests that maliciously chosen permutation matrices in the key generation algorithm may allow to leak secret values.

For preventing backdoors from a theoretical viewpoint, Bellare, Paterson and Rogaway [2] introduced the watchdog model. However, applying the watchdog model to McEliece does not result in a practical encryption scheme.

Our Contribution. We propose the first SETUP mechanism for McEliece. For didactic reasons, we first address a usual Vanilla Niederreiter version of McEliece, that uses the parity check matrix of a code C as secret key. The randomness for generating C comes from the output of a PRG applied to some secret seed δ.

The public key is a randomized and permuted basis of C. A malicious adversary $\mathcal{A}$ may now backdoor the key generation process of a user $\mathcal{U}$ by encoding an encryption of δ (under $\mathcal{A}$'s public key $\mathsf{pk}_{\mathcal{A}}$) into $\mathcal{U}$'s public key $\mathsf{pk}_{\mathcal{U}}$ using a different permutation of C. We show that the resulting backdoored keys are indistinguishable from ordinary McEliece keys under some mild assumption. This indistinguishability even holds when our SETUP mechanism, $\mathsf{pk}_{\mathcal{A}}$, and the secret code C are known. Thus, there is no way to check for the user $\mathcal{U}$ whether the generated secret/public key pair has been backdoored as long as $\mathcal{U}$ only has black-box access to the key generation and cannot inspect the implementation. In the terminology of Young and Yung we therefore provide a *strong* SETUP.

However, if the user $\mathcal{U}$ knows in addition the secret seed δ, then $\mathcal{U}$ can identify backdoored keys. The reason is that the randomness for transforming the secret key $\mathsf{sk}_{\mathcal{U}}$ into the public key $\mathsf{pk}_{\mathcal{U}}$ usually also comes from the PRG output on δ. Thus, δ already fully determines the public key given the secret key. So $\mathcal{U}$ may rerun the secret/public key generation from the verifiable randomness provided by δ to check for the validity of a key pair.

Thus, if the seed δ is included into $\mathcal{U}$'s secret key $\mathsf{sk}_{\mathcal{U}}$, then our backdoor mechanism is detectable from $\mathsf{sk}_{\mathcal{U}}$. In the terminology of Young and Yung we therefore provide a *weak* SETUP for McEliece when δ is part of the secret key since the backdoor still cannot be detected given only the public key $\mathsf{pk}_{\mathcal{U}}$.

As a main result, we then show that our SETUP backdoor mechanism easily transfers from our Vanilla McEliece scheme to *Classic McEliece* [1], the 4th round NIST standardization candidate. This might at first sight come as a surprise, since our SETUP uses the permutation to embed the backdoor, while Classic McEliece does not permute the entries of C. However, we observe that Classic McEliece inherently includes a permutation that defines the Goppa code, which can be used analogously for our SETUP. Since the proposal [1] requires to store δ as part of the secret key, our construction yields a weak SETUP for Classic McEliece, but turns into a strong SETUP if an implementer chooses to deviate from the specification and deletes δ after key generation. This also emphasizes the importance of making the seed δ a mandatory part of the secret key when specifying any McEliece-based cryptosystem. Our SETUP mechanism applies to the non-compressed key format described in the Classic McEliece submission, not to the compressed formats.

Last but not least, we show that a backdoor implementer $\mathcal{A}$ may use McEliece itself for encrypting δ, thereby securing our backdoor even in the presence of quantum computers.

Implementer's Advice. Our results show that inclusion of the secret δ efficiently protects against strong SETUP backdoor mechanisms, though not against weak SETUPs. Thus, our results strongly suggest including δ into the secret key. This enables users to verify the absence of our SETUP mechanism in black-box implementations of McEliece key generation with other (trusted) implementations.

We would like to stress that storing δ is not necessary for McEliece functionality. The original purpose of δ is to provide a small piece of randomness, from which one can efficiently derive the full McEliece secret/public key pairs. To this end, standards usually recommend to store δ. Our work shows another strong benefit of storing δ, since δ serves as a short proof for the correct, non-backdoored, deterministic derivation of the secret/public key pair.

In general, open-source implementations and code reviews are recommended for establishing trust in cryptographic implementations. However, code reviews are not always feasible or sufficient in practice. In these cases, access to δ provides an efficiently verifiable witness of a correct key generation with respect to the specification.

Open Problems. Since we describe the first SETUP backdoor mechanism for code-based cryptography, one might wonder whether our SETUP transfers without much effort to other code-based schemes like BIKE or HQC. However, BIKE/HQC both use cyclic codes, whose structure seems to prevent a direct application of our method. It remains an open problem to derive weak/strong SETUP mechanisms in the cyclic setting.

Paper Organization. In Sect. 2 we give an introduction to McEliece and the SETUP backdoor mechanism of Young and Yung [15], Sect. 3 provides the strong SETUP mechanism for Vanilla McEliece (without storing δ), as well as the backdoor identification when δ is provided in the secret key. In Sect. 4 we provide the necessary modifications to our SETUP for Classic McEliece. Eventually, in Sect. 5 we show how to use McEliece to hide the encryption of δ in a user's public key. Appendix A contains a simpler but (instructively) flawed backdoor construction.

2 Background

2.1 McEliece and Binary Goppa Codes

McEliece uses a binary linear $[n, k]$-code C, i.e., $C \subset \mathbf{F}_2^n$ is a subspace of dimension k. C may be described by a generator matrix $G \in \mathbf{F}_2^{k \times n}$, or equivalently by a so-called parity check matrix $H \in \mathbf{F}_2^{(n-k) \times n}$ whose kernel is C.

Due to efficiency reasons, all modern instantiations of McEliece use a parity check matrix, usually called the Niederreiter version of McEliece. While our

SETUP backdoor mechanism for Vanilla McEliece from Sect. 3 works for any code, our SETUP mechanism from Sect. 4 also uses properties of the binary Goppa codes that are used in the *Classic McEliece* scheme [1].

Thus, let us briefly recall the parity check matrix of a binary Goppa code. Let $\mathbf{F}_{2^m}$ be a binary field. Choose $\alpha_1, \ldots, \alpha_n$ distinct from $\mathbf{F}_{2^m}$, and an irreducible Goppa polynomial $g \in \mathbf{F}_{2^m}[x]$ of degree t. This defines a linear length-n code C with minimal distance at least $2t + 1$ and parity check matrix

$$
H = \begin{pmatrix} 1 & 1 & \cdots & 1 \\ \alpha_1 & \alpha_2 & \cdots & \alpha_n \\ \vdots & & \ddots & \\ \alpha_1^{t-1} & \alpha_2^{t-1} & \cdots & \alpha_n^{t-1} \end{pmatrix} \begin{pmatrix} g(\alpha_1) & 0 & \cdots & 0 \\ 0 & g(\alpha_2) & \cdots & 0 \\ \vdots & & \ddots & \\ 0 & 0 & \cdots & g(\alpha_n) \end{pmatrix}^{-1}
$$

$$
= \begin{pmatrix} \frac{1}{g(\alpha_1)} & \frac{1}{g(\alpha_2)} & \cdots & \frac{1}{g(\alpha_n)} \\ \frac{\alpha_1}{g(\alpha_1)} & \frac{\alpha_2}{g(\alpha_2)} & \cdots & \frac{\alpha_n}{g(\alpha_n)} \\ \vdots & & \ddots & \\ \frac{\alpha_1^{t-1}}{g(\alpha_1)} & \frac{\alpha_2^{t-1}}{g(\alpha_2)} & \cdots & \frac{\alpha_n^{t-1}}{g(\alpha_n)} \end{pmatrix}.
$$

Notice that $H \in \mathbf{F}_{2^m}^{t \times n}$. If we write the elements of H in an $\mathbf{F}_2$-basis, then we end up with an $(mt \times n)$-matrix, i.e., C is a $k \geq n - mt$ dimensional subspace of $\mathbf{F}_2^n$.

2.2   SETUP Mechanism

SETUP (Secretly Embedded Trapdoor with Universal Protection) mechanisms were introduced by Young and Yung [14,15]. A SETUP mechanism transforms a cryptosystem Π into a backdoored cryptosystem Π' for a malicious backdoor holder $\mathcal{A}$ with asymmetric key pair $(\mathsf{sk}_{\mathcal{A}}, \mathsf{pk}_{\mathcal{A}})$. This transformation fulfills the following properties.

1. *The input to functions in Π' agrees with the specification of inputs to Π.*
   This property ensures the compatibility of Π and Π'.
2. *Π' is still efficient and uses $\mathsf{Enc}_{\mathsf{pk}_{\mathcal{A}}}$ (and possibly other functions as well).*
3. *$\mathsf{Dec}_{\mathsf{sk}_{\mathcal{A}}}$ is not part of Π' and is only known to $\mathcal{A}$.*
   This prevents the use of symmetric schemes and guarantees $\mathcal{A}$ exclusive access to the backdoor, assuming that $\mathcal{A}$'s used asymmetric scheme is secure. In particular, the legitimate user is not able to decrypt the backdoor information, even with access to the implementation of Π'.
4. *The output of algorithms in Π' is compatible with the specification of outputs of algorithms in Π. At the same time, it contains information efficiently derivable by $\mathcal{A}$ only.*
   The output of Π' needs to be compatible to Π in the sense that e.g. a ciphertext created with an encryption function from Π' must be decryptable by the corresponding decryption function in Π. While maintaining this compatibility, output of Π' additionally needs to contain information that only the adversary can derive efficiently.

Moreover, SETUP mechanisms can be grouped into categories of different strength. We focus only on the *weak* and *strong* SETUP from [15].

Weak SETUP. The output of Π and Π' are polynomially indistinguishable, except for $\mathcal{A}$ and the legitimate user $\mathcal{U}$ of the implementation. Thus, in a weak SETUP, $\mathcal{U}$ may identify with the help of the generated secret key $\mathsf{sk}_{\mathcal{U}}$ from Π' the existence of a backdoor. All users knowing only $\mathsf{pk}_{\mathcal{U}}$ and $\mathsf{pk}_{\mathcal{A}}$ cannot identify a backdoor in $\mathcal{U}$'s key, i.e. all users except $\mathcal{U}$ and $\mathcal{A}$.

Strong SETUP. The output of Π and Π' are polynomially indistinguishable, except for $\mathcal{A}$. Thus, a user $\mathcal{U}$ cannot recognize any backdoors, even when $\mathcal{U}$ knows the SETUP mechanism and $\mathsf{pk}_{\mathcal{A}}$.

We will formalize the notions for weak and strong SETUP in Sect. 3, and especially for proving Theorem 1.

3   Backdooring Vanilla McEliece

Recall that for didactic reasons we first define some generic McEliece system in Niederreiter form, called *Vanilla McEliece*. Our Vanilla McEliece scheme has the advantage that it does not rely on specifics of the underlying code, and as opposed to Classic McEliece explicitly uses a permutation matrix P, in which we embed our strong SETUP mechanism.

Let us start by defining Vanilla McEliece's key generation algorithm.

3.1   Key Generation for Vanilla McEliece

In the key generation process of Vanilla McEliece, see also Fig. 1, the secret parity check matrix $H \in \mathbf{F}_2^{(n-k) \times n}$ of a binary linear $[n, k]$-code C is scrambled by a random invertible linear transformation $S \in \mathbf{F}_2^{(n-k) \times (n-k)}$ and a random permutation matrix $P \in \mathbf{F}_2^{n \times n}$. The resulting public key is $\mathsf{pk} = SHP \in \mathbf{F}_2^{(n-k) \times n}$, and the secret key is $\mathsf{sk} = (C, S, H, P)$. It is important to stress that the randomness for constructing C, S, H, P is chosen from the output of a PRG $G(\cdot)$ applied to a short random seed δ, say of 256 bits. Thus a small seed δ completely determines sk and allows compact storage of the secret key.

The invertible matrix S does not affect the code C. The matrix P permutes the coordinates of C, resulting in a code equivalent to C. From a security perspective, the transformations S, P are supposed to completely hide the structure of the underlying C. The security of McEliece is based on pk behaving like a random parity check matrix, for which the *syndrome decoding problem* is hard.

3.2   Vanilla McEliece Strong SETUP

Our SETUP mechanism for Vanilla McEliece manipulates the key generation in such a way that the keys are indistinguishable from legitimate keys, but

KGen$_V(1^n)$

---

1 : $\boldsymbol{\delta} \leftarrow_\$ \{0,1\}^s$

2 : $\boldsymbol{r} := G(\boldsymbol{\delta}) \;/\!/\; G$ is a PRG

3 : Generate C with parity check matrix H from $\boldsymbol{r}$.

4 : Compute random S, P from $\boldsymbol{r}$.

5 : **return** sk $:= (C, S, H, P)$, pk $:= SHP$

Fig. 1. Vanilla McEliece key generation

knowledge of a secret backdoor allows an adversary to recover the secret key from the corresponding public key. This is achieved by encrypting the random seed $\boldsymbol{\delta}$ using a public-key encryption scheme $\Pi_{\mathcal{A}}$ of the adversary's choice with the public key pk$_{\mathcal{A}}$ to obtain a ciphertext $\boldsymbol{c} \leftarrow_\$ \mathsf{Enc}_{\mathsf{pk}_{\mathcal{A}}}(\boldsymbol{\delta}) \in \mathbf{F}_2^\ell$. Then $\boldsymbol{c}$ is embedded in the random permutation P such that it can be recovered just from the public key.

Encoding via Permutation. Let us denote by $P^{(n)} \subset \mathbf{F}_2^{n \times n}$ the set of n-dimensional permutation matrices, so $|P^{(n)}| = n!$. We write a permutation $\pi : \{1, \ldots, n\} \rightarrow \{1, \ldots, n\}$ as $\pi = (\pi_1, \ldots, \pi_n)$ with $\pi_i = \pi(i)$. Let $\boldsymbol{e}_i$ be the i-th unit vector, written in column form. Then we define the permutation matrix $P_\pi \in P^{(n)}$ corresponding to π as

$$P_\pi = \left(\boldsymbol{e}_{\pi(1)} \ldots \boldsymbol{e}_{\pi(n)} \right).$$

We use an efficiently computable bijection from Kreher and Stinson [6] (Algorithms 2.15 and 2.16, see also Fig. 2),

$$f_n : \{0, 1, \ldots, n! - 1\} \rightarrow P^{(n)},$$

that maps numbers to permutation matrices, and vice versa.

We use f_n to encode $\boldsymbol{c} \leftarrow_\$ \mathsf{Enc}_{\mathsf{pk}_{\mathcal{A}}}(\boldsymbol{\delta}) \in \mathbf{F}_2^\ell$ as a permutation. Notice that the algorithms from Fig. 2 efficiently compute f_n and f_n^{-1} both in time $\mathcal{O}\left(n^2\right)$.

Idea of Our Vanilla McEliece Backdoor. Our backdoored key generation $\widetilde{\mathsf{KGen}}_V$ is described in Fig. 3.

The parity check matrix H and the invertible matrix S are generated from the random seed $\boldsymbol{\delta}$ as in the non-backdoored key generation KGen_V from Fig. 1.

We assume w.l.o.g. that the columns of H are pairwise distinct, otherwise the code C defined by H has minimal distance at most 2 and is not suitable for McEliece. Therefore, SH also has pairwise distinct columns. Thus, we can unambiguously sort the columns of SH in lexicographic order $<_{\text{lex}}$. Let $P' \in P^{(n)}$ be the permutation that realizes this sorting.

Using standard rejection sampling, we expand $\boldsymbol{c} \leftarrow_\$ \mathsf{Enc}_{\mathsf{pk}_{\mathcal{A}}}(\boldsymbol{\delta}) \in \mathbf{F}_2^\ell$ to a bit representation of a number $a \in \{0, 1, \ldots, n! - 1\}$. Notice that $\widetilde{\mathsf{KGen}}_V$ requires

$$\ell \leq \log_2(n!), \tag{1}$$

$f_n(a)$	$f_n^{-1}(P)$
1: $\pi_n := 1$	1: Let $\pi = (\pi_1, \ldots, \pi_n)$ with $P = P_\pi$.
2: **for** $j = 1..n - 1$ **do**	2: $a := 0$
3: $d := \big(a \bmod (j+1)!\big)/j!$	3: **for** $j = 1..n$ **do**
4: $a := a - d \cdot j!$	4: $a := a + (\pi_j - 1)(n - j)!$
5: $\pi_{n-j} := d + 1$	5: **for** $i = j + 1..n$
6: **for** $i = n - j + 1..n$ **do**	6: **if** $\pi_i > \pi_j$ **then**
7: **if** $\pi_i > d$ **then**	7: $\pi_i := \pi_i - 1$
8: $\pi_i := \pi_i + 1$	8: **fi**
9: **fi**	9: **endfor**
10: **endfor**	10: **endfor**
11: **endfor**	11: **return** a
12: **return** $P_{(\pi_1, \ldots, \pi_n)}$	

Fig. 2. Algorithms for computing f_n and its inverse f_n^{-1}

$\widetilde{\mathsf{KGen}}_\mathsf{V}(1^n, \mathsf{pk}_\mathcal{A})$

1: $\boldsymbol{\delta} \leftarrow\!\!_\$ \{0,1\}^s$

2: $\boldsymbol{r} := G(\boldsymbol{\delta})$

3: Generate C with parity check matrix H from $\boldsymbol{r}$.

4: Compute random S from $\boldsymbol{r}$.

5: Find permutation P' with $\mathsf{Col}_1(SHP') <_{\text{lex}} \cdots <_{\text{lex}} \mathsf{Col}_n(SHP')$.

6: **repeat** // Rejection sampling of $a \in \{0, 1, \ldots, n! - 1\}$

7:      $\boldsymbol{c} \leftarrow\!\!_\$ \mathsf{Enc}_{\mathsf{pk}_\mathcal{A}}(\boldsymbol{\delta}) \in \mathbf{F}_2^\ell$

8:      $\boldsymbol{s} \leftarrow\!\!_\$ \{0,1\}^{\lceil \log_2 n! \rceil - \ell}$

9:      $\boldsymbol{c}' := \boldsymbol{c} \| \boldsymbol{s}$ and $a := \sum_{i=1}^{\lceil \log_2 n! \rceil} c_i' 2^{i-1}$

10: **until** $a < n!$

11: $P := f_n(a)$ and $\widetilde{P} := P'P$

12: **return** $\widetilde{\mathsf{sk}} := (C, S, H, \widetilde{P}), \widetilde{\mathsf{pk}} := SH\widetilde{P}$

Fig. 3. Backdoored Vanilla McEliece key generation.

which is easily met for many encryptions Enc. See Sect. 5, where we realize Enc with McEliece encryption itself.

If we further assume that $\boldsymbol{c}$ is uniformly distributed in $\mathbf{F}_2^\ell$, then a is uniform in $\{0, 1, \ldots, n! - 1\}$ and hence $P = f_n(a)$ is uniform in $P^{(n)}$. This implies that $\widetilde{P} = P'P$ is uniform in $P^{(n)}$.

Secret Key Recovery. Notice that our backdoored key generation algorithm $\widetilde{\mathsf{KGen}}_V$ from Fig. 3 generates public keys of the form $\widetilde{\mathsf{pk}} := SH\widetilde{P} = SHP'P$, where SHP' has lexicographically sorted columns.

This enables *anybody* to efficiently compute P. We then derive $a = f_n^{-1}(P)$, from which we can recover $c = \mathsf{Enc}_{\mathsf{pk}_\mathcal{A}}(\delta)$. This enables the adversary $\mathcal{A}$ to recover δ using $\mathsf{Dec}_{\mathsf{sk}_\mathcal{A}}$. One then basically reruns $\widetilde{\mathsf{KGen}}_V$ to recover the backdoored secret key $\widetilde{\mathsf{sk}}$. The details are given in Fig. 4.

$\underline{\text{RECOVER}_V(\mathsf{sk}_\mathcal{A}, \widetilde{\mathsf{pk}})}$

1 : Find permutation P with $\mathsf{Col}_1(\widetilde{\mathsf{pk}}P^{-1}) <_{\text{lex}} \cdots <_{\text{lex}} \mathsf{Col}_n(\widetilde{\mathsf{pk}}P^{-1})$.

2 : $a := f_n^{-1}(P)$. Write $a = \sum_{i=1}^{\lceil \log_2 n! \rceil} c_i' 2^{i-1}$.

3 : $c := c_1' \ldots c_\ell'$

4 : $\delta := \mathsf{Dec}_{\mathsf{sk}_\mathcal{A}}(c)$

5 : $r := G(\delta)$

6 : Generate C with parity check H from r.

7 : Compute random S from r.

8 : Find permutation P' with $\mathsf{Col}_1(SHP') <_{\text{lex}} \cdots <_{\text{lex}} \mathsf{Col}_n(SHP')$.

9 : $\widetilde{P} := P'P$

10 : **return** $\widetilde{\mathsf{sk}} = (C, S, H, \widetilde{P})$

Fig. 4. Vanilla McEliece secret key recovery

Proof of Strong SETUP. Let us first check that our backdoor mechanism for McEliece indeed satisfies the SETUP definition of [15] from Subsect. 2.2.

1. *The input to functions in backdoored McEliece agrees with the specification of inputs to McEliece.*
   All domains remain unchanged.
2. *Backdoored McEliece is still efficient and uses $\mathsf{Enc}_{\mathsf{pk}_\mathcal{A}}$ (and possibly other functions as well).*
   Our $\widetilde{\mathsf{KGen}}_V(1^n)$ applies $\mathsf{Enc}_{\mathsf{pk}_\mathcal{A}}$, which we assume to be efficient. Since c' is uniformly distributed in $\{0,1\}^{\lceil \log_2 n! \rceil}$, a is uniform in $\{0, \ldots, 2^{\lceil \log_2 n! \rceil} - 1\}$, so $\Pr[a < n!] = n!/2^{\lceil \log_2 n! \rceil} \geq n!/2^{\log_2 n!+1} = 1/2$. Therefore, the expected number of samples is at most 2, making the rejection sampling efficient. Since $f_n(a)$ and P' are also efficiently computable, our modification remains efficient.
3. $\mathsf{Dec}_{\mathsf{sk}_\mathcal{A}}$ *is not part of backdoored McEliece and is only known by $\mathcal{A}$.*
   We solely use $\mathsf{Dec}_{\mathsf{sk}_\mathcal{A}}$ in $\text{RECOVER}_V(\mathsf{sk}_\mathcal{A}, \widetilde{\mathsf{pk}})$.
4. *The output of algorithms in backdoored McEliece is compatible with the specification of outputs of algorithms in McEliece. At the same time, it contains information efficiently derivable for $\mathcal{A}$ only.*

The output of our backdoored McEliece scheme is fully compatible with the original McEliece scheme, in particular the original decryption function works on the backdoored key pairs $(\widetilde{\mathsf{pk}}, \widetilde{\mathsf{sk}})$. Moreover, our $\widetilde{\mathsf{pk}}$ allows to recover the full secret key $\widetilde{\mathsf{sk}}$ using $\textsc{Recover}_V(\mathsf{sk}_A, \widetilde{\mathsf{pk}})$.

It remains to show that our backdoor mechanism provides a *strong* SETUP for Vanilla McEliece. As the schemes only differ with regard to their key generation, it suffices to show that secret and public keys $(\mathsf{sk}, \mathsf{pk})$ and $(\widetilde{\mathsf{sk}}, \widetilde{\mathsf{pk}})$ output by their respective key generation algorithms are polynomially indistinguishable for anyone who knows pk_A—but not sk_A.

Recall that we used the randomness of $c \leftarrow_\$ \mathsf{Enc}_{\mathsf{pk}_A}(\delta) \in \mathbf{F}_2^\ell$ to derive a random P. In the high-level idea, we showed that uniformly distributed c lead to uniformly distributed P. Therefore, we want our ciphertexts c to be indistinguishable from random bit strings even given the adversary's public key pk_A.

This is captured more formally by the following definition.

Definition 1. *Let $\Pi = (\mathsf{KGen}, \mathsf{Enc}, \mathsf{Dec})$ be a public-key encryption scheme with ciphertexts $c \in \mathbf{F}_2^\ell$. For any algorithm $A^{\mathcal{O}}$ with oracle access to $\mathcal{O}$, define its advantage $\mathsf{Adv}_\Pi^{\mathsf{IND\$-CPA}}(A)$ to be*

$$\left| \Pr\left[A^{\mathsf{Enc}_{\mathsf{pk}}(\cdot)}(\mathsf{pk}) = 1 \,\Big|\, (\mathsf{sk}, \mathsf{pk}) \leftarrow_\$ \mathsf{KGen} \right] - \Pr\left[A^{\$(\cdot)}(\mathsf{pk}) = 1 \,\Big|\, (\mathsf{sk}, \mathsf{pk}) \leftarrow_\$ \mathsf{KGen} \right] \right|.$$

Here the oracle $\mathsf{Enc}_{\mathsf{pk}}(\cdot)$ on input m returns $c \leftarrow_\$ \mathsf{Enc}_{\mathsf{pk}}(m)$, and $\$(\cdot)$ returns a uniformly random $c \leftarrow_\$ \{0,1\}^\ell$ on any input. Π provides indistinguishability from random bits under a chosen plaintext attack, in short IND\$-CPA, if for any ppt adversary A with access to an oracle, $\mathsf{Adv}_\Pi^{\mathsf{IND\$-CPA}}(A)$ is negligible.

It is not hard to see that IND\$-CPA implies IND-CPA. The IND\$-CPA notion has been considered in [10] in the context of symmetric encryption. In Sect. 5 we show that a variant of the McEliece cryptosystem provides IND\$-CPA under reasonable assumptions.

Theorem 1. *Assume that the adversary's public-key encryption scheme $\mathsf{Enc}_{\mathsf{pk}_A}$ is IND\$-CPA and pk_A is publicly known. Then original keys $(\mathsf{sk}, \mathsf{pk}) \leftarrow_\$ \mathsf{KGen}(1^n)$ and backdoored keys $(\widetilde{\mathsf{sk}}, \widetilde{\mathsf{pk}}) \leftarrow_\$ \widetilde{\mathsf{KGen}}(1^n, \mathsf{pk}_A)$ are polynomially indistinguishable. Therefore, our algorithms $\widetilde{\mathsf{KGen}}_V(1^n, \mathsf{pk}_A)$ and $\textsc{Recover}_V(\mathsf{sk}_A, \widetilde{\mathsf{pk}})$ define a strong SETUP mechanism for Vanilla McEliece.*

Proof. For any ppt distinguisher D, we define D's advantage $\mathsf{Adv}_{\widetilde{\mathsf{KGen}}, \mathsf{KGen}}^{\mathsf{KeyDistinguish}}(D)$ for distinguishing original from backdoored keys as

$$\left| \Pr\left[D(\widetilde{\mathsf{sk}}, \widetilde{\mathsf{pk}}, \mathsf{pk}_A) = 1 \,\Big|\, (\widetilde{\mathsf{sk}}, \widetilde{\mathsf{pk}}) \leftarrow_\$ \widetilde{\mathsf{KGen}}_V(1^n, \mathsf{pk}_A) \right] \right.$$
$$\left. - \Pr\left[D(\mathsf{sk}, \mathsf{pk}, \mathsf{pk}_A) = 1 \mid (\mathsf{sk}, \mathsf{pk}) \leftarrow_\$ \mathsf{KGen}_V(1^n) \right] \right|.$$

Now consider the IND\$-CPA game described in Definition 1 where the oracle $\mathcal{O}_{\mathsf{IND\$-CPA}}$ is either $\mathsf{Enc}_{\mathsf{pk}_A}(\cdot)$ or $\$(\cdot)$ and we have to decide which one. In Fig. 5, we use D to construct an adversary $A_D^{\mathcal{O}_{\mathsf{IND\$-CPA}}}$ against the IND\$-CPA game. Here, the algorithm $\widetilde{\mathsf{KGen}}_{\mathsf{V}}(1^n, \mathcal{O}_{\mathsf{IND\$-CPA}})$ is the same as $\widetilde{\mathsf{KGen}}_{\mathsf{V}}(1^n)$ from Fig. 3, with the only difference that $c \leftarrow_\$ \mathcal{O}_{\mathsf{IND\$-CPA}}(\delta)$ is sampled from the given oracle on input δ in step 7.

$A_D^{\mathcal{O}_{\mathsf{IND\$-CPA}}}(1^n, \mathsf{pk}_{\mathcal{A}})$

---

1 : $(\widetilde{\mathsf{sk}}, \widetilde{\mathsf{pk}}) \leftarrow \widetilde{\mathsf{KGen}}_{\mathsf{V}}(1^n, \mathcal{O}_{\mathsf{IND\$-CPA}})$, where we compute $c \leftarrow_\$ \mathcal{O}_{\mathsf{IND\$-CPA}}(\delta) \in \mathbf{F}_2^\ell$

2 : **return** $b \leftarrow_\$ D(\widetilde{\mathsf{sk}}, \widetilde{\mathsf{pk}}, \mathsf{pk}_{\mathcal{A}})$

Fig. 5. Adversary against IND\$-CPA game constructed from D

In case $\mathcal{O}_{\mathsf{IND\$-CPA}} = \mathsf{Enc}_{\mathsf{pk}_{\mathcal{A}}}$, we perfectly simulate $\widetilde{\mathsf{KGen}}_{\mathsf{V}}(1^n, \mathsf{pk}_{\mathcal{A}})$. Hence

$$\Pr\left[A_D^{\mathsf{Enc}_{\mathsf{pk}}(\cdot)}(1^n, \mathsf{pk}_{\mathcal{A}}) = 1\right] = \Pr\left[D(\widetilde{\mathsf{sk}}, \widetilde{\mathsf{pk}}, \mathsf{pk}_{\mathcal{A}}) = 1 \,\middle|\, (\widetilde{\mathsf{sk}}, \widetilde{\mathsf{pk}}) \leftarrow_\$ \widetilde{\mathsf{KGen}}_{\mathsf{V}}(1^n, \mathsf{pk}_{\mathcal{A}})\right]$$

Now suppose $\mathcal{O}_{\mathsf{IND\$-CPA}} = \$(\cdot)$. In this case, $\widetilde{\mathsf{KGen}}_{\mathsf{V}}(1^n, \mathcal{O}_{\mathsf{IND\$-CPA}})$ computes a uniformly distributed c and therefore also a uniform permutation. This differs from the output distribution of $\mathsf{KGen}_{\mathsf{V}}$ only in the fact that $\mathsf{KGen}_{\mathsf{V}}$ generates P from $r = G(\delta)$. Since G is a PRG, we obtain

$$\left|\Pr\left[A_D^{\$(\cdot)}(1^n, \mathsf{pk}_{\mathcal{A}}) = 1\right] - \Pr\left[D(\mathsf{sk}, \mathsf{pk}, \mathsf{pk}_{\mathcal{A}}) = 1 \,\middle|\, (\mathsf{sk}, \mathsf{pk}) \leftarrow_\$ \mathsf{KGen}_{\mathsf{V}}(1^n)\right]\right| \le \mathsf{negl}(n).$$

Putting all this together and using that $\mathsf{Adv}_{\Pi_{\mathcal{A}}}^{\mathsf{IND\$-CPA}}\left(A_D^{\mathcal{O}_{\mathsf{IND\$-CPA}}}\right) \le \mathsf{negl}(n)$ by assumption, we deduce that $\mathsf{Adv}_{\widetilde{\mathsf{KGen}}, \mathsf{KGen}}^{\mathsf{KeyDistinguish}}(D) \le \mathsf{negl}(n)$.   □

3.3   From Strong to Weak SETUP

Recall that in the original McEliece key generation, we derive all randomness from a random seed δ and hence a key pair $(\mathsf{sk}, \mathsf{pk})$ is solely determined by δ. Thus, inclusion of δ into the secret key allows for a simple verification check of the validity of a key pair, thereby preventing our strong SETUP mechanism.

Denote by $\widetilde{\mathsf{KGen}}_{\mathsf{V}}^{\delta}$ the same algorithm as $\widetilde{\mathsf{KGen}}_{\mathsf{V}}$ with the only difference that the random seed δ is also included in $\widetilde{\mathsf{sk}}$.

Theorem 2. *Algorithms* $\widetilde{\mathsf{KGen}}_{\mathsf{V}}^{\delta}(1^n, \mathsf{pk}_{\mathcal{A}})$ *and* $\mathrm{RECOVER}_{\mathsf{V}}(\mathsf{sk}_{\mathcal{A}}, \widetilde{\mathsf{pk}})$ *define a weak SETUP mechanism for Vanilla McEliece.*

Proof. Let $(\widetilde{\mathsf{sk}}, \widetilde{\mathsf{pk}}) \leftarrow \widetilde{\mathsf{KGen}}_{\mathsf{V}}^{\delta}(1^n, \mathsf{pk}_{\mathcal{A}})$ with $\widetilde{\mathsf{sk}} = (C, S, H, \widetilde{P}, \delta)$. Run $\widetilde{\mathsf{KGen}}_{\mathsf{V}}$ with randomness $r := G(\delta)$, let the output be $\mathsf{sk} = (C, S, H, P)$. We conclude that $\widetilde{\mathsf{sk}}$ is backdoored if and only if $P \ne \widetilde{P}$.

Thus, we can decide via our secret key $\widetilde{\mathsf{sk}}$ whether our scheme has been backdoored. Since $\widetilde{\mathsf{KGen}_\mathsf{V}}^{\delta}$ and $\widetilde{\mathsf{KGen}_\mathsf{V}}$ differ only by the format of $\widetilde{\mathsf{sk}}$, by Theorem 1 our scheme still provides a weak SETUP mechanism.   □

Remark 1. Vanilla/Classic McEliece uses pseudorandomness from a PRG output to construct its secret key. One might think that constructing the secret key from true randomness only makes the scheme more secure. However, our results show that the reproducibility feature of pseudorandomness provides an effective way for detecting backdoors, a feature that cannot be realized by true randomness.

4   How to Backdoor Classic McEliece

In this section, we show that the strategy of embedding a backdoor in the secret permutation P from Sect. 3 also transfers to *Classic McEliece*.

Changes from Vanilla to Classic McEliece. A simplified version $\mathsf{KGen}_\mathsf{C}^{\delta}$ of the Classic McEliece key generation is outlined in Fig. 6. The main differences to the Classic McEliece specification are that we do not explicitly describe in detail how the Goppa code is derived from the seed, and that we leave out components of sk that are not relevant to our construction. As in Vanilla McEliece one also uses a seed δ to compute the randomness r for the Goppa code C and its parity check matrix H. However as opposed to Vanilla McEliece, Classic McEliece does not involve a random invertible S, and further completely omits the use of a permutation matrix P. Instead, let S be the *deterministic* Gaussian elimination matrix that sends H to the unique reduced row-echelon form

$$SH = \begin{bmatrix} I_{n-k} \| T \end{bmatrix}.$$

To this end, we assume that the first $n-k$ columns of H define a full rank matrix. Cases with a slightly relaxed condition can also be handled by some parameter sets of Classic McEliece, but our backdoor remains applicable as these parameter sets perform additional swaps on the α_i of the code to create the same structure $\begin{bmatrix} I_{n-k} \| T \end{bmatrix}$.

The reason for choosing S as above is that the public key $\mathsf{pk} = T$ is a matrix in $\mathbf{F}_2^{(n-k) \times k}$, thus saving $n - k$ columns in comparison to Vanilla McEliece for efficiency reasons. $\mathsf{KGen}_\mathsf{C}^{\delta}$ outputs C and δ as secret key. The Classic McEliece NIST submission also includes in sk a random string used for implicit rejection in case decapsulation fails and some additional data that is only relevant for compression purposes; otherwise the key formats are identical, and so for simplicity we refer to $\mathsf{KGen}_\mathsf{C}^{\delta}$ as the original Classic McEliece key generation. For key compression, Classic McEliece also defines multiple truncation levels of sk, where access to the seed δ is required to regenerate the removed elements. Our construction will yield a weak SETUP only for the uncompressed representation of sk. Finally, we also consider a modified version KGen_C of the Classic McEliece key generation that does not include the seed in the secret key for which we obtain a strong SETUP.

At first sight, it seems that the absence of P prevents the direct applicability of our SETUP technique from Sect. 3. Moreover, the deterministic S does not allow for backdoor manipulations either. However, we show in the following that the definition of the Goppa code C already implicitly introduces a permutation P, to which we apply a backdoor mechanism analogous to Sect. 3.

$\mathsf{KGen_C}(1^n)$ respectively $\mathsf{KGen_C^\delta}(1^n)$

---

1 : $\quad \delta \leftarrow_\$ \{0,1\}^s$

2 : $\quad r := G(\delta)$

3 : $\quad$ Compute from r Goppa code $C = (g(x), \alpha_1, \ldots, \alpha_n)$ with distinct α_i
$\quad\quad$ and parity check matrix H.

4 : $\quad$ Use Gaussian elimination S to compute $SH = \begin{bmatrix} I_{n-k} \| T \end{bmatrix}$.

5 : $\quad$ **return** $\mathsf{sk} := \begin{cases} C & \text{for } \mathsf{KGen_C}(1^n) \\ (\delta, C) & \text{for } \mathsf{KGen_C^\delta}(1^n) \end{cases}$, $\mathsf{pk} := T$

Fig. 6. Simplified representation of the Classic McEliece key generation $\mathsf{KGen_C^\delta}$ and a modification $\mathsf{KGen_C}$ that does not include the seed in the secret key.

Idea of Backdoored Key Generation. Recall from Subsect. 2.1 that the parity check matrix of a binary Goppa code is of the form

$$H = \begin{pmatrix} \frac{1}{g(\alpha_1)} & \frac{1}{g(\alpha_2)} & \cdots & \frac{1}{g(\alpha_n)} \\ \frac{\alpha_1}{g(\alpha_1)} & \frac{\alpha_2}{g(\alpha_2)} & \cdots & \frac{\alpha_n}{g(\alpha_n)} \\ \vdots & & \ddots & \\ \frac{\alpha_1^{t-1}}{g(\alpha_1)} & \frac{\alpha_2^{t-1}}{g(\alpha_2)} & \cdots & \frac{\alpha_n^{t-1}}{g(\alpha_n)} \end{pmatrix}.$$

Here, the $\alpha_i \in \mathbf{F}_{2^m}$ are random, distinct field elements. Note that the i-th column h_i of H depends on α_i only. Thus, a random choice of the α_i already induces a random permutation of the columns. Moreover, we may use our SETUP mechanism from Sect. 3 that modifies the permutation to encode the encryption of δ in the public key by modifying the order of the α_i. Due to manipulation of the order of the α_i, this SETUP mechanism is limited to the fully expanded representation of sk and does not apply to the compressed key formats mentioned above.

In our backdoored key generation algorithm from Fig. 7 we permute only the last k columns of the parity check matrix which constitute the (backdoored) public key.

$\widetilde{\mathsf{KGen}}_{\mathsf{C}}(1^n, \mathsf{pk}_{\mathcal{A}})$ respectively $\widetilde{\mathsf{KGen}}_{\mathsf{C}}^{\delta}(1^n, \mathsf{pk}_{\mathcal{A}})$

---

1 : $\delta \leftarrow\!\!\$ \{0,1\}^s$

2 : $r := G(\delta)$

3 : Compute from r Goppa code $C = (g(x), \alpha_1, \ldots, \alpha_n)$ with distinct α_i
     and parity check matrix H.

4 : Use Gaussian elimination S to compute $SH = [I_{n-k} \| T]$.

5 : Find permutation P' with $\mathsf{Col}_1(TP') <_{\text{lex}} \cdots <_{\text{lex}} \mathsf{Col}_k(TP')$.

6 : **repeat**   // Rejection sampling of $a \in \{0, 1, \ldots, k! - 1\}$

7 : $c \leftarrow\!\!\$ \mathsf{Enc}_{\mathsf{pk}_{\mathcal{A}}}(\delta) \in \mathbf{F}_2^\ell$

8 : $s \leftarrow\!\!\$ \{0,1\}^{\lceil \log_2 k! \rceil - \ell}$

9 : $c' := c\|s$ and $a := \sum_{i=1}^{\lceil \log_2 k! \rceil} c_i' 2^{i-1}$

10 : **until** $a < k!$

11 : Set $P := f_k(a)$

12 : Set $\widetilde{P} := \begin{pmatrix} I_{n-k} & \mathbf{0} \\ \mathbf{0} & P'P \end{pmatrix}$.

13 : Compute $\widetilde{C} := \big(g(x), (\alpha_1, \ldots, \alpha_n) \cdot \widetilde{P}\big)$.

14 : **return** $\widetilde{\mathsf{sk}} := \begin{cases} \widetilde{C} & \text{for } \widetilde{\mathsf{KGen}}_{\mathsf{C}}(1^n, \mathsf{pk}_{\mathcal{A}}) \\ (\delta, \widetilde{C}) & \text{for } \widetilde{\mathsf{KGen}}_{\mathsf{C}}^{\delta}(1^n, \mathsf{pk}_{\mathcal{A}}) \end{cases}$, $\widetilde{\mathsf{pk}} := TP'P$

Fig. 7. Backdoored classic McEliece key generation

Classic McEliece Secret Key Recovery. In Fig. 8, we detail the secret key recovery.

The correctness of our $\mathrm{RECOVER}_{\mathsf{C}}(\mathsf{sk}_{\mathcal{A}}, \widetilde{\mathsf{pk}})$ follows analogously to the discussion in Subsect. 3.2.

Analogously to Theorem 1 and Theorem 2 we obtain a weak/strong SETUP for Classic McEliece, depending on whether we include δ into sk or not.

Theorem 3. *Assume that the adversary's public-key encryption scheme* $\mathsf{Enc}_{\mathsf{pk}_{\mathcal{A}}}$ *is IND\$-CPA and* $\mathsf{pk}_{\mathcal{A}}$ *is publicly known. Then original keys* $(\mathsf{sk}, \mathsf{pk}) \leftarrow\!\!\$ \mathsf{KGen}_{\mathsf{C}}(1^n)$ *and backdoored keys* $(\widetilde{\mathsf{sk}}, \widetilde{\mathsf{pk}}) \leftarrow\!\!\$ \widetilde{\mathsf{KGen}}_{\mathsf{C}}(1^n, \mathsf{pk}_{\mathcal{A}})$ *are polynomially indistinguishable. Therefore, our algorithm* $\widetilde{\mathsf{KGen}}_{\mathsf{C}}$ *in combination with* $\mathrm{RECOVER}_{\mathsf{C}}$ *defines a weak SETUP mechanism for Classic McEliece, and* $\widetilde{\mathsf{KGen}}_{\mathsf{C}}^{\delta}$ *defines a strong SETUP mechanism for a modification of Classic McEliece that does not include the PRG-seed* δ *in the user's secret key* sk.

$\text{RECOVER}_{\text{C}}(\mathsf{sk}_{\mathcal{A}}, \widetilde{\mathsf{pk}})$

---

1 : Find permutation P with $\mathsf{Col}_1(\widetilde{\mathsf{pk}}P^{-1}) <_{\text{lex}} \cdots <_{\text{lex}} \mathsf{Col}_k(\widetilde{\mathsf{pk}}P^{-1})$.

2 : $a := f_k^{-1}(P)$. Write $a = \sum_{i=1}^{\lceil \log_2 k! \rceil} c_i 2^{i-1}$.

3 : $c := c_1' \ldots c_\ell'$

4 : $\delta := \mathsf{Dec}_{\mathsf{sk}_{\mathcal{A}}}(c)$

5 : $r := G(\delta)$

6 : Compute from r Goppa code $C = (g(x), \alpha_1, \ldots, \alpha_n)$ with distinct α_i and parity check matrix H.

7 : Use Gaussian elimination S to compute $SH = \left[I_{n-k} \| T \right]$.

8 : Find permutation P' with $\mathsf{Col}_1(TP') <_{\text{lex}} \cdots <_{\text{lex}} \mathsf{Col}_k(TP')$.

9 : Set $\widetilde{P} := \begin{pmatrix} I_{n-k} & 0 \\ 0 & P'P \end{pmatrix}$.

10 : Compute $\widetilde{C} := \left(g(x), (\alpha_1, \ldots, \alpha_n) \cdot \widetilde{P} \right)$.

11 : **return** $\widetilde{\mathsf{sk}} := \widetilde{C}$

Fig. 8. Classic McEliece secret key recovery

5 How to Use McEliece Encryption Against Classic McEliece

We propose to use a variant of the McEliece cryptosystem for the adversary's encryption algorithm Enc. Our scheme can be used to backdoor Classic McEliece for all parameter sets proposed in the NIST submission.

IND\$-CPA McEliece Encryption. As adversary $\mathcal{A}$'s Enc we use the *Randomized Niederreiter Cryptosystem* from [9]. Randomized Niederreiter public keys are scrambled $(n - k) \times n$ parity check matrices of some binary Goppa codes with minimal distance at least $2t + 1$, just as in our Vanilla McEliece scheme. Let n_1, n_2 with $n_1 + n_2 = n$ and define $t_i = \lfloor \frac{n_i t}{n} \rfloor$ for $i = 1, 2$. We take messages from $\mathcal{M}_{\text{RN}} = \{m \in \mathbf{F}_2^{n_2} \mid \mathsf{wt}(m) = t_2\}$, and pad them by a randomly chosen bitstring from $\mathcal{P}_{\text{RN}} = \{r \in \mathbf{F}_2^{n_1} \mid \mathsf{wt}(r) = t_1\}$. The padded message $e = (m \| r) \in \mathbf{F}_2^n$ is an error vector of weight at most t, for which we compute the so-called syndrome $e \cdot \mathsf{pk}^T$.

The key generation and encryption algorithm are detailed in Fig. 9.

Clearly, in order to achieve IND-CPA security, the syndrome decoding problem for the code with $(n - k) \times n_1$ parity check matrix that encodes the randomness r needs to be hard. Note that this code has dimension at least $k_1 := n_1 - (n-k)$. Proposition 2 of [9] shows that under the standard assumptions that public keys pk are indistinguishable from random matrices, and that syndrome decoding of random linear $[n_1, k_1, t_1]$-codes is hard, Randomized Niederreiter provides IND-CPA.

$\mathsf{KGen}_{\mathrm{RN}}(1^n)$	$\mathsf{Enc}_{\mathrm{RN}}(1^n, \mathsf{pk}, m)$
1 : Generate random Goppa code C	1 : $r \leftarrow\!\$ \, \mathcal{P}_{\mathrm{RN}}$
with parity check matrix $H \in \mathbf{F}_2^{(n-k)\times n}$	2 : $e := m\|r$
2 : Generate random invertible $S \in \mathbf{F}_2^{(n-k)\times(n-k)}$	3 : $\mathbf{return}\ c := e \cdot \mathsf{pk}^T$
and permutation matrix $P \in \mathbf{F}_2^{n\times n}$	
3 : $\mathbf{return}\ \mathsf{sk} := (C, S, H, P),\ \mathsf{pk} := SHP$	

Fig. 9. Randomized Niederreiter key generation and encryption for messages $m \in \mathcal{M}_{\mathrm{RN}}$

Actually, the authors of [9] prove an even stronger property, called *admissibility* (see Definition 5 in [9]). It is easily seen that admissibility does not only imply IND-CPA, but even IND\$-CPA from Definition 1. Thus, according to Theorems 1 and 3, Randomized Niederreiter yields a strong SETUP mechanism if δ is not part of the secret, and a weak SETUP mechanism otherwise.

Application to Classic McEliece. For our concrete instantiation of Randomized Niederreiter, we propose to use the Goppa codes from the highest category 5 of the Classic McEliece submission, for which $n = 8192$, $k = 6528$ and $t = 128$. We need to pick n_2 large enough such that $|\mathcal{M}_{\mathrm{RN}}| = \binom{n_2}{t_2} \geq 2^{256}$ so that we are able to encrypt all possible 256-bit strings δ using some suitable encoding $\{0,1\}^{256} \to \mathcal{M}_{\mathrm{RN}}$. It is easily checked that the choice $n_2 = 2250$ and hence $t_2 = \lfloor \frac{n_2 t}{n} \rfloor = 35$ suffices. The ciphertext size is $\ell = n - k = 1664$. Table 1 shows that this is significantly smaller than $\log_2(k!)$ for all Classic McEliece parameter sets of given code dimension k, thus satisfying our necessary condition from Eq. 1.

Table 1. Parameters for Classic McEliece and the number of bits $\lceil \log_2(k!) \rceil$ for encoding a random permutation P

Target instance	Category	n	k	$\lceil \log_2(k!) \rceil$
kem/mceliece348864	1	3488	2720	27117
kem/mceliece460896	3	4608	3360	34520
kem/mceliece6688128	5	6688	5024	54528
kem/mceliece6960119	5	6960	5413	59332
kem/mceliece8192128	5	8192	6528	73316

A   Appendix: A Simpler (But Flawed) SETUP Mechanism

We consider the Vanilla McEliece key generation and describe a simpler attempt at constructing a backdoor. This construction does not even yield a weak SETUP because the backdoor can be efficiently detected by just considering the public keys. The distinguisher may be interesting in its own right and is also described below.

A.1   A Flawed SETUP

A description of the original and our simpler (but flawed) backdoored key generation $\widetilde{\mathsf{KGen}}_{\mathsf{v}}^{\mathsf{F}}$ can be found in Fig. 10.

The matrices S and H are generated exactly as in the non-backdoored scheme. The key difference is that instead of applying a random permutation P, we choose a permutation $\widetilde{P}$ that permutes the columns of pk such that pk's first row contains the ciphertext $c \in \mathbf{F}_2^\ell$. This is done by choosing the permutation matrix as the combination of a purely random P and a permutation P' that sends the bits of c to the desired coordinates.

$\mathsf{KGen}_{\mathsf{v}}(1^n)$

---

1 : $\delta \leftarrow\!\!\$ \{0,1\}^s$

2 : $r := G(\delta)$

3 :   Generate C with parity check matrix H from r.

4 :   Compute random S, P from r.

5 :   **return** sk $:= (C, S, H, P)$, pk $:= (SHP)$

$\widetilde{\mathsf{KGen}}_{\mathsf{v}}^{\mathsf{F}}(1^n, \mathsf{pk}_\mathcal{A})$

---

1 : $\delta \leftarrow\!\!\$ \{0,1\}^s$

2 : $c \leftarrow\!\!\$ \mathsf{Enc}_{\mathsf{pk}_\mathcal{A}}(\delta) \in \mathbf{F}_2^\ell$

3 : $r := G(\delta)$

4 :   Generate C with parity check matrix H from r.

5 :   Compute random S, P from r.

6 :   Find P' with $\mathrm{Row}_1(SHPP') \in \{c\} \times \mathbf{F}_2^{n-\ell}$.

7 : $\widetilde{P} := PP'$

8 :   **return** $\widetilde{\mathsf{sk}} := (C, S, H, \widetilde{P}), \widetilde{\mathsf{pk}} := SH\widetilde{P}$

Fig. 10. Original and backdoored Vanilla McEliece key generation

Notice that $\widetilde{\mathsf{KGen}}_{\mathsf{v}}^{\mathsf{F}}$ works provided that

1. $c \in \mathbb{F}_2^\ell$ can be encoded in the first row $v = \mathsf{Row}_1(SHP)$ of the public key, and
2. P' is efficiently computable.

We briefly sketch why these statements hold. Regarding the first statement, notice that $c \in \mathbb{F}_2^\ell$ can be encoded in the first row of the public key if the Hamming weight of v lies in the interval $[\ell, n - \ell]$. A simple Chernoff bound shows that under reasonable assumptions (such as $\ell \leq \frac{1}{4}n$), the probability that this holds is exponentially close to 1.

Regarding the second statement, we can compute P' in an insertion-sort fashion: Iterating through the first ℓ entries of the first row of SHP from left to right, if an entry differs from the corresponding one in c, we swap this column with the first column to the right with the same entry in the first row.

A.2   The distinguisher

In order for the described backdoored keys to be indistinguishable from non-backdoored ones, it is clearly necessary that the ciphertexts of the adversary's encryption scheme look like random bitstrings. So let us assume that the adversary's scheme provides indistinguishability from random bits under a chosen plaintext attack (see Definition 1). Under this condition, does the described backdoored scheme provide a SETUP mechanism? Perhaps surprisingly, it turns out that it does not even provide a weak SETUP. To see this, for a public key pk sampled from KGen or $\widetilde{\mathsf{KGen}}_\mathsf{v}^\mathsf{F}$, we consider the random variables

$$X := \mathsf{wt}\,(v_1 \ldots v_\ell), \quad Y := \mathsf{wt}\,(v),$$

where $v = v_1 \ldots v_n := \mathsf{Row}_1(\mathsf{pk})$, and we make the following observation:

Lemma 1. *If* $(\mathsf{sk}, \mathsf{pk}) \leftarrow_\$ \widetilde{\mathsf{KGen}}_\mathsf{v}^\mathsf{F}$, *then* $X \mid Y = w \sim \mathsf{Binom}(\ell, \frac{1}{2})$.
  If $(\mathsf{sk}, \mathsf{pk}) \leftarrow_\$ \mathsf{KGen}_\mathsf{v}$, *then* $X \mid Y = w \sim \mathsf{Hypergeom}(n, w, \ell)$.

Proof. First suppose $(\mathsf{sk}, \mathsf{pk}) \leftarrow_\$ \widetilde{\mathsf{KGen}}_\mathsf{v}^\mathsf{F}$. Then the first ℓ entries of $\mathsf{Row}_1(\mathsf{pk})$ are given by an encryption $c \leftarrow_\$ \mathsf{Enc}_{\mathsf{pk}_\mathcal{A}}(\delta)$ of a random seed δ. Since $\mathsf{Enc}_{\mathsf{pk}_\mathcal{A}}$ provides random ciphertexts, c is uniformly distributed among all ℓ-bit strings (or at least computationally indistinguishable from it). Hence $X = \mathsf{wt}\,(c)$ is binomially distributed as required, independent of the Hamming weight of $\mathsf{Row}_1(\mathsf{pk})$.

Now suppose $(\mathsf{sk}, \mathsf{pk}) \leftarrow_\$ \mathsf{KGen}_\mathsf{v}$ where $\mathsf{sk} = (C, S, H, P)$. Observe that pk is obtained from SH by randomly permuting its columns. This means that the first ℓ entries of $\mathsf{Row}_1(\mathsf{pk})$ are obtained by randomly sampling without replacement from the entries in the first row of SH. Hence $X \mid \mathsf{wt}\,(\mathsf{Row}_1(SH)) = w \sim \mathsf{Hypergeom}(n, w, \ell)$. As permuting the columns of SH does not change the Hamming weight of its first row, we have $\mathsf{wt}\,(\mathsf{Row}_1(\mathsf{pk})) = \mathsf{wt}\,(\mathsf{Row}_1(SH))$. This implies the claim. $\square$

Hence the conditional distributions of $X \mid Y = w$ differ noticeably in the backdoored and non-backdoored case. A maximum-likelihood distinguisher can thus be used to distinguish backdoored from non-backdoored keys with non-negligible advantage.

This observation can be used to construct a distinguisher. Our distinguisher $\mathcal{D}$ described in Fig. 11 is inspired by Lemma 1 and requires only the public key and the ciphertext length of the adversary's encryption scheme. It is basically a maximum-likelihood distinguisher that, given a public key pk, considers the Hamming weight of the first ℓ bits of its first row. Depending on whether this ℓ-bit string has a higher probability of occurrence assuming $\mathsf{Binom}(\ell, \frac{1}{2})$ or $\mathsf{Hypergeom}(n, \mathsf{wt}\,(\mathsf{Row}_1(\mathsf{pk})), \ell)$ as the underlying distribution, the distinguisher outputs that the public key is backdoored or, respectively, non-backdoored.

Lemma 1 implies that the distinguishing advantage of $\mathcal{D}$ is given by the statistical distance[1] between the distributions $\mathsf{Hypergeom}(n, \mathsf{wt}\,(\mathsf{Row}_1(\mathsf{pk})), \ell)$ and $\mathsf{Binom}(\ell, \frac{1}{2})$. Notice that it depends on $\mathsf{wt}\,(\mathsf{Row}_1(\mathsf{pk}))$. It is minimal for $\mathsf{wt}\,(\mathsf{Row}_1(\mathsf{pk})) = \frac{n}{2}$, however even in this case it is far from negligible for reasonable n and ℓ occurring for practical McEliece parameter sets. For example, applying the Randomized Niederreiter scheme described in Sect. 5 to the highest Classic McEliece Category 5 parameter set (see Table 1), even in the favourable case that half the entries in the first row of the public key equal one respectively zero, the distinguishing advantage is about 0.071. It thus clearly does not even provide a weak SETUP because we can distinguish backdoored and non-backdoored keys from just the public keys.

Intuitively speaking, the problem with this attempt at a backdoor construction is the following: In the non-backdoored scheme, the distribution of the first

$\mathsf{D}\,(\mathsf{pk}, \ell)$

1: $n :=$ number of columns of pk

2: $r := \mathsf{Row}_1(\mathsf{pk})$

3: $c := r_1 \ldots r_\ell$

4: **if** $p^{\mathsf{Binom}}_{\ell, \frac{1}{2}}(\mathsf{wt}\,(c)) < p^{\mathsf{Hypergeom}}_{n, \mathsf{wt}(r), \ell}(\mathsf{wt}\,(c))$ **then**

5:      **return** NON-BACKDOORED

6: **else**

7:      **return** BACKDOORED

8: **fi**

Fig. 11. Distinguishing backdoored and non-backdoored public keys. $p^{\mathsf{Binom}}_{\ell, \frac{1}{2}}$ and $p^{\mathsf{Hypergeom}}_{n, w, \ell}$ denote the probability mass functions of the binomial respectively hypergeometric distribution.

---

[1] The *statistical distance* between two discrete distributions with probability mass functions p and q defined over the same set $\mathcal{X}$ is given by $d(p, q) = \frac{1}{2}\sum_{x \in \mathcal{X}} |p(x) - q(x)|$.

ℓ bits of the first row of pk is in fact dependent on the Hamming weight of the entire row. For example, if there happen to be in total more ones than zeros in the first row of pk or equivalently of the associated SH, then applying a random permutation to the columns of SH also results in a bias towards more ones than zeros in the first ℓ bits. This is in contrast with the backdoored scheme for which the first ℓ bits of the first row of the resulting pk are always uniformly distributed since they are completely determined by the ciphertext c — which is indistinguishable from a random bitstring by assumption.

References

1. Albrecht, M.R., et al.: Classic McEliece: conservative code-based cryptography (2020). https://classic.mceliece.org/nist/mceliece-20201010.pdf
2. Bellare, M., Paterson, K.G., Rogaway, P.: Security of symmetric encryption against mass surveillance. In: Garay, J.A., Gennaro, R. (eds.) CRYPTO 2014. LNCS, vol. 8616, pp. 1–19. Springer, Heidelberg (2014). https://doi.org/10.1007/978-3-662-44371-2_1
3. Bernstein, D.J., Lange, T., Niederhagen, R.: Dual EC: a standardized back door. In: Ryan, P.Y.A., Naccache, D., Quisquater, J.-J. (eds.) The New Codebreakers. LNCS, vol. 9100, pp. 256–281. Springer, Heidelberg (2016). https://doi.org/10.1007/978-3-662-49301-4_17
4. Classic McEliece Comparison Task Force: Classic McEliece vs. NTS-KEM (2018). https://classic.mceliece.org/nist/vsntskem-20180629.pdf
5. Crépeau, C., Slakmon, A.: Simple backdoors for RSA key generation. In: Joye, M. (ed.) CT-RSA 2003. LNCS, vol. 2612, pp. 403–416. Springer, Heidelberg (2003). https://doi.org/10.1007/3-540-36563-X_28
6. Kreher, D.L., Stinson, D.R.: Combinatorial Algorithms: Generation, Enumeration, and Search. CRC Press (1999)
7. Kwant, R., Lange, T., Thissen, K.: Lattice Klepto - turning post-quantum crypto against itself. In: Adams, C., Camenisch, J. (eds.) SAC 2017. LNCS, vol. 10719, pp. 336–354. Springer, Cham (2018). https://doi.org/10.1007/978-3-319-72565-9_17
8. Loidreau, P., Sendrier, N.: Weak keys in the McEliece public-key cryptosystem. IEEE Trans. Inf. Theory **47**(3), 1207–1211 (2001). https://doi.org/10.1109/18.915687
9. Nojima, R., Imai, H., Kobara, K., Morozov, K.: Semantic security for the McEliece cryptosystem without random oracles. Des. Codes Crypt. **49**, 289–305 (2008). https://doi.org/10.1007/s10623-008-9175-9
10. Rogaway, P.: Nonce-based symmetric encryption. In: Roy, B., Meier, W. (eds.) FSE 2004. LNCS, vol. 3017, pp. 348–358. Springer, Heidelberg (2004). https://doi.org/10.1007/978-3-540-25937-4_22
11. Simmons, G.J.: The prisoners' problem and the subliminal channel. In: Chaum, D. (ed.) CRYPTO 1983, pp. 51–67. Plenum Press, New York (1983)
12. Simmons, G.J.: The subliminal channel and digital signatures. In: Beth, T., Cot, N., Ingemarsson, I. (eds.) EUROCRYPT 1984. LNCS, vol. 209, pp. 364–378. Springer, Heidelberg (1985). https://doi.org/10.1007/3-540-39757-4_25
13. Yang, Z., Xie, T., Pan, Y.: Lattice Klepto revisited. In: Sun, H.M., Shieh, S.P., Gu, G., Ateniese, G. (eds.) ASIACCS 2020, pp. 867–873. ACM Press (2020). https://doi.org/10.1145/3320269.3384768

14. Young, A., Yung, M.: The dark side of "Black-Box" cryptography or: should we trust capstone? In: Koblitz, N. (ed.) CRYPTO 1996. LNCS, vol. 1109, pp. 89–103. Springer, Heidelberg (1996). https://doi.org/10.1007/3-540-68697-5_8

15. Young, A., Yung, M.: Kleptography: using cryptography against cryptography. In: Fumy, W. (ed.) EUROCRYPT 1997. LNCS, vol. 1233, pp. 62–74. Springer, Heidelberg (1997). https://doi.org/10.1007/3-540-69053-0_6

16. Young, A., Yung, M.: Kleptography from standard assumptions and applications. In: Garay, J.A., De Prisco, R. (eds.) SCN 2010. LNCS, vol. 6280, pp. 271–290. Springer, Heidelberg (2010). https://doi.org/10.1007/978-3-642-15317-4_18

LRPC Codes with Multiple Syndromes: Near Ideal-Size KEMs Without Ideals

Carlos Aguilar-Melchor[1], Nicolas Aragon[2], Victor Dyseryn[3(✉)],
Philippe Gaborit[3], and Gilles Zémor[4]

[1] SandboxAQ, Palo Alto, CA, USA
[2] CNRS, Inria, IRISA, Université de Rennes, Rennes, France
[3] XLIM, Université de Limoges, Limoges, France
`victor.dyseryn_fostier@unilim.fr`
[4] Institut de Mathématiques de Bordeaux, UMR 5251, Bordeaux, France

Abstract. We introduce a new rank-based key encapsulation mechanism (KEM) with public key and ciphertext sizes around 3.5 Kbytes each, for 128 bits of security, without using ideal structures. Such structures allow to compress objects, but give reductions to specific problems whose security is potentially weaker than for unstructured problems. To the best of our knowledge, our scheme improves in size upon all the existing unstructured post-quantum lattice or code-based algorithms such as FrodoKEM or Classic McEliece. Our technique, whose efficiency relies on properties of rank metric, is to build upon existing Low Rank Parity Check (LRPC) code-based KEMs and to send multiple syndromes in one ciphertext, allowing to reduce the parameters and still obtain an acceptable decoding failure rate. Our system relies on the hardness of the Rank Support Learning problem, a well-known variant of the Rank Syndrome Decoding problem. The gain on parameters is enough to significantly close the gap between ideal and non-ideal constructions. It also enables to choose an error weight close to the rank Gilbert-Varshamov bound, which is a relatively harder zone for algebraic attacks.

Keywords: Rank-based cryptography · Code-based cryptography · Post-quantum cryptography · Rank Support Learning · LRPC codes

1 Introduction and Previous Work

In recent years and especially since the 2017 NIST call for proposals on post-quantum cryptography, there has been a burst of activity in this field. Recent publications, such as the Barbulescu *et al.* attack against the small characteristic discrete logarithm problem [12], stress the importance of having a wide diversity of cryptographic systems before the emergence of large and fault-tolerant quantum computers.

The most common algorithms in post-quantum cryptography are lattice-based or code-based. Code-based cryptography relies on difficult problems related to error-correcting codes embedded in Hamming metric spaces (often

© The Author(s), under exclusive license to Springer Nature Switzerland AG 2022
J. H. Cheon and T. Johansson (Eds.): PQCrypto 2022, LNCS 13512, pp. 45–68, 2022.
https://doi.org/10.1007/978-3-031-17234-2_3

over small fields $\mathbb{F}_q$). Lattice-based cryptography is mainly based on the study of q-ary lattices, which can be seen as codes over rings of type $\mathbb{Z}/q\mathbb{Z}$ (for large q), embedded in Euclidean metric spaces.

In this paper we study a rank-based cryptosystem. Rank-based cryptography is similar to code-based cryptography, with the difference that the error-correcting codes are embedded in a rank-metric space (often over a prime order field extension).

In rank metric, the practical difficulty of usual decoding problems grows very quickly with parameter size, which makes it very appealing for cryptography. This metric was introduced by Delsarte and Gabidulin [23], along with Gabidulin codes which are a rank-metric equivalent of Reed-Solomon codes. Since then, rank-metric codes have been used for multiple applications such as coding theory and cryptography.

Among the different cryptographic primitives, rank-based cryptography literature is mainly focused around encryption schemes, even if rank metric is relevant to produce small size and general purpose digital signatures, such as Durandal [9]. Until recently, the main approach to build cryptosystems based on rank-metric decoding problems was masking Gabidulin codes [25] in different ways and using the McEliece (or Niederreiter) setting with these codes. Most cryptosystems based on this idea were broken by attacks which exploit the particular structure of Gabidulin codes [16,22,24,32,33]. A similar situation exists in the Hamming case for which most cryptosystems based on Reed-Solomon codes have been broken for a similar reason: these codes are so structured that they are difficult to mask and there is always some structural information leak.

To solve this difficulty, rank-based cryptosystems designers have either produced schemes without masking [2] or proposed to use LRPC codes which are easier to mask. The latter are the foundations of the new cryptosystem presented in this paper.

LRPC codes were first introduced in [27] and are a family of rank-metric error-correcting codes which admit a parity matrix whose coordinates generate a low rank vector space. They have a strong decoding power, and can be seen as the rank-metric equivalent to Hamming-metric MDPC codes, which are for example featured in third-round NIST candidate BIKE [6].

In their ideal form, LRPC codes are the main building block of the second-round NIST candidate ROLLO [8]. This candidate was not selected for the third round due to algebraic attacks [14,15], which significantly reduced the security of the parameters proposed in the original submissions. NIST encouraged further study on rank-metric cryptosystems [3], but these attacks have not been improved. The NIST standardization process has improved the scientific community understanding of LRPC cryptosystems and of the associated attacks, meanwhile there were two points which still could be improved.

A first point was related to constant time implementations which were unsatisfactory and for which a recent paper [18] showed how it was possible to drastically improve their performances. A second point was the Decoding Failure Rate (DFR). Indeed, LRPC parameters led to quite efficient cryptosystems for DFRs around 2^{-30}, but for DFRs below 2^{-128} there was a significant efficiency drop, as to obtain such DFRs the codes needed to be quite long. The present paper shows how to avoid larger code lengths while still obtaining very low DFRs. This results in a significant improvement of the associated cryptosystems, both for the structured and unstructured case, without compromising a precise analysis of the DFR.

A usual technique to reduce public key and ciphertext sizes in cryptosystems is to introduce structure in the underlying algebraic objects. This is done in general by introducing some extra ideal, module, or ring structure [2,6,11,30]. However, adding structure comes at the cost of losing reductions to difficult problems in the more general form. A hypothesis must be made: that the structure does not set the stage for better attacks than for the unstructured, general, problem.

When compared to structured finalist and alternate candidates to the NIST PQC standardization, using the standard communication metric (public key + ciphertext size), our ideal scheme is more efficient than BIKE [6] and HQC [1] (at least 1.4 times shorter for 128 bits of security), but somewhat less than structured lattice approaches (roughly 1.4 times larger for 128 bits of security) and significantly less than SIKE.

Using again the communication metric, our schemes perform very well in the unstructured setting. Among the finalist and alternate candidates, only two candidates do not use any ideal-like structure: FrodoKEM [5] for lattice-based cryptography and Classic McEliece [4] for code-based cryptography. A proposal of an unstructured code-based KEM was also introduced after the beginning of the NIST project, called Loong.CCAKEM [38]. Our non-ideal proposal compares advantageously to the three of them (2.8 times shorter than FrodoKEM for 128 bits of security).

Description of Our Technique. The usual approach to build a cryptosystem based on LRPC codes is to send a syndrome $s = He$ as a ciphertext where both e and H are of low rank weight and, to decrypt, use a Rank Support Recovery algorithm to recover the support of e from the support of the product He. The main obstacle to reduce the parameters for such cryptosystems is not the threat of cryptanalytic attacks but the DFR. In order for the Rank Support Recovery algorithm to work, the syndrome s has to be large enough so as to generate the full product of supports of H and e.

As [26] and [38] did, we use multiple syndromes $s_1, \ldots, s_\ell$ of same error support. The decoding of multiple syndromes that result from errors that share the same support can also be referred to as the decoding of interleaved codes. Interleaved LRPC codes and their decoding were studied in [35]. Furthermore, the idea of using interleaved codes for Hamming-based cryptosystems was introduced in [21] and for rank-based cryptosystems in [36]. Our main result is to show that this approach, in the context of LRPC codes, can solve decryption failure rate issues that affected previous schemes and thus reduce significantly key and ciphertext size, as the Rank Support Recovery algorithm gets more coordinates to recover the product of supports. As compared to [35], we give a more analysis of the DFR formula. Indeed, while intuitive at a first glance, the proof that multiple syndromes reduce the probability of failure is quite technical and led us to formulate a general result on the product of two random homogeneous matrices.

Sending multiple syndromes leads naturally to reducing the security of our KEM to the Rank Support Learning (RSL) problem [9,26,38], which implies that our approach is specific to rank-metric and cannot be used for Hamming-based cryptosystems. Indeed, in a Hamming metric context, the complexity of the Support Learning problem decreases way faster with the number of given syndromes than its rank-metric counterpart, and thus—with a direct application of our approach—it is not possible in Hamming metric to obtain parameter sets that have a practical interest and are secure.

Contributions of the Paper. We present in this paper three contributions:

- A new LRPC code-based key encapsulation mechanism built upon the multiple syndrome approach that significantly improves decoding. We give an unstructured version of our KEM that achieves a competitive size of around 3.5 Kbytes each for the public key and ciphertext. We also give an ideal version to reduce the sizes even further.
- A proof that with our new approach, small weight parameters r and d of the LRPC code can be chosen higher and even very close to the rank Gilbert-Varshamov bound $d_{RGV} = \mathcal{O}(n)$, whereas for a LRPC code-based cryptosystem these values have to be in $\mathcal{O}(\sqrt{n})$. When target weights increase, algebraic attacks become less effective and can even be more costly than combinatorial attacks.
- A probabilistic result on the support generated by the coordinates of a product matrix UV where U and V are two random homogeneous matrices of low weight. This result happens to be the cornerstone of the efficiency of our KEM but is also general enough to be applicable elsewhere in cryptography or in other fields.

Organization of the Paper. The paper is organized as follows: Sect. 2 recalls basic facts about the rank-metric and the corresponding difficult problems, Sect. 3 gives a background on LRPC codes and their decoding, Sect. 4 introduces a new KEM using the multiple-syndrome technique to decode LRPC codes, Sect. 5 proves the IND-CPA property of the KEM, Sect. 6 is concerned with parameters for our KEMs.

2   Background on Rank Metric Codes

2.1   General Definitions

Let $\mathbb{F}_q$ denote the finite field of q elements where q is the power of a prime and let $\mathbb{F}_{q^m}$ denote the field of q^m elements seen as the extension of degree m of $\mathbb{F}_q$.

$\mathbb{F}_{q^m}$ is also an $\mathbb{F}_q$ vector space of dimension m, we denote by capital letters the $\mathbb{F}_q$-subspaces of $\mathbb{F}_{q^m}$ and by lower-case letters the elements of $\mathbb{F}_{q^m}$.

We denote by $\langle x_1, \ldots, x_n \rangle$ the $\mathbb{F}_q$-subspace generated by the elements $(x_1, \ldots, x_n) \in \mathbb{F}_{q^m}^n$.

Vectors are denoted by bold lower-case letters and matrices by bold capital letters (e.g. $\boldsymbol{x} = (x_1, \ldots, x_n) \in \mathbb{F}_{q^m}^n$ and $\boldsymbol{M} = (m_{ij})_{\substack{1 \leqslant i \leqslant k \\ 1 \leqslant j \leqslant n}} \in \mathbb{F}_{q^m}^{k \times n}$).

Let $P \in \mathbb{F}_q[X]$ be a polynomial of degree n. We can identify the vector space $\mathbb{F}_{q^m}^n$ with the ring $\mathbb{F}_{q^m}[X]/\langle P \rangle$, by mapping $\boldsymbol{v} = (v_0, \ldots, v_{n-1})$ to $\Psi(\boldsymbol{v}) = \sum_{i=0}^{n-1} v_i X^i$. For $\boldsymbol{u}, \boldsymbol{v} \in \mathbb{F}_{q^m}^n$, we define their product similarly as in $\mathbb{F}_{q^m}[X]/\langle P \rangle$: $\boldsymbol{w} = \boldsymbol{uv} \in \mathbb{F}_{q^m}^n$ is the only vector such that $\Psi(\boldsymbol{w}) = \Psi(\boldsymbol{u})\Psi(\boldsymbol{v}) \mod P$. In order to lighten the formula, we will omit the symbol Ψ in the future.

If S is a finite set, we denote by $x \xleftarrow{\$} S$ the fact that x is chosen uniformly at random amongst S.

The number of $\mathbb{F}_q$-subspaces of dimension r of $\mathbb{F}_{q^m}$ is given by the Gaussian coefficient

$$\begin{bmatrix} m \\ r \end{bmatrix}_q = \prod_{i=0}^{r-1} \frac{q^m - q^i}{q^r - q^i}.$$

Definition 1 (Rank metric over $\mathbb{F}_{q^m}^n$). *Let $\boldsymbol{x} = (x_1, \ldots, x_n) \in \mathbb{F}_{q^m}^n$ and let $(b_1, \ldots, b_m) \in \mathbb{F}_{q^m}^m$ be a basis of $\mathbb{F}_{q^m}$ over $\mathbb{F}_q$. Each coordinate x_j is associated to a vector of $\mathbb{F}_q^m$ in this basis: $x_j = \sum_{i=1}^m m_{ij} b_i$. The $m \times n$ matrix associated to $\boldsymbol{x}$ is given by $\boldsymbol{M}(\boldsymbol{x}) = (m_{ij})_{\substack{1 \leqslant i \leqslant m \\ 1 \leqslant j \leqslant n}}$.*

The rank weight $\|\boldsymbol{x}\|$ of $\boldsymbol{x}$ is defined as the rank of $\boldsymbol{M}(\boldsymbol{x})$. This definition does not depend on the choice of the basis. The associated distance $d(\boldsymbol{x}, \boldsymbol{y})$ between elements $\boldsymbol{x}$ and $\boldsymbol{y}$ in $\mathbb{F}_{q^m}^n$ is defined by $d(\boldsymbol{x}, \boldsymbol{y}) = \|\boldsymbol{x} - \boldsymbol{y}\|$.

The support of $\boldsymbol{x}$, denoted $\mathrm{Supp}(\boldsymbol{x})$, is the $\mathbb{F}_q$-subspace of $\mathbb{F}_{q^m}$ generated by the coordinates of $\boldsymbol{x}$: $\mathrm{Supp}(\boldsymbol{x}) \stackrel{def}{=} \langle x_1, \ldots, x_n \rangle$. We have $\dim \mathrm{Supp}(\boldsymbol{x}) = \|\boldsymbol{x}\|$.

Definition 2 ($\mathbb{F}_{q^m}$-linear code). *An $\mathbb{F}_{q^m}$-linear code $\mathcal{C}$ of dimension k and length n is a subspace of dimension k of $\mathbb{F}_{q^m}^n$ seen as a rank metric space. The notation $[n, k]_{q^m}$ is used to denote its parameters.*

The code $\mathcal{C}$ can be represented by two equivalent ways:

- *by a generator matrix $\boldsymbol{G} \in \mathbb{F}_{q^m}^{k \times n}$. Each row of $\boldsymbol{G}$ is an element of a basis of $\mathcal{C}$,*

$$\mathcal{C} = \{\boldsymbol{x}\boldsymbol{G}, \boldsymbol{x} \in \mathbb{F}_{q^m}^k\}.$$

- *by a parity-check matrix $\boldsymbol{H} \in \mathbb{F}_{q^m}^{(n-k) \times n}$. Each row of $\boldsymbol{H}$ determines a parity-check equation verified by the elements of $\mathcal{C}$:*

$$\mathcal{C} = \{\boldsymbol{x} \in \mathbb{F}_{q^m}^n : \boldsymbol{H}\boldsymbol{x}^T = \boldsymbol{0}\}.$$

We say that $\boldsymbol{G}$ (respectively $\boldsymbol{H}$) is under systematic form if and only if it is of the form $(\boldsymbol{I}_k | \boldsymbol{A})$ (respectively $(\boldsymbol{I}_{n-k} | \boldsymbol{B})$).

2.2   Ideal Codes

To describe an $[n, k]_{q^m}$ linear code, we can give a systematic generator matrix or a systematic parity-check matrix. In both cases, the number of bits needed to represent such a matrix is $k(n - k)m \lceil \log_2 q \rceil$. To reduce the size of a representation of a code, we introduce ideal codes. They are a generalization of double circulant codes by choosing a polynomial P to define the quotient-ring $\mathbb{F}_{q^m}[X]/(P)$. More details about this construction can be found in [10].

Definition 3 (Ideal codes). *Let $P(X) \in \mathbb{F}_q[X]$ be a polynomial of degree n and $g_1, g_2 \in \mathbb{F}_{q^m}^k$. Let $G_1(X) = \sum_{i=0}^{k-1} g_{1i} X^i$ and $G_2(X) = \sum_{j=0}^{k-1} g_{2j} X^j$ be the polynomials associated respectively to g_1 and g_2. We call the $[2k, k]_{q^m}$ ideal code $\mathcal{C}$ of generator (g_1, g_2) the code with generator matrix*

$$
G = \begin{pmatrix}
G_1(X) \mod P & G_2(X) \mod P \\
XG_1(X) \mod P & XG_2(X) \mod P \\
\vdots & \vdots \\
X^{k-1}G_1(X) \mod P & X^{k-1}G_2(X) \mod P
\end{pmatrix}.
$$

More concisely, we have $\mathcal{C} = \{(xg_1 \mod P, xg_2 \mod P), x \in \mathbb{F}_{q^m}^k\}$. We will often omit mentioning the polynomial P if there is no ambiguity.

We usually require g_1 to be invertible, in which case the code admits the systematic form, $\mathcal{C} = \{(x, xg), x \in \mathbb{F}_{q^m}^k\}$ with $g = g_1^{-1} g_2 \mod P$.

2.3   Difficult Problems in Rank Metric

Rank Syndrome Decoding and Ideal Variant

Problem 1 (Rank Syndrome Decoding). On input $(H, s) \in \mathbb{F}_{q^m}^{(n-k) \times n} \times \mathbb{F}_{q^m}^{(n-k)}$, the Rank Syndrome Decoding Problem $\mathrm{RSD}_{n,k,r}$ is to compute $e \in \mathbb{F}_{q^m}^n$ such that $He^{\mathsf{T}} = s^{\mathsf{T}}$ and $\|e\| = r$.

In [29] it is proven that the Syndrome Decoding problem in the Hamming metric, which is a well-known NP-Hard problem, is probabilistically reduced to the RSD problem. Moreover, the RSD problem can be seen as a structured version of the NP-hard MinRank problem [17], indeed the MinRank problem is equivalent to the RSD problem replacing $\mathbb{F}_{q^m}$-linear codes by $\mathbb{F}_q$-linear codes. The variant of this problem for ideal codes is as follows.

Problem 2 (Ideal-Rank Syndrome Decoding). Let $P \in \mathbb{F}_q[X]$ a polynomial of degree k. On input $(h, \sigma) \in \mathbb{F}_{q^m}^k \times \mathbb{F}_{q^m}^k$, the Ideal-Rank Syndrome Decoding Problem $\mathrm{IRSD}_{2k,k,r}$ is to compute $x = (x_1, x_2) \in \mathbb{F}_{q^m}^{2k}$ such that $x_1 + x_2 h = \sigma \mod P$ and $\|x\| = r$.

Since h and P define a systematic parity-check matrix of a $[2k, k]_{q^m}$ ideal code, the IRSD problem is a particular case of the RSD problem. Although this problem is theoretically easier than the RSD problem, in practice the best algorithms for solving both these problems are the same.

Rank Support Learning. The following problem was introduced in [26]. It is similar to the RSD problem, the difference is that instead of having one syndrome, we are given several syndromes of errors of same support and the goal is to find this support. The security of RSL is considered to be similar to RSD for a small number of syndromes. More details about the security of RSL are provided in Sect. 5. The RSL problem also has an ideal variant called IRSL.

Problem 3. **Rank Support Learning (RSL)** [26] On input $(\boldsymbol{H}, \boldsymbol{S}) \in \mathbb{F}_{q^m}^{(n-k) \times n} \times \mathbb{F}_{q^m}^{\ell \times (n-k)}$, the Rank Support Learning Problem $\mathsf{RSL}_{n,k,r,\ell}$ is to compute a subspace E of $\mathbb{F}_{q^m}$ of dimension r, such that there exists a matrix $\boldsymbol{V} \in E^{\ell \times n}$ such that $\boldsymbol{H}\boldsymbol{V}^{\mathsf{T}} = \boldsymbol{S}^{\mathsf{T}}$.

Decisional Problems. For all the problems RSD, IRSD, RSL and IRSL defined above, we can give a decisional version whose goal is to distinguish (for the example of RSD) between a random input $(\boldsymbol{H}, \boldsymbol{s})$ or an actual syndrome input $(\boldsymbol{H}, \boldsymbol{H}\boldsymbol{e}^{\mathsf{T}})$. We denote these decisional versions DRSD, DIRSD, DRSL and DIRSL. The reader is referred to [10] for more details about decisional problems.

3 LRPC Codes and their Decoding

3.1 Low Rank Parity Check Codes

LRPC codes were introduced in [27]. They are the equivalent of MDPC codes from the Hamming metric. They have a strong decoding power and a weak algebraic structure, therefore they are well suited codes for cryptography.

Definition 4 (LRPC codes). *Let* $\boldsymbol{H} = (h_{ij})_{\substack{1 \leqslant i \leqslant n-k \\ 1 \leqslant j \leqslant n}} \in \mathbb{F}_{q^m}^{(n-k) \times n}$ *be a full-rank matrix such that its coordinates generate an* $\mathbb{F}_q$-*subspace* $F = \langle h_{ij} \rangle_{\mathbb{F}_q}$ *of small dimension* d.

Let $\mathcal{C}$ *be the code with parity-check matrix* $\boldsymbol{H}$. *By definition,* $\mathcal{C}$ *is an* $[n, k]_{q^m}$ *LRPC code of dual weight* d. *Such a matrix* $\boldsymbol{H}$ *is called a homogeneous matrix of weight* d *and support* F.

We can now define ideal LRPC codes similarly to our definition of ideal codes.

Definition 5 (Ideal LRPC codes). *An ideal LRPC code of dual weight* d *is an ideal* $[2k, k]_{q^m}$ *code whose parity matrix* $\boldsymbol{H}$ *is an ideal matrix generated by two polynomials* $(\boldsymbol{h}_1, \boldsymbol{h}_2) \in (F^k)^2$ *with* F *a subspace of* $\mathbb{F}_{q^m}$ *of dimension* d.

3.2 A Basic Decoding Algorithm

Problem 4 (Decoding LRPC codes). Given $\boldsymbol{H} = (h_{ij})_{\substack{1 \leqslant i \leqslant n-k \\ 1 \leqslant j \leqslant n}} \in \mathbb{F}_{q^m}^{(n-k) \times n}$ a parity-check matrix of an LRPC code such that $h_{ij} \in F$ a subspace of $\mathbb{F}_{q^m}$ of dimension d, a syndrome $\boldsymbol{s} \in \mathbb{F}_{q^m}^{n-k}$, and an integer r, the problem is to find a subspace E of dimension at most r such that there exists $\boldsymbol{e} \in E^n$, $\boldsymbol{H}\boldsymbol{e}^{\mathsf{T}} = \boldsymbol{s}^{\mathsf{T}}$.

Traditionally the decoding operation consists in finding not only the error support E but also the exact vector e. However, in that case it is only a trivial algebraic computation to find the vector e when E is known, that is why we confuse both.

We denote by EF the subspace generated by the product of the elements of E and F:

$$EF = \langle \{ef, e \in E, f \in F\}\rangle$$

In the typical case $\dim EF = rd$. For the considered parameters, it can happen that $\dim EF < rd$, but this case is also covered without modification.

A basic decoding algorithm is described in Algorithm 1. In the case where the syndrome s is indeed generated by He^T where e is in a support E, the coordinates of s are in a product space EF. The general idea of the algorithm is to use the fact that we know a parity-check matrix H of the LRPC code such that each of its coordinates h_{ij} belongs to an $\mathbb{F}_q$-subspace F of $\mathbb{F}_{q^m}$ of small dimension d, hence the subspace $S = \langle s_1, \ldots, s_{n-k} \rangle$ generated by the coordinates of the syndrome enables one to recover the whole product space EF. The knowledge of both EF and F enables to recover E. This approach is very similar to the classical decoding procedure of BCH codes for instance, where one recovers the error-locator polynomial, which gives the support of the error.

Algorithm 1: Rank Support Recovery (RSR) algorithm

Data: $F = \langle f_1, \ldots, f_d \rangle$ an $\mathbb{F}_q$-subspace of $\mathbb{F}_{q^m}$,

   $s = (s_1, \cdots, s_{n-k}) \in \mathbb{F}_{q^m}^{(n-k)}$ a syndrome of an error e of weight r
   and of support E

Result: A candidate for the vector space E

//Part 1: Compute the vector space EF

1 Compute $S = \langle s_1, \cdots, s_{n-k} \rangle$

//Part 2: Recover the vector space E

2 $E \leftarrow \bigcap_{i=1}^{d} f_i^{-1} S$

3 **return** E

Notation. For all i we denote S_i the space $f_i^{-1}S$.

Probability of Failure. There are two cases for which the decoding algorithm can fail:

- $S \subsetneq EF$, the syndrome coordinates do not generate the entire space EF, or
- $E \subsetneq S_1 \cap \cdots \cap S_d$, the chain of intersections generates a space of larger dimension than E.

From [10] we have that the probability of the first failure case $S \subsetneq EF$ is less than $q^{rd-(n-k)-1}$. In [8], under the assumption that the S_i behave as random subspaces containing E (which is validated by simulations), it is proven that the probability of the second failure case $E \subsetneq S_1 \cap \cdots \cap S_d$ is less than $q^{-(d-1)(m-rd-r)}$. This leads to the following proposition from [8]:

Proposition 1. *The Decoding Failure Rate of Algorithm 1 is bounded from above by:*

$$q^{-(d-1)(m-rd-r)} + q^{rd-(n-k)-1}$$

Computational Cost of Decoding. According to [10], the computational cost of the decoding algorithm is in $\mathcal{O}(4r^2d^2m + n^2r)$ operations in the base field $\mathbb{F}_q$.

There is an improved version of this decoding algorithm which was presented in [10]. However, we do not need these improvements in the present document.

3.3 LRPC Codes Indistinguishability

LRPC codes are easy to hide since we only need to reveal their systematic parity-check matrix. Due to their weak algebraic structure, it is hard to distinguish an LRPC code in its systematic form and a random systematic matrix. We can now introduce formally this problem, on which LRPC cryptosystems, and thus ours, are based.

Problem 5 (LRPC codes decisional problem - LRPC). Given a matrix $\boldsymbol{H} \in \mathbb{F}_{q^m}^{(n-k) \times k}$, distinguish whether the code $\mathcal{C}$ with the parity-check matrix $(\boldsymbol{I}_{n-k} | \boldsymbol{H})$ is a random code or an LRPC code of weight d.

The problem can also be stated as: distinguish whether $\boldsymbol{H}$ was sampled uniformly at random or as $\boldsymbol{A}^{-1}\boldsymbol{B}$ where the matrices $\boldsymbol{A}$ (of size $n - k \times n - k$) and $\boldsymbol{B}$ (of size $n - k \times k$) have the same support of small dimension d. The structured variant of the above problem follows immediately.

Problem 6 (Ideal LRPC codes decisional problem - ILRPC). Given a polynomial $P \in \mathbb{F}_q[X]$ of degree n and a vector $\boldsymbol{h} \in \mathbb{F}_{q^m}^n$, distinguish whether the ideal code $\mathcal{C}$ with the parity-check matrix generated by $\boldsymbol{h}$ and P is a random ideal code or an ideal LRPC code of weight d.

Again, the problem can also be stated as: distinguish whether $\boldsymbol{h}$ was sampled uniformly at random or as $\boldsymbol{x}^{-1}\boldsymbol{y} \bmod P$ where the vectors $\boldsymbol{x}$ and $\boldsymbol{y}$ have the same support of small dimension d.

The hardness of these decisional problems is presented in Sect. 5.

4 LRPC with Multiple Syndromes

4.1 General Idea

The decoding algorithm presented in the previous section has a probability of failure whose main component is $q^{rd-(n-k)-1}$ (see Proposition 1) so it forces one to have a large n in an LRPC-cryptosystem in order to obtain a DFR below 2^{-128}. To overcome this constraint, we made the observation that when several syndromes with same error support $(\boldsymbol{s}_1, ..., \boldsymbol{s}_\ell)$ were used in the decoding algorithm, the DFR was decreasing. This fact is the cornerstone of our new cryptosystem. We describe below the associated decoding problem.

Problem 7 (Decoding LRPC codes with mutliple syndromes). Given $\boldsymbol{H} \in \mathbb{F}_{q^m}^{(n-k) \times n}$ a parity-check matrix of an LRPC code of dimension d and support $F \subset \mathbb{F}_{q^m}$, a set of ℓ syndromes $\boldsymbol{s}_i \in \mathbb{F}_{q^m}^{n-k}$ for $1 \leqslant i \leqslant \ell$, and an integer r, the problem is to find a subspace E of dimension at most r such that there exists an error matrix $\boldsymbol{V} \in E^{n \times \ell}$ satisfying $\boldsymbol{HV} = \boldsymbol{S}$ where the i-th column of $\boldsymbol{S}$ is equal to $\boldsymbol{s}_i^{\mathsf{T}}$.

In order to solve this decoding problem, we introduce the Rank Support Recovery algorithm with multiple syndromes (Algorithm 2). It is exactly the same as Algorithm 1, but several columns are given to compute the syndrome space S. Intuitively, because the syndrome matrix $\boldsymbol{HV}$ has $(n-k) \times \ell$ coordinates inside the space EF of dimension rd, we would expect the Decoding Failure Rate of this new algorithm to be approximately $q^{rd-(n-k)\ell}$. Actually, because the coordinates of $\boldsymbol{HV}$ are not independent between each other, the result is not trivially established and requires technical lemmas which are presented in Appendix A.

Algorithm 2: Rank Support Recovery (RSR) algorithm with multiple syndromes

---

   Data: $F = \langle f_1, ..., f_d \rangle$ an $\mathbb{F}_q$-subspace of $\mathbb{F}_{q^m}$, $\boldsymbol{S} = (s_{ij}) \in \mathbb{F}_{q^m}^{(n-k) \times \ell}$ the ℓ
       syndromes of error vectors of weight r and support E
   Result: A candidate for the vector space E
   //Part 1: Compute the vector space EF
1 Compute $S = \langle s_{11}, \cdots, s_{(n-k)\ell} \rangle$
   //Part 2: Recover the vector space E
2 $E \leftarrow \bigcap_{i=1}^{d} f_i^{-1} S$
3 **return** E

In the following subsection, we describe our new scheme and its ideal variant, then study the Decoding Failure Rate.

4.2   Description of the Scheme (LRPC-MS)

Definition 6. *A Key Encapsulation Mechanism KEM = (KeyGen, Encap, Decap) is a triple of probabilistic algorithms together with a key space $\mathcal{K}$. The key generation algorithm KeyGen generates a pair of public and secret keys (pk, sk). The encapsulation algorithm Encap uses the public key pk to produce an encapsulation c and a key $K \in \mathcal{K}$. Finally Decap, using the secret key sk and an encapsulation c, recovers the key $K \in \mathcal{K}$, or fails and returns $\perp$.*

Our scheme contains a hash function G modeled as a random oracle.

– KeyGen(1^λ):
   • choose uniformly at random a subspace F of $\mathbb{F}_{q^m}$ of dimension d and sample an couple of homogeneous matrices of same support $U = (A|B) \xleftarrow{\$} F^{(n-k) \times (n-k)} \times F^{(n-k) \times k}$ such that A is invertible.
   • compute $\boldsymbol{H} = (\boldsymbol{I}_{n-k} | \boldsymbol{A}^{-1}\boldsymbol{B})$.

- define pk $= \boldsymbol{H}$ and sk $= (\boldsymbol{F}, \boldsymbol{A})$.
- Encap(pk):
  - choose uniformly at random a subspace E of $\mathbb{F}_{q^m}$ of dimension r and sample a matrix $\boldsymbol{V} \xleftarrow{\$} E^{n \times \ell}$.
  - compute $\boldsymbol{C} = \boldsymbol{H}\boldsymbol{V}$.
  - define $K = G(E)$ and return $\boldsymbol{C}$.
- Decap(sk):
  - compute $\boldsymbol{S} = \boldsymbol{A}\boldsymbol{C} \ (= \boldsymbol{U}\boldsymbol{V})$
  - recover $E \leftarrow \mathsf{RSR}(F, \boldsymbol{S}, r)$ (Algorithm 2).
  - return $K = G(E)$ or $\perp$ (if RSR failed).

We need to have a common representation of a subspace of dimension r of $\mathbb{F}_{q^m}$. The natural way is to choose the unique matrix $\boldsymbol{M} \in \mathbb{F}_q^{r \times m}$ of size $r \times m$ in its reduced row echelon form such that the rows of $\boldsymbol{M}$ are a basis of E.

An informal description of this scheme can be found in Fig. 1. We deal with the semantic security of the KEM in Sect. 5.

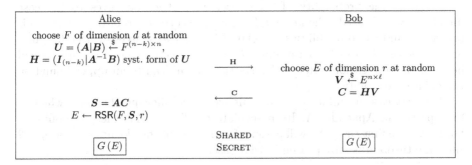

Fig. 1. Informal description of our new key encapsulation mechanism LRPC-MS. $\boldsymbol{H}$ constitutes the public key.

4.3 Description of the Scheme with Ideal Structure (ILRPC-MS)

An informal description of this scheme is found in Fig. 2. As for the non-ideal scheme, we deal with the semantic security of the KEM in Sect. 5.

4.4 Decoding Failure Rate of Our Scheme

The Decoding Failure Rate (DFR) of our scheme is the probability of failure of the Rank Support Recovery algorithm with multiple syndromes described in Algorithm 2. As stated in Sect. 3.2, the two cases that can provoke a failure of the algorithm are:

- $S \subsetneq EF$, the coordinates of the matrix $\boldsymbol{U}\boldsymbol{V}$ do not generate the entire space EF, or

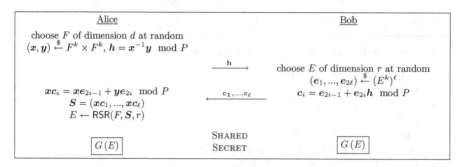

Fig. 2. Informal description of our new key encapsulation mechanism with ideal structure ILRPC-MS. h constitutes the public key.

- $E \subsetneq S_1 \cap \cdots \cap S_d$, the chain of intersections generate a space of larger dimension than E.

To study the probability of each case, we restrict ourselves to the case $\dim(EF) = rd$. Indeed, when $\dim(EF) < rd$, the correctness of the algorithm is preserved, and the probabilities associated to the two sources of decoding failures are lower than in the case $\dim(EF) = rd$, since all the vector spaces will be of smaller dimensions. Hence this restriction will lead to an upper bound on the failure probability.

The first case of failure can be dealt with the following theorem, which is fully proven in Appendix A. Its immediate corollary yields the probability of failure for the first case. We will assume for the rest of this document that $q = 2$ since the theorem is only proven in that case.

Theorem 1. *For $q = 2$, $n_1 + n_2 \leq n$ and for U and V random variables chosen uniformly in $F^{n_1 \times n}$ and $E^{n \times n_2}$ respectively, $\mathbb{P}(\mathrm{Supp}\,(UV) \neq EF) \leq (n_1 + 1)q^{rd - n_1 n_2}$*

Corollary 1. *For $q = 2$, $k \geq \ell$ and for U and V random variables chosen uniformly in $F^{(n-k) \times n}$ and $E^{n \times \ell}$ respectively, the probability that the syndrome space S computed by the algorithm $\mathsf{RSR}(F, UV, r)$ is not equal to EF is bounded by above by $(n - k + 1)q^{rd - (n-k)\ell}$*

As for the second failure case, $E \subsetneq S_1 \cap \cdots \cap S_d$, we apply again the upper-bound $q^{-(d-1)(m-rd-r)}$, used in Sect. 3 for Proposition 1. This leads to the following proposition:

Proposition 2. *For $q = 2$, $k \geq \ell$ and for U and V random variables chosen uniformly in $F^{(n-k) \times n}$ and $E^{n \times \ell}$ respectively, the Decoding Failure Rate of Algorithm 2 $\mathsf{RSR}(F, UV, r)$ is bounded from above by:*

$$q^{-(d-1)(m-rd-r)} + (n - k + 1)q^{rd - (n-k)\ell}$$

This proposition extends immediately to the ideal case without modifications.

4.5 Impact on the Asymptotic Range of Parameters

By reducing the decoding failure rate, the multiple syndrome approach fundamentally changes the zone of parameters that we consider for our cryptosystem.

In previous LRPC code-based cryptosystems, the decoding failure rate imposed the choice of r and d to be below $\sqrt{n}$ because of the need for $rd < n-k$ (cf. Proposition 1).

In this work, we can choose r and d bigger than $\sqrt{n}$. To simplify the rest of the analysis we will consider half-rate codes only, for which $k = n/2$. We will show that it is even asymptotically possible to choose r and d on the rank Gilbert-Varshamov bound d_{RGV}.

The DFR formula leads to the choice of a large ℓ such that when m and n tend to infinity, $rd = n\ell/2 + o(1)$. Because we chose $r = d = d_{RGV}$, we get

$$\ell \sim \frac{2d_{RGV}^2}{n}$$

When applying the asymptotic formula of d_{RGV} ([9], §2.4) to the case $k = n/2$, we get $d_{RGV} \le n/2$. As a result, we obtain that ℓ is asymptotically upper bounded by $d_{RGV} = r$. To the best of our knowledge, the range where $\ell \le r$ is a hard parameter range for which the RSL problem has no known polynomial attacks. In practice, for the parameters considered at the end of this document, when choosing r and d on the Gilbert-Varshamov bound, ℓ has to be chosen slightly greater than r and the RSL problem is still in a difficult zone.

The fact that we can choose r and d on the rank Gilbert-Varshamov bound has two major implications:

- Algebraic attacks against the RSD problem are more difficult when r gets closer to d_{RGV}.
- The secret parity check matrix U is homogeneous of weight d_{RGV} so the minimal distance of the dual of the resulting LRPC code is about d_{RGV}, just like a random code. It gives more confidence in the indistinguishably of the public matrix H (LRPC problem).

Our proposal is the only code-based cryptosystem with structural masking that has such an interesting property for the distinguishing problem.

5 Security

5.1 Definitions

We define the IND-CPA-security of a KEM formally via the following experiment, where Encap_0 returns a valid pair c^*, K^*, and Encap_1 returns a valid c^* and a random K^*.

Indistinguishability under Chosen Plaintext Attack: This notion states that an adversary should not be able to efficiently guess which key is encapsulated.

$$\begin{array}{|l|}
\hline
\mathbf{Exp}_{\mathcal{E},\mathcal{A}}^{ind-b}(\lambda) \\
\hline
\text{1. param} \leftarrow \mathsf{Setup}(1^{\lambda}) \\
\text{2. } (\mathsf{pk},\mathsf{sk}) \leftarrow \mathsf{KeyGen}(\mathsf{param}) \\
\text{3. } (c^*, K^*) \leftarrow \mathsf{Encap}_b(\mathsf{pk}) \\
\text{4. } b' \leftarrow \mathcal{A}(\mathrm{GUESS} : c^*, K^*) \\
\text{5. RETURN } b' \\
\hline
\end{array}$$

Definition 7 (IND-CPA Security). *A key encapsulation scheme KEM is* IND-CPA-*secure if for every PPT (probabilistic polynomial time) adversary $\mathcal{A}$, we have that*

$$\mathsf{Adv}_{\mathsf{KEM}}^{indcpa}(\mathcal{A}) := |\Pr[\text{IND-CPA}_{\mathsf{real}}^{\mathcal{A}} \Rightarrow 1] - \Pr[\text{IND-CPA}_{\mathsf{rand}}^{\mathcal{A}} \Rightarrow 1]|$$

is negligible.

5.2 IND-CPA Proof

Unstructured LRPC-MS

Theorem 2. *Under the hardness of the LRPC (Problem 5) and $DRSL_{k,n,r,\ell}$ (Problem 3) problems, the KEM presented in Sect. 4.2 is indistinguishable against Chosen Plaintext Attack in the Random Oracle Model.*

Proof. We are going to proceed in a sequence of games. The simulator first starts from the real scheme. First we replace the public key matrix by a random matrix, and then we use the ROM to solve Rank Support Learning.

We start from the normal game G_0: We generate the public key $\boldsymbol{H}$ honestly, as well as $\boldsymbol{E}$, and $\boldsymbol{C}$.

- In game G_1, we now replace $\boldsymbol{H}$ by a random matrix, the rest is identical to the previous game. From an adversary point of view, the only difference is the distribution of $\boldsymbol{H}$, which is either generated at random, or the systematic form of a low weight parity matrix. This is exactly the *LRPC codes decisional* problem, hence

$$\mathsf{Adv}_{\mathcal{A}}^{G_0} \leq \mathsf{Adv}_{\mathcal{A}}^{G_1} + \mathsf{Adv}_{\mathcal{A}}^{\mathsf{LRPC}}.$$

- In game G_2, we now proceed as earlier except we receive $\boldsymbol{H}, \boldsymbol{C}$ from a Rank Support Learning challenger. After sending $\boldsymbol{C}$ to the adversary, we monitor the adversary queries to the Random Oracle, and pick a random one that we forward as our simulator answer to the $DRSL_{k,n,r,\ell}$ problem. Either the adversary was able to predict the random oracle output, or with probably $1/q_G$, we picked the query associated with the support E (by q_G we denote the number of queries to the random oracle G), hence

$$\mathsf{Adv}_{\mathcal{A}}^{G_1} \leq 2^{-\lambda} + 1/q_G \cdot \mathsf{Adv}_{\mathcal{A}}^{\mathsf{DRSL}}$$

which leads to the conclusion.

Ideal LRPC-MS. For the ideal version of our scheme, the security proof is exactly the same except that ideal versions of hard problems appear. The IND-CPA property follows immediately.

Theorem 3. *Under the hardness of problems ILRPC and DIRSL$_{k,n,r,\ell}$, the KEM presented in Sect. 4.2 is indistinguishable against Chosen Plaintext Attack in the Random Oracle Model.*

The maximal value of ℓ for which DIRSL$_{k,n,r,\ell}$ is hard is way lower than its non-ideal counterpart. Indeed, a single ideal syndrome can be expanded in k traditional syndromes by performing ideal rotations. That is why the value of ℓ is lower in the parameter sets for the ideal version.

5.3   Known Attacks

As an RSL challenge is an RSD challenge with multiple syndromes, it is possible to try to solve RSL in two ways, either one takes only one syndrome to build an RSD challenge and attacks RSD, or one attacks RSL with all the information in the challenge. In order to define the parameter sets for our schemes we therefore have to consider the best attacks against both RSD and RSL. At last we recall a specific attack against the LRPC problem.

There are two main types of attacks for solving the generic RSD problem: combinatorial attacks and algebraic attacks. For cryptographic parameters the best attacks are usually the recent algebraic attacks, but it may also depend on parameters, sometimes combinatorial attacks can be better.

Combinatorial Attacks Against RSD. The best combinatorial attacks for solving the RSD problem on a random $[n, k]$ code over $\mathbb{F}_{q^m}$ for a rank weight d as described in [7] have complexity (for ω the linear algebra exponent):

$$\min((n - k)^{\omega} m^{\omega} q^{(d-1)(k+1)}, (km)^{\omega} q^{d\lceil \frac{km}{n} \rceil - m}) \tag{1}$$

The first term of the min typically corresponds to the case where $m \geq n$, the second term corresponds to the case where $m \leq n$, but still it can happen that this term is better than the first one, when $m \geq n$ but close to n. A detailed description of the complexity of the second term is given in [7].

Algebraic Attacks Against RSD. The general idea of algebraic attacks is to rewrite an RSD instance as a system of multivariate polynomial equations and to find a solution to this system.

For a long time, algebraic attacks were less efficient than combinatorial ones. Recent results improved the understanding of these attacks. The best algebraic attacks against RSD can be found in [15] and have complexity (for ω the linear algebra exponent):

$$q^{ar} m \binom{n - k - 1}{r} \binom{n - a}{r}^{\omega - 1} \tag{2}$$

operations in $\mathbb{F}_q$. a is defined as the smallest integer such that the condition $m\binom{n-k-1}{r} \geq \binom{n-a}{r} - 1$ is fulfilled.

On the Security of the RSL Problem. The difficulty of solving an instance of the $\mathsf{RSL}_{n,k,r,N}$ problem depends on the number N of samples. Clearly, for $N = 1$, the RSL problem is exactly the RSD problem with parameters (n, k, r), which is probabilistically reduced to the NP-hard syndrome decoding problem in the Hamming metric in [29]. When $N \geqslant nr$, the RSL problem is reduced to linear algebra, as stated in [26] where this problem was first introduced.

This raises the question of the security of the RSL problem in the case $1 < N < nr$. In [26] the authors relate this problem to the one of finding a codeword of rank r in a code of same length and dimension containing q^N words of this weight, and conjecture that the complexity of finding such a codeword gets reduced by at most a factor q^N compared to the case $N = 1$. They also observe that in practice, the complexity gain seems lower, likely due to the fact that said codewords are deeply correlated.

There have been recent improvements on the complexity of the RSL problem. In [19] the authors show that the condition $N \leqslant kr$ should be met in order to avoid a subexponential attack. We chose our parameters to fulfill this condition.

In [13], the authors propose to solve the RSL problem in the case $N \leq kr$ using an algebraic approach. Our parameters – in particular the number ℓ of syndromes – are chosen so as to resist these recent algebraic attacks.

On the Security of the LRPC Problem. Given $\boldsymbol{H} \in \mathbb{F}_{q^m}^{(n-k) \times k}$ such that $(\boldsymbol{I}_{n-k} | \boldsymbol{H})$ is the parity-check matrix of a code $\mathcal{C}$, the problem of distinguishing LRPC codes is to decide whether $\mathcal{C}$ is a random code or an LRPC code.

The best known attack against this problem for almost ten years [28] consists in using the underlying homogeneous structure of the LRPC code to find a codeword of weight d in a $[n - \lfloor \frac{n-k}{d} \rfloor, n - k - \lfloor \frac{n-k}{d} \rfloor]_{q^m}$ subcode $\mathcal{C}'$ of the dual code $\mathcal{C}^{\perp}$ generated by $(\boldsymbol{I}_{n-k} | \boldsymbol{H})$ rather than a codeword of weight d in the $\mathcal{C}^{\perp}$ $[n, n - k]$ code. Then one can consider the previously described algebraic or combinatorial attacks for this slightly smaller code (but for the same weight d).

6 Parameters

Choice of Parameters. In Sect. 5, the security of the protocol is reduced to the LRPC and DRSL problems (or their ideal variants). The best known attacks on these problems are thus used to define our parameters. We also chose our parameters in order to have the Decoding Failure Rate (DFR) below or very close to $2^{-\lambda}$, where λ is the security parameter, using Proposition 2. We only considered parameters with $k \geq \ell$ as required by these propositions.

Size of Parameters. One may use seeds to represent the random data in order to decrease the keysize. We use the NIST seed expander with 40 bytes long seeds.

The public key pk is composed of a matrix of size $(n - k) \times n$ in a systematic form, so its size is $\lceil \frac{k(n-k)m}{8} \rceil$ bytes. The size is reduced to $\lceil \frac{(n-k)m}{8} \rceil$ bytes in the ideal case. The secret key sk is composed of two random matrices that can be generated from a seed, so its size is 40 bytes. The ciphertext ct is composed of a matrix of size $(n - k) \times \ell$, so its size is $\left\lceil \frac{(n-k)\ell m}{8} \right\rceil$ bytes. The shared secret ss is composed of $K = G(E)$, so its size is 64 bytes.

Parameters are given in Table 1. The "structure" column indicates whether this parameter uses unstructured (random) matrices or ideal ones. The number indicated in the "DFR" column is actually $-\log_2(\text{DFR})$.

Table 1. Parameters for our unstructured and ideal LRPC-MS cryptosystem. The security is expressed in bits and sizes are expressed in bytes.

Instance	Structure	q	n	k	m	r	d	ℓ	Security	DFR	pk size	ct size	pk + ct
LRPC-MS-128	Random	2	34	17	113	9	10	13	128	126	4,083	3,122	7,205
LRPC-MS-192	Random	2	42	21	151	11	11	15	192	190	8,324	5,946	14,270
ILRPC-MS-128	Ideal	2	94	47	83	7	8	4	128	126	488	1,951	2,439
ILRPC-MS-192	Ideal	2	188	89	109	9	8	3	192	189	1,213	3,638	4,851

Comparison with Other Unstructured Cryptosystems. We compare our cryptosystem to other structured and unstructured proposals. Our comparison metric is the usual TLS-oriented communication size (public key + ciphertext).

For Loong.CCAKEM [38], we consider only the third set of parameters since the other sets of parameters have an error weight below 6 and thus are vulnerable to algebraic attacks. For Loidreau cryptosystem, we consider the parameters presented in the conclusion of [34] which take into account the recent improvements on algebraic attacks. For both cryptosystems mentioned in this paragraph, parameters were not available (N/A) for 192 bits of security (Table 2).

Table 2. Comparison of sizes of unstructured KEMs (left table) and structured code-based KEMs (right table). The sizes represent the sum of public key and ciphertext expressed in bytes.

Instance	128 bits	192 bits
LRPC-MS	7,205	14,270
Loong.CCAKEM-III	18,522	N/A
FrodoKEM	19,336	31,376
Loidreau cryptosystem	36,300	N/A
Classic McEliece	261,248	524,348

Instance	128 bits	192 bits
ILRPC-MS	2,439	4,851
BIKE	3,113	6,197
HQC	6,730	13,548

Performance. Indicative performance measurements of an implementation of some of the LRPC-MS cryptosystem parameters are given in Appendix B.

7   Conclusion and Future Work

We provided a proof that, using multiple syndromes on rank-metric key encapsulation mechanisms, it is possible to obtain unexpectedly low decoding failure rates with efficient parameters. As a result, it is possible to obtain KEMs with small ciphertext and public key sizes even without ideal structure. We provide an IND-CPA proof for our scheme, whose security relies on the hardness of the DRSL and LRPC distinguishing problems.

A possible future work could be to provide a state of the art implementation of this scheme both in software and hardware. Another improvement could be to perform algebraic computation to find the right space E even when the RSR algorithm computes a space strictly bigger. This would lead to a gain on the m parameter. Finally, our approach could also be extended to other rank-based cryptosystems that do not assume the hardness of the LRPC distinguishing problem, and only relies on DRSD, such as Ouroboros [20].

Appendix

A   Dimension of the Support of the Product of Homogeneous Matrices

In this section we prove the following theorem, which is required to prove the correctness of the multi-syndrome approach presented in Sect. 4. We fix E and F subspaces of $\mathbb{F}_{q^m}$ of dimension r and d respectively such that EF is of dimension rd. Remember that we have $q = 2$ all along the proof.

Theorem 1. *For $q = 2$, $n_1 + n_2 \leq n$ and for U and V random variables chosen uniformly in $F^{n_1 \times n}$ and $E^{n \times n_2}$ (respectively), $\mathbb{P}(\mathrm{Supp}(UV) \neq EF) \leq (n_1 + 1)q^{rd - n_1 n_2}$*

A first idea which may come to mind when trying to prove this theorem would be to use the Leftover Hash Lemma [31] (LHL) in order to prove that the statistical distribution of UV is ε-close to the uniform statistical distribution on $EF^{n_1 \times n_2}$. However, the total number of different couples (U, V) is equal to $\dim F^{n_1 n} \dim E^{n_2 n} = rd^n r^{n_2} d^{n_1}$ and the number of matrices in $EF^{n_1 \times n_2}$ is $rd^{n_1 n_2}$. In a usual code-based cryptography setting where $n_1 \approx n_2 \approx n/2$ and $r \approx d$, we get that $rd^n r^{n_2} d^{n_1} \ll rd^{n_1 n_2}$ therefore we cannot expect to use the LHL.

At first sight, this is quite an issue, as proving the statement of our theorem without standard statistical arguments can be quite complex, or impossible. The rest of the section presents a five stage proof of the theorem (main body and 4 lemmas), using algebraic arguments. Our approach is to study the distribution of $\phi(UV)$ for a linear form ϕ on EF. We show that the distribution of $\phi(UV)$ is uniform in a subspace of $\mathbb{F}_2^{n_1 \times n_2}$ whose dimension is depending on the rank of ϕ viewed as a tensor in $E \otimes F$ and on a simple condition on matrix U.

A.1 Preliminary Results on Binary Matrices

Lemma 1. *For a uniformly random binary matrix M of size $m \times n$ with $m \leq n$ and for $0 < i \leq m$, $\mathbb{P}(\mathrm{Rank}(M) = m - i) \leq 2^{i(m-n)}$.*

Proof. Let S be a subspace of $\{0,1\}^m$ of dimension $m - i$. The number of such possible subspaces is $\binom{m}{i}_2 \leq 2^{im}$.

For a uniformly random binary $m \times n$ matrix M, since the n columns of M are independent, $\mathbb{P}(\mathrm{Supp}(M) \subset S) = 2^{-in}$. Then:

$$\mathbb{P}(\mathrm{Rank}(M) = m - i) \leq \mathbb{P}(\mathrm{Rank}(M) \leq m - i)$$
$$\leq \mathbb{P}(\bigcup_S \mathrm{Supp}(M) \subset S)$$
$$\leq \sum_S \mathbb{P}(\mathrm{Supp}(M) \subset S)$$
$$\leq 2^{i(m-n)}$$

$\square$

Definition 8. *For $s > 0$, let R_s be the random variable defined as the rank of a uniformly random binary matrix of size $n_1 \times ns$.*

Lemma 2. *For $n_2 > 0$, $\mathbb{E}(2^{-n_2 R_1}) \leq (n_1 + 1)2^{-n_1 n_2}$.*

Proof.

$$\mathbb{E}(2^{-n_2 R_1}) = \sum_{i=0}^{n_1} 2^{-n_2 i} \mathbb{P}(R_1 = i)$$
$$= 2^{-n_1 n_2} \mathbb{P}(R_1 = n_1) + \sum_{i=0}^{n_1 - 1} 2^{-n_2 i} \mathbb{P}(R_1 = i)$$
$$\leq 2^{-n_1 n_2} + \sum_{i=1}^{n_1} 2^{-n_2(n_1 - i)} \mathbb{P}(R_1 = n_1 - i)$$
$$\leq 2^{-n_1 n_2} + \sum_{i=1}^{n_1} 2^{-n_2(n_1 - i)} 2^{i(n_1 - n)} \qquad \text{(Lemma 1)}$$
$$\leq 2^{-n_1 n_2} + \sum_{i=1}^{n_1} 2^{i(n_2 + n_1 - n) - n_1 n_2}$$
$$\leq 2^{-n_1 n_2} + \sum_{i=1}^{n_1} 2^{-n_1 n_2} \qquad (n \geq n_1 + n_2)$$
$$\leq (n_1 + 1)2^{-n_1 n_2}$$

$\square$

Since $R_1 \overset{\mathcal{L}}{\leq} R_s$, we get an immediate corollary.

Corollary 2. *For $n_2 > 0$ and for $s > 0$, $\mathbb{E}(2^{-n_2 R_s}) \leq (n_1 + 1)2^{-n_1 n_2}$.*

A.2 Proof of Theorem 1

We first fix ϕ a non-zero linear form from EF to $\mathbb{F}_q$ and we will study the probabibilty that $\text{Supp}(\boldsymbol{UV}) \subset \ker(\phi)$. For a vector $\boldsymbol{x} = (x_1, ..., x_i) \in (EF)^i$, we will note $\phi(\boldsymbol{x})$ the vector $(\phi(x_1), ..., \phi(x_i))$. We use the similar abuse of notation for $\phi(\boldsymbol{X})$ when $\boldsymbol{X}$ is a matrix.

Let ϕ_b be the non-zero bilinear form

$$\phi_b : E \times F \to \mathbb{F}_2$$
$$(e, f) \mapsto \phi(ef).$$

Let $s = \text{Rank}(\phi_b)$ be the rank of this bilinear form. Then there exists a basis $(e_1, \ldots, e_r)$ of E and a basis $(f_1, \ldots, f_d)$ of F in which the matrix representation of ϕ_b is

$$\begin{pmatrix} \boldsymbol{I}_s & 0 \\ 0 & 0 \end{pmatrix}$$

In the product basis of EF

$$(e_1, \ldots, e_r) \otimes (f_1, \ldots, f_d) = (e_1 f_1, ..., e_1 f_d, e_2 f_1, ..., e_r f_1, ..., e_r f_d)$$

the expression of ϕ is very simple. For $x = \sum_{\substack{1 \le i \le n \\ 1 \le j \le n}} x_{ij} e_i f_j$ we have

$$\phi(x) = \sum_{1 \le i \le s} x_{ii}.$$

Let $\boldsymbol{u} = (u_1, \ldots, u_n)$ be a vector of F^n and consider the map

$$E^n \to \mathbb{F}_2$$
$$\boldsymbol{v} = (v_1, \ldots v_n)^{\mathsf{T}} \mapsto \phi(\boldsymbol{uv}) = \phi(u_1 v_1 + \cdots + u_n v_n).$$

For $i = 1 \ldots n$, write $u_i = \sum_{j=1}^{d} u_{ij} f_j$ the decomposition of u_i along the basis of F $(f_1, \ldots, f_d)$. Similarly write $v_i = \sum_{j=1}^{r} v_{ij} e_j$ the decomposition of v_i along the basis of E $(e_1, \ldots, e_r)$. We clearly have:

$$\phi(\boldsymbol{uv}) = \sum_{\substack{1 \le i \le n \\ 1 \le j \le s}} u_{ij} v_{ij}. \tag{3}$$

Now let $\boldsymbol{U}$ be an $n_1 \times n$ matrix of elements in F. Define $\boldsymbol{U}^s$ to be the $n_1 \times sn$ binary matrix obtained from $\boldsymbol{U}$ by replacing every one of its rows $\boldsymbol{u}$ by its expansion

$$u_{11}, \ldots, u_{1s}, u_{21}, \ldots, u_{2s}, \ldots u_{n1}, \ldots, u_{ns}$$

as defined in (3). It follows that we have:

Lemma 3. *Let* $s = \text{Rank}(\phi_b)$, $\boldsymbol{U}$ *be an* $n_1 \times n$ *matrix of elements in* F *and let* φ_U *be the map*

$$\varphi_U : E^n \to \mathbb{F}_2^{n_1}$$
$$\boldsymbol{v} \mapsto \phi(\boldsymbol{Uv}).$$

The rank of the map φ_U *is equal to the rank of the* $n_1 \times sn$ *binary matrix* $\boldsymbol{U}^s$.

Corollary 3. *For U a random variable chosen uniformly in $F^{n_1 \times n}$, $\mathrm{Rank}(\varphi_U) \overset{\mathcal{L}}{=} R_s$ where s is the rank of ϕ_b.*

Now that we know the probability distribution of the rank of φ_U, we will give a probability on $\mathrm{Supp}(UV)$ depending on this rank.

Lemma 4. *Let U such that the above-defined φ_U is of rank $0 \leq i \leq n_1$. Then for V a random variable chosen uniformly in $E^{n \times n_2}$, $\mathbb{P}(\mathrm{Supp}(UV) \subset \ker(\phi)) \leq q^{-in_2}$*

Proof. Let $H = Im(\varphi_U)$ Let $V = (v_1, ..., v_{n_2})$ the columns of V.
φ_U is a surjective homomorphism of finite abelian groups E^n and H, so according to Theorem 8.5 in [37], for all i, Uv_i is uniformly distributed. Thus because the columns of V are independent, $\phi(UV)$ is uniformly distributed in H^{n_2}.
As a result, because $\mathrm{Supp}(UV) \subset \ker(\phi)$ if and only if $\phi(UV) = 0$, $\mathbb{P}(\mathrm{Supp}(UV) \subset \ker(\phi)) \leq 1/|H^{n_2}| = q^{-in_2}$. $\qquad\square$

Lemma 5. *For a non-null linear form ϕ of EF, $\mathbb{P}(\mathrm{Supp}(UV) \subset \ker(\phi)) \leq \mathbb{E}(2^{-n_2 R_1})$*

Proof. Let $s > 0$ be the rank of ϕ_b.

$$\mathbb{P}(\mathrm{Supp}(UV) \subset \ker(\phi)) = \sum_{i=0}^{n_1} \mathbb{P}(\mathrm{Supp}(UV) \subset \ker(\phi)\,|\, \mathrm{Rank}(\varphi_U) = i)\, \mathbb{P}(\mathrm{Rank}(\varphi_U) = i)$$

$$\leq \sum_{i=0}^{n_1} 2^{-in_2} \mathbb{P}(\mathrm{Rank}(\varphi_U) = i) \qquad \text{(Lemma 4)}$$

$$\leq \mathbb{E}(2^{-n_2\, \mathrm{Rank}(\varphi_U)})$$

$$\leq \mathbb{E}(2^{-n_2 R_s}) \qquad \text{(Corollary 3)}$$

$$\leq \mathbb{E}(2^{-n_2 R_1}) \qquad \text{(Corollary 2)}$$

$\qquad\square$

Proof (of Theorem 1).

$$\mathbb{P}(\mathrm{Supp}(UV) \neq EF) = \mathbb{P}(\bigcup_{\phi \in EF^* \setminus \{0\}} \mathrm{Supp}(UV) \subset \ker(\phi))$$

$$\leq \sum_{\phi \in EF^* \setminus \{0\}} \mathbb{P}(\mathrm{Supp}(UV) \subset \ker(\phi))$$

$$\leq \sum_{\phi \in EF^* \setminus \{0\}} \mathbb{E}(2^{-n_2 R_1}) \qquad \text{(Lemma 5)}$$

$$\leq 2^{rd}\, \mathbb{E}(2^{-n_2 R_1})$$

$$\leq (n_1 + 1) 2^{rd - n_1 n_2} \qquad \text{(Lemma 2)}$$

$\qquad\square$

B   Performance

This section provides indicative performance measurements of an implementation of some of the LRPC-MS cryptosystem parameters. Benchmarks were realized on an Intel® Core™ i7-11850H CPU by averaging 1000 executions (Table 3).

Table 3. Performances of our LRPC-MS cryptosystems in thousands of CPU cycles.

Instance	KeyGen	Encap	Decap
LRPC-MS-128	383	137	3,195
ILRPC-MS-128	214	107	1,213

As for other code-based schemes, the decapsulation algorithm has a higher computational cost than key generation and encapsulation. Note however, that our implementation does not yet benefit from the techniques of [18]. These techniques improved the decapsulation performance by a factor 15 (for 128 bits of security) with respect to the existing (and simpler to adapt) implementations we used as a basis for our benchmarking.

References

1. Aguilar Melchor, C., et al.: HQC. Round 3 Submission to the NIST Post-Quantum Cryptography Call (2021). https://pqc-hqc.org/
2. Aguilar Melchor, C., et al.: Rank quasi cyclic (RQC). First round submission to the NIST post-quantum cryptography call (2017). https://pqc-rqc.org/
3. Alagic, G., et al.: Status report on the second round of the NIST post-quantum cryptography standardization process. US Department of Commerce, NIST (2020)
4. Albrecht, M.R., et al.: Classic McEliece: conservative code-based cryptography. Third round submission to the NIST post-quantum cryptography call (2020). https://classic.mceliece.org/
5. Alkim, E., et al.: FrodoKEM - learning with errors key encapsulation. Third round submission to the NIST post-quantum cryptography call (2021). https://frodokem.org/
6. Aragon, N., et al.: BIKE (2017). https://bikesuite.org/, NIST Round 1 submission for Post-Quantum Cryptography
7. Aragon, N., Gaborit, P., Hauteville, A., Tillich, J.P.: A new algorithm for solving the rank syndrome decoding problem. In: Proceedings of the IEEE ISIT (2018)
8. Aragon, N., et al.: ROLLO (merger of Rank-Ouroboros, LAKE and LOCKER). Second round submission to the NIST post-quantum cryptography call (2019). https://pqc-rollo.org/
9. Aragon, N., Blazy, O., Gaborit, P., Hauteville, A., Zémor, G.: Durandal: a rank metric based signature scheme. In: Ishai, Y., Rijmen, V. (eds.) EUROCRYPT 2019. LNCS, vol. 11478, pp. 728–758. Springer, Cham (2019). https://doi.org/10.1007/978-3-030-17659-4_25

10. Aragon, N., Gaborit, P., Hauteville, A., Ruatta, O., Zémor, G.: Low rank parity check codes: new decoding algorithms and applications to cryptography. IEEE Trans. Inf. Theory **65**(12), 7697–7717 (2019)
11. Avanzi, R., et al.: Crystals-kyber. Third round submission to the NIST post-quantum cryptography call (2021). https://pq-crystals.org/kyber/
12. Barbulescu, R., Gaudry, P., Joux, A., Thomé, E.: A heuristic quasi-polynomial algorithm for discrete logarithm in finite fields of small characteristic. In: Nguyen, P.Q., Oswald, E. (eds.) EUROCRYPT 2014. LNCS, vol. 8441, pp. 1–16. Springer, Heidelberg (2014). https://doi.org/10.1007/978-3-642-55220-5_1
13. Bardet, M., Briaud, P.: An algebraic approach to the rank support learning problem. In: Cheon, J.H., Tillich, J.-P. (eds.) PQCrypto 2021 2021. LNCS, vol. 12841, pp. 442–462. Springer, Cham (2021). https://doi.org/10.1007/978-3-030-81293-5_23
14. Bardet, M., et al.: An algebraic attack on rank metric code-based cryptosystems. In: Canteaut, A., Ishai, Y. (eds.) EUROCRYPT 2020. LNCS, vol. 12107, pp. 64–93. Springer, Cham (2020). https://doi.org/10.1007/978-3-030-45727-3_3
15. Bardet, M., et al.: Improvements of algebraic attacks for solving the rank decoding and MinRank problems. In: Moriai, S., Wang, H. (eds.) ASIACRYPT 2020. LNCS, vol. 12491, pp. 507–536. Springer, Cham (2020). https://doi.org/10.1007/978-3-030-64837-4_17
16. Berger, T., Loidreau, P.: Designing an efficient and secure public-key cryptosystem based on reducible rank codes. In: Canteaut, A., Viswanathan, K. (eds.) INDOCRYPT 2004. LNCS, vol. 3348, pp. 218–229. Springer, Heidelberg (2004). https://doi.org/10.1007/978-3-540-30556-9_18
17. Buss, J.F., Frandsen, G.S., Shallit, J.O.: The computational complexity of some problems of linear algebra. J. Comput. Syst. Sci. **58**(3), 572–596 (1999)
18. Chou, T., Liou, J.H.: A constant-time AVX2 implementation of a variant of ROLLO. IACR Trans. Cryptographic Hardw. Embed. Syst. 152–174 (2022)
19. Debris-Alazard, T., Tillich, J.-P.: Two attacks on rank metric code-based schemes: RankSign and an IBE scheme. In: Peyrin, T., Galbraith, S. (eds.) ASIACRYPT 2018. LNCS, vol. 11272, pp. 62–92. Springer, Cham (2018). https://doi.org/10.1007/978-3-030-03326-2_3
20. Deneuville, J.-C., Gaborit, P., Zémor, G.: Ouroboros: a simple, secure and efficient key exchange protocol based on coding theory. In: Lange, T., Takagi, T. (eds.) PQCrypto 2017. LNCS, vol. 10346, pp. 18–34. Springer, Cham (2017). https://doi.org/10.1007/978-3-319-59879-6_2
21. Elleuch, M., Wachter-Zeh, A., Zeh, A.: A public-key cryptosystem from interleaved Goppa codes. arXiv preprint arXiv:1809.03024 (2018)
22. Faure, C., Loidreau, P.: A new public-key cryptosystem based on the problem of reconstructing p–polynomials. In: Ytrehus, Ø. (ed.) WCC 2005. LNCS, vol. 3969, pp. 304–315. Springer, Heidelberg (2006). https://doi.org/10.1007/11779360_24
23. Gabidulin, E.M.: Theory of codes with maximum rank distance. Problemy Peredachi Informatsii **21**(1), 3–16 (1985)
24. Gabidulin, E.M.: Attacks and counter-attacks on the GPT public key cryptosystem. Des. Codes Cryptogr. **48**(2), 171–177 (2008)
25. Gabidulin, E.M., Paramonov, A.V., Tretjakov, O.V.: Ideals over a non-commutative ring and their application in cryptology. In: Davies, D.W. (ed.) EUROCRYPT 1991. LNCS, vol. 547, pp. 482–489. Springer, Heidelberg (1991). https://doi.org/10.1007/3-540-46416-6_41

26. Gaborit, P., Hauteville, A., Phan, D.H., Tillich, J.-P.: Identity-based encryption from codes with rank metric. In: Katz, J., Shacham, H. (eds.) CRYPTO 2017. LNCS, vol. 10403, pp. 194–224. Springer, Cham (2017). https://doi.org/10.1007/978-3-319-63697-9_7

27. Gaborit, P., Murat, G., Ruatta, O., Zémor, G.: Low rank parity check codes and their application to cryptography. In: Proceedings of the Workshop on Coding and Cryptography WCC, vol. 2013 (2013)

28. Gaborit, P., Ruatta, O., Schrek, J., Zémor, G.: New results for rank-based cryptography. In: Pointcheval, D., Vergnaud, D. (eds.) AFRICACRYPT 2014. LNCS, vol. 8469, pp. 1–12. Springer, Cham (2014). https://doi.org/10.1007/978-3-319-06734-6_1

29. Gaborit, P., Zémor, G.: On the hardness of the decoding and the minimum distance problems for rank codes. IEEE Trans. Inform. Theory **62**(12), 7245–7252 (2016)

30. Hoffstein, J., Pipher, J., Silverman, J.H.: NTRU: a ring-based public key cryptosystem. In: Buhler, J.P. (ed.) ANTS 1998. LNCS, vol. 1423, pp. 267–288. Springer, Heidelberg (1998). https://doi.org/10.1007/BFb0054868

31. Impagliazzo, R., Levin, L.A., Luby, M.: Pseudo-random generation from one-way functions. In: Proceedings of the Twenty-First Annual ACM Symposium on Theory of Computing, pp. 12–24 (1989)

32. Legeay, M.: Permutation decoding: towards an approach using algebraic properties of the σ-subcode. In: Augot, D., Canteaut, A. (eds.) WCC 2011, pp. 193–202 (2011)

33. Overbeck, R.: Structural attacks for public key cryptosystems based on Gabidulin codes. J. Cryptol. **21**(2), 280–301 (2008)

34. Pham, B.D.: Étude et conception de nouvelles primitives de chiffrement fondées sur les codes correcteurs d'erreurs en métrique rang. Ph.D. thesis, Rennes 1 (2021)

35. Renner, J., Jerkovits, T., Bartz, H.: Efficient decoding of interleaved low-rank parity-check codes. In: 2019 XVI International Symposium Problems of Redundancy in Information and Control Systems (REDUNDANCY), pp. 121–126. IEEE (2019)

36. Renner, J., Puchinger, S., Wachter-Zeh, A.: Interleaving Loidreau's rank-metric cryptosystem. In: 2019 XVI International Symposium Problems of Redundancy in Information and Control Systems (REDUNDANCY), pp. 127–132. IEEE (2019)

37. Shoup, V.: A Computational Introduction to Number Theory and Algebra. Cambridge University Press, Cambridge (2009)

38. Wang, L.P.: Loong: a new IND-CCA-secure code-based KEM. In: 2019 IEEE International Symposium on Information Theory (ISIT), pp. 2584–2588. IEEE (2019)

Interleaved Prange: A New Generic Decoder for Interleaved Codes

Anmoal Porwal, Lukas Holzbaur, Hedongliang Liu, Julian Renner, Antonia Wachter-Zeh, and Violetta Weger[(✉)]

Institute for Communications Engineering, Technical University of Munich, Munich, Germany
{anmoal.porwal,lukas.holzbaur,lia.liu,julian.renner, antonia.wachter-zeh,violetta.weger}@tum.de

Abstract. Due to the recent challenges in post-quantum cryptography, several new approaches for code-based cryptography have been proposed. For example, a variant of the McEliece cryptosystem based on interleaved codes was proposed. In order to deem such new settings secure, we first need to understand and analyze the complexity of the underlying problem, in this case the problem of decoding a random interleaved code. A simple approach to decode such codes, would be to randomly choose a vector in the row span of the received matrix and run a classical information set decoding algorithm on this erroneous codeword. In this paper, we propose a new generic decoder for interleaved codes, which is an adaption of the classical idea of information set decoding by Prange and perfectly fits the interleaved setting. We then analyze the cost of the new algorithm and compare it to the other approaches.

Keywords: Information set decoding · Interleaved codes · Code-based cryptography

1 Introduction

Code-based cryptography is one of the most promising and prominent candidates for post-quantum cryptography, which is reflected in the NIST standardization process [7]. Although the third round of submissions has already been completed, and the classical McEliece system [3] has been chosen as a finalist, there are still many open challenges in the area. For example the search for efficient and secure signature schemes [17], but also the compelling task of reducing the key sizes of the original McEliece system. For this reason, researchers have proposed several alternatives to the classical scheme of McEliece, not only by changing the underlying code family, but also by considering different settings, for example by employing the rank metric [1,2], the Lee metric [6,12,24] or by using interleaved codes. The latter approach has been proposed in [8,11,20]. The simple reasoning behind this proposal is that an interleaved code has a larger error-correction capability than a non-interleaved code.

A codeword of an ℓ-interleaved code is an $\ell \times n$ matrix over $\mathbb{F}_q$, where each row is a codeword of a constituent linear code of blocklength n over $\mathbb{F}_q$. In this work,

© The Author(s), under exclusive license to Springer Nature Switzerland AG 2022
J. H. Cheon and T. Johansson (Eds.): PQCrypto 2022, LNCS 13512, pp. 69–88, 2022.
https://doi.org/10.1007/978-3-031-17234-2_4

we consider the decoding problem for *homogeneous* interleaved codes, where the same constituent code is used for all the rows.

An interleaved code $\mathcal{C}_\ell$ is especially well-suited for channels that are prone to burst errors, where t burst errors can be modeled as the addition of an $\ell \times n$ matrix $\mathbf{E}$ with t non-zero columns to a codeword in $\mathcal{C}_\ell$. In this case, we say that $\mathbf{E}$ has column weight t.

A generic decoder for any linear interleaved code was proposed in [9,16]. When the interleaving order ℓ is at least the number of column errors t, this decoder guarantees to correct (efficiently) any full-rank error of column weight up to $d - 2$, where d is the minimum distance of the constituent code. This decoder was generalized in [10,21] and guarantees to decode any error $\mathbf{E}$ of column weight t if $2t - \mathrm{rk}(\mathbf{E}) \leq d - 2$ and does so with low complexity of $t - \mathrm{rk}(\mathbf{E})$ is small. However, there is no known efficient decoder for interleaved codes with an arbitrary constituent code when $\ell \ll t$. In fact, it can be shown that the corresponding decisional problem, called Interleaved Decoding (ID) problem, is at least as hard as the decisional Syndrome Decoding (SD) problem.

This fact implies that interleaved codes are a well-suited alternative for code-based cryptography. It is therefore of interest to understand and analyze the complexity of decoding a generic interleaved code not only from a coding-theoretic perspective, but also in order to assess the security of code-based cryptosystems based on interleaved codes.

In this paper, we consider algorithms for the ID problem when $\ell \ll t < d$ for arbitrary linear constituent codes. We can categorize the generic decoding algorithms for interleaved codes into three types:

1. Algorithms that reduce the problem to the classical SD problem.
2. Algorithms that reduce the problem to a low-weight codeword finding (CF) problem.
3. Algorithms that do not reduce the problem to either CF or SD. We present one such novel algorithm inspired by Prange's information set decoder [19].

We remark that we will be content with finding just a subset of the t error positions since then the problem reduces to a much easier problem as the complexity is exponential in t.

The classical algorithm of Prange [19] can be described as picking k columns of the generator matrix $\mathbf{G}$, where the algorithm is successful if the corresponding positions are error-free, i.e., their complement of $n - k$ positions contains the support of the error. Alternatively, one can pick $k + 1$ columns from $\left[\begin{smallmatrix} \mathbf{G} \\ \mathbf{r} \end{smallmatrix} \right]$ where $\mathbf{r}$ is the received word and check whether the $(k + 1) \times (k + 1)$ submatrix formed by these columns is rank-deficient. This formulation allows for a generalization to interleaved codes, which is the main idea of our algorithm Interleaved Prange: we pick $k + \ell$ columns of $\left[\begin{smallmatrix} \mathbf{G} \\ \mathbf{R} \end{smallmatrix} \right]$ where $\mathbf{R}$ is an $\ell \times n$ matrix containing the ℓ received words as rows, and check if the rank of the $(k + \ell) \times (k + \ell)$ submatrix formed by these columns is less than $k + \ell$. The main contribution of this paper is the proposal and the analysis of the new decoding algorithm Interleaved Prange.

This paper is structured as follows. In Sect. 2 we introduce the notation and results for interleaved codes which are essential for the remainder of the paper.

We present the three types of interleaved decoding algorithms in Sect. 3 together with their corresponding complexity analysis. We then compare their asymptotic cost in Sect. 3.5. Finally, we conclude this paper in Sect. 4.

2   Preliminaries

For a prime power q, let $\mathbb{F}_q$ denote the finite field with q elements. We denote matrices and vectors by bold capital, respectively lower case letters. For $k \leq n$ positive integers and a matrix $\mathbf{G} \in \mathbb{F}_q^{k \times n}$ we denote by $\langle \mathbf{G} \rangle$ its rowspan, by $\mathbf{G}^\top$ the transposed matrix and by $\mathrm{rk}(\mathbf{G})$ its rank. For a vector $\mathbf{x} \in \mathbb{F}_q^n$, we denote by $\mathrm{supp}(\mathbf{x})$ its support, that is the indices of the non-zero entries of $\mathbf{x}$. Similarly for a matrix $\mathbf{X} \in \mathbb{F}_q^{k \times n}$ we denote by $\mathrm{supp}(\mathbf{X})$ the indices of the non-zero columns. We will denote by $\mathrm{wt}(\mathbf{x})$ the Hamming weight of the vector $\mathbf{x} \in \mathbb{F}_q^n$, that is the size of its support. For a matrix $\mathbf{X} \in \mathbb{F}_q^{k \times n}$ we will denote by $\mathrm{wt}(\mathbf{X})$ the number of non-zero columns of $\mathbf{X}$. We will denote by $|\mathcal{S}|$ the cardinality of a set $\mathcal{S}$. The set of all integers between 1 and n is denoted by $[1, n]$. Finally, for a set $\mathcal{I} \subseteq [1, n]$ of size r and a matrix $\mathbf{G} \in \mathbb{F}_q^{k \times n}$, we denote by $\mathbf{G}_\mathcal{I} \in \mathbb{F}_q^{k \times r}$ the matrix consisting of all columns of $\mathbf{G}$ indexed by $\mathcal{I}$.

A linear subspace $\mathcal{C} \subseteq \mathbb{F}_q^n$ of dimension k is called a linear code of length n and dimension k. We call this an $[n, k]_q$ code of rate $R = \frac{k}{n}$. For a linear code $\mathcal{C} \subseteq \mathbb{F}_q^n$ we can also define its minimum distance to be

$$d(\mathcal{C}) = \min\{\mathrm{wt}(\mathbf{c}) \mid c \in \mathcal{C}, \mathbf{c} \neq 0\}.$$

An $[n, k]_q$ linear code can be represented either through a generator matrix $\mathbf{G} \in \mathbb{F}_q^{k \times n}$, which has the code as image, or through a parity-check matrix $\mathbf{H} \in \mathbb{F}_q^{(n-k) \times n}$, which has the code as right kernel. For any $\mathbf{x} \in \mathbb{F}_q^n$, we call $\mathbf{s} = \mathbf{x}\mathbf{H}^\top \in \mathbb{F}_q^{n-k}$ the syndrome of $\mathbf{x}$.

It is well known that random codes of large blocklength over $\mathbb{F}_q$ achieve with high probability the minimum distance given by the Gilbert-Varshamov bound, that is

$$\delta = \frac{d(n)}{n} = H_q^{-1}(1 - R),$$

where we denote by H_q the q-ary entropy function.

Definition 1. *Let $\mathcal{C} \subseteq \mathbb{F}_q^n$ be a linear code of dimension k with generator matrix $\mathbf{G} \in \mathbb{F}_q^{k \times n}$. The homogeneous interleaved code of interleaving order ℓ of $\mathcal{C}$ is defined as*

$$\mathcal{C}_\ell = \{\mathbf{C} \in \mathbb{F}_q^{\ell \times n} \mid \mathbf{C} = \mathbf{M}\mathbf{G}, \mathbf{M} \in \mathbb{F}_q^{\ell \times k}\}.$$

Thus, the codewords of an interleaved code are $\ell \times n$ matrices. Let $\mathbf{H}$ be a parity-check matrix of $\mathcal{C}$ and consider the interleaved code $\mathcal{C}_\ell$. The syndrome of $\mathbf{X} \in \mathbb{F}_q^{\ell \times n}$ is then given by

$$\mathbf{S} = \mathbf{X}\mathbf{H} \in \mathbb{F}_q^{\ell \times (n-k)}.$$

Decoding an interleaved code with an arbitrary constituent code can be seen as the following problem.

Problem 1 (Interleaved Syndrome Decoding (ISD) Problem). Let $\ell \geq 2$ be a positive integer. Given $\mathbf{H} \in \mathbb{F}_q^{(n-k) \times n}$, $\mathbf{S} \in \mathbb{F}_q^{\ell \times (n-k)}$, and $t \in \mathbb{N}$, decide if there exists a matrix $\mathbf{E} \in \mathbb{F}_q^{\ell \times n}$ of column weight at most t, such that $\mathbf{H}\mathbf{E}^\top = \mathbf{S}^\top$.

This problem is equivalent to the Interleaved Decoding (ID) problem.

Problem 2 (Interleaved Decoding (ID) Problem). Given $\mathbf{G} \in \mathbb{F}_q^{k \times n}$, $\mathbf{R} \in \mathbb{F}_q^{\ell \times n}$, and $t \in \mathbb{N}$, decide if there exists a matrix $\mathbf{E} \in \mathbb{F}_q^{\ell \times n}$ of column weight at most t, such that each row of $\mathbf{R} - \mathbf{E}$ is in $\langle \mathbf{G} \rangle$.

This problem can be shown to be NP-hard by a reduction from the Hamming-metric SD problem, which has been proven to be NP-complete in [4,5].

Problem 3 (Hamming Syndrome Decoding (SD) Problem). Given $\mathbf{H} \in \mathbb{F}_q^{(n-k) \times n}$, $\mathbf{s} \in \mathbb{F}_q^{n-k}$, and $t \in \mathbb{N}$, decide if there exists a $\mathbf{e} \in \mathbb{F}_q^n$ of weight at most t, such that $\mathbf{s} = \mathbf{e}\mathbf{H}^\top$.

Theorem 1. *The Interleaved Syndrome Decoding Problem (Problem 1) is NP-complete.*

Proof. We show the NP-hardness of Problem 1 by a reduction from the classical Hamming SD. For this, take a random instance $\mathbf{H} \in \mathbb{F}_q^{(n-k) \times n}$, $\mathbf{s} \in \mathbb{F}_q^{n-k}$ and $t \in \mathbb{N}$ of the Hamming SD. Now define $\mathbf{S} = \begin{pmatrix} \mathbf{s} \\ \vdots \\ \mathbf{s} \end{pmatrix} \in \mathbb{F}_q^{\ell \times (n-k)}$. Assume we have an oracle for Problem 1.

- If the answer is 'yes' on the input $\mathbf{H}, \mathbf{S}, t$, then this is also the correct answer to the Hamming SD. In fact, if there exists $\mathbf{E} \in \mathbb{F}_q^{\ell \times n}$, such that $\mathbf{H}\mathbf{E}^\top = \mathbf{S}^\top$ and at most t columns of $\mathbf{E}$ are non-zero, then any column, e.g., the first column $\mathbf{e}$, of $\mathbf{E}$ is a solution to the Hamming SD, as $\mathbf{H}\mathbf{e} = \mathbf{s}$ and $\mathrm{wt}(\mathbf{e}) \leq t$.
- If the oracle returns 'no' on the input $\mathbf{H}, \mathbf{S}, t$, then this is also the correct answer to the Hamming SD. In fact, if there was a solution $\mathbf{e}$ to the Hamming SD then $\mathbf{E} = \begin{pmatrix} \mathbf{e} \\ \vdots \\ \mathbf{e} \end{pmatrix}$ would have been a solution to the interleaved SD.

Finally, we remark that for any candidate $\mathbf{E}$ we can check in polynomial time, whether $\mathbf{E}$ is a solution to the interleaved SD. Thus, the problem is also in NP. $\square$

3 Decoding Algorithms

In this section we present three types of generic decoding algorithms for interleaved codes. That is, given $\mathbf{G} \in \mathbb{F}_q^{k \times n}$, $\mathbf{R} \in \mathbb{F}_q^{\ell \times n}$, and $t \in \mathbb{N}$, these algorithms find a matrix $\mathbf{E} \in \mathbb{F}_q^{\ell \times n}$ of column weight at most t, such that each row of $\mathbf{R} - \mathbf{E}$ is in $\langle \mathbf{G} \rangle$.

In the following, we assume that $\mathbf{G} \in \mathbb{F}_q^{k \times n}$ and a set of error positions $\mathcal{T} \subseteq [1, n]$ of size t is chosen uniformly at random. Then ones takes a $\ell \times n$ zero matrix $\mathbf{E}$ and sets each column at these t error positions equal to a random vector in $\mathbb{F}_q^\ell$. Thus $\mathbf{E}_{\mathcal{T}}$ is a random matrix in $\mathbb{F}_q^{\ell \times t}$, and $\mathbf{E}$ is a random matrix in $\mathbb{F}_q^{\ell \times n}$ of column weight at most t. Finally, we choose $\mathbf{M} \in \mathbb{F}_q^{\ell \times k}$ uniformly at random and compute the received matrix $\mathbf{R} = \mathbf{C} + \mathbf{E}$ where $\mathbf{C} = \mathbf{MG}$. Thus, we assume that at least one solution to the ID problem exists.

For interleaved cryptosystems, t is typically close to the minimum distance of $\mathbf{G}$ which we denote by d.

3.1 SD-Based Algorithms

The most straightforward way to solve the ID problem is to simply pick a random non-zero vector $\mathbf{r}$ in the rowspan of $\mathbf{R}$ and solve the resulting SD problem with the parity-check matrix $\mathbf{H} \in \mathbb{F}_q^{(n-k) \times n}$ of the constituent code and the syndrome $\mathbf{s} = \mathbf{r}\mathbf{H}^\top \in \mathbb{F}_q^{n-k}$. Since information set decoding (ISD) attacks are the best known algorithms to solve the SD problem, we call this *Random* $\langle ISD \rangle$ (where $\langle ISD \rangle$ can be any ISD algorithm such as Prange, Stern [23], etc.).

Algorithm 1: Random ISD

Input: A generator matrix $\mathbf{G} \in \mathbb{F}_q^{k \times n}$ of $\mathcal{C}$ and a received matrix
$\qquad \mathbf{R} = \mathbf{C} + \mathbf{E} \in \mathbb{F}_q^{\ell \times n}$ where $\mathrm{wt}(\mathbf{E}) = t$.
Output: A nonempty subset $\mathcal{U} \subseteq \mathrm{supp}(\mathbf{E})$.

1 Compute a parity-check matrix $\mathbf{H} \in \mathbb{F}_q^{(n-k) \times n}$ of $\mathcal{C}$.
2 Pick a non-zero $\mathbf{r} \in \langle \mathbf{R} \rangle$ at random.
3 Compute $\mathbf{s} = \mathbf{r}\mathbf{H}^\top$.
4 Use an ISD algorithm that can find errors $\mathbf{e}$ of any weight belonging to some
   fixed subset of $[1, t]$ and run it with inputs $\mathbf{H}, \mathbf{s}$.
5 **if** *the ISD algorithm outputs an error* $\mathbf{e}$ **then**
6 $\quad \mid$ Return $\mathrm{supp}(\mathbf{e})$.

Before proceeding, we mention that in order to compute the work factor, there are two rather subtle ways to run Random $\langle ISD \rangle$. The first way is that we get a (1) random ciphertext $\mathbf{R}$, then (2) pick a random non-zero row $\mathbf{r}$ from $\langle \mathbf{R} \rangle$ and then finally (3) run one iteration of our ISD algorithm on it. If this iteration does not succeed, then we go back to step (1) and start again by generating a new random ciphertext $\mathbf{R}$. In the second method the difference is that on subsequent iterations we go back to step (2) instead. That is we *stay* with the same ciphertext $\mathbf{R}$ through all our iterations until success. Our analysis below follows the first way. While the second way might seem more appropriate to use one can show that its workfactor is an upper bound to the workfactor of the first method (by an application of the HM-AM inequality). Furthermore the workfactor of the second method is also much harder to analyze than the first.

(We also remark that this sort of consideration also applies to our analysis of Interleaved Prange where the first interpretation is applicable.)

If the success probability of the employed ISD algorithm of finding an error of weight v is denoted by $P(v)$, then the success probability of the Random $\langle \mathrm{ISD} \rangle$ approach is given by

$$\sum_{v=0}^{t} \frac{\binom{t}{v}(q-1)^v}{q^t} \cdot P(v).$$

Note that $P(v)$ is simply zero for all those error weights v which the chosen ISD algorithm is not designed to solve for. Here $\binom{t}{v}\frac{(q-1)^v}{q^t}$ denotes the probability that the chosen $\mathbf{r}$ has an error $\mathbf{e}$ of weight v. In fact, by choosing a random codeword $\mathbf{r} \in \langle \mathbf{R} \rangle$, this results in an error vector $\mathbf{e}$ which is a random linear combination of the rows of $\mathbf{E} \in \mathbb{F}_q^{\ell \times n}$ and thus when $\mathbf{e}$ is restricted to the t error positions it looks like a vector drawn uniformly at random from $\mathbb{F}_q^t$. Note that this approach comes with a failure probability as the errors generally have weight greater than the unique decoding radius of $\mathbf{G}$. However, this probability is expected to be very small as the error weights are less than the minimum distance of $\mathbf{G}$.

For the complexity analysis, let us consider first that we employ the ISD algorithm of Prange [19]. This algorithm has a success probability of

$$P(v) = \binom{n-k}{v}\binom{n}{v}^{-1}.$$

Hence the success probability of Random Prange is given by

$$\sum_{v=0}^{t} \frac{\binom{t}{v}(q-1)^v}{q^t}\binom{n-k}{v}\binom{n}{v}^{-1}.$$

To get an upper bound on the asymptotic complexity of Random Prange, we can give a lower bound on the success probability, e.g., by considering just the term in the summation where $v = t\frac{q-1}{q}$ (a reasonable choice since this is the most likely error weight in the chosen $\mathbf{r}$, i.e., this v maximizes $\binom{t}{v}\frac{(q-1)^v}{q^t}$).

In order to give an asymptotic complexity, we first consider the parameters k, t as functions in n and define

$$R = \lim_{n \to \infty} \frac{k(n)}{n},$$

$$T = \lim_{n \to \infty} \frac{t(n)}{n} = H_q^{-1}(1-R).$$

To ease the notation, we also introduce the asymptotics of the binomial coefficient, denoted by

$$H(F, G) := \lim_{n \to \infty} \frac{1}{n} \log_q \left(\binom{f(n)}{g(n)}\right)$$

$$= F \log_q(F) - G \log_q(G) - (F-G) \log_q(F-G),$$

where $f(n), g(n)$ are integer-valued functions such that $\lim\limits_{n\to\infty} \frac{f(n)}{n} = F$ and $\lim\limits_{n\to\infty} \frac{g(n)}{n} = G$. Thus, we get the following upper bound.

Proposition 1. *The asymptotic complexity of Random Prange on an ℓ-interleaved random code over $\mathbb{F}_q$ with length n and dimension k is given by at most $q^{ne_P(R,q)}$, where*

$$e_P(R,q) = H(1, T(q-1)/q) - H(1-R, T(q-1)/q).$$

If we employ Stern's ISD algorithm [23], we get a slight improvement. However, note that Stern's algorithm (at least in its conventional formulation) only solves the SD problem for a fixed error weight w. If instead in each iteration we run Stern t times for all error weights $w \in [1,t]$, this gives us a straightforward extension of the algorithm that works for all errors with weights in $[1,t]$. While this of course increases the cost of one iteration, it turns out that asymptotically the cost remains the same and since this formulation can only improve the probability of success of Random Stern, we will consider this version.

The cost of Random Stern's algorithm is in $\mathcal{O}(I \cdot C)$, where I is the expected number of iterations and C the cost of one iteration. This is given by

$$I = \left(\sum_{v=0}^{t} \frac{\binom{t}{v}(q-1)^v}{q^t} \binom{(k+\ell_v')/2}{w_v'/2}^2 \binom{n-k-\ell_v'}{v-w_v'} \binom{n}{v}^{-1} \right)^{-1}$$

$$C = \sum_{v=1}^{t} C_v \text{ where } C_v = \binom{(k+\ell_v')/2}{w_v'/2} q^{w_v'/2} + \binom{(k+\ell_v')/2}{w_v'/2}^2 q^{w_v'-\ell'},$$

where $0 \le w_v' \le \min\{k+\ell', v\}, 0 \le \ell_v' \le n-k$ are the internal parameters of Stern's algorithm that can be optimized individually for each of the t runs to give the lowest cost.

To get an upper bound on the asymptotic complexity of Random Stern, we again just consider the $v_0 = t\frac{q-1}{q}$ term in the summation in I's formula. For this let us consider additionally the parameters w_{v_0}' and ℓ_{v_0}' as functions in n and define

$$W' = \lim_{n\to\infty} \frac{w_{v_0}'(n)}{n},$$

$$L' = \lim_{n\to\infty} \frac{\ell_{v_0}'(n)}{n}.$$

Proposition 2. *The asymptotic complexity of Random Stern on an ℓ-interleaved random code over $\mathbb{F}_q$ with length n and dimension k is given by at most $q^{ne_S(R,q)}$, where*

$$\begin{aligned}
e_S(R,q) = {} & H(1, T(q-1)/q) - 2H((R+L')/2, W'/2) \\
& - H(1-R-L', T(q-1)/q - W') \\
& + \max\{H((R+L')/2, W'/2) + W'/2, \\
& \quad 2H((R+L')/2, W'/2) + W' - L'\}.
\end{aligned}$$

Finally, we can utilize the fact, that an attacker has the knowledge of q^ℓ instances of the syndrome decoding problem. Such a scenario has first been considered in [13]. Following an unpublished idea, attributed to Bleichenbacher, Sendrier considered in DOOM [22] the scenario where many instances are decoded simultaneously and the solution for only one is needed. More in details, if N denotes the number of instances and γ denotes the previous workfactor, e.g. of Stern's algorithm, then DOOM has a cost of

$$\max\{\gamma/\sqrt{N}, \gamma^{2/3}\},$$

depending on how large N is. In fact, if $\gamma/\sqrt{N} \leq N$ the workfactor of the new algorithm is given by $\gamma^{2/3}$ and else it costs $\gamma/\sqrt{N}$.

In our interleaved scenario, we can assume that an attacker has the knowledge of q^ℓ instances from the rowspan of the received matrix $\mathbf{R}$. Thus, if we denote by γ_S the cost of Stern's algorithm on one of these instances, then applying DOOM to our scenario has a cost of

$$\max\{\gamma_S/\sqrt{q^\ell}, \gamma_S^{2/3}\}.$$

This leads to the following exponent in the asymptotic cost.

Proposition 3. *The asymptotic complexity of DOOM using Stern on an ℓ-interleaved random code over $\mathbb{F}_q$ with length n and dimension k is given by at most $q^{n e_D(R,q)}$, where*

$$e_D(R, q) = \max\{e_S(R, q) - L/2, 2/3 e_S(R, q)\},$$

where $e_S(R, q)$ is the exponent of the asymptotic cost of random Stern 4.

3.2   CF-Based Algorithms

A different approach is the following. Having received the matrix $\mathbf{R}$, note that the code generated by $\mathbf{G}' = [\frac{\mathbf{G}}{\mathbf{R}}]$ is the same as the code generated by $[\frac{\mathbf{G}}{\mathbf{E}}]$. Thus the problem reduces to finding a low-weight codeword in the code $\langle \mathbf{G}' \rangle$ of dimension $k + \ell$.

Let us denote by $\mathbf{H}' \in \mathbb{F}_q^{(n-(k+\ell)) \times n}$ a parity-check matrix of the code $\langle \mathbf{G}' \rangle$.

Algorithm 2: CF-based Algorithm

Input: A generator matrix $\mathbf{G} \in \mathbb{F}_q^{k \times n}$ and a received matrix $\mathbf{R} = \mathbf{C} + \mathbf{E} \in \mathbb{F}_q^{\ell \times n}$
      where $\langle \mathbf{E} \rangle$ has minimum distance d_E.

Output: A nonempty subset $\mathcal{U} \subseteq \mathrm{supp}(\mathbf{E})$

1 Compute the parity-check matrix $\mathbf{H}' \in \mathbb{F}_q^{(n-k-\ell) \times n}$ of the code $\langle \mathbf{G}' \rangle$.

2 Use a CF algorithm with inputs $\mathbf{H}'$ and weight d_E to find a codeword $\mathbf{e}$ of weight w in $\langle \mathbf{G}' \rangle$.

3 Return $\mathbf{e}$.

Algorithm 2 gives a framework of finding a codeword from $\langle \mathbf{E} \rangle$ by using a low-weight codeword finding algorithm as a subroutine. The complexity of this approach is the same as the complexity of the CF algorithm used for finding low-weight codewords in the code $\langle \mathbf{G}' \rangle$. For example one might employ the well-known ISD algorithm by Stern.

We remark that differently from our description of the other two algorithms, we assume that the minimum distance d_{E} of the error matrix $\mathbf{E}$ is available. For interleaved cryptosystems, this is a parameter that is published and is usually chosen to be as large as possible to give the system a high security level. For large blocklengths and random $\mathbf{E}$ we can assume this distance is close to the Gilbert-Varshamov bound, as we do for the asymptotic analysis below.

The asymptotic complexity of this algorithm is exactly given by the asymptotic complexity of Stern's algorithm on a code of dimension $k + \ell$ and a target weight w, which is the minimum distance of $\langle \mathbf{E} \rangle$. For this recall that we have the internal parameters $0 \le w' \le \min\{k + \ell + \ell', w\}, 0 \le \ell' \le n - k - \ell$. We define

$$W' = \lim_{n \to \infty} \frac{w'(n)}{n},$$

$$L' = \lim_{n \to \infty} \frac{\ell'(n)}{n},$$

$$T = \lim_{n \to \infty} \frac{t(n)}{n} = H_q^{-1}(1 - R),$$

$$W = \lim_{n \to \infty} \frac{w(n)}{n} = H_q^{-1}(1 - \ell/t)T.$$

Proposition 4. *The asymptotic complexity of the CF approach on an ℓ-interleaved random code over $\mathbb{F}_q$ with length n and dimension k is given by at most $q^{nec(R,q)}$, where*

$$\begin{aligned}
e_C(R, q) = {} & H(1, T) - 2H((R + L + L')/2, W'/2) \\
& - H(1 - R - L - L', W - W') \\
& + \max\{H((R + L + L')/2, W'/2) + W'/2, \\
& \quad 2H((R + L + L')/2, W'/2) + W' - L'\}.
\end{aligned}$$

3.3 Novel Approach: Interleaved Prange

We propose a new algorithm (Algorithm 3) inspired by the classical attack of Prange. Note that Prange's algorithm can be described as choosing $k+1$ columns in $\begin{bmatrix} \mathbf{G} \\ \mathbf{r} \end{bmatrix}$ where $\mathbf{r}$ is the received word and checking whether the $(k + 1) \times (k + 1)$ submatrix formed at these positions is rank deficient. This formulation can neatly be generalized to interleaved codes, where we pick $k + \ell$ columns in $\begin{bmatrix} \mathbf{G} \\ \mathbf{R} \end{bmatrix}$ and check if the rank of the $(k + \ell) \times (k + \ell)$ submatrix formed at these positions is less than $k + \ell$.

In more details, we choose a set $\mathcal{J} \subset [1, n]$ of size $k + \ell$, which contains an information set $\mathcal{I}$ for $\mathbf{G}$ (in other words, $\mathbf{G}_\mathcal{I}$ and hence $\mathbf{G}_\mathcal{J}$ has full rank). Let us denote again by $\mathbf{G}' := \begin{bmatrix} \mathbf{G} \\ \mathbf{R} \end{bmatrix}$ and check if the square submatrix $\mathbf{G}'_\mathcal{J}$ (the blue region in Fig. 1) is rank-deficient, that is

$$\text{rk} \left((\mathbf{G}')_\mathcal{J} \right) < k + \ell.$$

This can be split into two cases:

1. $\mathbf{E}_\mathcal{J}$ has linearly dependent rows (which implies $\mathbf{G}'_\mathcal{J}$ is rank deficient).
2. $\mathbf{E}_\mathcal{J}$ has linearly independent rows but $\mathbf{G}'_\mathcal{J}$ is still rank deficient.

In the first case, we succeed as at least one non-zero word in $\langle \mathbf{R} \rangle$ is error-free at these $k + \ell$ positions and so by performing the re-encoding step of Prange on such a word $\mathbf{r}$, we can find the error in this word, giving us a subset of the t error positions. A naive way to find such an $\mathbf{r}$ would be to do the re-encoding on all $q^\ell - 1$ non-zero words in $\langle \mathbf{R} \rangle$. However, this step will fail if we are in the second case. As it turns out, the second case is far more likely than the first, so this naive re-encoding approach will make the entire algorithm very inefficient. Instead we do the re-encoding for only those $\mathbf{r} \in \langle \mathbf{R} \rangle$ that actually belong to some linearly dependent set of rows in $\mathbf{G}'_\mathcal{J}$ which can be easily found by computing its left null space, i.e., the set $\{\mathbf{x} \in \mathbb{F}_q^{k+\ell} : \mathbf{x}\mathbf{G}'_\mathcal{J} = \mathbf{0}\}$. With this modification, the algorithm becomes efficient again, though perhaps at the expense of a more involved complexity analysis.

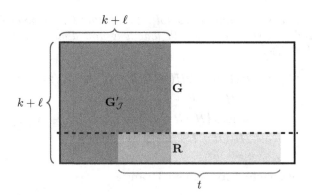

Fig. 1. Illustration of Interleaved Prange Algorithm.

Theorem 2. *The cost of Interleaved Prange on an ℓ-interleaved random code over $\mathbb{F}_q$ with length n and dimension k is in*

$$\mathcal{O} \left(P^{-1} C \right),$$

Algorithm 3: Interleaved Prange

Input: A generator matrix $\mathbf{G} \in \mathbb{F}_q^{k \times n}$ and a received matrix $\mathbf{R} = \mathbf{C} + \mathbf{E} \in \mathbb{F}_q^{\ell \times n}$
    where $\mathbf{E}$ has at most t non-zero columns.
Output: A nonempty subset $\mathcal{U} \subseteq \mathrm{supp}(\mathbf{E})$.

1   Choose $\mathcal{J} \subset [1, n]$ of size $k + \ell$ such that $\mathrm{rk}(\mathbf{G}_{\mathcal{J}}) = k$.
2   **if** $\mathrm{rk}(\mathbf{G}'_{\mathcal{J}}) < k + \ell$ **then**
3   **for** *each* $\mathbf{x} \in \mathbb{F}_q^{k+\ell} \setminus \{\mathbf{0}\}$ *in the left null space of* $\mathbf{G}'_{\mathcal{J}}$ **do**
4   **if** $\mathrm{wt}(\mathbf{xG}') \le t$ **then return** $\mathrm{supp}(\mathbf{xG}')$.
5   **end**
6   **else**
7   Go back to step 1.

---

where

$$P = \sum_{i=0}^{\min\{t, k+\ell\}} \frac{\binom{n-t}{k+\ell-i}\binom{t}{i}}{\binom{n}{k+\ell}} \cdot \left(1 - \prod_{j=0}^{\ell-1}(1 - q^{j-i}) \right),$$

denotes the success probability and

$$C = (k+\ell)^3 + \prod_{j=0}^{k-1}(1 - q^{j-k}) 16 \sum_{p=1}^{\ell} q^{-p^2+p})(k+\ell)(n - k - \ell)$$

denotes the cost of one iteration.

Proof. This algorithm succeeds whenever the chosen set $\mathcal{J}$ is such that the rows of $\mathbf{E}_{\mathcal{J} \cap \mathcal{T}}$ are linearly dependent and that $\mathbf{G}_{\mathcal{J}}$ has rank k. Since the latter is true with high probability, we will assume this probability is one. Let i denote $|\mathcal{J} \cap \mathcal{T}|$, i.e., the number of error positions in the set $\mathcal{J}$. Since $\mathbf{E}_{\mathcal{J} \cap \mathcal{T}}$ has the distribution of a random matrix in $\mathbb{F}_q^{\ell \times i}$, the probability that $\mathbf{E}_{\mathcal{J} \cap \mathcal{T}}$ has linearly dependent rows is given by,

$$\left(1 - \prod_{j=0}^{\ell-1}(1 - q^{j-i}) \right).$$

Next, we weight this term with the probability that exactly i errors land in $\mathcal{J}$ and form the summation over all possible i, giving us

$$P = \sum_{i=0}^{\min\{t, k+\ell\}} \frac{\binom{n-t}{k+\ell-i}\binom{t}{i}}{\binom{n}{k+\ell}} \cdot \left(1 - \prod_{j=0}^{\ell-1}(1 - q^{j-i}) \right).$$

Hence, we will need P^{-1} many iterations until we succeed. Among these non-successful iterations, we could either have that $\mathbf{G}'_{\mathcal{J}}$ was not rank deficient, which costs $\mathcal{O}((k + \ell)^3)$ due to the Gaussian elimination to check $\mathbf{G}'_{\mathcal{J}}$'s rank (step 2) or we have that $\mathbf{G}'_{\mathcal{J}}$ was indeed rank deficient but $\mathbf{E}_{\mathcal{J}}$ had linearly independent rows. In this second case we incur the additional cost of step 3 since only after that we will recognize that $\mathbf{E}_{\mathcal{J}}$ did not have linearly dependent rows. Note that step 3 consists of computing the left null space of $\mathbf{G}'$ and then performing q^p re-encoding steps where p is the dimension of this space. The left null space can be found using Gaussian elimination and thus has the same cost as the rank-check in step 2 (in fact, it is possible to find the null space with effectively no additional work from this step).

In order to compute the cost of doing the q^p re-encodings, assume $\mathbf{E}_{\mathcal{J}}$ has linearly independent rows. Let $P(p)$ denote the probability that $\mathbf{G}'_{\mathcal{J}}$ has rank deficiency p, i.e., $\mathrm{rk}(\mathbf{G}'_{\mathcal{J}}) = k + \ell - p$ where $p \in [1, \ell]$ (since $\mathcal{J}$ is chosen such that $\mathrm{rk}(\mathbf{G}_{\mathcal{J}}) = k$). Thus p is the dimension of the left null space of $\mathbf{G}'$. Then the workfactor of the re-encoding is given by

$$C' = \sum_{p=1}^{\ell} P(p) q^p \alpha$$

where $\alpha \in \mathcal{O}((k + \ell)(n - k - \ell))$ is the cost of a single re-encoding step.

To compute $P(p)$, we make use of the following result: if V is an n-dimensional vector space over $\mathbb{F}_q$ and U is an m-dimensional subspace in V, then the number of k-dimensional subspaces W over $\mathbb{F}_q$ with $\dim(W \cap U) = d$ is given by

$$\begin{bmatrix} n - m \\ k - d \end{bmatrix}_q \begin{bmatrix} m \\ d \end{bmatrix}_q q^{(m-d)(k-d)},$$

where $\begin{bmatrix} a \\ b \end{bmatrix}_q$ denotes the Gaussian binomial coefficient.

Since the number of $\mathbf{G}'_{\mathcal{J}}$ with rank deficiency p is given by the number of $\mathbf{E}_{\mathcal{J} \cap \mathcal{T}}$ of rank ℓ times the number of $\mathbf{G}_{\mathcal{J}}$ of rank k such that $\dim(\langle \mathbf{E}_{\mathcal{J} \cap \mathcal{T}} \rangle \cap \langle \mathbf{G}_{\mathcal{J}} \rangle) = p$, we get

$$\prod_{j=0}^{\ell-1}(q^i - q^j) \prod_{j=0}^{k-1}(q^k - q^j) \begin{bmatrix} \ell \\ p \end{bmatrix}_q \begin{bmatrix} k \\ k - p \end{bmatrix}_q q^{(\ell-p)(k-p)},$$

where the first term counts the number of rank ℓ matrices $\mathbf{E}_{\mathcal{J} \cap \mathcal{T}}$, the second term is the number of ways of picking an ordered basis of a k-dimensional subspace and the third term counts the number of k-dimensional subspaces (i.e. $\langle \mathbf{G}_{\mathcal{J}} \rangle$) inside a $k + \ell$ dimensional space whose intersection with a fixed ℓ-dimensional subspace (i.e. $\langle \mathbf{E}_{\mathcal{J} \cap \mathcal{T}} \rangle$) has dimension p.

Dividing this by the total number of possible $\mathbf{G}'_{\mathcal{J}}$, i.e.,

$$q^{(k+\ell)k} \prod_{j=0}^{\ell-1}(q^i - q^j),$$

we get the probability

$$P(p) = \prod_{j=0}^{k-1} \frac{q^k - q^j}{q^{k+\ell}} \begin{bmatrix} \ell \\ p \end{bmatrix}_q \begin{bmatrix} k \\ k - p \end{bmatrix}_q q^{(\ell-p)(k-p)}.$$

Hence the workfactor of one iteration is given by $C = \beta + C'$ where $\beta \in \mathcal{O}((k+\ell)^3)$ and

$$
\begin{aligned}
C' &= \sum_{p=1}^{\ell} P(p) q^p \alpha \\
&= \prod_{j=0}^{k-1} \left(1 - q^{j-k}\right) q^{-\ell k} \sum_{p=0}^{\ell} \begin{bmatrix} \ell \\ p \end{bmatrix}_q \begin{bmatrix} k \\ k-p \end{bmatrix}_q q^{(\ell-p)(k-p)} q^p \alpha \\
&\leq \prod_{j=0}^{k-1} (1 - q^{j-k}) q^{-\ell k} \sum_{p=1}^{\ell} 16 q^{\ell k - p^2 + p} \alpha \\
&= \prod_{j=0}^{k-1} (1 - q^{j-k}) 16 \sum_{p=1}^{\ell} q^{-p^2 + p} \alpha,
\end{aligned}
$$

where we used that

$$
q^{(a-b)b} \leq \begin{bmatrix} a \\ b \end{bmatrix}_q \leq 4 q^{(a-b)b}.
$$

$\square$

Again, we will give an upper bound on the asymptotic cost. For this it is enough to consider a lower bound on the success probability P, as

$$
\lim_{n\to\infty} \frac{1}{n} \log_q(C) = \lim_{n\to\infty} \frac{1}{n} \log_q \left((k+\ell)^3 + \prod_{j=0}^{k-1}(1 - q^{j-k}) 16 \sum_{p=1}^{\ell} q^{-p^2+p} \alpha \right)
$$

$$
\leq \lim_{n\to\infty} \frac{1}{n} \log_q((k+\ell)^3 + \ell 16(k+\ell)(n-k-\ell)) = 0.
$$

Note that the success probability can be written as

$$
P = \sum_{i=0}^{\min\{t, k+\ell\}} Q_i,
$$

for

$$
Q_i = \frac{\binom{n-t}{k+\ell-i}\binom{t}{i}}{\binom{n}{k+\ell}} \cdot \left(1 - \prod_{j=0}^{\ell-1}(1 - q^{j-i})\right).
$$

To get a lower bound, we use that $\sum_{i=0}^{\min\{t,k+\ell\}} Q_i \geq Q_{\ell-1}$, that is we just consider

$$
Q_{\ell-1} = \binom{n-t}{k+1}\binom{t}{\ell-1}\binom{n}{k+\ell}^{-1}.
$$

Since the interleaving order ℓ is usually very small compared to n, we set

$$
L = \lim_{n\to\infty} \frac{\ell(n)}{n} = \frac{T}{\alpha},
$$

for some positive integer $2 < \alpha$.

Proposition 5. *The asymptotic complexity of Interleaved Prange on an ℓ-interleaved random code over $\mathbb{F}_q$ with length n and dimension k is given by at most $q^{ne_I(R,q)}$, where*

$$e_I(R,q) = H(1, R+L) - H(1-T, R) - H(T, L) + \min\{H(R+L, R), L\}.$$

3.4   Recognizing Failures

In all the above algorithms, there is a certain probability that the returned set of positions is not a subset of the original error positions $\mathcal{T}$. For SD-based algorithms, this can happen because any non-zero word in $\langle \mathbf{E} \rangle$ generally has an error of weight greater than the unique decoding radius of $\mathbf{G}$. For CF-based algorithms or interleaved Prange, it is possible for a word with support not in $\mathcal{T}$ to exist in $\mathbf{G}' = [\begin{smallmatrix} \mathbf{G} \\ \mathbf{R} \end{smallmatrix}]$. This is because a word from $\langle \mathbf{E} \rangle$ might combine with a codeword from $\langle \mathbf{G} \rangle$ to yield a word that has weight less than t. While the probability of this happening is expected to very small, it is still important to handle this case.

Following an idea of Jean-Pierre Tillich (personal communication), we can recognize these cases with high probability. This idea is similar to the algorithm in [18], which attacks the KKS signature scheme [14,15]. The algorithm exploits the fact that there is a secret subcode of a publicly known code, which has many low-weight codewords with support centered in a small subset. Similarly for us, we have that $\langle \mathbf{G}' \rangle$ has the secret subcode $\langle \mathbf{E} \rangle$ which has many low-weight codewords centered in a subset of size t. We now describe the algorithm in more detail.

Suppose our algorithm finds a low-weight $\mathbf{x}$ and we want to determine if its support $\mathcal{U}$ is a subset of $\mathcal{T}$. We shorten the code $\langle \mathbf{G}' \rangle$ with respect to the complement of $\mathcal{U}$ and then calculate its dimension. In other words, we calculate the dimension of the code $\mathcal{C}_s = \{c_\mathcal{U} \mid c \in \langle \mathbf{G}' \rangle \text{ and } c_{[1,n] \setminus \mathcal{U}} = \mathbf{0}\}$. If $\mathcal{U} \not\subseteq \mathcal{T}$, then we can expect that a large part of $\mathcal{T}$ is outside $\mathcal{U}$ and hence we should expect the dimension of $\mathcal{C}_s$ to be zero. On the other hand, suppose $\mathcal{U} \subseteq \mathcal{T}$. Then for a random $\mathbf{E}$, any non-zero $x \in \langle \mathbf{E} \rangle$ is expected to be of weight $\frac{q-1}{q} t$ which is close to t for even moderate q. Thus we should expect very few positions of $\mathcal{T}$ to be left outside $\mathcal{U}$ and so the dimension should be greater than zero (more precisely this will be true if less than ℓ positions of $\mathcal{T}$ are outside $\mathcal{U}$).

An alternative method is also available that works well for $q = 2$. If we puncture $\langle \mathbf{G}' \rangle$ in supp($\mathbf{e}$), we can run a CF algorithm on the punctured code and look for a codeword of weight at most $t - w$. If $\mathbf{e}$ was indeed in $\langle \mathbf{E} \rangle$, then the CF algorithm should succeed in finding such a word. However it seems possible that this check succeeds even when supp($\mathbf{e}$) is not in $\mathcal{T}$. But as $w \geq t/2$ it is very unlikely that the punctured code in the support of a 'wrong' codeword $\mathbf{e}$ still contains codewords of low weight. In fact, if $\mathbf{e} \notin \langle \mathbf{E} \rangle$, then we are left with many positions of supp($\mathbf{E}$) after puncturing and it is very unlikely for such a punctured code to contain a codeword of weight $t - w \leq t/2$.

The first method is clearly a polynomial time check. The second method, while having an exponential cost, is still much less work than the main algorithm which tries to find a word of a much larger error weight. Further, since we expect these failure cases to be rare, incorporating any of the above two methods should not affect the overall complexity.

3.5   Comparison

In order to compare the different algorithms, we fix $q = 7$ and ℓ the interleaving order to be such that $L = \lim_{n \to \infty} \frac{\ell(n)}{n} = T/\alpha$, for $\alpha \in \{5, 10, 20, 30\}$. These choices of α are motivated from the proposed parameters in cryptosystems, e.g. compare to Table 3. In addition, we denote by $R^* = \operatorname{argmax}_{0 \leq R \leq 1} (e(R, q))$. We have two different approaches for the comparison. The first one is to take $\frac{1}{n} \log_q(\cdot)$ of the actual cost of the algorithms computed for large n, which seem to converge rather quickly, thus Fig. 2 and Table 1 gives a very accurate plot of the complexities in this case.

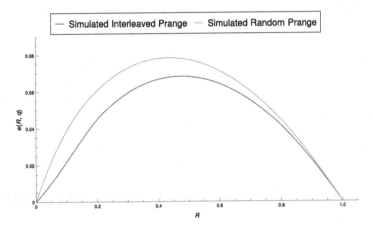

Fig. 2. Simulated asymptotic cost of the algorithms for $q = 7$ and $\ell = t/20$.

Table 1. Comparison of simulated asymptotic cost of different algorithms for $q = 7$ and $\ell = t/20$.

Algorithm	$e(R^*, q)$	R^*	T
Simulated Interleaved Prange	0.06832	0.475	0.254
Simulated Random Prange	0.07848	0.437	0.280

The second approach is using the presented upper bounds on the asymptotic complexity, which can be seen in Fig. 3, 4, 5 and Table 2. In Table 2, note that Random Prange as well as Random Stern do not depend on the different choices of α. We can observe that the Interleaved Prange algorithm outperforms DOOM for small choices of α, i.e., up to $\alpha = 20$, while after that point DOOM starts outperforming Interleaved Prange. In general, for small ℓ, it appears that CF-based algorithms have a lower complexity than Interleaved Prange and SD-based algorithms because SD-based algorithms generally solve the problem for a larger error weight than CF-based ones (but only in a slightly larger code). On the other hand, for large ℓ, namely at $\ell = t/5$, we could observe that Interleaved Prange outperforms even CF-based algorithms.

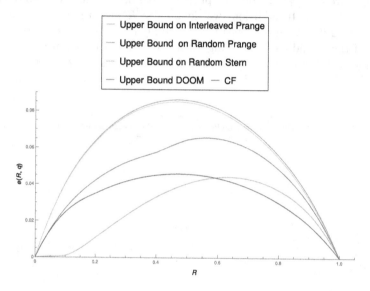

Fig. 3. Upper bounds on the asymptotic cost of the algorithms for $q = 7$ and $\ell = t/5$.

Both approaches show the same predicted behaviour, that is Interleaved Prange has a much lower complexity than the straightforward approach of SD for small α. Note that in the simulated asymptotics we did not compare also to Random Stern, as the improvement on Random Prange is only marginal.

Regarding the finite regime cost, we omit to state the cumbersome formulae in the paper and instead provide an updated table for the parameters of the cryptosystem [11] in Table 3. In Table 3 SL stands for security level, d_E is the minimum distance of $\langle \mathbf{E} \rangle$, r is the degree of the irreducible Goppa polynomial, m is the extension degree and WF_{CFS}, WF_{IP}, WF_{RP} stands for the workfactor of the CF-approach using Stern, Interleaved Prange and Random Prange, respectively. The cryptosystem is based on interleaved Goppa codes. We assume that arithmetic in $\mathbb{F}_q$ has a logarithmic cost.

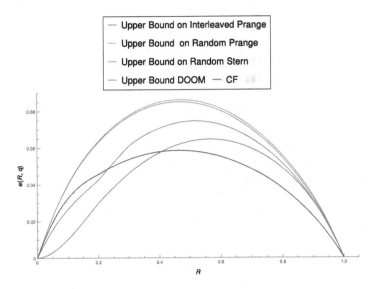

Fig. 4. Upper bounds on the asymptotic cost of the algorithms for $q = 7$ and $\ell = t/10$.

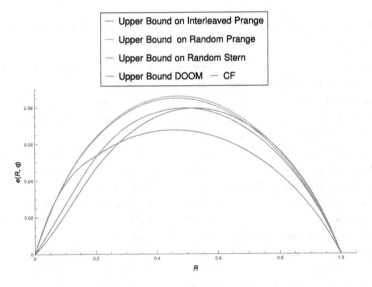

Fig. 5. Upper bounds on the asymptotic cost of the algorithms for $q = 7$ and $\ell = t/20$.

The Mathematica code for the asymptotic complexity, as well as a SAGE code for the finite regime cost can be found in https://doi.org/10.5281/zenodo.6988687.

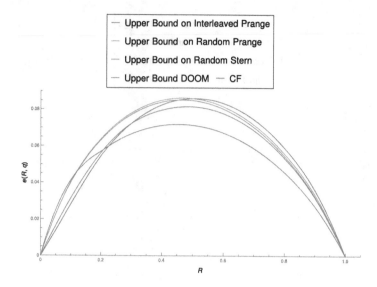

Fig. 6. Upper bounds on the asymptotic cost of the algorithms for $q = 7$ and $\ell = t/30$.

Table 2. Comparison of the asymptotic cost of the different algorithms for $q = 7$ and different α.

α	Algorithm	$e(R^*, q)$	R^*	T	Internal parameters
5	Upper Bound Interleaved Prange	0.04415	0.631	0.158	
	Upper Bound DOOM	0.06557	0.561	0.198	$w' = 0.0041, \ell' = 0.0152$
	CF Using Stern	0.04574	0.471	0.257	$w' = 0.0017, \ell' = 0.0069$
10	Upper Bound Interleaved Prange	0.06471	0.565	0.196	
	Upper Bound DOOM	0.07466	0.516	0.227	$w' = 0.0040, \ell' = 0.0147$
	CF Using Stern	0.05861	0.462	0.263	$w' = 0.0019, \ell' = 0.0076$
20	Upper Bound Interleaved Prange	0.07961	0.524	0.222	
	Upper Bound DOOM	0.07969	0.493	0.242	$w' = 0.0040, \ell' = 0.0144$
	CF Using Stern	0.06777	0.455	0.268	$w' = 0.0022, \ell' = 0.0087$
30	Upper Bound Interleaved Prange	0.08621	0.468	0.259	
	Upper Bound DOOM	0.08144	0.484	0.248	$w' = 0.0039, \ell' = 0.0143$
	CF Using Stern	0.07176	0.453	0.269	$w' = 0.0021, \ell' = 0.0081$
	Upper Bound Random Prange	0.08621	0.468	0.259	
	Upper Bound Random Stern	0.08510	0.465	0.261	$w' = 0.0038, \ell' = 0.0139$

Table 3. New security level for the proposed parameters in [11].

Old SL	WF$_{CFS}$	WF$_{IP}$	WF$_{RP}$	q	m	r	n	k	ℓ	t_{pub}	d_{E}
128	94.37	127.23	135.31	3	8	100	2130	1330	7	131	59
128	117.80	126.47	136.65	4	6	90	1580	1040	7	105	68
128	114.29	128.23	139.91	5	5	100	1290	790	7	109	73
256	204.60	229.45	237.59	3	8	180	4300	2860	7	236	123
256	169.57	246.59	256.80	4	7	240	3760	2080	7	280	135
256	184.90	246.70	258.65	5	6	200	3200	2000	7	218	121

4   Conclusion

In this paper we presented several algorithms that decode a random homogeneous ℓ-interleaved code, which also work for the missing case $\ell \ll t$. Two of these algorithms come from a straight-forward reduction to known ISD and CF algorithms in the classical case. In addition to those algorithms, we also presented a new generic decoding algorithm for interleaved codes, namely Interleaved Prange, which is an adaption of Prange's classical idea to the interleaved setting. We provided a complexity analysis and compared the asymptotic costs of the considered algorithms.

Acknowledgements. The sixth author is supported by the Swiss National Science Foundation grant number 195290. The authors are thankful to Jean-Pierre Tillich for helpful discussions on the failure probability of the CF approach.

References

1. Melchor, C.A., et al.: ROLLO- Rank-Ouroboros, LAKE & LOCKER. NIST PQC Call for Proposals (2020). Round 2 Submission
2. Melchor, C.A., et al.: Rank Quasi-Cyclic (RQC). NIST PQC Call for Proposals (2020). Round 2 Submission
3. Albrecht, M.R., et al.: Classic McEliece: Conservative Code-Based Cryptography. NIST PQC Call for Proposals (2020). Round 3 Submission
4. Barg, A.: Some new NP-complete coding problems. Problemy Peredachi Informatsii **30**(3), 23–28 (1994)
5. Berlekamp, E., McEliece, R., Van Tilborg, H.: On the inherent intractability of certain coding problems (corresp.). IEEE Trans. Inf. Theory **24**(3), 384–386 (1978)
6. Chailloux, A., Debris-Alazard, T., Etinski, S.: Classical and quantum algorithms for generic syndrome decoding problems and applications to the Lee metric. In: Cheon, J.H., Tillich, J.-P. (eds.) PQCrypto 2021 2021. LNCS, vol. 12841, pp. 44–62. Springer, Cham (2021). https://doi.org/10.1007/978-3-030-81293-5_3
7. Chen, L., et al.: Report on post-quantum cryptography, vol. 12. US Department of Commerce, National Institute of Standards and Technology (2016)
8. Elleuch, M., Wachter-Zeh, A., Zeh, A.: A public-key cryptosystem from interleaved Goppa codes. arXiv preprint arXiv:1809.03024 (2018)

9. Haslach, C., Han Vinck, A.J.: A decoding algorithm with restrictions for array codes. IEEE Trans. Inf. Theory **45**(7), 2339–2344 (1999)

10. Haslach, C., Han Vinck, A.J.: Efficient decoding of interleaved linear block codes. In: 2000 IEEE International Symposium on Information Theory (Cat. No. 00CH37060), p. 149. IEEE (2000)

11. Holzbaur, L., Liu, H., Puchinger, S., Wachter-Zeh, A.: On decoding and applications of interleaved Goppa codes. In: 2019 IEEE International Symposium on Information Theory (ISIT), pp. 1887–1891. IEEE (2019)

12. Horlemann-Trautmann, A.-L., Weger, V.: Information set decoding in the Lee metric with applications to cryptography. Adv. Math. Commun. **15**(4) (2021)

13. Johansson, T., Jonsson, F.: On the complexity of some cryptographic problems based on the general decoding problem. IEEE Trans. Inf. Theory **48**(10), 2669–2678 (2002)

14. Kabatianskii, G., Krouk, E., Smeets, B.: A digital signature scheme based on random error-correcting codes. In: Darnell, M. (ed.) Cryptography and Coding 1997. LNCS, vol. 1355, pp. 161–167. Springer, Heidelberg (1997). https://doi.org/10.1007/BFb0024461

15. Kabatiansky, G., Krouk, E., Semenov, S.: Error Correcting Coding and Security for Data Networks: Analysis of the Superchannel Concept. Wiley, Hoboken (2005)

16. Metzner, J.J., Kapturowski, E.J.: A general decoding technique applicable to replicated file disagreement location and concatenated code decoding. IEEE Trans. Inf. Theory **36**(4), 911–917 (1990)

17. Moody, D.: The beginning of the end: the first NIST PQC standards (2022). https://csrc.nist.gov/Presentations/2022/the-beginning-of-the-end-the-first-nist-pqc-standa

18. Otmani, A., Tillich, J.-P.: An efficient attack on all concrete KKS proposals. In: Yang, B.-Y. (ed.) PQCrypto 2011. LNCS, vol. 7071, pp. 98–116. Springer, Heidelberg (2011). https://doi.org/10.1007/978-3-642-25405-5_7

19. Prange, E.: The use of information sets in decoding cyclic codes. IRE Trans. Inf. Theory **8**(5), 5–9 (1962)

20. Renner, J., Puchinger, S., Wachter-Zeh, A.: Interleaving Loidreau's rank-metric cryptosystem. In: 2019 XVI International Symposium Problems of Redundancy in Information and Control Systems (REDUNDANCY), pp. 127–132. IEEE (2019)

21. Roth, R.M., Vontobel, P.O.: Coding for combined block-symbol error correction. IEEE Trans. Inf. Theory **60**(5), 2697–2713 (2014)

22. Sendrier, N.: Decoding one out of many. In: Yang, B.-Y. (ed.) PQCrypto 2011. LNCS, vol. 7071, pp. 51–67. Springer, Heidelberg (2011). https://doi.org/10.1007/978-3-642-25405-5_4

23. Stern, J.: A method for finding codewords of small weight. In: Cohen, G., Wolfmann, J. (eds.) Coding Theory 1988. LNCS, vol. 388, pp. 106–113. Springer, Heidelberg (1989). https://doi.org/10.1007/BFb0019850

24. Weger, V., Khathuria, K., Horlemann, A.-L., Battaglioni, M., Santini, P., Persichetti, E.: On the hardness of the Lee syndrome decoding problem. Adv. Math. Commun. (2022)

A Study of Error Floor Behavior
in QC-MDPC Codes

Sarah Arpin[1], Tyler Raven Billingsley[2], Daniel Rayor Hast[3], Jun Bo Lau[4],
Ray Perlner[5], and Angela Robinson[5(✉)]

[1] Department of Mathematics, University of Colorado Boulder, Boulder, USA
[2] Department of Mathematics, Rose-Hulman Institute of Technology,
Terre Haute, USA
[3] Department of Mathematics and Statistics, Boston University, Boston, USA
[4] Department of Mathematics, University of California San Diego,
San Diego, USA
[5] Computer Security Division, National Institute of Standards and Technology,
Gaithersburg, USA
angela.robinson@nist.gov

Abstract. We present experimental findings on the decoding failure
rate (DFR) of BIKE, a fourth-round candidate in the NIST Post-
Quantum Standardization process, at the 20-bit security level. We select
parameters according to BIKE design principles and conduct a series
of experiments. We directly compute the average DFR on a range of
BIKE block sizes and identify both the waterfall and error floor regions
of the DFR curve. We then study the influence on the average DFR of
three sets $\mathcal{C}$, $\mathcal{N}$, and $2\mathcal{N}$ of near-codewords—vectors of low weight that
induce syndromes of low weight—defined by Vasseur in 2021. We find
that error vectors leading to decoding failures have small maximum support intersection with elements of these sets; further, the distribution of
intersections is quite similar to that of sampling random error vectors
and counting the intersections with $\mathcal{C}$, $\mathcal{N}$, and $2\mathcal{N}$. Our results indicate
that these three sets are not sufficient in classifying vectors expected to
cause decoding failures. Finally, we study the role of syndrome weight on
the decoding behavior and conclude that the set of error vectors that lead
to decoding failures differ from random vectors by having low syndrome
weight.

Keywords: BIKE · Error-correcting codes · McEliece · PQC ·
QC-MDPC

1 Introduction

In 2016, the U.S. National Institute of Standards and Technology (NIST)
announced a Post-Quantum Cryptography (PQC) standardization process
aimed at updating NIST's public-key cryptographic standards to include post-
quantum cryptography, that is, cryptographic algorithms that are thought to be

© The Author(s), under exclusive license to Springer Nature Switzerland AG 2022
J. H. Cheon and T. Johansson (Eds.): PQCrypto 2022, LNCS 13512, pp. 89–103, 2022.
https://doi.org/10.1007/978-3-031-17234-2_5

secure against attacks by a quantum computer. One of the remaining code-based candidates in the NIST PQC Standardization process is BIKE, a cryptosystem based on quasi-cyclic moderate density parity check (QC-MDPC) codes.

The BIKE cryptosystem was originally designed for ephemeral use, that is in settings where a KEM key pair is generated for every key exchange. The requirement for BIKE to be used ephemerally provides a countermeasure to a reaction attack by GJS [10] wherein an attacker can use knowledge of messages that lead to decoding failures to recover the private key of a scheme. During the second and third round of the NIST PQC process, BIKE proposed parameter sets that were designed to provide security in the static-key setting [1], that is, a setting where KEM key pairs can be reused for several key exchanges. In fact all the parameter sets in the third round specification of BIKE are designed to be secure in the static-key setting, although they do not formally claim to be secure in this setting. While security in the ephemeral setting can be provided by a scheme meeting the weaker IND-CPA security notion, security in a static-key setting requires a scheme meeting the stronger IND-CCA2 security notion. Achieving IND-CCA2 security requires that BIKE's decoder has a sufficiently low decoding failure rate (DFR), both because the security proof of BIKE in the IND-CCA2 setting assumes a low DFR, and because if a QC-MDPC cryptosystem with a sufficiently high DFR is used in the static-key setting, it would allow an attacker to perform the GJS attack with a high probability of success.

By design, it is not feasible to directly compute an average DFR for BIKE at cryptographically relevant security levels. It is possible to measure DFRs for smaller code sizes and then use extrapolation methods to estimate the DFR for larger parameters [9,17]. One must consider the phenomenon known as the *error floor* region of DFR curves to avoid an underestimate of DFR for larger code sizes. It is known that for LDPC and MDPC codes, the logarithm of the DFR drops significantly faster than linearly, and then linearly as the signal-to-noise ratio is increased [15,21]. Thus a typical DFR curve contains a concave *waterfall* region followed by a near-linear *error floor* region. One must accurately predict the error floor of a DFR curve to accurately predict the DFR for cryptographically relevant code sizes.

The error floor regions for low density parity check (LDPC) codes have been extensively analyzed in the literature. These are codes which can be defined by parity check matrices $H_{k \times n}$ with row Hamming weight on the order of $O(1)$, or up to $O(\log(2n))$. For each parity check matrix, there is a corresponding bipartite graph, known as a Tanner graph. Much analysis of iterative LDPC decoding behavior focuses on properties of Tanner graph representations of the code [4,14–16,24], such as identifying *stopping sets* and *trapping sets*.

Recent work [22,23] has considered several factors affecting the DFR of QC-MPDC codes: choice of decoder [17,20], classes of weak keys, and sets of problematic error patterns. It was noted that error vectors with a small Hamming distance from problematic error patterns—error vectors of low weight that emit syndromes of low weight—are significant contributors to the error floors of QC-

MDPC codes and it was concluded that these vectors were rare enough to not affect the overall DFR predictions for higher code sizes.

In this work, we examine the error floor behavior of QC-MDPC codes and focus on a scaled-down version of BIKE. Existing analysis of the DFR for BIKE [9,17] relies on extrapolations based only on modifying the block size, but this analysis is only accurate if an upper bound can be established for the DFR at which the transition to error floor behavior occurs (see e.g. Assumption 3 on page 7 of [17]). Vasseur's thesis uses experiments with error vectors based on known classes of codewords and near-codewords to give an upper bound for the transition DFR. We try to directly measure the transition point and see if it can be modeled based on the known contributions to error floor behavior described in Vasseur's thesis, but we cannot directly measure the transition point for cryptographic size parameters, since that transition occurs at too low a DFR. We use the Black-Grey-Flip decoder [9], the recommended BIKE decoder as of the time of writing, and filter out any keys belonging to the classes of weak keys defined by [22]. We consider the three sets of *near codewords* as defined in [22] and find that error vectors that lead to decoding failures have small (between 2 and 8 bits) support intersections with elements of this set. We conclude that error vectors that emit syndromes of low weight are significant contributors to decoding failures, but are not fully captured by the sets of near codewords defined in [22].

2 Background

2.1 Coding Theory and QC-MDPC Codes

Throughout this document, let $\mathbb{F}_2$ denote the finite field of two elements. For $r \in \mathbb{N}$, $x \in \mathbb{F}_2^r$, let $|x|$ denote the Hamming weight of x. For two vectors $x, y \in \mathbb{F}_2^r$, let $x \star y = (x_0 \cdot y_0, x_1 \cdot y_1, \ldots, x_{r-1} \cdot y_{r-1})$ denote the Schur product. Let $\mathcal{C}(n, k)$ be a binary linear code, $n, k \in \mathbb{N}$. Then $\mathcal{C} \colon \mathbb{F}_2^k \to \mathbb{F}_2^n$ maps information words to codewords and the set of 2^k codewords forms a k-dimensional vector space of $\mathbb{F}_2^n$. Let $\mathcal{B} = \{b_0, b_1, \ldots, b_{k-1}\}$ be a basis for this subspace, $b_i \in \mathbb{F}_2^n$. Then the code $\mathcal{C}$ can be described by a generator matrix

$$G = \begin{bmatrix} b_0 \\ b_1 \\ \vdots \\ b_{k-1} \end{bmatrix}.$$

The code can equivalently be described by a parity check matrix $H \in \mathbb{F}_2^{n-k \times n}$ which is a generator matrix for the dual code $\mathcal{C}^\perp = \{x \in \mathbb{F}_2^n : \forall c \in \mathcal{C}, x \cdot c = 0\}$. Thus the following relationship holds: $HG^T = 0 \in \mathbb{F}_2^{k \times n-k}$. For any vector $y \in \mathbb{F}_2^n$, and parity check matrix H, the matrix-vector product $Hy^T = s \in \mathbb{F}_2^{n-k}$ is known as the syndrome. For any y such that $Hy^T = 0 \in \mathbb{F}_2^{n-k}$, y is a codeword (i.e., $y \in \mathcal{C}$).

A $v \times v$ circulant matrix is a square matrix such that each row r_{i+1} is one shift to the right of the previous row r_i for $i \in \{0, 1, \ldots, v-1\}$. The ring of $v \times v$ circulant matrices over $\mathbb{F}_2$ is isomorphic to the polynomial ring $\mathbb{F}_2[x]/\langle x^v + 1 \rangle$. A quasi-cyclic (QC) matrix is a block sum of circulant matrices.

2.2   BIKE

Bit-flipping Key Encapsulation (BIKE) is a cryptosystem based on binary linear codes with quasi-cyclic structure and moderately sparse private keys [1]. The private key $H \in \mathbb{F}_2^{r \times 2r}$ is composed of two circulant blocks: H_0, H_1 of size $r \times r$ with r prime and such that $x^r - 1$ has only two irreducible factors modulo 2. The columns of H have weight d and the rows h_i of H are such that $|h_i| = w = 2d$ for all $i \in \{0, \ldots, r-1\}$. MDPC code parameters satisfy row weight $w \approx \sqrt{n}$ for n the length of the code.

At a high level, the public-key encryption system underlying the BIKE KEM is composed of three algorithms: key generation, encryption, and decryption. The key generation algorithm generates a private key $H = [H_0 | H_1] \in \mathbb{F}_2^{r \times 2r}$ and public key H' is H in systematic form ($H' = H_0^{-1} H$). To encrypt a message m, a sender must encode m into a vector e of suitable weight t, then compute the syndrome $H' e^T = s$. The receiver decrypts by decoding the syndrome s using the secret key H and a predefined syndrome decoding algorithm. The recommended BIKE syndrome decoder as of the time of writing is the Black-Grey-Flip decoder [9].

Let λ denote the security parameter and let H denote a BIKE secret key. The security of BIKE depends on the inability of an attacker to break (variants of) the syndrome decoding problem(s). The best known attacks are information set decoding (ISD) algorithms, first introduced in 1962 by Prange [13] and later improved in dozens of works yielding small change in the overall asymptotic cost. (See [5,12,19] for a non-exhaustive list). Thus, for BIKE to achieve λ bits of security against the best known ISD attacks [7], the BIKE team determined that

$$\lambda \approx t - \frac{1}{2} \log_2 r \approx w - \log_2 r$$

where r denotes the circulant block size of H, w denotes the row weight of H, and t denotes the weight of the error vector in which a message is encoded [1].

2.3   Weak Keys and Near Codewords

For security level λ, the average decoding failure rate $\text{DFR}_{\mathcal{D},\mathcal{H}}$ for an IND-CCA secure cryptosystem should be $\leq 2^{-\lambda}$ where $\mathcal{D}$ denotes the decoder and $\mathcal{H}$ the key space. A set $\mathcal{W} \subset \mathcal{H}$ of keys is said to be *weak* if:

$$\frac{|\mathcal{W}|}{|\mathcal{H}|} \text{DFR}_{\mathcal{D},\mathcal{W}} > 2^{-\lambda} \geq \text{DFR}_{\mathcal{D},\mathcal{H}}.$$

In [22, Chapter 15], Vasseur identifies three types of *weak keys* for the BIKE cryptosystem:

- **Type I:** keys with many consecutive nonzero bits in the rows of one of the cyclic blocks, first identified by [8].
- **Type II:** keys with nonzero bits at many regular intervals in the rows of one of the cyclic blocks.
- **Type III:** keys with many intersections between the columns of the two cyclic blocks.

It is known that some sets of vectors are more likely to cause decoding failures than on average. A (u, v)-*near codeword* for a parity-check matrix H is an error vector e with Hamming weight u whose syndrome $s = He^T$ has weight v [11]. When u, v are small, these near codewords can be likely to cause decoding failures [15]. Based on the structure of BIKE, Vasseur defines three sets with small u, v as follows:

- $\mathcal{C}$: vectors which form the rows of the generator matrix $G = [H_1^T | H_0^T]$; these are codewords of weight w for the secret key $H = [H_0 | H_1]$.
- $\mathcal{N}$: the set of (d, d)-near codewords of the form $(v_0, \mathbf{0})$ or $(\mathbf{0}, v_1)$, where $\mathbf{0} \in \mathbb{F}_2^r$ and v_i is a row of the circulant block H_i of the parity check matrix.
- $2\mathcal{N}$: the set of vectors formed by sums of two vectors in $\mathcal{N}$. Due to the small chance of cancellation, one may consider the set $2\mathcal{N}$ as $(w - \epsilon_0, w - \epsilon_1)$-near codewords for some small $\epsilon_i \geq 0, i \in \{0, 1\}$.

3 Methods

Cryptographically relevant DFRs are too low ($< 2^{-128}$) to directly measure; it is only possible to measure DFRs for smaller code sizes, then use extrapolation methods to estimate the DFR to larger parameters. Some examples of this approach can be found in [8,9,18]. In this ongoing work, we begin by analyzing the decoding behavior for BIKE parameter sets targeting 20 bits of security in several experiments.

Parameters were selected according to BIKE design principles with the maximum error weight t reduced to prevent any inadvertent increase in decoding failures. Initial selected parameters are as follows: $(r, w, t, \lambda) = (523, 30, 18, 20)$. Later we include $389 \leq r \leq 827$ for prime r such that $x^r - 1$ has only two irreducible factors modulo 2.

We use the Black-Grey-Flip (BGF) decoder in all experiments. We used the original threshold selection function, defined in section 2.5.1 of the BIKE v1.0 specification [2], to compute the bit-flip threshold for all instances. The affine threshold functions in the current version of BIKE are derived from this original threshold rule. We precomputed the values used in the threshold function and stored them in a hash table for ease of computation.

Vasseur identifies three classes of weak keys that impede decoding (see Sect. 2.3 for the definitions of these classes) and describes an algorithm for filtering out weak keys [22, Algorithm 15.3]. We implement this algorithm and use it to reject weak keys. The definition of weak key depends on a parameter T, which

Vasseur sets to 10 for BIKE parameters in the cryptographically relevant range ($\lambda \geq 128$). (Note that smaller values of T mean that more keys are excluded.)

We instead use $T = 3$ for the weak key threshold, the smallest value of T for which finding non-weak keys is feasible. This is justified by the following empirical observation: If we set $T = 4$, the decoding failure rate increases enormously; for example, an experiment with $(r, T) = (587, 4)$ observed a DFR on the order of 2^{-8}, compared to around 2^{-20} for $(r, T) = (587, 3)$. Thus, to measure the DFR for non-weak keys, we must set $T = 3$.

We use the Boston University Shared Computing Cluster [6], a heterogeneous Linux-based computing cluster with approximately 21000 cores, to run SageMath implementations of the BGF decoder [1,9] in all experiments. The experiments yielded a graph with both the waterfall and error floor regions for our parameter set in addition to many explicit examples of decoding failures that can be used for future analysis. All raw data and the decoder used for this paper are available at [3].

4   Average DFR over Full Message Space

We first compute an average DFR for all suitable block lengths r as follows. For r in Table 1, we sample a random key H, rejecting any *weak keys of types I, II, III* [22], a random vector e of weight t, compute $s = He^T$, run BGF decoder on input (H, s), and record the total number of failures. This procedure is run N times where N varies flexibly ($N \in \{10^3, 10^4, 10^5, 10^6, 10^7, 10^8\}$) to ensure there are enough decoding failures at each r for robust statistical analysis. In the waterfall region, fewer decoding trials were needed to get a statistically adequate number of decoding failures. As r increased, the number of trials needed increased. For $r > 587$, decoding failures were exceptionally sparse. Since these computations get quite expensive and the log-DFR rate was decreasing only linearly for $r > 587$, we chose not to continue increasing the number of trials. The error vectors tested in the DFR experiment all had weight 18. The results of this experiment are displayed in Table 1 and plotted with best fit curves in Fig. 1.

We define a decoding failure as any instance where, on input (H, s), where s is of the form $s = He^T$, the syndrome decoder output e' is such that $He'^T \neq s$ or $e' \neq e$. The experiment was also designed to record any decoding instances where $He'^T = s$ and $e' \neq e$, but none were discovered.

5   DFR on $\mathcal{A}_{t,\ell}(\mathcal{S})$ Sets

Vasseur identified and studied the influence of the proximity of error vectors to any $\mathcal{S} \in \{\mathcal{C}, \mathcal{N}, 2\mathcal{N}\}$, described in Sect. 2.3, on the DFR [22]. To quantify how close certain error vectors are to such a set $\mathcal{S} \in \{\mathcal{C}, \mathcal{N}, 2\mathcal{N}\}$, Vasseur introduces the set

$$\mathcal{A}_{t,\ell}(\mathcal{S}) = \{v \in \mathbb{F}_2^{2r} : |v \star c| = \ell \text{ for some } c \in \mathcal{S}\},$$

Table 1. Decoding failure rates for r-values such that $389 \leq r \leq 827$, r is prime, and $x^r - 1$ has only two irreducible factors modulo 2. The data was computed using the parameters and methods described above.

r	Decoding failures	Decoding trials	$\log_2(\text{DFR})$
389	939	10^3	-0.09
419	680	10^3	-0.56
421	652	10^3	-0.62
443	3289	10^4	-1.60
461	1172	10^4	-3.09
467	850	10^4	-3.56
491	1524	10^5	-6.04
509	380	10^5	-8.04
523	946	10^6	-10.05
541	164	10^6	-12.57
547	70	10^6	-13.80
557	177	10^7	-15.79
563	108	10^7	-16.50
587	128	10^8	-19.58
613	61	10^8	-20.64
619	60	10^8	-20.67
653	37	10^8	-21.37
659	35	10^8	-21.45
661	37	10^8	-21.37
677	24	10^8	-21.99
701	20	10^8	-22.25
757	8	10^8	-23.58
827	7	10^8	-23.77

where t is the error vector weight and ℓ is the number of overlaps with an element of $\mathcal{S}$. To convert ℓ to a distance, for $v \in A_{t,\ell}(\mathcal{S})$ we define

$$\delta(v) = |c| + t - 2\ell$$

where c is a vector in $\mathcal{S}$ with $|v \star c| = \ell$. For δ low (equivalently, ℓ high), decoding failures are extremely common; see Fig. 2 for evidence at the 20-bit security level.

It is natural to consider the extent to which $A_{t,\ell}(\mathcal{S})$ for some ℓ and some $\mathcal{S} \in \{\mathcal{C}, \mathcal{N}, 2\mathcal{N}\}$ captures vectors which cause decoding failures. Our simulations indicate that it is extremely unlikely for a typical decoding failure vector to be in $A_{t,\ell}(\mathcal{S})$ for any $\mathcal{S}$ with a high ℓ. We define the *max overlap* of a decoding failure vector v with a $A_{t,\ell}(\mathcal{S})$ set for fixed $\mathcal{S}$ to be the largest value of ℓ for which $v \in A_{t,\ell}(\mathcal{S})$. Using experimental data from $r = 587, N = 10^8$ we recorded

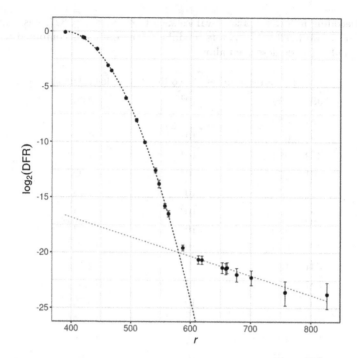

Fig. 1. Decoding failure rates as in Table 1 on a semi-log graph, with a quadratic best fit (blue) in the waterfall region $r < 587$ and a linear best fit (red) in the error floor region $r \geq 587$. (Color figure online)

128 total decoding failures and stored the 128 random error vectors that led to decoding failure. The relationship between these decoding failure vectors and the sets S is shown below; see Fig. 3a. We also repeated experiments for $r = 613$ and $r = 619$ with $N = 10^8$, recording 61 and 60 decoding failures, respectively. See Figs. 4 and 5 for this data.

Although the maximum value of ℓ is $t = 18$, the recorded values of ℓ never exceed 10. In fact, cases of $\ell = 10$ are quite rare. The values of ℓ recorded in experiments with vectors involved in decoding failures are greater than those of randomly sampled vectors, but it is expected that near-codewords and codewords of low weight overwhelmingly influence decoding failures in the error floor region [11]. From our results, it appears that only a minority of the error vectors producing a decoding failure are unusually close to a near-codeword or codeword of low weight. More analysis is needed to assess the relationships between the special sets S and decoding failures.

Notice that vectors close to a set S also have low syndrome weight; see Fig. 6. Moreover, as ℓ decreases, the syndrome weights approach the average.

From this, we are motivated to analyze to what extent syndrome weight predicts decoding failures.

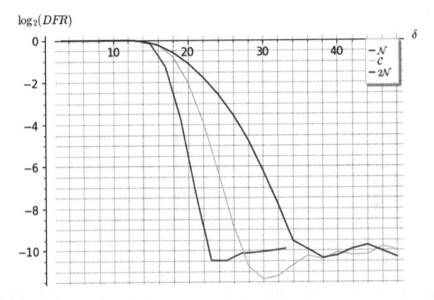

Fig. 2. 20-bit security DFR versus δ for near-codeword sets $\mathcal{C}, \mathcal{N}, 2\mathcal{N}$ for $r = 523$

6   Distribution of Syndrome Weight

We investigate the syndrome weights of error vectors causing decoding failures and compare them with those of generic vectors.

Figure 7 and Fig. 8 are obtained by generating 10^3 instances of non-weak parity check matrices H, random error vectors e, and then we compute the average weight of their syndromes $s = He^T$. For the ones causing decoding failures, we extract the information from our DFR computations containing the corresponding parity check matrices and error vectors and then we compute the average weight of their syndromes.

We observe that the syndrome weights of generic vectors tend to follow a normal distribution while the error vectors causing decoding failures have syndrome weights that are more concentrated around the mean, which we hypothesise to be lower than that of the generic vectors; see Fig. 8 for the case $r = 587$, where we compare the syndrome weights of the 128 vectors which caused decoding failures with the syndrome weights of the 10^5 randomly generated vectors of the same weight $t = 18$.

Figure 8 displays histograms of the syndrome weights of generic vectors and error vectors causing decoding failures for $r = 587$. Similarly, for the ten r values with $509 \leq r \leq 653$, we use data from the previous DFR computation and an additional 10^3 simulations of random error vectors to compare their syndrome weights. Using this data, we explore whether or not there is convincing evidence that the syndrome weights of error vectors causing decoding failures are lower than those of generic vectors. The null hypothesis is that there is no difference between the two groups in consideration while the alternative hypothesis is that

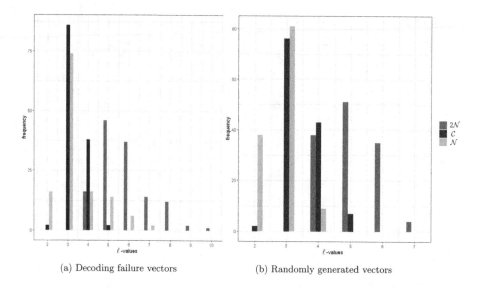

(a) Decoding failure vectors   (b) Randomly generated vectors

Fig. 3. For the 128 vectors v with $r = 587$, $d = 15$, $t = 18$ which caused decoding failures, we compute the distances from the sets $\mathcal{C}, \mathcal{N}, 2\mathcal{N}$ as measured by the maximum number of intersections with an element of these sets. Here, $\ell := |v \star c|$ for $c \in \mathcal{C}, \mathcal{N}, 2\mathcal{N}$. We do the same computation for 128 randomly generated vectors under the same parameters.

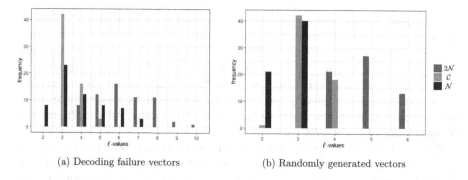

(a) Decoding failure vectors   (b) Randomly generated vectors

Fig. 4. For the 61 vectors v with $r = 613$, $d = 15$, $t = 18$ which caused decoding failures, we compute the distances from the sets $\mathcal{C}, \mathcal{N}, 2\mathcal{N}$ as measured by the maximum number of intersections with an element of these sets. Here, $\ell := |v \star c|$ for $c \in \mathcal{C}, \mathcal{N}, 2\mathcal{N}$. We do the same computation for 61 randomly generated vectors under the same parameters.

the generic vectors have higher syndrome weights. Both data come from random, independent sampling and have data sets with more than 30 observations. The difference in sample means may be modeled using a t-distribution. For each r, one could compute the point estimates $m_{\text{generic}} - m_{\text{DF}}$ of population difference $\mu = \mu_{\text{generic}} - \mu_{\text{DF}}$ and standard errors of the point estimate

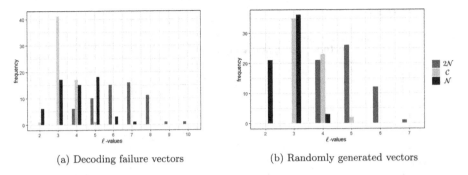

(a) Decoding failure vectors   (b) Randomly generated vectors

Fig. 5. For the 60 vectors v with $r = 619, d = 15, t = 18$ which caused decoding failures, we compute the distances from the sets $\mathcal{C}, \mathcal{N}, 2\mathcal{N}$ as measured by the maximum number of intersections with an element of these sets. Here, $\ell := |v \star c|$ for $c \in \mathcal{C}, \mathcal{N}, 2\mathcal{N}$. We do the same computation for 60 randomly generated vectors under the same parameters.

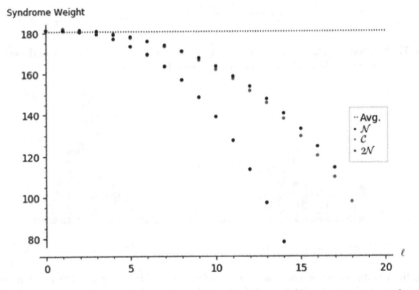

Fig. 6. Syndrome weight of error vectors in $\mathcal{A}_{t,\ell}(\mathcal{S})$ as ℓ (the maximum number of overlaps with an element of the set $\mathcal{S}$) varies, for $r = 587, t = 18$. Average syndrome weight for an error vector of weight $t = 18$ was approximately 180.712, plotted as the dotted horizontal line.

$$SE = \sqrt{\frac{\sigma_{\text{generic}}^2}{N_{\text{generic}}} + \frac{\sigma_{\text{DF}}^2}{N_{\text{DF}}}}.$$

With this information, one could compute the test statistic for this (one-tailed) test by the formula $T = \frac{\mu - 0}{SE}$. Using either a t-table or statistics software, we can find appropriate degrees of freedom and from there, the p-value, for each

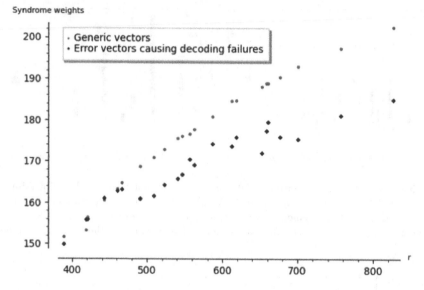

Fig. 7. Syndrome weights of random vectors with $t = 18$ (red circles) and vectors causing decoding failures (blue diamonds). (Color figure online)

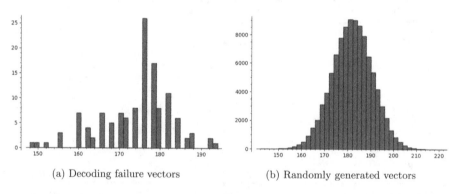

(a) Decoding failure vectors   (b) Randomly generated vectors

Fig. 8. A comparison of syndrome weights for $r = 587$ between the 128 error vectors which were found to be involved in decoding failures and 10^5 random vectors. Vertical axis is frequency, and horizontal axis is syndrome weight.

r. Our conclusion is that for the sixteen r-values in the range $509 \leq r \leq 827$, the p-value is less than the significance value $\alpha = 0.01$, and therefore we reject the null hypothesis, i.e., syndrome weights of error vectors causing decoding failures are lower than those of generic vectors. A general summary of the test statistic values $m_{\text{generic}} - m_{\text{DF}}$ and the corresponding p-values can be found in Table 2.

Table 2. Hypothesis test results for $509 \leq r \leq 827$, with the corresponding test statistic values and p-values, indicating the vectors causing decoding failures do have lower syndrome weights than generic vectors for $509 \leq r \leq 701$, notably a selection of r-values where the waterfall region meets the error floor in the DFR graph of Fig. 1.

r	$m_{\text{generic}} - m_{\text{DF}}$	p
509	9.29	<0.00001
523	8.60	<0.00001
541	9.79	<0.00001
547	9.29	<0.00001
557	6.20	<0.00001
563	8.61	<0.00001
587	6.56	<0.00001
613	10.92	<0.00001
619	8.86	<0.00001
653	15.99	<0.00001
659	11.49	<0.00001
661	9.40	<0.00001
677	14.45	<0.00001
701	17.58	<0.00001
757	16.25	0.00278
827	17.53	0.00002

7 Conclusion

In order to claim IND-CCA2 security with confidence for the proposed parameter sets of the BIKE cryptosystem, it is necessary to demonstrate that the BIKE decoder fails with cryptographically low probability on honestly generated ciphertexts. Such a low decoding failure rate cannot be directly measured, but is instead estimated by extrapolation from parameters with directly measurable decoding failure rates. In order for this analysis to be accurate, one must account for error floor behavior.

In our analysis of the BIKE cryptosystem at the 20-bit security level, we find that vectors which cause decoding failures have lower than average syndrome weight. However, identifying where these low syndrome weight vectors come from is still an open question. In [22,23], Vasseur proposes three classes of low syndrome weight vectors: $\mathcal{C}$, $\mathcal{N}$, and $2\mathcal{N}$. Vasseur also describes sets $\mathcal{A}_{t,\ell}(S)$ of vectors which are close to the sets $S \in \{\mathcal{C}, \mathcal{N}, 2\mathcal{N}\}$. In our work, while we do find that Vasseur's sets do contain many vectors that cause decoding failures, we do not find that these classes of vectors are responsible for the bulk of the decoding failures.

It therefore remains for future work to identify further classes of error vectors that might account for the observed decoding failures in our experiments.

If these can be identified it may be possible to predict error floor behavior for larger parameters, and thereby identify parameter sets that have a sufficiently low decoding failure rate to be used for IND-CCA2 security in the BIKE cryptosystem.

Acknowledgements. We would like to thank Valentin Vasseur for helpful discussions and code for reproducing experimental data, Paolo Santini for providing us with an initial SageMath implementation of the BGF decoder, and the anonymous reviewers for helpful feedback and suggestions.

This collaboration was initiated during the Rethinking Number Theory 2 (RNT2) Workshop. Funding for RNT2 came from the Number Theory Foundation and the University of Wisconsin-Eau Claire Department of Mathematics. This work was supported in part by the Simons Collaboration on Arithmetic Geometry, Number Theory, and Computation (Simons Foundation grant #550023).

References

1. Aragon, N., et al.: BIKE: bit flipping key encapsulation - spec v4.2 (2021). https://bikesuite.org/files/v4.2/BIKE_Spec.2021.07.26.1.pdf
2. Aragon, N., et al.: BIKE: bit flipping key encapsulation - spec v1.0 (2017). https://bikesuite.org/files/BIKE.2017.11.30.pdf
3. Arpin, S., Billingsley, T.R., Hast, D.R., Lau, J.B., Perlner, R., Robinson, A.: Raw data and decoder for the paper "A study of error floor behavior in QC-MDPC codes". https://github.com/HastD/BIKE-error-floor. Accessed 23 May 2022
4. Baldi, M.: QC-LDPC Code-Based Cryptography. SECE, Springer, Cham (2014). https://doi.org/10.1007/978-3-319-02556-8
5. Becker, A., Joux, A., May, A., Meurer, A.: Decoding random binary linear codes in $2^{n/20}$: how $1 + 1 = 0$ improves information set decoding. In: Pointcheval, D., Johansson, T. (eds.) EUROCRYPT 2012. LNCS, vol. 7237, pp. 520–536. Springer, Heidelberg (2012). https://doi.org/10.1007/978-3-642-29011-4_31
6. Boston University Shared Computing Cluster. https://www.bu.edu/tech/support/research/computing-resources/scc/. Accessed 18 Feb 2022
7. Canto Torres, R., Sendrier, N.: Analysis of information set decoding for a sub-linear error weight. In: Takagi, T. (ed.) PQCrypto 2016. LNCS, vol. 9606, pp. 144–161. Springer, Cham (2016). https://doi.org/10.1007/978-3-319-29360-8_10
8. Drucker, N., Gueron, S., Kostic, D.: On constant-time QC-MDPC decoders with negligible failure rate. In: Baldi, M., Persichetti, E., Santini, P. (eds.) CBCrypto 2020. LNCS, vol. 12087, pp. 50–79. Springer, Cham (2020). https://doi.org/10.1007/978-3-030-54074-6_4
9. Drucker, N., Gueron, S., Kostic, D.: QC-MDPC decoders with several shades of gray. In: Ding, J., Tillich, J.-P. (eds.) PQCrypto 2020. LNCS, vol. 12100, pp. 35–50. Springer, Cham (2020). https://doi.org/10.1007/978-3-030-44223-1_3
10. Guo, Q., Johansson, T., Stankovski, P.: A key recovery attack on MDPC with CCA security using decoding errors. In: Cheon, J.H., Takagi, T. (eds.) ASIACRYPT 2016. LNCS, vol. 10031, pp. 789–815. Springer, Heidelberg (2016). https://doi.org/10.1007/978-3-662-53887-6_29
11. MacKay, D.J.C., Postol, M.S.: Weaknesses of Margulis and Ramanujan-Margulis low-density parity-check codes. Electron. Notes Theor. Comput. Sci. **74**, 97–104 (2003). MFCSIT 2002, The Second Irish Conference on the Mathematical Foundations of Computer Science and Information Technology

12. May, A., Meurer, A., Thomae, E.: Decoding random linear codes in $\tilde{\mathcal{O}}(2^{0.054n})$. In: Lee, D.H., Wang, X. (eds.) ASIACRYPT 2011. LNCS, vol. 7073, pp. 107–124. Springer, Heidelberg (2011). https://doi.org/10.1007/978-3-642-25385-0_6
13. Prange, E.: The use of information sets in decoding cyclic codes. IRE Trans. Inf. Theory **8**(5), 5–9 (1962)
14. Price, A., Hall, J.: A survey on trapping sets and stopping sets. arXiv e-prints (2017)
15. Richardson, T.: Error floors of LDPC codes. In: Proceedings of the 41st Annual Allerton Conference on Communication, Control, and Computing, pp. 1426–1435 (2003)
16. Richter, G.: Finding small stopping sets in the Tanner graphs of LDPC codes. In: 4th International Symposium on Turbo Codes and Related Topics, pp. 1–5 (2006)
17. Sendrier, N., Vasseur, V.: About low DFR for QC-MDPC decoding. Cryptology ePrint Archive, Paper 2019/1434 (2019). https://eprint.iacr.org/2019/1434
18. Sendrier, N., Vasseur, V.: On the decoding failure rate of QC-MDPC bit-flipping decoders. In: Ding, J., Steinwandt, R. (eds.) PQCrypto 2019. LNCS, vol. 11505, pp. 404–416. Springer, Cham (2019). https://doi.org/10.1007/978-3-030-25510-7_22
19. Stern, J.: A method for finding codewords of small weight. In: Cohen, G., Wolfmann, J. (eds.) Coding Theory 1988. LNCS, vol. 388, pp. 106–113. Springer, Heidelberg (1989). https://doi.org/10.1007/BFb0019850
20. Tillich, J.-P.: The decoding failure probability of MDPC codes. In: 2018 IEEE International Symposium on Information Theory (ISIT), pp. 941–945. IEEE (2018)
21. Vasić, B., Chilappagari, S.K., Nguyen, D.V.: Failures and error floors of iterative decoders, chapter 6. In: Declerq, D., Fossorier, M., Biglieri, E. (eds.) Academic Press Library in Mobile and Wireless Communications, pp. 299–341. Academic Press, Oxford (2014)
22. Vasseur, V.: Post-quantum cryptography: a study of the decoding of QC-MDPC codes. Ph.D. thesis, Université de Paris (2021)
23. Vasseur, V.: QC-MDPC codes DFR and the IND-CCA security of BIKE. Cryptology ePrint Archive, Paper 2021/1458 (2021). https://eprint.iacr.org/2021/1458
24. Wang, C.-C., Kulkarni, S.R., Vincent Poor, H.: Finding all small error-prone substructures in LDPC codes. IEEE Trans. Inform. Theory **55**(5), 1976–1999 (2009)

Multivariate Cryptography
and the MinRank Problem

Improvement of Algebraic Attacks for Solving Superdetermined MinRank Instances

Magali Bardet[(⊠)] and Manon Bertin

LITIS, University of Rouen Normandie, Rouen, France
magali.bardet@univ-rouen.fr, manon.bertin@etu.univ-rouen.fr

Abstract. The MinRank (MR) problem is a computational problem that arises in many cryptographic applications. In Verbel et al. [24], the authors introduced a new way to solve superdetermined instances of the MinRank problem, starting from the bilinear Kipnis-Shamir (KS) modeling. They use linear algebra on specific Macaulay matrices, considering only multiples of the initial equations by one block of variables, the so called "kernel" variables. Later, Bardet et al. [7] introduced a new Support Minors modeling (SM), that consider the Plücker coordinates associated to the kernel variables, *i.e.* the maximal minors of the Kernel matrix in the KS modeling.

In this paper, we give a complete algebraic explanation of the link between the (KS) and (SM) modelings (for any instance). We then show that superdetermined MinRank instances can be seen as easy instances of the SM modeling. In particular, we show that performing computation at the smallest possible degree (the "first degree fall") and the smallest possible number of variables is not always the best strategy. We give complexity estimates of the attack for generic random instances.

We apply those results to the DAGS cryptosystem, that was submitted to the first round of the NIST standardization process. We show that the algebraic attack from Barelli and Couvreur [8], improved in Bardet et al. [5], is a particular superdetermined MinRank instance. Here, the instances are not generic, but we show that it is possible to analyse the particular instances from DAGS and provide a way to select the optimal parameters (number of shortened positions) to solve a particular instance.

Keywords: Post-quantum cryptography · MinRank problem · Algebraic attack · DAGS cryptosystem

1 Introduction

The MinRank Problem. The MinRank problem was first mentioned in [12] where its NP-completeness was also proven. It is a central problem in algebraic cryptanalysis, starting with the Kipnis and Shamir modeling [18] for the HFE encryption scheme. The MinRank problem is very simple to state:

© The Author(s), under exclusive license to Springer Nature Switzerland AG 2022
J. H. Cheon and T. Johansson (Eds.): PQCrypto 2022, LNCS 13512, pp. 107–123, 2022.
https://doi.org/10.1007/978-3-031-17234-2_6

Problem 1 (Homogeneous MinRank problem).
   Input: a target rank $r \in \mathbb{N}$ and K matrices $\mathbf{M}_1, \ldots, \mathbf{M}_K \in \mathbb{F}_q^{m \times n}$.
   Output: field elements $x_1, x_2, \ldots, x_K \in \mathbb{F}_q$, not all zero, such that

$$\mathrm{Rank}\left(\mathbf{M_x} \overset{\mathrm{def}}{=} \sum_{i=1}^{K} x_i \mathbf{M}_i \right) \leqslant r.$$

It plays a central role in public key cryptography. Many multivariate schemes are strongly related to the hardness of this problem, as in [18,20–22]. The 3rd round NIST post-quantum competition finalist Rainbow [14], or alternate GeMSS [13] suffered attacks based on the MinRank problem [3,9,10,23].

In code-based cryptography, the MinRank problem is exactly the decoding problem for matrix codes in rank metric. The two submissions ROLLO and RQC [1,2], from the 2nd round of the NIST post-quantum competition, have been attacked using algebraic cryptanalysis in [6,7]. Their security analysis relies on the decoding problem for $\mathbb{F}_{q^m}$-linear rank-metric codes, which can actually be reduced to the MinRank problem.

This is of great importance for cryptographic purposes to design algorithms that solve efficiently algebraic modeling for the MinRank problem, and to understand their complexity.

Algebraic Modeling. There has been a lot of recent progress in the algebraic modeling and solving of the MinRank problem. We start by recalling the first modeling, namely the Kipnis-Shamir (KS) modeling. Note that it implicitly assumes that the $n - r$ first columns of the small-rank matrix $\mathbf{M_x}$ we are looking for are linearly dependent from the last r ones. In this paper, we will assume that we are looking for a matrix $\mathbf{M_x}$ of rank *exactly* r (this can be achieved by looking for increasing ranks, starting from $r = 1$), and that the last r columns of $\mathbf{M_x}$ are linearly independent (it is true up to a permutation of the columns, and for random matrices it is true with high probability). We will see later that this last assumption is not mandatory.

Modeling 1 (Kipnis-Shamir Modeling [18]**).** *Consider a MinRank instance* $(\mathbf{M}_1, \ldots, \mathbf{M}_K) \in \mathbb{F}_q^{m \times n}$ *with target rank* r. *Then, the MR problem can be solved by finding* $x_1, \ldots, x_K \in \mathbb{F}_q^K$, *and* $\mathbf{C} = (c_{i,j}) \in \mathbb{F}_q^{r \times (n-r)}$ *such that*

$$\left(\sum_{i=1}^{K} x_i \mathbf{M}_i \right) \begin{pmatrix} \mathbf{I}_{n-r} \\ \mathbf{C} \end{pmatrix} = \mathbf{0}_{m \times (n-r)}. \tag{KS}$$

The $m(n-r)$ *equations are bilinear in the* K *linear variables* $\mathbf{x} = (x_1, \ldots, x_K)$ *and the* $r(n-r)$ *entries of the formal matrix* $\mathbf{C} = (c_{i,j})_{i,j}$, *refered to as the kernel variables.*

It is clear that a matrix has rank $\leq r$ if and only if its right kernel has dimension at least $n - r$, so that any solution of the MinRank problem is a solution of (KS).

The complexity of solving a generic bilinear system has been studied in [15, 17], and gives an upper bound for the KS system, but this estimate wildly overestimates the experimental results.

The matrix $\mathbf{M_x}$ has rank $\leq r$ if and only if all its minors of size $r+1$ are zero. This modeling has been presented and analysed in [16, 17]. Under the assumption that the last r columns of $\mathbf{M_x}$ are linearly independent, it is sufficient to consider minors involving columns in sets $T = \{t\} \cup \{n-r+1..n\}$ with $1 \leq t \leq n-r$, as it means that the last r columns generate the column vector space. The notation $|\mathbf{M}|_{J,T}$ represents the determinant of the submatrix of $\mathbf{M}$ where we keep only rows in J and columns in T.

Modeling 2 (Minors Modeling). *Let $(\mathbf{M}_1,\ldots,\mathbf{M}_K) \in \mathbb{F}_q^{m \times n}$ be a MinRank instance with target rank r. Then, the MR problem can be solved by finding $x_1,\ldots,x_K \in \mathbb{F}_q^K$ such that*

$$\left\{ |\mathbf{M_x}|_{J,T} = 0, \forall J \subset \{1..m\}, \#J = r+1, \forall T = \{t\} \cup \{n-r+1..n\} \subset \{1..n\} \right\}.$$
(Minors)

Recently, a new modeling has been introduced in [7], that is at the moment the most efficient one from the complexity point of view. It uses two ideas, that we will separate in two modelings: the first idea is that (KS) means that the vector space with generator matrix $\mathbf{M_x}$ is orthogonal to the one with generator matrix $(\mathbf{I}_{n-r} \; \mathbf{C}^\top)$. It is then straightforward to see that any row of $\mathbf{M_x}$ belongs to the dual space with generator matrix $(-\mathbf{C} \; \mathbf{I}_r)$. This leads to:

Modeling 3 (Support Minor Modeling-C [7]). *Let $(\mathbf{M}_1,\ldots,\mathbf{M}_K) \in \mathbb{F}_q^{m \times n}$ be a MinRank instance with target rank r. Then, the MR problem can be solved by finding $x_1,\ldots,x_K \in \mathbb{F}_q^K$, and $\mathbf{C} = (c_{i,j})_{1 \leq i \leq r, 1 \leq j \leq n-r} \in \mathbb{F}_q^{r \times (n-r)}$ such that*

$$\left\{ \left| \begin{pmatrix} \mathbf{r}_i \\ -\mathbf{CI}_r \end{pmatrix} \right|_{*,T} = 0, \forall T \subset \{1..n\}, \#T = r+1, \text{ and } \mathbf{r}_i \text{ row of } \mathbf{M_x} \right\}. \quad \text{(SM-C)}$$

The $m\binom{n}{r+1}$ equations are bi-homogeneous with bi-degree $(1,r)$ in the K linear variables $\mathbf{x} = (x_1,\ldots,x_K)$ and the $r(n-r)$ entries of the formal matrix $\mathbf{C} = (c_{i,j})_{i,j}$, refered to as the kernel variables.

Note that in (SM-C), the entries of $\mathbf{C}$ appear only as maximal minors of $(-\mathbf{CI}_r)$. This leads to the second idea from [7], which consists in using the Plücker coordinates: we replace each $|(-\mathbf{CI}_r)|_{*,T}$, that is a polynomial of degree $\#T = r$ in the entries of $\mathbf{C}$, by a new variable c_T using the injective Plücker map, see [11, p. 6].

$$p: \{\mathcal{W} \subset \mathbb{F}_q^n : \dim(\mathcal{W}) = r\} \to \mathbb{P}^N(\mathbb{F}_q) \qquad (N = \binom{n}{r} - 1)$$
$$\mathbf{C} \mapsto (c_T)_{T \subset \{1..n\}, \#T = r}.$$

Modeling 4 (Support Minor Modeling-c_T [7]). *Let $(\mathbf{M}_1, \ldots, \mathbf{M}_K) \in \mathbb{F}_q^{m \times n}$ be a MinRank instance with target rank r. Then, the MR problem can be solved by finding $x_1, \ldots, x_K \in \mathbb{F}_q^K$, and $(c_T)_{T \subset \{1..n\}, \#T=r} \subset \mathbb{F}_q^{\binom{n}{r}}$ such that*

$$\left\{ \sum_{t \in T} (\mathbf{M_x})_{i,t} c_{T \setminus \{t\}} = 0, \forall T \subset \{1..n\}, \#T = r + 1, \ and \ i \in \{1..m\} \right\}. \quad \text{(SM)}$$

The $m\binom{n}{r+1}$ equations are bilinear in the K linear variables $\mathbf{x} = (x_1, \ldots, x_K)$ and the $\binom{n}{r}$ minor variables c_T, for all $T \subset \{1..n\}, \#T = r$.

The benefit of introducing such coordinates to describe a vector space rather than a matrix describing a basis is that contrarily to the matrix representation, a vector space W has unique Plücker coordinates associated to it. This is not the case of the matrix representation of a vector space: if the rows of a matrix $\mathbf{C}$ generate the vector space, then the rows of $\mathbf{AC}$ generate the same vector space for any invertible $\mathbf{A} \in GL(r, \mathbb{F}_q)$. For our algebraic system, this brings the benefit of reducing the number of solutions of the system: there are several solutions $\mathbf{C}$ to the algebraic system (SM-C), that correspond to one unique solution to (SM). As already pointed out in [7], it is also extremely beneficial for the computation to replace polynomials $|(-\mathbf{CI}_r|_{*,T}$ with $r!$ terms of degree r in the entries of $\mathbf{C}$ by single variables c_T's in $\mathbb{F}_q$. We will use (SM-C) for the theoretical analysis of the link between the various modelings, and (SM) for the computational solving.

Contributions. As a first contribution, we show that the first three systems are related, more precisely

Proposition 1. *The set of equations (KS) is included in the set of equations (SM-C), and the ideals generated by the SM-C and KS equations are equal. Equations Minors (Minors modeling) are included in the ideal generated by KS.*

This proposition applies to any instance, without particular hypothesis.

Note that Eq. (Minors) contain only the linear variables, hence the ideals cannot be equal.

This proposition is not only interesting on the theoretical point of view, but it also allows to understand different computational strategies and to select the best one. A discussion is provided in 1.

In [24], Verbel et al. analyse degree falls occuring during a Gröbner basis computation of (KS), and show that for overdetermined systems this can occur before degree $r+2$, which is the general case. As a second contribution, we show that these degree falls are in fact equations from SM-C. Using the Plücker coordinates in (SM) allows to drastically reduce the size of the considered matrices. Moreover, we give example to show that minimising the degree and number of equations is not always the best strategy for optimising the solving complexity.

Finally, we revisit the DAGS cryptosystem [4], that was a 1st round candidate to the NIST post-quantum standardization process, and was attacked by Barelli and Couvreur [8]. We show that the attack is in fact a MinRank attack, and describe the structure of this non-random superdetermined MinRank instance. This precise understanding of the problem makes it possible to choose the right parameters for an optimal attack.

2 Notation and Preliminaries

Vectors are denoted by lower case boldface letters such as $\mathbf{x}$, $\mathbf{e}$ and matrices by upper case letters $\mathbf{C}$, $\mathbf{M}$. The all-zero vector of length ℓ is denoted by $\mathbf{0}_\ell$. The j-th coordinate of a vector $\mathbf{x}$ is denoted by x_j and the submatrix of a matrix $\mathbf{C}$ formed from the rows in I and columns in J by $\mathbf{C}_{I,J}$. When I (*resp. J*) represents all the rows (*resp.* columns), we may use the notation $\mathbf{C}_{*,J}$ (*resp.* $\mathbf{C}_{I,*}$). We simplify $\mathbf{C}_{i,*} = \mathbf{C}_{\{i\},*}$ (*resp.* $\mathbf{C}_{*,j} = \mathbf{C}_{*,\{j\}}$) for the i-th row of $\mathbf{C}$ (*resp.* j-th column of $\mathbf{C}$) and $c_{i,j} = \mathbf{C}_{\{i\},\{j\}}$ for the entry in row i and column j. Finally, $|\mathbf{C}|$ is the determinant of a matrix $\mathbf{C}$, $|\mathbf{C}|_{I,J}$ is the determinant of the submatrix $\mathbf{C}_{I,J}$ and $|\mathbf{C}|_{*,J}$ the one of $\mathbf{C}_{*,J}$. The transpose of a matrix $\mathbf{C}$ is $\mathbf{C}^\top$.

The all-one vector of size n is denoted by $\mathbb{1}_n = (1, \ldots, 1)$.

To simplify the presentation, we restrict ourselves to a field of characteristic 2, but the results are valid for any characteristic, the only difference being the occurrence of a $\pm$ sign before each formula.

For any matrix $\mathbf{A}$ of size $q \times r$ with $r \leq q$, and any set $J \subset \{1..q\}$ of size $r + 1$, we define the vector $\mathbf{V}_J(\mathbf{A})$ of length q whose jst entry is 0 if $j \notin J$ and $|\mathbf{A}|_{J\setminus\{j\},*}$ for $j \in J$. For $\mathbf{A}$ of size $r \times q$ with $r \leq q$ we define $\mathbf{V}_J(\mathbf{A}) \stackrel{\text{def}}{=} \mathbf{V}_J(\mathbf{A}^\top)$.

Using Laplace expansion along a column, it is clear that for any vector $\mathbf{a}$ of length q we have

$$\mathbf{V}_J(\mathbf{A})\mathbf{a}^\top = \left|(\mathbf{a}^\top \, \mathbf{A})\right|_{J,*}. \tag{1}$$

We denote by $vec_{row}(\mathbf{A})$ (*resp.* $vec_{col}(\mathbf{A})$) the vertical vector formed by concatenating successives rows (*resp.* cols) of $\mathbf{A}$. We have the formula

$$vec_{row}(\mathbf{AXY}) = (\mathbf{A} \otimes \mathbf{Y}^\top)vec_{row}(\mathbf{X}) \tag{2}$$
$$vec_{col}(\mathbf{AXY}) = (\mathbf{Y}^\top \otimes \mathbf{A})vec_{col}(\mathbf{X})$$

where $\mathbf{A} \otimes \mathbf{B} \stackrel{\text{def}}{=} (a_{i,j}\mathbf{B})_{i,j}$ is the Kronecker product of two matrices $\mathbf{A} = (a_{i,j})_{i,j}$ and $\mathbf{B}$.

For a system $\mathcal{F} = \{f_1, \ldots, f_M\}$ of bilinear equations in two sets of variables $\mathbf{x} = (x_j)_{1 \leq j \leq n_x}$ and $\mathbf{y} = (y_\ell)_{1 \ell l \leq n_y}$, it is usual to consider the associated Jacobian matrices:

$$Jac_{\mathbf{x}}(\mathcal{F}) = \left(\frac{\partial f_i}{\partial x_j}\right)_{i=1..M, j=1..n_x}, \qquad Jac_{\mathbf{y}}(\mathcal{F}) = \left(\frac{\partial f_i}{\partial y_\ell}\right)_{i=1..M, \ell=1..n_y}.$$

For homogeneous bilinear systems they satisfy the particular relation:

$$Jac_{\mathbf{x}}(\mathcal{F})\mathbf{x}^\top = \left(f_1 \cdots f_M\right)^\top$$

and any vector in the left kernel of a Jacobian matrix is a syzygy of the system. Moreover, $Jac_{\mathbf{x}}$ is a matrix whose entries are linear form in the variables $\mathbf{y}$, and Cramer's rule show that the left kernel of $Jac_{\mathbf{x}}$ contains vectors $\mathbf{V}_T(Jac_{\mathbf{x}}(\mathcal{F})_{T,*})$ using the notation from (1) for all $T \subset \{1..M\}$ of size $n_y + 1$. Generically those vectors generate the left kernel. For affine systems, we consider the jacobian matrix associated to the homogeneous part of highest degree of the system, and any syzygy for this part, that is not a syzygy of the entire system leads to a degree fall.

3   Relations Between the Various Modelings

This section applies to any MinRank instance without any specific hypothesis.

The KS modeling consists in bilinear equations in two blocks of variables $\mathbf{x}$ and $\mathbf{C}$, whereas the SM-C modeling contains equations of degree 1 in $\mathbf{x}$ and r in $\mathbf{C}$, the variables $\mathbf{C}$ appearing only as maximal minors of $(-\mathbf{C}\ \mathbf{I}_r)$.

In the case of the KS modeling, it has been noticed in [24], and later [7, Lemma1] that the jacobian matrices have a very particular shape: if we write $\mathbf{M}_{\mathbf{x}} = \left(\mathbf{M}_{\mathbf{x}}^{(1)}\ \mathbf{M}_{\mathbf{x}}^{(2)}\right)$ with $\mathbf{M}_{\mathbf{x}}^{(1)}$ of size $m \times (n - r)$ and $\mathbf{M}_{\mathbf{x}}^{(2)}$ of size $m \times r$, and in the same way we write each $\mathbf{M}_i = \left(\mathbf{M}_i^{(1)}\ \mathbf{M}_i^{(2)}\right)$, then the homogeneous part of highest degree of the system is $\mathbf{M}_{\mathbf{x}}^{(2)}\mathbf{C}$, and its Jacobian matrices are, if we take the variables and equations in row/column order:

$$Jac_{x_i}\left(vec_{row}\left(x_i\mathbf{M}_i^{(2)}\mathbf{C}\right)\right) = vec_{row}\left(\mathbf{M}_i^{(2)}\mathbf{C}\right) = (\mathbf{I}_m \otimes \mathbf{C}^\top)\, vec_{row}\left(\mathbf{M}_i^{(2)}\right)$$

$$Jac_{\mathbf{x}}\left(vec_{row}\left(\mathbf{M}_{\mathbf{x}}^{(2)}\mathbf{C}\right)\right) = (\mathbf{I}_m \otimes \mathbf{C}^\top)\left(vec_{row}\left(\mathbf{M}_1^{(2)}\right) \ldots vec_{row}\left(\mathbf{M}_K^{(2)}\right)\right)$$

$$Jac_{vec_{col}(\mathbf{C})}\left(vec_{col}\left(\mathbf{M}_{\mathbf{x}}^{(2)}\mathbf{C}\right)\right) = \mathbf{I}_{n-r} \otimes \mathbf{M}_{\mathbf{x}}^{(2)} \qquad (3)$$

The jacobian matrix in $\mathbf{C}$ admits a left kernel that contains the following vectors:

$$\mathbf{e}_i \otimes \mathbf{V}_J(\mathbf{M}_{\mathbf{x}}^{(2)}) \text{ for any } J \subset \{1..p\}, \#J = r + 1, 1 \leq i \leq n - r, \qquad (4)$$

where $\mathbf{e}_i$ is the ith row of $\mathbf{I}_{n-r}$. As a consequence, the ideal generated by the (KS) equations contains the equations

$$(\mathbf{e}_i \otimes \mathbf{V}_J(\mathbf{M}_{\mathbf{x}}^{(2)}))vec_{col}(\mathbf{M}_{\mathbf{x}}\begin{pmatrix}\mathbf{I}_{n-r}\\\mathbf{C}\end{pmatrix}) = (\mathbf{e}_i \otimes \mathbf{V}_J(\mathbf{M}_{\mathbf{x}}^{(2)}))vec_{col}(\mathbf{M}_{\mathbf{x}}1)$$

$$= \mathbf{V}_J(\mathbf{M}_{\mathbf{x}}^{(2)})\mathbf{M}_{\mathbf{x}}^{(1)}\mathbf{e}_i^\top (\text{ thanks to (2))}$$

$$= |\mathbf{M}_{\mathbf{x}}|_{J,\{i\}\cup\{n-r+1..n\}} (\text{ thanks to (1))}.$$

Those are precisely the (Minors) equations.

The jacobian matrix in $\mathbf{x}$ admits a left kernel that contains the vectors

$$\mathbf{e}_\ell \otimes \mathbf{V}_J(\mathbf{C}) \text{ for any } J \subset \{1..n - r\}, \#J = r + 1, 1 \leq \ell \leq m. \qquad (5)$$

The ideal generated by the (KS) equations contains the equations

$$(\mathbf{e}_\ell \otimes \mathbf{V}_J(\mathbf{C}))vec_{row}(\mathbf{M}_{\mathbf{x}}^{(1)}) = \mathbf{e}_\ell \mathbf{M}_{\mathbf{x}}^{(1)} \mathbf{V}_J(\mathbf{C})^\top = \mathbf{V}_J(\mathbf{C})(\mathbf{M}_{\mathbf{x}}^{(1)}{}_{\ell,*})^\top$$

$$= \left| \left((\mathbf{M}_{\mathbf{x}}^{(1)}{}_{\ell,*})^\top \ \mathbf{C}^\top \right) \right|_{J,*} = \left| \begin{pmatrix} \mathbf{M}_{\mathbf{x}}^{(1)}{}_{\ell,*} \\ \mathbf{C} \end{pmatrix} \right|_{*,J}.$$

They are exactly the (SM-C) equations for $J \subset \{1..n-r\}$. They have a degree r in the kernel variables $c_{i,j}$.

In [24], the authors propose to solve (any) instances of KS by considering particular elements in the left kernel of the Jacobian matrix in $\mathbf{x}$ for some degree $1 \leq d \leq r-1$. This is done by considering all combination of the polynomials with coefficients

$$\mathbf{e}_\ell \otimes \mathbf{V}_J(\mathbf{C}_{T,*}) \tag{6}$$

for any $d \in \{1..r\}$, $J \subset \{1..n-r\}$, $\#J = d+1$, $T \subset \{1..r\}$, $\#T = d$ and $\ell \in \{1..m\}$. The authors in [24, Theorem 2] construct a matrix $\mathbf{B}_J$ whose left kernel contains elements related to the left kernel of the Jacobian matrix in $\mathbf{x}$. The key remark is that the equations they consider are

$$(\mathbf{e}_\ell \otimes \mathbf{V}_J(\mathbf{C}_{T,*}))vec_{row}\left(\mathbf{M}_{\mathbf{x}} \begin{pmatrix} \mathbf{I}_{n-r} \\ \mathbf{C} \end{pmatrix}\right) = \mathbf{e}_\ell \mathbf{M}_{\mathbf{x}} \begin{pmatrix} \mathbf{I}_{n-r} \\ \mathbf{C} \end{pmatrix} \mathbf{V}_J(\mathbf{C}_{T,*})^\top$$

$$= \left| \begin{pmatrix} \mathbf{r}_\ell \\ -\mathbf{C}\mathbf{I}_r \end{pmatrix} \right|_{*,T'}$$

for $T' = J \cup (\{n-r+1..n\} \backslash (T+n-r)) \subset \{1..n\}$ of size $r+1$. The equations have indeed a degree d in the kernel variables $c_{i,j}$.

Note that for $d = 0$, for $T' = \{\ell\} \cup \{n-r+1..n\}$ the equation $\left| \begin{pmatrix} \mathbf{r}_\ell \\ -\mathbf{C}\mathbf{I}_r \end{pmatrix} \right|_{*,T'}$ is the ℓth KS equation, and we get all SM equations. As a consequence, we have proven Proposition 1.

Remark 1. In the light of the previous results, we can understand more precisely the behavior of a generic Gröbner basis (GB) algorithm with a graded monomial ordering and a Normal selection strategy run on (KS) or (SM-C). As (SM-C) contains (KS) directly into the system, computing a GB on (SM-C) will also compute all equations that would be computed by (KS). On the other hand, when computing a GB for (KS), the algorithm will produce all equations (SM-C) by multiplying by monomials in $\mathbf{C}$, hence we can expect many syzygies during a GB computation on (SM-C).

This encourages to compute with (SM-C), but to look only at multiple of the equations by the x_i's variables, which is the strategy proposed in [7]. Adding to this the change of variable that consider any minor of $\mathbf{C}$ as a variable removes the hardness of computing with high degree polynomials (as the new variables have degree 1 instead of a polynomial of degree d with $d!$ coefficients for the minor).

4   Complexity of Solving Superdetermined Systems

Superdetermined MinRank instances are defined in [24] as MinRank instances where $K < rm$. In the light of the previous section, it is now clear that [24] considers for any $0 \le d \le r$ the equations

$$\mathcal{E}(d) \stackrel{\text{def}}{=} \left\{ E_{J,T,\ell} \stackrel{\text{def}}{=} \mathbf{e}_\ell \mathbf{M_x} \begin{pmatrix} \mathbf{I}_{n-r} \\ \mathbf{C} \end{pmatrix} \mathbf{V}_J (\mathbf{C}_{T,*})^\top : \begin{matrix} \forall J \subset \{1..n-r\}, \#J = d+1, \\ \forall T \subset \{1..r\}, \#T = d, \\ \forall \ell \in \{1..m\} \end{matrix} \right\}. \quad (7)$$

and search for linear combination that will produce degree falls. We can rewrite the equations

$$E_{J,T,\ell} = \left| \begin{pmatrix} \mathbf{r}_\ell \\ \mathbf{CI}_r \end{pmatrix} \right|_{*,T'} \quad \text{with } T' = J \cup (\{n-r+1..n\} \backslash (T+n-r)) \subset \{1..n\}$$

$$= \sum_{i=1}^{K} \sum_{j \in J} (\mathbf{M}_i^{(1)})_{\ell,j} x_i \, |\mathbf{C}|_{T,J \backslash \{j\}} + \sum_{i=1}^{K} \sum_{s \notin T} (\mathbf{M}_i^{(2)})_{\ell,s} x_i \, |\mathbf{C}|_{T \cup \{s\}, J} \, .$$

We have a total of $\sum_{d=0}^{r} m \binom{n-r}{d+1} \binom{r}{d} = m \binom{n}{r+1}$ equations in $\sum_{d=0}^{r} K \binom{n-r}{d} \binom{r}{d} = K \binom{n}{r}$ variables described by

$$\mathcal{V}(d) \stackrel{\text{def}}{=} \{ x_i \, |\mathbf{C}|_{T,J} \}_{i=1..K, \#J=d, \#T=d}, \quad \mathcal{V}(r+1) = \emptyset.$$

The system can be solved by linearization by constructing the associated Macaulay matrix: its rows are indexed by J, T, ℓ (with $\#J = d+1$, $\#T = d$) and its columns by i, J', T' (with $\#J' = d = \#T'$), and the coefficient in row (J, T, l) and column (i, J', T') corresponds to the coefficient of $E_{J,T,\ell}$ in the monomial $x_i \, |\mathbf{C}|_{T',J'}$. We can sort the columns by decreasing degree, i.e. consider first monomials in $\mathcal{V}(r)$, up to $\mathcal{V}(0)$ that are the K variables x_i, see Fig. 1. Then finding linear combination of the equations that produce degree falls can be done by computing the echelon form of the Macaulay matrix. For a set of rows in $\mathcal{E}(d)$, we have $m \binom{n-r}{d+1} \binom{r}{d}$ equations in $K \binom{n-r}{d+1} \binom{r}{r+1} + K \binom{n-r}{d} \binom{r}{d}$ monomials, and we get generically a degree fall under the condition

$$m \binom{n-r}{d+1} \binom{r}{d} \ge K \binom{n-r}{d+1} \binom{r}{d+1}$$

which is Corollary 5 in [24], and the first part of the Macaulay matrix with columns in $\mathcal{V}(d+1)$ is, up to a good choice of the ordering of rows and columns, a block of diagonal matrices $\mathbf{B}_J$ as described in [24].

The best complexity estimates comes from the (SM) modeling, when considering the minors $|\mathbf{C}|_{T,J}$ as new variables. Equation (7) contains $m \binom{n}{r+1}$ equations in K variables x_i and $\binom{n}{r}$ variables that are minors of $(-\mathbf{CI}_r)$. Hence the system can be solved whenever $m \binom{n}{r+1} \ge K \binom{n}{r}$ by linearization, i.e. $m(n-r) \ge K(r+1)$. After linearization, we get with overwhelming probability $\#\mathcal{V}(0) - 1 = m - 1$ linear equations in the x_i's only.

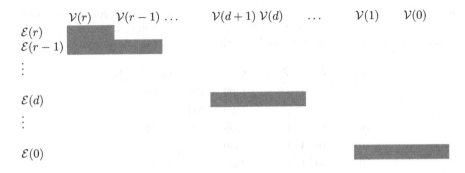

Fig. 1. Shape of the Macaulay matrix associated to Eq. (7). The columns correspond to equations in $\mathcal{V}(d)$, the rows to equations $\mathcal{E}(d)$. Gray cells correspond to non-zero part of the matrix.

As always, it is possible to improve computation by puncturing the matrix $\mathbf{M_x}$ (taking only sufficiently many columns so that we keep an overdetermined system), or by hybrid approach (performing an exhaustive search on some columns of $\mathbf{C}$, at the cost of q^{ar} operation in $\mathbb{F}_q$ for a columns). It is also possible, as in [7, Eq. (23) p. 19], to compute equations at higher degree b in x_i. For instance, at $b = 2$ we can multiply all equations in (SM) by x_i's variables, and we get for each set $\mathcal{E}(d)$ of equations:

$$m\binom{n}{r+1}K - \binom{n}{r+2}\binom{m+1}{2} \text{ equations,} \quad \binom{n}{r}\binom{K+1}{2} \text{ monomials.} \quad (8)$$

For instance, Table 1 compares the (SM) system with previous results from [24]. For $r = 5$, the ratio between equations and monomials in (SM) is smaller than 1, so that we cannot expect to solve by linearization directly. Computing at $b = 2$ would produce 14400 equations in 13860 variables of degree less than or equal to 7 in $(\mathbf{x}, \mathbf{C})$. Note that the last entry for $r = 6$ would theoretically require to go up to $b = 5$ with matrices of size 427350.

However, [24] suggest that we can have a closer look at the shape of the equations and maybe find a better complexity for some very overdetermined instances.

Hence, for a fixed $d \in \{0..r\}$, the set $\mathcal{E}(d)$ contains $m\binom{n-r}{d+1}\binom{r}{d}$ equations with $K\binom{n-r}{d}\binom{r}{d}$ monomials $\mathcal{V}(d)$ of bidegree $(1, d)$ and $K\binom{n-r}{d+1}\binom{r}{d+1}$ variables $\mathcal{V}(d+1)$ of bidegree $(1, d+1)$. In [24], the authors determine the first degree fall in KS by looking for the smallest d for which we have more equations in $\mathcal{E}(d)$ than variables in $\mathcal{V}(d+1)$. This produces $\text{Rank}(\mathcal{E}(d)) - \#\mathcal{V}(d+1)$ degree fall, but it is not clear how to end the computation. If there is more equations than variables, i.e.

$$m\binom{n-r}{d+1}\binom{r}{d} \geqslant K\binom{n-r}{d+1}\binom{r}{d+1} + K\binom{n-r}{d}\binom{r}{d} - 1$$

Table 1. Size of matrices on (SM) for a MinRank instance with $K = 10$ matrices of size $m \times n$, for various r. n can be decreased by puncturing the matrices to get a speedup. The results have been verified experimentally on random instances.

m	n	K	r	$\frac{m(n-r)}{K(r+1)}$	n_{eq}	n_{vars}	n_{rows} in [24]
10	10	10	2	2.6	1200	450	1530
10	5	10	2	1	100	100	
10	10	10	3	1.75	2100	1200	20240
10	7	10	3	1	350	350	
10	10	10	4	1.2	2520	2100	38586
10	9	10	4	1	1260	1260	
10	10	10	5	**0.8**	2100	2520	341495

then with overwhelming probability, the linear system is full rank (its kernel has dimension 1 as the system is homogeneous in $\mathbf{x}$) and a non-zero element in the kernel of the Macaulay matrix gives a value for each variable $x_i |\mathbf{C}|_{T,J}$. It is then straightforward to deduce x_i/x_{i_0} from two values $x_i |\mathbf{C}|_{T,J}$ and $x_{i_0} |\mathbf{C}|_{T,J}$. On the other hand, if

$$K \binom{n-r}{d+1}\binom{r}{d+1} \leq m \binom{n-r}{d+1}\binom{r}{d}$$

and

$$m \binom{n-r}{d+1}\binom{r}{d} < K \binom{n-r}{d+1}\binom{r}{d+1} + K \binom{n-r}{d}\binom{r}{d} - 1$$

then it is necessary to add new equations to end the computation. It can be done by consider equations of "higher degree". If each minor of $\mathbf{C}$ is taken as a variable, it doesn't add a computational burden. We can solve as soon as we can get sufficiently many blocks of equations $\mathcal{E}(d)$ such that we get more equations than columns. Experimental results are presented Table 2 on the same parameters as [24, Table 2]. For instance for a MinRank problem with 12×12 matrices and a target rank $r = 4$, the authors in [24] solve at degree $d = 4$ in $58\,s$, whereas it is more interesting to consider equations in $\mathcal{E}(3..4)$ that have degree up to 5, without considering equations of degree 2..3. Note that if we puncture too much the matrices, for instance by taking only $n = 8$ columns, then we do not have any more an overdetermined SM system, and solving it now require to produce more equations, for instance by considering $b = 2$. In this case, we get a system of 5880 equations in 5460 and we can solve, but this will be more costly than solving with $n = 9$.

Remark 2. There is an asymmetry between m and n in the modelings. It is always possible to exchange m and n by considering the transpose of the matrices, but it is not clear in general which problem will be easier ($m > n$ or $m < n$). For instance, for $K = 10$, $r = 2$ we can have the following behaviors: for $m = 6, n = 7$ the Macaulay matrix up to $d = r$ has size 210×210, whereas for $m = 7$, $n = 6$ it is not possible to solve at $b = 1$ (the Macaulay matrix has dimension 140×150).

Table 2. Experimental size of matrices on SM for a MinRank instance with $K = 12$ matrices of size 12×12, for various r. It is possible to puncture the codes, by considering only $n = \kappa + r$ columns of the matrices. We consider only systems for which SM solves at $b = 1$. The second row gives the size of a submatrix of blocks $\mathcal{E}(d)$ for some d that solves the problem faster.

r	κ	d	size	time	[24]	r	κ	d	size	time	[24]
4	8	0..4	9504×5940	5.6 s	58 s	5	7	0..5	11088×9504	11 s	756 s
		3..4	4032×3528	2.4 s				2..4	9660×9072	9.6 s	
	7	0..4	5544×3960	2.1 s	38 s	6	0..5		5544×5544	3.1 s	367s
	6	0..4	3024×2520	0.74 s	21 s						
		2..4	2232×2220	0.52 s							
	5	0..4	1512×1512	0.23 s	13 s						

We need to go to $b = 2$ and solve a matrix of size 980×825. On the contrary, for $m = 10$, $n = 6$, the Macaulay matrix has dimension 160×140 ($d = 1..2$), whereas for $m = 6$, $n = 10$, the Macaulay matrix for $d = r$ has size 336×280.

However, as the number of equations is a multiple of m, the best solution is often with $m \geq n$.

5   Application to DAGS

DAGS scheme [4] is a key encapsulation mechanism (KEM) based on quasi-dyadic alternant codes that was submitted to the first round of the NIST standardization process for a quantum resistant public key algorithm. It suffered from an algebraic attack [8] that efficiently recovers the private key, and was improved in [5]. Here, we show that the DAGS algebraic modeling is in fact a MinRank problem. However, the previous complexity results do not apply, as those MinRank instances have a structure, that can be used to understand more precisely the complexity.

5.1   Principle of the Attack

We recall some elements of the scheme. DAGS is based on the McEliece scheme and uses Quasi-Dyadic Generalized Srivastava codes, which are a subfamily of alternant codes. The structure of such codes is what allowed DAGS to be attacked [5,8].

The idea of the key-recovery attack leading to the modeling presented here is to find a subcode of the public code. The attack was proposed in two versions: a combinatorial one that uses brute force to find the subcode, and an algebraic one that relies on solving a polynomial system. The complexity of the combinatorial version is easy to compute, however the numbers of calculations remains too high to be done in practice. On the contrary, the algebraic attack is more efficient but its complexity is harder to estimate.

We focus on the second version and explain the principle. We begin by computing the invariant subcode of the public code of the scheme. Then, we search for a subcode of this invariant code by solving a bilinear system built from public parts of the scheme. Finally, we can recover the support and multiplier of the original alternant code.

In the next subsection, we explain how the system we want to solve is built.

5.2   Original Modeling

Let $\mathscr{C}_{\mathsf{pub}}$ be the DAGS public code, $\mathbf{H}_{\mathsf{pub}}$ be the public key of the scheme, which is a parity-check matrix of $\mathscr{C}_{\mathsf{pub}}$, and let $\mathbf{G}_{\mathsf{pub}}$ be its generator matrix.

We refer to [19, Chap. 12] for the definition of alternant codes. DAGS codes are quasi-dyadic alternant codes over $\mathbb{F}_{q^m}$, with q a power of 2 and $m = 2$. To build the system we need to understand the construction of quasi-dyadic alternant codes, that are alternant codes for which the support $\mathbf{x}$ and the multiplier $\mathbf{y}$ have a particular structure.

Definition 1. *Let $\gamma \geqslant 1$ and $n = 2^{\gamma} n_0$. The support $\mathbf{x} \in \mathbb{F}_{q^m}^n$ of a quasi-dyadic alternant code of order 2^{γ} is constructed from $(b_1, \ldots, b_{\gamma}) \in \mathbb{F}_{q^m}^{\gamma}$ that are linearly independent over $\mathbb{F}_2$, and $\tau = (\tau_1, \ldots, \tau_{n_0}) \in \mathbb{F}_{q^m}^{n_0}$ as*

$$\mathbf{x} \stackrel{def}{=} \tau \otimes \mathbb{1}_{2^{\gamma}} + \mathbb{1}_{n_0} \otimes \mathbf{g},$$

where $\mathbf{g} \stackrel{def}{=} (g)_{g \in \mathbb{G}}$ is a vector of all 2^{γ} elements of the group $\mathbb{G} = \langle b_1, \ldots, b_{\gamma} \rangle_{\mathbb{F}_2}$ which is the vector space generated by the elements (b_i) over $\mathbb{F}_2$.

The elements τ_i are randomy drawn from $\mathbb{F}_{q^m}$ such that the cosets $\tau_i + \mathbb{G}$ are pairwise disjoint.

For instance for $\gamma = 2$, we can choose $\mathbf{g} = (0, b_1, b_2, b_1 + b_2) = b_1(0, 1, 0, 1) + b_2(0, 0, 1, 1)$. For $\gamma = 3$ we take $\mathbf{g} = (0, b_1, b_2, b_1 + b_2, b_3, b_1 + b_3, b_2 + b_3, b_1 + b_2 + b_3) = b_1(0, 1, 0, 1, 0, 1, 0, 1) + b_2(0, 0, 1, 1, 0, 0, 1, 1) + b_3(0, 0, 0, 0, 1, 1, 1, 1)$. In general, one possible order for $\mathbf{g}$ is given by $\mathbf{g} = \sum_{i=1}^{\gamma} b_i \mathbf{e}_i$ where

$$\mathbf{e}_i \stackrel{def}{=} (\mathbf{0}_{2^{i-1}}, \mathbb{1}_{2^{i-1}}, \mathbf{0}_{2^{i-1}}, \mathbb{1}_{2^{i-1}}, \ldots) = \mathbb{1}_{2^{\gamma-i}} \otimes (0, 1) \otimes \mathbb{1}_{2^{i-1}}.$$

The group $\mathbb{G}$ acts by translation on $\mathbb{F}_{q^m}$, and its action induces a permutation of the code $\mathscr{C}_{\mathsf{pub}}$. This is what allows the DAGS system to have reduced public keys: the public matrix $\mathbf{G}_{\mathsf{pub}}$ is formed by blocks of size 2^{γ} where each row of the block is deduced from the first row by one of the permutation induced by $\mathbb{G}$.

The attack in [8] introduces the *invariant subcode* $\mathscr{C}_{\mathsf{pub}}^{\mathbb{G}}$ with respect to $\mathbb{G}$ of $\mathscr{C}_{\mathsf{pub}}$, which is defined as

Definition 2. *The invariant code of $\mathscr{C}_{\mathsf{pub}}$ is defined by:*

$$\mathscr{C}_{\mathsf{pub}}^{\mathbb{G}} = \{\mathbf{c} \in \mathscr{C}_{\mathsf{pub}} | \forall (i, j) \in \{0..n_0 - 1\} \times \{1..2^{\gamma}\}, c_{i2^{\gamma}+j} = c_{i2^{\gamma}+1}\}.$$

The invariant subcode has dimension $k_0 = k/2^\gamma$ where k is the dimension of $\mathscr{C}_{\mathsf{pub}}$. Its generator matrix $\mathbf{G}_{\mathsf{inv}}$ is easy to compute from $\mathbf{G}_{\mathsf{pub}}$: each block of 2^γ rows of $\mathbf{G}_{\mathsf{pub}}$ gives one row of $\mathbf{G}_{\mathsf{inv}}$ by summation. The entries of $\mathbf{G}_{\mathsf{pub}}$ are then repeated by blocks of size 2^γ, so that we can define a matrix $\tilde{\mathbf{G}} \in \mathbb{F}_{q^m}^{k_0 \times n_0}$ satisfying $\mathbf{G}_{\mathsf{inv}} = \tilde{\mathbf{G}} \otimes \mathbb{1}_{2^\gamma}$.

We introduce the component-wise product called Schur product:

Definition 3. *The* Schur product *of two codes $\mathscr{A}$ and $\mathscr{B} \subseteq \mathbb{F}_q^n$ corresponds to the code generated by all the component-wise products of one codeword from $\mathscr{A}$ and one codeword of $\mathscr{B}$:*

$$\mathscr{A} \star \mathscr{B} = \langle \mathbf{a} \star \mathbf{b} \mid \mathbf{a} \in \mathscr{A}, \mathbf{b} \in \mathscr{B} \rangle_{\mathbb{F}_q}$$

The attack in [8] amounts to find $\mathscr{D}$, an unknown subcode of $\mathscr{C}_{\mathsf{pub}}{}^{G}$ such that $\mathbf{x}$ is orthogonal to $\mathscr{D} \star \mathscr{C}_{\mathsf{pub}}{}^{\perp}$. This leads to following system with 2 unknowns, $\mathscr{D}$ and $\mathbf{x}$:

$$\mathbf{G}_{\mathscr{D} \star \mathscr{C}_{\mathsf{pub}}{}^{\perp}} \cdot \mathbf{x}^\top = 0 \qquad (9)$$

Algebraically, a generator matrix for $\mathscr{D} \star \mathscr{C}_{\mathsf{pub}}{}^{\perp}$ can be written with high probability as

$$\left((\mathbf{I}_{k_0 - c}\ \mathbf{U}) \cdot \mathbf{G}_{inv} \right) \star \mathbf{H}_{pub} \qquad (10)$$

with c the codimension of $\mathscr{D}$ in the invariant subcode $\mathscr{C}_{\mathsf{pub}}{}^{G}$. If we can not express the system like that, we just need to take another generator matrix for the invariant subcode of $\mathscr{C}_{\mathsf{pub}}$. This finally leads to the original modeling:

$$\left((\mathbf{I}_{k_0 - c}\ \mathbf{U})\ \mathbf{G}_{inv} \star \mathbf{H}_{pub} \right) \mathbf{x}^\top = 0 \qquad (11)$$

where $\mathbf{U}$ is a matrix of unknowns of size $(k_0 - c) \times c$, $\mathbf{G}_{inv} = \tilde{\mathbf{G}} \otimes \mathbb{1}_{2^\gamma}$ and $\tilde{\mathbf{G}}$ is a public invariant matrix of size $k_0 \times n_0$, $\mathbf{H}_{pub}$ is the public parity-check matrix, and $\mathbf{x} = \tau \otimes \mathbb{1}_{2^\gamma} + \sum_{i=1}^{\gamma} b_i \mathbb{1}_{n_0} \otimes \mathbf{e}_i \in \mathbb{F}_{q^m}^n$ is a vector of unknowns $\tau = (\tau_1, \ldots, \tau_{n_0})$ and $(b_1, \ldots, b_\gamma)$.

Remark 3. As explained in [8], any affine map $\mathbf{x} \to a\mathbf{x} + b$ for $a \in \mathbb{F}_{q^m}^*, b \in \mathbb{F}_{q^m}$ preserves the quasi-dyadic structure of the code, and leaves the code invariant, so that it is always possible to search among all possible $\mathbf{x}$ for the ones that satisfy $b_1 = 1$ and $\tau_{n_0} = 0$. Moreover, the vector $\mathbf{x}^q$, hence $\mathrm{Tr}(\mathbf{x}) \overset{\text{def}}{=} \mathbf{x} + \mathbf{x}^q$ are also solution of the system (11), so that $\mathrm{Tr}(b_2)^{-1}\mathrm{Tr}(\mathbf{x})$ is a solution with $\tau_{n_0} = 0$, $b_1 = 0$ and $b_2 = 1$ (as $\mathrm{Tr}(a) = 0$ for $a \in \mathbb{F}_q$ when $m = 2$).

Remark 4. As explained in [5], there is a lot of redundancy among the equations. We avoid that by considering only one out of every 2^γ rows in $\mathbf{H}_{\mathsf{pub}}$.

5.3   Modeling Update

A simple (but fastidious, see Appendix A) computation allows to write the system as a MinRank instance with matrices of size $(n_0 - k_0) \times k_0$, when $\tilde{\mathbf{G}} = (\mathbf{I}_{k_0}\ \mathbf{G})$

is taken in systematic form:

$$\left(\sum_{i=1}^{k_0} \tau_i \mathbf{M}_i + \sum_{j=1}^{n_0-k_0} \tau_{j+k_0} \mathbf{M}_{j+k_0} + \sum_{b=2}^{\gamma} b_i \mathbf{H}_i\right)\begin{pmatrix} \mathbf{I}_{k_0-c} \\ \mathbf{U}^\top \end{pmatrix} = \mathbf{0} \qquad (12)$$

$$\text{with } \mathbf{M}_i = \left(\mathbf{0}_{i-1}\ (\mathbf{G}_{\{i\},*})^\top\ \mathbf{0}_{k_0-i}\right) \forall 1 \leq i \leq k_0$$

$$\mathbf{M}_{j+k_0} = \begin{pmatrix} \mathbf{0}_{j-1} \\ (\mathbf{G}_{*,\{j\}})^\top \\ \mathbf{0}_{n_0-k_0-j} \end{pmatrix} \forall 1 \leq j \leq n_0 - k_0$$

$$\mathbf{H}_i = \mathbf{H}_{\mathsf{pub}}(\mathbf{I}_{n_0} \otimes \mathbf{e}_i^\top)_{*,\{1..k_0\}} \forall 2 \leq i \leq \gamma$$

It is clear that the matrices $\mathbf{M}_i$ from DAGS instances are not random, and in practice we have more degree falls than expected. On the other hand, the part concerning the variables b_i with matrices $\mathbf{H}_i$ seems to behave like a random system. Note also that experimentally we find that the system always produces 3 solutions. However, this is small enough to be able to recover the good one from the kernel of the Macaulay matrix, as only one belong to the finite field $\mathbb{F}_q$.

Proposition 2. *For the DAGS modeling, the Macaulay matrix associated to the set of equations $\mathcal{E}(d)$ has size $N_{rows} \times N_{cols} = (n_0 - k_0)\binom{k_0-c}{d+1}\binom{c}{d} \times (n_0 - k_0 - 1 + c + \gamma - 1)\binom{k_0-c}{d+1}\binom{c}{d+1}$, but its rank is*

$$\mathrm{Rank}(\mathcal{E}(d)) = \min\left(N_{rows}, \binom{k_0-c}{d+1}\left((n_0-k_0)\binom{c-1}{d} + \binom{c}{d+1}d\right)\right)$$

Note that it is always possible to use shortened codes on a_0 positions, that amounts to consider codes with parameters $(n_0 - a_0, k_0 - a_0)$.

The first sets of parameters were given in the specifications of the scheme. They are shown in Table 3. Experimental results in [5] give a solution of the system DAGS_3 in degree 4 with linear algebra on a matrix of size $725,895 \times 671,071$. It is improved by shortening the system up to $k_0 - a_0 - c = 4$ with a matrix of size $103,973 \times 97,980$ and a computation lasting 70 s. All results presented here allows to choose to shorten the system to $k_0 - a_0 - c = 5$ instead of 4, as for 4 the system does not leads directly to linear equations, and it reduces the computation to linear algebra on a matrix of size 2772 by 4284 that last only few seconds.

Table 3. DAGS original sets of parameters

Security level	q	n_0	k_0	γ	c	$k_0 - a_0 - c$	Matrix size	Rank	Time
DAGS_1 (128)	2^5	52	26	4	4	4	1456×2520	1322	3.5 s
DAGS_3 (192)	2^6	38	16	4	4	5	2772×4284	2540	8.8 s
DAGS_5 (256)	2^6	33	11	2	2	3	220×310	194	0.0 s

Conclusion

We have presented the link between the different modelings for the MinRank problem. This allows a more accurate understanding of the best strategy to solve MinRank instances.

We have shown that superdetermined MinRank instances are instances for which (SM) solves at $b = 1$, and that the maximal degree in the computations is not the best parameter to use to optimize the computation.

We have also presented the DAGS attack as a particular superdetermined MinRank one, and how the accurate study of the involved matrices allows to find the best strategy.

Acknowledgements. This work has been supported by the French ANR project CBCRYPT (ANR-17-CE39-0007).

A   Appendix

We want to reduce (11) to a MinRank problem (12). We start from (11):

$$\left(\left(\mathbf{I}_{k_0-c}\ \mathbf{U}\right)(\tilde{\mathbf{G}} \otimes \mathbb{1}_{2^\gamma}) \star \mathbf{H}_{pub}\right)\mathbf{x}^\top = 0.$$

Using the fact that $(\mathbf{A} \star \mathbf{B})\mathbf{a}^\top = 0$ is equivalent to $(\mathbf{A} \star \mathbf{a})\mathbf{B}^\top = 0$, that $\mathbf{A} \otimes \mathbf{a} = \mathbf{A}(\mathbf{I} \otimes \mathbf{a})$ and $(\mathbf{AB}) \star \mathbf{a} = \mathbf{A}(\mathbf{B} \star \mathbf{a})$, it can be rewritten

$$\left(\mathbf{I}_{k_0-c}\ \mathbf{U}\right)\tilde{\mathbf{G}}((\mathbf{I}_{n_0} \otimes \mathbb{1}_{2^\gamma}) \star \mathbf{x}){\mathbf{H}_{pub}}^\top = 0$$

Now we can use the relations $(\mathbf{A} \otimes \mathbf{a}) \star (\mathbf{b} \otimes \mathbf{x}) = (\mathbf{A} \star \mathbf{b}) \otimes (\mathbf{a} \star \mathbf{x})$, $\tau \star \mathbf{I} = \mathrm{Diag}(\tau)$ and $\mathbf{A} \otimes \mathbf{a} = \mathbf{A}(\mathbf{I} \otimes \mathbf{a})$ to simplify

$$(\mathbf{I}_{n_0} \otimes \mathbb{1}_{2^\gamma}) \star \mathbf{x} = (\mathbf{I}_{n_0} \otimes \mathbb{1}_{2^\gamma}) \star \left(\tau \otimes \mathbb{1}_{2^\gamma} + \sum_{i=1}^{\gamma} b_i \mathbb{1}_{n_0} \otimes \mathbf{e}_i\right)$$

$$= (\tau \star \mathbf{I}_{n_0}) \otimes \mathbb{1}_{2^\gamma} + \sum_{i=1}^{\gamma} b_i(\mathbf{I}_{n_0} \otimes \mathbf{e}_i)$$

$$= \mathrm{Diag}(\tau)(\mathbf{I}_{n_0} \otimes \mathbb{1}_{2^\gamma}) + \sum_{i=1}^{\gamma} b_i(\mathbf{I}_{n_0} \otimes \mathbf{e}_i)$$

We can now define $\tilde{\mathbf{H}}_i = \mathbf{H}_{\mathsf{pub}}(\mathbf{I}_{n_0} \otimes \mathbf{e}_i{}^\top)$ and $\tilde{\mathbf{H}} = \mathbf{H}_{\mathsf{pub}}(\mathbf{I}_{n_0} \otimes \mathbb{1}_{2^\gamma}{}^\top)$ and we get the system

$$\left(\mathbf{I}_{k_0-c}\ \mathbf{U}\right)\tilde{\mathbf{G}}\left(\mathrm{Diag}(\tau)\tilde{\mathbf{H}}^\top + \sum_{i=1}^{\gamma} b_i\tilde{\mathbf{H}}_i{}^\top\right) = 0,$$

$$\left(\tilde{\mathbf{H}}\,\mathrm{Diag}(\tau)\tilde{\mathbf{G}}^\top + \sum_{i=1}^{\gamma} b_i\tilde{\mathbf{H}}_i\tilde{\mathbf{G}}^\top\right)\begin{pmatrix}\mathbf{I}_{k_0-c} \\ \mathbf{U}^\top\end{pmatrix} = 0$$

We now simplify the products using the remark that $\tilde{\mathbf{H}}$ is the parity-check matrix corresponding to $\tilde{\mathbf{G}} = (\mathbf{I}_{k_0}\mathbf{G})$: $\tilde{\mathbf{H}} = (\mathbf{G}^\top \mathbf{I}_{n_0-k_0})$, and that $\tilde{\mathbf{H}}_i = (\mathbf{H}_i \mathbf{0}_{n_0-k_0})$ contains columns of zeros on the last $n_0 - k_0$ positions. This gives (12).

References

1. Aguilar Melchor, C., et al.: Rank quasi cyclic (RQC). Second Round submission to NIST Post-Quantum Cryptography call (2020). https://pqc-rqc.org
2. Aragon, N., et al.: ROLLO (merger of rank-ouroboros, LAKE and LOCKER). Second round submission to the NIST post-quantum cryptography call (2019). https://pqc-rollo.org
3. Baena, J., Briaud, P., Cabarcas, D., Perlner, R.A., Smith-Tone, D., Verbel, J.A.: Improving support-minors rank attacks: applications to GeMSS and Rainbow. IACR Cryptol. ePrint Arch., Accepted for Publication in CRYPTO 2022, p. 1677 (2021). https://eprint.iacr.org/2021/1677
4. Banegas, G., et al.: DAGS: key encapsulation for dyadic GS codes (2017). https://csrc.nist.gov/CSRC/media/Projects/Post-Quantum-Cryptography/documents/round-1/submissions/DAGS.zip. First round submission to the NIST post-quantum cryptography call
5. Bardet, M., Bertin, M., Couvreur, A., Otmani, A.: Practical algebraic attack on DAGS. In: Baldi, M., Persichetti, E., Santini, P. (eds.) CBC 2019. LNCS, vol. 11666, pp. 86–101. Springer, Cham (2019). https://doi.org/10.1007/978-3-030-25922-8_5
6. Bardet, M., et al.: An algebraic attack on rank metric code-based cryptosystems. In: Canteaut, A., Ishai, Y. (eds.) EUROCRYPT 2020. LNCS, vol. 12107, pp. 64–93. Springer, Cham (2020). https://doi.org/10.1007/978-3-030-45727-3_3, http://arxiv.org/abs/1910.00810
7. Bardet, M., et al.: Improvements of algebraic attacks for solving the rank decoding and MinRank problems. In: Moriai, S., Wang, H. (eds.) ASIACRYPT 2020. LNCS, vol. 12491, pp. 507–536. Springer, Cham (2020). https://doi.org/10.1007/978-3-030-64837-4_17, https://arxiv.org/abs/2002.08322v4
8. Barelli, É., Couvreur, A.: An efficient structural attack on NIST submission DAGS. In: Peyrin, T., Galbraith, S. (eds.) ASIACRYPT 2018. LNCS, vol. 11272, pp. 93–118. Springer, Cham (2018). https://doi.org/10.1007/978-3-030-03326-2_4
9. Beullens, W.: Improved cryptanalysis of UOV and rainbow. In: Canteaut, A., Standaert, F.-X. (eds.) EUROCRYPT 2021. LNCS, vol. 12696, pp. 348–373. Springer, Cham (2021). https://doi.org/10.1007/978-3-030-77870-5_13
10. Beullens, W.: Breaking Rainbow takes a weekend on a laptop. IACR Cryptol. ePrint Arch. (2022). https://eprint.iacr.org/2022/214
11. Bruns, W., Vetter, U.: Determinantal Rings. LNCS, vol. 1327. Springer, Heidelberg (1988). https://doi.org/10.1007/BFb0080378
12. Buss, J.F., Frandsen, G.S., Shallit, J.O.: Computational complexity of some problems of linear algebra. J. Comput. System Sci. **58**(3), 572–596 (1999)
13. Casanova, A., Faugère, J., Macario-Rat, G., Patarin, J., Perret, L., Ryckeghem, J.: GeMSS: a great multivariate short signature. Second round submission to the NIST post-quantum cryptography call (2019). https://csrc.nist.gov/Projects/post-quantum-cryptography/round-2-submissions/GeMSS-Round2.zip
14. Ding, J., Chen, M.S., Petzoldt, A., Schmidt, D., Yang, B.Y.: Rainbow. Second round submission to the NIST post-quantum cryptography call (2019). https://csrc.nist.gov/Projects/post-quantum-cryptography/round-2-submissions/Rainbow-Round2.zip
15. Faugère, J.C., Safey El Din, M., Spaenlehauer, P.J.: Gröbner bases of bihomogeneous ideals generated by polynomials of bidegree (1,1): algorithms and complexity. J. Symb. Comput. **46**(4), 406–437 (2011)

16. Faugère, J.C., Safey El Din, M., Spaenlehauer, P.J.: On the complexity of the generalized minrank problem. J. Symb. Comput. **55**, 30–58 (2013). https://doi.org/10.1016/j.jsc.2013.03.004

17. Faugère, J., Safey El Din, M., Spaenlehauer, P.: Computing loci of rank defects of linear matrices using Gröbner bases and applications to cryptology. In: International Symposium on Symbolic and Algebraic Computation, ISSAC 2010, Munich, Germany, 25–28 July 2010, pp. 257–264 (2010). https://doi.org/10.1145/1837934.1837984

18. Kipnis, A., Shamir, A.: Cryptanalysis of the HFE public key cryptosystem by relinearization. In: Wiener, M. (ed.) CRYPTO 1999. LNCS, vol. 1666, pp. 19–30. Springer, Heidelberg (1999). https://doi.org/10.1007/3-540-48405-1_2

19. MacWilliams, F.J., Sloane, N.J.A.: The Theory of Error-Correcting Codes, 5th edn. North-Holland, Amsterdam (1986)

20. Patarin, J.: Hidden fields equations (HFE) and isomorphisms of polynomials (IP): two new families of asymmetric algorithms. In: Maurer, U. (ed.) EUROCRYPT 1996. LNCS, vol. 1070, pp. 33–48. Springer, Heidelberg (1996). https://doi.org/10.1007/3-540-68339-9_4

21. Petzoldt, A., Chen, M.-S., Yang, B.-Y., Tao, C., Ding, J.: Design principles for HFEv- based multivariate signature schemes. In: Iwata, T., Cheon, J.H. (eds.) ASIACRYPT 2015, Part I. LNCS, vol. 9452, pp. 311–334. Springer, Heidelberg (2015). https://doi.org/10.1007/978-3-662-48797-6_14

22. Porras, J., Baena, J., Ding, J.: ZHFE, a new multivariate public key encryption scheme. In: Mosca, M. (ed.) PQCrypto 2014. LNCS, vol. 8772, pp. 229–245. Springer, Cham (2014). https://doi.org/10.1007/978-3-319-11659-4_14

23. Tao, C., Petzoldt, A., Ding, J.: Efficient key recovery for all HFE signature variants. In: Malkin, T., Peikert, C. (eds.) CRYPTO 2021, Part I. LNCS, vol. 12825, pp. 70–93. Springer, Cham (2021). https://doi.org/10.1007/978-3-030-84242-0_4

24. Verbel, J., Baena, J., Cabarcas, D., Perlner, R., Smith-Tone, D.: On the complexity of "Superdetermined" minrank instances. In: Ding, J., Steinwandt, R. (eds.) PQCrypto 2019. LNCS, vol. 11505, pp. 167–186. Springer, Cham (2019). https://doi.org/10.1007/978-3-030-25510-7_10

A New Fault Attack on UOV Multivariate Signature Scheme

Hiroki Furue[1]($\boxtimes$), Yutaro Kiyomura[2], Tatsuya Nagasawa[1], and Tsuyoshi Takagi[1]

[1] Department of Mathematical Informatics, The University of Tokyo, Tokyo, Japan
`furue-hiroki261@g.ecc.u-tokyo.ac.jp`
[2] NTT Social Informatics Laboratories, Tokyo, Japan

Abstract. The unbalanced oil and vinegar signature scheme (UOV), which is one of the multivariate signature schemes, is expected to be secure against quantum attacks. To achieve cryptosystem security in a practical manner, we need to deal with security against physical attacks such as fault attacks, which generate computational errors to lead to security failures. In this study, we propose a new fault attack on UOV using faults occurring on the secret key. The proposed attack first recovers a part of the linear map of the secret key by utilizing faults occurring on the secret key, and then transforms the public key system. As a result, the proposed attack reduces a given public key system into one with fewer variables than the original system. After applying our proposed attack, the secret key can be recovered with less complexity than the original system by using an existing key recovery attack. Our simulation results show that, for two practical parameter sets satisfying 100-bit security, the proposed attack can reduce the given system into one with only 90-bit security with a probability of approximately $80 \sim 90\%$. We also show that the proposed attack achieves a smaller resulting system than the above case with lower probability, and that such a system can be broken even more efficiently.

Keywords: Post-quantum cryptography · Multivariate public key cryptography · UOV · Fault attack

1 Introduction

Currently used public key cryptosystems such as RSA and ECC can be broken in polynomial time using Shor's algorithm [22], which is a quantum computer algorithm. Thus, the amount of research conducted on post-quantum cryptography (PQC), which is secure against quantum computing attacks, has been accelerating. Indeed, the U.S. National Institute for Standards and Technology (NIST) has initiated a PQC standardization project [19]. Among various PQC candidates, multivariate public key cryptography (MPKC) is one of the main categories. MPKCs are cryptosystems constructed based on the difficulty of solving

© The Author(s), under exclusive license to Springer Nature Switzerland AG 2022
J. H. Cheon and T. Johansson (Eds.): PQCrypto 2022, LNCS 13512, pp. 124–143, 2022.
https://doi.org/10.1007/978-3-031-17234-2_7

a system of multivariate quadratic polynomial equations over a finite field (the multivariate quadratic (MQ) problem). The MQ problem is NP-complete [13] and is thus likely to be secure against quantum computers.

The unbalanced oil and vinegar signature scheme (UOV) is a multivariate signature scheme proposed by Kipnis et al. [15]. UOV has withstood various types of attacks since 1999 and thus is considered to achieve sufficient security. In addition, UOV is a well-established signature scheme owing to its short signature and brief execution time. Indeed, several studies [5,7,8,24] have presented efficient implementations of UOV and Rainbow [9], the latter of which is a multilayer UOV variant selected as a third-round finalist in the NIST PQC project [20]. Concretely, the public key of UOV is a quadratic map $\mathcal{P}$ constructed using $\mathcal{P} = F \circ T$ with an invertible quadratic map $\mathcal{F}$ and a linear map $\mathcal{T}$, which make up the secret key. In [2] and [3], Beullens recently proposed some attacks on UOV and Rainbow, the intersection, rectangular MinRank, and simple attacks. The rectangular MinRank and simple attacks do not work on the plain UOV, and by choosing the parameters properly, UOV can be secure against the intersection attack.

To achieve the security of a cryptosystem in a practical manner, we need to consider not only the weaknesses of the cryptographic protocols but also those of the devices implementing the cryptosystems. Physical attacks utilize information gained from the implementation of a computer system. As an example of such attacks on UOV-type signature schemes, a correlation power analysis attack was proposed at CHES 2018 [21]. Furthermore, among various physical attacks, fault attacks aim to stress the cryptographic device and generate computational errors, leading to a security failure of the cryptosystem. As fault attacks on UOV or its variants, some attacks combining information leakage through computational errors and algebraic measures have been proposed. Hashimoto et al. proposed two fault attacks at PQCrypto 2011 [14]. One attack is applicable to MPKCs with the public key $\mathcal{P} = S \circ F \circ T$, where an invertible quadratic map $\mathcal{F}$ and two linear maps S and T make up the secret key. This attack utilizes a fault that changes the coefficients of unknown terms in $\mathcal{F}$ and recovers the secret linear map S. This can be applied to Rainbow owing to its construction of the public and secret keys. The other fault attack in [14] is one in which the attacker fixes parameters chosen at random during the signature generation step. This attack weakens the security of UOV-like schemes such as UOV and Rainbow. These attacks proposed by Hashimoto et al. were complemented by [17] and [23], who analyzed how to apply them to UOV and Rainbow. Furthermore, at ACM CCS 2020 [18], Mus et al. proposed *QuantumHammer*, which is a fault attack on LUOV [4], a variant of UOV using a subfield. This attack utilizes faults occurring on the secret key, similar to the first attack described in [14]. The authors demonstrated a full key recovery for LUOV-7-57-197 with a bit-tracing phase of less than 4 h and an algebraic phase of 49 h. Note that these proposed fault attacks on UOV do not utilize the recently proposed intersection algebraic attack.

Although several fault attacks on UOV or its variants have been proposed, a fault attack on plain UOV using faults occurring on the secret key $\mathcal{F}$ and $\mathcal{T}$ has yet to be proposed. The attack on the central map described in [14] cannot be applied to UOV because the secret key of the scheme is composed of a quadratic map $\mathcal{F}$ and a linear map $\mathcal{T}$, unlike Rainbow. Indeed, at COSADE 2019 [17], the authors confirmed that the first attack described in [14] does not work on UOV. Furthermore, the attack detailed in [18] also does not work on UOV because it utilizes the fact that the secret key of LUOV is over the finite field of two elements.

Our Contributions. In this study, we propose a new fault attack on the plain UOV scheme. To the best of our knowledge, this is the first fault attack on UOV that causes faults on the secret key $\mathcal{F}$ and $\mathcal{T}$. The proposed attack transforms the public key system into a UOV system with fewer variables than the original. The secret key can then be fully recovered from this smaller system by using existing key recovery attacks on UOV. It should be noted that our attack model mainly follows the model used in [14].

In the proposed attack, we assume that the fault caused on the secret key randomly changes the coefficient of the secret key, which is composed of the central map $\mathcal{F}$ and linear map $\mathcal{T}$. In UOV with n variables and m equations, the numbers of coefficients of $\mathcal{F}$ and $\mathcal{T}$ are estimated as $O(m \cdot n^2)$ and $O(n^2)$, respectively, and thus we utilize the faults caused on the central map $\mathcal{F}$. The proposed attack is mainly composed of two steps:

1. Recover a part of $\mathcal{T}$ utilizing faults.
2. Transform the public key system $\mathcal{P}$.

The first step utilizes a fault occurring on the quadratic map $\mathcal{F}$. Some of the rows of the representation matrix of $\mathcal{T}$ are recovered from the computational error generated using the signing oracle several times, which generates a signature using the secret key with a fault. This step is iterated for each new fault unless a new fault is generated on $\mathcal{T}$. Subsequently, using a part of $\mathcal{T}$ recovered in the first step, the second step reduces the given public key system into one with fewer variables than the original. For the resulting smaller system obtained by executing the proposed attack, existing key recovery attacks can clearly be conducted with a smaller complexity than that of the key recovery attack on the original system.

In this paper, we simulated the proposed attack on two parameter sets $(q, v, m) = (16, 60, 39)$ and $(256, 50, 33)$ satisfying 100-bit security, and then confirmed the size of the public key system transformed by the proposed attack. As a result, there are five fewer variables of the resulting system than the original system with a probability of approximately 80–90%, and this resulting system can be broken using manipulations of smaller than 90-bits by applying a Kipnis-Shamir or intersection attack. Furthermore, we can obtain a smaller resulting system than the above case with a smaller probability, and such a system can be broken even more efficiently. For example, in the case of $(q, v, m) = (256, 50, 33)$, the secret key can be recovered with smaller manipulations, i.e., 81.3 bits with 68.0% probability, 63.2 bits with 46.2% probability, and 40.6 bits with 26.2% probability. Finally, in Subsect. 4.3 below, we confirm that the proposed attack works even when the number of faults is limited. For the parameter set $(q, v, m) = (16, 60, 39)$, the secret key of the resulting system of the proposed attack with one, two, or three faults is recovered by 93.1-, 85.1-, or 77.1-bit manipulations with 41.4%, 17.1%, or 7.1% probability, respectively.

Organizations. In Sect. 2, we review the construction of multivariate signature schemes, UOV, some attacks conducted on UOV, and fault attacks on UOV or its variants. Section 3 describes the details of the proposed attack, and Sect. 4 shows how to apply existing key recovery attacks after executing the proposed attack and how the proposed attack behaves on actual parameter sets. Finally, in Sect. 5, we provide some concluding remarks.

2   Preliminaries

In this section, we first describe the MQ problem and general signature schemes based on this problem. Subsequently, we review the construction of UOV [15] and some attacks applied to it. Finally, we recall some existing fault attacks on UOV or its variants.

2.1   Multivariate Signature Schemes

Let $\mathbb{F}_q$ be a finite field with q elements, and let n and m be two positive integers. For a system of quadratic polynomials $\mathcal{P} = (p_1(\mathbf{x}), \ldots, p_m(\mathbf{x}))$ in n variables over $\mathbb{F}_q$, the problem of obtaining a solution $\mathbf{x} \in \mathbb{F}_q^n$ to $\mathcal{P}(\mathbf{x}) = \mathbf{0}$ is called the MQ problem. Garey and Johnson [13] proved that this problem is NP-complete if $n \approx m$, and is thus considered to have the potential to resist quantum computer attacks.

Next, we briefly describe the construction of general multivariate signature schemes. First, an easily invertible quadratic map $\mathcal{F} = (f_1, \ldots, f_m) : \mathbb{F}_q^n \to \mathbb{F}_q^m$, called a *central map*, is generated. Next, two invertible linear maps $\mathcal{T} : \mathbb{F}_q^n \to \mathbb{F}_q^n$ and $\mathcal{S} : \mathbb{F}_q^m \to \mathbb{F}_q^m$ are randomly chosen to hide the structure of $\mathcal{F}$. These two linear maps $\mathcal{S}$ and $\mathcal{T}$ can be seen as two matrices in $\mathbb{F}_q^{m \times m}$ and $\mathbb{F}_q^{n \times n}$. The public key $\mathcal{P}$ is then provided as a polynomial map,

$$\mathcal{P} = \mathcal{S} \circ \mathcal{F} \circ \mathcal{T} : \mathbb{F}_q^n \to \mathbb{F}_q^m, \tag{1}$$

and the secret key comprises $\mathcal{S}$, $\mathcal{F}$, and $\mathcal{T}$. The signature is generated as follows: Given a message $\mathbf{m} \in \mathbb{F}_q^m$ to be signed, compute $\mathbf{m}_1 = \mathcal{S}^{-1}(\mathbf{m})$, and obtain a solution $\mathbf{m}_2$ to the equation $\mathcal{F}(\mathbf{x}) = \mathbf{m}_1$. This gives the signature $\mathbf{s} = \mathcal{T}^{-1}(\mathbf{m}_2) \in \mathbb{F}_q^n$ for the message $\mathbf{m}$. Verification is applied by confirming whether $\mathcal{P}(\mathbf{s}) = \mathbf{m}$.

2.2 Unbalanced Oil and Vinegar Signature Scheme

In this subsection, UOV is described. Let v be a positive integer and $n = v + m$. For variables $\mathbf{x} = (x_1, \ldots, x_n)$ over $\mathbb{F}_q$, we call $x_1, \ldots, x_v$ *vinegar variables* and $x_{v+1}, \ldots, x_n$ *oil variables*.

In UOV, a central map $\mathcal{F} = (f_1, \ldots, f_m) : \mathbb{F}_q^n \to \mathbb{F}_q^m$ is designed such that each f_k $(k = 1, \ldots, m)$ is a quadratic polynomial of the form

$$f_k(x_1, \ldots, x_n) = \sum_{i=1}^{v} \sum_{j=i}^{n} \alpha_{i,j}^{(k)} x_i x_j \tag{2}$$

where $\alpha_{i,j}^{(k)} \in \mathbb{F}_q$. By using a randomly chosen linear map $\mathcal{T} : \mathbb{F}_q^n \to \mathbb{F}_q^n$, the public key map $\mathcal{P} : \mathbb{F}_q^n \to \mathbb{F}_q^m$ is computed using $\mathcal{P} = \mathcal{F} \circ \mathcal{T}$. The linear map $\mathcal{S}$ in Eq. (1) is not required because it does not help hide the structure of $\mathcal{F}$ in UOV. Indeed, the secret key is composed of only two maps $\mathcal{F}$ and $\mathcal{T}$. It should be noted that we here omit linear and constant terms of $\mathcal{F}$ and constant terms of $\mathcal{T}$ for simplicity.

Next, we describe the inversion of the central map $\mathcal{F}$. When we find $\mathbf{x} \in \mathbb{F}_q^n$ satisfying $\mathcal{F}(\mathbf{x}) = \mathbf{y}$ for a given $\mathbf{y} \in \mathbb{F}_q^m$, we first choose random values $a_1, \ldots, a_v$ in $\mathbb{F}_q$ as the values of the vinegar variables. We can then easily obtain a solution for the equation $\mathcal{F}(a_1, \ldots, a_v, x_{v+1}, \ldots, x_n) = \mathbf{y}$, because this is a linear system of m equations in m oil variables. If there is no solution to this equation, we choose new random values $a_1', \ldots, a_v'$, and repeat the above procedure. By using this inversion approach, we can execute the signing process described in Subsect. 2.1.

Finally, we introduce some matrices representing the public and secret keys of UOV. For each polynomial p_i of the public key $\mathcal{P}$, there exists an $n \times n$ matrix P_i such that $p_i(\mathbf{x}) = \mathbf{x}^\top \cdot P_i \cdot \mathbf{x}$. Similarly, an $n \times n$ matrix F_i can be taken for each f_i with $1 \leq i \leq m$, and an $n \times n$ matrix T is defined to satisfy $\mathcal{T}(\mathbf{x}) = T \cdot \mathbf{x}$. In general, these matrices P_i and F_i are taken as symmetric matrices if q is odd, and are taken as upper triangular matrices if q is even. For these representation matrices, based on Eq. (2), F_i can be considered as follows:

$$\begin{pmatrix} *_{v \times v} & *_{v \times m} \\ *_{m \times v} & 0_{m \times m} \end{pmatrix}.$$

Furthermore, from $\mathcal{P} = \mathcal{F} \circ \mathcal{T}$, we have

$$P_i = T^\top F_i T, \quad (i = 1, \ldots, m).$$

2.3 Attacks on UOV

A straightforward approach to attacking UOV is finding a signature $\mathbf{s}$ satisfying $\mathcal{P}(\mathbf{s}) = \mathbf{m}$ for a given public key $\mathcal{P}$ and a message $\mathbf{m}$. A direct attack tries to solve this MQ system using an algorithm such as XL [6] or a Gröbner based approach such as F_4 [11] and F_5 [12].

Several attacks that aim to recover the secret key have also been proposed. The attacker can sign any message after the secret key is recovered, and we call such attacks *key recovery attacks*. In the following, we review three key recovery attacks, the Kipnis-Shamir attack [16], a reconciliation attack [10], and an intersection attack [2]. All of these attacks are constructed for the purpose of obtaining the subspace $\mathcal{T}^{-1}(\mathcal{O})$ of $\mathbb{F}_q^n$, where $\mathcal{O}$ is the oil subspace defined as

$$\mathcal{O} := \left\{ (0, \ldots, 0, \alpha_1, \ldots, \alpha_m)^\top \mid \alpha_i \in \mathbb{F}_q \right\}.$$

This subspace $\mathcal{T}^{-1}(\mathcal{O})$ can induce the secret linear map $\mathcal{T}$ or an equivalent linear map $\mathcal{T}' : \mathbb{F}_q^n \to \mathbb{F}_q^n$ such that every component of $\mathcal{P} \circ \mathcal{T}'^{-1}$ has the form of Eq. (2).

Kipnis-Shamir Attack. To obtain $\mathcal{T}^{-1}(\mathcal{O})$, the Kipnis-Shamir attack chooses two invertible matrices W_i, W_j from the set of linear combinations of the representation matrices $P_1, \ldots, P_m$ for the public key. We then compute the invariant subspace of $W_i^{-1}W_j$, and a part of the subspace $\mathcal{T}^{-1}(\mathcal{O})$ is probabilistically recovered. The complexity of the Kipnis-Shamir attack is estimated as

$$O\left(q^{v-m-1} \cdot m^4\right). \tag{3}$$

Reconciliation Attack. The reconciliation attack treats a vector y of $\mathcal{T}^{-1}(\mathcal{O})$ as variables and solves the quadratic system $y^\top P_i y = 0$ $(i = 1, \ldots, m)$. Here, the number of dimensions of $\mathcal{T}^{-1}(\mathcal{O})$ is m, and thus if we impose affine constraints, we then solve a system of m equations in $n - m = v$ variables and still have a solution with high probability. However, the parameters of UOV are set to satisfy $v > m$ for the security against the Kipnis-Shamir attack, and in this case the system of $y^\top P_i y = 0$ has a large number of solutions. Therefore, to determine a solution uniquely, we need to solve the following system to find multiple vectors $y_1, \ldots, y_k$ of $\mathcal{T}^{-1}(\mathcal{O})$:

$$\begin{cases} y_i^\top P_i y_j = 0 & (1 \le i \le m, 1 \le j \le k) \\ y_j^\top P_i y_\ell = 0 & (1 \le i \le m, 1 \le j < \ell \le k) \end{cases}.$$

However, this attack will usually not outperform a direct attack because the number of variables to be solved increases.

Intersection Attack. In [2], Beullens proposed a new attack against UOV, called an intersection attack. For an integer k satisfying $k < \frac{v}{v-m}$, let $L_1, \ldots, L_k$ be k invertible matrices randomly chosen from a set of linear combinations of the representation matrices $P_1, \ldots, P_m$ for the public key. This attack then solves the following equations for $\mathbf{y} \in \mathbb{F}_q^n$:

$$\begin{cases} (L_j^{-1}\mathbf{y})^\top P_i (L_j^{-1}\mathbf{y}) = 0 & (1 \le i \le m, 1 \le j \le k) \\ (L_j^{-1}\mathbf{y})^\top P_i (L_\ell^{-1}\mathbf{y}) = 0 & (1 \le i \le m, 1 \le j < \ell \le k) \end{cases}.$$

The solution space obtained from the above equation has $km - (k-1)v$ dimensions. Thus, its complexity is equivalent to that of solving the quadratic system with $n - (km - (k-1)v) = kv - (k-1)m$ variables and $\binom{k+1}{2}m - 2\binom{k}{2}$ equations owing to its linear dependency. The value of k is generally chosen such that the complexity of solving the above system takes the minimum value under the condition of $k < \frac{v}{v-m}$. Note that, when $v \geq 2m$, the intersection attack becomes a probabilistic algorithm.

2.4   Existing Fault Attacks on UOV or Its Variant

This subsection mainly recalls two fault attacks on multivariate signatures proposed by Hashimoto et al. [14] and the attack on LUOV [4] proposed by Mus et al. [18].

Hashimoto et al. proposed a fault attack on the stepwise triangular system (STS) and big field (BF) type signatures that have the public and secret keys of the form (1). This attack causes a fault to change the coefficients of unknown terms in the secret key $\mathcal{S}$, $\mathcal{F}$, and $\mathcal{T}$. In the case of the STS type, if the fault is caused on the central map $\mathcal{F}$, the attacker can recover a part of $\mathcal{S}$ directly from a message and signature pair given by the faulty central map. The authors also show that the probability that the fault will successfully change $\mathcal{F}$ is sufficiently high. In [17], the authors complementary investigated the behavior of this attack on UOV and Rainbow and confirmed it does not work on UOV owing to the construction of the secret key.

Furthermore, Hashimoto et al. proposed another attack that creates faults on the randomly chosen values in the process of the signature generation. For UOV and its variant, this attack can recover a part of $\mathcal{T}$. Regarding this attack on UOV and Rainbow, Krämer and Loiero discussed a special case in [17], whereas Shim and Koo investigated the algebraic part in detail in [23].

In [18], Mus et al. proposed *QuantumHammer* for use on LUOV [4], whose secret keys, like those of UOV, are composed of a central map $\mathcal{F}$ and a linear map $\mathcal{T}$. This attack combines a bit tracing phase, which causes faults on the linear map $\mathcal{T}$ and recovers a part of $\mathcal{T}$, with an algebraic phase, which recovers the remaining part of $\mathcal{T}$. The authors demonstrated a full key recovery for LUOV with $(q, v, m) = (7, 197, 57)$ using a bit-tracing phase of less than $4\,h$ and an algebraic phase of $49\,h$.

3   New Fault Attack on UOV

In this section, we propose a new fault attack on UOV. The proposed attack utilizes faults generated on the secret key, particularly on the central map $\mathcal{F}$. After describing our attack model in Subsect. 3.1, we describe the details of the proposed attack in Subsect. 3.2.

3.1 Attack Model

This subsection describes our attack model. We suppose that the coefficients of the secret key, $\mathcal{F}$ and $\mathcal{T}$, are stored in the device as fixed parameters used in UOV. In our proposed attack, we deal with the case in which the attacker causes a fault to change a coefficient, $\mathcal{F}$ or $\mathcal{T}$, of the secret key. The proposed attack is then constructed under the following assumptions:

- One fault changes one coefficient of the secret key, $\mathcal{F}$ or $\mathcal{T}$.
- A coefficient changed by a fault is randomly chosen.
- The attacker cannot know the location of the fault.
- Coefficients changed by the faults do not return to the original values (even if new faults are injected).

It should be noted that our attack model mainly follows that used in fault attacks on the secret key proposed in [14].

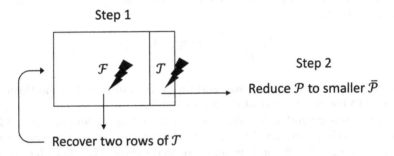

Step 1

Step 2

Reduce $\mathcal{P}$ to smaller $\bar{\mathcal{P}}$

Recover two rows of $\mathcal{T}$

Fig. 1. Rough description of the proposed attack

3.2 Description

This subsection describes the details of the proposed attack. Our proposed attack mainly consists of the following two steps (Fig. 1):

1. Some rows of the representation matrix T for the secret key are recovered utilizing faults.
2. The public key system $\mathcal{P}$ is reduced to a UOV public key system $\bar{\mathcal{P}}$ with fewer variables than the original system.

The resulting system with fewer variables can be broken with smaller complexity using existing key recovery attacks. In the following, for any vector $\mathbf{v} \in \mathbb{F}_q^a$ with $a \in \mathbb{N}$, $(\mathbf{v})_b$ with $b \in \{1, \ldots, a\}$ denotes the b-th element of $\mathbf{v}$.

Partial Recovery of $\mathcal{T}$. Herein, because, the data sizes of $\mathcal{F}$ and $\mathcal{T}$ are estimated as $O(\log(q) \cdot m \cdot n^2)$ and $O(\log(q) \cdot n^2)$, respectively, and thus a random fault is generated on the central map $\mathcal{F}$ with high probability, we consider a case in which the first fault is generated on $\mathcal{F}$. Concretely, we suppose that the coefficient $\alpha_{i,j}^{(k)}$ in Eq. (2) is changed into $\bar{\alpha}_{i,j}^{(k)}$ with $\alpha_{i,j}^{(k)} \neq \bar{\alpha}_{i,j}^{(k)}$. The central map with the fault is then denoted by $\mathcal{F}'$.

For each fault occurring on $\mathcal{F}$, the row vector recovery step is described as follows:

1. Iterate the following three steps N times
   (a) Randomly choose $\mathbf{m}_\ell \in \mathbb{F}_q^m$.
   (b) Obtain $\mathbf{s}_\ell = \mathcal{T}^{-1} \circ \mathcal{F}'^{-1}(\mathbf{m}_\ell)$ using the signing oracle with the fault.
   (c) $\delta_\ell = \mathcal{P}(\mathbf{s}_\ell) - \mathbf{m}_\ell$.
2. Solve the following linear system in $\{y_{p,r}\}_{1 \leq p \leq r \leq n}$

$$\sum_{p \leq r} (\mathbf{s}_\ell)_p (\mathbf{s}_\ell)_r y_{p,r} = \bar{\delta}_\ell \qquad (1 \leq \ell \leq N), \tag{4}$$

where $\bar{\delta}_\ell$ is the only nonzero element of δ_ℓ. (If $\delta_\ell = \mathbf{0}$, then $\bar{\delta}_\ell = 0$.)
3. For the solution $\{z_{p,r}\}_{1 \leq p \leq r \leq n}$ of Eq. (4), find two vectors $(a_1, \ldots, a_n)$ and $(b_1, \ldots, b_n)$ satisfying

$$\begin{cases} a_i b_j + a_j b_i = z_{i,j} & (i < j) \\ a_i b_i = z_{i,i} \end{cases}. \tag{5}$$

As a result, two vectors $(a_1, \ldots, a_n)$ and $(b_1, \ldots, b_n)$ obtained in the third step correspond to the row vectors of the secret key $\mathcal{T}$.

The first step generates N pairs of two vectors $\mathbf{s}_\ell \in \mathbb{F}_q^n$ and $\delta_\ell \in \mathbb{F}_q^m$. These pairs are generated through the following three steps: First, a message $\mathbf{m}_\ell$ is randomly chosen in $\mathbb{F}_q^m$. Second, we input $\mathbf{m}_\ell$ to the signing oracle with the faulty central map $\mathcal{F}'$ and receive $\mathbf{s}_\ell$ as an output. Third, we compute the difference δ_ℓ between $\mathcal{P}(\mathbf{s}_\ell)$ and $\mathbf{m}_\ell$. These manipulations are iterated N times. For each $1 \leq \ell \leq N$, we then have

$$\begin{aligned} \delta_\ell &= (\mathcal{F} \circ \mathcal{T})(\mathbf{s}_\ell) - (\mathcal{F}' \circ \mathcal{T})(\mathbf{s}_\ell) \\ &= (\mathcal{F} - \mathcal{F}') \circ \mathcal{T}(\mathbf{s}_\ell) \\ &= \left(0, \ldots, 0, \left(\alpha_{i,j}^{(k)} - \bar{\alpha}_{i,j}^{(k)} \right) \cdot (\mathcal{T}(\mathbf{s}_\ell))_i \cdot (\mathcal{T}(\mathbf{s}_\ell))_j, 0, \ldots, 0 \right), \end{aligned}$$

and thus, if $(\mathcal{T}(\mathbf{s}_\ell))_i \neq 0$ and $(\mathcal{T}(\mathbf{s}_\ell))_j \neq 0$, then δ_ℓ has the only nonzero k-th element. This is because $\mathcal{F}$ and $\mathcal{F}'$ only differ in the coefficient of $x_i x_j$ of f_k. Here, let $\bar{\delta}_\ell \in \mathbb{F}_q$ be the nonzero element of δ_ℓ (if $\delta_\ell = \mathbf{0}$, then $\bar{\delta}_\ell = 0$), and $t_{i,j}$ be the (i,j)-element of the representation matrix T for the secret key. We then hold

$$\begin{aligned} \bar{\delta}_\ell &= \left(\alpha_{i,j}^{(k)} - \bar{\alpha}_{i,j}^{(k)} \right) \cdot \left(\sum_p t_{i,p}(\mathbf{s}_\ell)_p \right) \cdot \left(\sum_r t_{j,r}(\mathbf{s}_\ell)_r \right) \\ &= \left(\alpha_{i,j}^{(k)} - \bar{\alpha}_{i,j}^{(k)} \right) \sum_{p \leq r} (\mathbf{s}_\ell)_p (\mathbf{s}_\ell)_r \begin{cases} (t_{i,p} t_{j,r} + t_{j,p} t_{i,r}) & (p \neq r) \\ t_{i,p} t_{j,p} & (p = r) \end{cases}. \end{aligned} \tag{6}$$

In the second step, we introduce new $n(n + 1)/2$ variables $\{y_{p,r}\}_{1 \leq p \leq r \leq n}$ such that every component $y_{p,r}$ corresponds to $(t_{i,p}t_{j,r} + t_{j,p}t_{i,r})$ in the case of $p \neq r$ and $t_{i,p}t_{j,p}$ in the case of $p = r$, as in Eq. (6). We then generate a linear system of N equations (4) in $n(n+1)/2$ variables $\{y_{p,r}\}_{1 \leq p \leq r \leq n}$. Here, although equation (4) is clearly deduced from Eq. (6), we omit the part of $\alpha_{i,j}^{(k)} - \bar{\alpha}_{i,j}^{(k)}$ from Eq. (6) because recovering a multiple of row vectors of T is sufficient. If we set $N = n(n+1)/2$, then the solution is determined uniquely with high probability. When a linear system has some solutions, we add a new linear equation obtained using a new pairing of s_ℓ and δ_ℓ until the solution is uniquely determined.

Subsequently, from the solution $\{z_{p,r}\}_{1 \leq p \leq r \leq n}$ of Eq. (4), we generate two vectors $(a_1, \ldots, a_n)$ and $(b_1, \ldots, b_n)$ satisfying Eq. (5), as in the definition of $\{y_{p,r}\}_{1 \leq p \leq r \leq n}$. Specifically, these two vectors can be found as follows:

1. $a_1 = 1$.
2. $b_1 = z_{1,1}$.
3. Find a_2 and b_2 solving

$$\begin{cases} a_1b_2 + a_2b_1 = z_{1,2} \\ a_2b_2 = z_{2,2} \end{cases}.$$

4. For $3 \leq i \leq n$, find a_i and b_i solving

$$\begin{cases} a_1b_i + a_ib_1 = z_{1,i} \\ a_2b_i + a_ib_2 = z_{2,i} \end{cases}.$$

Then, $(a_1, \ldots, a_n)$ and $(b_1, \ldots, b_n)$ clearly correspond to constant multiples of two row vectors of T from Eq. (6).

After executing the manipulations described above for the first fault, we cause another fault on the secret key and recover two row vectors of T again by applying a similar method if a new fault also occurs on $\mathcal{F}$. As the main difference from the first fault, δ_ℓ may have several nonzero elements owing to the previous faults. Herein, we suppose that, for the i-th fault with $1 \leq i < \bar{i}$ caused on $\mathcal{F}$, we obtain $\{z_{p,r}^{(i)}\}_{1 \leq p \leq r \leq n}$ by solving Eq. (4), and k_i then denotes the index in which δ_ℓ has a nonzero element. Then, after generating the $\bar{i}$-th fault, for a new pairing of s_ℓ and δ_ℓ, by subtracting $\left(\sum_{p \leq r} (s_\ell)_p (s_\ell)_r z_{p,r}^{(i)} \right) e_{k_i}$ from δ_ℓ for every $1 \leq i < \bar{i}$, δ_ℓ becomes a vector with one nonzero element, as in the first fault case. Based on this manipulation, the same recovery approach as the first fault case can be applied. Note that if a recovered row vector of T is dependent on one of the row vectors already recovered, it indicates that the same vector is recovered in a duplicate manner.

These manipulations are iterated until n independent row vectors are recovered or a new fault is caused on T, which can be easily confirmed because δ_ℓ has many nonzero elements even after subtracting $\left(\sum_{p \leq r} (s_\ell)_p (s_\ell)_r z_{p,r}^{(i)} \right) e_{k_i}$.

Reduction to Smaller UOV. Herein, we assume that α row vectors $(a_1^{(i)}, \ldots, a_n^{(i)})$ with $1 \leq i \leq \alpha$ are recovered in the first step, and each

$(a_1^{(i)}, \ldots, a_n^{(i)})$ corresponds to the β_i-th row of T. This reduction step is then described as follows:

1. For $i = 1, \ldots, \alpha$ do
   (a) $(b_1, \ldots, b_n) := (a_1^{(i)}, \ldots, a_n^{(i)}) \cdot T_1 \cdots T_{i-1}$,
   (b) Choose k_i from $\{k' \notin \{k_1, \ldots, k_{i-1}\} \mid b_{k'} \neq 0\}$,
   (c) $T_i \in \mathbb{F}_q^{n \times n}$ is taken as follows:

$$
T_i := \begin{array}{c} \\ k_i \\ \\ \end{array} \overset{\displaystyle k_i}{\left(\begin{array}{ccccccc} & I & & & & O & \\ -\frac{b_1}{b_{k_i}} & \cdots & -\frac{b_{k_i-1}}{b_{k_i}} & 1 & -\frac{b_{k_i+1}}{b_{k_i}} & \cdots & -\frac{b_n}{b_{k_i}} \\ & O & & & & I & \end{array} \right)}. \tag{7}
$$

2. Substitute 0 for $\{x_k \mid k \in \{k_1, \ldots, k_\alpha\}\}$ in $\mathcal{P}(T_1 \cdots T_\alpha \cdot \mathbf{x})$.

It should be noted that the first part of this reduction step mainly originates from [14].

First, for $(a_1^{(1)}, \ldots, a_n^{(1)})$ obtained in Subsect. 3.2, we take the matrix T_1 to transform the β_1-th row of T. We then choose one nonzero element $a_{k_1}^{(1)}$ from $(a_1^{(1)}, \ldots, a_n^{(1)})$ and take a matrix T_1 following Eq. (7). We then have

$$
T \cdot T_1 = \begin{array}{c} \\ \\ \beta_1 \\ \\ \end{array} \overset{\displaystyle k_1}{\left(\begin{array}{c} * \\ 0 \cdots 0 * 0 \cdots 0 \\ * \end{array} \right)}.
$$

We iterate such processes for all α row vectors obtained in the first step. It should be noted that, because the β_i-th row of T has already been transformed by $T_1 \cdots T_{i-1}$, we need to multiply $T_1 \cdots T_{i-1}$ to $(a_1^{(i)}, \ldots, a_n^{(i)})$ from the right side before choosing k_i and setting T_i. As a result, when we let $T' := T_1 \cdots T_\alpha$, the $\beta_1, \ldots, \beta_\alpha$ rows of T are eliminated by multiplying T' from the right side. Indeed, if we take two $n \times n$ permutation matrices A_1 and A_2 satisfying

$$
A_1 \cdot (1 \cdots m)^\top = (\beta_1 \cdots \beta_\alpha * \cdots *)^\top
$$
$$
(1 \cdots m) \cdot A_2 = (k_1 \cdots k_\alpha * \cdots *),
$$

then we have

$$
A_1 \cdot (T \cdot T') \cdot A_2 = \begin{pmatrix} I_\alpha & 0_{\alpha \times (n-\alpha)} \\ B_1 & B_2 \end{pmatrix}, \tag{8}
$$

where B_1 and B_2 are $(n - \alpha) \times \alpha$ and $(n - \alpha) \times (n - \alpha)$ matrices, respectively.

Subsequently, the second part reduces the transformed public key system $\mathcal{P}(T' \cdot \mathbf{x})$ into a UOV public key system with fewer variables than the original. In this part, we substitute 0 for $x_{k_1}, \ldots, x_{k_\alpha}$ in $\mathcal{P}(T' \cdot \mathbf{x})$. Here, we denote the remaining $n - \alpha$ variables $\bar{\mathbf{x}} = (\bar{x}_1, \ldots, \bar{x}_{n-\alpha})$ such that

$$
A_2^{-1} \cdot \mathbf{x} = A_2^\top \cdot \mathbf{x}
$$
$$
= (x_{\beta_1} \cdots x_{\beta_\alpha} \, \bar{x}_1 \cdots \bar{x}_{n-\alpha})^\top ,
$$

and denote by $\bar{\mathcal{P}} = (\bar{p}_1(\bar{\mathbf{x}}), \ldots, \bar{p}_m(\bar{\mathbf{x}}))$ the resulting public key system obtained by executing the second part. With two permutation matrices in Eq. (8), we assume that $A_1^{-\top} \cdot F_i \cdot A_1^{-1}$ is written in the following forms:

$$
A_1^{-\top} \cdot F_i \cdot A_1^{-1} = \begin{pmatrix} C_1 & C_2 \\ C_3 & C_4 \end{pmatrix},
$$

where C_1, C_2, C_3, and C_4 are $\alpha \times \alpha$, $\alpha \times (n - \alpha)$, $(n - \alpha) \times \alpha$, and $(n - \alpha) \times (n - \alpha)$ matrices, respectively. We then have

$$
\begin{aligned}
&p_i(T' \cdot \mathbf{x}) \\
&= (T \cdot T' \cdot \mathbf{x})^\top \cdot F_i \cdot (T \cdot T' \cdot \mathbf{x}), \\
&= (A_2^{-1} \cdot \mathbf{x})^\top \cdot (A_1 \cdot T \cdot T' \cdot A_2)^\top \cdot (A_1^{-\top} \cdot F_i \cdot A_1^{-1}) \cdot (A_1 \cdot T \cdot T' \cdot A_2) \cdot (A_2^{-1} \cdot \mathbf{x}),
\end{aligned}
$$

and thus it holds that

$$
\begin{aligned}
&\bar{p}_i(\bar{\mathbf{x}}) \\
&= (0, \ldots, 0, \bar{\mathbf{x}}^\top) \begin{pmatrix} I_\alpha & 0_{\alpha \times (n-\alpha)} \\ B_1 & B_2 \end{pmatrix}^\top \begin{pmatrix} C_1 & C_2 \\ C_3 & C_4 \end{pmatrix} \begin{pmatrix} I_\alpha & 0_{\alpha \times (n-\alpha)} \\ B_1 & B_2 \end{pmatrix} (0, \ldots, 0, \bar{\mathbf{x}}^\top)^\top \\
&= \bar{\mathbf{x}}^\top \begin{pmatrix} 0_{\alpha \times (n-\alpha)} \\ B_2 \end{pmatrix}^\top \begin{pmatrix} C_1 & C_2 \\ C_3 & C_4 \end{pmatrix} \begin{pmatrix} 0_{\alpha \times (n-\alpha)} \\ B_2 \end{pmatrix} \bar{\mathbf{x}} \\
&= \bar{\mathbf{x}}^\top \cdot B_2 \cdot C_4 \cdot B_2 \cdot \bar{\mathbf{x}}.
\end{aligned}
$$

In the above equation, because A_1^{-1} is also a permutation matrix, C_4 can be seen as a representation matrix of the central map of UOV with $n - \alpha$ variables. Therefore, we can regard $\bar{\mathcal{P}}$ as the public key system of UOV in $n - \alpha$ variables. Furthermore, if, among $\beta_1, \ldots, \beta_\ell$, the v' elements are in the set of $\{1, \ldots, v\}$ and the m' elements are in the set of $\{v + 1, \ldots, n\}$, then $\bar{\mathcal{P}}$ is the UOV public key with $v - v'$ vinegar variables and $m - m'$ oil variables owing to the structure of A_1^{-1}.

4   Analysis of Our Proposed Attack

As we described in Sect. 3, we obtain a smaller UOV public key system $\bar{\mathcal{P}}$ with $v - v'$ vinegar and $m - m'$ oil variables with $v' + m' = \alpha$ using our proposed attack. This section first explains the method of applying existing key recovery attacks to $\bar{\mathcal{P}}$. Next, we show the results of our simulations in our attack model and the behavior of the proposed attack under the condition that the number of faults is limited to small values.

4.1   Application of Key Recovery Attacks

In this subsection, we describe how to recover the secret key from the resulting smaller system $\bar{\mathcal{P}}$ with $v - v'$ vinegar variables and $m - m'$ oil variables obtained by the proposed attack described in Sect. 3. In the resulting system $\bar{\mathcal{P}}$, key recovery attacks on UOV can be executed with a smaller complexity in most cases. As the reason why the direct attack cannot be conducted with a smaller complexity, no pre-image of $\bar{\mathcal{P}}$ exists with high probability because the number $m - m'$ of the oil variables is smaller than the number m of equations if $m' > 0$.

As stated in Subsect. 2.3, key recovery attacks on UOV aim to recover $\mathcal{T}^{-1}(\mathcal{O})$, where $\mathcal{O}$ is the oil subspace. If we obtain a vector $\mathbf{a} \in \mathbb{F}_q^{n-\alpha}$ by applying key recovery attacks on $\bar{\mathcal{P}}$, then we can obtain a vector in $\mathcal{T}^{-1}(\mathcal{O})$ by concatenating $\mathbf{a}$ with 0 for $x_{k_1}, \ldots, x_{k_\alpha}$ and multiplying $T_1 \cdots T_\alpha$ from the construction of $\bar{\mathcal{P}}$. Note that, using key recovery attacks on $\bar{\mathcal{P}}$, we only obtain at most $m - m'$ independent vectors of $\mathcal{T}^{-1}(\mathcal{O})$. However, in most cases, after some basis of $\mathcal{T}^{-1}(\mathcal{O})$ is obtained, it becomes easy to recover the remaining basis of $\mathcal{T}^{-1}(\mathcal{O})$. The proposed attack described in Sect. 3 can be clearly executed in polynomial time, and thus the complexity of the attack is dominated by that of the key recovery attacks. In the following, we apply two key recovery attacks, the Kipnis-Shamir attack [16] and intersection attack [2] because they are particularly effective for our chosen parameter sets in Subsect. 4.2. Note that the attacker here cannot know the number of vinegar and oil variables of $\bar{\mathcal{P}}$.

Kipnis-Shamir Attack. The Kipnis-Shamir attack can be executed without the number of vinegar and oil variables, and thus we can simply apply the Kipnis-Shamir attack on $\bar{\mathcal{P}}$. From Eq. (3), the complexity of the Kipnis-Shamir attack on $\bar{\mathcal{P}}$ is estimated as

$$O\left(q^{(v-v')-(m-m')-1} \cdot (m - m')^4\right). \tag{9}$$

Because v' is larger than m' with high probability, as stated in Subsect. 4.2, this attack will be applied with a smaller complexity than that of the Kipnis-Shamir attack on the original system.

Intersection Attack. By contrast, the intersection attack generally requires the number of vinegar and oil variables. As described in Subsect. 2.3, for UOV with v vinegar variables, o oil variables, and m equations, the intersection attack solves an MQ system of $\binom{k+1}{2}m - 2\binom{k}{2}$ equations in $kv - (k-1)o$ variables for an integer $k < \frac{v}{v-o}$. (We here distinguish the number o of oil variables and the number m of equations unlike Subsect. 2.3.) The above value $kv - (k-1)o$ is determined by subtracting the dimension $ko - (k-1)v$ of the solution subspace from the number $n = v + o$ of variables to be solved. However, the attacker here only knows the value of $\alpha = v' + m'$ and does not know each value of v' and m', and thus the dimensions of the solution space and the value of k for the optimal complexity cannot be correctly conjectured before solving the system.

In the following, we introduce a way to execute the intersection attack on $\bar{\mathcal{P}}$. First, the attacker assumes that $v' = \alpha$ and $m' = 0$, and then conducts the intersection attack by choosing the optimal $k < \frac{v-\alpha}{(v-\alpha)-m}$ and supposing that the dimension of the solution space is $km - (k-1)(v-\alpha)$, namely, the number of variables to be solved is

$$(v + m - \alpha) - (km - (k-1)(v-\alpha)) = k(v-\alpha) - (k-1)m.$$

If there exists no solution for the above system, we then assume that $v' = \alpha - 1$ and $m' = 1$, and solve the system by supposing that the solution space is $k(m-1) - (k-1)(v-\alpha+1)$ for $k < \frac{v-\alpha+1}{(v-\alpha+1)-(m-1)}$. In this way, we iterate the decrease in v' and increase in m' until we obtain a solution. We can then find a solution in which we correctly assume the values of v' and m', which will dominate the complexity because the number of variables is larger than that of the previous case. In conclusion, the complexity of the intersection attack on $\bar{\mathcal{P}}$ is estimated as that of solving an MQ system of $\binom{k+1}{2}m - 2\binom{k}{2}$ equations in $k(v - v') - (k-1)(m - m')$ variables for $k < \frac{v-v'}{(v-v')-(m-m')}$. If we set $N = k(v - v') - (k-1)(m - m')$ and $M = \binom{k+1}{2}m - 2\binom{k}{2}$, by considering the hybrid approach [1,25] with Wiedemann XL [26], the complexity of solving the above system is given as

$$\min_{k} \left(O\left(q^k \cdot 3 \cdot \binom{N-k}{2} \cdot \binom{D+N-k}{D}^2 \right) \right), \tag{10}$$

where D is the degree of the first non-positive term of $(1 - z)^{M-N+k}(1 + z)^M$.

Remark 1. This remark indicates that the proposed attack can be executed more efficiently when the secret key $\mathcal{T}$ is limited to a specific compact form. It is known that the secret linear map $\mathcal{T}$ can be restricted to a special form [7]:

$$T = \begin{pmatrix} I_{v \times v} & T' \\ 0_{m \times v} & I_{m \times m} \end{pmatrix}, \tag{11}$$

where T' is a $v \times m$ matrix, and such a compact form is often used for efficiency.

Although the proposed attack assumes that $\mathcal{T}$ is a randomly chosen line map, it can be clearly applied to UOV with a compact $\mathcal{T}$. For each row vector obtained in the recovery step, we can identify which row of T in the form of (11) that the recovered vector corresponds to. We then dismiss vectors corresponding to the last m rows, which are unit vectors, and transform only v' row vectors during the reduction step. By doing so, the proposed attack gives the public key system of UOV with $v - v'$ vinegar variables and m oil variables. The complexity of the Kipnis-Shamir attack can then be given as

$$O\left(q^{(v-v')-m-1} \cdot m^4\right).$$

Furthermore, we can simply apply the intersection attack, which solves an MQ system of $\binom{k+1}{2}m - 2\binom{k}{2}$ equations in $k(v - v') - (k - 1)m$ variables for $k < \frac{v-v'}{(v-v')-m}$. These complexities are clearly smaller than that of the proposed attack on UOV with a plain $\mathcal{T}$, as estimated above.

4.2 Simulations of Our Proposed Attack

This subsection describes how our proposed algorithm transforms the given public key system and the complexity of key recovery attacks on the resulting system for two practical parameter sets $(q, v, m) = (16, 60, 39)$ and $(256, 50, 33)$ satisfying 100-bit security. These parameter sets are chosen such that the public key and signature sizes reach the smallest values unless the complexity of the direct attack, Kipnis-Shamir attack [16], reconciliation attack [10], or intersection attack [2] is smaller than 100 bits.

Table 1. With two parameters $(q, v, m) = (16, 60, 39)$ and $(256, 50, 33)$ satisfying 100-bit security, for each difference between the numbers of variables of the public key system $\mathcal{P}$ and the resulting system $\bar{\mathcal{P}}$ of the proposed attack ($= v' + m'$), the probability of its occurrence, the average rate of v' to $v' + m'$, and the average number of faults used in the attack

$(q, v, m) =$ $(16, 60, 39)$	The difference between the numbers of variables of $\mathcal{P}$ and $\bar{\mathcal{P}}$				
	0~4	5~9	10~19	20~29	30~
Probability	15.4%	9.5%	22.6%	19.8%	32.7%
$v'/(v' + m')$	–	0.68	0.70	0.71	0.69
The number of faults	1.9	4.8	8.7	14.8	33.9
$(q, v, m) =$ $(256, 50, 33)$	The difference between the numbers of variables of $\mathcal{P}$ and $\bar{\mathcal{P}}$				
	0~4	5~9	10~19	20~29	30~
Probability	18.8%	13.2%	21.8%	20.0%	26.2%
$v'/(v' + m')$	–	0.73	0.71	0.70	0.68
The number of faults	1.9	4.8	8.7	15.7	32.1

We simulated our proposed attack 1000 times for each parameter set. Table 1 shows the occurrence probabilities, the average rate of v' to $v' + m'$, and the average number of faults occurring in the attack for each difference in the numbers of variables of $\mathcal{P}$ and $\bar{\mathcal{P}}$, which is equal to $v' + m'$. For example, with the parameter set $(q, v, m) = (16, 60, 39)$, $v' + m'$ falls within the range of 5 to 9 with a 9.5% probability, and in this case, the average value of $v'/(v' + m')$ and the number of faults are 0.68 and 4.8, respectively. From this table, we can confirm that, by using the proposed fault attack, we can obtain $\bar{\mathcal{P}}$ with 5 fewer variables than the original system with a probability of approximately 80–90%, and $\bar{\mathcal{P}}$ with 10 fewer variables with a probability of approximately 70%. Furthermore, Table 1 shows that v' is larger than m' in most cases because, for each fault, either one of the first v rows and one of the last m rows, or two of the first v rows are recovered during the recovery step described in Subsect. 3.2 owing to equation (2). In addition, the number of faults used in the proposed attack clearly increases with the increase in the difference in the numbers of variables of $\mathcal{P}$ and $\bar{\mathcal{P}}$.

Table 2. With the two parameter sets $(q, v, m) = (16, 60, 39)$ and $(256, 50, 33)$ satisfying 100-bit security, the complexities of the Kipnis-Shamir (KS) and intersection (Int) attacks breaking the resulting system $\bar{\mathcal{P}}$ of the proposed attack when the parameters (v', m') of the proposed attack are set to $(4, 1)$, $(7, 3)$, $(14, 6)$, or $(21, 9)$

Parameter (100 bits) (q, v, m)	Attack	$(v' + m', v', m')$			
		$(5, 4, 1)$	$(10, 7, 3)$	$(20, 14, 6)$	$(30, 21, 9)$
$(16, 60, 39)$	KS Eq. (9)	89.0	84.7	68.2	51.6
	Int Eq. (10)	105.8	97.6	75.8	59.9
$(256, 50, 33)$	KS Eq. (9)	124.0	115.6	83.0	50.3
	Int Eq. (10)	89.5	81.3	63.2	40.6

Subsequently, for the two parameter sets satisfying 100-bit security, herein we estimate the complexity of the Kipnis-Shamir and intersection attacks on the resulting system $\bar{\mathcal{P}}$ of the proposed attack. As indicated in Table 2, we choose four values, 5, 10, 20, and 30, for $v' + m'$, which is equal to the difference between the numbers of variables of $\mathcal{P}$ and $\bar{\mathcal{P}}$. In addition, we set (v', m') as $(4, 1)$, $(7, 3)$, $(14, 6)$, and $(21, 9)$ in each case owing to the rate of v' to $v' + m'$ shown in Table 1. Table 2 shows the bit complexities of the Kipnis-Shamir and intersection attacks, where for example the complexity of the Kipnis-Shamir attack on $\bar{\mathcal{P}}$ with $(q, v, m) = (16, 60, 39)$ and $(v', m') = (4, 1)$ is 89.0 bits. This table indicates that, by choosing the optimal attack among the two key recovery attacks, the secret key can be recovered from $\bar{\mathcal{P}}$ with less complexity than the claimed security level in each case. Along with the results shown in Table 1, for $(q, v, m) = (16, 60, 39)$, the Kipnis-Shamir attack can be applied with smaller manipulations than 89.0 bits with 84.6% probability, since $v' + m' \geq 5$ with a probability of $100 - 15.4 = 84.6\%$. Similarly, for $(q, v, m) = (16, 60, 39)$, the secret key can be recovered with smaller manipulations than 84.7 bits with 75.1% probability, 68.2 bits with 52.5% probability, and 51.6 bits with 32.7% probability. For the case of $(q, v, m) =$

$(256, 50, 33)$, the secret key can be recovered with smaller manipulations than 89.5 bits with 81.2% probability, 81.3 bits with 68.0% probability, 63.2 bits with 46.2% probability, and 40.6 bits with 26.2% probability. These results indicate a trade-off between the complexity of recovering the secret key and the probability that it will occur.

Table 3. For the parameter $(q, v, m) = (16, 60, 39)$ satisfying 100-bit security, the values of v' and m', the probability of such occurrence, and the complexity of the Kipnis-Shamir attack on the resulting system $\bar{\mathcal{P}}$ obtained from Eq. (9) when a fault occurs once, twice, and three times, respectively.

Faults						
1	(v', m')	(1,1)	(2,0)	(0,0)		
	Probability	52.9%	41.4%	5.7%		
	$\log_2$(complexity)	101.0	**93.1**	101.1		
2	(v', m')	(3,1)	(2,2)	(4,0)	(0,0)	Other
	Probability	43.8%	28.0%	17.1%	5.7%	5.4%
	$\log_2$(complexity)	**93.0**	100.8	**85.1**	101.1	
3	(v', m')	(4,2)	(5,1)	(3,3)	(6,0)	Other
	Probability	34.8%	27.2%	14.8%	7.1%	16.1%
	$\log_2$(complexity)	**92.8**	**85.0**	100.7	**77.1**	

4.3   Limited Faults Cases

In this subsection, we consider applying our proposed attack in a case in which the number of faults is limited. Table 3 shows the results of the proposed attack on the parameter set $(q, v, m) = (16, 60, 39)$ under the conditions in which a fault occurs once, twice, and three times. For each case, we show the probability of occurrence and the complexity of the Kipnis Shamir attack on the resulting system with $v - v'$ vinegar variables and $m - m'$ oil variables for each set of v' and m'. Herein, we choose the Kipnis-Shamir attack because it is more efficient than the intersection attack, as indicated from Table 2. Note that we dismiss the case in which rows of T are recovered in duplicate during the recovery step of the proposed attack, which occurs with negligible probability.

As a result, in a case in which a fault occurs once, the secret key is recovered with a smaller complexity of 93.1 bits in comparison to the claimed security level when $(v', m') = (2, 0)$ with a probability of 41.4%. In the case of two faults, the system is less secure when $(v', m') = (3, 1)$ and $(4, 0)$ with a total probability of 60.9%, and in the case of three faults, the system is less secure when $(v', m') = (4, 2)$, $(5, 1)$, and $(6, 0)$ with a total probability of 69.1%. These results indicate that the proposed approach weakens the security of UOV even when the number of faults is limited.

5   Conclusion

In this paper, we proposed a new fault attack on UOV, which is a multivariate signature scheme. This is the first fault attack on UOV that uses faults occurring on the secret key.

Our proposed attack is mainly composed of two steps: We recover some row vectors of the secret linear map $\mathcal{T}$ using faults generated on the central map $\mathcal{F}$, and transform the public key system. Given a UOV public key system with v vinegar variables and m oil variables, the resulting system of the proposed attack is a UOV system with $v - v'$ vinegar variables and $m - m'$ oil variables, where v' and m' are determined based on the faults. In this paper, we also showed that the existing key recovery attacks on UOV, i.e., Kipnis-Shamir and intersection attacks, can be applied to the resulting proposed attack system with smaller complexity than that on the original system.

Moreover, we simulated the proposed attack on two parameter sets satisfying 100-bit security. For example, in the case of $(q, v, m) = (256, 50, 33)$, the secret key can be recovered with smaller manipulations of 89.5, 81.3, or 63.2 bits with a probability of 84.6%, 68.0%, or 46.2%, respectively. We also confirmed that the proposed attack works even when the number of faults is limited. In the case of one, two, and three faults, the secret key of the resulting system can be recovered through 93.1-, 85.1-, and 77.1-bit manipulations with a feasible probability of 41.4%, 17.1%, and 7.1%, respectively.

It should be noted that a naive countermeasure against the proposed attack would be to check whether the secret key is faulty, and if so, to avoid generating the signature, as described in [14]. This countermeasure will be practical in online scenario since the verification of UOV is known to be so efficient.

Acknowledgements. This work was supported by JST CREST Grant Number JPMJCR2113, Japan, and JSPS KAKENHI Grant Number JP21J20391, Japan.

References

1. Bettale, L., Faugère, J.-C., Perret, L.: Hybrid approach for solving multivariate systems over finite fields. J. Math. Crypto. **3**, 177–197 (2009)
2. Beullens, W.: Improved cryptanalysis of UOV and rainbow. In: Canteaut, A., Standaert, F.-X. (eds.) EUROCRYPT 2021. LNCS, vol. 12696, pp. 348–373. Springer, Cham (2021). https://doi.org/10.1007/978-3-030-77870-5_13
3. Beullens, W.: Breaking rainbow takes a weekend on a laptop. IACR Cryptology ePrint Archive: Report 2022/385 (2022)
4. Beullens, W., Preneel, B.: Field lifting for smaller UOV public keys. In: Patra, A., Smart, N.P. (eds.) INDOCRYPT 2017. LNCS, vol. 10698, pp. 227–246. Springer, Cham (2017). https://doi.org/10.1007/978-3-319-71667-1_12
5. Bogdanov, A., Eisenbarth, T., Rupp, A., Wolf, C.: Time-area optimized public-key engines: $\mathcal{MQ}$-cryptosystems as replacement for elliptic curves? In: Oswald, E., Rohatgi, P. (eds.) CHES 2008. LNCS, vol. 5154, pp. 45–61. Springer, Heidelberg (2008). https://doi.org/10.1007/978-3-540-85053-3_4

6. Courtois, N., Klimov, A., Patarin, J., Shamir, A.: Efficient algorithms for solving overdefined systems of multivariate polynomial equations. In: Preneel, B. (ed.) EUROCRYPT 2000. LNCS, vol. 1807, pp. 392–407. Springer, Heidelberg (2000). https://doi.org/10.1007/3-540-45539-6_27

7. Czypek, P., Heyse, S., Thomae, E.: Efficient implementations of MQPKS on constrained devices. In: Prouff, E., Schaumont, P. (eds.) CHES 2012. LNCS, vol. 7428, pp. 374–389. Springer, Heidelberg (2012). https://doi.org/10.1007/978-3-642-33027-8_22

8. Chen, A.I.-T., et al.: SSE implementation of multivariate PKCs on modern x86 CPUs. In: Clavier, C., Gaj, K. (eds.) CHES 2009. LNCS, vol. 5747, pp. 33–48. Springer, Heidelberg (2009). https://doi.org/10.1007/978-3-642-04138-9_3

9. Ding, J., Schmidt, D.: Rainbow, a new multivariable polynomial signature scheme. In: Ioannidis, J., Keromytis, A., Yung, M. (eds.) ACNS 2005. LNCS, vol. 3531, pp. 164–175. Springer, Heidelberg (2005). https://doi.org/10.1007/11496137_12

10. Ding, J., Yang, B.-Y., Chen, C.-H.O., Chen, M.-S., Cheng, C.-M.: New differential-algebraic attacks and reparametrization of rainbow. In: Bellovin, S.M., Gennaro, R., Keromytis, A., Yung, M. (eds.) ACNS 2008. LNCS, vol. 5037, pp. 242–257. Springer, Heidelberg (2008). https://doi.org/10.1007/978-3-540-68914-0_15

11. Faugère, J.-C.: A new efficient algorithm for computing Gröbner bases (F4). J. Pure Appl. Algebra 139(1–3), 61–88 (1999)

12. Faugère, J.-C.: A new efficient algorithm for computing Gröbner bases without reduction to zero (F5). In: ISSAC 2002, pp. 75–83. ACM (2002)

13. Garey, M.-R., Johnson, D.-S.: Computers and Intractability: A Guide to the Theory of NP-Completeness. W. H. Freeman (1979)

14. Hashimoto, Y., Takagi, T., Sakurai, K.: General fault attacks on multivariate public key cryptosystems. In: Yang, B.-Y. (ed.) PQCrypto 2011. LNCS, vol. 7071, pp. 1–18. Springer, Heidelberg (2011). https://doi.org/10.1007/978-3-642-25405-5_1

15. Kipnis, A., Patarin, J., Goubin, L.: Unbalanced oil and vinegar signature schemes. In: Stern, J. (ed.) EUROCRYPT 1999. LNCS, vol. 1592, pp. 206–222. Springer, Heidelberg (1999). https://doi.org/10.1007/3-540-48910-X_15

16. Kipnis, A., Shamir, A.: Cryptanalysis of the oil and vinegar signature scheme. In: Krawczyk, H. (ed.) CRYPTO 1998. LNCS, vol. 1462, pp. 257–266. Springer, Heidelberg (1998). https://doi.org/10.1007/BFb0055733

17. Krämer, J., Loiero, M.: Fault attacks on UOV and rainbow. In: Polian, I., Stöttinger, M. (eds.) COSADE 2019. LNCS, vol. 11421, pp. 193–214. Springer, Cham (2019). https://doi.org/10.1007/978-3-030-16350-1_11

18. Mus, K., Islam, S., Sunar, B.: QuantumHammer: a practical hybrid attack on the LUOV signature scheme. In: CCS 2020, pp. 1071–1084. ACM (2020)

19. NIST: Post-quantum cryptography CSRC. https://csrc.nist.gov/Projects/post-quantum-cryptography/post-quantum-cryptography-standardization

20. NIST: Status report on the second round of the NIST post-quantum cryptography standardization process. NIST Internal Report 8309, NIST (2020)

21. Park, A., Shim, K.-A., Koo, N., Han, D.-G.: Side-channel attacks on post-quantum signature schemes based on multivariate quadratic equations - rainbow and UOV -. IACR Trans. Cryptogr. Hardw. Embed. Syst. 2018(3), 500–523 (2018)

22. Shor, P.W.: Polynomial-time algorithms for prime factorization and discrete logarithms on a quantum computer. SIAM J. Comput. 26(5), 1484–1509 (1997)

23. Shim, K.-A., Koo, N.: Algebraic fault analysis of UOV and Rainbow with the leakage of random vinegar values. IEEE Trans. Inf. Forensics Secur. 15, 2429–2439 (2020)

24. Shim, K.-A., Lee, S., Koo, N.: Efficient implementations of Rainbow and UOV using AVX2. IACR Trans. Cryptogr. Hardw. Embed. Syst. **2022**(1), 245–269 (2022)
25. Yang, B.-Y., Chen, J.-M., Courtois, N.T.: On asymptotic security estimates in XL and Gröbner bases-related algebraic cryptanalysis. In: Lopez, J., Qing, S., Okamoto, E. (eds.) ICICS 2004. LNCS, vol. 3269, pp. 401–413. Springer, Heidelberg (2004). https://doi.org/10.1007/978-3-540-30191-2_31
26. Yang, B.-Y., Chen, O.C.-H., Bernstein, D.J., Chen, J.-M.: Analysis of QUAD. In: Biryukov, A. (ed.) FSE 2007. LNCS, vol. 4593, pp. 290–308. Springer, Heidelberg (2007). https://doi.org/10.1007/978-3-540-74619-5_19

MR-DSS – Smaller MinRank-Based (Ring-)Signatures

Emanuele Bellini[1], Andre Esser[1], Carlo Sanna[2], and Javier Verbel[1(✉)]

[1] Technology Innovation Institute, Abu Dhabi, UAE
{emanuele.bellini,andre.esser,javier.verbel}@tii.ae
[2] Politecnico di Torino, Torino, Italy
carlo.sanna@polito.it

Abstract. In the light of NIST's announced reopening of the call for digital signature proposals in 2023 due to lacking diversity, there is a strong need for constructions based on other established hardness assumptions. In this work we construct a new post-quantum secure digital signature scheme based on the *MinRank* problem, a problem with a long history of applications in cryptanalysis that led to a strong belief in its hardness. Initially following a design by Courtois (Asiacrypt '01) based on the Fiat–Shamir transform, we make use of several recent developments in the design of sigma protocols to reduce signature size and improve efficiency. This includes the recently introduced *sigma protocol with helper* paradigm (Eurocrypt '19) and combinations with *cut-and-choose* techniques (CCS '18). Moreover, we introduce several improvements to the core of the scheme to further reduce its signature size.

As a second contribution, we formalize the natural extension of our construction to a ring signature scheme and show that it achieves desired anonymity and unforgeability guarantees. Our ring signature is characterized by a sublinear scaling of the signature size in the number of users. Moreover, we achieve competitive practical signature sizes for moderate amount of users in comparison to recent ring signature proposals.

Keywords: Fiat–Shamir · MinRank · Post-quantum signature · Ring signature · Sigma protocols

1 Introduction

The NIST standardization process for post-quantum secure cryptographic schemes is in transition to its fourth round. While the process for post-quantum secure KEMs is progressing well, the process for digital signatures suffers from a lack of diversity among the hardness assumptions of the remaining candidates. In particular, the remaining signature schemes are either based on structured lattices or symmetric primitives [40]. Although, both foundations have

C. Sanna is a member of GNSAGA of INdAM, and of CrypTO, the group of Cryptography and Number Theory of Politecnico di Torino.

J. H. Cheon and T. Johansson (Eds.): PQCrypto 2022, LNCS 13512, pp. 144–169, 2022.
https://doi.org/10.1007/978-3-031-17234-2_8

desirable attributes, the security guarantees of structured lattice-based schemes have recently been challenged [39] and schemes based on symmetric primitives, while generally secure, suffer from performance issues [40]. For this reason, NIST announced that it will reopen the call for digital signature schemes in early 2023, making the study of schemes based on other established hardness assumptions an important and urgent task.

In this work we propose a new post-quantum secure digital signature scheme based on the so-called MinRank problem, which was introduced in 1999 by Buss, Frandsen, and Shallit [21]. Roughly speaking, the MinRank problem asks to find a low-rank linear combination of some given matrices over a finite field. The MinRank problem is an attractive candidate for post-quantum cryptography for multiple reasons. First, it is entirely based on linear algebra computations, allowing constructions to benefit from the long line of research in optimizing the involved operations [3,36,47]. Also, the MinRank problem has been extensively studied due to its applications in cryptanalysis [14,19,20,22,35,41,45,48], where faster algorithms for solving the MinRank problem usually imply improved attacks on the involved schemes. This relation has established a strong belief in the hardness of the MinRank problem over the last decades. Furthermore, there are no quantum attacks known that go beyond straightforward quantum search applications. However, there has been very limited work on cryptographic primitives based on this problem. To the best of our knowledge, the only construction based on the hardness of the MinRank problem is a sigma protocol from 2001 due to Courtois [23].

Sigma protocols implement zero-knowledge proofs of knowledge (PoK). These constructions allow a prover to prove to a verifier that he knows a secret object x, which satisfies a certain relation, without revealing any information about x. For example, x might be the secret key corresponding to a known public key or, as in the protocol of Courtois, the solution to a publicly-known MinRank instance. Sigma protocols do not reach perfect soundness, i.e., a cheating prover not knowing x might be able to convince the verifier that he actually knows x. If a cheating prover is able to convince the verifier with probability p, then p is called the soundness error of the protocol.

It is well known that a sigma protocol that offers security against passive attacks can be transformed into a digital signature scheme, secure in the random oracle model, by using the Fiat–Shamir transform. A straightforward application of this transformation to Courtois' protocol results in a digital signature scheme with not particularly desirable parameters. However, starting from Courtois' initial protocol, we adopt recent techniques in the design of sigma-protocols to reduce the soundness error of the construction. Combining this with several modifications and improvements to the original protocol, we are able to derive a new digital signature scheme with significantly reduced signature and public key sizes.

Another major advantage of our construction is that it naturally extends to ring-signatures. A ring-signature allows a signer to sign a message on behalf of a group of users, called a *ring*. A verifier is then able to verify the signature as usual, but can not identify the signer among all members of the ring. The performance of those schemes is usually a function depending on the number of users in the ring. There exist constant size ring-signatures [2,25], however, none of those are post-quantum secure. Our scheme is characterized by a sublinear scaling of the signature size in the number of users and allowing to achieve competitive practical parameters.

1.1 Related Work

Signature schemes constructed from sigma protocols have a long standing history (e.g. [1,11,12,30,38,42,46,49]). A main advantage of such constructions is that they do not require a trapdoor-relation. This makes it possible to base their security on presumably hard instances of the underlying problem. However, a common drawback is usually a larger signature size due to necessary repetitions of the protocol when applying the Fiat–Shamir transformation. These repetitions reduce the (high) soundness error of the sigma protocol from p to $p^R \leq 2^{-\lambda}$, where R is the number of repetitions and λ the security parameter.

Multiple recent works try to lower the initial soundness error, to reduce the amount of repetitions. Katz et al. [34] have constructed a zero knowledge PoK using the *MPC-in-the-head* paradigm [33] in combination with a preprocessing stage to distribute some auxiliary information to the participants. The protocol extends to an arbitrary number of users n resulting in a sigma protocol with soundness error $\frac{1}{n}$. Beullens [17] then generalized the approach from Katz, Kolesnikov and Wang [34] by introducing the *sigma protocol with helper* paradigm. Here, the sigma protocol uses a trusted third party, called the *helper*, to provide some auxiliary information to the verifier, which similarly results in a lower soundness error of the construction. Eventually, the helper is removed using a *cut-and-choose* technique. The helper paradigm and independent similar techniques to lower the soundness error have recently led to efficient zero-knowledge-based signature schemes [28,29,32].

1.2 Contribution

We construct a post-quantum secure digital signature scheme based on the Min-Rank problem, which we call *MR-DSS*. Our construction obtains about half the signature size and slightly more than half the public key size of a straightforward application of the Fiat–Shamir transform to the sigma protocol by Courtois.

From a design point of view, we follow the sigma protocol with helper paradigm of Beullens. By introducing the helper we reduce the soundness error of Courtois' protocol from $\frac{2}{3}$ to $\frac{1}{2}$. We then use a cut-and-choose technique from [34] to remove the helper. This results in a sigma protocol with very low soundness error, mitigating the need for multiple iterations when applying the Fiat–Shamir transform. We further introduce several improvements to Courtois' protocol reducing its communication complexity and, implicitly, the signature size. Overall, we are able to decrease the signature size by a factor of roughly 2.

Further we formalize the natural extension of our scheme to ring signatures. The possibility of such an extension was already observed by Courtois [23]. However, he did neither formalize the resulting scheme nor argue about its security or determine its parameters. We show that the extension of our scheme matches the security definitions of ring-signatures given by Bender, Katz, and Morselli [13]. Moreover, the ring signature scheme is characterized by a sublinear scaling of the signature size in the amount of users, leading to particularly good practical signature sizes, especially for moderate amounts of users.

Outline. In Sect. 2 we cover used notations and definitions, followed by a recap of basic properties of sigma protocols with helpers and commitment schemes. Subsequently, in Sect. 3 we recall the initial sigma protocol from Courtois. In the following Sect. 4 we then describe our new scheme, including an analysis of its public key and signature size as well as suggested parameters. Eventually, Sect. 5 covers our extension of the scheme to ring-signatures.

Concurrent Work. Recently, Santoso et al. [44] independently proposed a variation of Courtois' sigma protocol that achieves soundness probability $\frac{1}{2}$. They adapt challenge space and responses to lower the soundness. However, their approach yields only slight improvements (in the magnitude of bytes) over Courtois' signature size. Moreover, the authors disregard the size of the initial commitments in their analysis of the communication complexity. Taking commitment sizes into account they achieve no improvement over Courtois. We give more details on this in Appendix C.

2   Preliminaries

For each prime power q, we let $\mathbb{F}_q$ denote the finite field of q elements. For positive integers m and n, we write $M_{m,n}(\mathbb{F}_q)$ for the vector space of $m \times n$ matrices with entries in $\mathbb{F}_q$, and $GL_n(\mathbb{F}_q)$ for the group of invertible matrices in $M_{n,n}(\mathbb{F}_q)$. We let λ denote the security parameter. We use standard Landau notation for complexity statements and write log for the logarithm in base 2.

Let us define the *MinRank* problem. By MinRank we refer to the search version of the MinRank problem over finite fields defined as follows.

Definition 1 (MinRank problem).

- *Parameters: Positive integers q, m, n, k, r with q a prime power.*
- *Instance: $(k+1)$-tuple $\boldsymbol{M}$ of matrices $M_0; M_1, \ldots, M_k \in M_{m,n}(\mathbb{F}_q)$.*
- *Solution: $\alpha \in \mathbb{F}_q^k$ such that $E := M_0 + \sum_{i=1}^{k} \alpha_i M_i$ has rank less than or equal to r.*

2.1 Sigma Protocols with Helper

Sigma protocols with helper were recently introduced by Beullens [17]. Informally, a sigma protocol with helper extends a sigma protocol by adding a trusted party, which is called the *helper*. This trusted party runs a setup algorithm based on a random seed at the beginning of each execution of the protocol. The helper then sends the seed value to the prover and some auxiliary information to the verifier. The formal definition of a sigma protocol with helper is the following.

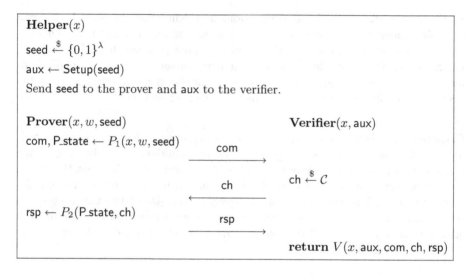

Fig. 1. Structure of a sigma protocol with helper.

Definition 2 (Sigma protocol with helper). *A protocol is a sigma protocol with helper for a relation $\mathcal{R}$ with challenge space $\mathcal{C}$ if it is of the form of Fig. 1 and satisfies the following properties:*

- *Completeness: If all parties follow the protocol on input $(x, w) \in \mathcal{R}$, then the verifier always accepts.*
- *2-Special soundness: From an adversary that outputs with significant probability two valid transcripts $(x, \mathsf{aux}, \mathsf{com}, \mathsf{ch}, \mathsf{rsp})$ and $(x, \mathsf{aux}, \mathsf{com}, \mathsf{ch}', \mathsf{rsp}')$, with $\mathsf{ch} \neq \mathsf{ch}'$ and where $\mathsf{aux} = \mathsf{Setup}(\mathsf{seed})$ for some seed values (unknown to the extractor), one can efficiently extract a witness w such that $(x, w) \in \mathcal{R}$.*
- *Special honest-verifier zero-knowledge: There exists a probabilistic polynomial-time simulator that takes as input x, a random seed, and a random challenge ch; and outputs a transcript $(x, \mathsf{aux}, \mathsf{com}, \mathsf{ch}, \mathsf{rsp})$, with $\mathsf{aux} = \mathsf{Setup}(\mathsf{seed})$, that is computationally indistinguishable from the probability distribution of transcripts of an honest execution of the protocol on input (x, w) for some w such that $(x, w) \in \mathcal{R}$, conditioned on the auxiliary information being equal to aux and the challenge being equal to ch.*

Every sigma protocol with helper can be transformed into a standard sigma protocol by a *cut-and-choose* approach, which we outline in Sect. 4.2.

2.2 Commitment Schemes

In our constructions we assume the existence of a non-interactive commitment function $\mathsf{Com} : \{0,1\}^\lambda \times \{0,1\}^* \to \{0,1\}^{2\lambda}$, which takes as input a pair (r, m) consisting of λ random bits r and an arbitrary message m, and returns a commitment of 2λ bits. The function Com is assumed to be *computational hiding*, which informally means that the commitments do not reveal anything about the committed message, and *computational binding*, which informally states that it should not be possible to find a different message m' that leads to the same commitment. The formal definitions of these properties are given in Appendix A. In practice, Com can be implemented by a cryptographic secure hash function.

3 The Sigma Protocol of Courtois

Let us briefly recall the sigma protocol of Courtois [23] for a zero-knowledge proof of knowledge of the solution α to an instance of the MinRank problem. It follows a three-pass design with challenge space $\{0, 1, 2\}$ and achieves a soundness error of $\frac{2}{3}$. The protocol is based on an additive masking of the solution vector α with some random vector β. Initially, the prover commits to the matrices

$$N_1 = \sum_{i=1}^{k} \beta_i M_i \quad \text{and} \quad N_2 = M_0 + \sum_{i=1}^{k} (\alpha_i + \beta_i) M_i = N_1 + E,$$

where E is the matrix of rank less than r from the underlying MinRank problem. Then challenges 1 and 2 lead to revealing either β or $\alpha + \beta$, which enables the verifier to check that the prover followed the protocol for the computation of either N_1 or N_2. In case of challenge equal to 0, the prover sends to the verifier two matrices Z_1 and Z_2, which are obtained by multiplicatively and additively masking N_1 and N_2 with the matrices S, T and X. Then the verifier checks that $\mathrm{rank}(Z_2 - Z_1) \leq r$, which implies that $\mathrm{rank}(N_2 - N_1) \leq r$, i.e., that α is a solution to the MinRank problem. See Fig. 2 for a formal description of the protocol.

4 Improved MinRank-Based Signature Scheme

In this section, we present an improved signature scheme based on the MinRank problem. The scheme is constructed in three steps. First, in Sect. 4.1, we give a sigma protocol with helper for a zero-knowledge proof of knowledge of the solution to an instance of the MinRank problem. Second, the helper is removed using a cut-and-choose technique, detailed in Sect. 4.2, to obtain a standard sigma protocol. Eventually, the sigma protocol is converted to a signature scheme by a standard application of the Fiat–Shamir transform.

Furthermore, in Sect. 4.3 we give several improvements to our initial design, reducing the communication complexity and, implicitly, the signature size.

Prover(M, α) **Verifier**(M)

$S \xleftarrow{\$} \mathrm{GL}_n(\mathbb{F}_q), \; T \xleftarrow{\$} \mathrm{GL}_m(\mathbb{F}_q)$

$X \xleftarrow{\$} \mathrm{M}_{m,n}(\mathbb{F}_q), \; \beta \xleftarrow{\$} \mathbb{F}_q^k$

$E \leftarrow M_0 + \sum_{i=1}^{k} \alpha_i M_i$

$N_1 \leftarrow \sum_{i=1}^{k} \beta_i M_i, \; N_2 \leftarrow N_1 + E$

$Z_i \leftarrow TN_iS + X \quad (i = 1, 2)$

$r_0, r_1, r_2 \xleftarrow{\$} \{0,1\}^\lambda \times \{0,1\}^\lambda \times \{0,1\}^\lambda$

$\mathsf{com}_0 \leftarrow \mathsf{Com}\big(r_0, (S, T, X)\big)$

$\mathsf{com}_i \leftarrow \mathsf{Com}\big(r_i, Z_i\big) \quad (i = 1, 2)$

$\mathsf{com} \leftarrow (\mathsf{com}_0, \mathsf{com}_1, \mathsf{com}_2)$

$\xrightarrow{\quad \mathsf{com} \quad}$

$\xleftarrow{\quad \mathsf{ch} \quad} \qquad \mathsf{ch} \xleftarrow{\$} \{0, 1, 2\}$

if $\mathsf{ch} = 0$ **then**

    $\mathsf{rsp} \leftarrow (r_1, r_2, Z_1, Z_2)$

if $\mathsf{ch} = 1$ **then**

    $\mathsf{rsp} \leftarrow (r_0, r_1, S, T, X, \beta)$

if $\mathsf{ch} = 2$ **then**

    $\mathsf{rsp} \leftarrow (r_0, r_2, S, T, X, \alpha + \beta)$

$\xrightarrow{\quad \mathsf{rsp} \quad}$

                 if $\mathsf{ch} = 0$ **then**

                     return $\big(\mathsf{Com}(r_1, Z_1) = \mathsf{com}_1\big)$

                         $\wedge \big(\mathsf{Com}(r_2, Z_2) = \mathsf{com}_2\big)$

                         $\wedge \big(\mathrm{rank}(Z_2 - Z_1) \leq r\big)$

                 if $\mathsf{ch} \in \{1, 2\}$ **then**

                     Recompute Z_{ch} from rsp

                     return $(S, T$ are invertible$)$

                         $\wedge \big(\mathsf{Com}(r_0, (S, T, X)) = \mathsf{com}_0\big)$

                         $\wedge \big(\mathsf{Com}(r_{\mathsf{ch}}, Z_{\mathsf{ch}}) = \mathsf{com}_{\mathsf{ch}}\big)$

Fig. 2. The sigma protocol of Courtois for ZK proof of MinRank.

4.1 Sigma Protocol with Helper for ZK Proof of MinRank

On a high level, we use the helper as a trusted third party to provide the *non-secret-key dependent* commitments. This allows us to decrease the challenge space to $\{0, 1\}$, since the prover has to commit only to a single value. For challenge 1 the prover then allows the verifier to check that he followed the protocol when computing the commitment, while for challenge 0 he proves his knowledge of the solution to the MinRank problem.

More precisely, the helper provides the non-secret-key dependent commitments com_0 and com_1 of Fig. 2. He then sends those commitments to the verifier

Helper(M)

seed $\xleftarrow{\$} \{0,1\}^\lambda$

Generate $S \in \mathrm{GL}_n(\mathbb{F}_q)$, $T \in \mathrm{GL}_m(\mathbb{F}_q)$, $X \in \mathrm{M}_{m,n}(\mathbb{F}_q)$, and $\beta \in \mathbb{F}_q^k$ from seed.

Generate $r_0 \xleftarrow{\$} \{0,1\}^\lambda$ and $r_1 \xleftarrow{\$} \{0,1\}^\lambda$ from seed

$N_1 \leftarrow \sum_{i=1}^k \beta_i M_i$

$\mathsf{com}_0 \leftarrow \mathsf{Com}(r_0, (S, T, X))$

$\mathsf{com}_1 \leftarrow \mathsf{Com}(r_1, TN_1S + X)$

$\mathsf{aux} \leftarrow (\mathsf{com}_0, \mathsf{com}_1)$

Send seed to the prover and aux to the verifier.

Prover(M, α, seed)		**Verifier**(M, aux)

Regenerate S, T, X, β, r_0, and r_1 from seed.

Recompute N_1.

$N_2 \leftarrow N_1 + E$, $Z_i = TN_iS + X$ $(i = 1, 2)$

$r_2 \xleftarrow{\$} \{0,1\}^\lambda$, $\mathsf{com}_2 \leftarrow \mathsf{Com}(r_2, TN_2S + X)$ $\xrightarrow{\mathsf{com}_2}$

$\xleftarrow{\mathsf{ch}}$ $\mathsf{ch} \xleftarrow{\$} \{0,1\}$

if $\mathsf{ch} = 0$ **then**

    $\mathsf{rsp} \leftarrow (r_1, r_2, Z_1, Z_2)$

if $\mathsf{ch} = 1$ **then**

    $\mathsf{rsp} \leftarrow \big(r_0, r_2, (S, T, X), \alpha + \beta\big)$ $\xrightarrow{\mathsf{rsp}}$

        if $\mathsf{ch} = 0$ **then**

            return $\big(\mathsf{Com}(r_1, Z_1) = \mathsf{com}_1\big)$

            $\wedge \big(\mathsf{Com}(r_2, Z_2) = \mathsf{com}_2\big)$

            $\wedge \big(\mathrm{rank}(Z_2 - Z_1) \leq r\big)$

        if $\mathsf{ch} = 1$ **then**

            Recompute N_2, Z_2 from rsp

            $N_2 \leftarrow M_0 + \sum_{i=1}^k (\alpha_i + \beta_i)M_i$

            $Z_2 \leftarrow TN_2S + X$

            return $(S, T$ are invertible$)$

            $\wedge \big(\mathsf{Com}(r_0, (S, T, X)) = \mathsf{com}_0\big)$

            $\wedge \big(\mathsf{Com}(r_2, Z_2) = \mathsf{com}_2\big)$

Fig. 3. Structure of a sigma protocol with helper for ZK proof of MinRank.

and the used randomness to the prover. The prover only needs to provide the key-dependent commitment com_2, after recomputing the helper-generated data from the given randomness seed. The challenge space reduces to $\{0,1\}$, since the helper-provided commitment does not have to be challenged. Analogously to before, in case of challenge 1 the prover reveals the masked secret $\alpha + \beta$, allowing the re-computation of N_2, while for challenge 0 he answers with Z_1 and Z_2 allowing to verify his knowledge of the MinRank solution. Our full protocol is detailed in Fig. 3.

Theorem 1 (MinRank with Helper). *Let* Com *be a commitment scheme which is computational binding and hiding. Then the protocol detailed in Fig. 3* *satisfies Definition 2 for sigma protocols with helper for challenge space* $\mathcal{C} = \{0, 1\}$.

Proof. We have to prove that the protocol of Fig. 3 fulfills the notions of completeness, 2-special soundness, and special honest-verifier zero-knowledge given in Definition 2. In the following, we let $\mathsf{rsp} = (r_0, r_2, Y, \gamma)$ denote the response for challenge $\mathsf{ch} = 1$. In particular, an honest prover sends $Y := (Y_1, Y_2, Y_3) = (S, T, X)$ and $\gamma = \alpha + \beta$.

Completeness. If all parties follow the protocol, then it is clear that the verifier accepts, since

$$\operatorname{rank}(Z_2 - Z_1) = \operatorname{rank}\big(T(N_2 - N_1)S\big) = \operatorname{rank}(N_2 - N_1) = \operatorname{rank}(E) \le r.$$

2-Special Soundness. Suppose that an adversary knows two valid transcripts

$$(\boldsymbol{M}, \mathsf{aux}, \mathsf{com}, \mathsf{ch}, \mathsf{rsp}) \quad \text{and} \quad (\boldsymbol{M}, \mathsf{aux}, \mathsf{com}, \mathsf{ch}', \mathsf{rsp}')$$

with $\mathsf{ch} \ne \mathsf{ch}'$ and where $\mathsf{aux} = \mathsf{Setup}(\mathsf{seed})$ for some value of seed, which is unknown to the adversary. We have to prove that the adversary can efficiently compute a solution to $\boldsymbol{M}$.

Without loss of generality, assume that $\mathsf{ch} = 1$ and $\mathsf{ch}' = 0$. Since the verifier accepts the response rsp, we have that $\mathsf{com}_0 = \mathsf{Com}(r_0, Y)$ and

$$\mathsf{com}_2 = \mathsf{Com}\big(r, Y_2(M_0 + \textstyle\sum_{i=1}^{k} \gamma_i M_i)Y_1 + Y_3\big).$$

From the computational binding property of the commitment we now conclude that $Y = (S, T, X)$ since $\mathsf{Com}(r_0, Y) = \mathsf{com}_0 = \mathsf{Com}\big(r_0, (S, T, X)\big)$.

Moreover, from the verifier accepting the response rsp', we know that $\mathsf{com}_2 = \mathsf{Com}(r, Z_2')$. Thus, we find analogously that

$$\mathsf{Com}\big(r, T(M_0 + \textstyle\sum_{i=1}^{k} \gamma_i M_i)S + X\big) = \mathsf{com}_2 = \mathsf{Com}(r, Z_2'),$$

implying $Z_2' = T(M_0 + \sum_{i=1}^{k} \gamma_i M_i)S + X$. Further, by the helper behaving honestly we know that $\mathsf{com}_1 = \mathsf{Com}(r_1, T\sum_{i}^{k} \beta_i M_i S + X)$ while the verifier only accepts rsp' if $\mathsf{com}_1 = \mathsf{Com}(r_1, Z_1')$, giving $Z_1' = T(\sum_{i=1}^{k} \beta_i M_i)S + X$.

In turn, this gives that

$$\begin{aligned} Z_2' - Z_1' &= \big(T(M_0 + \textstyle\sum_{i=1}^{k} \gamma_i M_i)S + X\big) - \big(T(\textstyle\sum_{i=1}^{k} \beta_i M_i)S + X\big) \\ &= T\big(M_0 + \textstyle\sum_{i=1}^{k} (\gamma_i - \beta_i)M_i\big)S = T\big(M_0 + \textstyle\sum_{i=1}^{k} \delta_i M_i\big)S, \end{aligned}$$

where $\delta := \gamma - \beta \in \mathbb{F}_q^k$. Since $Y = (S, T, X)$ is known, we can compute δ by solving the linear system

$$\textstyle\sum_{i=1}^{k} \delta_i M_i = Y_2^{-1}(Z_2' - Z_1')Y_1^{-1} - M_0.$$

Finally, from the verifier accepting rsp' we know that $\operatorname{rank}(Z_2' - Z_1') \le r$ which implies

$$\operatorname{rank}\big(M_0 + \textstyle\sum_{i=1}^{k} \delta_i M_i\big) = \operatorname{rank}\big(T\big(M_0 + \textstyle\sum_{i=1}^{k} \delta_i M_i\big)S\big) = \operatorname{rank}(Z_2' - Z_1') \le r,$$

thus δ is a solution to the instance $\boldsymbol{M}$.

Special Honest-Verifier Zero-Knowledge. Define a simulator that takes as input M, a random seed seed, and a random challenge ch; and outputs a valid transcript $(M, \text{aux}, \widetilde{\text{com}}_2, \text{ch}, \widetilde{\text{rsp}})$ computed as follows:

1. Generate $S, T, X, \beta, N_1, r_0, r_1, \text{com}_0, \text{com}_1, \text{aux}$ from seed as a honest helper would do.
2. If ch $= 1$ then pick a random $r \in \{0,1\}^\lambda$ and a random $\widetilde{\gamma} \in \mathbb{F}_q^k$, and set $\widetilde{N}_2 = M_0 + \sum_{i=1}^k \widetilde{\gamma}_i M_i$, $\widetilde{\text{com}}_2 = \text{Com}(r, T\widetilde{N}_2 S + X)$, and $\widetilde{\text{rsp}} = (r, r_0, (S, T, X), \widetilde{\gamma})$.
3. If ch $= 0$ then pick a random $r \in \{0,1\}^\lambda$ and a random $R \in M_{m,n}(\mathbb{F}_q)$ of rank r, and set $\widetilde{Z}_2 = T(N_1 + R)S + X$, $\widetilde{\text{com}}_2 = \text{Com}(r, \widetilde{Z}_2)$, and $\widetilde{\text{rsp}} = (r, r_1, TN_1 S + X, \widetilde{Z}_2)$.

Then, by construction, $(M, \text{aux}, \widetilde{\text{com}}_2, \text{ch}, \widetilde{\text{rsp}})$ is a valid transcript where $\widetilde{\text{rsp}}$ is uniformly distributed in

$$\{0,1\}^\lambda \times \{0,1\}^\lambda \times \text{GL}_n(\mathbb{F}_q) \times \text{GL}_m(\mathbb{F}_q) \times M_{m,n}(\mathbb{F}_q) \times \mathbb{F}_q^k$$
$$\cup \{0,1\}^\lambda \times \{0,1\}^\lambda \times \{(U, V) : U, V \in M_{m,n}(\mathbb{F}_q), \text{rank}(U - V) = r\}.$$

Since also rsp is uniformly distributed in the above set, we get that rsp and $\widetilde{\text{rsp}}$ follow the same distribution. Moreover, $\widetilde{\text{com}}_2$ is completely determined by $\widetilde{\text{rsp}}$ in the same way that com_2 is completely determined by rsp. This implies that the transcripts $(M, \text{aux}, \widetilde{\text{com}}_2, \text{ch}, \text{rsp})$ and $(M, \text{aux}, \text{com}, \text{ch}, \text{rsp})$ follow the same distribution.

Eventually, since the commitment $\text{com}_{1-\text{ch}}$ is never opened, by the computational hiding property of the commitment the transcripts are indistinguishable. $\square$

4.2 Removing the Helper

In order to remove the helper, we use a cut-and-choose technique of Katz et al. [34] that proceeds as follows. The prover computes several setups and sends all generated auxiliary information to the verifier. The verifier then chooses a certain amount of the setups to execute, i.e., run the normal protocol based on the seeds of the chosen setups. Additionally, the prover sends all seeds belonging to the setups that are not executed to the verifier, allowing him to check that those setups have been computed honestly.

More precisely, we let the prover compute s setups and the verifier has to choose a subset of τ setups to execute. We illustrate this procedure schematically in Fig. 4. Now, if the soundness error of a single execution of the protocol with helper is p then the soundness error of the whole construction becomes

$$p_\tau := \max_{0 \leq i \leq \tau} \frac{\binom{s-i}{\tau-i} p^{\tau-i}}{\binom{s}{\tau}}. \tag{1}$$

Therefore assume that the prover computed a total of i setups dishonestly to provide valid responses in the online phase. Since the prover discloses all seeds

---

Prover(x, w) **Verifier**(x)

for $i \in \{1, \ldots, s\}$ do

  $\text{seed}_i \xleftarrow{\$} \{0,1\}^{\lambda}$

  $(\text{com}_{0,i}, \text{com}_{1,i}) \leftarrow \text{Setup}(\text{seed}_i)$

  $\text{aux}_i = (\text{com}_{0,i}, \text{com}_{1,i})$

  $\text{com}_{2,i} \leftarrow P_1(x, w, \text{seed}_i)$

end for

$$\xrightarrow{\text{aux}_i, \text{com}_{2,i}, \forall i}$$

$\qquad\qquad\qquad\qquad\qquad\qquad\qquad I \subseteq \{1, \ldots, s\},\ |I| = \tau$

$$\xleftarrow{I, \text{ch}_i,\ \forall i \in I} \qquad \text{ch}_i \xleftarrow{\$} \mathcal{C},\ \forall i \in I$$

$\text{rsp}_i \leftarrow P_2(x, w, \text{seed}_i, \text{ch}_i),\ \forall i \in I$

$$\xrightarrow[\text{seed}_i,\ \forall i \notin I]{\text{rsp}_i,\ \forall i \in I}$$

$\qquad\qquad\qquad\qquad\qquad\qquad$ for $i \in \{1, \ldots, s\} \setminus I$ do

$\qquad\qquad\qquad\qquad\qquad\qquad\qquad$ if $\text{aux}_i \neq \text{Setup}(\text{seed}_i)$ then

$\qquad\qquad\qquad\qquad\qquad\qquad\qquad\qquad$ **return false**

$\qquad\qquad\qquad\qquad\qquad\qquad$ **return** $\bigwedge_{i \in I} V(x, \text{aux}_i, \text{com}_{2,i}, \text{ch}_i, \text{rsp}_i)$

Fig. 4. Sigma protocol obtained by removing the helper from the protocol in Fig. 3. P_1, P_2 and V relate to the actions performed by the prover and verifier in Fig. 3 respectively.

belonging to setups that have not been executed, the cheating can only be hidden from the verifier if all these i setups are executed. The probability for this to happen is $\binom{s-i}{\tau-i} / \binom{s}{\tau}$. Now, the prover still needs to provide valid responses for the $\tau - i$ executed and honestly computed setups, in which he succeeds with probability $p^{\tau-i}$. For a more formal proof we refer to [10].

4.3 Further Improvements

In order to reduce the communication complexity of the sigma protocol of Fig. 4, we apply various improvements outlined in the following.

Merkle-Tree. First, we combine the $\text{com}_{2,i}$ in a Merkle-tree, with $\text{com}_{2,i}$ being the i-th leaf of the tree, where we label the root of the tree ρ. Then instead of sending $\text{com}_{2,i}, \forall i$, we only send ρ as a commitment. Later we then provide missing nodes of the tree to the verifier to be able to recompute the root ρ.

Seed-Tree. Similarly, we optimize the transmission of the seeds by using a seed-tree that expands an initial root into two seeds via a hash function. From there every node of the tree is expanded in a similar fashion, until the tree reaches a depth of $\lceil \log s \rceil$, i.e., it contains at least s leaves. Now we declare seed_i to be the

i-th leaf of that tree. The transmission of the seeds then only requires to reveal a certain (fewer) number of nodes of the tree.

Single Initial Commitment. Instead of initially sending the root of the Merkle-tree ρ together with all aux_i's as commitment, we just send a single commitment $com := Com(\rho, aux_1, \dots, aux_n)$. Later we then provide the missing inputs similar to the missing nodes of the Merkle-tree so that the verifier can recompute com.

Sending a Rank-r Matrix. In the case of challenge equal to 0 instead of sending Z_1, Z_2 as response, we send $Z_1, Z_1 - Z_2$. Note, that the response still carries the same information. However, the benefit lies in $Z_1 - Z_2$ being a rank-r matrix, which for small r has a shorter description length. Precisely, we can write $Z_1 - Z_2 = XY$, where X is an $m \times r$ matrix and Y an $r \times n$ matrix. Hence, instead of sending the entries of Z_2, we can send the entries of X and Y, which requires to transmit $(m + n)r \log q$ bits instead of $mn \log q$ bits, i.e., we obtain an improvement as long as $r < mn/(m + n)$.

4.4 Public Key Size

The public key of the scheme is the MinRank instance M. Courtois [23] generates $M_0, \dots, M_{k-1}$ from an initial seed and chooses M_k such that there exists a solution to the MinRank instance. Precisely, for a random matrix $E \in M_{m,n}(\mathbb{F}_q)$ of rank r and a random secret key $\alpha \in \mathbb{F}_q^k$ with $\alpha_k \neq 0$, he lets

$$M_k := \alpha_k^{-1} \left(-E + M_0 + \sum_{i=1}^{k-1} \alpha_i M_i \right).$$

The public key then consists of the seed and M_k and, thus, has a size of $\lambda + mn \log q$ bits. We improve on this by showing that any generic MinRank instance can be transformed into a canonical form which yields a shorter description length for its matrices.

More precisely, let L be the $(k + 1) \times mn$ matrix whose i-th row consists of the entries of M_i in row-major order, for $i = 1, \dots, k$ and whose $(k + 1)$-th row is formed by the entries of M_0. Now, row operations on L correspond to linear transformations of the variables α_i, i.e., we can apply elementary row operations without affecting the existence of a solution. Hence, we assume

$$L = \left(\begin{matrix} I \\ 0 \dots 0 \end{matrix} \middle| L' \right), \tag{2}$$

where I is the $k \times k$ identity matrix. Here, we restrict to keys where the first k columns and k rows of L form a matrix of full rank. However, since we consider random instances this is a constant fraction of the whole keyspace.

The public key is now generated as follows. First, from a random seed of λ bits, generate the first k rows of L', from which the matrices $M_1, \dots, M_k$ can be derived following Eq. (2). Then generate a random $m \times n$ matrix E of rank r, a random $\beta \in \mathbb{F}_q^k$, and compute $F := E - \sum_{i=1}^k \beta_i M_i$. Finally, let $f_1, \dots, f_k$ be the first k entries of F in row-major order, and let $M_0 := F - \sum_{i=1}^{k} f_i M_i$ and $\alpha_i := \beta_i + f_i$ for $i = 1, \ldots, k$. This ensures that the last row of L starts with k zeros. The compressed public key now consists of the seed and the last $mn - k$ entries of M_0 (the first k entries are all zero) and so its size is $\lambda + (mn - k) \log q$ bits.

4.5 Signature Size

The signature size after the Fiat–Shamir transform is determined by the communication size of messages send from the prover to the verifier. For our improved version of the protocol (see Sect. 4.3) this communication includes:

1. initial commitment of size 2λ,
2. missing nodes of the Merkle-tree to compute ρ,
3. seed values seed_i for $i \notin I$,
4. missing auxiliary information aux_i to compute $\mathsf{com} := \mathsf{Com}(\rho, \mathsf{aux}_1, \ldots, \mathsf{aux}_n)$,
5. responses rsp_i for $i \in I$.

In the online phase the verifier can compute all τ values $\mathsf{com}_{2,i}$ for $i \in I$. Hence, due to the usage of a Merkle-tree, the prover needs to send at most $\lceil \tau \log \frac{s}{\tau} \rceil$ tree-nodes, each of size 2λ, to allow the verifier the re-computation of the root ρ. Similarly, the usage of the seed-tree requires the prover to reveal at most $\lceil \tau \log \frac{s}{\tau} \rceil$ nodes of the tree, each of size λ, to enable the verifier to recompute all $s - \tau$ seeds seed_i for $i \notin I$.

These seeds allow to compute $\mathsf{aux}_i := (\mathsf{com}_{0,i}, \mathsf{com}_{1,i})$ for $i \notin I$. Further in the online phase the verifier can compute one of either $\mathsf{com}_{0,i}$ or $\mathsf{com}_{1,i}$ for $i \in I$. In order to finally re-compute com the verifier, now, misses τ values $\mathsf{com}_{j,i}$, not obtained in the online phase, which have to be provided by the prover, corresponding to $\tau \cdot 2\lambda$ bits of communication.

Eventually the average size of each of the τ responses is

$$|\mathsf{rsp}| = \underbrace{\frac{(mn + r(m+n)) \log q}{2}}_{\mathsf{ch}=0} + \underbrace{\frac{\lambda + k \log q}{2}}_{\mathsf{ch}=1}.$$

Indeed, in the case of $\mathsf{ch} = 0$ the response is composed of one $m \times n$ matrix and one rank-r $(m \times n)$-matrix over $\mathbb{F}_q$; while in the case of $\mathsf{ch} = 1$ it consists of the seed used to derive the matrices (S, T, X) and a vector of length k over $\mathbb{F}_q$.

In total we find a communication complexity of

$$C := \underbrace{2\lambda}_{1)} + \underbrace{3\lambda \left\lceil \log \frac{s}{\tau} \right\rceil}_{2) + 3)} + \underbrace{\tau \cdot 2\lambda}_{4)} + \underbrace{\tau \cdot |\mathsf{rsp}|}_{5)}, \tag{3}$$

while the soundness of the protocol is p_τ detailed in Eq. (1).

4.6   Parameters

In this section, we propose parameters for our signature scheme targeting NIST's security categories I, III, and V and detail the corresponding signature and public key sizes.

We estimate the security of our parameters by using the recent hybrid-MinRank approach from [6]. Given $0 \leq a \leq n$, this hybrid-MinRank approach reduces the cost of solving a rank-r MinRank problem with K matrices in $M_{m,n}(\mathbb{F}_q)$ to the cost of solving q^{ar} smaller instances with only $K - am$ matrices in $M_{m,n-a}(\mathbb{F}_q)$ and rank r. The complexity of the smaller instances is estimated by using the kernel-search algorithm [31], the Support-Minors modeling [4], and the big-k algorithm [24][1]. Notice that we do not consider the Kipnis-Shamir [35], and Minors [27] modelings, since it was recently proven that these modelings are less efficient than Support-Minors [5].

The complexity of the aforementioned algorithms depends on the linear algebra constant $2 \leq \omega \leq 3$, where the complexity of multiplying two $n \times n$ matrices is $O(n^\omega)$. All our bit security estimates are done for the conservative choice of $\omega = 2$. Also, we assume that multiplying two elements in $\mathbb{F}_q$ costs $(\log q)^2$ bit operations. Table 1 states the parameter sets for our scheme targeting the different security categories. The column KS contains the complexity of the kernel-search algorithm, while SM indicates the complexity of the Support-Minors modeling. The value of a inside the parenthesis shows the hybridization parameter of the hybrid-MinRank approach from [6].

Avoiding Random Solutions. Further, it is known that a set of k' randomly chosen matrices in $M_{m,n}(\mathbb{F}_q)$, in expectation, does not to span a rank r matrix when $k' < (m-r)(n-r)$ [24, Sec. 24.2]. Hence we enforce $k+1 < (m-r)(n-r)$ in order to avoid random solutions to the underlying MinRank problem.

Table 1. Estimated bit-security of proposed parameter sets using $\omega = 2$.

Category	λ	q	m	n	k	r	KS(a)	SM(a)	big-k(a)
I	128	16	14	14	108	4	144(6)	146(6)	150(0)
III	192	16	17	17	130	6	209(6)	207(6)	251(0)
V	256	16	20	20	208	6	281(9)	274(9)	312(0)

Table 2 gives the signature and public key sizes obtained for the proposed parameters. We compare our scheme to the original scheme by Courtois. Here, we obtain an optimal signature size of our scheme for cut-and-choose parameters $\tau = \lambda$ and $s = 2\lambda$ (compare to Sect. 4.2). For this choice, using Merkle- and seed-trees (as described in Sect. 4.3) yields signature size improvements (only) on average.

---

[1] The big-k algorithms is called big-m in [24].

Nevertheless, our scheme improves significantly on Courtois' design. In terms of signature size we, e.g., obtain a reduction by a factor of 2.18 for category III, while achieving a public key reduction by 1.62 using the improvement described in Sect. 4.4.

Table 2. Signature sizes (in kilobytes) and public key sizes (in bytes) for suggested parameters of our new scheme in comparison to Courtois' scheme. The signature size of our scheme is computed by setting $\tau = \lambda$ and $s = 2\lambda$ in Eq. (3)

Category	Signature (kB)		Public key (B)	
	Courtois	New	Courtois	New
I	55	24	114	60
III	118	54	169	104
V	221	97	232	128

Note that the nature of the MinRank problem involves the transmission of matrices between the corresponding parties, which leads in general to larger signatures compared to schemes that only involve vector exchanges. Nevertheless, the signature size of our construction gets close to being competitive to other NIST PQC candidates that are not based on structured problems. As for example to those of SPHINCS$^+$, which achieves roughly $17\,\mathrm{kB}$ signatures for category I.

5   MinRank-Based Ring Signatures

In the following we formalize the extension of our MinRank-based signature scheme to ring-signatures. We follow the formalism and the security definitions for ring signatures given by Bender, Katz, and Morselli [13]. We refer as a *ring* (of users) to a list of public keys $R = (\mathsf{pk}_1, \ldots, \mathsf{pk}_u)$. The formal definition of a ring signature scheme is given in Appendix B. An essential property of a ring signature scheme is that no coordination between the potential users of the scheme is needed. First, anyone can generate keys independently using Gen. Second, at the time of signing a message msg, a particular user holding a secret key sk uses its own public key along with any set of $u - 1$ public keys from other users to create a ring R and computes $\sigma \leftarrow \mathsf{Sign}_{\mathsf{sk}}(\mathsf{msg}, \mathsf{R})$. Anyone knowing R can verify the signature σ of the message msg, and guarantee that msg was signed by someone holding a secret key with corresponding public key in R. In the following we refer to the holder of sk as the *signer*.

A desired property of a ring signature scheme is to preserve the *anonymity* of the signer, i.e., informally speaking, the verifier can not identify the signer among all members of R. Another fundamental security property is the *unforgeability* for fixed rings. Roughly speaking, for a given ring R, without knowing any of the secret keys corresponding to public keys in R, an adversary is not able to produce a valid signature. Formal definitions of those security properties are given in Appendix B.1.

5.1   Extending to Ring Signatures

Let us briefly outline the idea of how to extend our signature scheme to a ring-signature scheme. The public key of each user is a matrix R, while the instance M (the public key of our regular signature scheme) is now a public parameter of the ring-signature scheme. Each user crafts R, such that he knows a linear combination of the M_i's that added to R yields a low-rank matrix, i.e., he knows a solution to the instance (M, R), which defines his secret key. Recall that a ring is defined as u public keys $\mathsf{R} := (R_1, R_2, \ldots, R_u)$. A ring signature is obtained by invoking the signing function of our regular scheme with (M, R) as public key and the known solution as private-key.

Formal Definition of the Scheme. In the following we let MR-Sign and MR-Verify denote the signing and verification function of our signature scheme outlined in Sect. 4. Further, let $M := (M_0, M_1, \ldots, M_k) \in \left(M_{m,n}(\mathbb{F}_q)\right)^{k+1}$ be a public parameter of the scheme (generated from some public Initseed $\in \{0,1\}^\lambda$). In the following R is the public-key corresponding to secret-key α and the ring is $\mathsf{R} = (R_1, \ldots, R_u)$.

$\mathsf{Gen}(1^\lambda)$:

1. Choose random secret key $\alpha := (\alpha_1, \ldots, \alpha_k) \in \mathbb{F}_q^k$,
2. Set the public key to $R = -\left(M_0 + \sum_{i=1}^{k} \alpha_i M_i\right) + E$, where $E \in \mathbb{F}_q^{m \times n}$ is a randomly chosen rank r matrix.
3. Output (R, α)

$\mathsf{Sign}_\alpha(\mathsf{msg}, \mathsf{R})$:

1. Set $\gamma \leftarrow (\alpha, \varepsilon_j)$, where $\varepsilon_j \in \mathbb{F}_q^u$ denotes the j-th canonical vector.
2. Output MR-$\mathsf{Sign}_\gamma(\mathsf{msg})$

$\mathsf{Verify}_\mathsf{R}(\mathsf{msg}, \sigma)$:

1. Output MR-$\mathsf{Verify}_{\widetilde{M}}(\mathsf{msg}, \sigma)$, where $\widetilde{M} := (M, \mathsf{R})$

The proof of correctness as well as the proofs of our scheme fulfilling the security notions of anonymity with regard to adversarially-chosen keys and unforgeability against fixed rings is given in Appendix B.2.

5.2   Parameters of the Scheme

Next we derive parameter sets for our constructed ring signature scheme. Therefore, we need to make some observations on the security of the constructed instances. Let us start with a remark on the amount of users a certain parameter set can support.

Limitation on the Number of Users. A given parameter set for our MinRank-based ring signature scheme can not afford an unlimited number of users. This is because for a ring of size u we can forge a signature by solving a MinRank instance with $u + k + 1$ matrices in $M_{m,n}(\mathbb{F}_q)$. Such an instance turns easy if $u + k + 1$ is big enough. By using the big-k algorithm [23] one solves any MinRank problem with parameters (m, n, k', r) in polynomial time $\text{Poly}(m, n, k')$ as long as $k' \geq m(n - r)$. Hence in both cases, i.e., for the one-user and the ring version of our scheme we make sure that

$$k' < m(n - r). \tag{4}$$

Still, in the case $k' < m(n - r)$, the attacker can succeed with probability $q^{k' - m(n-r)}$. Hence, the complexity of the algorithm becomes

$$q^{m(n-r)-k'} \cdot \text{Poly}(m, n, k').$$

We take this attack into account when deriving parameters. Further, we enforce $u + k + 1 \leq (m - r)(n - r)$ in order to avoid random solutions to the underlying MinRank problem.

Attack Scenarios. To forge a signature for a given ring $R := (R_1, R_2, \ldots, R_u)$ one has to solve an instance of the rank-r MinRank problem with matrices $(\boldsymbol{M}, R) \subset M_{m,n}(\mathbb{F}_q)$, where $\boldsymbol{M} := (M_0; M_1, \ldots, M_k)$ is the fixed set of matrices of the scheme. We consider two attack scenarios. First, due to the construction of our ring signature, one can fix to zero the coefficients of all but one matrix in R and still the remaining problem has a solution. That is, for any $1 \leq i \leq u$, the rank-r MinRank problem defined on the $k+1$ matrices $M_0 + R_i, M_1, \ldots, M_k$ has a solution. Finding this solution corresponds to solving a MinRank instance with parameters $(q, m, n, k + 1, r)$. In the second scenario the attacker aims at finding a solution to the instance $M_0, M_1, \ldots, M_k, R_1, \ldots, R_i$, for $2 \leq i \leq u$ which has i solutions. We then take the minimum time complexity obtained in both scenarios to derive the bit complexity.

Table 3 shows a list of parameters for our ring signature achieving NIST category I security.

5.3 Public Key and Signature Size

Suppose we have a ring with u users. The public key size for a ring of u users is given by

$$\lambda + u \cdot mn \log q.$$

This means that the public key size is linear in the number of users u.

The signature size is given by $f(m, n, k+u, r, q)$, where $f(m, n, k, r, q)$ denotes the signature size with one user and parameters (m, n, k, r, q). Asymptotically we find

Table 3. Suggested parameters for our ring signature an their estimated bit-security.

# users	8	16	32	64	128	256	512	1024	4096
q	16	16	16	16	16	16	16	16	16
m	16	16	18	20	23	29	36	46	81
n	16	16	18	20	23	29	36	46	81
k	102	102	102	124	158	216	320	340	560
r	5	5	6	6	6	7	7	9	12
bit-security	143	143	146	146	143	147	151	144	155

Table 4. Ring signature size (in kilobytes) of our ring signature in comparison to recent proposals.

#users	2^3	2^4	2^5	2^6	2^7	2^8	2^{10}	2^{12}	Assumption	Security
MRr-DSS	27	27	32	36	45	64	145	422	MinRank	Cat. I
KKW [34]	-	-	-	250	-	-	-	456	LowMC	Cat. V
Raptor [37]	10	-	-	81	-	333	1290	5161	MSIS/MLWE	100 bit
EZSLL [26]	19	-	-	31	-	-	-	148	MSIS/MLWE	Cat. II
Falafl [15]	30	-	-	32	-	-	-	35	MSIS/MLWE	Cat. I
Calamari [15]	5	-	-	8	-	-	-	14	CSIDH	128 bit (60 bit)
LESS [8]	11	-	-	14	-	-	-	20	Code equiv.	128 bit

$$\frac{f(m, n, k+u, r, q)}{f(m, n, k, r, q)} = \mathcal{O}\left(\frac{\lambda/\log q + mn + k + u}{\lambda/\log q + mn + k}\right) = \mathcal{O}\left(\frac{mn + k + u}{mn + k}\right),$$

assuming that $\frac{\lambda}{\log q} = \mathcal{O}(mn)$. Since we know from Eq. (4) that $k < mn$ we achieve a signature size that scales with the number of users u roughly as $\mathcal{O}\left(\frac{u}{mn}\right)$. Note that as long as mn is a function in u that tends to infinity for growing u, this corresponds to a sublinear scaling. Moreover, for practical parameters the large denominator allows us to achieve a competitive signature size for low to moderate amounts of users.

Table 4 states the signature sizes of our ring signature *MRr-DSS* achieved for different amounts of ring sizes using the parameters detailed in Table 3. We compare our parameters to various recent developments. Note that parameters for NIST category I are not available for all designs, so we also indicate the achieved security level.

The most compact ring signatures are obtained by the *Calamari* construction of Beullens, Katsumata, and Pintore [15], which follows a group-action-based construction similar to classical discrete logarithm based schemes. However, there is some doubt about the quantum security of its hardness assumption. Moreover, the chosen parameters offer at most 60 bits of quantum security employing NIST metrics [43]. Recently, Barenghi et al. [8] adapted the same idea but instantiated the group action via the code equivalence problem. However, despite recent efforts [9,16] motivated by cryptographic constructions [7,8,18], the code equivalence problem has not yet reached the same level of cryptanalytic maturity as the MinRank problem.

Apart from group action based constructions, for a large number of users the *Falafl* scheme [15] yields the best signature size, due to its logarithmic dependence on the ring size.

However, for low to moderate amounts of users ($\leq 2^7$) our scheme yields competitive performance. Even though some of the considered schemes might achieve (slightly) lower signature sizes in this regime, those are all based on structured lattice-based assumptions. Our scheme yields a solid alternative to this trend by being based on the hardness of random instances of a non-structured problem.

A   Commitment Scheme

In this section we give the formal definition of a computation hiding and computation binding commitment scheme.

Definition 3 (Computational hiding). *We say that* Com *is computationally hiding if for all polynomial time algorithms* $\mathcal{A}$, *and every pair of messages* m, m' *the advantage* $\mathsf{Adv}^{\text{hiding}}_{\mathsf{Com}}(\mathcal{A}, m, m')$ *is a negligible function of the security parameter* λ, *where*

$$\mathsf{Adv}^{\text{hiding}}_{\mathsf{Com}}(\mathcal{A}, m, m') := \left| \Pr_{\text{bits} \xleftarrow{\$} \{0,1\}^\lambda} \left[\mathcal{A}\big(\mathsf{Com}(\text{bits}, m)\big) = 1 \right] - \Pr_{\text{bits} \xleftarrow{\$} \{0,1\}^\lambda} \left[\mathcal{A}\big(\mathsf{Com}(\text{bits}, m')\big) = 1 \right] \right|.$$

Definition 4 (Computational binding). *We say that* Com *is computationally binding if for all polynomial time algorithms* $\mathcal{A}$, *the advantage* $\mathsf{Adv}^{\text{binding}}_{\mathsf{Com}}(\mathcal{A})$ *is a negligible function of the security parameter* λ, *where*

$$\mathsf{Adv}^{\text{binding}}_{\mathsf{Com}}(\mathcal{A}) = \Pr\left[\mathsf{Com}(\text{bits}, m) = \mathsf{Com}(\text{bits}', m') \mid (\text{bits}, m, \text{bits}', m') \leftarrow \mathcal{A}(1^\lambda) \right].$$

B   Ring Signatures

In the following we give the formal definition of a ring signature scheme.

Definition 5 (Ring signature scheme). *A ring signature scheme is a triple of polynomial time algorithms* (*Gen*, *Sign*, *Verify*) *that generates keys, sign a message, and verify the signature of a message, respectively. Formally:*

- *Gen*(1^λ) *outputs a key pair* (pk, sk), *where* pk *denotes the public key and* sk *its corresponding secret key.*
- *Sign*$_{\mathsf{sk}_i}$(*msg*, R) *outputs a signature* σ *of the message* *msg* *with respect to the ring* $R = (\mathsf{pk}_1, \ldots, \mathsf{pk}_u)$. *Here it is assumed that: (1)* $(\mathsf{pk}_i, \mathsf{sk}_i)$ *is a valid key-pair output by* Gen; *(2)* $|R| \geq 2$; *and (3) each public key in the ring is distinct.*
- *Verify*$_R$(*msg*, σ) *verifies a signature* σ *of the message* *msg* *with respect to* R.

We say that a ring signature scheme is correct if it satisfy the following correct-ness condition: for every λ and for every set of outputs $\{(\mathsf{pk}_i, \mathsf{sk}_i)\}_{i=1}^{u}$ of $\mathsf{Gen}(1^{\lambda})$ it holds

$$\mathsf{Verify}_R(\mathit{msg}, \mathsf{Sign}_{\mathsf{sk}_i}(\mathit{msg}, R)) = 1,$$

where $R = (\mathsf{pk}_1, \ldots, \mathsf{pk}_u)$.

B.1 Security Definitions

Next we give the security definitions for ring signatures following Bender, Katz, and Morselli [13].

Definition 6 (Anonymity w.r.t adversarially-chosen keys). *Let $(\mathsf{Gen}, \mathsf{Sign}, \mathsf{Verify})$ be a ring signature scheme, $u(\cdot)$ a polynomial, and let $\mathcal{A}$ be a PPT adversary. Consider the following game:*

1. *The key pairs $\{(\mathsf{pk}_i, \mathsf{sk}_i)\}_{i=1}^{u(\lambda)}$ are generated using $\mathsf{Gen}(1^{\lambda})$, and the set of public keys $S := \{\mathsf{pk}_i\}_{i=1}^{u(\lambda)}$ is given to $\mathcal{A}$.*
2. *$\mathcal{A}$ is given access to an oracle $\mathsf{OSign}(\cdot, \cdot, \cdot)$ such that for every R and $1 \leq i \leq u(\lambda)$ it holds $\mathsf{OSign}(i, \mathit{msg}, R) := \mathsf{Sign}_{\mathsf{sk}_i}(\mathit{msg}, R)$, where $\mathsf{pk}_i \in R$.*
3. *$\mathcal{A}$ outputs a message msg and a ring R that contains at least two public keys $\mathsf{pk}_{i_0}, \mathsf{pk}_{i_1} \in S$.*
4. *A challenge signature $\sigma \leftarrow \mathsf{Sign}_{\mathsf{sk}_{i_b}}(\mathit{msg}, R)$, where $b \xleftarrow{\$} \{0, 1\}$ is a random bit, is given to $\mathcal{A}$.*
5. *$\mathcal{A}$ outputs a bit b', and it succeeds if $b' = b$.*

We say $(\mathsf{Gen}, \mathsf{Sign}, \mathsf{Verify})$ achieves Anonymity w.r.t adversarially-chosen keys if, for any PPT $\mathcal{A}$ and any polynomial $u(\cdot)$, the success probability of $\mathcal{A}$ in the aforementioned game is negligibly close to $\frac{1}{2}$.

Note that in contrast to the weaker security notion of *basic anonymity* the property of *anonymity w.r.t adversarially-chosen keys* allows the adversary to inject own public keys in R. This holds for the usage of the oracle in step 2 as well as when providing the challenge data in step 3.

Definition 7 (Unforgeability against fixed-ring attacks). *We say that a ring signature $(\mathsf{Gen}, \mathsf{Sign}, \mathsf{Verify})$ is unforgeable against fixed-ring attacks if for any PPT adversary $\mathcal{A}$ and for any polynomial $u(\cdot)$, the probability that $\mathcal{A}$ succeeds in the following game is negligible:*

1. *The key pairs $\{(\mathsf{pk}_i, \mathsf{sk}_i)\}_{i=1}^{u(\lambda)}$ are generated using $\mathsf{Gen}(1^{\lambda})$, and the set of public keys $R := \{\mathsf{pk}_i\}_{i=1}^{u(\lambda)}$ is given to $\mathcal{A}$.*
2. *$\mathcal{A}$ is given access to a signing oracle $\mathsf{OSign}(\cdot, \cdot)$, where $\mathsf{OSign}(i, \mathit{msg})$ outputs $\mathsf{Sign}_{\mathsf{sk}_i}(\mathit{msg}, R)$.*
3. *$\mathcal{A}$ outputs $(\mathit{msg}^*, \sigma^*)$, and succeeds if $\mathsf{Verify}(\mathit{msg}^*, \sigma^*) = 1$ and also $\mathcal{A}$ never made a query of the form $\mathsf{OSign}(*, \mathit{msg}^*)$.*

B.2   Proofs

In the following we prove the correctness, anonymity, and unforgeability of our ring-signature scheme defined in Sect. 5.1.

Correctness. Let ε_i be the i-th canonical vector in $\mathbb{F}_q^u$ and sk_i denote the secret key of the i-th user in the ring R. Clearly, $\gamma_i := (\mathsf{sk}_i, \varepsilon_i)$ is a solution to the MinRank problem defined on $\widetilde{M} := (M, \mathsf{R})$. The correctness of the ring signature scheme now follows from the correctness of our basic signature scheme by observing that

$$\mathsf{Verify}_\mathsf{R}\big(\mathsf{msg}, \mathsf{Sign}_{\mathsf{sk}_i}(\mathsf{msg}, \mathsf{R})\big) = \mathsf{MR\text{-}Verify}_{\widetilde{M}}\big(\mathsf{msg}, \mathsf{MR\text{-}Sign}_{\gamma_i}(\mathsf{msg})\big).$$

Anonymity w.r.t Adversarially-Chosen Keys. We proof anonymity w.r.t adversarially-chosen keys in the random oracle model by showing the existence of a simulator that, without knowing any of the secret keys corresponding to one of the public keys in the ring, can produce signatures that are indistinguishable from signatures build by a legitimate user.

First note that from the HVZK property of our sigma protocol in the random oracle model it follows that there exists a simulator $\mathcal{S}'$ which is able to provide values σ' indistinguishable from legitimate signatures produced with MR-Sign. To construct $\mathcal{S}'$ we simply follow the Fiat–Shamir transform but using the simulator $\mathcal{S}$ of our sigma protocol whenever a valid transcript is needed.

Now, recall that the signing operation of our ring signature is a call to MR-Sign with adapted public-key (M, R), where

$$\mathsf{Sign}_{\mathsf{sk}_i}(\mathsf{msg}, \mathsf{R}) = \mathsf{MR\text{-}Sign}_{\mathsf{sk}_i'}(\mathsf{msg}).$$

Therefore we can use $\mathcal{S}'$ as a simulator to obtain values σ' which are indistinguishable from legitimate ring signatures.

Now, let G_0 denote the game described in Definition 6. We modify step 4 in G_0 to define a new game G_1. Instead of $\sigma \leftarrow \mathsf{Sign}_{\mathsf{sk}_{i_b}}(\mathsf{msg}, \mathsf{R})$, the output of step 4 in G_1 is $\sigma' \leftarrow \mathcal{S}'(\mathsf{msg}, \mathsf{R})$. Notice G_0 and G_1 are indistinguishable games. Hence, the advantage of any adversary $\mathcal{A}$ against G_0 and G_1 is the same. Also, the challenge σ' given in G_1 does not depend on the bit b chosen in step 3. Therefore, the advantage of an adversary $\mathcal{A}$ against game G_1 is zero.

Unforgeability Against Fixed-Ring Attacks. Forging a signature for a fixed ring R, i.e., winning the game given in Definition 7, directly reduces to forging a signature for MR-Sign with public-key (M, R). The unforgeability for MR-Sign now follows from the Fiat–Shamir transform applied to the sigma protocol and its HVZK property.

C   A Note on Santoso et al.'s Scheme

The parameters given by Santoso et al. [44] to obtain a security level of λ bits are shown in Table 5.

Table 5. Parameter sets proposed in [44].

Parameter set	λ	q	n	m	k	r
A	128	2	26	26	208	13
B	192	2	33	33	330	17
C	256	2	39	39	468	20

Missing Commitments in the Signature Size. The authors of [44] disregard the size of the initial commitments in their analysis of the communication complexity. Taking commitment sizes into account (2λ bits for each hash, to be collision-resistant) the signature size of [44] is given by

$$\lambda \left(\frac{29}{2}\lambda + mn \log q + \frac{k}{2} \log q \right). \tag{5}$$

While the signature size of Courtiois' scheme is given by

$$\frac{\lambda}{\log(3/2)} \left(\frac{20}{3}\lambda + \frac{2}{3}mn \log q + \frac{2}{3}k \log q \right). \tag{6}$$

Random Solutions. As stated in Sect. 4.6, a random instance of the MinRank problem with parameters (q, n, m, k, r) has, in expectation, $n_{sol} := q^{k-(m-r)(n-r)}$ solutions. Some algorithms, as e.g., the kernel search algorithm, can directly benefit from multiple solutions by obtaining a speed-up of magnitude $n_{sol} > 1$ in those cases. It turns out that the parameter sets given in [44] contain a large amount of solutions, affecting security.

New Security Estimates and Signature Size. Table 6 shows the bit-security of the kernel search algorithm for parameters suggested in [44]. Note that all the parameter sets are far below the claimed bit-security, which is 128 for set A, 192 for set B, and 256 for set C. Also, observe that the signature size is larger than the one of standard Courtois for all suggested parameters.

Table 6. Bit-security and signature size for parameter sets proposed in [44].

Parameters set	Algorithm	Bit-security	Courtois' signature size using Eq. (6)	Santoso et al.'s signature size given in [44]	Santoso et al.'s signature size using Eq. (5)
A	Kernel search	88	38.54 KB	18.81 KB	41.19 KB
B	Kernel search	121	89.19 KB	44.50 KB	94.64 KB
C	Kernel search	159	162.01 KB	82.15 KB	170.84 KB

References

1. Abdalla, M., An, J.H., Bellare, M., Namprempre, C.: From identification to signatures via the Fiat-Shamir transform: minimizing assumptions for security and forward-security. In: Knudsen, L.R. (ed.) EUROCRYPT 2002. LNCS, vol. 2332, pp. 418–433. Springer, Heidelberg (2002). https://doi.org/10.1007/3-540-46035-7_28

2. Au, M.H., Liu, J.K., Susilo, W., Yuen, T.H.: Secure ID-based linkable and revocable-iff-linked ring signature with constant-size construction. Theoret. Comput. Sci. **469**, 1–14 (2013)

3. Bard, G.V.: Accelerating cryptanalysis with the method of four Russians. Cryptology ePrint Archive (2006)

4. Bardet, M., et al.: Improvements of algebraic attacks for solving the rank decoding and MinRank problems. In: Moriai, S., Wang, H. (eds.) ASIACRYPT 2020. LNCS, vol. 12491, pp. 507–536. Springer, Cham (2020). https://doi.org/10.1007/978-3-030-64837-4_17

5. Bardet, M., Bertin, M.: Improvement of algebraic attacks for solving superdetermined MinRank instances. CoRR abs/2208.01442 (2022). https://doi.org/10.48550/arXiv.2208.01442

6. Bardet, M., Briaud, P., Bros, M., Gaborit, P., Tillich, J.P.: Revisiting algebraic attacks on MinRank and on the rank decoding problem. Cryptology ePrint Archive, Paper 2022/1031 (2022). https://eprint.iacr.org/2022/1031

7. Barenghi, A., Biasse, J.-F., Persichetti, E., Santini, P.: LESS-FM: fine-tuning signatures from the code equivalence problem. In: Cheon, J.H., Tillich, J.-P. (eds.) PQCrypto 2021 2021. LNCS, vol. 12841, pp. 23–43. Springer, Cham (2021). https://doi.org/10.1007/978-3-030-81293-5_2

8. Barenghi, A., Biasse, J.F., Ngo, T., Persichetti, E., Santini, P.: Advanced signature functionalities from the code equivalence problem. Int. J. Comput. Math. Comput. Syst. Theory **7**(2), 112–128 (2022)

9. Barenghi, A., Biasse, J.F., Persichetti, E., Santini, P.: On the computational hardness of the code equivalence problem in cryptography. Cryptology ePrint Archive (2022)

10. Baum, C., Nof, A.: Concretely-efficient zero-knowledge arguments for arithmetic circuits and their application to lattice-based cryptography. In: Kiayias, A., Kohlweiss, M., Wallden, P., Zikas, V. (eds.) PKC 2020. LNCS, vol. 12110, pp. 495–526. Springer, Cham (2020). https://doi.org/10.1007/978-3-030-45374-9_17

11. Bellini, E., Caullery, F., Gaborit, P., Manzano, M., Mateu, V.: Improved Veron identification and signature schemes in the rank metric. In: IEEE International Symposium on Information Theory, pp. 1872–1876 (2019)

12. Bellini, E., Gaborit, P., Hasikos, A., Mateu, V.: Enhancing code based zero-knowledge proofs using rank metric. In: Krenn, S., Shulman, H., Vaudenay, S. (eds.) CANS 2020. LNCS, vol. 12579, pp. 570–592. Springer, Cham (2020). https://doi.org/10.1007/978-3-030-65411-5_28

13. Bender, A., Katz, J., Morselli, R.: Ring signatures: stronger definitions, and constructions without random oracles. J. Cryptol. **22**(1), 114–138 (2009)

14. Beullens, W.: Improved cryptanalysis of UOV and rainbow. In: Canteaut, A., Standaert, F.-X. (eds.) EUROCRYPT 2021. LNCS, vol. 12696, pp. 348–373. Springer, Cham (2021). https://doi.org/10.1007/978-3-030-77870-5_13

15. Beullens, W., Katsumata, S., Pintore, F.: Calamari and Falafl: logarithmic (linkable) ring signatures from isogenies and lattices. In: Moriai, S., Wang, H. (eds.)

ASIACRYPT 2020. LNCS, vol. 12492, pp. 464–492. Springer, Cham (2020). https://doi.org/10.1007/978-3-030-64834-3_16

16. Beullens, W.: Not enough LESS: an improved algorithm for solving code equivalence problems over $\mathbb{F}_q$. In: Dunkelman, O., Jacobson, Jr., M.J., O'Flynn, C. (eds.) SAC 2020. LNCS, vol. 12804, pp. 387–403. Springer, Cham (2021). https://doi.org/10.1007/978-3-030-81652-0_15

17. Beullens, W.: Sigma protocols for MQ, PKP and SIS, and fishy signature schemes. In: Canteaut, A., Ishai, Y. (eds.) EUROCRYPT 2020. LNCS, vol. 12107, pp. 183–211. Springer, Cham (2020). https://doi.org/10.1007/978-3-030-45727-3_7

18. Biasse, J.-F., Micheli, G., Persichetti, E., Santini, P.: LESS is more: code-based signatures without syndromes. In: Nitaj, A., Youssef, A. (eds.) AFRICACRYPT 2020. LNCS, vol. 12174, pp. 45–65. Springer, Cham (2020). https://doi.org/10.1007/978-3-030-51938-4_3

19. Billet, O., Gilbert, H.: Cryptanalysis of rainbow. In: De Prisco, R., Yung, M. (eds.) SCN 2006. LNCS, vol. 4116, pp. 336–347. Springer, Heidelberg (2006). https://doi.org/10.1007/11832072_23

20. Briaud, P., Tillich, J.-P., Verbel, J.: A polynomial time key-recovery attack on the Sidon cryptosystem. In: AlTawy, R., Hülsing, A. (eds.) SAC 2021. LNCS, vol. 13203, pp. 419–438. Springer, Cham (2022). https://doi.org/10.1007/978-3-030-99277-4_20

21. Buss, J.F., Frandsen, G.S., Shallit, J.O.: The computational complexity of some problems of linear algebra. J. Comput. Syst. Sci. **58**(3), 572–596 (1999)

22. Cabarcas, D., Smith-Tone, D., Verbel, J.A.: Key recovery attack for ZHFE. In: Lange, T., Takagi, T. (eds.) PQCrypto 2017. LNCS, vol. 10346, pp. 289–308. Springer, Cham (2017). https://doi.org/10.1007/978-3-319-59879-6_17

23. Courtois, N.T.: Efficient zero-knowledge authentication based on a linear algebra problem MinRank. In: Boyd, C. (ed.) ASIACRYPT 2001. LNCS, vol. 2248, pp. 402–421. Springer, Heidelberg (2001). https://doi.org/10.1007/3-540-45682-1_24

24. Courtois, N.T.: La sécurité des primitives cryptographiques basées sur des problèmes algébriques multivariables: MQ, IP, MinRank, HFE. Ph.D. thesis, Université de Paris 6 - Pierre et Marie Curie (2001)

25. Dodis, Y., Kiayias, A., Nicolosi, A., Shoup, V.: Anonymous identification in ad hoc groups. In: Cachin, C., Camenisch, J.L. (eds.) EUROCRYPT 2004. LNCS, vol. 3027, pp. 609–626. Springer, Heidelberg (2004). https://doi.org/10.1007/978-3-540-24676-3_36

26. Esgin, M.F., Zhao, R.K., Steinfeld, R., Liu, J.K., Liu, D.: MatRiCT: efficient, scalable and post-quantum blockchain confidential transactions protocol. In: Proceedings of the 2019 ACM SIGSAC Conference on Computer and Communications Security, pp. 567–584 (2019)

27. Faugère, J.C., Safey El Din, M., Spaenlehauer, P.J.: Computing loci of rank defects of linear matrices using Gröbner bases and applications to cryptology. In: Proceedings of the 2010 International Symposium on Symbolic and Algebraic Computation, ISSAC 2010, pp. 257–264 (2010)

28. Feneuil, T., Joux, A., Rivain, M.: Shared permutation for syndrome decoding: new zero-knowledge protocol and code-based signature. Cryptology ePrint Archive (2021)

29. Feneuil, T., Joux, A., Rivain, M.: Syndrome decoding in the head: shorter signatures from zero-knowledge proofs. Cryptology ePrint Archive (2022)

30. Gaborit, P., Schrek, J., Zémor, G.: Full cryptanalysis of the Chen identification protocol. In: Yang, B.-Y. (ed.) PQCrypto 2011. LNCS, vol. 7071, pp. 35–50. Springer, Heidelberg (2011). https://doi.org/10.1007/978-3-642-25405-5_3

31. Goubin, L., Courtois, N.T.: Cryptanalysis of the TTM cryptosystem. In: Okamoto, T. (ed.) ASIACRYPT 2000. LNCS, vol. 1976, pp. 44–57. Springer, Heidelberg (2000). https://doi.org/10.1007/3-540-44448-3_4

32. Gueron, S., Persichetti, E., Santini, P.: Designing a practical code-based signature scheme from zero-knowledge proofs with trusted setup. Cryptography **6**(1), 5 (2022)

33. Ishai, Y., Kushilevitz, E., Ostrovsky, R., Sahai, A.: Zero-knowledge proofs from secure multiparty computation. SIAM J. Comput. **39**(3), 1121–1152 (2009)

34. Katz, J., Kolesnikov, V., Wang, X.: Improved non-interactive zero knowledge with applications to post-quantum signatures. In: Proceedings of the ACM Conference on Computer and Communications Security, pp. 525–537 (2018)

35. Kipnis, A., Shamir, A.: Cryptanalysis of the HFE public key cryptosystem by relinearization. In: Wiener, M. (ed.) CRYPTO 1999. LNCS, vol. 1666, pp. 19–30. Springer, Heidelberg (1999). https://doi.org/10.1007/3-540-48405-1_2

36. Linton, S., Nebe, G., Niemeyer, A., Parker, R., Thackray, J.: A parallel algorithm for Gaussian elimination over finite fields. arXiv preprint arXiv:1806.04211 (2018)

37. Lu, X., Au, M.H., Zhang, Z.: Raptor: a practical lattice-based (linkable) ring signature. In: Deng, R.H., Gauthier-Umaña, V., Ochoa, M., Yung, M. (eds.) ACNS 2019. LNCS, vol. 11464, pp. 110–130. Springer, Cham (2019). https://doi.org/10.1007/978-3-030-21568-2_6

38. Lyubashevsky, V.: Fiat-Shamir with aborts: applications to lattice and factoring-based signatures. In: Matsui, M. (ed.) ASIACRYPT 2009. LNCS, vol. 5912, pp. 598–616. Springer, Heidelberg (2009). https://doi.org/10.1007/978-3-642-10366-7_35

39. MATZOV: Report on the security of LWE: improved dual lattice attack (2022)

40. Moody, D., et al.: Status report on the second round of the NIST post-quantum cryptography standardization process (2020)

41. Moody, D., Perlner, R., Smith-Tone, D.: Key recovery attack on the cubic ABC simple matrix multivariate encryption scheme. In: Avanzi, R., Heys, H. (eds.) SAC 2016. LNCS, vol. 10532, pp. 543–558. Springer, Cham (2017). https://doi.org/10.1007/978-3-319-69453-5_29

42. Ohta, K., Okamoto, T.: A digital multisignature scheme based on the Fiat-Shamir scheme. In: Imai, H., Rivest, R.L., Matsumoto, T. (eds.) ASIACRYPT 1991. LNCS, vol. 739, pp. 139–148. Springer, Heidelberg (1993). https://doi.org/10.1007/3-540-57332-1_11

43. Peikert, C.: He gives C-Sieves on the CSIDH. In: Canteaut, A., Ishai, Y. (eds.) EUROCRYPT 2020. LNCS, vol. 12106, pp. 463–492. Springer, Cham (2020). https://doi.org/10.1007/978-3-030-45724-2_16

44. Santoso, B., Ikematsu, Y., Nakamura, S., Yasuda, T.: Three-pass identification scheme based on MinRank problem with half cheating probability. https://arxiv.org/abs/2205.03255

45. Smith-Tone, D., Verbel, J.: A rank attack against extension field cancellation. In: Ding, J., Tillich, J.-P. (eds.) PQCrypto 2020. LNCS, vol. 12100, pp. 381–401. Springer, Cham (2020). https://doi.org/10.1007/978-3-030-44223-1_21

46. Stern, J.: A new identification scheme based on syndrome decoding. In: Stinson, D.R. (ed.) CRYPTO 1993. LNCS, vol. 773, pp. 13–21. Springer, Heidelberg (1994). https://doi.org/10.1007/3-540-48329-2_2

47. Strassen, V., et al.: Gaussian elimination is not optimal. Numer. Math. **13**(4), 354–356 (1969)

48. Tao, C., Petzoldt, A., Ding, J.: Efficient key recovery for all HFE signature variants. In: Malkin, T., Peikert, C. (eds.) CRYPTO 2021. LNCS, vol. 12825, pp. 70–93. Springer, Cham (2021). https://doi.org/10.1007/978-3-030-84242-0_4
49. Véron, P.: Improved identification schemes based on error-correcting codes. Appl. Algebra Eng. Commun. Comput. **8**(1), 57–69 (1996)

IPRainbow

Ryann Cartor[1]([⊠]), Max Cartor[2], Mark Lewis[2], and Daniel Smith-Tone[2,3]

[1] School of Mathematical and Statistical Sciences, Clemson University,
Clemson, SC, USA
`rcartor@clemson.edu`
[2] Department of Mathematics, University of Louisville, Louisville, KY, USA
`{maxwell.cartor,mark.lewis.2}@louisville.edu`
[3] National Institute of Standards and Technology, Gaithersburg, MD, USA
`daniel.smith@nist.gov`

Abstract. The Rainbow signature scheme is the only multivariate scheme listed as a finalist in round 3 of the NIST post-quantum standardization process. A few recent attacks, including the intersection attack, rectangular MinRank attacks, and the "simple attack," have changed this landscape; leaving questions about the viability of this scheme for future application.

The purpose of this paper is to analyze the possibility of repairing Rainbow by adding an internal perturbation modifier and to compare its performance with that of UOV at the same security level. While the costly internal perturbation modifier was originally designed with encryption in mind, the use of schemes with performance characteristics similar to Rainbow is most interesting for applications in which short signatures or fast verification is a necessity, while signing can be done offline. We find that Rainbow can be made secure while achieving smaller keys, shorter signatures and faster verification times than UOV, but this advantage comes at significant cost in terms of signing time.

Keywords: Multivariate cryptography · Rainbow · MinRank

1 Introduction

As the world marches toward a future of widespread quantum computing, the need for secure post-quantum cryptosystems is imperative. One branch of post-quantum cryptography is multivariate cryptography. Multivariate cryptosystems are based on the MQ problem, which is the problem of solving a system of nonlinear equations over a finite field. The Rainbow signature scheme is the only multivariate cryptosystem among the round 3 finalists of the National Institute for Standards and Technology (NIST) Post Quantum Standardization process [18].

The first massively multivariate cryptosystem published in the west was C^*, introduced in 1988 by Matsumoto and Imai [17]. This encryption scheme is an example of a big-field scheme, which makes use of computations in both a

This work was partially supported by a grant from the Simons Foundation (712530, DCST).

base field and an extension field. Given a base field $\mathbb{F}_q$ and an extension field $\mathbb{K}$, C^* will have an $\mathbb{F}_q$-quadratic central map $F : \mathbb{K} \rightarrow \mathbb{K}$, whose structure is hidden by function composition. C^* was broken by Patarin in 1995 [19] with the introduction of linearization equations, which exploits a linear relationship between plain text and ciphertext vectors. Many modifiers were introduced after the break of C^* in the hopes of repairing the scheme, including minus, projection and internal perturbation modifiers, see [9,21,22]. The security of this family of modifiers is discussed in [6].

Another avenue of study is to consider small-field cryptosystems, which are multivariate schemes that work over only one field, $\mathbb{F}_q$. Patarin introduced the small field scheme Oil and Vinegar [20] as a new possible multivariate signature scheme. The Oil and Vinegar scheme consists of two different types of variables, specifically oil variables and vinegar variables. In the original presentation of the scheme, the number of oil variables was equal to the number of vinegar variables. Cryptanlysis from Kipnis and Shamir [16] showed this parameterization to be insecure, which lead to the Unbalanced Oil and Vinegar scheme (UOV) which necessitates that the number of vinegar variables is much larger than the number of oil variables.

The Rainbow Signature scheme [11] is an extension of the UOV signature scheme that consists of layers of UOV central maps. Despite the relatively large size of public keys associated with the Rainbow scheme, its short signatures and high degree of computational efficiency in verification make it an attractive choice for many applications, such as verified/secure boot and certificate transparency.

Following the support minors advance in MinRank methodology, see [1], new attacks in [3], and more significantly [4], have reduced the security of Rainbow below their claimed NIST security levels, rendering the scheme significantly less efficient. The critical insight of these attacks is that information about the secret key can be encoded in equations in the public variable set and combined with the public equations, resulting in a significant enhancement of a direct algebraic attack targeting a hidden subspace.

In this paper, we introduce the variant "IPRainbow", which adds an internal perturbation modifier to the Rainbow central map. This perturbation of the private key disrupts the above attacks by decoupling the new relations from the public equations; specifically, the public equations are satisfied by a vector in the secret subspace with low probability, corrupting the attack mechanism. We analyze the security and efficiency of this new scheme in comparison with UOV. We show that it is still possible for Rainbow to outperform UOV in terms of verification speed, signature size and public key size; however, these enhancements come at a significant cost in signing time.

2   UOV and Rainbow

2.1   Oil and Vinegar

The Oil and Vinegar signature scheme was introduced in [20] as a response to Patarin's linearization equations in [19], which broke the first multivariate cryptosystem C^*. The scheme consists of two types of variables over a finite field $\mathbb{F}_q$, namely oil and vinegar variables. Furthermore, the number of oil variables and the number of vinegar variables were equal in the original parameterization. Kipnis and Shamir broke this balanced Oil and Vinegar scheme in [16], so we now only consider the case of Unbalanced Oil and Vinegar (UOV), where the number of vinegar variables is sufficiently large enough that the statistical attacks of [15] and the intersection attack from [3] are infeasible.

Let $\mathbf{x} = (x_1, \ldots, x_v, x_{v+1}, \ldots, x_n) \in \mathbb{F}_q^n$. We will call $x_1, \ldots, x_v$ the vinegar variables whereas $x_{v+1}, \ldots, x_n$ will denote the oil variables. We define the following central map $F = (f_1, \ldots, f_{v+1})$, where each f is of the form:

$$f(\mathbf{x}) = \sum_{i=1}^{v} \sum_{j=i}^{v} \alpha_{ij} x_i x_j + \sum_{i=1}^{v} \sum_{j=v+1}^{n} \beta_{ij} x_i x_j + \sum_{i=1}^{n} \gamma_i x_i + \delta$$

To create the public key equations P we compose F with an invertible affine map $T : \mathbb{F}_q^n \to \mathbb{F}_q^n$ to get $P = F \circ T$. Notice that although F is a quadratic map, F is linear on the oil variables. Therefore, inversion of the central map is completed by choosing random values in $\mathbb{F}_q$ for each of the vinegar variables. Each equation is then set equal to zero and Gaussian Elimination is used to solve for the remaining oil variables. If no solution is found, choose different values for the vinegar variables. Repeat this process until a solution is found.

2.2   Rainbow

The Rainbow signature scheme was first introduced in [11]. Rainbow can be thought of a banded construction of UOV, where Rainbow consists of L different UOV layers. Rainbow is the only multivariate signature scheme to make it into the finalists of the third round of the NIST standardization process [18], but the scheme has recently faced substantial attacks from [3] and [4].

To create a Rainbow signature scheme, we will still consider input vectors of the form $\mathbf{x} = (x_1, \ldots, x_n) \in \mathbb{F}_q^n$, but now each layer of Rainbow will contain a different number of vinegar variables. Consider a sequence of integer values $0 < v_1 < v_2 < \cdots < v_L < n$, and corresponding sets of variables $V_1 = \{x_1, \ldots, x_{v_1}\}, V_2 = \{x_1 \ldots, x_{v_1}, \ldots, x_{v_2}\}, \ldots, V_L = \{x_1, \ldots, x_{v_L}\}$ that contain the vinegar variables for the 1st, 2nd, ..., and Lth layers, respectively. Note that the oil variables in layer ℓ will contain $O_\ell = \{x_{v_\ell+1}, \ldots, x_n\}$. Furthermore $V_1 \subset V_2 \subset \cdots \subset V_L$, whereas $O_L \subset \cdots \subset O_2 \subset O_1$.

Each layer ℓ will be composed of $n - v_\ell$ equations, which is also the number of oil variables in that layer. A polynomial in the ℓth layer will have the form:

$$f_\ell(\mathbf{x}) = \sum_{i=1}^{v_\ell} \sum_{j=1}^{v_\ell} \alpha_{ij\ell} x_i x_j + \sum_{i=1}^{v_\ell} \sum_{j=v_\ell+1}^{n} \beta_{ij\ell} x_i x_j + \sum_{i=1}^{n} \gamma_{i\ell} x_i + \delta_\ell$$

The public key is then formed by composing the central map with two affine maps, $P = U \circ F \circ T$. The Rainbow parameterization proposed in the current submission [10] to NIST's standardization process utilizes $L = 2$ layers, as is historically typical. Also, in order to speed up key generation, by convention we consider only homogeneous polynomials f_i (Fig. 1).

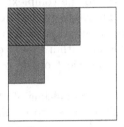

Layer 1 Rainbow Map   Layer 2 Rainbow Map

Fig. 1. These diagrams represent the matrices corresponding to the central map of a Rainbow scheme with two layers. White areas represent entries of the matrix that are zero, whereas gray areas correspond to possibly nonzero entries. The lined gray areas correspond to coefficients on the quadratic vinegar terms, and solid gray areas correspond to mixed vinegar and oil coefficients.

To invert the central map $F = f^{(1)}, \ldots, f^{(n)}$ we choose values for the first layer vinegar variables $x_1, \ldots, x_{v_1}$ and substitute these values into the first layer maps $f^{(1)}, \ldots, f^{(o_1)}$. Then we solve the resulting linear system in the first layer oil variables $x_{v_1+1}, \ldots, x_{v_2}$. Next we substitute the values of these variables into the central maps $f^{(v+1)}, \ldots, f^{(n)}$ and solve similarly for the remaining variables, $x_{v_2+1}, \ldots, x_n$.

3 Known Attacks of Rainbow

3.1 Background

MinRank attacks have proven to be highly effective against multivariate schemes. We can define the MinRank problem as follows:

Problem 1 (MinRank Problem). *Given matrices $A_1, \ldots, A_k \in \mathbb{F}_q^{n \times m}$ and $r \in \mathbb{N}$, decide if there exists a linear combination $y_1, \ldots, y_k \in \mathbb{F}_q$ (not all zero) such that*

$$rank \left(\sum_{i=1}^{k} y_i A_i \right) \leq r.$$

The MinRank attack was first introduced in [14] as the first effective attack on the multivariate scheme HFE. This first iteration of the MinRank attack is commonly called the Kipnis-Shamir (KS) attack. Other methods have since followed, including minors modeling and support minors modeling [2,13]. The goal of MinRank attacks is to try to find linear combinations of the public matrices that result in a matrix with low rank. This is useful against schemes like HFE and C^* as the central map has low rank, thus the attacker can find an equivalent key. The MinRank attack is also applicable to Rainbow, since the first layer maps exhibit a rank defect.

The complexity of MinRank attacks are tied to the complexity of polynomial solvers, such as the XL algorithm of [8]. These algorithms create a larger generating set by generating higher degree equations through monomial multiplication. The first degree fall of the XL-style algorithm should occur at the degree corresponding to the first non-positive coefficient of the corresponding Hilbert Series.

We briefly explain the idea of the support minors modeling of [2], see [2] for the details. The support minors system from [2] involves two variable sets, the so-called "minor" variables, whereas the above variables are given the moniker "linear". As mentioned in [24] with more details following in [23], the additivity of Hilbert Series can be generalized to a multi-series respecting disparate variable sets. Due to the large number of the minor variables, we may restrict ourselves to consider the algebra of degree one in the minor variables and graded with respect to the degree of the linear variables. In this way, we can "forget" the minor variables and recover a univariate series.

In [2], the coefficients of this series for degree b where m' columns are used is derived. Specifically, the degree b coefficient is given by

$$\sum_{i=0}^{b}(-1)^i\binom{m'}{o_2+i}\binom{n+i-1}{i}\binom{n+b-i-1}{b-i}.$$

Note that we must include all n matrices. Thus we obtain the series

$$G(t) = \sum_{b=0}^{\infty}\sum_{i=0}^{b}(-1)^i\binom{m'}{o_2+i}\binom{n+i-1}{i}\binom{n+b-i-1}{b-i}t^b.$$

Given that the solving bi-degree is $(1,b)$, it follows that the support-minors algorithm solves a MinRank instance of k many $n \times m$ matrices with a target rank r with an estimated cost of

$$3(k-1)(r+1)\binom{m'}{r}^2\binom{k+b-2}{b}^2$$

field multiplications. Note that it is sometimes more efficient to increase b if it is possible to use a smaller m'.

3.2 Rectangular MinRank Attack

In this section, we describe the attack presented in [3]. The public key of a multivariate cryptosystem is a set of m nonlinear equations in n variables. We can consider the quadratic form of each equation f_i, which will be an $n \times n$ matrix $\mathbf{F}_i$ of the form:

$$f_i(\mathbf{x}) = \mathbf{x}\mathbf{F}_i\mathbf{x}^\top.$$

It is often useful to consider the public or private key of a multivariate scheme with m equations in n variables as a single 3-tensor. In this vein, consider the Rainbow public and private keys as 3-tensors of dimension $n \times n \times m$. In particular, consider Fig. 2, where the white represents zero coordinates and the gray represents nonzero coordinates. Given a vector from O_2, the multiplication of the public key with this oil vector will result in a matrix with nonzero elements only in the upper $(v + o_1) \times o_2$ coordinates.

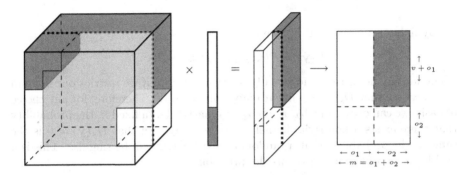

Fig. 2. Multiplication of a Rainbow public key by a vector in O_2.

Thus, if we can find a linear combination of the public key equations such that

$$\text{rank}\left(\sum_{i=1}^{n-o_2+1} y_i \mathbf{P}_i \right) \le o_2,$$

then it is probable that $\mathbf{y} \in O_2$. This instance of the MinRank problem requires $n - o_2 + 1$ different $n \times m$ matrices with a target rank of o_2.

3.3 Simple Attack

The Simple attack of [4] breaks the Rainbow I parameters quite efficiently. The technique can also be used in conjunction with the Rectangular MinRank attack to significantly impact security for the higher security parameters, Rainbow III and Rainbow V as well. The attack introduces a new strategy to find vectors in O_2, which then can be used to remove the outer layer of the Rainbow public key, leaving us with a small instance of UOV.

The Simple attack will make use of the discrete differential of the public key, defined as

$$P'(\mathbf{x}, \mathbf{y}) = P(\mathbf{x} + \mathbf{y}) - P(\mathbf{x}) - P(\mathbf{y}).$$

We denote $W := P(O_1)$, $\dim(O_2) = \dim(W) = o_2$. From analysis in [3], we know that for $\mathbf{y} \in O_2$, $P'(\mathbf{x}, \mathbf{y}) \in W$ for any $\mathbf{x} \in \mathbb{F}_q^n$. This structure is illustrated in Fig. 3.

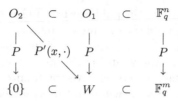

Fig. 3. Structure of nested subspaces.

By fixing a random $\mathbf{x} \in \mathbb{F}_q^n$, we can define

$$D_{\mathbf{x}}(\mathbf{y}) = P(\mathbf{x} + \mathbf{y}) - P(\mathbf{x}) - P(\mathbf{y}),$$

where for any nonzero $\mathbf{x}$ and $\mathbf{y} \in O_2$, $D_{\mathbf{x}}(\mathbf{y}) \in W$. So, if we restrict our domain to O_2, we see that $D_{\mathbf{x}}|_{O_2}$ is a linear map from O_2 to W. Therefore, for any choice of basis, we can express $D_{\mathbf{x}}|_{O_2}$ as an $o_2 \times o_2$ matrix. For a fixed $\mathbf{x}$, the probability that there exists a nontrivial kernel vector $\mathbf{y} \in O_2$ such that $D_{\mathbf{x}}(\mathbf{y}) = 0$ is the same as the probability that a random $o_2 \times o_2$ matrix will be singular. This is a well known problem and gives us the probability

$$1 - \prod_{i=0}^{o_2-1} (1 - q^{i-o_2}),$$

which for large q is approximately q^{-1}. This leads to the strategy of guessing a random vector $\mathbf{x}$ and trying to find a solution to the system of equations

$$\begin{cases} D_{\mathbf{x}}(\mathbf{y}) = 0 \\ P(\mathbf{y}) = 0. \end{cases}$$

If we can find such a $\mathbf{y}$, then it is likely that $\mathbf{y} \in O_2$. If we cannot find such a $\mathbf{y}$, choose a different $\mathbf{x}$ and repeat the process.

Once we have a vector $\mathbf{y} \in O_2$, we can generate a subspace of W by computing

$$\langle P'(\mathbf{e}_1, \mathbf{y}), \cdots, P'(\mathbf{e}_n, \mathbf{y}) \rangle \subseteq W.$$

Analysis from [4] shows that with high probability the generated space will be equal to W. This gives us access to a subspace of, if not the entirety of, the secret space W. Given this information, we can create a map V that allows us to find the secret space O_2. We define V to be the change of variables such that

$$V \circ P(\mathbf{x}) = \begin{cases} P_1(\mathbf{x}) \\ P_2(\mathbf{x}) \end{cases}$$

where $P_1 : \mathbb{F}_q^n \to \mathbb{F}_q^{m-o_2}$ and $P_2 : \mathbb{F}_q^n \to \mathbb{F}_q^{o_2}$. From here, we can find the kernel of the map

$$\mathbf{x} \mapsto \begin{pmatrix} P'(\mathbf{e}_1, \mathbf{x}) \\ \vdots \\ P'(\mathbf{e}_n, \mathbf{x}) \end{pmatrix}.$$

With high probability, the kernel of this map will be O_2. Beullens completes the attack using another change of variable map. Let $U : \mathbb{F}_q^n \to \mathbb{F}_q^n$ send the last o_2 coordinates to O_2 and then consider

$$V \circ P \circ U(\mathbf{x}) = \begin{cases} F_1(\mathbf{x}) \\ F_2(\mathbf{x}) \end{cases}.$$

It is shown in [4] that finding a preimage P is equivalent to finding a preimage of F, and finding a preimage of F_1 gives a preimage of F. F_1 is a system of $m - o_2$ equations that has the structure of a UOV public key with $n - o_2$ variables and an oil space of dimension $m - o_2$. Given this smaller UOV system, the remainder of the attack is to solve a system of m equations in $n - m$ unknowns. Under the assumption that this system is semi-regular, it can be solved with an XL-style algorithm at degree

$$d_{sr} = \min_d \left\{ [t^d] \frac{(1 - t^2)^m}{(1 - t)^{n-m}} \leq 0 \right\}.$$

In such a case, the complexity of the attack is dominated by the cost of the block Wiedemann [7] step in the XL algorithm. This cost is well known to be

$$3 \binom{n - m - 1 + d_{sr}}{d_{sr}} \binom{n - m + 1}{2},$$

where $\binom{n-m-1+d_{sr}}{d_{sr}}$ is the number of monomials (i.e., the dimension of the square Macaulay submatrix), and $\binom{n-m+1}{2}$ is the number of nonzero entries in each row of the Macaulay matrix.

The Simple attack of [4] can be combined with the Rectangular MinRank attack of [3]. We may construct a Hilbert series in this case by pasting together the rectangular MinRank support minors system with the two systems

$$D_{\mathbf{x}}(\mathbf{y}) = \mathbf{0}, \text{ and}$$
$$P(\mathbf{y}) = \mathbf{0}.$$

The latter two systems involve the same variable set, thus we obtain the Hilbert series

$$\frac{(1 - t)^m (1 - t^2)^m}{(1 - t)^n} = \frac{(1 - t^2)^m}{(1 - t)^{n-m}}.$$

To obtain the Hilbert series for the entire system, we merely add the relations in the already present variables. Under the assumption of semi-regularity of the resulting system, we obtain the series

$$(1 - t)^m (1 - t^2)^m G(t),$$

where $G(t)$ is as described in Sect. 3.1. This is a similar result to what was observed in [3].

4   IPRainbow

4.1   Description of IPRainbow

We will consider the internal perturbation (IP) modifier, see [9], applied to the Rainbow scheme. The IP modifier can be described as follows. Let $Q : \mathbb{F}_q^n \rightarrow \mathbb{F}_q^m$ be a set of m quadratic equations where q_i denotes the ith equation. Given a public key $P : \mathbb{F}_q^n \rightarrow \mathbb{F}_q^m$ whose i^{th} equation is denoted p_i we create the internally perturbed public key $\tilde{P}(\mathbf{x})$ by defining

$$\tilde{p}_i(\mathbf{x}) = p_i(\mathbf{x}) + q_i(\mathbf{x})$$

for each $0 < i \leq m$. The support dimension of IP will be denoted as s.

To define IPRainbow, we will keep the layer 1 central maps the same and internally perturb the 2nd layer maps. Specifically, we will consider an internally perturbed 2nd layer homogeneous equation of the form:

$$f(\mathbf{x}) = \sum_{i=1}^{v_2} \sum_{j=1}^{v_2} \alpha_{ij} x_i x_j + \sum_{i=1}^{v_2} \sum_{j=v_2+1}^{n} \beta_{ij} x_i x_j + \sum_{i=v_2+1}^{v_2+s} \sum_{j=v_2+1}^{v_2+s} \mu_{ij} x_i x_j,$$

see Algorithm 1 in Appendix A. The matrix representations of the central maps are illustrated in Fig. 4.

Layer 1 Rainbow Map.

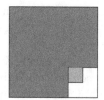

Layer 2 Rainbow Map.

Fig. 4. The first layer maps remain the same as the unmodified Rainbow first layer maps. Now we consider a $s \times s$ submatrix of the oil times oil section of the second layer map that is nonzero and denoted as light gray.

Given an unmodified Rainbow public key, we know that for any $\mathbf{x} \in \mathbb{F}_q^n$ such that $T\mathbf{x} \in O_2$, $P(\mathbf{x}) = 0$. Now, given the IPModifier, the O_2 space is not a subspace of the kernel. Indeed, an O_2 vector is in the kernel of Q with probability approximately q^{-s}.

Inversion is similar to the process of inversion for Rainbow. One randomly assigns values to the first layer vinegar variables, $x_1, \ldots, x_{v_1}$ and uses the first layer maps to solve for the first layer oil variables, $x_{v_1+1}, \ldots, x_{v_2}$. To invert the second layer maps, they are evaluated at $x_1, \ldots, x_{v_2}$ to recover o_2 equations in o_2 variables. These equations are quadratic, however, only s variables occur in quadratic terms, thus by Gaussian elimination, we may recover a system of s quadratic equations in s variables whose resolution by standard Gröbner basis techniques allows for the remaining variables to be linearly solved, see Algorithm 2 in Appendix A.

4.2   Security Analysis

Simple Attack. The simple attack of [4] remains applicable to IPRainbow, with some slight differences. Note that the matrix structure of $D_{\mathbf{x}}$ remains the same as in the case of Rainbow. Thus, with probability roughly q^{-1} the linear map defined by $D_{\mathbf{x}}$ contains an O_2 vector $\mathbf{y}$ in its left kernel. For our new IPRainbow scheme, an oil vector in the kernel of $D_{\mathbf{x}}$ may not necessarily be in the kernel of the public key. Given that the second layer maps contain quadratic summands in s of the second layer oil variables, we expect the simple attack of [4] to proceed with probability roughly q^{-s-1} (See Lemma 1).

Lemma 1. *For sufficiently small s, the linear map $D_{\mathbf{x}}$ has an O_2 vector $\mathbf{y}$ in its left kernel that satisfies $P(\mathbf{y}) = \mathbf{0}$ with probability approximately q^{-s-1}.*

Proof. Let $\mathbf{y}$ be an O_2 vector satisfying $P(\mathbf{y}) = \mathbf{0}$. First, note that there are $\binom{s+1}{2}$ homogeneous quadratic monomials in the variables $y_{v_2+1}, \dots, y_{v_2+s}$. Since the m unperturbed 2nd layer maps vanish at $\mathbf{y}$, the possibly nonzero terms of the perturbed second layer maps involve precisely these monomials. Thus, the probability that all of these monomials are zero (and hence $y_{v_2+i} = 0$ for i from 1 to s) is bounded below by the probability that this set of m equations has rank $\binom{s+1}{2}$, which is

$$\mathfrak{p}_r = \frac{\prod_{i=0}^{\binom{s+1}{2}-1} q^m - q^i}{q^{m\binom{s+1}{2}}} = \prod_{i=0}^{\binom{s+1}{2}-1} 1 - q^{i-m}.$$

Next, we work under the condition that the values $y_{v_2+1}, \dots, y_{v_2+s}$ are all zero and determine the probability that such an O_2 vector is in the left kernel of $D_{\mathbf{x}}$. This probability is the same as the probability that there exists a nontrivial kernel vector of $D_{\mathbf{x}}$ restricted to this $o_2 - s$-dimensional subspace of O_2. This restricted linear map, which we may represent as a random $(o_2 - s) \times o_2$ matrix over $\mathbb{F}_q$, is of full rank with probability

$$\mathfrak{p}_k = \frac{\prod_{i=0}^{o_2-s-1} q^{o_2} - q^i}{q^{o_2(o_2-s)}} = \prod_{i=0}^{o_2-s-1} 1 - q^{i-o_2},$$

Finally, by Markov's inequality, the probability that there is at least a one-dimensional subspace W of O_2 in the left kernel of $D_{\mathbf{x}}$ such that $P(\mathbf{y}) = \mathbf{0}$ for all $\mathbf{y} \in W$ is then bounded by q^{-1} times the expected number of such vectors. We then note that the dominant term in the second expression is bounded by $(1 - \mathfrak{p}_r) + (1 - \mathfrak{p}_k)$, which is approximately q^{-s-1} for sufficiently small s. □

We further remark that the constraint on s being small is not very strict. Even if s is such that $1 < \mathfrak{p}_r, \mathfrak{p}_k$, there is still a rank condition that must be satisfied for such a vector to exist in the kernel of $D_\mathbf{x}$. Thus, we find that the above probability estimate is accurate even when $\binom{s+1}{2}$ is somewhat larger than m, a fact we have verified experimentally.

Rectangular MinRank Attack. As is the case with Rainbow, the Simple attack of [4] can be combined with the Rectangular MinRank attack of [3]. As the attack still involves the finding a second layer oil variable and uses the property that such a vector satisfies the public equations, Lemma 1 applies, and we find that the complexity of the combined Rectangular MinRank attack costs a factor of approximately q^s times more for IPRainbow than for Rainbow. Thus, the complexity of the enhanced Rectangular MinRank Attack is given by

$$3q^{s+1}(n - m - 1)(o_2 + 1)\binom{m'}{r}^2\binom{n - m + b - 3}{b}^2$$

field multiplications, where $m' \leq m$ and b are chosen to optimize the attack.

Intersection Attack. In addition to the Simple attack and Rectangular Min-Rank attacks, Beullens also enhanced the Rainbow Band Separation attack of [12] and the tighter analysis of [23] with what he calls the Intersection Attack, see [3]. Once again, this attack relies on finding vectors in O_2 that satisfy the public polynomials. Therefore, once again, Lemma 1 applies and the complexity of these attacks is increased by a factor of about q^s. Even in the case that $n = 3m$, this attack is not the limiting attack.

4.3 Efficiency and Key Size

The complexity of the signing procedure is dominated by the complexity of the Gröbner basis algorithm used to solve the s-quadratic terms introduced in the IP modifier. Since the security of IPRainbow is exponential in s with base q, we choose $q = 257$ so that s can remain small for the fastest inversion. Figure 5 compares the efficiency of IPRainbow with comparable UOV parameters. These estimates were computed with unoptimized implementations using the MAGMA Computer Algebra System,[1] see [5], on a 2.4 GHz Quad-Core Intel Core i5 processor.

We find that it is easy to achieve secure parameters of IPRainbow with smaller keys and smaller signatures. While it is possible to set parameters so that IPRainbow verification is faster than UOV, in all of the experiments we performed the signing times for these instances are very costly, to the point of possibly being disqualifying even for applications using offline signing. Still, it is important to note that our data seem a bit noisy and better implementation can make the relationship between key size and verification time tighter.

---

[1] Any mention of commercial products does not indicate endorsement by NIST.

Scheme-(q, o_1, o_2, v, s)	Signing time	Verif. time	Key size	Sign. size	Security
UOV-$(257, 47, 0, 71, 0)$	0.750ms	0.370ms	330.2KB	118	144.5
IPRainbow-$(257, 32, 32, 32, 9)$	13700ms	0.370ms	298.2KB	96	145
IPRainbow-$(257, 32, 32, 36, 8)$	1976.5ms	0.380ms	323.4KB	100	144.3
IPRainbow-$(257, 32, 32, 38, 7)$	491ms	0.440ms	336.4KB	102	142.4
IPRainbow-$(257, 32, 36, 44, 6)$	127ms	0.510ms	430.6KB	112	143.1
UOV-$(257, 71, 0, 107, 0)$	138ms	1.190ms	1131.9KB	178	205.5
IPRainbow-$(257, 32, 42, 68, 9)$	16552ms	0.850ms	751.9KB	142	207.1
IPRainbow-$(257, 32, 48, 70, 8)$	4579ms	1.100ms	906.6KB	150	206.8
IPRainbow-$(257, 32, 48, 76, 7)$	987ms	1.020ms	980.4KB	156	206.9
IPRainbow-$(257, 32, 50, 84, 6)$	269ms	1.440ms	1137.4KB	166	206.9
UOV-$(257, 97, 0, 146, 0)$	5.240ms	4.630ms	2854.1KB	243	271
UOV-$(257, 98, 0, 147, 0)$	5.320ms	4.670ms	2931.3KB	245	275
IPRainbow-$(257, 36, 64, 112, 9)$	22026ms	2.390ms	2259.4KB	212	272
IPRainbow-$(257, 36, 64, 122, 8)$	29597ms	2.460ms	2477KB	222	271
IPRainbow-$(257, 36, 64, 135, 7)$	1123ms	5.300ms	2774.9KB	235	271.5
IPRainbow-$(257, 36, 66, 148, 6)$	298ms	5.280ms	3202.5KB	250	272.4

Fig. 5. Parameters targeting NIST security levels I, III and V.

5   Conclusion

In the past year and a half, the new attacks from Beullens have significantly improved the cryptanalysis of Rainbow and have rendered it less efficient than UOV. As the motivation of Rainbow was originally to create a more efficient scheme based on the oil-vinegar structure, these attacks are particularly problematic for Rainbow.

Still, the appeal of schemes such as Rainbow is their ability to provide low cost for applications that are not dominated by investment in public key transmission. Such applications are naturally amenable to offline signing, so a penalty in the cost of inversion may be acceptable if there is sufficient benefit in verification speed or signature size.

As we have shown, the implementation of the IP modifier on Rainbow adds solid theoretical protection from these new attacks at the cost of a significant increase in the complexity of inversion. Our data indicate that it is indeed feasible to salvage an advantage in verification time, key size and signature size at the cost of additional signing time. The next step for future work is optimizing this construction and determining the market for such a product.

Acknowledgements. The authors would like to thank Kyle Salyer for his help on this project.

A   Algorithms

Below are the key generation and central map inversion algorithms of IPRainbow.

Algorithm 1. IPRainbowKeyGen

Input: IPRainbow Parameters (q, v_1, o_1, o_2, s)
Output: IPRainbow Key Pair (sk, pk)
1: Set $m := o_1 + o_2, n := m + v_1$
2: $\mathcal{T}, \mathcal{U} \leftarrow GL(n, \mathbb{F}_q)$
3: $\mathcal{F} \leftarrow \text{RainbowMap}(q, v_1, o_1, o_2)$
4: $\mathcal{Q} \leftarrow \text{IPModifier}(s)$
5: $\mathcal{P} = \mathcal{T} \circ (\mathcal{F} + Q) \circ \mathcal{U}$
6: $sk = (\mathcal{T}, \mathcal{F}, \mathcal{Q}, \mathcal{U})$
7: $pk = \mathcal{P}$
8: **return** (sk, pk)

Algorithm 2. Inversion of IPRainbow Central Map

Input: IPRainbow central map $\mathcal{F} + \mathcal{Q} = (f_{v_1+1}, \ldots, f_m)$, vector $\mathbf{x} \in \mathbb{F}^m$
Output: $\mathbf{y} \in \mathbb{F}^n$ with $\tilde{\mathcal{F}}(\mathbf{y}) = \mathbf{x}$
1: $y_1, \ldots, y_{v_1} \xleftarrow{\$} \mathbb{F}_q$
2: $\tilde{f}_i := f_i(y_1, \ldots, y_{v_1})$ for $i \in \{v_1 + 1, \ldots, m\}$.
3: $y_{v_1+1}, \ldots, y_{v_2} := \text{GaussElim}(\tilde{f}_{v_1+1}, \ldots, \tilde{f}_m)$.
4: $\hat{f}_j := \tilde{f}_j(y_{v_1+1}, \ldots, y_{v_2})$ for $j \in \{v_2 + 1, \ldots, m\}$.
5: $g_1, \ldots, g_s := \text{GaussElim}(\hat{f}_{v_2+1}, \ldots, \hat{f}_m)$.
6: $y_{v_2+1}, \ldots, y_n := \text{PolySolve}(g_1, \ldots, g_s)$.
7: $\mathbf{y} := y_1, \ldots, y_{v_1}, y_{v_1+1}, \ldots, y_{v_2}, y_{v_2+1}, \ldots, y_n$.
8: **return** $\mathbf{y}$.

References

1. Bardet, M., et al.: An algebraic attack on rank metric code-based cryptosystems. In: Canteaut, A., Ishai, Y. (eds.) EUROCRYPT 2020, Part III. LNCS, vol. 12107, pp. 64–93. Springer, Cham (2020). https://doi.org/10.1007/978-3-030-45727-3_3
2. Bardet, M., et al.: Improvements of algebraic attacks for solving the rank decoding and MinRank problems. In: Moriai, S., Wang, H. (eds.) ASIACRYPT 2020, Part I. LNCS, vol. 12491, pp. 507–536. Springer, Cham (2020). https://doi.org/10.1007/978-3-030-64837-4_17
3. Beullens, W.: Improved cryptanalysis of UOV and rainbow. In: Canteaut, A., Standaert, F.-X. (eds.) EUROCRYPT 2021, Part I. LNCS, vol. 12696, pp. 348–373. Springer, Cham (2021). https://doi.org/10.1007/978-3-030-77870-5_13

4. Beullens, W.: Breaking rainbow takes a weekend on a laptop (2022). https://eprint.iacr.org/2022/214.pdf
5. Bosma, W., Cannon, J., Playoust, C.: The magma algebra system I: the user language. J. Symb. Comput. **24**(3–4), 235–265 (1997)
6. Cartor, R., Smith-Tone, D.: All in the c* family. Des. Codes Cryptogr. **88**(6), 1023–1036 (2020)
7. Coppersmith, D.: Solving homogeneous linear equations over GF(2) via block Wiedemann algorithm. Math. Comput. **62**(205), 333–350 (1994)
8. Courtois, N., Klimov, A., Patarin, J., Shamir, A.: Efficient algorithms for solving overdefined systems of multivariate polynomial equations. In: Preneel, B. (ed.) EUROCRYPT 2000. LNCS, vol. 1807, pp. 392–407. Springer, Heidelberg (2000). https://doi.org/10.1007/3-540-45539-6_27
9. Ding, J.: A new variant of the Matsumoto-Imai cryptosystem through perturbation. In: Bao, F., Deng, R., Zhou, J. (eds.) PKC 2004. LNCS, vol. 2947, pp. 305–318. Springer, Heidelberg (2004). https://doi.org/10.1007/978-3-540-24632-9_22
10. Ding, J., Chen, M.-S., Petzoldt, A., Schmidt, D., Yang, B.-Y.: Rainbow. NIST CSRC (2020). https://csrc.nist.gov/Projects/post-quantum-cryptography/round-3-submissions
11. Ding, J., Schmidt, D.: Rainbow, a new multivariable polynomial signature scheme. In: Ioannidis, J., Keromytis, A., Yung, M. (eds.) ACNS 2005. LNCS, vol. 3531, pp. 164–175. Springer, Heidelberg (2005). https://doi.org/10.1007/11496137_12
12. Ding, J., Yang, B.-Y., Chen, C.-H.O., Chen, M.-S., Cheng, C.-M.: New differential-algebraic attacks and reparametrization of rainbow. In: Bellovin, S.M., Gennaro, R., Keromytis, A., Yung, M. (eds.) ACNS 2008. LNCS, vol. 5037, pp. 242–257. Springer, Heidelberg (2008). https://doi.org/10.1007/978-3-540-68914-0_15
13. Faugère, J.-C., Levy-dit-Vehel, F., Perret, L.: Cryptanalysis of MinRank. In: Wagner, D. (ed.) CRYPTO 2008. LNCS, vol. 5157, pp. 280–296. Springer, Heidelberg (2008). https://doi.org/10.1007/978-3-540-85174-5_16
14. Kipnis, A., Shamir, A.: Cryptanalysis of the HFE public key cryptosystem by relinearization. In: Wiener, M. (ed.) CRYPTO 1999. LNCS, vol. 1666, pp. 19–30. Springer, Heidelberg (1999). https://doi.org/10.1007/3-540-48405-1_2
15. Kipnis, A., Patarin, J., Goubin, L.: Unbalanced oil and vinegar signature schemes. In: Stern, J. (ed.) EUROCRYPT 1999. LNCS, vol. 1592, pp. 206–222. Springer, Heidelberg (1999). https://doi.org/10.1007/3-540-48910-X_15
16. Kipnis, A., Shamir, A.: Cryptanalysis of the oil and vinegar signature scheme. In: Krawczyk, H. (ed.) CRYPTO 1998. LNCS, vol. 1462, pp. 257–266. Springer, Heidelberg (1998). https://doi.org/10.1007/BFb0055733
17. Matsumoto, T., Imai, H.: Public quadratic polynomial-tuples for efficient signature-verification and message-encryption. In: Barstow, D., et al. (eds.) EUROCRYPT 1988. LNCS, vol. 330, pp. 419–453. Springer, Heidelberg (1988). https://doi.org/10.1007/3-540-45961-8_39
18. National Institute of Standards and Technology. Post-quantum cryptography, round 3 submissions (2022)
19. Patarin, J.: Cryptanalysis of the matsumoto and imai public key scheme of Eurocrypt'88. In: Coppersmith, D. (ed.) CRYPTO 1995. LNCS, vol. 963, pp. 248–261. Springer, Heidelberg (1995). https://doi.org/10.1007/3-540-44750-4_20
20. Patarin, J.: The oil and vinegar signature scheme. Presented at the Dagstuhl Workshop on Cryptography, September 1997
21. Patarin, J., Goubin, L.: Trapdoor one-way permutations and multivariate polynomials. In: Han, Y., Okamoto, T., Qing, S. (eds.) ICICS 1997. LNCS, vol. 1334, pp. 356–368. Springer, Heidelberg (1997). https://doi.org/10.1007/BFb0028491

22. Patarin, J., Goubin, L., Courtois, N.: *C*, and *HM*: variations around two schemes of T. Matsumoto and H. Imai. In: Ohta, K., Pei, D. (eds.) ASIACRYPT 1998. LNCS, vol. 1514, pp. 35–50. Springer, Heidelberg (1998). https://doi.org/10.1007/3-540-49649-1_4

23. Perlner, R.A., Smith-Tone, D.: Rainbow band separation is better than we thought. IACR Cryptology ePrint Archive, p. 702 (2020)

24. Yang, B.-Y., Chen, J.-M.: Theoretical analysis of XL over small fields. In: Wang, H., Pieprzyk, J., Varadharajan, V. (eds.) ACISP 2004. LNCS, vol. 3108, pp. 277–288. Springer, Heidelberg (2004). https://doi.org/10.1007/978-3-540-27800-9_24

2F - A New Method for Constructing Efficient Multivariate Encryption Schemes

Daniel Smith-Tone[1,2(✉)]

[1] Department of Mathematics, University of Louisville, Louisville, KY, USA
`daniel.smith@nist.gov`
[2] National Institute of Standards and Technology, Gaithersburg, MD, USA

Abstract. The Support Minors method of solving the MinRank problem has contributed to several new cryptanalyses of post-quantum cryptosystems including some of the most efficient multivariate cryptosystems. While there are a few viable multivariate schemes that are secure against rank methods, the most prominent schemes, particularly for encryption, are not particularly efficient.

In this article we present a new generic construction for building efficient multivariate encryption schemes. Such schemes can be built from maps having rank properties that would otherwise be damaging, but are immune to traditional rank attack. We then construct one such efficient multivariate encryption scheme and show it to be about 100 times faster than other secure multivariate encryption schemes in the literature.

Keywords: Multivariate cryptography · MinRank · Encryption

1 Introduction

In the past two years there have been several new advances in cryptanalysis that have significantly impacted the efficiency of various post-quantum cryptosystems. In particular, there has been a dramatic change in the power and variety of attacks exploiting rank properties of cryptosystems.

These new attacks rely on creative instances or more efficient modeling of the MinRank problem. The MinRank problem is the generic problem of finding a low rank linear combination of a collection of matrices.

In the rank-metric code-based regime, the basic problem of rank syndrome decoding is exactly an instance of MinRank. While it was previously assumed that the asymptotically most efficient attack on such schemes is the so-called support-trapping method, see [1], the new support minors technique of [2] not only significantly outperforms support-trapping asymptotically, but greatly reduces the efficiency of secure instances of these schemes. Schemes such as ROLLO [3] suffered a roughly square root security reduction.

This work was partially supported by a grant from the Simons Foundation (712530, DCST).

J. H. Cheon and T. Johansson (Eds.): PQCrypto 2022, LNCS 13512, pp. 185–201, 2022.
https://doi.org/10.1007/978-3-031-17234-2_10

In the multivariate arena, new MinRank instances have been found that have significantly changed the security level of prominent schemes. The rectangular MinRank attack of [4] reduces the security of Rainbow and is made possible by the efficiency of support minors modeling. Even in conjunction with the new "simple attack" of [5], the support minors technique supporting the rectangular MinRank attack is required for the cryptanalysis of larger parameters. While the new MinRank instances found in GeMSS, see [6], reduce the security level even with the minors technique, see [7], MinRank attacks powered by the support minors modeling make the HFEv- framework infeasible for practical use, see [8].

These results along with numerous other rank-based attacks on encryption and signature schemes, see [9–12], show that MinRank methods are a major obstacle to overcome in the construction of secure and efficient schemes. Thus we are in need of a method to side-step MinRank attacks.

Our Contributions. We offer a new method for generating multivariate encryption schemes that are immune from rank attacks. The technique exploits the fact that modulus switching induces a nonlinear action over finite fields. We find that we can take essentially any multivariate encryption primitive and apply a modulus switching hack that we call 2F (since two fields of differing characteristic are used) to mask rank properties and construct an efficient encryption scheme. As an exercise, we construct from a primitive that is insecure against four different attacks (two rank-based, one differential and one algebraic) a new multivariate encryption scheme and show that the new 2F version is secure against these attacks.

The paper is organized as follows. In Sect. 2, we present some historical schemes that have relevance to our construction. Next, in Sect. 3, we introduce the generic 2F construction and verify its correctness. Then in Sect. 4, we introduce a prototype 2F scheme chosen to illustrate the effects on security the 2F construction has. Section 5 then provides a detailed security analysis highlighting the impact of the construction on every known attack surface. We then suggest parameters for the 128-bit and 143-bit security levels in Sect. 6, drawing performance comparisons with other secure multivariate encryption schemes in the literature. Finally, we conclude, reflecting on the changes we have seen in the design approach to multivariate cryptography and noting directions for future work.

2   Multivariate Encryption Schemes

In this section we describe the relevant historical schemes that motivate and power our new construction as well as schemes to which we want to draw comparison. We introduce them in order of their development and mention the known results on these schemes in the literature.

2.1   HFE

The HFE cryptosystem presented in [13] is a "big field" scheme in the lineage of C^*, see [14]. Such schemes rely on the vector space structure of finite extension fields to create vector-valued maps whose nonlinear component is derived from multiplication in the extension field.

Let $\mathbb{F}_q$ be a finite field with q elements, let $\mathbb{K}$ be a degree n extension of $\mathbb{F}_q$, and let $\phi : \mathbb{F}_q^n \to \mathbb{K}$ be an $\mathbb{F}_q$-vector space isomorphism. An HFE polynomial of degree bound D is a polynomial $f : \mathbb{K} \to \mathbb{K}$ of the form

$$f(X) = \sum_{q^i + q^j \leq D} \alpha_{ij} X^{q^i + q^j} + \sum_{q^i \leq D} \beta_i X^{q^i} + \gamma,$$

where $\alpha_{ij}, \beta_i, \gamma \in \mathbb{K}$. We note that since the ith and jth Frobenius powers are $\mathbb{F}_q$-linear, f is $\mathbb{F}_q$-quadratic. The HFE public key is then given by

$$P(\mathbf{x}) = T \circ \phi^{-1} \circ f \circ \phi \circ U(\mathbf{x}),$$

where U and T are $\mathbb{F}_q$-linear or $\mathbb{F}_q$-affine maps, see Fig. 1.

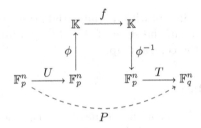

Fig. 1. The HFE scheme. Given the $\mathbb{F}_q$-quadratic map f, the $\mathbb{F}_q$-vector space isomorphism ϕ, and $\mathbb{F}_q$-linear maps U, and T, we construct the vector-valued function $P : \mathbb{F}_q^n \to \mathbb{F}_q^n$.

One may use the plain HFE as a public key encryption scheme. Encryption is accomplished by evaluating the public key at an encoding of the plaintext while decryption is performed by inverting each of the private maps sequentially. The inversion of the central map can be performed efficiently by using Berlekamp's algorithm, see [15], as long as D is fairly small.

There are a few attacks that make HFE inefficient. The first attack on HFE was [16]. An improvement on this technique in [9] modeled a MinRank instance with matrices over the small field with solutions in the large field and solved that instance with the minors modeling technique. The same MinRank instance was later found to be more efficiently solvable by once again returning to the Kipnis-Shamir method with variables defined over the extension field in [17]. The new attack on GeMSS, see [7], exploits a new MinRank instance associated with the structure of the HFE public key, but for naked HFE instances has the same complexity as the above attack. Finally, the new method for using support minors for MinRank instances with solutions in extension fields of [8] significantly reduces the complexity of attacking HFE and renders it too inefficient for use.

2.2 SQUARE

The SQUARE multivariate encryption scheme, see [18], is a big field scheme using a simple monomial map that is two-to-one and that employs the projection modifier, the idea of fixing certain variables before the publication of the key to alter its algebraic properties. The SQUARE central map can be seen as an odd field HFE map but with degree bound 2 and no affine component.

Specifically, choose an odd characteristic field $\mathbb{F}_q$ and let $\mathbb{K}$ be a degree $n+p$ extension of $\mathbb{F}_q$. Let $f : \mathbb{K} \to \mathbb{K}$ be defined by $f(X) = X^2$. Let $T : \mathbb{F}_q^{n+p} \to \mathbb{F}_q^{n+p}$ be an invertible linear map and let $U : \mathbb{F}_q^n \to \mathbb{F}_q^{n+p}$ be an injection. We then generate a public key $P = T \circ \phi^{-1} \circ f \circ \phi \circ U$, where $\phi : \mathbb{F}_q^{n+p} \to \mathbb{K}$ is a $\mathbb{F}_q$-vector space isomorphism.

We note that unlike the case of HFE where most elements in the range of the central map have a unique preimage, the map f above is a 2-to-1 map. Thus, some sort of padding of the plaintext is necessary to ensure uniqueness of preimages.

SQUARE was broken in [19] with a differential attack similar to that of [20]. We note also that attacks in the style of [7–9,17] also break SQUARE due to the very low Q-rank of the central map.

2.3 ABC Simple Matrix

The ABC Simple Matrix Encryption scheme of [21] uses the structure of a matrix algebra instead of an extension field to obtain its nonlinear central map. A modified version of this scheme was published in [22] to repair a high decryption failure rate of the original that leaked information about the secret key. Another version with a cubic public key was introduced in [23].

Fix parameters $s \leq r$ and set $n = rs$. Let $\mathbf{A}$ be an $r \times s$ matrix of random linear forms in n variables and let $\mathbf{B}$ and $\mathbf{C}$ be $s \times u$ and $s \times v$ matrices of random linear forms, respectively, where u and v are additional parameters of the system. We construct the quadratic map $F : \mathbb{F}_q^{rs} \to \mathbb{F}_q^{r(u+v)}$ by vectorizing the matrix product $\mathbf{A} [\mathbf{B}\ \mathbf{C}]$. The public key P is then computed by composing with linear transformations U and T.

As before, encryption is achieved by simply evaluating the public key at an encoding of the plaintext. To invert the central map, one parses the preimage of the ciphertext under T into an $r \times (u + v)$ matrix $\mathbf{V}$, sets $\mathbf{W}$ to be a formal left inverse of $\mathbf{A}$ consisting of rs unknowns w_{ij} and computes the product $\mathbf{WV}$. Since $\mathbf{W}$ is a left inverse of $\mathbf{A}$, this product must produce $[\mathbf{B}\ \mathbf{C}]$ evaluated at $U(\mathbf{x})$. This equality produces a system of $s(u + v)$ equations that are linear in $2rs$ unknowns, the values w_{ij} and the values x_i. Via Gaussian elimination, all of the variables w_{ij} can be eliminated to produce $s(u + v) - rs$ linear equations in the rs unknown values x_i. Since this system has a small dimensional solution space, these relations can be used to transform the public key into a system with very few unknowns that can be solved directly to reveal the preimage.

Several attacks are known to affect the security of the ABC scheme. The first attack that broke security claims was [24]. The attack revealed that there exist rank $2s$ maps in the span of the public quadratic forms and outlined an algebraic/combinatorial attack that was more efficient than the designers anticipated. Subsequently, in [25] it was shown that the cubic scheme was vulnerable to a similar attack and is less efficient than the quadratic scheme. These attacks on the cubic version were further improved in [26]. Most recently, it was shown in [11] that increasing r relative to s decreases security against rank attacks at the same rate that it decreases the decryption failure rate, thus showing that there are fundamental limits to the efficiency of any such scheme.

2.4   PCBM

The PCBM multivariate encryption scheme, see [27] is a relatively new encryption scheme with similar algebraic structure to HFERP, see [28], but with a wildly different approach to parametrization. PCBM is currently the fastest published multivariate encryption scheme targeting CCA security that remains secure at the 128-bit level.

Fix q and n and let C be a random k-dimensional subspace of $\mathbb{F}_q^n$. Let $\mathbf{H}$ be an $(n-k) \times n$ matrix whose right kernel is C. Given k random $n \times (n-k)$ matrices $\mathbf{A}_i$, we form the products $\mathbf{B}_i = \mathbf{A}_i\mathbf{H}$. Then define the polynomial

$$f_i(\mathbf{x}) = \mathbf{x}\mathbf{B}_i\mathbf{x}^\top + \mathbf{x}\mathbf{L}_i,$$

where $\mathbf{L}_i$ is a random $n \times 1$ matrix.

Note that for any $\mathbf{x} \in \mathbb{F}_q^n$, the value $\mathbf{H}\mathbf{x}^\top$ uniquely identifies the coset of C in $\mathbb{F}_q^n$ containing $\mathbf{x}$. This value is encoded in extra polynomials g_i via a small instance of EFLASH or PFLASH, see [29,30]. Finally, a large number of random quadratic equations h_i are included. The public key is then given by

$$P(\mathbf{x}) = T \circ (F\|G\|H) \circ U,$$

where T is affine, U is an affine embedding not intersecting C, $F = [f_i]$, $G = [g_i]$ and $H = [h_i]$.

Inversion is accomplished sequentially with the most interesting step being the inversion of F. Once the coset to which $\mathbf{x}$ belongs is extracted from G, it is easy to derive $\mathbf{x}$ by solving a linear system. Specifically, if $\mathbf{x} = \mathbf{x}' + \widehat{\mathbf{x}}$, where $\widehat{\mathbf{x}} \in C$ and $\mathbf{x}'$ is a coset representative derived from G we have that

$$f_i(\mathbf{x}) = (\mathbf{x}' + \widehat{\mathbf{x}}) \mathbf{B}_i (\mathbf{x}'^\top + \widehat{\mathbf{x}}^\top) + (\mathbf{x}' + \widehat{\mathbf{x}})\mathbf{L}_i^\top = \mathbf{x}'\mathbf{B}_i\mathbf{x}'^\top + \widehat{\mathbf{x}}\mathbf{B}_i\mathbf{x}'^\top + (\mathbf{x}' + \widehat{\mathbf{x}})\mathbf{L}_i^\top,$$

for all i and thus we can solve linearly for $\widehat{\mathbf{x}}$ and $\mathbf{x}$.

The natural ways to attack this structure relate to searching for the large subspace C and MinRank methods attacking either the low rank, in general

$2(n-k)$, maps of F or by attacking the low Q-rank map G. The very large number of random maps H added mitigates these risks though, and the check equations that H provides makes PCBM have a very low decryption failure rate.

3   2F Modulus Switching

The first post-quantum cryptosystem to employ modulus switching was NTRU, see [31]. There, independent reduction modulo two coprime integers was used to mix and unmix operations in two polynomial rings.

While the original NTRU proposal was probabilistic in nature, with appropriate restrictions on the parameters, perfect correctness can be assured, such as is the case for the NIST Round 3 finalist NTRU, see [32]. The same analogy will hold with the 2F construction as well. In the following, we present a perfectly correct version of 2F but comment that we may select parameters to construct a probabilistic version as well.

Let p and q be primes with q much larger than p. Let $F : \mathbb{F}_p^n \to \mathbb{F}_p^n$ be an efficiently invertible and computationally injective quadratic function. In particular, we may consider F to be any public key of a multivariate encryption scheme over a prime field. Let $T : \mathbb{F}_q^n \to \mathbb{F}_q^n$ be an invertible linear map and let ι be the map that casts a function on $\mathbb{F}_p^n$ as a function on $\mathbb{F}_q^n$ with the same coefficients considered as least absolute residues lying in $\mathbb{F}_q$. The 2F version of the map F is then $\widetilde{F} : \mathbb{F}_q^n \to \mathbb{F}_q^n$ (with domain restricted to $(-\frac{p}{2}, \frac{p}{2})^n$) defined by

$$\widetilde{F} = T \circ \iota(F).$$

The reason this simple modulus-switching transformation changes the algebraic properties of the function is that ι is neither $\mathbb{F}_p$-linear nor $\mathbb{F}_q$-linear. A key observation is that even ι modulo p is not $\mathbb{F}_p$-linear since reduction is first computed modulo q and then modulo p. Thus, in general, $\widetilde{F} \neq T' \circ F$ for any $\mathbb{F}_p$-linear function T'.

First, we must show that the inversion process succeeds; that is, we must show that finding a preimage under T, reducing modulo p, and, finally computing a preimage under F produces a preimage of $\widetilde{F}$. This discussion establishes the necessary relationship between the sizes of p and q for the inversion of $\widetilde{F}$ to depend only on the ability to invert F.

Theorem 1. *Let p and q be odd primes, let $F : \mathbb{F}_p^n \to \mathbb{F}_p^n$ be a homogeneous quadratic map and let $T : \mathbb{F}_q^n \to \mathbb{F}_q^n$ be an invertible $\mathbb{F}_q$-linear transformation. If*

$$q > \frac{(p-1)^3}{4}\binom{n+1}{2},$$

then $\mathbf{y} = T \circ \iota(F)(\mathbf{x})$ *if and only if* $T^{-1}(\mathbf{y}) \ (mod\ p) = F(\mathbf{x})$

Proof. Clearly, $T^{-1}(\mathbf{y}) = \iota(F)(\mathbf{x})$. It remains to be shown that $\iota(F)(\mathbf{x}) \ (mod\ p)$ is the same as $F(\mathbf{x})$.

To accomplish the above task, we first consider computing the value of a coordinate function F_i over the integers. Since the least residue value of each coordinate of $\mathbf{x}$ is bounded in absolute value by $\frac{p-1}{2}$, as are the coefficients of F_i, each monomial has a least residue bounded in absolute value by $\frac{(p-1)^3}{8}$. As there are $\binom{n+1}{2}$ such monomials in F_i, the value calculated as an integer is bounded in absolute value by $\frac{(p-1)^3}{8}\binom{n+1}{2}$. Since this quantity is less than $\frac{q}{2}$, no reduction modulo q occurs in the computation of F_i. Therefore $\iota(F)(\mathbf{x})$ equals $F(\mathbf{x})$ over the integers, and thus reduced modulo p has the same value as $F(\mathbf{x})$.

Recall that valid decryption for any encryption scheme requires that a ciphertext has a unique preimage. Injective functions satisfy this property with probability 1; however, many encryption schemes are based on functions that are not injective, but satisfy some weaker property. We describe two such properties below.

Definition 1. *A finite family $\mathcal{F}$ of functions $F : A \to B$ on the finite sets A and B is statistically injective with bound p if given $G \xleftarrow{\mathcal{U}} \mathcal{F}$,*

$$\mathcal{P}\left(\exists a \neq a_0 \in A \text{ with } G(a) = G(a_0)\right) \leq p.$$

The family $\mathcal{F}$ is computationally injective with bound p if given $G \xleftarrow{\mathcal{U}} \mathcal{F}$ and $a_0 \xleftarrow{\mathcal{U}} A$,

$$\mathcal{P}\left(\exists a \in A \setminus \{a_0\} \text{ with } G(a) = G(a_0)\right) \leq p.$$

A good example of a statistically injective family of functions is the collection of public keys for the PCBM encryption scheme, see [27]. It is estimated in [27] that the probability that a uniformly sampled PCBM$(148, 149, 113, 37, 12, 414)$ public key is an injective function is approximately $1 - 2^{-200}$; thus, since decryption failure can only occur when a ciphertext has multiple preimages, PCBM may be used to target CCA security.

For an example of a computationally injective family of functions, consider the collection of public keys with parameters $(q, n, m) = (3, 140, 226)$ of the HFERP encryption scheme, see [28, Section 7]. There the bound for computational injectivity (and therefore a bound on the probability that a randomly generated ciphertext has multiple preimages) is about 2^{-136}, though the probability that a given public key is an injective function is quite low. Due to Theorem 1, we have that injectivity as well as computational and statistical injectivity are preserved by the 2F construction.

Corollary 1. *Let p and q be primes, let $F : \mathbb{F}_p^n \to \mathbb{F}_p^n$ be a homogeneous quadratic map and let $T : \mathbb{F}_q^n \to \mathbb{F}_q^n$ be an invertible $\mathbb{F}_q$-linear transformation. If*

$$q > \frac{(p-1)^3}{4}\binom{n+1}{2},$$

then $P = T \circ \iota(F)$ is injective if and only if F is injective. Under the same condition, P is computationally (or statistically) injective if and only if F is computationally (or statistically) injective.

We note here that it may be desirable for efficiency to choose a smaller value of q than the one mentioned above. There are two clear motivations for such a choice.

First, the output distributions for fixed quadratic forms are typically far narrower than the theoretical limit given by the bound above. Thus it is possible to pick a far smaller q that still has a very low, or even zero, decryption failure rate.

Second, it is not necessary to have the plaintext space be all of $\mathbb{F}_p^n$. For example, we could insist that valid plaintexts lie in $\{-1, 0, 1\}^n$, in which case we can use a much larger p and still utilize a smaller q for which the natural analogue of Theorem 1 still holds. In this latter case, the output distribution of a fixed quadratic form is even narrower, so there is room for further optimization of q if we allow a small decryption failure rate from the 2F construction.

4   An Instance of 2F Multivariate Encryption

As an exercise, we construct and demonstrate 2FSQUARE, the 2F version of the SQUARE encryption scheme, see [18], without projection. Since SQUARE can be broken by numerous methods, see [8,9,33], this choice offers the best chance for future cryptanalysis and advancement in this line of research.

Let p be an odd prime and fix a positive integer n. Let q be a prime larger than $\frac{(p-1)^3}{4}\binom{n+1}{2}$. Let $\mathbb{K}$ be a degree n extension of $\mathbb{F}_p$ and let $\phi : \mathbb{F}_p^n \to \mathbb{K}$ be an $\mathbb{F}_p$-vector space isomorphism. Select an invertible linear transformation $U : \mathbb{F}_p^n \to \mathbb{F}_p^n$ and define $F : \mathbb{F}_p^n \to \mathbb{F}_p^n$ by

$$F(\mathbf{x}) = \phi^{-1}(\phi(U(\mathbf{x}))^2).$$

Select another invertible linear transformation $T : \mathbb{F}_q^n \to \mathbb{F}_q^n$ and define

$$P(\mathbf{x}) = T \circ \iota(F)(\mathbf{x}),$$

where ι be the map that casts a function on $\mathbb{F}_p^n$ as a function on $\mathbb{F}_q^n$ with the same coefficients considered as least absolute residues lying in $\mathbb{F}_q$. See Fig. 2 for a visual description of P.

Encryption is accomplished by evaluating the public key P at the plaintext $\mathbf{x}$. Decryption is accomplished by inverting T, reducing the result modulo p and inverting F. For the latter step, some redundancy must be built into the domain of F to produce unique preimages as was already the case for SQUARE.

5   Security Analysis

The 2F construction adds a nonlinear modification to a multivariate cryptosystem, so we expect it to change the algebraic properties such as rank that we normally use to cryptanalyze multivariate cryptosystems. We verify the security of 2FSQUARE against the typical attacks we use on multivariate schemes in this section. In addition to analyzing what structure is taken away by the 2F construction, we analyze the structure added by 2F at the end of the section.

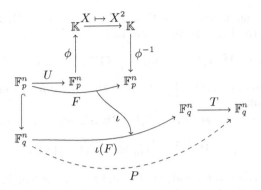

Fig. 2. The 2FSQUARE scheme. Given the $\mathbb{F}_p$-vector space isomorphism ϕ, $\mathbb{F}_p$-linear map U, $\mathbb{F}_q$-linear map T and the modulus switching map ι, we construct the vector-valued function $P : \mathbb{F}_p^n \to \mathbb{F}_q^n$. The inclusion of $\mathbb{F}_p^n$ into $\mathbb{F}_q^n$ is understood to coordinatewise map the least absolute residue $a \in \mathbb{F}_p$ to least absolute residue $a \in \mathbb{F}_q$.

5.1 MinRank Attacks

The SQUARE cryptosystem is vulnerable to two different types of rank attacks. The historically first such attack originated in the work of Kipnis and Shamir, see [16], and was improved in [9].

Note that we may represent elements of $\mathbb{K}$ as n-dimensional vectors over $\mathbb{F}_p$. Then the $\mathbb{F}_p$-vector space isomorphism ϕ can be expressed as a matrix over $\mathbb{F}_p$. In particular, if θ is a primitive element for $\mathbb{K}$ over $\mathbb{F}_p$, then we can represent ϕ via right multiplication by the matrix

$$\mathbf{M} = \begin{bmatrix} 1 & 1 & \cdots & 1 \\ \theta & \theta^p & \cdots & \theta^{p^{n-1}} \\ \theta^2 & \theta^{2p} & \cdots & \theta^{2p^{n-1}} \\ \vdots & \vdots & \ddots & \vdots \\ \theta^{(n-1)} & \theta^{(n-1)p} & \cdots & \theta^{(n-1)p^{n-1}} \end{bmatrix},$$

given that the vector representations of elements in $\mathbb{K}$ is relative to the same basis, $\{1, \theta, \theta^2, \ldots, \theta^{(n-1)}\}$.

Letting $G(X) = X^2$, and setting $\mathbf{G}^{*i}$ to be the matrix representation of the ith Frobenius power of G, we have that

$$G(X)^{p^i} = \begin{bmatrix} X & X^p & \cdots & X^{p^{(n-1)}} \end{bmatrix} \mathbf{G}^{*i} \begin{bmatrix} X \\ X^p \\ \vdots \\ X^{p^{(n-1)}} \end{bmatrix}.$$

The matrix $\mathbf{G}^{*i}$ has only one nonzero value, a 1 in the ith row and column.

Let $\mathbf{U}$ be the matrix representation of U and set $\mathbf{S} = \mathbf{UM}$. We may then note that if $\mathbf{H}_i$ is the ith quadratic form in $H = \phi^{-1} \circ G \circ \phi \circ U$, we have

$$\begin{bmatrix} \mathbf{H}_0 \ \mathbf{H}_1 \ \cdots \ \mathbf{H}_{n-1} \end{bmatrix} (\mathbf{M} \otimes \mathbf{I}_n) = \begin{bmatrix} \mathbf{SG}^{*0}\mathbf{S}^\top \ \cdots \ \mathbf{SG}^{*(n-1)}\mathbf{S}^\top \end{bmatrix}. \tag{1}$$

Since $\mathbf{G}^{*0}$, for example, has rank 1, there is thus a $\mathbb{K}$-linear combination of the matrices $\mathbf{H}_i$ of rank 1.

Notice that the public key of 2FSQUARE is given in matrix form by

$$\begin{bmatrix} \mathbf{P}_0 \ \mathbf{P}_1 \ \cdots \ \mathbf{P}_{n-1} \end{bmatrix} = \begin{bmatrix} \widetilde{\mathbf{H}}_0 \ \widetilde{\mathbf{H}}_1 \ \cdots \ \widetilde{\mathbf{H}}_{n-1} \end{bmatrix} (\mathbf{T} \otimes \mathbf{I}_n), \tag{2}$$

where $\mathbf{T}$ is the matrix representation of T and $\mathbf{P}_i$ are the matrix representations of the public quadratic forms. Critically, T is $\mathbb{F}_q$-linear, and so not $\mathbb{F}_p$-linear. Thus there is a $\mathbb{K}$-linear combination of $\mathbb{F}_q$-linear combinations of the $\mathbf{P}_i$ that has low rank as a $\mathbb{K}$-valued matrix. This combination does not correspond to a linear combination over any ring, and so the rank property is broken. We verified experimentally for small instances that the smallest rank in the span of the public matrices is high over $\mathbb{F}_p$, $\mathbb{F}_q$ and $\mathbb{K}$.

The second kind of rank attack affecting SQUARE is that of [7]. This rank attack is also based on Eq. (1). The attack works by finding a row of $\mathbf{S}^{-1}$ and reconstructing $\mathbf{S}$ by Frobenius relations. Specifically, if $\mathbf{s} = \begin{bmatrix} s_0 \ s_1 \ \dots \ s_{n-1} \end{bmatrix}$ is the first row of $\mathbf{S}^{-1}$, then the matrix $\mathbf{Z}$ whose ith row is given by $\mathbf{sH}_i$ has rank 1. This rank condition induces a system of equations on the unknown coefficients of $\mathbf{s}$ which can be solved at low degree, in fact, at degree 2 in this case.

Again, the $\mathbb{F}_q$-linear map T present in Eq. (2) halts the attack. Since the relationship between the public matrices $\mathbf{P}_i$ and $\mathbf{G}^{*i}$ is not linear with respect to any ring, the rank condition present in the $\mathbf{H}_i$ is not echoed by the public matrices. Once again, we have verified this property experimentally.

5.2   Differential

Another class of attack against which SQUARE is vulnerable is the attack based on differential symmetry. This attack is the one that first broke SQUARE, see [19].

Recall that the discrete differential of any function $F(x)$ is merely the associated bilinear function $DF(a, x) = F(a + x) - F(a) - F(x) + F(0)$. We may examine the differential over the small field where the function of interest is vector-valued, or over the large field in which our function is the monomial map $G(X) = X^2$. In the latter case, the differential is $DG(A, X) = 2AX$.

Given any element β of the extension field $\mathbb{K}$, we see that the differential satisfies a symmetric multiplicative symmetry

$$DG(\beta A, X) + DG(A, \beta X) = 2\beta DG(A, X).$$

Passing this relation to the small field and incorporating U we obtain the linear differential symmetry

$$DH(\mathbf{M}_\beta \mathbf{Ua}, \mathbf{Ux}) + DH(\mathbf{Ua}, \mathbf{M}_\beta \mathbf{Ux}) = 2\mathbf{M}_\beta DH(\mathbf{Ua}, \mathbf{Ux}),$$

where $H = \phi^{-1} \circ G \circ \phi$.

For the original SQUARE cryptosystem the linear transformation T was $\mathbb{F}_p$-linear, and then there is an easy way to translate the above relation into a relation on the public key. This relation can then be used to complete an attack on SQUARE by the same technique as [33]. Due to the fact that T is not $\mathbb{F}_p$-linear, however, the symmetric application of an $\mathbb{F}_p$-linear map corresponding to multiplication by an element of $\mathbb{K}$ in the correct basis is not equivalent to the composition of a linear map with the public differential over any ring. Thus, 2FSQUARE is immune from differential attack as well.

5.3   Direct

In [34], the authors present evidence that the analysis of EFLASH, see [29], against direct message recovery attacks is incomplete. Specifically, they show that low Q-rank relations in the extension field correspond to low degree syzygies in the direct attack. This observation offers another method of cryptanalysis against SQUARE as an instance of EFLASH with special parameters.

Note, however, that the observation of [34] relies on relations induced by the Frobenius automorphisms of $\mathbb{K}$ "passing through" the output transformation in the sense that there exists an $\mathbb{F}_p$ linear map L such that L composed with T is equal to T composed with the Frobenius automorphism. As before, since T is not $\mathbb{F}_p$-linear in 2FSQUARE, this property fails to hold, thus, 2FSQUARE does not have the anomalous low degree syzygies observed in [34]. We have experimentally verified for small instances that the first fall degree matches the semi-regular degree.

The best method for effecting a direct attack on a balanced multivariate system is called the hybrid approach. First the attacker guesses the values of k variables. Then some polynomial system solver is used to solve the resulting system.

The type of polynomial system solver that is optimal depends on many parameters including the density of the equations, the number of variables and the solving degree. Typically denser systems for which the solving degree is lower benefit from Gröbner basis solvers powered by F4, see [35]. Systems with a larger number of variables or less dense systems or that require a higher operating degree do not benefit as greatly from the normalization step in F4 and can therefore benefit from the lower memory costs, see [8], of the XL algorithm [36]. For parameters of cryptographic interest, we expect that XL variants will be the most effective.

Notice that the system must be solved over $\mathbb{F}_q$, and so we are not able to add the normal field equations. Still, we may add equations of the form

$$g_i(x_i) = \prod_{j=\frac{1-p}{2}}^{\frac{p-1}{2}} (x_i - j),$$

which perform the same role as $\mathbb{F}_p$ field equations when solving over $\mathbb{F}_q$.

Thus, under the standard semi-regular assumption, the complexity of the hybrid direct attack with k guesses will then be

$$\text{Complexity}_{\text{direct}} = 3p^k \binom{n+1}{2} \binom{n+d}{d}^2 \tag{3}$$

$\mathbb{F}_q$ operations, where d is the smallest degree with a nonpositive coefficient in the series expansion of

$$\mathcal{H}(t) = \frac{(1-t^2)^n (1-t^p)^{n-k}}{(1-t)^{n-k}}.$$

Note that each such field operation will cost $2(\log_2 q^2 + \log_2 q)$ bit operations.

5.4   Lattice Attacks

While it seems that all of the standard multivariate attacks are made less efficient by the 2F construction, some structure is added to the public key. Notice that there exist $\mathbb{F}_q$-linear combinations of the public key that are polynomials with small coefficients, bounded in size by $\frac{p-1}{2}$. This observation is the basis for an attack based on lattices.

Notice that, analogous to the NTRU lattice, we may construct the lattice given by the rowspace of

$$\begin{bmatrix} \frac{p}{q}\mathbf{I}_n & \mathbf{P} \\ \mathbf{0} & q\mathbf{I}_{\binom{n+1}{2}} \end{bmatrix},$$

where $\mathbf{P}$ is the matrix whose ith row is the ordered list of monomial coefficients of the ith public equation P_i. Notice that there exists a vector $\mathbf{w}$ with entries in $\mathbb{F}_q$ such that $\mathbf{t}_i \| \mathbf{w}$ multiplied by the above matrix is $\frac{p}{q}\mathbf{t}_i$ concatenated with the list of monomial coefficients of $H_i \circ U$, where $\mathbf{t}_i$ is the ith row of T^{-1}. Thus, we expect that the shortest vector in this dimension $d = \binom{n+1}{2} + n$ lattice to be among these vectors.

All coordinates of this short vector lie in the interval $(-p/2, p/2)$ with at least $\binom{n+1}{2}$ of them taking integral values, and so the expected length is well-approximated by $s = \sqrt{(p^2-1)d/12}$. In contrast the expected length of the shortest vector in a random lattice of dimension d and volume $V = p^n q^{d-2n}$ is approximately $np^{n/d}q^{1-2n/d}/2\sqrt{\pi e}$.

We may follow the core-SVP methodology of [37] to estimate the complexity of solving this SVP instance conservatively ignoring some polynomial overhead. Following the geometric series assumption, we suppose that the length of the ith Gram-Schmidt basis vector is given by $\|\mathbf{b}_i^*\| = \delta^{d-2i-1}V^{1/d}$, where $\delta = ((\pi b)^{1/b}b/2\pi e)^{1/2(b-1)}$. The BKZ block size is then the smallest b for which the projected length $s\sqrt{b/d}$ is bounded by $\|\mathbf{b}_{d-b}^*\|$. The classical core-SVP hardness of this problem instance is then computed as

$$\text{Complexity}_{\text{core-SVP}} = 2^{0.292b}. \tag{4}$$

Of course, we may change the disparity in the length of the shortest vector in the above lattice and the value suggested by the Gaussian heuristic by bringing the values of p and q closer, either by introducing a nonzero decryption failure rate, by restricting the plaintext space or both, as discussed in Sect. 3. Thus, the 2F construction has the strength to address any vulnerability arising from some future lattice attack by adjusting these parameters in such a way as to make the vectors associated with the secret key not be among the shortest vectors in the lattice. The optimization of these strategies as well as other lattice attacks is an interesting direction to further study.

6 Parameters and Performance

As discussed in Sect. 5, the best known attacks on 2FSQUARE are the direct attack and the lattice attack. We find that for $p = 3$ the disparity in the length between the shortest vector in the lattice of Subsect. 5.4 and the Gaussian heuristic is sufficiently small and the dimension sufficiently large that the limiting attack is the direct attack. In contrast, for $p = 7$ the shortest vector is much smaller than would be implied by the Gaussian heuristic and the lattice attack then offers an advantage. Thus, we may select parameters based on the formula (3) for $p = 3$ and based on formula (4) for $p = 7$. To be careful, we assume that one bit of information is leaked in the form of the parity of some coordinate of the plaintext. We do this because the central map of SQUARE is a two-to-one function and 1-bit of redundant information is necessary to specify a unique preimage. For 128-bit security, we may select $p = 3$, $q = 6653$ and $n = 81$ or $p = 7$, $q = 344,749$ and $n = 54$. Targeting NIST level I security, see [38], we may select $p = 3$, $q = 8377$ and $n = 91$ or $p = 7$, $q = 449,287$ and $n = 64$. We summarize the complexity of attacks at these security levels in Table 1.

Table 1. Complexity of known attacks at the 128-bit and 143-bit (corresponding to NIST level I) security levels.

Scheme	Sec.	k	Direct	b	core-SVP
2FSQUARE(3, 6653, 81)	128	43	128	463	135
2FSQUARE(3, 8377, 91)	143	46	143	700	204
2FSQUARE(7, 130411, 69)	128	18	169	360	105
2FSQUARE(7, 145861, 73)	143	20	176	412	120

We made a proof-of-concept implementation on the MAGMA Computer Algebra System,[1] see [39], to make a comparison to other secure multivariate encryption schemes, see [21,27]. We find that our simple implementation is dramatically faster at the same security level, even when compared with optimized code. Still,

---

[1] Any mention of commercial products does not indicate endorsement by NIST.

MAGMA's implementation of the `Sqrt` command for finite fields is extremely efficient, so we suspect that an optimized implementation will not significantly outperform this one. The results of these experiments are recorded in Table 2.

Table 2. Public key, message and ciphertext sizes, decryption failure rate and encryption and decryption performance of multivariate encryption schemes at the best available comparison to the 128-bit security level.

Scheme	Sec.	PK	pt	ct	Enc.(ms)	Dec.(ms)	DFR
ABC(2^8,384,760)	128	54863KB	384B	760B	502	545	2^{-32}
PCBM(149,414)	128	743KB	149b	414b	13	743	2^{-350}
2FSQ(3, 6653, 81)	128	417KB	162b	129B	1.5	0.4	0
2FSQ(3, 8377, 91)	143	606KB	182b	148B	1.2	0.5	0
2FSQ(7, 130411, 69)	128	346KB	207b	147B	1.0	2.6	0
2FSQ(7, 145861, 73)	143	413KB	219b	157B	1.1	2.8	0

7   Conclusion

In the aftermath of several significant advances in cryptanalysis, there are several new directions to explore to find secure post-quantum schemes. These new schemes have motivations coming from avoiding rank attacks as well as importing ideas from other areas in cryptography.

In the area of multivariate digital signatures the new Mayo scheme of [40] introduces a method of creating oil-vinegar style maps, see [41], that can have more balance between the number of variables and number of equations. The Q modifier of [42] introduces a new method inspired by the relinearization algorithm of [16] to construct structured instances of UOV that have a more efficient inversion. While the recent result [43] shows that the latter scheme has limits on how long the keys can be used statically, both schemes appear to be secure for now.

The PCBM multivariate encryption scheme, inspired by linear codes, see [27], establishes a new way of parameterizing a multivariate encryption scheme similar to HFERP, see [28], but far more efficient. Now the 2F construction provides a new way, inspired by the modulus switching of NTRU, to build secure and very efficient multivariate encryption schemes.

While the above digital signature schemes take inspiration from established knowledge in multivariate cryptography, the encryption schemes mentioned are derived from examining code-based and lattice-based ideas. In all cases, however, there is a motivation to build a more efficient scheme that does not have exploitable rank properties.

In particular, both the Q-modifier and the 2F construction are generic and attempt to nonlinearly modify a given multivariate primitive. This genericity means that there is a multitude of possible schemes that may be derived from these constructions that may have disparate security properties. This fact suggests that there may be an enticing direction in which this work can progress aside from advancing new targets for cryptanalysis; namely, we may work in the attempt to build new multivariate schemes based on the 2F construction with other profitable modifications.

References

1. Gaborit, P., Ruatta, O., Schrek, J.: On the complexity of the rank syndrome decoding problem. CoRR abs/1301.1026 (2013)
2. Bardet, M., et al.: Improvements of algebraic attacks for solving the rank decoding and MinRank problems. In: Moriai, S., Wang, H. (eds.) ASIACRYPT 2020, Part I. LNCS, vol. 12491, pp. 507–536. Springer, Cham (2020). https://doi.org/10.1007/978-3-030-64837-4_17
3. Melchor, C.A., et al.: ROLLO - Rank-Ouroboros, Lake & LOcker. Submission to the NIST's Post-quantum Cryptography Standardization Process (2019)
4. Beullens, W.: Improved cryptanalysis of UOV and rainbow. In: Canteaut, A., Standaert, F.-X. (eds.) EUROCRYPT 2021, Part I. LNCS, vol. 12696, pp. 348–373. Springer, Cham (2021). https://doi.org/10.1007/978-3-030-77870-5_13
5. Beullens, W.: Breaking rainbow takes a weekend on a laptop. IACR Cryptology ePrint Archive, p. 214 (2022)
6. Casanova, A., Faugere, J.C., Macario-Rat, G., Patarin, J., Perret, L., Ryckeghem, J.: GeMSS - A Great Multivariate Short Signature. Submission to the NIST's Post-quantum Cryptography Standardization Process (2020)
7. Tao, C., Petzoldt, A., Ding, J.: Efficient key recovery for all HFE signature variants. In: Malkin, T., Peikert, C. (eds.) CRYPTO 2021, Part I. LNCS, vol. 12825, pp. 70–93. Springer, Cham (2021). https://doi.org/10.1007/978-3-030-84242-0_4
8. Baena, J., Briaud, P., Cabarcas, D., Perlner, R.A., Smith-Tone, D., Verbel, J.A.: Improving support-minors rank attacks: applications to GeMSS and rainbow. IACR Cryptology ePrint Archive, p. 1677 (2021)
9. Bettale, L., Faugère, J., Perret, L.: Cryptanalysis of HFE, multi-HFE and variants for odd and even characteristic. Des. Codes Cryptogr. **69**(1), 1–52 (2013)
10. Vates, J., Smith-Tone, D.: Key recovery attack for all parameters of HFE-. In: Lange, T., Takagi, T. (eds.) PQCrypto 2017. LNCS, vol. 10346, pp. 272–288. Springer, Cham (2017). https://doi.org/10.1007/978-3-319-59879-6_16
11. Apon, D., Moody, D., Perlner, R., Smith-Tone, D., Verbel, J.: Combinatorial rank attacks against the rectangular simple matrix encryption scheme. In: Ding, J., Tillich, J.-P. (eds.) PQCrypto 2020. LNCS, vol. 12100, pp. 307–322. Springer, Cham (2020). https://doi.org/10.1007/978-3-030-44223-1_17
12. Ding, J., Perlner, R., Petzoldt, A., Smith-Tone, D.: Improved cryptanalysis of HFEv- via projection. In: Lange, T., Steinwandt, R. (eds.) PQCrypto 2018. LNCS, vol. 10786, pp. 375–395. Springer, Cham (2018). https://doi.org/10.1007/978-3-319-79063-3_18
13. Patarin, J.: Hidden fields equations (HFE) and isomorphisms of polynomials (IP): two new families of asymmetric algorithms. In: Maurer, U. (ed.) EUROCRYPT 1996. LNCS, vol. 1070, pp. 33–48. Springer, Heidelberg (1996). https://doi.org/10.1007/3-540-68339-9_4

14. Matsumoto, T., Imai, H.: Public quadratic polynomial-tuples for efficient signature-verification and message-encryption. In: Barstow, D., et al. (eds.) EUROCRYPT 1988. LNCS, vol. 330, pp. 419–453. Springer, Heidelberg (1988). https://doi.org/10.1007/3-540-45961-8_39

15. Berlekamp, E.R.: Factoring polynomials over large finite fields. Math. Comput. **24**(111), 713–735 (1970)

16. Kipnis, A., Shamir, A.: Cryptanalysis of the HFE public key cryptosystem by relinearization. In: Wiener, M. (ed.) CRYPTO 1999. LNCS, vol. 1666, pp. 19–30. Springer, Heidelberg (1999). https://doi.org/10.1007/3-540-48405-1_2

17. Verbel, J., Baena, J., Cabarcas, D., Perlner, R., Smith-Tone, D.: On the complexity of "superdetermined" minrank instances. In: Ding, J., Steinwandt, R. (eds.) PQCrypto 2019. LNCS, vol. 11505, pp. 167–186. Springer, Cham (2019). https://doi.org/10.1007/978-3-030-25510-7_10

18. Clough, C., Baena, J., Ding, J., Yang, B.-Y., Chen, M.: Square, a new multivariate encryption scheme. In: Fischlin, M. (ed.) CT-RSA 2009. LNCS, vol. 5473, pp. 252–264. Springer, Heidelberg (2009). https://doi.org/10.1007/978-3-642-00862-7_17

19. Billet, O., Macario-Rat, G.: Cryptanalysis of the square cryptosystems. In: Matsui, M. (ed.) ASIACRYPT 2009. LNCS, vol. 5912, pp. 451–468. Springer, Heidelberg (2009). https://doi.org/10.1007/978-3-642-10366-7_27

20. Dubois, V., Fouque, P.-A., Shamir, A., Stern, J.: Practical cryptanalysis of SFLASH. In: Menezes, A. (ed.) CRYPTO 2007. LNCS, vol. 4622, pp. 1–12. Springer, Heidelberg (2007). https://doi.org/10.1007/978-3-540-74143-5_1

21. Tao, C., Diene, A., Tang, S., Ding, J.: Simple matrix scheme for encryption. In: Gaborit, P. (ed.) PQCrypto 2013. LNCS, vol. 7932, pp. 231–242. Springer, Heidelberg (2013). https://doi.org/10.1007/978-3-642-38616-9_16

22. Tao, C., Xiang, H., Petzoldt, A., Ding, J.: Simple matrix - a multivariate public key cryptosystem (MPKC) for encryption. Finite Fields Their Appl. **35**, 352–368 (2015)

23. Ding, J., Petzoldt, A., Wang, L.: The cubic simple matrix encryption scheme. In: Mosca, M. (ed.) PQCrypto 2014. LNCS, vol. 8772, pp. 76–87. Springer, Cham (2014). https://doi.org/10.1007/978-3-319-11659-4_5

24. Moody, D., Perlner, R., Smith-Tone, D.: An asymptotically optimal structural attack on the ABC multivariate encryption scheme. In: Mosca, M. (ed.) PQCrypto 2014. LNCS, vol. 8772, pp. 180–196. Springer, Cham (2014). https://doi.org/10.1007/978-3-319-11659-4_11

25. Moody, D., Perlner, R., Smith-Tone, D.: Key recovery attack on the cubic ABC simple matrix multivariate encryption scheme. In: Avanzi, R., Heys, H. (eds.) SAC 2016. LNCS, vol. 10532, pp. 543–558. Springer, Cham (2017). https://doi.org/10.1007/978-3-319-69453-5_29

26. Moody, D., Perlner, R., Smith-Tone, D.: Improved attacks for characteristic-2 parameters of the cubic ABC simple matrix encryption scheme. In: Lange, T., Takagi, T. (eds.) PQCrypto 2017. LNCS, vol. 10346, pp. 255–271. Springer, Cham (2017). https://doi.org/10.1007/978-3-319-59879-6_15

27. Smith-Tone, D., Tone, C.: A multivariate cryptosystem inspired by random linear codes. Finite Fields Their Appl. **69**, 101778 (2021)

28. Ikematsu, Y., Perlner, R., Smith-Tone, D., Takagi, T., Vates, J.: HFERP - a new multivariate encryption scheme. In: Lange, T., Steinwandt, R. (eds.) PQCrypto 2018. LNCS, vol. 10786, pp. 396–416. Springer, Cham (2018). https://doi.org/10.1007/978-3-319-79063-3_19

29. Cartor, R., Smith-Tone, D.: EFLASH: A new multivariate encryption scheme. In: Cid, C., Jacobson, M., Jr. (eds.) SAC 201. LNCS, pp. 281–299. Springer, Cham (2018). https://doi.org/10.1007/978-3-030-10970-7_13

30. Ding, J., Dubois, V., Yang, B.-Y., Chen, O.C.-H., Cheng, C.-M.: Could SFLASH be repaired? In: Aceto, L., Damgård, I., Goldberg, L.A., Halldórsson, M.M., Ingólfsdóttir, A., Walukiewicz, I. (eds.) ICALP 2008. LNCS, vol. 5126, pp. 691–701. Springer, Heidelberg (2008). https://doi.org/10.1007/978-3-540-70583-3_56

31. Hoffstein, J., Pipher, J., Silverman, J.H.: NTRU: a ring-based public key cryptosystem. In: Buhler, J.P. (ed.) ANTS 1998. LNCS, vol. 1423, pp. 267–288. Springer, Heidelberg (1998). https://doi.org/10.1007/BFb0054868

32. Chen, C., et al.: NTRU. Submission to the NIST's Post-quantum Cryptography Standardization Process (2020)

33. Smith-Tone, D.: Practical cryptanalysis of k-ary C^*. In: Ding, J., Tillich, J.-P. (eds.) PQCrypto 2020. LNCS, vol. 12100, pp. 360–380. Springer, Cham (2020). https://doi.org/10.1007/978-3-030-44223-1_20

34. Øygarden, M., Felke, P., Raddum, H., Cid, C.: Cryptanalysis of the multivariate encryption scheme EFLASH. In: Jarecki, S. (ed.) CT-RSA 2020. LNCS, vol. 12006, pp. 85–105. Springer, Cham (2020). https://doi.org/10.1007/978-3-030-40186-3_5

35. Faugere, J.C.: A new efficient algorithm for computing grobner bases (f4). J. Pure Appl. Algebra **139**, 61–88 (1999)

36. Courtois, N., Klimov, A., Patarin, J., Shamir, A.: Efficient algorithms for solving overdefined systems of multivariate polynomial equations. In: Preneel, B. (ed.) EUROCRYPT 2000. LNCS, vol. 1807, pp. 392–407. Springer, Heidelberg (2000). https://doi.org/10.1007/3-540-45539-6_27

37. Alkim, E., Ducas, L., Pöppelmann, T., Schwabe, P.: Post-quantum key exchange - a new hope. In: Holz, T., Savage, S. (eds.) 25th USENIX Security Symposium, USENIX Security 2016, Austin, TX, USA, 10–12 August 2016, pp. 327–343. USENIX Association (2016)

38. Submission requirements and evaluation criteria for the post-quantum cryptography standardization process. NIST CSRC (2016). http://csrc.nist.gov/groups/ST/post-quantum-crypto/documents/call-for-proposals-final-dec-2016.pdf

39. Bosma, W., Cannon, J., Playoust, C.: The magma algebra system I: the user language. J. Symb. Comput. **24**(3–4), 235–265 (1997)

40. Beullens, W.: MAYO: practical post-quantum signatures from oil-and-vinegar maps. In: AlTawy, R., Hülsing, A. (eds.) SAC 2021. LNCS, vol. 13203, pp. 355–376. Springer, Cham (2022). https://doi.org/10.1007/978-3-030-99277-4_17

41. Kipnis, A., Patarin, J., Goubin, L.: Unbalanced oil and vinegar signature schemes. In: Stern, J. (ed.) EUROCRYPT 1999. LNCS, vol. 1592, pp. 206–222. Springer, Heidelberg (1999). https://doi.org/10.1007/3-540-48910-X_15

42. Smith-Tone, D.: New practical multivariate signatures from a nonlinear modifier. In: Cheon, J.H., Tillich, J.-P. (eds.) PQCrypto 2021 2021. LNCS, vol. 12841, pp. 79–97. Springer, Cham (2021). https://doi.org/10.1007/978-3-030-81293-5_5

43. Hashimoto, Y.: On the modifier Q for multivariate signature schemes. IACR Cryptology ePrint Archive, p. 1046 (2021)

Quantum Algorithms, Attacks
and Models

Quantum Attacks on Lai-Massey Structure

Shuping Mao[1,2], Tingting Guo[1,2], Peng Wang[1,2(✉)], and Lei Hu[1,2]

[1] State Key Laboratory of Information Security, Institute of Information Engineering,
CAS, Beijing, China
w.rocking@gmail.com

[2] School of Cyber Security, University of Chinese Academy of Sciences, Beijing, China

Abstract. Aaram Yun et al. considered that Lai-Massey structure has the same security as Feistel structure. However, Luo et al. showed that 3-round Lai-Massey structure can resist quantum attacks of Simon's algorithm, which is different from Feistel structure. We give quantum attacks against a typical Lai-Massey structure. The result shows that there exists a quantum CPA distinguisher against 3-round Lai-Massey structure and a quantum CCA distinguisher against 4-round Lai-Massey Structure, which is the same as Feistel structure. We extend the attack on Lai-Massey structure to quasi-Feistel structure. We show that if the combiner of quasi-Feistel structure is linear, there exists a quantum CPA distinguisher against 3-round balanced quasi-Feistel structure and a quantum CCA distinguisher against 4-round balanced quasi-Feistel Structure.

Keywords: Quantum attacks · Lai-Massey structure · Quasi-Feistel structure

1 Introduction

Quantum Attacks. With the rapid development of quantum computers, the security of classic algorithms has been challenged. Shor [31] found that both the large number decomposition problem and the discrete logarithm problem have quantum polynomial-time algorithms, which pose a serious threat to RSA and other mainstream asymmetric crypto algorithms. In symmetric cryptography, it has always been considered that the biggest threat comes from Grover's quantum search algorithm [12]. It can reduce the complexity of k bits exhaustive algorithm to $O\left(2^{k/2}\right)$.

In his seminal paper, Simon [32] answered the question of how to find the period of a periodic function in $O(n)$ quantum queries. Many structures and the most widely used modes of operation for authentication and authenticated encryption were attacked by using Simon's algorithm. For example, the attacks of 3-round [21], 4-round [17] Feistel structures, 3-round MISTY-L structure, 3-round MISTY-R structure [29], Even-Mansour structure, LRW structure, CBC-MAC, PMAC, GMAC, GCM, and OCB [19].

Leander and May combined Simon's Algorithm with Gover's algorithm, giving a quantum key-recovery attack on FX-construction [24], which caused a quantum CPA attack on 5-round Feistel structure [8], quantum CCA attack on 7-round Feistel-KF structure and 9-round Feistel-FK structure [17].

Supported by the NSFC of China (61732021) and the National Key R&D Program of China (2018YFB0803801 and 2018YFA0704704).

J. H. Cheon and T. Johansson (Eds.): PQCrypto 2022, LNCS 13512, pp. 205–229, 2022.
https://doi.org/10.1007/978-3-031-17234-2_11

Lai-Massey Structure. IDEA algorithm [22,23] was designed by Lai and Massey. Vaudenay [35] generalized the structure adopted by IDEA algorithm and proposed the Lai-Massey structure. Lai-Massey structure uses general addition and subtraction operations in a finite abelian group G and has an orthomorphism permutation $\sigma : G \to G$. σ has the orthomorphism property: σ and $x \mapsto \sigma(x) - x$ are both permutations. Based on Lai-Massey structure, FOX [18] (also known as "IDEA NXT") was produced. FOX uses XOR operation instead of general addition and subtraction operations, and it reifies σ as $\sigma(x_L, x_R) = (x_R, x_L \oplus x_R)$. In this paper, we attack the instantiated Lai-Massey structure used in FOX. The ith-round of Lai-Massey structure is shown in Fig. 1.

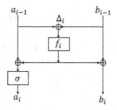

Fig. 1. The ith-round of Lai-Massey structure

Let $\mathrm{LM}_i(a_{i-1}, b_{i-1}) = (\sigma(a_{i-1} \oplus f_i(\Delta_i)), b_{i-1} \oplus f_i(\Delta_i))$, $\mathrm{LM}'_i(a_{i-1}, b_{i-1}) = (a_{i-1} \oplus f_i(\Delta_i), b_{i-1} \oplus f_i(\Delta_i))$. Then r-round Lai-Massey structure can be written as:

$$\mathrm{F_{rLM}} \stackrel{\text{def}}{=} (a_r, b_r) = \mathrm{LM}'_r \circ \mathrm{LM}_{r-1} \circ \cdots \circ \mathrm{LM}_1.$$

3-round and 4-round Lai-Massey structures are proven to be secure against chosen-plaintext attacks (CPAs) and chosen-ciphertext attacks (CCAs), respectively by Vaudenay et al. [35], like Feistel structure [9]. Luo, et al. [27] proved that 3 rounds (4 rounds) are necessary for CPA secure (CCA secure). Sui et al. [34] proved that 4-round Lai-Massey structure is CCA secure even if the adversary extra access to two internal rounds. Luo, et al. [28] proved beyond-birthday-bound for the CCA-security of many-round Lai-Massey scheme. Attacks like integral attacks [37,38], impossible differential cryptanalysis [7,13,39], collision-integral attacks [36], fault attacks [25], differential cryptanalysis [10,11], linear cryptanalysis [10], all-subkeys recovery attacks [16], imprimitivity attacks [3] were applied to block ciphers with Lai-Massey structure.

Quasi-Feistel Structure. Feistel structure is one of the most important block-cipher structures. Many block ciphers are designed by this scheme like DES [33], FEAL [30], SKIPJACK [1] and SIMON [4]. Michael Luby and Charles Rackoff [26] proved that 3-round Feistel structure is CPA secure, and 4-round Feistel structure is CCA secure if round functions are independent random functions. Zhang Liting et al. [41] extended those conclusions and proved that $k + 1$ rounds unbalanced Feistel networks with contracting functions(UFN-C) is CPA secure, $k + 2$ rounds UFN-C is CCA secure.

In [40], Aaram Yun et al. proposed quasi-Feistel structure and proved that Feistel structure and Lai-Massey structure are quasi-Feistel structures. They shown that the birthday security of $(2b-1)$-round and $(3b-2)$-round unbalanced quasi-Feistel ciphers with b branches against CPA and CCA attacks respectively.

In [29], Luo, et al. shown that 3-round Lai-Massey structure can resist the attacks of Simon's algorithm in quantum, which is different from Feistel structure. This leads to natural questions:

Do Lai-Massey structure and Feistel structure have the same number of rounds that can be attacked in quantum? Can the attacks be extended to quasi-Feistel structures?

Our Contributions. The contributions of this paper are listed as follows:

1. We show a quantum CPA distinguisher against 3-round Lai-Massey structure and a quantum CCA distinguisher against 4-round Lai-Massey structure with $O(n)$ quantum queries, where the input length of Lai-Massey structure is $2n$ bits. So Lai-Massey structure and Feistel structure have the same number of rounds that can be attacked efficiently in quantum, this makes it possible for quasi-Feistel structures to have similar security strength in quantum.
2. we give a quantum Grover-meet-Simon attack on 4-round Lai-Massey structure with $O(n2^{m/2})$ quantum queries, where m is the length of the key k_4 of the fourth round function f_4.
3. We extend the quantum attack on Lai-Massey structure to quasi-Feistel structure. We show that 3-rounds (4-round) balanced quasi-Feistel structure including Feistel structure and Lai-Massey structure with linear combiners can be attacked with $O(n)$ quantum queries in quantum CPA (CCA).

2 Preliminaries

2.1 Notation

Let $\mathcal{X}$ be a finite set. Let $\mathrm{Perm}(\mathcal{X})$ be the set of all permutations on $\mathcal{X}$. Let $x \xleftarrow{\$} \mathcal{X}$ denote selecting an element x from the set $\mathcal{X}$ uniformly and randomly. Let $\pi \xleftarrow{\$} \mathrm{Perm}(\mathcal{X})$ be a random permutation on $\mathcal{X}$. $\mathcal{X}^k$ denotes the set of all k-tuples of elements from $\mathcal{X}$. A block cipher keyed by K is a function $E_K \in \mathrm{Perm}(\mathcal{X})$. We call the input and output of E_K as plaintext and ciphertext respectively. Let $\mathrm{Func}(\mathcal{X}, \mathcal{Y})$ be the set of all functions $f : \mathcal{X} \to \mathcal{Y}$. We write $\mathrm{Func}(\mathcal{X}) \stackrel{\mathrm{def}}{=} \mathrm{Func}(\mathcal{X}, \mathcal{X})$.

Let $\mathcal{A}$ be an adversary. Let $\mathcal{A}^{f(\cdot)} \Rightarrow b$ (resp. $\mathcal{A}^{f(\odot)} \Rightarrow b$) denote an algorithm performs classical queries (resp. quantum queries) to oracle f and outputs b.

2.2 Pseudo-Random Permutation

In this paper, we consider the adversary $\mathcal{A}$ making **c**hosen-**p**laintext **a**ttack (CPA), i.e., $\mathcal{A}$ queries with plaintexts and get corresponding ciphertexts, or **c**hosen-**c**iphertext **a**ttack (CCA), i.e., $\mathcal{A}$ queries with plaintexts or ciphertexts and get corresponding ciphertexts or plaintexts. Let PRP-CPA and PRP-CPA denote the **p**seudo-**r**andom **p**ermutation (PRP) security under CPA and CCA respectively. Let qPRP-CPA and qPRP-CPA denote

the quantum PRP security under CPA and CCA respectively. We put the formal definitions as follows.

Definition 1 *(PRP-CPA/qPRP-CPA). Let $E : \mathcal{K} \times \mathcal{X} \to \mathcal{X}$ be a family of permutations indexed by the elements in $\mathcal{K}$, $g : \mathcal{X} \to \mathcal{X}$. Let $\mathcal{A}$ be a adversary. The PRP-CPA/qPRP-CPA advantage of $\mathcal{A}$ is defined as:*

$$\mathbf{Adv}_E^{prp\text{-}cpa/qprp\text{-}cpa}(\mathcal{A}) = \left| \Pr_{K \xleftarrow{\$} \mathcal{K}} \left[\mathcal{A}^{E_K(*)} \Rightarrow 1 \right] - \Pr_{g \xleftarrow{\$} \text{Perm}(\mathcal{X})} \left[\mathcal{A}^{g(*)} \Rightarrow 1 \right] \right|,$$

where we replace the $*$ symbol by $\cdot$ (classical) or $\odot$ (quantum).

Definition 2 *(PRP-CCA/qPRP-CCA). Let $E : \mathcal{K} \times \mathcal{X} \to \mathcal{X}$ be a family of permutations indexed by the elements in $\mathcal{K}$, $g : \mathcal{X} \to \mathcal{X}$. Let $\mathcal{A}$ be a adversary. The PRP-CCA/qPRP-CCA advantage of $\mathcal{A}$ is defined as:*

$$\mathbf{Adv}_E^{prp\text{-}cca/qprp\text{-}cca}(\mathcal{A}) = \left| \Pr_{K \xleftarrow{\$} \mathcal{K}} \left[\mathcal{A}^{E_K(*), E_K^{-1}(*)} \Rightarrow 1 \right] - \Pr_{g \xleftarrow{\$} \text{Perm}(\mathcal{X})} \left[\mathcal{A}^{g(*), g^{-1}(*)} \Rightarrow 1 \right] \right|,$$

where we replace the $*$ symbol by $\cdot$ (classical) or $\odot$ (quantum).

2.3   Quantum Algorithms

In this section, we present some quantum algorithms that will be applied in our attacks.

Simon's Algorithm.   Simon's algorithm is a quantum algorithm to recover the period of a periodic function with polynomial queries. It solves the Simon's problem.

Simon's problem [32]. Given a Boolean function $f : \{0,1\}^n \to \{0,1\}^m$, $x, y \in \{0,1\}^n$. x, y satisfied the condition $[f(x) = f(y)] \Leftrightarrow [x \oplus y \in \{0^n, s\}]$, s is non-zero and $s \in \{0,1\}^n$, the goal is to find s.

The steps of Simon's algorithm [32]:

1. Initialize the state of $2n$ qubits to $|0\rangle^{\otimes n}|0\rangle^{\otimes m}$;
2. Apply Hadamard transformation $H^{\otimes n}$ to the first n qubits to obtain quantum super-position $\frac{1}{\sqrt{2^n}} \sum_{x \in \{0,1\}^n} |x\rangle |0\rangle^{\otimes m}$;
3. A quantum query to the function f maps this to the state: $\frac{1}{\sqrt{2^n}} \sum_{x \in \{0,1\}^n} |x\rangle |f(x)\rangle$;
4. Measure the last m qubits to get the output z of $f(x)$, and the first n qubits collapse to $\frac{1}{\sqrt{2}}(|z\rangle + |z \oplus s\rangle)$;
5. Apply the Hadamard transform to the first n quantum again $H^{\otimes n}$, we can get $\frac{1}{\sqrt{2}} \frac{1}{\sqrt{2^n}} \sum_{y \in \{0,1\}^n} (-1)^{y \cdot z} (1 + (-1)^{y \cdot s}) |y\rangle$. If $y \cdot s = 1$ then the amplitude of $|y\rangle$ is 0. So measuring the state in the computational basis yields a random vector y such that $y \cdot s = 0$, which means that y must be orthogonal to s.

By repeating this step $O(n)$ times, $n - 1$ independent vectors y orthogonal to s can be obtained with high probability, then we can recover s with high probability by using linear algebra.

For $f : \{0,1\}^n \to \{0,1\}^n$ and $f(x \oplus s) = f(x)$, Kaplan [19] define:

$$\varepsilon(f, s) = \max_{t \in \{0,1\}^n \setminus \{0,s\}} \Pr_x[f(x) = f(x \oplus t)].$$

ε represents max probability of unwanted additional collisions that $f(x) = f(x \oplus t)$ where $t \notin \{0,1\}^n \setminus \{0,s\}$. The following theorem shows that Simon's algorithm can succeed even with additional collisions.

Theorem 1 [19]. *If $m = n$ and $\varepsilon(f, s) \leq p_0 < 1$, then Simon's algorithm returns s with cn queries, with probability at least $1 - \left(2 \left(\frac{1+p_0}{2}\right)^c\right)^n$.*

Guo et al. [14] shows Simon's conclusion holds for $m \neq n$ as well.

Grover's Algorithm. Grover's Algorithm can find a marked element from a set with an acceleration of the square root compared to classical computing. It solves the Grover's problem.

Grover's Problem. Given a Boolean function $f : \{0,1\}^n \to \{0,1\}$. Find a marked element x_0 from $\{0,1\}^n$ such that $f(x_0) = 1$.

The Steps of Grover's Algorithm [12]:

1. Initializing a n-bit register $|0\rangle^{\otimes n}$.
2. Apply Hadamard transformation $H^{\otimes n}$ to the first register to obtain quantum superposition $H^{\otimes n}|0\rangle = \frac{1}{\sqrt{2^n}} \sum_{x \in \{0,1\}^n} |x\rangle = |\varphi\rangle$.
3. Construct an Oracle $\mathcal{O} : |x\rangle \xrightarrow{\mathcal{O}} (-1)^{f(x)}|x\rangle$, if x is the correct state then $f(x) = 1$, otherwise $f(x) = 0$.
4. Apply Grover iteration for $R \approx \frac{\pi}{4}\sqrt{2^n}$ times: $[(2|\varphi\rangle\langle\varphi| - I)\mathcal{O}]^R|\varphi\rangle \approx |x_0\rangle$.
5. Return x_0.

Grover-Meet-Simon Algorithm. In 2017, Leander and May [24] combined Grover's algorithm with Simon's algorithm to attack FX construction [20]. Their main idea is to construct a function with two inputs based on FX, say $f(u, x)$. When the first input u equals to a special value k, the function has a hidden period s such that $f(k, x) = f(k, x \oplus s)$ for all x. Their combined algorithm use Grover's algorithm to search k, by running many independent Simon's algorithms to check whether the function is periodic or not, and recover both k and s in the end. The attack only costs $\mathcal{O}(2^{m/2}(m + n))$ quantum queries to FX, which is much less than the proved security up to $2^{\frac{m+n}{2}}$ queries [20], where m is the bit length of u, which is the key length of the underlying block cipher and n is the bit length of s, which is the block size.

3   Quantum Attacks on Lai-Massey Structures

3.1   Quantum Chosen-Plaintext Attack Against 3-Round Lai-Massey Structure

Figure 2 shows the 3-round Lai-Massey Structure, where f_1, f_2, f_3 are round functions and $\sigma(x_L, x_R) = (x_R, x_L \oplus x_R)$. We define $[a, b] \in \{0, 1\}^n$, where a, b represent the highest $n/2$ bits and the lowest $n/2$ bits respectively. Let $x_i, y_i \in \{0, 1\}^{n/2}, i = 1, 2, 3, 4$. The inputs of 3-round Lai-Massey structure can be written as $[x_1, x_2], [x_3, x_4]$, the outputs can be written as $[y_1, y_2], [y_3, y_4]$. a_i, b_i and $\Delta_i, i = 1, 2, 3$ are intermediate parameters as shown in Fig. 2.

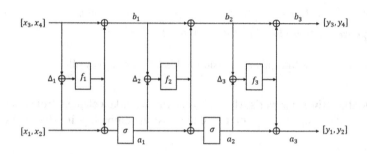

Fig. 2. 3-round Lai-Massey structure

Theorem 2. *If $f_i, i = 1, 2, 3$ are random functions, we can construct a quantum CPA distinguisher against 3-round Lai-Massey structure with $\sigma(x_L, x_R) = (x_R, x_L \oplus x_R)$ in $O(n)$ quantum queries by using Simon's algorithm.*

We first give some lemmas before proving Theorem 2. To attack 3-round Lai-Massey structure with Simon's algorithm, we will find a periodic function. Due to the complex structure of Lai-Massey, first we write the values of intermediate parameters.

For the 3-round Lai-Massey structure shown in the Fig. 2, the intermediate parameters are as follows

$a_1 = [x_2 \oplus f_{1R}(\Delta), x_1 \oplus x_2 \oplus f_{1L}(\Delta_1) \oplus f_{1R}(\Delta_1)],$

$b_1 = [x_3 \oplus f_{1L}(\Delta_1), x_4 \oplus f_{1R}(\Delta_1)],$

$a_2 = [x_1 \oplus x_2 \oplus f_{1L}(\Delta_1) \oplus f_{1R}(\Delta_1) \oplus f_{2R}(\Delta_2),$

$\quad\quad x_1 \oplus f_{1L}(\Delta_1) \oplus f_{2L}(\Delta_2) \oplus f_{2R}(\Delta_2)],$

$b_2 = [x_3 \oplus f_{1L}(\Delta_1) \oplus f_{2L}(\Delta_2), x_4 \oplus f_{1R}(\Delta_1) \oplus f_{2R}(\Delta_2)],$

$a_3 = [y_1, y_2]$

$\quad = [x_1 \oplus x_2 \oplus f_{1L}(\Delta_1) \oplus f_{1R}(\Delta_1) \oplus f_{2R}(\Delta_2) \oplus f_{3L}(\Delta_3),$

$\quad\quad x_1 \oplus f_{1L}(\Delta_1) \oplus f_{2L}(\Delta_2) \oplus f_{2R}(\Delta_2) \oplus f_{3R}(\Delta_3)]$

$b_3 = [y_3, y_4]$

$\quad = [x_3 \oplus f_{1L}(\Delta_1) \oplus f_{2L}(\Delta_2) \oplus f_{3L}(\Delta_3), x_4 \oplus f_{1R}(\Delta_1) \oplus f_{2R}(\Delta_2) \oplus f_{3R}(\Delta_3)],$

where

$$\Delta_1 = [x_1 \oplus x_3, x_2 \oplus x_4],$$
$$\Delta_2 = [x_2 \oplus x_3 \oplus f_{1L}(\Delta_1) \oplus f_{1R}(\Delta_1), x_1 \oplus x_2 \oplus x_4 \oplus f_{1L}(\Delta_1)],$$
$$\Delta_3 = [x_1 \oplus x_2 \oplus x_3 \oplus f_{1R}(\Delta_1) \oplus f_{2L}(\Delta_2) \oplus f_{2R}(\Delta_2),$$
$$x_1 \oplus x_4 \oplus f_{1L}(\Delta_1) \oplus f_{1R}(\Delta_1) \oplus f_{2L}(\Delta_2)].$$

Lemma 1. *Let* $x, x' \in \{0,1\}^{n/2}, b \in \{0,1\}$ *and* α_0, α_1 *be arbitrary two fixed different numbers in* $\{0,1\}^{n/2}$. *Let* $([x_1^{\alpha_b}, x_2^{\alpha_b}], [x_3^{\alpha_b}, x_4^{\alpha_b}]) \overset{def}{=} ([x \oplus \alpha_b, x'], [x, x' \oplus \alpha_b])$ *being the input of 3-round Lai-Massey structure with corresponding output* $([y_1^{\alpha_b}, y_2^{\alpha_b}], [y_3^{\alpha_b}, y_4^{\alpha_b}])$. *We can construct a periodic function* g_1 *from 3-round Lai-Massey structure with period* $s = f_1[\alpha_0, \alpha_0] \oplus f_1[\alpha_1, \alpha_1]$ *by letting*

$$g_1 : \{0,1\}^n \to \{0,1\}^{n/2}$$
$$[x, x'] \mapsto x_1^{\alpha_0} \oplus x_2^{\alpha_0} \oplus x_3^{\alpha_0} \oplus y_1^{\alpha_0} \oplus y_3^{\alpha_0} \oplus x_1^{\alpha_1} \oplus x_2^{\alpha_1} \oplus x_3^{\alpha_1} \oplus y_1^{\alpha_1} \oplus y_3^{\alpha_1}$$
$$g_1([x, x']) = f_{1R}[\alpha_0, \alpha_0] \oplus f_{2L}(\Delta_2^{\alpha_0}([x, x'])) \oplus f_{2R}(\Delta_2^{\alpha_0}([x, x']))$$
$$\oplus f_{1R}[\alpha_1, \alpha_1] \oplus f_{2L}(\Delta_2^{\alpha_1}([x, x'])) \oplus f_{2R}(\Delta_2^{\alpha_1}([x, x'])), \qquad (1)$$

where $\Delta_2^{\alpha_b}([x, x'])$ *denotes the value of intermediate parameter* Δ_2 *when the input of 3-round Lai-Massey structure is* $([x_1^{\alpha_b}, x_2^{\alpha_b}], [x_3^{\alpha_b}, x_4^{\alpha_b}])$ *and*

$$\Delta_2^{\alpha_b}([x, x']) = [x' \oplus x \oplus f_{1L}[\alpha_b, \alpha_b] \oplus f_{1R}[\alpha_b, \alpha_b], x \oplus f_{1L}[\alpha_b, \alpha_b]].$$

Proof. we show that g_1 is obviously a periodic function.

(a) $\Delta_2^{\alpha_b}([x, x']) = \Delta_2^{\alpha_b \oplus 1}([x, x'] \oplus s)$ holds for all $x, x' \in \{0,1\}^{n/2}$.
(b) $g_1([x, x'])$ has a period s deriving from (a). $\qquad \square$

Proof (Proof of Theorem 2). Now we have a periodic function g_1 with period $s = f_1[\alpha_0, \alpha_0] \oplus f_1[\alpha_1, \alpha_1]$. Actually, other t's $(t \neq s)$ may occur due to collisions, which may lead to misjudgments. Theorem 1 guarantees that Simon's algorithm can still succeed with probability $1 - \left(2\left(\frac{3}{4}\right)^c\right)^n$ if $\varepsilon(f, s) \leq p_0 < 1$. For 3-round Lai-Massey structure, the following certificate $\varepsilon(g_1, s) < \frac{1}{2}$:

Assuming $\varepsilon(g_1, s) \geq \frac{1}{2}$, then there is at least one $t \notin \{0, s\}$ such that $\Pr[g_1([x, x']) = g_1([x, x'] \oplus t)] \geq 1/2$. We denote f_{2L} or f_{2R} as f_{2*}. From Eq. (1) we have $\Pr\{f_{2*}[x' \oplus x \oplus u', x \oplus v'] = f_{2*}[x' \oplus t_R \oplus x \oplus t_L \oplus u', x \oplus t_L \oplus v']\} \geq \frac{1}{2}$, where u', v' are some parameters. That is, if $\varepsilon(g_1, s) \geq \frac{1}{2}$, then the probability that the permutation $f_{2*}[x' \oplus x \oplus u, x \oplus v]$ has a collision is greater than $\frac{1}{2}$. For different m_1, m_2, $\Pr\{f_{2*}[m_1' \oplus m_1 \oplus u, m_1 \oplus v] = f_{2*}[m_2' \oplus m_2 \oplus u, m_2 \oplus v]\} = \frac{1}{2^n}$, which is contradictory. Therefore $\varepsilon(g_1, s) < \frac{1}{2}$.

let $\mathcal{A}$ be an adversary, we write 3-round Lai-Massey structure as 3LM. For 3-round Lai-Massey structure, we can construct a period function g_1 with period s, and $g_1([x, x']) = g_1([x, x'] \oplus s)$. In the first query we ask x, and then we ask $x \oplus s$. If $\mathcal{A}$ is asking about 3-round Lai-Massey structure, then the outputs are the same. If $\mathcal{A}$ is asking about random permutation, then the outputs are different. So $\mathbf{Adv}_{3LM}^{qprp-cpa}(\mathcal{A}) = 1 - \left(2\left(\frac{3}{4}\right)^c\right)^n - \frac{1}{2^{n/2}}$. If we choose $c \geq 3/(1-p_0)$, the error decreases exponentially with n. So if $c \geq 6$, $\mathbf{Adv}_{3LM}^{qprp-cpa}(\mathcal{A}) = 1 - \frac{1}{2^{n/2}}$.

$\qquad \square$

3.2   Quantum Chosen-Ciphertext Attack Against 4 Round Lai-Massey Structure

For 4-round Lai-Massey Structure, let f_1, f_2, f_3, f_4 be round functions and $\sigma(x_L, x_R) = (x_R, x_L \oplus x_R)$. Let $x_i, y_i, n_i, z_i, x'_i \in \{0,1\}^{n/2}$, $i = 1, 2, 3, 4$. To attack 4-round Lai-Massey Structure in CCA model, our attack strategy is as follows.

- Query the 4-round Lai- Massey structure with inputs $([x_1, x_2], [x_3, x_4])$s and get corresponding outputs $([y_1, y_2], [y_3, y_4])$s;
- Xor $([y_1, y_2], [y_3, y_4])$s with $([n_1, n_2], [n_3, n_4])$ and get $([z_3, z_4], [z_1, z_2])$;
- Query the inverse of 4-round Lai- Massey structure with inputs $([z_1, z_2], [z_3, z_4])$s and get corresponding outputs $([x'_1, x'_2], [x'_3, x'_4])$s;
- Construct a periodic function g_2 based on x'_1, x'_2, x'_3, x'_4s.
- Apply the periodicity of g_2 to distinguish 4-round Lai-Massey structure from a random permutation.

Let a_i, b_i, a'_i, b'_i and $\Delta_i, \Delta'_i, i = 1, 2, 3, 4$ be intermediate parameters as shown in Fig. 3. In the following, we show the formulation.

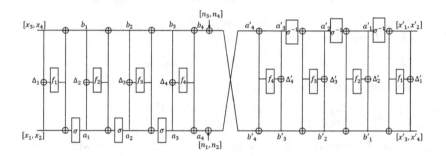

Fig. 3. The encryption and decryption process of 4-round Lai-Massey structure

Theorem 3. *If $f_i, i = 1, 2, 3, 4$ are random functions, we can construct a quantum CCA distinguisher against 4-round Lai-Massey Structure with $\sigma(x_L, x_R) = (x_R, x_L \oplus x_R)$ in $O(n)$ quantum queries by using Simon's algorithm.*

We first give a lemma before proving Theorem 3. To show a quantum CCA distinguisher against 4-round Lai-Massey Structure with Simon's algorithm, we will find a periodic function based the function showed in Fig. 3.

Intermediate parameters $a_i, b_i, \Delta_j, i = 1, 2; j = 1, 2, 3$ are the same as Sect. 3.1. Intermediate parameters $a_3, b_3, a_4, b_4, \Delta_4$ are shown as follows. Other intermediate parameters $a'_i, b'_i, \Delta'_i, i = 1, 2, 3, 4$ with respect to $[z_1, z_2], [z_3, z_4]$ are showed in in Appendix A.

$$a_3 = [x_1 \oplus f_{1L}(\Delta_1) \oplus f_{2L}(\Delta_2) \oplus f_{2R}(\Delta_2) \oplus f_{3R}(\Delta_3),$$
$$x_2 \oplus f_{1R}(\Delta_1) \oplus f_{2L}(\Delta_2) \oplus f_{3L}(\Delta_3) \oplus f_{3R}(\Delta_3)],$$
$$b_3 = [x_3 \oplus f_{1L}(\Delta_1) \oplus f_{2L}(\Delta_2) \oplus f_{3L}(\Delta_3), x_4 \oplus f_{1R}(\Delta_1) \oplus f_{2R}(\Delta_2) \oplus f_{3R}(\Delta_3)],$$

$$a_4 = [y_1, y_2]$$
$$= [x_1 \oplus f_{1L}(\Delta_1) \oplus f_{2L}(\Delta_2) \oplus f_{2R}(\Delta_2) \oplus f_{3R}(\Delta_3) \oplus f_{4L}(\Delta_4),$$
$$x_2 \oplus f_{1R}(\Delta_1) \oplus f_{2L}(\Delta_2) \oplus f_{3R}(\Delta_3) \oplus f_{3L}(\Delta_3) \oplus f_{4R}(\Delta_4)],$$
$$b_4 = [y_3, y_4]$$
$$= [x_3 \oplus f_{1L}(\Delta_1) \oplus f_{2L}(\Delta_2) \oplus f_{3L}(\Delta_3) \oplus f_{4L}(\Delta_4),$$
$$x_4 \oplus f_{1R}(\Delta_1) \oplus f_{2R}(\Delta_2) \oplus f_{3R}(\Delta_3) \oplus f_{4R}(\Delta_4)].$$

where

$$\Delta_4 = [x_1 \oplus x_3 \oplus f_{2R}(\Delta_2) \oplus f_{3L}(\Delta_3) \oplus f_{3R}(\Delta_3),$$
$$x_2 \oplus x_4 \oplus f_{2L}(\Delta_2) \oplus f_{2R}(\Delta_2) \oplus f_{3L}(\Delta_3)].$$

Let $n_1 \oplus n_3 = 0, n_2 \oplus n_4 = 0$. After the whole process of 4-round Lai-Massey structure shown in the Fig. 3, the outputs $[x_1', x_2'], [x_3', x_4']$ can be expressed with $[x_1, x_2], [x_3, x_4]$:

$$x_1' = x_1 \oplus n_1 \oplus f_{1L}(\Delta_1) \oplus f_{2L}(\Delta_2) \oplus f_{2R}(\Delta_2) \oplus f_{3R}(\Delta_3)$$
$$\oplus f_{1L}(\Delta_1') \oplus f_{2L}(\Delta_2') \oplus f_{2R}(\Delta_2') \oplus f_{3R}(\Delta_3'),$$
$$x_2' = x_2 \oplus n_2 \oplus f_{1R}(\Delta_1) \oplus f_{2L}(\Delta_2) \oplus f_{3R}(\Delta_3) \oplus f_{3L}(\Delta_3)$$
$$\oplus f_{1R}(\Delta_1') \oplus f_{2L}(\Delta_2') \oplus f_{3R}(\Delta_3') \oplus f_{3L}(\Delta_3'),$$
$$x_3' = x_3 \oplus n_3 \oplus f_{1L}(\Delta_1) \oplus f_{2L}(\Delta_2) \oplus f_{3L}(\Delta_3) \oplus f_{1L}(\Delta_1') \oplus f_{2L}(\Delta_2') \oplus f_{3L}(\Delta_3'),$$
$$x_4' = x_4 \oplus n_4 \oplus f_{1R}(\Delta_1) \oplus f_{2R}(\Delta_2) \oplus f_{3R}(\Delta_3) \oplus f_{1R}(\Delta_1') \oplus f_{2R}(\Delta_2') \oplus f_{3R}(\Delta_3'),$$

where

$$\Delta_3' = \Delta_3 \oplus [n_2, n_1 \oplus n_4],$$
$$\Delta_2' = \Delta_2 \oplus [f_{3R}(\Delta_3) \oplus f_{3R}(\Delta_3') \oplus n_2 \oplus n_3,$$
$$f_{3L}(\Delta_3) \oplus f_{3R}(\Delta_3) \oplus f_{3L}(\Delta_3') \oplus f_{3R}(\Delta_3') \oplus n_1],$$
$$\Delta_1' = \Delta_1 \oplus [f_{2R}(\Delta_2) \oplus f_{3R}(\Delta_3) \oplus f_{3L}(\Delta_3) \oplus f_{2R}(\Delta_2') \oplus f_{3L}(\Delta_3') \oplus f_{3R}(\Delta_3'),$$
$$f_{2R}(\Delta_2) \oplus f_{2L}(\Delta_2) \oplus f_{3L}(\Delta_3) \oplus f_{2L}(\Delta_2') \oplus f_{2R}(\Delta_2') \oplus f_{3L}(\Delta_3')].$$

Lemma 2. *Let $x, x' \in \{0,1\}^{n/2}, b \in \{0,1\}$ and α_0, α_1 be arbitrary two fixed different numbers in $\{0,1\}^{n/2}$. Let $([x_1^{\alpha_b}, x_2^{\alpha_b}], [x_3^{\alpha_b}, x_4^{\alpha_b}]) \stackrel{def}{=} ([x \oplus \alpha_b, x'], [x, x' \oplus \alpha_b])$ being the input of the function in Fig. 3 based on 4-round Lai-Massey structure and its inverse with corresponding output $([x_1'^{\alpha_b}, x_2'^{\alpha_b}], [x_3'^{\alpha_b}, x_4'^{\alpha_b}])$ when $n_1 = n_2 = n_3 = n_4 = \alpha_0 \oplus \alpha_1$. We an construct a periodic function g_2 from 4-round Lai-Massey structure with period $s = f_1[\alpha_0, \alpha_0] \oplus f_1[\alpha_1, \alpha_1]$ by letting*

$$g_2 : \{0,1\}^n \rightarrow \{0,1\}^{n/2}$$
$$[x, x'] \mapsto x_1'^{\alpha_0} \oplus x_3'^{\alpha_0} \oplus x_1'^{\alpha_1} \oplus x_3'^{\alpha_1}$$
$$g_2([x, x']) = f_{2R}(\Delta_2'^{\alpha_0}([x,x'])) \oplus f_{2R}(\Delta_2'^{\alpha_0}([x,x'])) \oplus f_{2R}(\Delta_2'^{\alpha_1}([x,x']))$$
$$\oplus f_{2R}(\Delta_2'^{\alpha_1}([x,x'])) \oplus f_{3R}(\Delta_3'^{\alpha_0}([x,x'])) \oplus f_{3R}(\Delta_3'^{\alpha_0}([x,x']))$$
$$\oplus f_{3R}(\Delta_3'^{\alpha_1}([x,x'])) \oplus f_{3R}(\Delta_3'^{\alpha_1}([x,x'])) \oplus f_{3L}(\Delta_3'^{\alpha_0}([x,x']))$$
$$\oplus f_{3L}(\Delta_3'^{\alpha_0}([x,x'])) \oplus f_{3L}(\Delta_3'^{\alpha_1}([x,x'])) \oplus f_{3L}(\Delta_3'^{\alpha_1}([x,x']))$$
$$\oplus \alpha_0 \oplus \alpha_1,$$

where $\Delta_2^{\alpha_b}([x,x'])$, $\Delta_2'^{\alpha_b}([x,x'])$, $\Delta_3^{\alpha_b}([x,x'])$, and $\Delta_3'^{\alpha_b}([x,x'])$ denote the values of intermediate parameters Δ_2, Δ_2', Δ_3, and Δ_3' respectively when the input of the function in Fig. 3 is $([x_1^{\alpha_b}, x_2^{\alpha_b}], [x_3^{\alpha_b}, x_4^{\alpha_b}])$.

Proof. For $i = 2, 3$, we let

$$h_i([x, x'])$$
$$\overset{\text{def}}{=} f_i\left(\Delta_i^{\alpha_0}([x, x'])\right) \oplus f_i\left(\Delta_i'^{\alpha_0}([x, x'])\right) \oplus f_i\left(\Delta_i^{\alpha_1}([x, x'])\right) \oplus f_i\left(\Delta_i'^{\alpha_1}([x, x'])\right).$$

Then we will clearly show that g_2 is a periodic function step by step.

(a) $\Delta_2^{\alpha_b}([x, x']) = \Delta_2^{\alpha_b \oplus 1}([x, x'] \oplus s)$ holds for all $x, x' \in \{0, 1\}^{n/2}$ the same as Lemma 1.

(b) $\Delta_3^{\alpha_b}([x, x']) = \Delta_3'^{\alpha_b \oplus 1}([x, x'] \oplus s)$ holds for all $x, x' \in \{0, 1\}^{n/2}$. We have

$$\Delta_3^{\alpha_b}([x, x']) = [x' \oplus \alpha_b \oplus f_{1R}[\alpha_b, \alpha_b] \oplus f_{2L}(\Delta_2^{\alpha_b}([x, x'])) \oplus f_{2R}(\Delta_2^{\alpha_b}([x, x'])),$$
$$x \oplus x' \oplus f_{1L}[\alpha_b, \alpha_b] \oplus f_{1R}[\alpha_b, \alpha_b] \oplus f_{2L}(\Delta_2^{\alpha_b}([x, x']))],$$
$$\Delta_3'^{\alpha_b}([x, x']) = \Delta_3^{\alpha_b}([x, x']) \oplus [\alpha_0 \oplus \alpha_1, 0].$$

Thus we get $\Delta_3^{\alpha_b}([x, x']) = \Delta_3'^{\alpha_b \oplus 1}([x, x'] \oplus s)$ deriving from (a).

(c) $h_3([x, x'])$ has a period s deriving from (b).

(d) $\Delta_2'^{\alpha_b}([x, x']) = \Delta_2'^{\alpha_b \oplus 1}([x, x'] \oplus s)$ holds for all $x, x' \in \{0, 1\}^{n/2}$. We have

$$\Delta_2'^{\alpha_b}([x, x']) = \Delta_2^{\alpha_b}([x, x']) \oplus [f_{3R}\left(\Delta_3^{\alpha_b}([x, x'])\right) \oplus f_{3R}\left(\Delta_3'^{\alpha_b}([x, x'])\right),$$
$$f_{3L}\left(\Delta_3^{\alpha_b}([x, x'])\right) \oplus f_{3L}\left(\Delta_3'^{\alpha_b}([x, x'])\right) \oplus f_{3R}\left(\Delta_3^{\alpha_b}([x, x'])\right)$$
$$\oplus f_{3R}\left(\Delta_3'^{\alpha_b}([x, x'])\right) \oplus \alpha_0 \oplus \alpha_1].$$

Thus $\Delta_2'^{\alpha_b}([x, x']) = \Delta_2'^{\alpha_b \oplus 1}([x, x'] \oplus s)$ deriving from (a) and (b).

(e) $h_2([x, x'])$ has a period s deriving from (d).

(f) $g_2([x, x'])$ has a period s. We have

$$g_2([x, x']) = h_{2R}([x, x']) \oplus h_{3R}([x, x']) \oplus h_{3L}([x, x']) \oplus \alpha_0 \oplus \alpha_1.$$

Thus we get $g_2([x, x'])$ has a period s deriving from (c) and (e).   □

Proof (Proof of Theorem 3). When the period is not unique, that is, Simon's algorithm satisfies the approximate commitment, there is $\varepsilon(g_2, s) < \frac{1}{2}$, the probability of getting the correct s is at least $1 - \left(2\left(\frac{3}{4}\right)^c\right)^n$.

Let $\mathcal{A}$ be an Adversary, we write 4-round Lai-Massey structure as 4LM. Similar to the proof of Theorem 2, We have $\mathbf{Adv}_{4LM}^{\text{qprp-cpa}}(\mathcal{A}) = 1 - \left(2\left(\frac{3}{4}\right)^c\right)^n - \frac{1}{2^{n/2}}$. If we choose $c \geq 6$, $\mathbf{Adv}_{4LM}^{\text{qprp-cpa}}(\mathcal{A}) = 1 - \frac{1}{2^{n/2}}$.

□

3.3 Quantum Key-Recovery Attack on 4-Round Lai-Massey Structure

Figure 4 shows the 4-round Lai-Massey Structure, where f_1, f_2, f_3, f_4 are round functions and $\sigma(x_L, x_R) = (x_R, x_L \oplus x_R)$. a_i, b_i and $\Delta_i, i = 1, 2, 3, 4$ are intermediate parameters as shown in Fig. 4. Let $x_i, y_i, z_i \in \{0, 1\}^{n/2}, i = 1, 2, 3, 4$. Let the inputs of 4-round Lai-Massey Structure be $[x_1, x_2], [x_3, x_4]$, the outputs be $[z_1, z_2], [z_3, z_4]$, and the immediate parameters after 3-round Lai-Massey be $[y_1, y_2], [y_3, y_4]$.

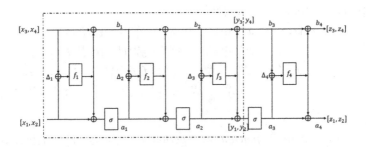

Fig. 4. 4-round Lai-Massey structure

To recover the partial key of 4-round Lai-Massey structure in CPA model, our strategy is as follows.

- Query the 4-round Lai- Massey structure with inputs $([x_1, x_2], [x_3, x_4])$s and get corresponding outputs $([z_1, z_2], [z_3, z_4])$s;
- Guess the key k_4 of f_4 as k;
- Given the value of the outputs $([z_1, z_2], [z_3, z_4])$s of 4-round Lai- Massey structure and key k, compute the value of immediate parameters after 3-round Lai-Massey $([y_1, y_2], [y_3, y_4])$s as $([y_1(k), y_2(k)], [y_3(k), y_4(k)])$s through the reverse of the last round Lai-Massey;
- Construct function $g_3(k, \cdot)$ based on $x_1, x_2, x_3, x_4, y_1(k), y_2(k), y_3(k), y_4(k)$s the same as $g1$ in Lemma 1 when attacking 3-round Lai-Massey.
- If $g_3(k, \cdot)$ is a periodic function, then k is the correct key k_4 of f_4; Or it doesn't hold by the randomness of f_4.

Thus we can recover key k_4 and $g_3(k_4, \cdot)$ is a periodic function. However, when replacing above 4-round Lai- Massey structure with random permutation, g_3 isn't a periodic any more. So we can distinguish 4-round Lai-Massey Structure from a random permutation. In the following, we show the formulation.

Theorem 4. *If $f_i, i = 1, 2, 3, 4$ are random functions, the length of the key k_4 of f_4 is m bits. We can give a quantum Grover-meet-Simon attack on 4-round Lai- Massey structure with $\sigma(x_L, x_R) = (x_R, x_L \oplus x_R)$ with $O(n2^{m/2})$ quantum queries in quantum CPA.*

We first give a lemma before proving Theorem 4.

Lemma 3. *If $f_i, i = 1, 2, 3, 4$ are random functions, the length of the key k_4 of f_4 is m bits. Let $x, x' \in \{0,1\}^{n/2}, b \in \{0,1\}$ and α_0, α_1 be arbitrary two fixed different numbers in $\{0,1\}^{n/2}$. Let $([x_1^{\alpha_b}, x_2^{\alpha_b}], [x_3^{\alpha_b}, x_4^{\alpha_b}]) \stackrel{def}{=} ([x \oplus \alpha_b, x'], [x, x' \oplus \alpha_b])$ being the input of 4-round Lai-Massey structure with corresponding output $([z_1^{\alpha_b}, z_2^{\alpha_b}], [z_3^{\alpha_b}, z_4^{\alpha_b}])$. And let $([y_1^{\alpha_b}(k), y_2^{\alpha_b}(k)], [y_3^{\alpha_b}(k), y_4^{\alpha_b}(k)])$ be the immediate parameters when reverse the last round of 4-round Lai-Massey with a guessed key k of f_4. We construct a function g_3 from 4-round Lai-Massey structure by letting*

$$g_3 : \{0,1\}^m \times \{0,1\}^n \to \{0,1\}^{n/2}$$
$$k, [x, x'] \mapsto x_1^{\alpha_0} \oplus x_2^{\alpha_0} \oplus x_3^{\alpha_0} \oplus y_1^{\alpha_0}(k) \oplus y_3^{\alpha_0}(k) \oplus$$
$$x_1^{\alpha_1} \oplus x_2^{\alpha_1} \oplus x_3^{\alpha_1} \oplus y_1^{\alpha_1}(k) \oplus y_3^{\alpha_1}(k)$$
$$g_3(k, [x, x']) = z_1^{\alpha_0} \oplus z_2^{\alpha_0} \oplus z_3^{\alpha_0} \oplus f_{4R}([z_1^{\alpha_0} \oplus z_3^{\alpha_0}, z_2^{\alpha_0} \oplus z_4^{\alpha_0}])$$
$$\oplus z_1^{\alpha_1} \oplus z_2^{\alpha_1} \oplus z_3^{\alpha_1} \oplus f_{4R}([z_1^{\alpha_1} \oplus z_3^{\alpha_1}, z_2^{\alpha_1} \oplus z_4^{\alpha_1}])$$
$$\oplus \alpha_0 \oplus \alpha_1.$$

Then $g_3(k_4, \cdot)$ is a periodic function with period $s = f_1[\alpha_0, \alpha_0] \oplus f_1[\alpha_1, \alpha_1]$ in its second component.

It is obviously that $g_3(k_4, [x, x']) = g_1([x, x'])$. By Lemma 1 we get the Lemma 3.

Proof (Proof of Theorem 4). Given quantum oracle to g_3 , k_4 and $f_1[\alpha_0, \alpha_0] \oplus f_1[\alpha_1, \alpha_1]$ could be computed with $O(n^2)$ qubits and about $2^{n/2}$ quantum queries. The details are provided in Appendix B. And Theorem 4 is proved.

$\square$

4   Lai-Massey and Quasi-Feistel Structures

4.1   Quasi-Feistel Structure

Aaram Yun et al. [40] proposed the notion of quasi-Feistel structure, which is an extension of Feistel structure and Lai-Massey structure. Combiner is an important notion in quasi-Feistel structure, we briefly recall the definitions.

Definition 3 [40] *(Combiner). A function $\Gamma : \mathcal{X} \times \mathcal{X} \times \mathcal{Y} \to \mathcal{X}$ is a combiner over $(\mathcal{X}, \mathcal{Y})$, if for $y \in \mathcal{X}, z \in \mathcal{Y}, x \mapsto \Gamma(x, y, z)$ is a permutation, and for $x \in \mathcal{X}, z \in \mathcal{Y}, y \mapsto \Gamma(x, y, z)$ is a permutation. We denote $\Gamma[[x \star y \mid z]] \stackrel{def}{=} \Gamma(x, y, z)$.*

Definition 4 [40] *(b-branched, r-round quasi-Feistel structure). Let $b > 1$ and $r \geq 1$ be fixed integers, and fix a b-combiner Γ over $\mathcal{X}$. Suppose that $P, Q : \mathcal{X}^b \to \mathcal{X}^b$ are permutations. Given r functions $f_1, ..., f_r : \mathcal{X}^{b-1} \to \mathcal{X}$, we define a function $\Psi = \Psi_{P,Q}^{b,r}(f_1, ..., f_r) : \mathcal{X}^b \to \mathcal{X}^b$ as follows; for $x = (x_1, x_2, ..., x_b) \in \mathcal{X}^b$, we compute $y = \Psi(x)$ by*

1. $(z_0, z_1, \ldots, z_{b-1}) \leftarrow P(x)$,
2. $z_{i+b-1} \leftarrow \Gamma[[z_{i-1} \star f_i(z_i \cdots z_{i+b-2}) \mid z_i \cdots z_{i+b-2}]]$ *for $i = 1, \ldots, r$.*
3. $y \leftarrow Q^{-1}(z_r, z_{r+1}, \ldots, z_{r+b-1})$.

Then Ψ is a permutation. For integer $b > 1$, we call Ψ a b-branched, r-round quasi-Feistel permutation for $f_1, ..., f_r$ with respect to (P, Q, Γ). If $\Psi^{b,r}$: Func $(\mathcal{X}^{b-1}, \mathcal{X})^r \rightarrow$ Perm $(\mathcal{X}^b)$. We call Ψ a b-branched, r-round quasi-Feistel structure for $f_1, ..., f_r$ with respect to (P, Q, Γ).

Note 1. Quasi-Feistel structure is *balanced* when $b = 2$, and *unbalanced* when $b > 2$. In our subsequent discussion, Feistel and Lai-Massey structures are both under the condition of $b = 2$.

Aaram Yun et al. [40] showed that Feistel and Lai-Massey structures are quasi-Feistel structures with different combiners when $b = 2$. The Lai-Massey structure version they used is given by Vaudenay [35].

Lemma 4 [40] *(Unbalanced). Feistel structure is a special case of the quasi-Feistel structure, and the combiner is $\Gamma[[x \star y \mid z]] = x \oplus y$.*

Lemma 5 [40]. *Lai-Massey structure is an instance of the quasi-Feistel structure. Let G be a finite abelian group, $\sigma : G \rightarrow G$. The underlying set $\mathcal{X}$ is the group G. $\tau(x) = \sigma(x) - x$. The combiner is $\Gamma[[x \star y \mid z]] = z + \tau(z - x + y + \tau^{-1}(z - x))$.*

4.2 Lai-Massey and Quasi-Feistel Structures

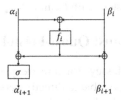

Fig. 5. The ith-round of Lai-Massey structure

First we write the combiner of Lai-Massey structure with $\sigma(x_L, x_R) = (x_R, x_L \oplus x_R)$. Note that our notation is slightly different from the above in order to match the definition of quasi-Feistel (Fig. 5).

Theorem 5. *The r-round Lai-Massey structure with $\sigma(x_L, x_R) = (x_R, x_L \oplus x_R)$ can be written as:*

$$\alpha_1 \leftarrow [x_1, x_2], \beta_1 \leftarrow [x_3, x_4].$$
$$\alpha_{i+1} \leftarrow [\alpha_{iR} \oplus f_{iR}(\alpha_i \oplus \beta_i), \alpha_{iL} \oplus \alpha_{iR} \oplus f_{iL}(\alpha_i \oplus \beta_i) \oplus f_{iR}(\alpha_i \oplus \beta_i)],$$
$$\beta_{i+1} \leftarrow [\beta_{iL} \oplus f_{iL}(\alpha_i \oplus \beta_i), \beta_{iR} \oplus f_{iR}(\alpha_i \oplus \beta_i)], i = 1...r,$$
$$y_L \leftarrow \alpha_{r+1}, y_R \leftarrow \beta_{r+1},$$
Return $y = (y_L, y_R)$.

The combiner of Lai-Massey structure is $\Gamma[[x \star y \mid z]] = \sigma(x) \oplus \sigma^{-1}(y) \oplus \sigma^{-1}(z)$.

Proof. Let $x = \alpha_{i-1} \oplus \beta_{i-1}, y = f_i(\alpha_i \oplus \beta_i), z_i = \alpha_i \oplus \beta_i, z_{i+1} = \alpha_{i+1} \oplus \beta_{i+1}$. Then

$$\alpha_{i+1} \oplus \beta_{i+1} = [\alpha_{iR} \oplus \beta_{iL} \oplus f_{iL}(\alpha_i \oplus \beta_i) \oplus f_{iR}(\alpha_i \oplus \beta_i), \alpha_{iL} \oplus \alpha_{iR} \oplus \beta_{iR} \oplus f_{iL}(\alpha_i \oplus \beta_i)].$$

Similarly, we can get $\alpha_i \oplus \beta_i$, which means that

$$z_{i+1} = [x_L \oplus \alpha_{i-1R} \oplus f_{i-1R}(\alpha_{i-1} \oplus \beta_{i-1}) \oplus y_L \oplus y_R,$$
$$\alpha_{i-1L} \oplus \beta_{i-1R} \oplus f_{i-1L}(\alpha_{i-1} \oplus \beta_{i-1}) \oplus f_{i-1R}(\alpha_{i-1} \oplus \beta_{i-1}) \oplus y_L]$$
$$= [z_{iL} \oplus z_{iR} \oplus x_R \oplus y_L \oplus y_R, z_{iL} \oplus x_L \oplus x_R \oplus y_L].$$

Hence, we may define the combiner by

$$\Gamma[[x \star y \mid z]] = [z_L \oplus z_R \oplus x_R \oplus y_L \oplus y_R, z_L \oplus x_L \oplus x_R \oplus y_L] = \sigma(x) \oplus \sigma^{-1}(y) \oplus \sigma^{-1}(z).$$

We can see that $x \mapsto \Gamma[[x \star y \mid z]]$ and $y \mapsto \Gamma[[x \star y \mid z]]$ are permutations. We give the following equivalent description of Lai-Massey structure: given the input $x = (\alpha_1, \beta_1)$.

Let $H(x, y) = (\sigma^{-1}(x) \oplus y, x \oplus y)$ and we can compute $(z_0, z_1) = H(\alpha_1, \beta_1)$. We calculate $z_2, ..., z_{r+1}$ by

$$z_{i+1} = \sigma(z_{i-1}) \oplus \sigma^{-1}(f_i(z_i)) \oplus \sigma^{-1}(z_i) = \Gamma[[z_{i-1} \star f_i(z_i) \mid z_i]].$$

We compute the output $(\alpha_{r+1}, \beta_{r+1})$ by $(\alpha_{r+1}, \beta_{r+1}) = H^{-1}(z_r, z_{r+1})$.   □

The result of Theorem 5 is consistent with Lemma 5.

5   Quantum Attacks Against Quasi-Feistel Structures

Since Feistel structure and Lai-Massey structure are quasi-Feistel structures, a problem of much interest is whether it is possible to directly perform quantum attacks on quasi-Feistel structures. Here we consider $b = 2$. The ith-round of quasi-Feistel structure is shown in Fig. 6.

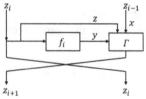   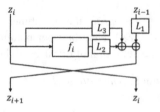

Fig. 6. ith-round of quasi-Feistel structure with $b = 2$.

Fig. 7. ith-round of quasi-Feistel structure with linear combiner and $b = 2$.

We only consider the case where the combiner Γ of quasi-Feistel structure is linear. Let A be a matrix of linear transformation. Then we write

$$\Gamma(x, y, z) = A \cdot \begin{bmatrix} x \\ y \\ z \end{bmatrix} = [A_1 \ A_2 \ A_3] \cdot \begin{bmatrix} x \\ y \\ z \end{bmatrix} \stackrel{\text{def}}{=} L_1(x) \oplus L_2(y) \oplus L_3(z),$$

According to Definition 3, L_1, L_2 are reversible. The ith-round of quasi-Feistel structure with linear combiner and $b = 2$ is shown in Fig. 7.

5.1 Quantum Chosen-Plaintext Attack Against 3-Round Quasi-Feistel Structure

Figure 8 shows the 3-round quasi-Feistel Structure with linear combiner and $b = 2$, where f_1, f_2, f_3 are round functions. For $b = 2$, the inputs are z_0, z_1 and the outputs are z_3, z_4 as we shown in Definition 4.

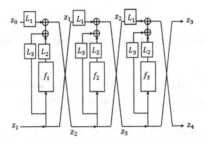

Fig. 8. 3-round quasi-Feistel structure with linear combiner and $b = 2$

Theorem 6. *If $f_i, i = 1, 2, 3$ are random functions, we can construct a quantum CPA distinguisher against 3-round balanced quasi-Feistel Structure in $O(n)$ queries by using Simon's algorithm.*

Proof. For inputs z_0, z_1, $z_i = L_1(z_{i-2}) \oplus L_2(f_{i-1}(z_{i-1})) \oplus L_3(z_{i-1}), i = 2, 3, 4$. let $z_0 = x, z_1 = \alpha_b$. We have

$$z_2^{\alpha_b}(x) = L_1(x) \oplus L_2(f_1(\alpha_b)) \oplus L_3(\alpha_b) = L_1[x \oplus L_1^{-1}L_2(f_1(\alpha_b)) \oplus L_1^{-1}L_3(\alpha_b)],$$

Then $z_3^{\alpha_b}(x) = L_1(\alpha_b) \oplus L_2(f_2(z_2^{\alpha_b})) \oplus L_3(z_2^{\alpha_b})$.

Lemma 6. *Let $x \in \{0,1\}^n, b \in \{0,1\}$ and α_0, α_1 be arbitrary two fixed different numbers in $\{0,1\}^n$. Let $(z_0^{\alpha_b}, z_1^{\alpha_b}) \stackrel{def}{=} (x, \alpha_b)$ being the input of 3-round balanced quasi-Feistel structure with corresponding output $(z_3^{\alpha_b}, z_4^{\alpha_b})$. We can construct a periodic function g_4 from 3-round balanced quasi-Feistel structure with period $s = L_1^{-1}L_2(f_1(\alpha_0)) \oplus L_1^{-1}L_2(f_1(\alpha_1)) \oplus L_1^{-1}L_3(\alpha_0) \oplus L_1^{-1}L_3(\alpha_1)$ by letting*

$$g_4 : \{0,1\}^n \to \{0,1\}^n$$
$$x \mapsto z_3^{\alpha_0}(x) \oplus z_3^{\alpha_1}(x)$$
$$g_4(x) = L_1(\alpha_0) \oplus L_2(f_2(z_2^{\alpha_0}(x))) \oplus L_3(z_2^{\alpha_0}(x))$$
$$\oplus L_1(\alpha_1) \oplus L_2(f_2(z_2^{\alpha_1}(x))) \oplus L_3(z_2^{\alpha_1}(x)),$$

where $z_2^{\alpha_b}(x)$ denotes the value of z_2 when the input of 3-round balanced quasi-Feistel structure is $(z_0^{\alpha_b}, z_1^{\alpha_b})$.

Proof. we show that g_4 is obviously a periodic function.

(a) $z_2^{\alpha_b}(x) = z_2^{\alpha_b \oplus 1}(x \oplus s)$ holds for all $x \in \{0,1\}^n$.

(b) $g_4(x)$ has a period s deriving from (a).   □

When the period is not unique, that is, Simon's algorithm satisfies the approximate commitment, there is $\varepsilon(g_4, s) < \frac{1}{2}$, the probability of getting the correct s is at least $1 - \left(2\left(\frac{3}{4}\right)^c\right)^n$. Let A be an Adversary, we write 3-round balanced quasi-Feistel structure as 3qF. We have $\mathbf{Adv}_{3qF}^{qprp\text{-}cpa}(A) = 1 - \left(2\left(\frac{3}{4}\right)^c\right)^n - \frac{1}{2^n}$. If we choose $c \geq 6$, $\mathbf{Adv}_{3qF}^{qprp\text{-}cpa}(A) = 1 - \frac{1}{2^n}$.   □

5.2   Quantum Chosen-Ciphertext Attack Against 4-Round Quasi-Feistel Structure

Figure 9 shows the attack progress of 4-round quasi-Feistel Structure with linear combiner and $b = 2$, where f_1, f_2, f_3, f_4 are round functions. $z_i, z_i', i = 0, ..., 4$ follow the definition in Definition 4.

Let the inputs of the encryption process be z_0, z_1, and the outputs be z_4, z_5. Let the inputs of the decryption process be z_4', z_5', and the outputs be z_0', z_1'. $z_4' = z_4 \oplus m_1$ and $z_5' = z_5 \oplus m_5$, where $m_j, j = 1, 2$ and z_i have the same length.

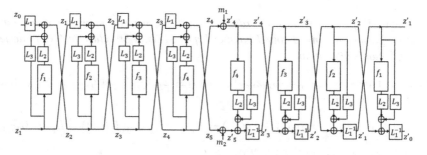

Fig. 9. The encryption and decryption progress of 4-round quasi-Feistel structure with linear combiner and $b = 2$

Theorem 7. *If $f_i, i = 1, 2, 3$ are random functions, 4-round balanced quasi-Feistel Structure can be attacked in $O(n)$ queries by using Simon's algorithm in quantum CCA.*

Proof. For the encryption process we have

$$z_i = L_1(z_{i-2}) \oplus L_2(f_{i-1}(z_{i-1})) \oplus L_3(z_{i-1}), i = 2, 3, 4, 5.$$

And for the decryption process we have

$$z_j' = L_1^{-1}[z_{j+2}' \oplus L_2(f_{j+1}(z_{j+1}')) \oplus L_3(z_{j+1}')], j = 0, 1, 2, 3.$$

Let $m_1 = 0$. Let $m_2 = L_1 L_1(\alpha_0) \oplus L_1 L_1(\alpha_1)$. So we can get

$$z_3' = z_3 \oplus L_1(\alpha_0 \oplus \alpha_1),$$

$$z_2' = z_2 \oplus L_1^{-1} L_2(f_3(z_3) \oplus f_3(z_3')) \oplus L_1^{-1} L_3 L_1(\alpha_0 \oplus \alpha_1),$$

$$z_1' = z_1 \oplus L_1^{-1} L_2(f_2(z_2) \oplus f_2(z_2')) \oplus L_1^{-1} L_3 L_1^{-1} L_2(f_3(z_3) \oplus f_3(z_3'))$$
$$\oplus \alpha_0 \oplus \alpha_1 \oplus L_1^{-1} L_3 L_1^{-1} L_3 L_1(\alpha_0 \oplus \alpha_1).$$

Lemma 7. *Let $x \in \{0,1\}^n$, $b \in \{0,1\}$ and α_0, α_1 be arbitrary two fixed different numbers in $\{0,1\}^n$. Let $(z_0^{\alpha_b}, z_1^{\alpha_b}) \overset{def}{=} (x, \alpha_b)$ being the input of the function in Fig. 9 based on 4-round balanced quasi-Feistel structure and its inverse with corresponding output $(z'^{\alpha_b}_0, z'^{\alpha_b}_1)$ when $m_1 = 0, m_2 = L_1 L_1(\alpha_0) \oplus L_1 L_1(\alpha_1)$. We an construct a periodic function g_5 from 4-round round balanced quasi-Feistel structure with period $s = L_1^{-1} L_2(f_1(\alpha_0)) \oplus L_1^{-1} L_2(f_1(\alpha_1)) \oplus L_1^{-1} L_3(\alpha_0) \oplus L_1^{-1} L_3(\alpha_1)$ by letting*

$$g_5 : \{0,1\}^n \to \{0,1\}^n$$

$$x \mapsto z'^{\alpha_0}_1(x) \oplus z'^{\alpha_1}_1(x) \oplus \alpha_0 \oplus \alpha_1$$

$$g_5(x) = L_1^{-1} L_2(f_2(z_2^{\alpha_0}(x)) \oplus f_2(z'^{\alpha_0}_2(x)) \oplus f_2(z_2^{\alpha_1}(x)) \oplus f_2(z'^{\alpha_1}_2(x)))$$

$$\oplus L_1^{-1} L_3 L_1^{-1} L_2(f_3(z_3^{\alpha_0}(x)) \oplus f_3(z'^{\alpha_0}_3(x)) \oplus f_3(z_3^{\alpha_1}(x)) \oplus f_3(z'^{\alpha_1}_3(x))),$$

where $z_2^{\alpha_b}(x), z'^{\alpha_b}_2(x), z_3^{\alpha_b}(x)$, and $z'^{\alpha_b}_3(x)$ denote the values of intermediate parameters z_2, z_2', z_3, and z_3' respectively when the input of the function in Fig. 9 is $(z'^{\alpha_b}_0, z'^{\alpha_b}_1)$.

Proof. For $i = 2, 3$, we let $h_i'(x) \overset{def}{=} f_i(z_i^{\alpha_0}(x)) \oplus f_i(z'^{\alpha_0}_i(x)) \oplus f_i(z_i^{\alpha_1}(x)) \oplus f_i(z'^{\alpha_1}_i(x))$. Then we will clearly show that g_5 is a periodic function step by step.

(a) $z_2^{\alpha_b}(x) = z_2^{\alpha_{b \oplus 1}}(x \oplus s)$ holds for all $x \in \{0,1\}^n$ the same as Lemma 6.
(b) $z_3^{\alpha_b}(x) = z'^{\alpha_{b \oplus 1}}_3(x \oplus s)$ holds for all $x \in \{0,1\}^n$. We have

$$z_3^{\alpha_b}(x) = L_1(\alpha_b) \oplus L_2(f_2(z_2^{\alpha_b})) \oplus L_3(z_2^{\alpha_b}),$$

$$z'^{\alpha_b}_3(x) = L_1(\alpha_{b \oplus 1}) \oplus L_2(f_2(z_2^{\alpha_b})) \oplus L_3(z_2^{\alpha_b}).$$

Thus we get $z_3^{\alpha_b}(x) = z'^{\alpha_{b \oplus 1}}_3(x \oplus s)$ deriving from (a).
(c) $h_3'(x)$ has a period s deriving from (b).
(d) $z'^{\alpha_b}_2(x) = z'^{\alpha_{b \oplus 1}}_2(x \oplus s)$ holds for all $x \in \{0,1\}^n$. We have

$$z'^{\alpha_b}_2(x) = z_2^{\alpha_b}(x) \oplus L_1^{-1} L_2(f_3(z_3^{\alpha_b}(x)) \oplus f_3(z'^{\alpha_b}_3(x))) \oplus L_1^{-1} L_3 L_1(\alpha_0 \oplus \alpha_1).$$

Thus $z'^{\alpha_b}_2(x) = z'^{\alpha_{b \oplus 1}}_2(x \oplus s)$ deriving from (a) and (b).
(e) $h_2'(x)$ has a period s deriving from (d).
(f) $g_5(x)$ has a period s. We have $g_5(x) = L_1^{-1} L_2(h_2'(x)) \oplus L_1^{-1} L_3 L_1^{-1} L_2(h_3'(x))$. Thus we get $g_5(x)$ has a period s deriving from (c) and (e). □

Proof (Proof of Theorem 7). Now we have $g_5(x) = g_5(x \oplus s)$ with period $s = L_1^{-1} L_2(f_1(\alpha_0)) \oplus L_1^{-1} L_2(f_1(\alpha_1)) \oplus L_1^{-1} L_3(\alpha_0) \oplus L_1^{-1} L_3(\alpha_1)$. When the period is not unique, that is, Simon's algorithm satisfies the approximate commitment, there is $\varepsilon(g_5, s) < \frac{1}{2}$, the probability of getting the correct s is at least $1 - \left(2\left(\frac{3}{4}\right)^c\right)^n$. Let A be an Adversary, we write 4-round balanced quasi-Feistel structure as 4qF. We have $\mathbf{Adv}_{4qF}^{qprp\text{-}cpa}(A) = 1 - \left(2\left(\frac{3}{4}\right)^c\right)^n - \frac{1}{2^n}$. If we choose $c \geq 6$, $\mathbf{Adv}_{4qF}^{qprp\text{-}cpa}(A) = 1 - \frac{1}{2^n}$. □

6 Conclusion and Discussion

There has been a discussion about whether the security of Lai-Massey structure and Feistel structure are the same. Aaram Yun et al. [40] proved that Feistel structure and Lai-Massey structure are quasi-Feistel structures and proved the birthday security of $(2b - 1)$ and $(3b - 2)$-round unbalanced quasi-Feistel networks with b branches against CPA and CCA attacks in classical. In [29], Luo, et al. shown that 3-round Lai-Massey structure can resist the attacks of Simon's algorithm in quantum, which is different from Feistel structure. According to Luo, this means that Lai-Massey structure and Feistel structure have a different number of rounds for CPA attacks in quantum, which also means that quasi-Feistel structures do not have similar security strength in quantum.

We first give quantum attacks on Lai-Massey structure used in FOX. We show that 3-round Lai-Massey structure can be attacked by using Simon's algorithm in $O(n)$ quantum queries against quantum CPA attacks, which is the same as Feistel structure. Then we give quantum CCA attacks on 4-round Lai-Massey structure, $O(n)$ quantum queries are sufficient to distinguish 4-round Lai-Massey structure from random permutation, which is the same as Feistel structure too. This makes us realize that quasi-Feistel structures may have similar security strength in quantum. So we give quantum attacks on quasi-Feistel structures and show that 3-round (4-round) balanced quasi-Feistel structure with linear combiners can be attacked with $O(n)$ quantum queries in quantum CPA(CCA).

For Lai-Massey structure, the version given by Vaudenay [35] used general operations in a finite group, and the version given by FOX [18] used XOR operation. In both versions, the operation used in σ and the remainder of Lai-Massey structure are the same. We consider that σ and the remainder of Lai-Massey structure use different operations, i.e., we use XOR operation in σ and general operations in the remainder of Lai-Massey structure. A problem of much interest is whether different operations can improve the security of Lai-Massey structure. If the security can be improved, another problem has been whether it is possible to resist quantum attacks as shown in [2].

Here we use quantum attacks that can make superposition queries. Quantum attacks work with classical queries and offline quantum computations can be further considered, as Bonnetain et al. did in [5].

Hosoyamada and Iwata [15] show that 4-round Feistel structure against sufficient qCPAs. More precisely, they prove that 4-round Feistel structure is secure up to $O(2^{n/3})$ quantum queries if the input length is $2n$ bits. We guess that the quantum security bound of 4-round Lai-Massey structure maybe $O(2^{n/3})$, too. But this still needs to be proved in the future.

Acknowledgement. Many thanks to the reviewers for their constructive comments during the review process. One of reviewers pointed out that the combiner Γ of balanced quasi-Feistel structure in Sect. 5 does not need to be all linear. After our verification, only L_1 needs to be linear. Specifically, if the combiner of quasi-Feistel structure is like $\Gamma(x, y, z) = L_1(x) \oplus F(y, z)$, where L_1 is linear and F is a function, there exists a quantum CPA distinguisher against 3-round balanced quasi-Feistel structure and a quantum CCA distinguisher against 4-round balanced quasi-Feistel Structure.

A   Intermediate Parameters in the Decryption Process of 4-round Lai-Massey Structure in Sect. 3.2

For the decryption process of 4-round Lai-Massey structure shown in the Fig. 3, we write the inputs as $[z_1, z_2], [z_3, z_4]$ and the outputs as $[x'_1, x'_2], [x'_3, x'_4]$. Intermediate parameters are as follows.

$$a'_4 = [z_1, z_2], b'_4 = [z_3, z_4],$$
$$a'_3 = [z_1 \oplus f_{4L}(\Delta'_4), z_2 \oplus f_{4R}(\Delta'_4)], b'_3 = [z_3 \oplus f_{4L}(\Delta'_4), z_4 \oplus f_{4R}(\Delta'_4)],$$
$$a'_2 = [z_1 \oplus z_2 \oplus f_{3L}(\Delta'_3) \oplus f_{4L}(\Delta'_4) \oplus f_{4R}(\Delta'_4), z_1 \oplus f_{3R}(\Delta'_3) \oplus f_{4L}(\Delta'_4)],$$
$$b'_2 = [z_3 \oplus f_{3L}(\Delta'_3) \oplus f_{4L}(\Delta'_4), z_4 \oplus f_{3R}(\Delta'_3) \oplus f_{4R}(\Delta'_4)],$$
$$a'_1 = [z_2 \oplus f_{2L}(\Delta'_2) \oplus f_{3L}(\Delta'_3) \oplus f_{3R}(\Delta'_3) \oplus f_{4R}(\Delta'_4),$$
$$\quad z_1 \oplus z_2 \oplus f_{2R}(\Delta'_2) \oplus f_{3L}(\Delta'_3) \oplus f_{4L}(\Delta'_4) \oplus f_{4R}(\Delta'_4)],$$
$$b'_1 = [z_3 \oplus f_{2L}(\Delta'_2) \oplus f_{3L}(\Delta'_3) \oplus f_{4L}(\Delta'_4), z_4 \oplus f_{2R}(\Delta'_2) \oplus f_{3R}(\Delta'_3) \oplus f_{4R}(\Delta'_4)],$$

where

$$\Delta'_4 = [z_1 \oplus z_3, z_2 \oplus z_4],$$
$$\Delta'_3 = [z_1 \oplus z_2 \oplus z_3 \oplus f_{4R}(\Delta'_4), z_1 \oplus z_4 \oplus f_{4L}(\Delta'_4) \oplus f_{4R}(\Delta'_4)],$$
$$\Delta'_2 = [z_2 \oplus z_3 \oplus f_{3R}(\Delta'_3) \oplus f_{4L}(\Delta'_4) \oplus f_{4R}(\Delta'_4),$$
$$\quad z_1 \oplus z_2 \oplus z_4 \oplus f_{3L}(\Delta'_3) \oplus f_{3R}(\Delta'_3) \oplus f_{4L}(\Delta'_4)],$$
$$\Delta'_1 = [z_1 \oplus z_3 \oplus f_{2R}(\Delta'_2) \oplus f_{3L}(\Delta'_3) \oplus f_{3R}(\Delta'_3),$$
$$\quad z_2 \oplus z_4 \oplus f_{2L}(\Delta'_2) \oplus f_{2R}(\Delta'_2) \oplus f_{3L}(\Delta'_3)].$$

Proof. Let $a'_4 = [z_1, z_2], b'_4 = [z_3, z_4]$. Intermediate parameters $a_i, b_i, \Delta_j, i = 1, 2, 3, 4$ are the same as Sect. 3.1 and Sect. 3.2.

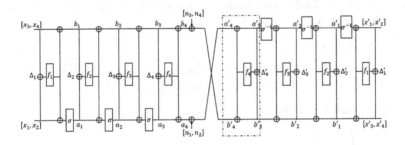

Fig. 10. The fourth round of the decryption progress of 4-round Lai-Massey structure

Lemma 8. *For the fourth round of the decryption progress of 4-round Lai-Massey structure (Fig. 10), intermediate parameters Δ'_4, a'_3, b'_3 can be expressed as:*

$$\Delta'_4 = [z_1 \oplus z_3, z_2 \oplus z_4],$$

$$a'_3 = [z_1 \oplus f_{4L}(\Delta'_4), z_2 \oplus f_{4R}(\Delta'_4)],$$
$$b'_3 = [z_3 \oplus f_{4L}(\Delta'_4), z_4 \oplus f_{4R}(\Delta'_4)].$$

Proof. According to the decryption progress of 4-round Lai-Massey structure, we can get the following system of equations

$$\begin{cases} \Delta'_4 = a'_3 \oplus b'_3, \\ a'_3 \oplus f_4(\Delta'_4) = a'_4, \\ b'_3 \oplus f_4(\Delta'_4) = b'_4. \end{cases}$$

Solving the system of equations gives the result.

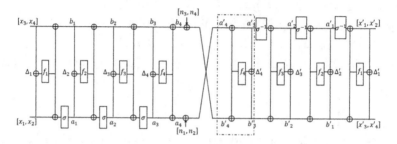

Fig. 11. The third round of the decryption progress of 4-round Lai-Massey structure

Lemma 9. *For the third round of the decryption progress of 4-round Lai-Massey structure (Fig. 11), intermediate parameters Δ'_3, a'_2, b'_2 can be expressed as:*

$$\Delta'_3 = a'_2 \oplus b'_2 = [z_1 \oplus z_2 \oplus z_3 \oplus f_{4R}(\Delta'_4), z_1 \oplus z_4 \oplus f_{4L}(\Delta'_4) \oplus f_{4R}(\Delta'_4)],$$
$$a'_2 = [z_1 \oplus z_2 \oplus f_{3L}(\Delta'_3) \oplus f_{4L}(\Delta'_4) \oplus f_{4R}(\Delta'_4), z_1 \oplus f_{3R}(\Delta'_3) \oplus f_{4L}(\Delta'_4)],$$
$$b'_2 = [z_3 \oplus f_{3L}(\Delta'_3) \oplus f_{4L}(\Delta'_4), z_4 \oplus f_{3R}(\Delta'_3) \oplus f_{4R}(\Delta'_4)].$$

Proof. According to the decryption progress of 4-round Lai-Massey structure, we can get the following system of equations

$$\begin{cases} \Delta'_3 = a'_2 \oplus b'_2, \\ a'_3 = [a'_{2R} \oplus f_{3R}(\Delta'_3), a'_{2L} \oplus a'_{2R} \oplus f_{3L}(\Delta'_3) \oplus f_{3R}(\Delta'_3)], \\ b'_3 = [b'_{2L} \oplus f_{3L}(\Delta'_3), b'_{2R} \oplus f_{3R}(\Delta'_3)]. \end{cases}$$

From Lemma 8 we can get:

$$\begin{cases} a'_{2R} \oplus f_{3R}(\Delta'_3) = z_1 \oplus f_{4L}(\Delta'_4), \\ a'_{2L} \oplus a'_{2R} \oplus f_{3L}(\Delta'_3) \oplus f_{3R}(\Delta'_3) = z_2 \oplus f_{4R}(\Delta'_4), \\ b'_{2L} \oplus f_{3L}(\Delta'_3) = z_3 \oplus f_{4L}(\Delta'_4), \\ b'_{2R} \oplus f_{3R}(\Delta'_3) = z_4 \oplus f_{4R}(\Delta'_4). \end{cases}$$

Solving the system of equations gives the result.

Lemma 10. *For the second round of the decryption progress of 4-round Lai-Massey structure, intermediate parameters Δ'_2, a'_1, b'_1 can be expressed as:*

$$\Delta_2' = [z_2 \oplus z_3 \oplus f_{3R}(\Delta_3') \oplus f_{4L}(\Delta_4') \oplus f_{4R}(\Delta_4'),$$
$$z_1 \oplus z_2 \oplus z_4 \oplus f_{3L}(\Delta_3') \oplus f_{3R}(\Delta_3') \oplus f_{4L}(\Delta_4')],$$
$$a_1' = [z_2 \oplus f_{2L}(\Delta_2') \oplus f_{3L}(\Delta_3') \oplus f_{3R}(\Delta_3') \oplus f_{4R}(\Delta_4'),$$
$$z_1 \oplus z_2 \oplus f_{2R}(\Delta_2') \oplus f_{3L}(\Delta_3') \oplus f_{4L}(\Delta_4') \oplus f_{4R}(\Delta_4')],$$
$$b_1' = [z_3 \oplus f_{2L}(\Delta_2') \oplus f_{3L}(\Delta_3') \oplus f_{4L}(\Delta_4'), z_4 \oplus f_{2R}(\Delta_2') \oplus f_{3R}(\Delta_3') \oplus f_{4R}(\Delta_4')].$$

Proof. According to the decryption progress of 4-round Lai-Massey structure, we can get the following system of equations

$$\begin{cases} \Delta_2' = a_1' \oplus b_1', \\ a_2' = [a_{1R}' \oplus f_{2R}(\Delta_2'), a_{1L}' \oplus a_{1R}' \oplus f_{2L}(\Delta_2') \oplus f_{2R}(\Delta_2')], \\ b_2' = [b_{1L}' \oplus f_{2L}(\Delta_2'), b_{1R} \oplus f_{2R}(\Delta_2')]. \end{cases}$$

From Lemma 9 we have:

$$\begin{cases} a_{1R}' \oplus f_{2R}(\Delta_2') = z_1 \oplus z_2 \oplus f_{3L}(\Delta_3') \oplus f_{4L}(\Delta_4') \oplus f_{4R}(\Delta_4'), \\ a_{1L}' \oplus a_{1R}' \oplus f_{2L}(\Delta_2') \oplus f_{2R}(\Delta_2') = z_1 \oplus f_{3R}(\Delta_3') \oplus f_{4L}(\Delta_4'), \\ b_{1L}' \oplus f_{2L}(\Delta_2') = z_3 \oplus f_{3L}(\Delta_3') \oplus f_{4L}(\Delta_4'), \\ b_{1R}' \oplus f_{2R}(\Delta_2') = z_4 \oplus f_{3R}(\Delta_3') \oplus f_{4R}(\Delta_4'). \end{cases}$$

Solving the system of equations gives the result.

Lemma 11. *For the first round of the decryption progress of 4-round Lai-Massey structure, intermediate parameters* Δ_1', $[x_1', x_2']$, $[x_3', x_4']$ *can be expressed as:*

$$\Delta_1' = [z_1 \oplus z_3 \oplus f_{2R}(\Delta_2') \oplus f_{3L}(\Delta_3') \oplus f_{3R}(\Delta_3'),$$
$$z_2 \oplus z_4 \oplus f_{2L}(\Delta_2') \oplus f_{2R}(\Delta_2') \oplus f_{3L}(\Delta_3')],$$
$$[x_1', x_2'] = [z_1 \oplus f_{1L}(\Delta_1') \oplus f_{2L}(\Delta_2') \oplus f_{2R}(\Delta_2') \oplus f_{3R}(\Delta_3') \oplus f_{4L}(\Delta_4'),$$
$$z_2 \oplus f_{1R}(\Delta_1') \oplus f_{2L}(\Delta_2') \oplus f_{3L}(\Delta_3') \oplus f_{3R}(\Delta_3') \oplus f_{4R}(\Delta_4'),$$
$$[x_3', x_4'] = [z_3 \oplus f_{1L}(\Delta_1') \oplus f_{2L}(\Delta_2') \oplus f_{3L}(\Delta_3') \oplus f_{4L}(\Delta_4'),$$
$$z_4 \oplus f_{1R}(\Delta_1') \oplus f_{2R}(\Delta_2') \oplus f_{3R}(\Delta_3') \oplus f_{4R}(\Delta_4')].$$

Proof. According to the decryption progress of 4-round Lai-Massey structure, we can get the following system of equations

$$\begin{cases} \Delta_1' = [x_1', x_2'] \oplus [x_3', x_4'], \\ a_1' = [x_2' \oplus f_{1R}(\Delta_1'), x_1' \oplus x_2' \oplus f_{1L}(\Delta_1') \oplus f_{1R}(\Delta_1')], \\ b_1' = b_0' \oplus f_1(\Delta_1') = [x_3' \oplus f_{1L}(\Delta_1'), x_4' \oplus f_{1R}(\Delta_1')]. \end{cases}$$

From Lemma 11 we have

$$\begin{cases} x_2' \oplus f_{1R}(\Delta_1') = z_2 \oplus f_{2L}(\Delta_2') \oplus f_{3L}(\Delta_3') \oplus f_{3R}(\Delta_3') \oplus f_{4R}(\Delta_4'), \\ x_1' \oplus x_2' \oplus f_{1L}(\Delta_1') \oplus f_{1R}(\Delta_1') = z_1 \oplus z_2 \oplus f_{2R}(\Delta_2') \oplus f_{3L}(\Delta_3') \oplus f_{4L}(\Delta_4') \oplus f_{4R}(\Delta_4'), \\ x_3' \oplus f_{1L}(\Delta_1') = z_3 \oplus f_{2L}(\Delta_2') \oplus f_{3L}(\Delta_3') \oplus f_{4L}(\Delta_4'), \\ x_4' \oplus f_{1R}(\Delta_1') = z_4 \oplus f_{2R}(\Delta_2') \oplus f_{3R}(\Delta_3') \oplus f_{4R}(\Delta_4'). \end{cases}$$

Solving the system of equations gives the result.

B   Proof of Theorem 4

Proof. First, we introduce a Theorem and a Lemma for subsequent proofs.

Theorem 8 [6] *(Brassard, Hoyer, Mosca and Tapp). Let A be any quantum algorithm on q qubits that uses no measurement. Let $B : \mathbb{F}_2^q \to \{0,1\}$ be a function that classifies outcomes of A as good or bad. Let $p > 0$ be the initial success probability that a measurement of $A|0\rangle$ is good. Set $t = \lceil \frac{\pi}{4\theta} \rceil$, where θ is defined via $\sin^2(\theta) = p$. Moreover, define the unitary operator $Q = -AS_0A^{-1}S_B$, where the operator S_B changes the sign of the good state:*

$$|x\rangle \mapsto \begin{cases} -|x\rangle & \text{if } B(x) = 1 \\ |x\rangle & \text{if } B(x) = 0 \end{cases}$$

while S_0 changes the sign of the amplitude only for the zero state $|0\rangle$. Then after the computation of $Q^t A|0\rangle$, a measurement yields well with probability a least $\max\{1 - p, p\}$.

Lemma 12 [24]. *Any state $|z_i\rangle = (-1)^{\langle u_i, x_i \rangle}|u_i\rangle$ is proper with probability at least $\frac{1}{2}$. Any set of $\ell = 2(n + \sqrt{n})$ states contains at least $n - 1$ proper states with probability greater than $\frac{4}{5}$.*

Let U_h be a quantum oracle as $|x_1, ..., x_l, 0\rangle \mapsto |x_1, ..., x_l, h(x_1, ..., x_l)\rangle$. If k_4 guessed right, then $g_3(k_4, [x, x']) = g_3(k_4, [x, x'] \oplus s)$. Let $h : \mathbb{F}_2^m \times \mathbb{F}_2^{n^l} \to \mathbb{F}_2^{(n/2)^l}$ with: $(k, [x_1, x_1'], ..., [x_l, x_l']) \mapsto g_3(k, [x_1, x_1'])||...||g_3(k, [x_l, x_l'])$. Then we can construct the following quantum algorithm A:

1. Initializing a $m + nl + nl/2$-qubit register $|0\rangle^{\otimes m+nl+nl/2}$.
2. Apply Hadamard transformation $H^{\otimes(m+nl)}$ to the first $m+nl$ qubits to obtain quantum superposition

$$H^{\otimes(m+nl)}|0\rangle = \frac{1}{\sqrt{2^{m+nl}}} \sum_{k \in \mathbb{F}_2^m, [x_1, x_1'], ..., [x_l, x_l'] \in \mathbb{F}_2^n} |k\rangle|[x_1, x_1']\rangle...|[x_l, x_l']\rangle|0, ..., 0\rangle.$$

3. Applying U_h:

$$\frac{1}{\sqrt{2^{m+nl}}} \sum_{k \in \mathbb{F}_2^m, [x_1, x_1'], ..., [x_l, x_l'] \in \mathbb{F}_2^n} |k\rangle|[x_1, x_1']\rangle...|[x_l, x_l']\rangle|h(k, [x_1, x_1'], ..., [x_l, x_l'])\rangle.$$

4. Apply Hadamard transformation to the qubits $|[x_1, x_1']\rangle...|[x_l, x_l']\rangle$:

$$|\varphi\rangle = \frac{1}{\sqrt{2^{m+2nl}}} \sum_{k \in \mathbb{F}_2^m, u_1, ..., u_l, [x_1, x_1'], ..., [x_l, x_l'] \in \mathbb{F}_2^n} |k\rangle(-1)^{\langle u_1, [x_1, x_1'] \rangle}|u_1\rangle \cdots (-1)^{\langle u_l, [x_l, x_l'] \rangle}$$

$$|u_l\rangle|h(k, [x_1, x_1'], ..., [x_l, x_l'])\rangle.$$

If k_4 is guessed right, the period s will orthogonal to all the $u_i, i = 1...l$. From Lemma 12, we choose $l = 2(n + \sqrt{n})$. Then we can construct a classifier $B : \mathbb{F}_2^{m+nl} \to \{0,1\}$ with a good subspace $|\varphi_1\rangle$ and a bad subspace $|\varphi_0\rangle$ as Definition 5. $|x\rangle$ in the good subspace if $B(x) = 1$. Let $|\varphi\rangle = |\varphi_1\rangle + |\varphi_0\rangle$. $|\varphi_1\rangle$ is the sum of basis states for which the right k_4. We can check it by whether $g_3(k, [x, x']) = g_3(k, [x, x'] \oplus s)$:

Definition 5. *Let* $\tilde{U} = \langle u_1, ..., u_l \rangle$ *be the linear span of all* u_i. *We define Classifier* $\mathcal{B} : \mathbb{F}_2^{m+nl} \mapsto \{0, 1\}$ *which maps* $(k, u_1, ..., u_l) \mapsto \{0, 1\}$.

1. *If* $\dim(\tilde{U}) \neq n - 1$, *output 0. Otherwise compute the unique period* s *by using Lemma 2 in* [24].
2. *For random* $[x, x']$, *if* $g_3(k, [x, x']) = g_3(k, [x, x'] \oplus s)$, *then output 1, otherwise output 0.*

Mearsure $|\varphi\rangle$ and the initial probability of the good state is:

$$p = \Pr[|k\rangle|u_1\rangle...|u_l\rangle \text{ is good}] = \Pr[k = k_4] \cdot \Pr[\mathcal{B}(k, u_1, ..., u_l) = 1 | k = k_4] \approx \frac{1}{2^m}.$$

Set $t = \lceil \frac{\pi}{4\theta} \rceil$, where θ is defined via $sin^2(\theta) = p$. Then $\theta \approx \arcsin(2^{-m/2}) \approx 2^{-m/2}$, $t \approx \lceil \frac{\pi}{4 \times 2^{-m/2}} \rceil \approx 2^{m/2}$. We define the unitary operator $Q = -\mathcal{A}S_0\mathcal{A}^{-1}S_{\mathcal{B}}$, where the operator $S_{\mathcal{B}}$ changes the sign of the good state:

$$|k\rangle|u_1\rangle...|u_l\rangle \mapsto \begin{cases} -|k\rangle|u_1\rangle...|u_l\rangle & \text{if } B(k, u_1, ..., u_l) = 1 \\ |k\rangle|u_1\rangle...|u_l\rangle & \text{if } B(k, u_1, ..., u_l) = 0. \end{cases}$$

S_0 changes the sign of the amplitude only for the zero state $|0\rangle$. Then after the computation of $Q^t\mathcal{A}|0\rangle$, according to the Theorem 8, a measurement yields good with probability a least $\max\{1 - p, p\} \approx 1 - \frac{1}{2^m}$.

References

1. Skipjack and kea algorithm specifications. Technical report, May 1998
2. Alagic, G., Russell, A.: Quantum-secure symmetric-key cryptography based on hidden shifts. In: Coron, J.-S., Nielsen, J.B. (eds.) EUROCRYPT 2017, Part III. LNCS, vol. 10212, pp. 65–93. Springer, Cham (2017). https://doi.org/10.1007/978-3-319-56617-7_3
3. Aragona, R., Civino, R.: On invariant subspaces in the Lai-Massey scheme and a primitivity reduction. Mediterr. J. Math. 18(4), 1–14 (2021)
4. Beaulieu, R., Shors, D., Smith, J., Treatman-Clark, S., Weeks, B., Wingers, L.: The SIMON and SPECK families of lightweight block ciphers. IACR Cryptol. ePrint Arch. 404 (2013). http://eprint.iacr.org/2013/404
5. Bonnetain, X., Hosoyamada, A., Naya-Plasencia, M., Sasaki, Yu., Schrottenloher, A.: Quantum attacks without superposition queries: the offline Simon's algorithm. In: Galbraith, S.D., Moriai, S. (eds.) ASIACRYPT 2019. LNCS, vol. 11921, pp. 552–583. Springer, Cham (2019). https://doi.org/10.1007/978-3-030-34578-5_20
6. Brassard, G., Høyer, P., Mosca, M., Tapp, A.: Quantum amplitude amplification and estimation. arXiv Quantum Physics (2000)
7. Derbez, P.: Note on impossible differential attacks. In: Peyrin, T. (ed.) FSE 2016. LNCS, vol. 9783, pp. 416–427. Springer, Heidelberg (2016). https://doi.org/10.1007/978-3-662-52993-5_21
8. Dong, X., Wang, X.: Quantum key-recovery attack on Feistel structures. Sci. China Inf. Sci. 61(10), 1–7 (2018). https://doi.org/10.1007/s11432-017-9468-y
9. Feistel, H.: Cryptography and computer privacy. Sci. Am. 228(5), 15–23 (1973)
10. Fu, L., Jin, C.: Differential and linear provable security of Lai-Massey scheme (in chinese) (2013)

11. Fu, L., Jin, C.: Practical security evaluation against differential and linear cryptanalyses for the Lai-Massey scheme with an SPS f-function. KSII Trans. Internet Inf. Syst. **8**(10), 3624–3637 (2014). https://doi.org/10.3837/tiis.2014.10.020

12. Grover, L.K.: A fast quantum mechanical algorithm for database search. In: 1996 Proceedings of the Twenty-Eighth Annual ACM Symposium on the Theory of Computing, pp. 212–219. ACM (1996). https://doi.org/10.1145/237814.237866

13. Guo, R., Jin, C.: Impossible differential cryptanalysis on Lai-Massey scheme. ETRI J. **36**(6), 1032–1040 (2014)

14. Guo, T., Wang, P., Hu, L., Ye, D.: Attacks on beyond-birthday-bound MACs in the quantum setting. In: Cheon, J.H., Tillich, J.-P. (eds.) PQCrypto 2021 2021. LNCS, vol. 12841, pp. 421–441. Springer, Cham (2021). https://doi.org/10.1007/978-3-030-81293-5_22

15. Hosoyamada, A., Iwata, T.: 4-round Luby-Rackoff construction is a qPRP: tight quantum security bound. Cryptology ePrint Archive, Report 2019/243 (2019). https://ia.cr/2019/243

16. Isobe, T., Shibutani, K.: Improved all-subkeys recovery attacks on FOX, KATAN and SHACAL-2 block ciphers. In: Cid, C., Rechberger, C. (eds.) FSE 2014. LNCS, vol. 8540, pp. 104–126. Springer, Heidelberg (2015). https://doi.org/10.1007/978-3-662-46706-0_6

17. Ito, G., Hosoyamada, A., Matsumoto, R., Sasaki, Yu., Iwata, T.: Quantum chosen-ciphertext attacks against feistel ciphers. In: Matsui, M. (ed.) CT-RSA 2019. LNCS, vol. 11405, pp. 391–411. Springer, Cham (2019). https://doi.org/10.1007/978-3-030-12612-4_20

18. Junod, P., Vaudenay, S.: FOX: a new family of block ciphers. In: Handschuh, H., Hasan, M.A. (eds.) SAC 2004. LNCS, vol. 3357, pp. 114–129. Springer, Heidelberg (2004). https://doi.org/10.1007/978-3-540-30564-4_8

19. Kaplan, M., Leurent, G., Leverrier, A., Naya-Plasencia, M.: Breaking symmetric cryptosystems using quantum period finding. In: Robshaw, M., Katz, J. (eds.) CRYPTO 2016. LNCS, vol. 9815, pp. 207–237. Springer, Heidelberg (2016). https://doi.org/10.1007/978-3-662-53008-5_8

20. Kilian, J., Rogaway, P.: How to protect DES against exhaustive key search. In: Koblitz, N. (ed.) CRYPTO 1996. LNCS, vol. 1109, pp. 252–267. Springer, Heidelberg (1996). https://doi.org/10.1007/3-540-68697-5_20

21. Kuwakado, H., Morii, M.: Quantum distinguisher between the 3-round Feistel cipher and the random permutation. In: Proceedings of the ISIT 2010, pp. 2682–2685. IEEE (2010). https://doi.org/10.1109/ISIT.2010.5513654

22. Lai, X.: On the design and security of block ciphers. Ph.D. thesis, ETH Zurich, Zürich, Switzerland (1992). https://d-nb.info/920912710

23. Lai, X., Massey, J.L.: A proposal for a new block encryption standard. In: Damgård, I.B. (ed.) EUROCRYPT 1990. LNCS, vol. 473, pp. 389–404. Springer, Heidelberg (1991). https://doi.org/10.1007/3-540-46877-3_35

24. Leander, G., May, A.: Grover meets Simon – quantumly attacking the FX-construction. In: Takagi, T., Peyrin, T. (eds.) ASIACRYPT 2017, Part II. LNCS, vol. 10625, pp. 161–178. Springer, Cham (2017). https://doi.org/10.1007/978-3-319-70697-9_6

25. Li, R., You, J., Sun, B., Li, C.: Fault analysis study of the block cipher FOX64. Multim. Tools Appl. **63**(3), 691–708 (2013). https://doi.org/10.1007/s11042-011-0895-x

26. Luby, M., Rackoff, C.: How to construct pseudorandom permutations from pseudorandom functions. SIAM J. Comput. **17**(2), 373–386 (1988). https://doi.org/10.1137/0217022

27. Luo, Y., Lai, X., Gong, Z.: Pseudorandomness analysis of the (extended) Lai-Massey scheme. Inf. Process. Lett. **111**(2), 90–96 (2010). https://doi.org/10.1016/j.ipl.2010.10.012

28. Luo, Y., Lai, X., Hu, J.: The pseudorandomness of many-round Lai-Massey scheme. J. Inf. Sci. Eng. **31**(3), 1085–1096 (2015). http://www.iis.sinica.edu.tw/page/jise/2015/201505_17.html

29. Luo, Y., Yan, H., Wang, L., Hu, H., Lai, X.: Study on block cipher structures against Simon's quantum algorithm (in Chinese). J. Cryptol. Res. **6**(5), 561–573 (2019)

30. Miyaguchi, S.: The FEAL-8 cryptosystem and a call for attack. In: Brassard, G. (ed.) CRYPTO 1989. LNCS, vol. 435, pp. 624–627. Springer, New York (1990). https://doi.org/10.1007/0-387-34805-0_59

31. Shor, P.W.: Algorithms for quantum computation: discrete logarithms and factoring. In: 1994 35th Annual Symposium on Foundations of Computer Science, pp. 124–134. IEEE Computer Society (1994). https://doi.org/10.1109/SFCS.1994.365700

32. Simon, D.R.: On the power of quantum computation. SIAM J. Comput. **26**(5), 1474–1483 (1997). https://doi.org/10.1137/S0097539796298637

33. U.S. Department of Commerce/National Institute of Standards, Technology: Data encryption standard (DES) (1977)

34. Sui, H., Wu, W., Zhang, L.: Round security of the Lai-Massey structure (in Chinese). J. Cryptol. Res. **1**, 28–40 (2014)

35. Vaudenay, S.: On the Lai-Massey scheme. In: Lam, K.-Y., Okamoto, E., Xing, C. (eds.) ASIACRYPT 1999. LNCS, vol. 1716, pp. 8–19. Springer, Heidelberg (1999). https://doi.org/10.1007/978-3-540-48000-6_2

36. Wu, W., Wei, H.: Collision-integral attack of reduced-round FOX (in Chinese). Acta Electron. Sinica **33**, 1307 (2005)

37. Wu, W., Zhang, W., Feng, D.: Improved integral cryptanalysis of FOX block cipher. IACR Cryptol. ePrint Arch. 292 (2005). http://eprint.iacr.org/2005/292

38. Wu, W., Zhang, W., Feng, D.: Integral cryptanalysis of reduced FOX block cipher. In: Won, D.H., Kim, S. (eds.) ICISC 2005. LNCS, vol. 3935, pp. 229–241. Springer, Heidelberg (2006). https://doi.org/10.1007/11734727_20

39. Wu, Z., Lai, X., Zhu, B., Luo, Y.: Impossible differential cryptanalysis of FOX. IACR Cryptol. ePrint Arch. 357 (2009). http://eprint.iacr.org/2009/357

40. Yun, A., Park, J.H., Lee, J.: On Lai-Massey and quasi-Feistel ciphers. Des. Codes Cryptogr. **58**(1), 45–72 (2011). https://doi.org/10.1007/s10623-010-9386-8

41. Zhang, L., Wu, W.: Pseudorandomness and super pseudorandomness on the unbalanced Feistel networks with contracting functions (in chinese). Chin. J. Comput. **32**(7), 1320–1330 (2009)

Sponge-Based Authenticated Encryption: Security Against Quantum Attackers

Christian Janson[1] and Patrick Struck[2([⊠])]

[1] Technische Universität Darmstadt, Darmstadt, Germany
christian.janson@cryptoplexity.de
[2] Universität Regensburg, Regensburg, Germany
patrick.struck@ur.de

Abstract. In this work, we study the security of sponge-based authenticated encryption schemes against quantum attackers. In particular, we analyse the sponge-based authenticated encryption scheme SLAE as put forward by Degabriele et al. (ASIACRYPT'19) due to its modularity. We show that the scheme achieves security in the post-quantum (QS1) setting in the quantum random oracle model by using the one-way to hiding lemma. Furthermore, we analyse the scheme in a fully-quantum (QS2) setting. There we provide a set of attacks showing that SLAE does not achieve ciphertext indistinguishability and hence overall does not provide the desired level of security.

1 Introduction

Authenticated encryption schemes with associated data (AEAD) [47] are the main employed cryptographic scheme when it comes to securing the communication between two parties who already share a secret key by ensuring both confidentiality and authenticity of the exchanged messages. Several works show that AEAD schemes can be constructed purely from sponges [21–24,35], which were initially introduced as a tool to construct cryptographic hash functions. Recent examples of such sponge-based AEAD schemes are ISAP [22,23] and SLAE [21]. Observe that these schemes are already analysed showing that they are even secure against side-channel leakage, however, their security against quantum adversaries has yet to be studied.

Unlike public key cryptography that is based on number theoretic problems, which is completely broken by Shor's algorithm [49], AEAD schemes are often assumed to be only mildly affected by Grover's algorithm [31], although this assumption turns out to be delusive in some cases [13]. To compensate this, usually one simply doubles the key length. This approach indeed works for many symmetric schemes in the standard model, namely those where their security proofs can be easily translated to one against quantum adversaries [50]. However, schemes that rely on random oracles [7] cannot be translated in a straightforward manner and hence require more attention. In particular, translating their security to hold against quantum adversaries requires a proof in the quantum random

J. H. Cheon and T. Johansson (Eds.): PQCrypto 2022, LNCS 13512, pp. 230–259, 2022.
https://doi.org/10.1007/978-3-031-17234-2_12

oracle model (QROM) [10], and it has recently been shown that proofs cannot always be translated from the ROM to the QROM [56]. In particular, this will also apply to sponge-based AEAD schemes where we typically model the block function that underlies the sponge construction as a random oracle and includes the schemes in [21–23].

The security of cryptographic primitives against quantum adversaries can nowadays be divided into two cases [27,37]. The first case corresponds to the setting of post-quantum security (usually abbreviated as QS1) where the adversary only has quantum computing power. This setting covers the scenario once the first large-scale quantum computer exists and corresponds to the setting described above which typically requires switching from the ROM to the QROM. The second case deals with the setting of quantum security (usually referred to as QS2) where protocol participants also have quantum computing power. This covers a scenario where quantum computers are ubiquitous but also earlier scenarios using more sophisticated attacks such as the *frozen smart-card* attack [28].

Observe that security in the QS2 setting is more involved since the adversary gets superposition access to the primitive, e.g., it can encrypt/sign messages in a superposition. Many schemes that are secure in the QS1 setting are however completely broken in the QS2 setting as is shown by a series of works [2,4,33,36,41,42,48]. Yet another difficulty in the QS2 setting is that there are many different security notions [1,12,14,15,25,28–30,43]. These notions use different approaches to formalise the idea of allowing the adversary to "encrypt/sign messages in a superposition" in order to obtain a security notion that translates the classical intuition of the corresponding security notion to the QS2 setting.

Our Contribution. In this work, we study the security of sponge-based authenticated encryption schemes against quantum attackers which has so far only received very little attention. In particular, we scrutinize the scheme SLAE as put forward by Degabriele et al. [21] in both settings, namely in the QS1 and QS2 setting. Observe that the beauty of SLAE is its simplicity in terms of their construction, i.e., SLAE is a N2-composition [44] of a symmetric key encryption scheme and a message authentication code. In particular, Degabriele et al. show that SLAE can be viewed in terms of smaller components (with slight improvements by [39]), i.e., the encryption scheme consists of a sponge-based pseudorandom function (PRF) and a sponge-based pseudorandom generator (PRG) while the MAC consists of the combination of a sponge-based hash function and a sponge-based PRF (a more detailed description can be found in Sect. 3). Note that our analysis does not only contribute towards the study of SLAE but rather also provides a QS1 and QS2 analysis of the core primitives themselves which is of independent interest. Note that SLAE is a leakage-resilient AEAD scheme. However, in this work we do not consider the leakage setting but rather use the scheme SLAE due to its simplicity in order to provide a thorough security analysis of sponge-based AEAD schemes and the employed core primitives in the QS1 and QS2 setting closing this gap in the literature.

In the QS1 setting, we are able to establish security for SLAE. In particular, by using the one-way to hiding lemma [3,53], we can show that the underlying building blocks, namely the sponge-based PRF and PRG are secure with respect to quantum adversaries. For the sponge-based hash function, we show that we can leverage existing results [18] to the construction specifics of SLAE. Finally, being equipped with the established results, we can overall establish security of SLAE in the QS1 setting.

In the QS2 setting, we analyse the ciphertext indistinguishability of SLAE. Unlike the QS1 setting, there are different notions for ciphertext indistinguishability in the QS2 setting which do not form a strict hierarchy. We consider the two strongest, incomparable notions by Gagliardoni et al. [28] and Mossayebi and Schack [43]. We extend these notions to the nonce-based setting and show that SLAE achieves neither of these notions by showing attacks. Finally, we argue that one may establish QS2 security in the sense of [12] of the generic construction that underlies SLAE. However, the security when studying the sponge-based construction is left as an open problem.

As mentioned above, we chose to analyse SLAE rather than other relevant sponge-based schemes due to its modularity. Since SLAE is based on a random transformation, we can leverage techniques for the QROM, whereas other sponge-based primitives are typically based on a random permutation. Our results yield post-quantum secure pseudorandom functions, pseudorandom generators, and hash functions all constructed entirely from sponges. Since these are fundamental cryptographic building blocks our contribution is more than just a post-quantum security proof for an AEAD scheme and can be applied elsewhere. In particular, it provides a starting point for proving post-quantum security of more practical schemes.

Related Work. Sponges were introduced by Bertoni et al. [8] as a tool to construct cryptographic hash functions which resulted in the hash function SHA-3. Since then, sponges were shown to be a versatile tool allowing not only the construction of hash functions but also primitives including authenticated encryption schemes [21–24,35].

Research in the realm of QS1 security of sponges mainly targets the security of hash functions. The first result addresses sponge-based hash functions based on random transformations or non-invertible random permutations [18]. The ultimate goal is a post-quantum proof for SHA-3 which is targeted both by Unruh [55][1] and Czajkowski [16] using Zhandry's compressed oracle technique [58]. Apart from that we are not aware of other works considering the QS1 security of sponge-based constructions.

In the QS2 setting, [20] studies the quantum indifferentiability of sponges and [19] analyses the quantum indistinguishability of sponge-based pseudorandom functions. The analysis in [19] uses keyed functions for the underlying block function which allow the adversary only classical access to these block functions while it has superposition access to the resulting pseudorandom function.

---

[1] Observe that the current version of the paper is flawed.

Soukharev et al. [51] study the generic composition paradigms for authenticated encryption in the QS2 setting according to the security notions put forth by Boneh and Zhandry [12]. However, their proof implicitly assumes that superposition queries by the adversary can be recorded which, at this point, was unclear how to do as was pointed out Chevalier et al. [15].

Structure of the Paper. In Sect. 2 and Appendix A, we provide the necessary notation and background. The general sponge construction and the particular instantiation SLAE is provided in Sect. 3. In Sect. 4, we provide a security analysis in the QS1 setting while in Sect. 5, we provide an analysis in the QS2 setting. We conclude the paper in Sect. 6 and provide proof details in Appendices B and C.

2 Preliminaries

2.1 Notation

For any positive integer $n \in \mathbb{N}$, we use $[n]$ to denote the set $\{1, \ldots, n\}$. For any two bit strings x and y of length n, $|x|$ denotes the size of x, $x \parallel y$ denotes their concatenation and by $x \cdot y = x_1 y_1 \oplus x_2 y_2 \oplus \ldots \oplus x_n y_n$ we denote their inner product. Furthermore, for a positive integer $k \leq |x|$, we use the notation $\lfloor x \rfloor_k$ to denote the string when truncated to its k least significant bits while $\lceil x \rceil^k$ denotes the string when truncated to its k most significant bits. We denote the set of bit strings of size n by $\{0,1\}^n$, and we denote by $\{0,1\}^*$ the set of all bit strings of finite length. By writing $x \leftarrow_\$ \mathcal{X}$, we denote the process of sampling at random a value from a finite set $\mathcal{X}$ and assigning it to x. We simply denote by $\mathsf{par}(x)$ the parity of x. Furthermore, we denote by $\mathcal{Y}^\mathcal{X}$ the set of all functions from $\mathcal{X}$ to $\mathcal{Y}$. We assume familiarity with the basics of quantum computation such as bra-ket notion for quantum states, e.g., $|x\rangle$, Hadamard operators, and measurements. For an in-depth discussion we refer to [46].

2.2 Definitions

Due to space restrictions, we provide basic definitions about authenticated encryption with associated data (AEAD) and message authentication codes (MAC) in Appendix A.

Pseudorandom Function. Next we define pseudorandom functions and their respective security.

Definition 1. *Let* $\mathcal{F} \colon \mathcal{K} \times \mathcal{X} \to \mathcal{Y}$ *be a deterministic function. We define the PRF advantage of an adversary* $\mathcal{A}$ *against* $\mathcal{F}$ *as*

$$\mathbf{Adv}_{\mathcal{F}}^{\mathsf{PRF}}(\mathcal{A}) = \left| \Pr_{\mathsf{K} \leftarrow_\$ \mathcal{K}}[\mathcal{A}^{\mathcal{F}(\mathsf{K}, \cdot)} \to 1] - \Pr_{\overline{\mathcal{F}} \leftarrow_\$ \mathcal{Y}^\mathcal{X}}[\mathcal{A}^{\overline{\mathcal{F}}(\cdot)} \to 1] \right|.$$

Pseudorandom Generator. Next we define a pseudorandom generator and its security. Observe that we specify a PRG with variable output length, where the length is specified as part of the input.

Definition 2. *Let $\mathcal{G}\colon \mathcal{S} \times \mathbb{N} \to \{0,1\}^*$ be a pseudorandom generator with associated seed space $\mathcal{S}$ and let $\ell \in \mathbb{N}$ define the PRG's output length. We define the PRG advantage of an adversary $\mathcal{A}$ against $\mathcal{G}$ as*

$$\mathbf{Adv}_{\mathcal{G}}^{\mathsf{PRG}}(\mathcal{A}) = \left| \Pr_{z \leftarrow \$ \, \mathcal{S}}[\mathcal{A}(\mathcal{G}(z, \ell)) \to 1] - \Pr_{R \leftarrow \$ \, \{0,1\}^\ell}[\mathcal{A}(R) \to 1] \right|.$$

Hash Function. Hash functions are a versatile cryptographic primitive that are efficiently computable functions that compress bit strings of arbitrary length to bit strings of fixed length. Hash functions do enjoy a variety of security properties and next we define collision resistance over a domain $\mathcal{X} = \{0,1\}^*$.

Definition 3. *Let $\mathcal{H}\colon \mathcal{X} \to \{0,1\}^w$ be a hash function constructed from a random transformation ρ. We define the collision-resistance advantage of an adversary $\mathcal{A}$ against $\mathcal{H}$ where the adversary has (quantum) oracle access to ρ as*

$$\mathbf{Adv}_{\mathcal{H}}^{\mathsf{CR}}(\mathcal{A}) = \Pr[(X_0, X_1) \leftarrow \$ \, \mathcal{A}^\rho : \mathcal{H}(X_0) = \mathcal{H}(X_1) \wedge X_0 \neq X_1 \wedge X_0, X_1 \in \mathcal{X}].$$

Since we consider hash functions in the QS1 and QS2 setting in this work, we require two additional properties when arguing about the security of a hash function, namely collapsing hash functions and zero-preimage resistance.

The collapsing property of hash functions is due to Unruh [54], who observed that collision resistance is not sufficient to construct commitment schemes secure against quantum adversaries.[2] Intuitively, a hash function is collapsing if an adversary can not distinguish between a measurement of the output (the hash value) and a measurement of the input. In [52, Lemma 25], Unruh shows that collapsing hash functions are also collision resistant. We present the formal definition of collapsing security in Appendix A.3.

Zero-preimage resistance states that it is infeasible for the adversary to output an element from the function's domain which evaluates to the zero string.

Definition 4. *Let $f^\rho\colon \{0,1\}^x \to \{0,1\}^y$ be a function. We define the zero-preimage resistance advantage of an adversary $\mathcal{A}$ against f^ρ where the adversary has (quantum) oracle access to ρ as*

$$\mathbf{Adv}_{f^\rho}^{\mathsf{ZP}}(\mathcal{A}) = \Pr[f^\rho(X) = 0^y : X \leftarrow \$ \, \mathcal{A}^\rho].$$

---

[2] In a nutshell, a quantum adversary can open a commitment to an arbitrary message but not to two different messages. Thus it breaks the binding property without finding a collision.

Quantum Random Oracle Model and One-way to Hiding Lemma. The quantum random oracle model (QROM) was formalised by Boneh et al. [10] extending the random oracle model (ROM) [7] to the quantum setting. The QROM has become the de-facto standard for analysing primitives which rely on random oracles. Boneh et al. [10] gave a separation between the ROM and the QROM, yet under non-standard assumptions. Recently, Yamakawa and Zhandry [56] provided a separation under standard assumptions. More precisely, let $H\colon \{0,1\}^n \to \{0,1\}^n$,[3] then the QROM allows a quantum adversary access to the unitary U_H that does the following

$$\sum_{x,y\in\{0,1\}^n} \alpha_{x,y} |x\rangle |y\rangle \mapsto \sum_{x,y\in\{0,1\}^n} \alpha_{x,y} |x\rangle |y \oplus H(x)\rangle .$$

We write $\mathcal{A}^H$ to denote that $\mathcal{A}$ has oracle access to H which means having access to an oracle performing the unitary above.

The one-way to hiding (O2H) lemma is a fundamental tool for proofs in the quantum random oracle model (QROM). It provides an upper bound on the distinguishing advantage of a quantum adversary between different random oracles when having superposition access to it. The first variant was given by Unruh [53]. Subsequently, variants achieving tighter bounds were given in [3,9, 40], yet at the cost of a more restricted applicability.

Below we recall the O2H lemma by Unruh [53], albeit in the formulation put forth by Ambainis et al. [3].

Lemma 5 (One-way to hiding (O2H) [3]). *Let $G, H\colon \mathcal{X} \to \mathcal{Y}$ be random functions, let z be a random bitstring, and let $\mathcal{S} \subset \mathcal{X}$ be a random set such that $\forall x \notin \mathcal{S}$, $G(x) = H(x)$. $(G, H, \mathcal{S}, z)$ may have arbitrary joint distribution. Furthermore, let $\mathcal{A}^H$ be a quantum oracle algorithm which queries H at most q times. Define an oracle algorithm $\mathcal{B}^H$ as follows: Pick $i \leftarrow_\$ [q]$. Run $\mathcal{A}_q^H(z)$ until just before its i-th query to H. Measure the query in the computational basis, and output the measurement outcome. Then it holds that*

$$\left|\Pr[\mathcal{A}^H(z) \to 1] - \Pr[\mathcal{A}^G(z) \to 1]\right| \le 2q\sqrt{\Pr[x \in \mathcal{S} \mid \mathcal{B}^H(z) \to x]}.$$

3 The Sponge Construction and SLAE

In this section, we provide the basic syntax about the sponge construction. Being equipped with the required syntax, we review SLAE which is a N2-based authenticated encryption scheme [44] based on the sponge construction. Recall that a N2-construction follows the Encrypt-then-MAC paradigm and SLAE is a refinement that builds a nonce-based AEAD scheme from a nonce-based symmetric key encryption scheme and a vector MAC.

---

[3] We assume that domain and co-domain are of the same size as it is the only case we are considering in this work.

3.1 Sponge Construction

The sponge construction has been introduced by Bertoni et al. [8] and has been used to build various cryptographic primitives. In Fig. 1, we provide an illustration of the plain sponge construction.

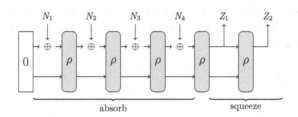

Fig. 1. Plain sponge using four rounds of absorbing and two rounds of squeezing.

The sponge construction consists of a so-called *absorbing* phase and a *squeezing* phase that is built upon a transformation ρ that is iteratively called on its input. This transformation basically maps strings of length n to strings of the same length, and in particular one can decompose n into two values $r + c$ where r is called the rate and c is called the capacity. After each iteration of the transformation we refer to its output as the state S. Furthermore, we usually refer to the leftmost r bits of the state as the outer part $\bar{S}$, which is equivalent to $\lceil S \rceil^r$, and we refer to the remaining c bits as the inner part $\hat{S}$, which is equivalent to $\lfloor S \rfloor_c$. In order to input some element N, this input is first padded to a non-zero multiple of the rate r. For this, we use an injective padding function **pad** to get $l \geq 1$ input blocks $N_1 \parallel N_2 \parallel \ldots \parallel N_l = \textbf{pad}(N)$. At the ith iteration, N_i is XORed with the outer part $\bar{S}$ before being inputted to the transformation, i.e., more formally $Y_i \leftarrow (N_i \oplus \bar{S}_i) \parallel \hat{S}_i$ and evaluating $S_{i+1} \leftarrow \rho(Y_i)$. In the squeezing phase, one can produce an output in one or more iterations obtaining r bits of output per iteration, i.e., more formally at the jth iteration the output Z_j is produced by $Z_j \leftarrow \bar{S}_j$.

3.2 The FGHF' Construction and SLAE

Degabriele et al. [21] provide a generic N2-construction [44] of a leakage-resilient authenticated encryption scheme with associated data called the FGHF' construction. In particular, they show that the encryption component can be constructed from a fixed-input length function family that retains pseudorandomness in the presence of leakage (F) combined with a (standard) pseudorandom generator (G) while the authentication component is built from a collision-resistant hash function (H) and a fixed-input length function family that retains both pseudorandomness and unpredictability in the presence of leakage (F'). Overall this yields a leakage-resilient AEAD scheme. Observe that Krämer and

$\text{SLAE-Enc}(K, N, A, M)$	$\text{SLFUNC}(K, N)$	$\text{SVHASH}(N, A, C)$
$C \leftarrow \text{SLENC}(K, N, M)$	$l \leftarrow \lceil \frac{|N|}{r} \rceil$	$S_0 \leftarrow 0^n$
$T \leftarrow \text{SLMAC}(K, (N, A, C))$	$Y_0 \leftarrow K$	$Y_0 \leftarrow (N \oplus \bar{S}_0) \parallel \hat{S}_0$
return (C, T)	**for** $i = 1..l$	$S_1 \leftarrow \rho(Y_0)$
	$\quad S_i \leftarrow \rho(Y_{i-1})$	$u \leftarrow \lceil \frac{|A|}{r} \rceil$
$\text{SLENC-Enc}(K, N, M)$	$\quad Y_i \leftarrow (N_i \oplus \bar{S}_i) \parallel \hat{S}_i$	**for** $i = 1..u$
	$S_{l+1} \leftarrow \rho(Y_l)$	$\quad Y_i \leftarrow (A_i \oplus \bar{S}_i) \parallel \hat{S}_i$
$z \leftarrow \text{SLFUNC}(K, N)$	**return** S_{l+1}	$\quad S_{i+1} \leftarrow \rho(Y_i)$
$Z \leftarrow \text{SPRG}(z, |M|)$		$\hat{S}_{u+1} \leftarrow \hat{S}_{u+1} \oplus (1 \parallel 0^{c-1})$
$C \leftarrow Z \oplus M$	$\text{SPRG}(z, y)$	$v \leftarrow \lceil \frac{|C|}{r} \rceil$
return C	$l \leftarrow \lceil \frac{y}{r} \rceil$	**for** $i = u+1..u+v$
	$S_0 \leftarrow z$	$\quad Y_i \leftarrow (C_{i-u} \oplus \bar{S}_i) \parallel \hat{S}_i$
$\text{SLMAC-T}(K, (N, A, C))$	**for** $i = 1..l$	$\quad S_{i+1} \leftarrow \rho(Y_i)$
	$\quad S_i \leftarrow \rho(S_{i-1})$	$h \leftarrow \lfloor S_{u+v+1} \rfloor_w$
$H \leftarrow \text{SVHASH}(N, A, C)$	$\quad Z_i \leftarrow \bar{S}_i$	**return** h
$T \leftarrow \text{SLFUNC}(K, H)$	$Z \leftarrow Z_1 \parallel \ldots \parallel Z_l$	
return T	**return** $\lfloor Z \rfloor_y$	

Fig. 2. Pseudocode of SLAE and the underlying components. We only provide the details of the encryption and tagging algorithms. Decryption and verification works in the obvious reversed way.

Struck [39] showed that leakage-resilient pseudorandom functions suffice to build the scheme of Degabriele et al. [21] dropping the unpredictability requirement.

Furthermore, Degabriele et al. [21] show that the generic construction FGHF' can be instantiated entirely from the sponge construction using a random transformation. Their particular sponge construction is called SLAE which is composed of a symmetric key encryption scheme SLENC and a MAC SLMAC according to the N2-construction. In particular, viewing each of the schemes in terms of their smaller components, Degabriele et al. build SLENC from a leakage-resilient function SLFUNC and a pseudorandom generator SPRG while SLMAC can be built from a collision-resistant hash function SVHASH and a leakage-resilient function SLFUNC, and a formal description is given in Fig. 2. Regarding the security of SLAE, they prove the security via a composition theorem for the N2-construction in the leakage setting as established by Barwell et al. [5].

However, the quantum resistance of SLAE has not been considered yet. In the following, we will scrutinize the SLAE construction in this regard and we set the respective leakage sets to be empty. Therefore, we analyse the construction in the standard setting without leakage.

4   Post-Quantum (QS1) Security

In this section we analyse the security of SLAE against quantum adversaries in the QS1 setting. The respective proofs of this Section can be found in Appendix B.

4.1   Security of SLFUNC

The sponge-based pseudorandom function SLFUNC is illustrated in Fig. 3 while the pseudocode can be found in Fig. 2. The function initialises the state of the sponge with the key and then absorbs the input, in case of SLAE the nonce N, r bits at a time. After the nonce has been absorbed, the output is obtained by applying the transformation ρ a final time and outputting the state. Note that the function outputs the full state rather than squeezing it over several rounds. That is also the reason why ρ is required to be a random transformation rather than a random permutation. Otherwise, an adversary could simply undo the transformation from the output by applying the inverse permutation. The theorem below gives a bound on distinguishing SLFUNC from a random function when having superposition access to the underlying random oracle ρ. The proof utilises the O2H lemma (cf. Lemma 5).

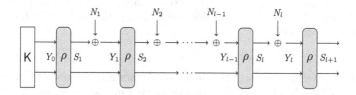

Fig. 3. Sponge-based pseudorandom function SLFUNC.

Theorem 6. *Let $\mathcal{F} = $ SLFUNC be the function displayed in Fig. 3. Then for any quantum adversary $\mathcal{A}$, making $q_{\mathcal{F}}$ (classical) queries to SLFUNC and q_ρ (quantum) queries to ρ, it holds that*

$$\mathbf{Adv}_{\mathrm{SLFUNC}}^{\mathrm{PRF}}(\mathcal{A}) \leq \frac{q_{\mathcal{F}}^2 + q_{\mathcal{F}}}{2^{n+1}} + 2q_\rho\sqrt{\frac{2^\nu}{2^n}}.$$

Proof. Let $l = \lceil\frac{\nu}{r}\rceil$ be the number of absorption steps and we assume for simplicity that ν is a multiple of the rate. We further recursively define sets $\mathcal{Y}_i$ as

$$\mathcal{Y}_0 = \{\mathsf{K}\} \qquad \text{and} \qquad \mathcal{Y}_i = \{R \parallel \lfloor\rho(x)\rfloor_c \mid R \in \{0,1\}^r, x \in \mathcal{Y}_{i-1}\}$$

for all $i \in \{1, \ldots, l\}$, i.e., $\mathcal{Y}_i$ is the set of all possible values that can occur as input to ρ while evaluating $\mathcal{F}(\mathsf{K}, \cdot)$. It follows that $|\mathcal{Y}_i| \leq 2^{ir}$ and, in particular, $|\mathcal{Y}_l| \leq 2^{lr} = 2^\nu$. Note that every input N defines a sequence of states $Y_0, Y_1, \ldots, Y_l$

that occur while evaluating the sponge. For an input N, let $Y_i[N]$ denote the state Y_i for this particular input, e.g., $Y_1[N] = (\lceil \rho(\mathsf{K}) \rceil^r \oplus N_1) \parallel \lfloor \rho(\mathsf{K}) \rfloor_c$, where $N = N_1 \parallel \ldots \parallel N_l$. In particular, for every input N it holds that $Y_0[N] = \mathsf{K}$.

We want to bound the following difference

$$\mathbf{Adv}^{\mathrm{PRF}}_{\mathrm{SLFunc}}(\mathcal{A}) = \left| \Pr_{\mathsf{K} \leftarrow \$ \, \mathcal{K}} [\mathcal{A}^{\mathcal{F}(\mathsf{K},\cdot),\rho} \to 1] - \Pr_{\overline{\mathcal{F}} \leftarrow \$ \, \mathcal{Y}^{\mathcal{X}}} [\mathcal{A}^{\overline{\mathcal{F}}(\cdot),\rho} \to 1] \right|.$$

In order to do this, we define the oracle ρ_*, where $\rho_*(Y_l[N]) = \overline{\mathcal{F}}(N)$ for all $Y_l[N] \in \mathcal{Y}_l$. That is, oracle ρ_* is reprogrammed on all final input states $Y_l[N]$ to output the output of a random function $\overline{\mathcal{F}}$ on the input N. Then it holds that

$$\left| \Pr_{\mathsf{K} \leftarrow \$ \, \mathcal{K}} [\mathcal{A}^{\mathcal{F}(\mathsf{K},\cdot),\rho} \to 1] - \Pr_{\overline{\mathcal{F}} \leftarrow \$ \, \mathcal{Y}^{\mathcal{X}}} [\mathcal{A}^{\overline{\mathcal{F}}(\cdot),\rho} \to 1] \right|$$

$$\leq \left| \Pr_{\mathsf{K} \leftarrow \$ \, \mathcal{K}} [\mathcal{A}^{\mathcal{F}(\mathsf{K},\cdot),\rho} \to 1] - \Pr_{\overline{\mathcal{F}} \leftarrow \$ \, \mathcal{Y}^{\mathcal{X}}} [\mathcal{A}^{\overline{\mathcal{F}}(\cdot),\rho_*} \to 1] \right|$$

$$+ \left| \Pr_{\overline{\mathcal{F}} \leftarrow \$ \, \mathcal{Y}^{\mathcal{X}}} [\mathcal{A}^{\overline{\mathcal{F}}(\cdot),\rho_*} \to 1] - \Pr_{\overline{\mathcal{F}} \leftarrow \$ \, \mathcal{Y}^{\mathcal{X}}} [\mathcal{A}^{\overline{\mathcal{F}}(\cdot),\rho} \to 1] \right|.$$

For the first difference on the right-hand side, the oracles are consistent in both cases. However, if the adversary finds a collision on the final input to ρ for $\mathrm{SLFunc}(\mathsf{K},\cdot)$, more precisely, two inputs N and N' such that $\lceil N \rceil^{\nu-r} \neq \lceil N' \rceil^{\nu-r}$ and $Y_l[N] = Y_l[N']$, then these two inputs will result in the same output for $\mathcal{F}$ and (most likely) different outputs for $\overline{\mathcal{F}}$. Finding such a collision is a counting argument over the number of queries to the function and an application of Gaussian summation. Hence, it follows that

$$\left| \Pr_{\mathsf{K} \leftarrow \$ \, \mathcal{K}} [\mathcal{A}^{\mathcal{F}(\mathsf{K},\cdot),\rho} \to 1] - \Pr_{\overline{\mathcal{F}} \leftarrow \$ \, \mathcal{Y}^{\mathcal{X}}} [\mathcal{A}^{\overline{\mathcal{F}}(\cdot),\rho_*} \to 1] \right| \leq \frac{q_{\overline{\mathcal{F}}}^2 + q_{\mathcal{F}}}{2^{n+1}}.$$

For the second difference, we can apply the O2H lemma (cf. Lemma 5) which yields

$$\left| \Pr_{\overline{\mathcal{F}} \leftarrow \$ \, \mathcal{Y}^{\mathcal{X}}} [\mathcal{A}^{\overline{\mathcal{F}}(\cdot),\rho_*} \to 1] - \Pr_{\overline{\mathcal{F}} \leftarrow \$ \, \mathcal{Y}^{\mathcal{X}}} [\mathcal{A}^{\overline{\mathcal{F}}(\cdot),\rho} \to 1] \right| \leq 2q_\rho \sqrt{\Pr[x \in \mathcal{Y}_l \mid \mathcal{B}^{\overline{\mathcal{F}}(\cdot),\rho} \to x]}.$$

Recall that $\mathcal{B}^{\overline{\mathcal{F}}(\cdot),\rho}$ simply runs $\mathcal{A}^{\overline{\mathcal{F}}(\cdot),\rho}$ and outputs the measurement outcome of a randomly chosen query to ρ. However, $\mathcal{A}$ has no information about the set $\mathcal{Y}_l$, hence we conclude with

$$2q_\rho \sqrt{\Pr[x \in \mathcal{Y}_l \mid \mathcal{B}^{\overline{\mathcal{F}}(\cdot),\rho} \to x]} \leq 2q_\rho \sqrt{\frac{|\mathcal{Y}_l|}{2^n}} \leq 2q_\rho \sqrt{\frac{2^\nu}{2^n}}.$$

Collecting everything yields

$$\mathbf{Adv}^{\mathrm{PRF}}_{\mathrm{SLFunc}}(\mathcal{A}) = \left| \Pr_{\mathsf{K} \leftarrow \$ \, \mathcal{K}} [\mathcal{A}^{\mathcal{F}(\mathsf{K},\cdot),\rho} \to 1] - \Pr_{\overline{\mathcal{F}} \leftarrow \$ \, \mathcal{Y}^{\mathcal{X}}} [\mathcal{A}^{\overline{\mathcal{F}}(\cdot),\rho} \to 1] \right|$$

$$\leq \frac{q_{\overline{\mathcal{F}}}^2 + q_{\mathcal{F}}}{2^{n+1}} + 2q_\rho \sqrt{\frac{2^\nu}{2^n}}.$$

$\square$

We would like to point out the following. The length of the nonce ν is typically of fixed size, e.g., in case of the NIST lightweight cryptography standardization process [45] the nonce is assumed to be 12 bytes long. In particular, ν will be much smaller than the size of the sponge n.

4.2 Security of SPRG

In this section we show that the sponge-based pseudorandom generator SPRG is secure against adversaries having superposition access to the underlying random oracle ρ. The PRG SPRG is displayed in Fig. 4 and the respective pseudocode is given in Fig. 2. The construction deviates from more common constructions for pseudorandom generators since it initialises the state of the sponge with the seed rather than absorbing it. The output is then generated by squeezing r bits at each iteration of the sponge. Similar to the previous section, the proof relies on the O2H lemma.

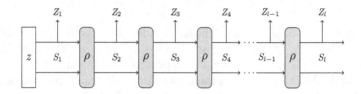

Fig. 4. Sponge-based pseudorandom generator SPRG.

Theorem 7. *Let* SPRG *be the pseudorandom generator displayed in Fig. 4. Then for any quantum adversary* $\mathcal{A}$, *making* q *(quantum) queries to* ρ, *and receiving an input of length* μ *it holds that*

$$\mathbf{Adv}_{\mathrm{SPRG}}^{\mathrm{PRG}}(\mathcal{A}) \leq \frac{2lq}{\sqrt{2^c}},$$

where $l = \lceil \frac{\mu}{r} \rceil$ *is the number of squeezing steps to obtain the required output length* μ.

Proof. Let $l = \lceil \frac{\mu}{r} \rceil$ be the number of squeezing steps. We assume, for sake of simplicity, that μ is a multiple of r. For a seed z, let $S_1, S_2, \ldots, S_l$ denote the sequence of states that occur during evaluation of the sponge, i.e., $S_i = \rho^{i-1}(z)$, where ρ^i corresponds to i consecutive evaluations of ρ. We want to bound the following difference

$$\mathbf{Adv}_{\mathrm{SPRG}}^{\mathrm{PRG}}(\mathcal{A}) = \left| \Pr_{z \leftarrow \$\, \mathcal{S}}[\mathcal{A}^\rho(Z) \to 1] - \Pr_{R \leftarrow \$\, \{0,1\}^\mu}[\mathcal{A}^\rho(R) \to 1] \right|,$$

where $Z = Z_1 \parallel \ldots \parallel Z_l = \mathrm{SPRG}(z, lr)$, i.e., obtaining an output of length lr using SPRG on seed z and $R = R_1 \parallel \ldots \parallel R_l$, such that $|Z_i| = |R_i| = r$.

We write $R_{[i,j]}$ for $R_i \parallel \ldots \parallel R_j$, the same for Z. In particular, $R_{[i,j]}$ for $i > j$ equals the empty string. In the following we leave out the probability spaces for readability. We obtain

$$\mathbf{Adv}_{\mathrm{SPRG}}^{\mathrm{PRG}}(\mathcal{A}) = \left| \Pr[\mathcal{A}^\rho(Z_{[1,l]}) \to 1] - \Pr[\mathcal{A}^\rho(R_{[1,l]}) \to 1] \right|$$

$$\leq \sum_{i=1}^{l} \left| \Pr[\mathcal{A}^\rho(R_{[1,i-1]} \parallel Z_{[i,l]}) \to 1] - \Pr[\mathcal{A}^\rho(R_{[1,i]} \parallel Z_{[i+1,l]}) \to 1] \right| .$$

We start with the first difference, that, after simple rewriting, is,

$$\left| \Pr[\mathcal{A}^\rho(Z_1 \parallel Z_{[2,l]}) \to 1] - \Pr[\mathcal{A}^\rho(R_1 \parallel Z_{[2,l]}) \to 1] \right|$$

$$\leq \left| \Pr[\mathcal{A}^\rho(Z_1 \parallel Z_{[2,l]}) \to 1] - \Pr[\mathcal{A}^{\rho_1}(R_1 \parallel Z_{[2,l]}) \to 1] \right|$$

$$+ \left| \Pr[\mathcal{A}^{\rho_1}(R_1 \parallel Z_{[2,l]}) \to 1] - \Pr[\mathcal{A}^\rho(R_1 \parallel Z_{[2,l]}) \to 1] \right| ,$$

where $\rho_1(R_1 \parallel [S_1]_c) = S_2$. Then it holds that the first difference above is 0, as the relation between R_1 and ρ_1 is the same as between Z_1 and ρ, and we merely need to bound the second difference, which only differs in the random oracle (ρ and ρ_1) at input $R_1 \parallel [S_1]_c$. Let $\mathcal{S}_1 = \{R_1 \parallel [S_1]_c\}$, then we can apply the O2H lemma (cf. Lemma 5) to obtain

$$\left| \Pr[\mathcal{A}^{\rho_1}(R_1 \parallel Z_{[2,l]}) \to 1] - \Pr[\mathcal{A}^\rho(R_1 \parallel Z_{[2,l]}) \to 1] \right|$$

$$\leq 2q\sqrt{\Pr[x \in \mathcal{S}_1 \mid \mathcal{B}^\rho(R_1 \parallel Z_{[2,l]}) \to x]}.$$

While $\mathcal{A}$ knows R_1, it has no information about $[S_1]_c$ (note that Z_i, for $i > 1$ provides no information about $\mathcal{S}_1$ due to ρ being one-way in the random oracle model). This yields

$$\Pr[x \in \mathcal{S}_1 \mid \mathcal{B}^\rho(R_1 \parallel Z_{[2,l]}) \to x] \leq \frac{|\mathcal{S}_1|}{2^c} \leq \frac{1}{2^c} .$$

The same argument applies to the other differences, where more and more r bit blocks of $\mathcal{A}$'s input are replaced with R_i. More precisely, we obtain

$$\left| \Pr[\mathcal{A}^\rho(R_{[1,i-1]} \parallel Z_{[i,l]}) \to 1] - \Pr[\mathcal{A}^\rho(R_{[1,i]} \parallel Z_{[i+1,l]}) \to 1] \right|$$

$$\leq 2q\sqrt{\Pr[x \in \mathcal{S}_i \mid \mathcal{B}^\rho(R_{[1,i]} \parallel Z_{[i+1,l]}) \to x]} \leq \frac{2q}{\sqrt{2^c}} ,$$

where $\mathcal{S}_i = \{R_i \parallel [S_i]_c\}$. Collecting everything then yields

$$\mathbf{Adv}_{\mathrm{SPRG}}^{\mathrm{PRG}}(\mathcal{A}) = \left| \Pr[\mathcal{A}^\rho(Z_{[1,l-1]}) \to 1] - \Pr[\mathcal{A}^\rho(R_{[1,l-1]}) \to 1] \right|$$

$$\leq \sum_{i=1}^{l} \left| \Pr[\mathcal{A}^\rho(R_{[1,i-1]} \parallel Z_{[i,l]}) \to 1] - \Pr[\mathcal{A}^\rho(R_{[1,i]} \parallel Z_{[i+1,l]}) \to 1] \right|$$

$$\leq \sum_{i=1}^{l} 2q\sqrt{\Pr[x \in \mathcal{S}_i \mid \mathcal{B}^\rho(R_{[1,i]} \parallel Z_{[i+1,l]}) \to x]} \leq \frac{2lq}{\sqrt{2^c}} .$$

$\square$

4.3   Security of SvHash

In this section we analyse the QS1 security of SvHash which we display in Fig. 5 and its respective pseudocode can be found in Fig. 2. Observe that in order to compute a hash digest, the internal state is initialised to an evaluation of the random transformation of a zero bit string of length n XORed with the passed nonce. Afterwards the padded associated data and padded ciphertext are absorbed blockwise. Degabriele et al. chose to employ a domain separation to separate the boundary between associated data and ciphertext consisting of XORing the string $1 \parallel 0^{c-1}$ to the inner state $\hat{S}$ as soon as the associated data has been absorbed. Observe that the domain separation can be viewed as a sponge construction with a rate increased by one bit. In this sense, an adversary $\mathcal{A}$ against SvHash with rate r and capacity c can be viewed as an adversary against the plain sponge-based hash function with rate $r+1$ and capacity $c-1$, where $\mathcal{A}$ guarantees that the $(r+1)$th bit of each input block is 0 except for the block which corresponds to absorbing the first ciphertext block. Hence a bound for the plain sponge-based hash function directly yields a bound for SvHash by accounting for the one bit loss in the capacity. The proof can be found in Appendix B.

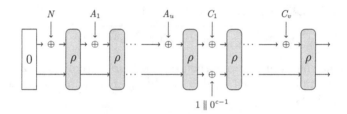

Fig. 5. Sponge-based Hash function SvHash.

Theorem 8. *Let SvHash be the hash function as displayed in Fig. 5. Then for any quantum adversary $\mathcal{A}$ making q (quantum) queries to ρ, it holds that*

$$\mathbf{Adv}^{\mathsf{CR}}_{\mathrm{SvHash}}(\mathcal{A}) \leq \sqrt{\varepsilon_1} + l \cdot \varepsilon_2 + \varepsilon_3 \,,$$

where $\varepsilon_1 \leq (q+1)^2 2^{-c+4}$, $\varepsilon_2 \leq q^3 \left(\frac{\delta'+324}{2^{c-1}} \right) + 7\delta \sqrt{\frac{3(q+4)^3}{2^c}}$ and $\varepsilon_3 \leq q^3 \left(\frac{\delta'+324}{2^{w+1}} \right) + 7\delta \sqrt{\frac{3(q+4)^3}{2^{w+2}}}$ with non-zero constants δ and δ' as well as $l = \lceil \frac{\mu}{r} \rceil$ where μ is the length of the (padded) message.

4.4   Security of SLAE

In this section we show that the IND-CPA and INT-CTXT security of the authenticated encryption scheme SLAE in the QS1 follows from the QS1 security of the underlying primitives SLFunc, SPrg, and SvHash. The proofs can be found in Appendix B.

IND-CPA *Security of* SLAE. IND-CPA security follows from SLFUNC and SPRG being a secure PRF and PRG, respectively. Theorem 9 first shows that SLFUNC and SPRG yield SLENC being IND-CPA-secure while Theorem 10 then establishes the IND-CPA security of SLAE.

Theorem 9. *Let* SLFUNC *be a pseudorandom function and* SPRG *a pseudorandom generator. Let further* SLENC *be the symmetric key encryption scheme constructed from* SLFUNC *and* SPRG *as shown in Fig. 2. For any quantum adversary* $\mathcal{A}$, *making* q_{Enc} *queries to its encryption oracle, against the* IND-CPA *security there exist adversaries* $\mathcal{A}_{prf}$ *and* $\mathcal{A}_{prg}$ *against* SLFUNC *and* SPRG, *respectively, such that*

$$\mathbf{Adv}_{\mathrm{SLENC}}^{\mathsf{IND\text{-}CPA}}(\mathcal{A}) \leq 2\,\mathbf{Adv}_{\mathrm{SLFUNC}}^{\mathsf{PRF}}(\mathcal{A}_{prf}) + 2q\,\mathbf{Adv}_{\mathrm{SPRG}}^{\mathsf{PRG}}(\mathcal{A}_{prg})\,.$$

Theorem 10. *Let* SLENC *be the symmetric key encryption scheme and* SLMAC *be a MAC. Let further* SLAE *be the authenticated encryption scheme constructed from* SLENC *and* SLMAC *as shown in Fig. 2. For any quantum adversary* $\mathcal{A}$, *making* q_{Enc} *queries to its encryption oracle, against the* IND-CPA *security there exists an adversary* $\mathcal{A}_{se}$, *such that*

$$\mathbf{Adv}_{\mathrm{SLAE}}^{\mathsf{IND\text{-}CPA}}(\mathcal{A}) \leq \mathbf{Adv}_{\mathrm{SLENC}}^{\mathsf{IND\text{-}CPA}}(\mathcal{A}_{se})\,.$$

INT-CTXT *Security of* SLAE. The INT-CTXT security follows from SLFUNC being a secure PRF and SVHASH being a collision-resistant hash function. In Theorem 11, we show that both yield a SUF-CMA-secure MAC SLMAC. Subsequently, Theorem 12 shows that the SUF-CMA security of SLMAC ensures INT-CTXT security of SLAE.

Theorem 11. *Let* SLFUNC *be a function and* SVHASH *a hash function. Let further* SLMAC *be the MAC constructed from* SLFUNC *and* SVHASH *as shown in Fig. 2. For any quantum adversary* $\mathcal{A}$, *making* q_T *queries to its tagging oracle and* q_F *to its forge oracle, against the* SUF-CMA *security there exist adversaries* $\mathcal{A}_{prf}$ *and* $\mathcal{A}_{hash}$ *against* SLFUNC *and* SVHASH, *respectively, such that*

$$\mathbf{Adv}_{\mathrm{SLMAC}}^{\mathsf{SUF\text{-}CMA}}(\mathcal{A}) \leq \mathbf{Adv}_{\mathrm{SLFUNC}}^{\mathsf{PRF}}(\mathcal{A}_{prf}) + \mathbf{Adv}_{\mathrm{SVHASH}}^{\mathsf{CR}}(\mathcal{A}_{hash}) + \frac{q_F}{2^\tau}\,.$$

Theorem 12. *Let* SLENC *be the symmetric key encryption scheme and* SLMAC *be a MAC. Let further* SLAE *be the authenticated encryption scheme constructed from* SLENC *and* SLMAC *as shown in Fig. 2. For any quantum adversary* $\mathcal{A}$, *making* q_E *queries to its encryption oracle and* q_F *queries to its forge oracle, against the* INT-CTXT *security there exists an adversary* $\mathcal{A}_{mac}$, *such that*

$$\mathbf{Adv}_{\mathrm{SLAE}}^{\mathsf{INT\text{-}CTXT}}(\mathcal{A}) \leq \mathbf{Adv}_{\mathrm{SLMAC}}^{\mathsf{SUF\text{-}CMA}}(\mathcal{A}_{mac})\,.$$

5   Quantum (QS2) Security

In this section we study the security of SLAE in the QS2 setting, where both the adversary and the challenger are quantum. Unlike the QS1 setting, the QS2 setting comes with several security notions. We analyse SLAE, or even more precisely its encryption component SLENC, with respect to the quantum security notions put forward in [12, 28, 43] providing positive and negative results.

5.1   QS2 Security Notions for SKE

Unlike the QS1 setting, there are several notions in the QS2 setting for encryption schemes. The first notion, called IND-qCPA, was presented by Boneh and Zhandry [12]. This notion allows the adversary superposition queries in the learning (qCPA) phase, while its challenge (IND) phase is restricted to classical queries. They further showed that simply allowing a quantum indistinguishability phase results in an unachievable security notion, called fqIND-CPA. More precisely, they consider a left-or-right oracle which performs the following

$$\sum_{x_0, x_1, y} \alpha_{x_0, x_1, y} |x_0\rangle |x_1\rangle |y\rangle \mapsto \sum_{x_0, x_1, y} \alpha_{x_0, x_1, y} |x_0\rangle |x_1\rangle |y \oplus \mathtt{Enc}(\mathsf{K}, x_b)\rangle \ .$$

This operator entangles the ciphertext register with one of the message registers. Boneh and Zhandry show how this entanglement can be exploited to determine the bit b, irrespectively of the underlying encryption scheme.

Later, Gagliardoni et al. [28] and Mossayebi and Schack [43] provided security notions which allow the challenge (IND) phase to be quantum while not suffering from the impossibility result from [12].

An exhaustive study of QS2 security notions for encryption schemes is given by Carstens et al. [14]. Their study includes the aforementioned notions, along with many variants differing in the number of queries during challenge resp. learning phase. They show, surprisingly, that the notions do not form a strict hierarchy. Instead, the notions by Gagliardoni et al. [28] and Mossayebi and Schack [43] are incomparable but, together, imply all other notions. To ensure security in the QS2 setting, schemes have to be analysed with respect to both of these notions.

Nonce-Respecting Adversaries in the QS2 Setting. Another question that arises for the security of SLAE, deals with the nonce selection. Typically, adversaries are assumed to be nonce-respecting, meaning that they never repeat a nonce. While this is well defined in both the classical as well as QS1 setting, there is no definition for such adversaries in the QS2 setting. Kaplan et al. [36] mention this problem and sidestep it by letting the game pick the nonce at random. Thus, they essentially switch to the weaker IV setting which is well-studied in the classical setting. In our adapted security notions, we let the adversary submit a nonce register along with its message(s). We observe that it is not necessary to observe nonces in superposition since all QS2 notions for encryption schemes [12,15,28,29,43] consider the randomness (in case of SLAE the nonce) to be classical.[4] To comply with this, we let the challenger measure the nonce register, thus ensuring a classical nonce, and reject a query if a nonce repeats.

5.2   Left-or-Right Security of SLEnc

The notion by Gagliardoni et al. [28] follows a left-or-right approach, similar to the one by Boneh and Zhandry [12], in which the adversary submits two

---

[4] The same applies to QS2 notions for MACs and signatures [1,11,12,25].

messages (possibly in superposition) and receives the encryption of one of the two. The main difference is that Gagliardoni et al. use type-2 operators which operate directly on the register (instead of XORing the output to a separate output register). These operators are more powerful than the corresponding type-1 operator and they can only be realised for functions that are reversible. Type-2 operators were first studied by Kashefi et al. [38] and have further been studied by Carstens et al. [14] for symmetric key encryption and by Gagliardoni et al. [29] for public key encryption.

More formally those operators can be formalised as follows. Let $\mathcal{F}\colon \{0,1\}^n \to \{0,1\}^n$ be a function. The type-1 operator for $\mathcal{F}$ is the unitary $U_{\mathcal{F}}^{(1)}$ that does the following

$$\sum_{x,y\in\{0,1\}^n} \alpha_{x,y} \ket{x}\ket{y} \mapsto \sum_{x,y\in\{0,1\}^n} \alpha_{x,y} \ket{x}\ket{y\oplus\mathcal{F}(x)} .$$

Observe that the realisation of $U_{\mathcal{F}}^{(1)}$ is efficient if $\mathcal{F}$ can be realised efficiently [46]. The type-2 operator for $\mathcal{F}$ is the unitary $U_{\mathcal{F}}^{(2)}$ that does the following

$$\sum_{x\in\{0,1\}^n} \alpha_x \ket{x} \mapsto \sum_{x} \alpha_x \ket{\mathcal{F}(x)} .$$

A realisation of a type-2 operator is, unlike for type-1 operators, not straightforward. Kashefi et al. [38] show that they can be realised using type-1 operators for both $\mathcal{F}$ and $\mathcal{F}^{-1}$. Gagliardoni et al. [28] use this to show that type-2 operators for symmetric key encryption schemes can be realised using type-1 operators for encryption and decryption (cf. Fig. 6).

Using type-2 operators, Gagliardoni et al. [28] bypass the impossibility result by Boneh and Zhandry [12]. Since the adversary only receives a ciphertext register, it can not exploit the entanglement between registers as was the case for fqIND-CPA.

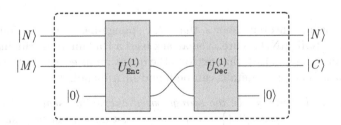

Fig. 6. Circuit for realising the type-2 operator $U_{\mathsf{Enc}}^{(2)}$ using type-1 operators $U_{\mathsf{Enc}}^{(1)}$ and $U_{\mathsf{Dec}}^{(1)}$ for Enc and Dec, respectively.

Below we define LoR-qIND security. This is the notion given in [28] restricted to a single challenge and no learning queries. The difference is that our notion allows the adversary to specify a register containing the nonce used for encryption. To ensure the usage of classical randomness, we let the challenger measure this register. We restrict ourselves to the weaker LoR-qIND notion, since we show below that SLAE does not even achieve this notion. Extension to the stronger LoR-qINDqCPA (allowing multiple challenges and learning queries) is straightforward by giving the adversary oracle access to a left-or-right oracle and a learning oracle implementing the type-2 encryption operator. The nonce-respecting property is ensured by letting the challenger reject queries for which the measurement of the nonce register yields an already measured nonce.

Definition 13. *Let* $\Sigma = (\text{Enc}, \text{Dec})$ *be symmetric key encryption scheme and the security game* LoR-qIND *be defined as in Fig. 7. For any adversary* $\mathcal{A}$ *we define its* LoR-qIND *advantage as*

$$\mathbf{Adv}_{\Sigma}^{\text{LoR-qIND}}(\mathcal{A}) = \left| 2 \Pr[\text{LoR-qIND}^{\mathcal{A}} \to 1] - 1 \right| .$$

LoR-qIND
$K \leftarrow_{\$} \mathcal{K}$
implement $U_{\text{Enc}}^{(2)}$ using K
$b \leftarrow_{\$} \{0,1\}$
$\lvert N \rangle_N, \lvert \varphi_0 \rangle_M, \lvert \varphi_1 \rangle_M \leftarrow_{\$} \mathcal{A}_1()$
Measure register $\lvert N \rangle_N$
trace out $\lvert \varphi_{1-b} \rangle$
$\lvert \psi \rangle \leftarrow U_{\text{Enc}}^{(2)}(\lvert N \rangle_N \lvert \varphi_b \rangle_M)$
$b' \leftarrow_{\$} \mathcal{A}_2(\lvert \psi \rangle)$
return $(b' = b)$

Fig. 7. Security notion LoR-qIND following [28].

The following theorem shows that the sponge-based encryption scheme SLENC is not LoR-qIND-secure. The attack uses a Hadamard distinguisher, following the one given in [28], that exploits the quantum insecurity of the one-time pad approach. The proof details can be found in Appendix C.

Theorem 14. *Let* SLENC *be the sponge-based encryption scheme displayed in Fig. 2 with message space* $\{0,1\}^\mu$. *Then there exist an adversary* $\mathcal{A}$ *such that*

$$\mathbf{Adv}_{\text{SLENC}}^{\text{LoR-qIND}}(\mathcal{A}) = 1 - \frac{1}{2^\mu} .$$

Observe that there is no security notion for AEAD schemes using type-2 operators. Both [28] and [29] only focus on encryption schemes. The obvious question is whether the MAC can be implemented using a type-2 operator. Regardless of this, we point out that the attack does not necessarily extend to SLAE. The reason is that the register containing the tag will be entangled which thwarts an attack by simply discarding the tag.

Note that the same attack applies to the encryption scheme underlying the sponge-based AEAD schemes ISAP [23] and its successor ISAP v2.0 [22].

5.3   Real-or-Random Security of SLENC

The notion by Mossayebi and Schack [43] follows a real-or-random approach, where the adversary submits only a single message (possibly in superposition) and receives back the message along with a ciphertext. The ciphertext is either the encryption of the submitted message or of the permuted message using a permutation picked at random. Usage of the permutation ensures that the number of messages in superposition is the same for both the submitted and permuted message. Mossayebi and Schack [43] also defined the corresponding security with respect to chosen ciphertext attacks. The relevance of this notion is questionable, as it assumes non-cheating adversaries, that do not try to decrypt the challenge ciphertext with its decryption oracle.

In this notion, there is only a single message register that will always be entangled with the ciphertext register. This bypasses the impossibility result by Boneh and Zhandry [12].

RoR-qIND

$K \leftarrow_\$ \mathcal{K}$

implement $U_{\text{Enc}}^{(1)}$ using K

$b \leftarrow_\$ \{0, 1\}$

$\pi \leftarrow_\$ \mathcal{P}(\{0, 1\}^\mu)$

$|N\rangle_N |M\rangle_M |C\rangle_C \leftarrow_\$ \mathcal{A}_1()$

Measure register $|N\rangle_N$

if $b = 0$

   $|\psi\rangle \leftarrow U_{\text{Enc}}^{(1)}(|N\rangle_N |M\rangle_M |C\rangle_C)$

if $b = 1$

   $|\psi\rangle \leftarrow ((id \otimes \pi^{-1} \otimes id) \circ U_{\text{Enc}}^{(1)} \circ (id \otimes \pi \otimes id))(|N\rangle_N |M\rangle_M |C\rangle_C)$

$b' \leftarrow_\$ \mathcal{A}_2(|\psi\rangle)$

return $(b' = b)$

Fig. 8. Security notion RoR-qIND following [43].

Below we define RoR-qIND security, where the adversary is restricted to a single challenge query and no learning query, again, extended by letting the adversary send a register with the nonce that is measured by the challenger.

Extension to RoR-qINDqCPA security works by providing the adversary a real-or-random challenge oracle and a learning oracle and reject queries where (measured) nonces repeat (Fig. 9).

Definition 15. *Let $\Sigma = (\mathrm{Enc}, \mathrm{Dec})$ be a symmetric key encryption scheme and the security game RoR-qIND be defined as in Fig. 8. For any adversary $\mathcal{A}$ we define its RoR-qIND advantage as*

$$\mathbf{Adv}_\Sigma^{\mathrm{RoR\text{-}qIND}}(\mathcal{A}) = \left|2\,\Pr[\mathrm{RoR\text{-}qIND}^{\mathcal{A}} \to 1] - 1\right|.$$

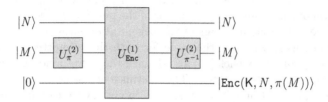

Fig. 9. Circuit for real-or-random security notion. The permutation π is applied if $b = 1$.

The following theorem shows that the sponge-based encryption scheme SLEnc is not RoR-qIND-secure. The attack follows [15] exploiting the outcome of a measurement in the Hadamard basis on two entangled registers. The full proof details can be found in the full version of the paper [34].

Theorem 16. *Let SLEnc be the sponge-based encryption scheme displayed in Fig. 2. Then there exist an adversary $\mathcal{A}$ such that*

$$\mathbf{Adv}_{\mathrm{SLEnc}}^{\mathrm{RoR\text{-}qIND}}(\mathcal{A}) = \frac{1}{2}.$$

5.4   IND-qCPA Security of SLAE and FGHF'

In Sect. 5.1, we have discussed various different security notions for symmetric key encryption schemes in the QS2 setting. So far we have shown that SLEnc is neither LoR-qIND nor RoR-qIND secure. Observe that the attacks also apply to the generic construction FGHF', as the weakness lies in the one-time pad (OTP) approach exploiting an inherent insecurity of the OTP against quantum attackers.

Observe that both the generic FGHF' construction as well as SLAE are stream ciphers. Following the results by Anand et al. [4], we obtain that both constructions are IND-qCPA secure which is a direct consequence from the established IND-CPA security in the QS1 sense.

6   Conclusion

In this work we have given both positive and negative results for the security of the sponge-based AEAD scheme SLAE. On the one hand, we have shown that SLAE as well as the underlying core primitives are post-quantum secure. On the other hand, we have shown that their quantum security is not fully clear yet. While SLAE, as well as the generic FGHF' construction, are easily seen to be not quantum secure for notions that allow challenge queries by the adversary to be in superposition, its quantum security with respect to IND-qCPA is still open. More precisely, we argued that its IND-qCPA security reduces to the quantum security of the underlying function SLFUNC via the generic FGHF' construction.

In the realm of quantum security, it is open to analyse the quantum security of the sponge-based function SLFUNC as well as addressing the quantum unforgeability of SLAE and its underlying MAC SLMAC. The reason is that the landscape of quantum unforgeability notions is still unclear as the existing notions [1,12,25,30] suffer from some drawbacks that allow for intuitive forgeries that are not covered by the notions.

Regarding the post-quantum security of SLAE, one can investigate whether tighter bounds can be achieved. Generally, our bounds establish for the first time post-quantum security for the AEAD scheme and the underlying primitives but they are rather conservative and there might be room for improvements. For example, for SLFUNC one may be able to use the semi-classical variant of the O2H lemma developed by Ambainis et al. [3] and for SPRG one may get tighter bounds by using the doubled-sided O2H lemma by Bindel et al. [9]. One can also consider an adaptive version, where the random oracle is reprogrammed only on the points that the adversary queries to its classical oracle.

Acknowledgements. We thank anonymous reviewers for their valuable comments on an earlier draft of this work. This work was funded by the Deutsche Forschungsgemeinschaft (DFG) – SFB 1119 – 236615297.

A   Additional Preliminaries

A.1   Authenticated Encryption

We begin with a definition of authenticated encryption schemes with associated data [6,47].

Definition 17. *An* authenticated encryption scheme with associated data (AEAD) $\texttt{AEAD} = (\texttt{Enc}, \texttt{Dec})$ *is a pair of efficient algorithms associated with key space* $\mathcal{K}$*, nonce space* $\mathcal{N}$*, associated-data space* $\mathcal{H}$*, message space* $\mathcal{M}$*, and ciphertext space* $\mathcal{C}$ *such that:*

- *The deterministic encryption algorithm* $\texttt{Enc}: \mathcal{K} \times \mathcal{N} \times \mathcal{H} \times \mathcal{M} \to \mathcal{C}$ *takes as input a secret key* K*, a nonce* N*, associated data* A*, and a message* M*. It outputs a ciphertext* C*.*

- *The deterministic decryption algorithm* $\mathrm{Dec}\colon \mathcal{K} \times \mathcal{N} \times \mathcal{H} \times \mathcal{C} \to \mathcal{M} \cup \{\bot\}$ *takes as input a secret key* K, *a nonce* N, *associated data* A, *and a ciphertext* C. *It outputs a message* M *or* $\bot$ *indicating an invalid ciphertext.*

We say that an AEAD scheme is correct, if for all $\mathsf{K} \in \mathcal{K}$, $N \in \mathcal{N}$, $A \in \mathcal{H}$ and $M \in \mathcal{M}$, it holds that $\mathrm{Dec}(\mathsf{K}, N, A, \mathrm{Enc}(\mathsf{K}, N, A, M)) = M$.

Throughout this work, we consider $\mathcal{K} = \{0,1\}^k$, $\mathcal{N} = \{0,1\}^\nu$, $\mathcal{H} = \{0,1\}^\alpha$, $\mathcal{M} = \{0,1\}^\mu$, and $\mathcal{C} = \{0,1\}^\gamma$.

Security of an AEAD scheme now demands that an adversary cannot distinguish encryptions of equal-length messages which corresponds to the usual CPA-security notion of encryption schemes. The formal description of the game can be found on the left side of Fig. 10. Additionally, security also demands that the adversary is not able to forge further valid ciphertexts which corresponds to an integrity notion on the ciphertext level. The formal description of the games can be found on the right side of Fig. 10.

IND-CPA	$\mathrm{Enc}(\mathsf{K}, N, A, M_0, M_1)$	INT-CTXT	$\mathrm{Enc}(\mathsf{K}, N, A, M)$
$\mathsf{K} \leftarrow_\$ \mathcal{K}$	**if** $\lvert M_0 \rvert \neq \lvert M_1 \rvert$ **then**	$\mathsf{K} \leftarrow_\$ \mathcal{K}$	**if** $(N, \cdot, \cdot) \in \mathcal{Q}$ **then**
$\mathcal{Q} \leftarrow \emptyset$	return $\bot$	$\mathcal{Q} \leftarrow \emptyset$	return $\bot$
$b \leftarrow_\$ \{0,1\}$	**if** $N \in \mathcal{Q}$ **then**	win $\leftarrow 0$	$C \leftarrow \mathrm{Enc}(\mathsf{K}, N, A, M)$
$b' \leftarrow_\$ \mathcal{A}^{\mathrm{Enc}(\mathsf{K},\cdot,\cdot,\cdot,\cdot)}$	return $\bot$	$\mathcal{A}^{\mathrm{Enc}(\mathsf{K},\cdot,\cdot,\cdot),\mathrm{Forge}(\mathsf{K},\cdot,\cdot,\cdot)}$	$\mathcal{Q} \leftarrow \mathcal{Q} \cup \{(N, A, C)\}$
return $(b' = b)$	$C \leftarrow \mathrm{Enc}(\mathsf{K}, N, A, M_b)$	return win	return C
	$\mathcal{Q} \leftarrow \mathcal{Q} \cup \{N\}$		
	return C		$\mathrm{Forge}(\mathsf{K}, N, A, C)$
			if $(N, A, C) \in \mathcal{Q}$ **then**
			return $\bot$
			$d \leftarrow \mathrm{Dec}(\mathsf{K}, N, A, C)$
			if $d \neq \bot$ **then**
			win $\leftarrow 1$
			return d

Fig. 10. Security games for AEAD.

Definition 18. *Let* AEAD *be an authenticated encryption scheme with associated data.*

- *For an adversary* $\mathcal{A}$, *making* q_E *queries to its encryption oracle, we define its* IND-CPA *advantage as*

$$\mathbf{Adv}_{\mathrm{AEAD}}^{\mathrm{IND\text{-}CPA}}(\mathcal{A}) = 2\Pr[\mathrm{IND\text{-}CPA}^{\mathcal{A}} \to 1] - 1.$$

- *For an adversary* $\mathcal{A}$, *making* q_E *and* q_F *queries to its encryption oracle and forge oracle, respectively, we define its* INT-CTXT *advantage as*

$$\mathbf{Adv}_{\mathrm{AEAD}}^{\mathrm{INT\text{-}CTXT}}(\mathcal{A}) = \Pr[\mathrm{INT\text{-}CTXT}^{\mathcal{A}} \to 1].$$

Symmetric Key Encryption. Observe that the definition of a symmetric key encryption (SKE) scheme is very close to the given about AEAD. Note that one can obtain a SKE scheme by analogously defining an encryption scheme which does not admit associated data as a part of its input in comparison to Definition 17.

Usually one defines CPA-security of a SKE scheme. Here the formalisation is again very close to the description in Fig. 10 with the modification of not including the associated data as an input to the encryption oracle.

A.2   Message Authentication Code

Next we will provide the basic definition of a message authentication code.

Definition 19. *A message authentication code (MAC)* $\mathtt{MAC} = (\mathtt{Tag}, \mathtt{Vfy})$ *is a pair of efficient algorithms associated with key space* $\mathcal{K}$ *and domain space* $\mathcal{X}$ *such that:*

- *The deterministic tagging algorithm* $\mathtt{Tag} \colon \mathcal{K} \times \mathcal{X} \to \{0,1\}^\tau$ *takes as input a key* K *and an element* X. *It returns a tag* T *of size* $\{0,1\}^\tau$.
- *The deterministic verification algorithm* $\mathtt{Vfy} \colon \mathcal{K} \times \mathcal{X} \times \{0,1\}^\tau \to \{0,1\}$ *takes as input a key* K, *an element* X, *and a tag* T *and outputs* 1 *indicating that the input is valid, or otherwise* 0.

We say that a MAC scheme is correct, *if for all* $\mathsf{K} \in \mathcal{K}$ *and any admissible input* $X \in \mathcal{X}$, *it holds that* $\mathtt{Vfy}(\mathsf{K}, X, \mathtt{Tag}(\mathsf{K}, X)) = 1$.

SUF-CMA	Tag(K, M)	Forge (K, M, T)
$\mathsf{K} \twoheadleftarrow_{\$} \mathcal{K}$	$T \leftarrow \mathtt{Tag}(\mathsf{K}, M)$	if $(M, T) \in \mathcal{Q}$ then
$\mathcal{Q} \leftarrow \emptyset$	$\mathcal{Q} \leftarrow \mathcal{Q} \cup \{(M, T)\}$	$\quad$ return $\perp$
win $\leftarrow 0$	return T	$d \leftarrow \mathtt{Vfy}(\mathsf{K}, M, T)$
$\mathcal{A}^{\mathtt{Tag}(\mathsf{K},\cdot),\mathtt{Forge}(\mathsf{K},\cdot,\cdot)}$		if $d = 1$ then
return win		$\quad$ win $\leftarrow 1$
		return d

Fig. 11. Security game for MAC.

Definition 20. *Let* $\mathtt{MAC}$ *be a message authentication code. We define the* SUF-CMA *advantage of an adversary* $\mathcal{A}$ *making at most* q_T *queries to its tag oracle and* q_F *many queries to its forge oracle as*

$$\mathbf{Adv}_{\mathtt{MAC}}^{\mathsf{SUF\text{-}CMA}}(\mathcal{A}) = \Pr[\mathsf{SUF\text{-}CMA}^{\mathcal{A}} \to 1],$$

where the respective game is depicted in Fig. 11.

A.3   Hash Function

In this section, we simply review the collapsing property of hash functions [54] in the formalisation of [18].

Definition 21. *For algorithms $\mathcal{A}$ and $\mathcal{B}$, consider the following games given in Fig. 12. There are quantum registers S and M, and $\mathcal{M}(M)$ is a measurement of M in the computational basis.*

For a set $\mathbf{m}$, we call an adversary $(\mathcal{A}, \mathcal{B})$ valid on $\mathbf{m}$ for H^{O} if and only if $\Pr[H^{\mathsf{O}}(m) = h \wedge m \in \mathbf{m}]$ when we run $(S, M, h) \leftarrow \mathcal{A}^{\mathsf{O}}()$ and measure M in the computational basis as m.

A function H is collapsing on $\mathbf{m}$ if and only if for any quantum-polynomial-time adversary $(\mathcal{A}, \mathcal{B})$ that is valid for H^{O} on $\mathbf{m}$ and $|\Pr[b = 1: \mathsf{Game}_1] - \Pr[b = 1: \mathsf{Game}_2]|$ is negligible.

Game₁	Game₂
$(S, M, h) \leftarrow \mathcal{A}^{\mathsf{O}}()$	$(S, M, h) \leftarrow \mathcal{A}^{\mathsf{O}}()$
$m \leftarrow \mathcal{M}(M)$	
$b \leftarrow \mathcal{B}^{\mathsf{O}}(S, M)$	$b \leftarrow \mathcal{B}^{\mathsf{O}}(S, M)$

Fig. 12. Collapsing games.

B   QS1 Proofs

B.1   Proof of Theorem 8

Proof. The above collision resistance bound can be obtained from a combination of results from Czajkowski et al. [17] and Unruh [52] with a slight modification that stems from the way SvHASH is constructed. Observe that the small modification is due to the interpretation that we consider a sponge-based hash function with the capacity being reduced by one bit and hence the rate being increased by one bit. We take care of this one bit loss when applying the following results.

A crucial property in the realm of hash functions in the post-quantum setting is called the collapsing property which is a strengthening of collision resistance and Unruh has showed in [52,54] that if a hash function is collapsing then this also implies that it is quantum collision resistant. Additionally, Czajkowski et al. [17,18] showed that if the underlying function of the sponge construction is a random transformation then the sponge construction is collapsing. Being equipped with their result, we can derive the required bound for our setting.

We will follow the proof strategy put forward by Czajkowski et al. [17, Theorem 33] to show that the sponge construction is collapsing. This requires to show that the inner state $\hat{S}$ is collapsing in the absorbing phase while the outer state

$\bar{S}$ is collapsing in the squeezing phase and that there are no zero-preimages in the inner state $\hat{S}$. Then using [52, Lemma 25] provides us with the implication that the sponge construction is then also collision resistant. It now remains to apply the above strategy appropriately to derive the bound.

We have that $l = \lceil \frac{\mu}{r} \rceil$ and by [17, Theorem 33], we know that the collapsing advantage is bounded by $\sqrt{\varepsilon_1} + l \cdot \varepsilon_2 + \varepsilon_3$, where ε_1 corresponds to the probability of finding zero-preimages, ε_2 corresponds to the collapsing advantage of the inner state and ε_3 corresponds to the collapsing advantage of the outer state, respectively. By applying [17, Lemma 19], we obtain that $\varepsilon_1 \le (q+1)^2 2^{-c+4}$. By a simple combination of [17, Lemma 32] and [52, Theorem 38], we can derive $\varepsilon_2 \le q^3 \left(\frac{\delta'+324}{2^{c-1}} \right) + 7\delta \sqrt{\frac{3(q+4)^3}{2^c}}$ and $\varepsilon_3 \le q^3 \left(\frac{\delta'+324}{2^{w+1}} \right) + 7\delta \sqrt{\frac{3(q+4)^3}{2^{w+2}}}$ where both δ and δ' are non-zero constants. Then by [52, Lemma 25], we have a tight reduction from collapsing to collision resistance and hence the same bound holds for the collision resistance of the sponge construction. □

B.2 Proof of Theorem 9

Proof. The proof can be obtained from [21] by dropping everything related to the leakage setting. It proceeds in two game hops. The first game hop replaces the function SLFUNC by a random function which can be straightforwardly bound by the PRF advantage of SLFUNC. More precisely, $\mathcal{A}_{prf}$ uses its own oracle for everything related to SLFUNC while simulating SPRG using (classical) queries to the random oracle ρ. All (quantum) queries by $\mathcal{A}$ to ρ are simply forwarded by $\mathcal{A}_{prf}$, as are the responses back to $\mathcal{A}$.

The second game hop replaces the output of SPRG by a random output. A standard hybrid argument [26] shows that this can be bound by the security of SPRG. The reduction $\mathcal{A}_{prg}$ picks a random query of $\mathcal{A}$ to its encryption oracle, where it uses its own input (either the output of SPRG or a random bit string) to encrypt the message. Prior queries are answered by XORing random bit string to the message while subsequent queries are answered by simulating SPRG using (classical) queries to ρ. All (quantum) queries by $\mathcal{A}$ to ρ are simply forwarded by $\mathcal{A}_{prg}$, as are the responses back to $\mathcal{A}$.

The resulting game yields identically distributed ciphertexts, irrespectively of the message. The factor 2 accounts for doing the game hops for both cases $b = 0$ and $b = 1$. □

B.3 Proof of Theorem 10

Proof. The proof proceeds by a simple reduction. In more detail, the reduction $\mathcal{A}_{se}$ picks a key for the MAC SLMAC. For every query to the encryption oracle by $\mathcal{A}$, $\mathcal{A}_{se}$ invokes its own encryption oracle and locally computes the tag of the ciphertext using (classical) queries to ρ before sending the ciphertext and the tag back to $\mathcal{A}$. Every (quantum) query by $\mathcal{A}$ to ρ is simply forwarded by $\mathcal{A}_{se}$. □

B.4   Proof of Theorem 11

Proof. We assume that all messages queried by $\mathcal{A}$ result in different hash values, otherwise, we obtain a simple reduction $\mathcal{A}_{hash}$ from the collision resistance of SvHASH.

Then the proof proceeds by a game hop in which SLFUNC is replaced by a random function. The reduction $\mathcal{A}_{prf}$ will invoke its own function to simulate the tagging and verification of SLMAC and (classical) queries to ρ to evaluate SvHASH. Every (quantum) query to ρ by $\mathcal{A}$ is simply forwarded by $\mathcal{A}_{prf}$.

The resulting game is bound by a simple counting argument that $\mathcal{A}$ predicts the output of a random function.   □

B.5   Proof of Theorem 12

Proof. The reduction $\mathcal{A}_{mac}$ picks a key for the symmetric key encryption scheme SLENC. For every query to the encryption oracle by $\mathcal{A}$, $\mathcal{A}_{mac}$ locally computes the ciphertext using (classical) queries to ρ and obtains the tag using its own tagging oracle. It then sends the ciphertext and the tag back to $\mathcal{A}$. For every forgery attempt by $\mathcal{A}$, $\mathcal{A}_{mac}$ queries the ciphertext and the tag as its own forgery attempt. If the tag verifies correctly, $\mathcal{A}_{mac}$ locally decrypts the ciphertext using the sampled key and (classical) queries to ρ and sends the message back to $\mathcal{A}$, otherwise, i.e., if the tag was invalid, $\mathcal{A}_{mac}$ simply returns $\perp$ to $\mathcal{A}$. Every (quantum) query by $\mathcal{A}$ to ρ is simply forwarded by $\mathcal{A}_{se}$.   □

C   QS2 Proofs

C.1   Proof of Theorem 14

Proof. We construct the following adversary $\mathcal{A} = (\mathcal{A}_1, \mathcal{A}_2)$. It picks a nonce $N \leftarrow_\$ \{0, 1\}^\nu$ and prepares the states $|\varphi_0\rangle = H |0^\mu\rangle = |+\rangle^{\otimes\mu}$ and $|\varphi_1\rangle = |0^\mu\rangle$. It outputs the state

$$|\varphi\rangle = |N\rangle \otimes |+\rangle^{\otimes\mu} \otimes |\varphi_1\rangle \ .$$

Upon receiving the state $|\psi\rangle$, $\mathcal{A}_2$ applies the Hadamard operator to it and measures the register. If the measurement output is 0^μ, $\mathcal{A}_0$ outputs 0, otherwise, it outputs 1.

Before analysing the different cases, note that measuring the nonce register as well as tracing out one of the message registers does not affect the other registers as they are all unentangled. Let us now start with the case distinctions.

If $b = 0$, the game encrypts the left message, i.e., the state

$$|\varphi\rangle = H |0^\mu\rangle = |+\rangle^{\otimes\mu} = \frac{1}{\sqrt{2^\mu}} \left(\sum_{x \in \{0,1\}^\mu} |x\rangle \right) \ .$$

$\mathcal{A}_2$ receives the state

$$|\psi\rangle = \frac{1}{\sqrt{2^\mu}} \left(\sum_{x \in \{0,1\}^\mu} |N\rangle |x \oplus \text{SPRG}(\text{SLFUNC}(\mathsf{K}, N))\rangle \right) = |\varphi\rangle \,,$$

i.e., the state $|\varphi\rangle$ is left unchanged. Application of the Hadamard operator therefore yields the state $|0^\mu\rangle$, for which the measurement outcome is 0^μ with probability 1. Thus we get

$$\Pr[\mathcal{A}^{\text{LoR-qIND}} \to 0 \,|\, b = 0] = 1 \,.$$

If $b = 1$, $\mathcal{A}_2$ receives the state

$$|\psi\rangle = |\text{Enc}(\mathsf{K}, N, 0^\mu)\rangle = |0^\mu \oplus \text{SPRG}(\text{SLFUNC}(\mathsf{K}, N))\rangle \,.$$

Application of the Hadamard operator yields

$$H \,|\psi\rangle = \frac{1}{\sqrt{2^\mu}} \left(\sum_{x \in \{0,1\}^\mu} (-1)^{x \cdot \text{SPRG}(\text{SLFUNC}(\mathsf{K},N))} \,|x\rangle \right) \,.$$

Measurement yields a random $x \in \{0,1\}^\mu$. Since $\mathcal{A}_2$ outputs 0 if and only if the measurement yields 0^μ, we obtain

$$\Pr[\mathcal{A}^{\text{LoR-qIND}} \to 0 \,|\, b = 1] = \frac{1}{2^\mu} \,.$$

Collecting everything yields

$$\begin{aligned}
\mathbf{Adv}^{\text{LoR-qIND}}(\mathcal{A}) &= \left| \Pr[\mathcal{A}^{\text{LoR-qIND}} \to 0 \,|\, b = 0] - \Pr[\mathcal{A}^{\text{LoR-qIND}} \to 0 \,|\, b = 1] \right| \\
&= 1 - \frac{1}{2^\mu} \,.
\end{aligned}$$

$\square$

References

1. Alagic, G., Majenz, C., Russell, A., Song, F.: Quantum-access-secure message authentication via blind-unforgeability. In: Canteaut, A., Ishai, Y. (eds.) EUROCRYPT 2020, Part III. LNCS, vol. 12107, pp. 788–817. Springer, Cham (2020). https://doi.org/10.1007/978-3-030-45727-3_27
2. Alagic, G., Russell, A.: Quantum-secure symmetric-key cryptography based on hidden shifts. In: Coron, J.-S., Nielsen, J.B. (eds.) EUROCRYPT 2017, Part III. LNCS, vol. 10212, pp. 65–93. Springer, Cham (2017). https://doi.org/10.1007/978-3-319-56617-7_3
3. Ambainis, A., Hamburg, M., Unruh, D.: Quantum security proofs using semiclassical oracles. In: Boldyreva, A., Micciancio, D. (eds.) CRYPTO 2019, Part II. LNCS, vol. 11693, pp. 269–295. Springer, Cham (2019). https://doi.org/10.1007/978-3-030-26951-7_10

4. Anand, M.V., Targhi, E.E., Tabia, G.N., Unruh, D.: Post-quantum security of the CBC, CFB, OFB, CTR, and XTS modes of operation. In: Takagi, T. (ed.) PQCrypto 2016. LNCS, vol. 9606, pp. 44–63. Springer, Cham (2016). https://doi.org/10.1007/978-3-319-29360-8_4

5. Barwell, G., Martin, D.P., Oswald, E., Stam, M.: Authenticated encryption in the face of protocol and side channel leakage. In: Takagi, T., Peyrin, T. (eds.) ASIACRYPT 2017, Part I. LNCS, vol. 10624, pp. 693–723. Springer, Cham (2017). https://doi.org/10.1007/978-3-319-70694-8_24

6. Bellare, M., Namprempre, C.: Authenticated encryption: relations among notions and analysis of the generic composition paradigm. In: Okamoto, T. (ed.) ASIACRYPT 2000. LNCS, vol. 1976, pp. 531–545. Springer, Heidelberg (2000). https://doi.org/10.1007/3-540-44448-3_41

7. Bellare, M., Rogaway, P.: Random oracles are practical: a paradigm for designing efficient protocols. In: Denning, D.E., Pyle, R., Ganesan, R., Sandhu, R.S., Ashby, V. (eds.) ACM CCS 1993, pp. 62–73. ACM Press, November 1993

8. Bertoni, G., Daemen, J., Peeters, M., Van Assche, G.: Sponge functions. In: ECRYPT Hash Workshop (2007)

9. Bindel, N., Hamburg, M., Hövelmanns, K., Hülsing, A., Persichetti, E.: Tighter proofs of CCA security in the quantum random oracle model. In: Hofheinz, D., Rosen, A. (eds.) TCC 2019, Part II. LNCS, vol. 11892, pp. 61–90. Springer, Cham (2019). https://doi.org/10.1007/978-3-030-36033-7_3

10. Boneh, D., Dagdelen, Ö., Fischlin, M., Lehmann, A., Schaffner, C., Zhandry, M.: Random oracles in a quantum world. In: Lee, D.H., Wang, X. (eds.) ASIACRYPT 2011. LNCS, vol. 7073, pp. 41–69. Springer, Heidelberg (2011). https://doi.org/10.1007/978-3-642-25385-0_3

11. Boneh, D., Zhandry, M.: Quantum-secure message authentication codes. In: Johansson, T., Nguyen, P.Q. (eds.) EUROCRYPT 2013. LNCS, vol. 7881, pp. 592–608. Springer, Heidelberg (2013). https://doi.org/10.1007/978-3-642-38348-9_35

12. Boneh, D., Zhandry, M.: Secure signatures and chosen ciphertext security in a quantum computing world. In: Canetti, R., Garay, J.A. (eds.) CRYPTO 2013, Part II. LNCS, vol. 8043, pp. 361–379. Springer, Heidelberg (2013). https://doi.org/10.1007/978-3-642-40084-1_21

13. Bonnetain, X., Hosoyamada, A., Naya-Plasencia, M., Sasaki, Yu., Schrottenloher, A.: Quantum attacks without superposition queries: the offline Simon's algorithm. In: Galbraith, S.D., Moriai, S. (eds.) ASIACRYPT 2019, Part I. LNCS, vol. 11921, pp. 552–583. Springer, Cham (2019). https://doi.org/10.1007/978-3-030-34578-5_20

14. Carstens, T.V., Ebrahimi, E., Tabia, G.N., Unruh, D.: On quantum indistinguishability under chosen plaintext attack. Cryptology ePrint Archive, Report 2020/596 (2020). https://eprint.iacr.org/2020/596

15. Chevalier, C., Ebrahimi, E., Vu, Q.-H.: On security notions for encryption in a quantum world. Cryptology ePrint Archive, Report 2020/237 (2020). https://eprint.iacr.org/2020/237

16. Czajkowski, J.: Quantum indifferentiability of SHA-3. IACR Cryptology ePrint Archive 2021/192 (2021)

17. Czajkowski, J., Groot Bruinderink, L., Hülsing, A., Schaffner, C., Unruh, D.: Post-quantum security of the sponge construction. Cryptology ePrint Archive, Report 2017/771 (2017). https://eprint.iacr.org/2017/771

18. Czajkowski, J., Groot Bruinderink, L., Hülsing, A., Schaffner, C., Unruh, D.: Post-quantum security of the sponge construction. In: Lange, T., Steinwandt, R. (eds.) PQCrypto 2018. LNCS, vol. 10786, pp. 185–204. Springer, Cham (2018). https://doi.org/10.1007/978-3-319-79063-3_9

19. Czajkowski, J., Hülsing, A., Schaffner, C.: Quantum indistinguishability of random sponges. In: Boldyreva, A., Micciancio, D. (eds.) CRYPTO 2019, Part II. LNCS, vol. 11693, pp. 296–325. Springer, Cham (2019). https://doi.org/10.1007/978-3-030-26951-7_11

20. Czajkowski, J., Majenz, C., Schaffner, C., Zur, S.: Quantum lazy sampling and game-playing proofs for quantum indifferentiability. Cryptology ePrint Archive, Report 2019/428 (2019). https://eprint.iacr.org/2019/428

21. Degabriele, J.P., Janson, C., Struck, P.: Sponges resist leakage: the case of authenticated encryption. In: Galbraith, S.D., Moriai, S. (eds.) ASIACRYPT 2019, Part II. LNCS, vol. 11922, pp. 209–240. Springer, Cham (2019). https://doi.org/10.1007/978-3-030-34621-8_8

22. Dobraunig, C., et al.: ISAP v2.0. IACR Trans. Symm. Cryptol. **2020**(S1), 390–416 (2020)

23. Dobraunig, C., Eichlseder, M., Mangard, S., Mendel, F., Unterluggauer, T.: ISAP - towards side-channel secure authenticated encryption. IACR Trans. Symm. Cryptol. **2017**(1), 80–105 (2017)

24. Dobraunig, C., Eichlseder, M., Mendel, F., Schläffer, M.: Ascon v1. 2. Submission to the CAESAR Competition (2016)

25. Doosti, M., Delavar, M., Kashefi, E., Arapinis, M.: A unified framework for quantum unforgeability. CoRR, abs/2103.13994 (2021)

26. Fischlin, M., Mittelbach, A.: An overview of the hybrid argument. Cryptology ePrint Archive, Report 2021/088 (2021). https://eprint.iacr.org/2021/088

27. Gagliardoni, T.: Quantum security of cryptographic primitives. Ph.D. thesis, Darmstadt University of Technology, Germany (2017)

28. Gagliardoni, T., Hülsing, A., Schaffner, C.: Semantic security and indistinguishability in the quantum world. In: Robshaw, M., Katz, J. (eds.) CRYPTO 2016, Part III. LNCS, vol. 9816, pp. 60–89. Springer, Heidelberg (2016). https://doi.org/10.1007/978-3-662-53015-3_3

29. Gagliardoni, T., Krämer, J., Struck, P.: Quantum indistinguishability for public key encryption. In: Cheon, J.H., Tillich, J.-P. (eds.) PQCrypto 2021 2021. LNCS, vol. 12841, pp. 463–482. Springer, Cham (2021). https://doi.org/10.1007/978-3-030-81293-5_24

30. Garg, S., Yuen, H., Zhandry, M.: New security notions and feasibility results for authentication of quantum data. In: Katz, J., Shacham, H. (eds.) CRYPTO 2017, Part III. LNCS, vol. 10402, pp. 342–371. Springer, Cham (2017). https://doi.org/10.1007/978-3-319-63715-0_12

31. Grover, L.K.: A fast quantum mechanical algorithm for database search. In: 28th ACM STOC, pp. 212–219. ACM Press, May 1996

32. Hosoyamada, A., Sasaki, Yu.: Quantum Demiric-Selçuk meet-in-the-middle attacks: applications to 6-round generic feistel constructions. In: Catalano, D., De Prisco, R. (eds.) SCN 2018. LNCS, vol. 11035, pp. 386–403. Springer, Cham (2018). https://doi.org/10.1007/978-3-319-98113-0_21

33. Ito, G., Hosoyamada, A., Matsumoto, R., Sasaki, Yu., Iwata, T.: Quantum chosen-ciphertext attacks against feistel ciphers. In: Matsui, M. (ed.) CT-RSA 2019. LNCS, vol. 11405, pp. 391–411. Springer, Cham (2019). https://doi.org/10.1007/978-3-030-12612-4_20

34. Janson, C., Struck, P.: Sponge-based authenticated encryption: security against quantum attackers. Cryptology ePrint Archive, Report 2022/139 (2022). https://eprint.iacr.org/2022/139

35. Jovanovic, P., Luykx, A., Mennink, B.: Beyond $2^{c/2}$ security in sponge-based authenticated encryption modes. In: Sarkar, P., Iwata, T. (eds.) ASIACRYPT 2014, Part I. LNCS, vol. 8873, pp. 85–104. Springer, Heidelberg (2014). https://doi.org/10.1007/978-3-662-45611-8_5

36. Kaplan, M., Leurent, G., Leverrier, A., Naya-Plasencia, M.: Breaking symmetric cryptosystems using quantum period finding. In: Robshaw, M., Katz, J. (eds.) CRYPTO 2016, Part II. LNCS, vol. 9815, pp. 207–237. Springer, Heidelberg (2016). https://doi.org/10.1007/978-3-662-53008-5_8

37. Kaplan, M., Leurent, G., Leverrier, A., Naya-Plasencia, M.: Quantum differential and linear cryptanalysis. IACR Trans. Symm. Cryptol. **2016**(1), 71–94 (2016). https://tosc.iacr.org/index.php/ToSC/article/view/536

38. Kashefi, E., Kent, A., Vedral, V., Banaszek, K.: Comparison of quantum oracles. Phys. Rev. A **65**(5), 050304 (2002)

39. Krämer, J., Struck, P.: Leakage-resilient authenticated encryption from leakage-resilient pseudorandom functions. In: Bertoni, G.M., Regazzoni, F. (eds.) COSADE 2020. LNCS, vol. 12244, pp. 315–337. Springer, Cham (2021). https://doi.org/10.1007/978-3-030-68773-1_15

40. Kuchta, V., Sakzad, A., Stehlé, D., Steinfeld, R., Sun, S.-F.: Measure-rewind-measure: tighter quantum random oracle model proofs for one-way to hiding and CCA security. In: Canteaut, A., Ishai, Y. (eds.) EUROCRYPT 2020, Part III. LNCS, vol. 12107, pp. 703–728. Springer, Cham (2020). https://doi.org/10.1007/978-3-030-45727-3_24

41. Kuwakado, H., Morii, M.: Quantum distinguisher between the 3-round feistel cipher and the random permutation. In: ISIT 2010 (2010)

42. Kuwakado, H., Morii, M.: Security on the quantum-type even-mansour cipher. In: ISITA 2012 (2012)

43. Mossayebi, S., Schack, R.: Concrete security against adversaries with quantum superposition access to encryption and decryption oracles. CoRR, abs/1609.03780 (2016)

44. Namprempre, C., Rogaway, P., Shrimpton, T.: Reconsidering generic composition. In: Nguyen, P.Q., Oswald, E. (eds.) EUROCRYPT 2014. LNCS, vol. 8441, pp. 257–274. Springer, Heidelberg (2014). https://doi.org/10.1007/978-3-642-55220-5_15

45. National Institute of Standards and Technology. Lightweight cryptography standardization process (2015)

46. Nielsen, M.A., Chuang, I.L.: Quantum Computation and Quantum Information: 10th Anniversary Edition, 10th edn. Cambridge University Press, New York (2011)

47. Rogaway, P.: Authenticated-encryption with associated-data. In: Atluri, V. (ed.) ACM CCS 2002, pp. 98–107. ACM Press, November 2002

48. Rötteler, M., Steinwandt, R.: A note on quantum related-key attacks. Inf. Process. Lett. **115**(1), 40–44 (2015)

49. Shor, P.W.: Algorithms for quantum computation: discrete logarithms and factoring. In: 35th FOCS, pp. 124–134. IEEE Computer Society Press, November 1994

50. Song, F.: A note on quantum security for post-quantum cryptography. In: Mosca, M. (ed.) PQCrypto 2014. LNCS, vol. 8772, pp. 246–265. Springer, Cham (2014). https://doi.org/10.1007/978-3-319-11659-4_15

51. Soukharev, V., Jao, D., Seshadri, S.: Post-quantum security models for authenticated encryption. In: Takagi, T. (ed.) PQCrypto 2016. LNCS, vol. 9606, pp. 64–78. Springer, Cham (2016). https://doi.org/10.1007/978-3-319-29360-8_5

52. Unruh, D.: Computationally binding quantum commitments. Cryptology ePrint Archive, Report 2015/361 (2015). https://eprint.iacr.org/2015/361

53. Unruh, D.: Revocable quantum timed-release encryption. J. ACM **62**(6), 1–76 (2015)

54. Unruh, D.: Computationally binding quantum commitments. In: Fischlin, M., Coron, J.-S. (eds.) EUROCRYPT 2016, Part II. LNCS, vol. 9666, pp. 497–527. Springer, Heidelberg (2016). https://doi.org/10.1007/978-3-662-49896-5_18

55. Unruh, D.: Compressed permutation oracles (and the collision-resistance of sponge/SHA3). Cryptology ePrint Archive, Report 2021/062 (2021). https://eprint.iacr.org/2021/062

56. Yamakawa, T., Zhandry, M.: Classical vs quantum random oracles. In: Canteaut, A., Standaert, F.-X. (eds.) EUROCRYPT 2021, Part II. LNCS, vol. 12697, pp. 568–597. Springer, Cham (2021). https://doi.org/10.1007/978-3-030-77886-6_20

57. Zhandry, M.: How to construct quantum random functions. In: 53rd FOCS, pp. 679–687. IEEE Computer Society Press, October 2012

58. Zhandry, M.: How to record quantum queries, and applications to quantum indifferentiability. In: Boldyreva, A., Micciancio, D. (eds.) CRYPTO 2019, Part II. LNCS, vol. 11693, pp. 239–268. Springer, Cham (2019). https://doi.org/10.1007/978-3-030-26951-7_9

Post-quantum Plaintext-Awareness

Ehsan Ebrahimi[1,2($\boxtimes$)] and Jeroen van Wier[2]

[1] Department of Computer Science, University of Luxembourg, Esch-sur-Alzette,
Luxembourg
ehsan.ebrahimi@uni.lu
[2] SnT, University of Luxembourg, Esch-sur-Alzette, Luxembourg

Abstract. In this paper, we formalize the plaintext-awareness notion in the superposition access model in which a quantum adversary may implement the encryption oracle in a quantum device and make superposition queries to the decryption oracle. Due to various possible ways an adversary can access the decryption oracles, we present six security definitions to capture the plaintext-awareness notion with respect to each way of access. We study the relationships between these definitions and present various implications and non-implications.

Classically, the strongest plaintext-awareness notion (PA2) accompanied by the indistinguishability under chosen-plaintext attack (IND-CPA) notion yields the indistinguishability under chosen-ciphertext attack (IND-CCA) notion. We show that the PA2 notion is not sufficient to show the above relation when targeting the IND-qCCA notion (Boneh-Zhandry definition, Crypto 2013). However, our proposed post-quantum PA2 notion with superposition decryption queries fulfils this implication.

Keywords: Plaintext-awareness · Post-quantum security · Public-key encryption

1 Introduction

Plaintext-awareness is the property of a public-key encryption scheme that guarantees the only way to feasibly create a ciphertext is using the encryption algorithm, similar to the unforgeability notion for symmetric-key schemes. This property guarantees that the creator of a ciphertext knows the corresponding plaintext, even without knowing the secret key. This becomes a powerful tool when constructing proofs of other security properties, as it effectively negates the need to provide the adversary with a decryption oracle. For example, plaintext-awareness allows us to boost security from IND-CPA to IND-CCA since the only difference between these security properties is the availability of a decryption oracle to the adversary. Plaintext-awareness is also a useful property in the setting of deniability, where one would often like a process between two parties to be simulatable by either party. Plaintext-awareness steps in here and guarantees that any ciphertext created in this simulation can be decrypted without

J. H. Cheon and T. Johansson (Eds.): PQCrypto 2022, LNCS 13512, pp. 260–285, 2022.
https://doi.org/10.1007/978-3-031-17234-2_13

the need of a secret key, as the plaintext is known by the ciphertext-creating party and can be extracted from the simulation. Lastly, plaintext-awareness can provide useful insight into why a scheme does or does not achieve a certain level of security. Clearly, it is a property that one would intuitively like to satisfy, as the natural way of creating ciphertexts is to use the encryption algorithm. When another way to craft ciphertext is available, i.e. when a scheme is not plaintext-aware, this might indicate a gap in security.

The plaintext-awareness notion was first introduced in the random oracle model by Bellare and Rogaway [4]. Vaguely speaking, their definition of plaintext-awareness implies the existence of an extractor algorithm which, given access to the random oracle queries, is able to decrypt any ciphertext outputted by the adversary. The main motivation to define this notion was to show the security of Optimal Asymmetric Encryption Padding (OAEP).

The definition in [4] does not take into account the possibility of eavesdropping the communication by the adversary. Subsequently in [2], a stronger definition of plaintext-awareness was introduced in the random oracle model. In [2], the adversary is able to eavesdrop some valid ciphertexts (through an oracle) and the extractor, given access to these ciphertexts and the random oracle queries made by the adversary, should be able to decrypt any ciphertext outputted by the adversary.

The first attempt to define a plaintext-awareness notion in the standard model was in [13], but, it needs to access a trusted third party. Later, Bellare and Palacio defined three levels of plaintext-awareness notions in the standard model (PA0, PA1, PA2) without the use of a third party [3]. In addition, they study the relations between these notions and IND-CCA notions.

The PA+1 notion, which lies between PA1 and PA2, was introduced by Dent [9]. Dent showed that an encryption scheme that is PA+1 and "simulatable" is PA2. Then he showed that the Cramer-Shoup encryption scheme is PA+1 and simulatable and therefore it satisfies the PA2 notion. This result is extended in the journal version [5]. A symmetric-key version of plaintext-awareness was considered in [1].

In this paper, we investigate the plaintext-awareness notion in the quantum setting. This includes adopting the plaintext-awareness notion to the superposition setting in which a quantum adversary is attacking a classical public-key encryption scheme.

1.1 Motivation

The plaintext-awareness notion is a strong security notion for public-key encryption schemes. It guarantees that the adversary is not able to generate a valid ciphertext without knowing the corresponding plaintext (called PA1). If we consider the possibility of eavesdropping the communication for the adversary, a stronger notion is considered. Namely, an adversary with the ability to eavesdrop on the communication is not able to generate a valid ciphertext without knowing the corresponding plaintext unless it obtains this ciphertext through eavesdropping (called PA2).

Since the advent of quantum algorithms that break some classical computational problems [19], there has been extensive research to construct post-quantum secure public-key encryption schemes[1]. This line of works varies from constructing public-key encryption schemes from quantum-hard assumptions [17,18] to considering stronger security notions for public-key encryption schemes [6]. (For instance, the IND-qCCA notion introduced in [6] in which a quantum adversary has superposition access to the decryption oracle.)

Traditionally, the PA2 plaintext-awareness notion, accompanied by the IND-CPA notion, is used to prove IND-CCA security. If we use public-key encryption schemes based on quantum-hard assumptions, we will get the same result in the presence of a quantum adversary as well (PA2 + IND-CPA implies IND-CCA in the presence of a quantum adversary). However, if one wants to achieve a stronger level of security (e.g. IND-qCCA security), the classical PA2 notion is not sufficient. In fact, we show that Classical PA2 + IND-qCPA does not imply IND-qCCA security (see Corollary 3.). Therefore, we need to formalize a stronger plaintext-awareness notion to achieve a security level of type IND-qCCA for public-key encryption schemes.

In addition, a post-quantum plaintext-awareness notion is used in a high-level manner in some existing security proofs in the literature without giving any formal treatment of the notion. For instance in [10], to show IND-qCCA security of plain OAEP transform in the quantum random oracle model, the adversary's inability in producing a valid ciphertext (without executing the encryption oracle or eavesdropping the communication) is crucial in the transition from Game 4 to Game 5 in their security proof. Note that this step will not hold with a classical PA2 notion since the adversary attacking in the sense of the IND-qCCA notion has superposition access to the decryption oracle. However, in the classical PA2 notion the adversary can only make classical decryption queries in order to generate a valid ciphertext. Formalizing a post-quantum plaintext-awareness notion will lead to more formal and accessible IND-qCCA security proofs. And currently, such a notion is not available in the literature.

And last but not least, a quantum adversary on input pk can implement the encryption oracle in his quantum device. So it is natural and necessary to investigate the effect of this stronger access to the encryption oracle on the plaintext-awareness notion. Currently, it is unknown if superposition access to the encryption oracle renders public-key encryption schemes not-plaintext-aware or it does not give a noticeable advantage to the ciphertext-creator adversary.

The overall conclusion is that formalizing and investigating the plaintext-awareness notion in the quantum setting seems a natural and necessary extension given the facts that: 1) a quantum adversary can have quantum access to the encryption oracle and the effect of this access to PA notions is unknown, 2) available plaintext-awareness notions are not sufficient to conclude stronger security notions like the IND-qCCA notion, 3) some post-quantum security proofs rely

---

[1] Along with NIST competition to standardize the post-quantum public-key encryption schemes.

on post-quantum plaintext-awareness notions in a high-level argument without any formal definition for PA notions in the quantum setting, etc.

1.2 Challenges and Our Contribution

Intuitively, we say a scheme is (classically) plaintext-aware if for any (ciphertext-creator) adversary $\mathcal{A}$, there exists a (plaintext-extractor) algorithm $\mathcal{A}^*$ that, when given access to the "view" of $\mathcal{A}$, is able to answer the decryption queries outputted by $\mathcal{A}$.

In the quantum setting, a quantum adversary on input pk can implement the encryption oracle in its quantum device, thus, the adversary can run the encryption oracle in superposition. At a first glance, it seems that the plaintext-awareness notion might not be possible to achieve when the adversary can execute the encryption oracle in superposition. Hypothetically, assume that an adversary $\mathcal{A}$ is able to access the encryption oracle by the "minimal-query model" [15], that is $|m\rangle \to |\text{Enc}(m;r)\rangle$ (where r is a classical value chosen uniformly at random from the randomness space), without using any ancillary registers. In this model, the adversary is able to generate a valid ciphertext without knowing its corresponding plaintext. Namely, the adversary queries the uniform superposition of all messages, $\sum |m\rangle$, to get the superposition of corresponding ciphertexts, $\sum |\text{Enc}(m;r)\rangle$. Now if the adversary measures the state $\sum |\text{Enc}(m;r)\rangle$, the result is a random valid ciphertext for which the algorithm $\mathcal{A}^*$ might not be able to decrypt.

Even though the minimal query model has been studied in many works [7,11,12,15], it is not a canonical quantum access model. For private-key encryption schemes, the implementation of this query model requires some ancillary quantum registers and a decryption query. In the public-key setting, the query model can be implemented for some public-key encryption schemes without knowledge of the secret key but with access to an ancillary register containing the randomness needed for the encryption [12]. These encryption schemes called "recoverable public-key encryption schemes" in [12]. Note that this implementation of the minimal query model requires an ancillary register to store the randomness, that is, $|r, m\rangle \to |r, \text{Enc}(m;r)\rangle$. Measuring the quantum state after the query fixes a randomness r and $c := \text{Enc}(m;r)$ and using this randomness r, $\mathcal{A}^*$ is able to recover m from c, that is, the adversary knows the corresponding plaintext of c and the attack sketched above does not work for this implementation.

In this paper, we consider the "standard query model" and not the minimal query model to formulate superposition access to the encryption oracle. For any classical function f, the standard way to implement this function in a quantum computer is $\mathbb{U}_f : |x, y\rangle \to |x, y \oplus f(x)\rangle$. So for an encryption oracle Enc_{pk}, we consider $\mathbb{U}_{\text{Enc}_{\text{pk}}} : |m, r, c\rangle \to |m, r, c \oplus \text{Enc}_{\text{pk}}(m;r)\rangle$. Clearly, this transformation is a unitary and an involution. In the above, we briefly discussed that available implementations of the minimal query model require some ancillary registers along with either a decryption query or access to the randomness register. Even though there is no implementation of the minimal query model without using ancillary registers ($|m\rangle \rightarrow |\text{Enc}_{\text{pk}}(m;r)\rangle$) and it might not be possible at all to implement the minimal query model without the use of ancillary registers (since a quantum operation is a unitary but the size of the ciphertext space is usually bigger than the size of the plaintext space and the operation $|m\rangle \rightarrow |\text{Enc}_{\text{pk}}(m;r)\rangle$ might not be a unitary), we give an argument below why it is not reasonable to consider the query model $|m\rangle \rightarrow |\text{Enc}_{\text{pk}}(m;r)\rangle$ to define plaintext-awareness notions.

Philosophical Reasoning. Note that in the public-key setting, the encryption oracle can be implemented in the standard way, so any effort conducted by the adversary to implement the query model $|m\rangle \rightarrow |\text{Enc}_{\text{pk}}(m;r)\rangle$ instead of implementing the encryption oracle as a standard query might be considered an intentional effort to forget the corresponding plaintext that is encrypted. Considering it from a different angle, let us consider this classical scenario in which the classical adversary encrypts a message m to obtain the ciphertext $c := \text{Enc}(m;r)$, then it permanently deletes m from its memory. Now, the adversary possesses a ciphertext c without knowing its corresponding plaintext. We argue that any effort by the adversary to implement the query model $|m\rangle \rightarrow |\text{Enc}_{\text{pk}}(m;r)\rangle$ lies in the "encrypt-then-forget" argument sketched above.

In addition, we need to propose a notion that captures the vague intuition that we established above: "a valid ciphertext that is not the output of a superposition execution of the encryption oracle". Note that a superposition query to the encryption oracle can contain an exponential number of ciphertexts and thus we cannot argue that the output of the adversary is not in this superposition of ciphertexts.

1.3   Our Contribution

In the superposition setting (when a classical public-key encryption scheme is attacked by a quantum adversary), we present various definitions. These definitions vary with respect to the following criteria:

- Number of decryption queries: one or many.
- Type of decryption queries: classical or quantum.
- Possibility of eavesdropping some ciphertexts.

Then, we study the relationship between these notions. Table 1 summarizes these notions and their relations with each other. In the abbreviation of notions, pq stands for post-quantum, C_{dec} stands for classical decryption queries, Q_{dec} stands for quantum decryption queries, PA0 is a notion with one decryption query and without the possibility of eavesdropping, PA1 is a notion with many decryption queries and without the possibility of eavesdropping and PA2 is a notion with many decryption queries and the possibility of eavesdropping. So for example, pqPA1-Q_{dec} is a notion in which the adversary is allowed to make many quantum decryption queries but is not allowed to eavesdrop ciphertexts.

Our notions are an adaptation of classical PA0, PA1, and PA2 notions in the standard model [3] to the quantum setting. Vaguely speaking, a public-key

Table 1. Implications and separations between definitions. An arrow in row n, column m indicates whether n implies or does not imply m. The superscript number next to an arrow indicates the number of the corresponding theorem. Arrows without a superscript follow by transitivity.

	pqPA2-Q_{dec}	pqPA2-C_{dec}	pqPA1-Q_{dec}	pqPA1-C_{dec}	pqPA0-Q_{dec}	pqPA0-C_{dec}
pqPA2-Q_{dec}		$\Rightarrow^{Theorem1}$	$\Rightarrow^{Theorem2}$	$\Rightarrow$	$\Rightarrow$	$\Rightarrow$
pqPA2-C_{dec}	$\not\Rightarrow^{Theorem4}$		$\Rightarrow$	$\Rightarrow^{Theorem1}$	$\not\Rightarrow^{Corollary2}$	$\Rightarrow$
pqPA1-Q_{dec}	$\not\Rightarrow$	$\not\Rightarrow^{Theorem5}$		$\Rightarrow^{Theorem1}$	$\Rightarrow^{Theorem3}$	$\Rightarrow$
pqPA1-C_{dec}	$\not\Rightarrow$	$\not\Rightarrow$	$\not\Rightarrow^{Theorem4}$		$\not\Rightarrow$	$\Rightarrow^{Theorem3}$
pqPA0-Q_{dec}	$\not\Rightarrow$	$\not\Rightarrow$	$\not\Rightarrow$	$\not\Rightarrow^{Theorem6}$		$\Rightarrow^{Theorem1}$
pqPA0-C_{dec}	$\not\Rightarrow$	$\not\Rightarrow$	$\not\Rightarrow$	$\not\Rightarrow$	$\not\Rightarrow^{Corollary1}$	

encryption scheme is plaintext-aware with respect to a class of adversaries if for any adversary $\mathcal{A}$ in the class, there exists a plaintext-extractor algorithm $\mathcal{A}^*$ that given access to the view of $\mathcal{A}$ is able to simulate the decryption algorithm without using the secret key. Classically, given access to the view of $\mathcal{A}$ is formalized by given $\mathcal{A}^*$ the access to the coin tosses of $\mathcal{A}$. In our paper, the adversaries are QPT algorithms and are able to generate randomness by doing some quantum operations. For instance, applying Hadamard to $|0\rangle$ and measuring the result in the computational basis gives a random bit. To formalize our notions, we give $\mathcal{A}^*$ the access to the internal quantum registers of $\mathcal{A}$.

For instance, we say a public-key encryption scheme is pqPA1-Q_{dec} if for any QPT ciphertext-creator adversary $\mathcal{A}$ that makes quantum queries to the decryption oracle, there exists a QPT plaintext-extractor algorithm $\mathcal{A}^*$ that given access to the internal registers of $\mathcal{A}$ can simulate the decryption queries. In more detail, the execution of $\mathcal{A}$ querying the decryption oracle is indistinguishable from the execution of $\mathcal{A}$ querying $\mathcal{A}^*$ for any QPT distinguisher $\mathcal{D}$.

For PA2 notions, the possibility of eavesdropping the communication is given to $\mathcal{A}$ by classical access to a randomized algorithm $\mathcal{P}$ (called a plaintext-creator) that upon receiving a query from $\mathcal{A}$ generates a message, encrypts it and sends the ciphertext to $\mathcal{A}$. (Since in the post-quantum setting the honest parties use the classical public-key encryption schemes to communicate, we do not consider the possibility of eavesdropping a superposition of ciphertexts in this paper.) Note that $\mathcal{A}^*$ does not have any access to the internal quantum registers of $\mathcal{P}$, so it might not be able to decrypt a ciphertext obtained from $\mathcal{P}$. The list of these ciphertexts is given to both the decryption oracle and $\mathcal{A}^*$ to return $\perp$ when one of these ciphertexts is submitted as a decryption query.

1.4 Organization

We present some preliminaries in Sect. 2. In Sect. 3, we define six possible definitions for the plaintext-awareness notion in the post-quantum setting. Section 4 discusses the relationships between notions. Finally, we discuss the achievability of our notions in Sect. 5.

2 Preliminaries

Any classical function $f : X \to Y$ can be implemented as a unitary operator $\mathbb{U}_f$ in a quantum computer where $\mathbb{U}_f : |x, y\rangle \to |x, y \oplus f(x)\rangle$ and it is clear that $\mathbb{U}_f^\dagger = \mathbb{U}_f$. A quantum adversary has standard oracle access to a classical function f if it can query the unitary $\mathbb{U}_f$. We refer the reader to Appendix A.2 for a short introduction to quantum computing. We refer to the class of quantum polynomial-time algorithms as QPT.

2.1 Definitions

We define a strong quantum-secure pseudo-random permutation as a permutation that is indistinguishable from a random permutation when the quantum adversary has superposition access to the permutation and its inverse.

Definition 1. *We say a permutation P a strong quantum-secure pseudo-random permutation if for any* QPT *adversary $\mathcal{A}$,*

$$|\Pr[b = 1 : b \leftarrow \mathcal{A}^{\mathbb{U}_P, \mathbb{U}_{P^{-1}}}] - \Pr[b = 1 : b \leftarrow \mathcal{A}^{\mathbb{U}_\pi, \mathbb{U}_{\pi^{-1}}}]| \le neg(\eta),$$

where π is a truly random permutation and η is the security parameter.

We define a public-key encryption scheme in the following.

Definition 2. *A public-key encryption scheme Π consists of three polynomial time (in the security parameter η) algorithms, (KGen, Enc, Dec), such that:*

1. KGen, *the key generation algorithm, is a probabilistic algorithm which on input 1^η outputs a pair of keys, $(\mathsf{pk}, \mathsf{sk}) \leftarrow \mathrm{KGen}(1^\eta)$, called the public key and the secret key for the encryption scheme, respectively.*
2. Enc, *the encryption algorithm, is a probabilistic algorithm which takes as input a public key pk and a message m from the message space and outputs a ciphertext $c \leftarrow \mathrm{Enc}_{\mathsf{pk}}(m)$. We may specify the randomness r that is used for computing c and write $c = \mathrm{Enc}_{\mathsf{pk}}(m; r)$.*
3. Dec, *the decryption algorithm, is a deterministic algorithm that takes as input a secret key sk and a ciphertext c and returns the message $m := \mathrm{Dec}_{\mathsf{sk}}(c)$. It is required that the decryption algorithm returns the original message, i.e., $\mathrm{Dec}_{\mathsf{sk}}(\mathrm{Enc}_{\mathsf{pk}}(m)) = m$, for every $(\mathsf{pk}, \mathsf{sk}) \leftarrow \mathrm{KGen}(1^\eta)$ and every m. The algorithm Dec returns $\perp$ if ciphertext c is not decryptable.*

We define a one-way public-key encryption scheme below. This is the minimal security requirement for an encryption scheme. This is needed for separation theorems between PA notions to exclude trivial encryption schemes, for example the identity encryption scheme that is defined as $\mathrm{Enc}_{\mathsf{pk}}(m) = m$, which are plaintext-aware with respect to any reasonable definition.

Definition 3. *We say a public-key encryption scheme* $\Pi = (\mathsf{KGen}, \mathsf{Enc}, \mathsf{Dec})$ *is one-way if for any* QPT *adversary* $\mathcal{A}$

$$\Pr[\mathcal{A}(\mathsf{pk}, c) = m : (\mathsf{pk}, \mathsf{sk}) \leftarrow \mathrm{KGen}(1^\eta), m \overset{\$}{\leftarrow} M, c \leftarrow \mathrm{Enc}_{\mathsf{pk}}(m)] \leq neg(\eta),$$

where M *is the message space.*

IND-qCPA and IND-qCCA. Here, we define a quantum IND-CPA and quantum IND-CCA notion used in this paper. Note that a quantum adversary can implement a public-key encryption algorithm in its quantum device since pk is public. To define IND-qCPA and IND-qCCA notions, we need to determine whether the challenge queries and decryption queries are classical or quantum. There are many quantum IND-CPA notions available in the literature [7] that include definitions with classical challenge queries and quantum challenge queries, on the other hand, there is only one definite quantum IND-CCA notion (called IND-qCCA) available in the literature that only allows classical challenge queries [6][2] the weakest quantum IND-CPA notion which, accompanied by our quantum PA2 notion, implies the IND-qCCA notion. We follow the definitions proposed in [6] by Boneh and Zhandry in this paper.

Definition 4. *We say an encryption scheme* Enc *is IND-qCPA secure if the following two games are indistinguishable for any* QPT *adversary* $\mathcal{X}$.

Game 0: $G_{\mathcal{X},0}^{qCPA}$
$$(\mathsf{pk}, \mathsf{sk}) \leftarrow \mathrm{KGen}(1^\eta), \qquad m_0, m_1 \leftarrow \mathcal{X}(\mathsf{pk}),$$
$$\mathrm{Enc}(m_0; r_0) \leftarrow Challenger(m_0, m_1), \ b \leftarrow \mathcal{X}(\mathsf{pk}, \mathrm{Enc}(m_0; r_0))$$

Game 1: $G_{\mathcal{X},1}^{qCPA}$
$$(\mathsf{pk}, \mathsf{sk}) \leftarrow \mathrm{KGen}(1^\eta), \qquad m_0, m_1 \leftarrow \mathcal{X}(\mathsf{pk}),$$
$$\mathrm{Enc}(m_1; r_1) \leftarrow Challenger(m_0, m_1), \ b \leftarrow \mathcal{X}(\mathsf{pk}, \mathrm{Enc}(m_1; r_1))$$

In other words, $|\Pr[G_{\mathcal{X},0}^{qCPA} = 1] - \Pr[G_{\mathcal{X},1}^{qCPA} = 1]| \leq neg(\eta)$ *for any* QPT *adversary* $\mathcal{X}$.

IND-qCCA. Here, a quantum adversary can query the encryption and decryption oracle on superposition of inputs but the challenge queries are classical. Let **List** be the list of ciphertexts obtained during the challenge phase. We say **List** is defined if at least one challenge query has been executed. We define a decryption algorithm $\mathrm{Dec}'_{(\mathsf{sk}, \mathbf{List})}$ as follows:

$$\mathrm{Dec}'_{(\mathsf{sk}, \mathbf{List})}(c) = \begin{cases} \perp & \text{if } \mathbf{List} \text{ is defined and } c \in \mathbf{List} \\ \mathrm{Dec}_{\mathsf{sk}}(c) & \text{otherwise} \end{cases}.$$

---

[2] There are some very recent research to define a quantum IND-CCA notion with quantum challenge queries (for instance [8,12]).

Definition 5. *We say an encryption scheme* Enc *is IND-qCCA secure if the following two games are indistinguishable for any* QPT *adversary* $\mathcal{X}$.

Game 0: $G_{\mathcal{X},0}^{qCCA}$

$$(\mathsf{pk},\mathsf{sk}) \leftarrow \mathrm{KGen}(1^\eta), \qquad\qquad m_0, m_1 \leftarrow \mathcal{X}^{\mathbb{U}_{\mathrm{Dec}_{\mathsf{sk}}}}(\mathsf{pk}),$$
$$\mathrm{Enc}(m_0; r_0) \leftarrow Challenger(m_0, m_1), \, b \leftarrow \mathcal{X}^{\mathbb{U}_{\mathrm{Dec}'_{(\mathsf{sk},\mathbf{List})}}}(\mathsf{pk}, \mathrm{Enc}(m_0; r_0))$$

Game 1: $G_{\mathcal{X},1}^{qCCA}$

$$(\mathsf{pk},\mathsf{sk}) \leftarrow \mathrm{KGen}(1^\eta), \qquad\qquad m_0, m_1 \leftarrow \mathcal{X}^{\mathbb{U}_{\mathrm{Dec}_{\mathsf{sk}}}}(\mathsf{pk}),$$
$$\mathrm{Enc}(m_1; r_1) \leftarrow Challenger(m_0, m_1), \, b \leftarrow \mathcal{X}^{\mathbb{U}_{\mathrm{Dec}'_{(\mathsf{sk},\mathbf{List})}}}(\mathsf{pk}, \mathrm{Enc}(m_1; r_1))$$

In other words, $|\Pr[G_{\mathcal{X},0}^{qCCA} = 1] - \Pr[G_{\mathcal{X},1}^{qCCA}]| \leq neg(\eta)$ *for any* QPT *adversary* $\mathcal{X}$.

We define a computationally hiding and binding commitment scheme in Appendix A.1.

3   Post-quantum Plaintext-Awareness

In this section, we define plaintext-awareness for classical encryption schemes in the presence of a quantum adversary. Let Q_{int} indicate the internal registers of the ciphertext-creator adversary $\mathcal{A}$. Note that Q_{int} includes the input, output and some ancillary registers of $\mathcal{A}$.

3.1   Post-quantum PA0, PA1

There are two possible cases to define PA0 and PA1. Namely, either $\mathcal{A}$'s goal is to output a classical ciphertext without knowing its corresponding plaintext or its goal is to output a superposition of ciphertexts where the corresponding quantum plaintext is unknown to $\mathcal{A}$. In the formulation of these two possible cases, the access to the decryption oracle will differ. Namely, either the adversary $\mathcal{A}$ has classical access to the decryption oracle or it has superposition access to the decryption oracle. In other words, to say that $\mathcal{A}$ is not able to output a valid classical (quantum) ciphertext unless it executes the encryption algorithm, there should be an algorithm $\mathcal{A}^*$ that can respond to classical (quantum) decryption queries given the internal registers of $\mathcal{A}$. That is, any valid ciphertext known to $\mathcal{A}$ can be decrypted if $\mathcal{A}^*$ has access to the internal register of $\mathcal{A}$.

Classical Decryption Queries. We define the definition using two games. In the real game, $\mathcal{A}$ given pk has access to the decryption oracle. In the fake game, the decryption queries will be answered with an algorithm $\mathcal{A}^*$ that has access to the internal register of $\mathcal{A}$. In both games, $\mathcal{A}$ outputs a quantum state in the end. We say a public-key encryption scheme is plaintext-aware if for any QPT adversary $\mathcal{A}$, there exists a QPT algorithm $\mathcal{A}^*$ such that the output of these two games is indistinguishable for any QPT distinguisher $\mathcal{D}$. Without loss of generality, we assume that the output of $\mathcal{D}$ is determined with a computational basis measurement. This computational indistinguishability definition for quantum states is common in the literature, for instance in Definition 1 in [16].

Game $G_{real}^{\mathsf{pqPA1\text{-}C_{dec}}}$. In this game, the ciphertext-creator adversary $\mathcal{A}$ given pk has classical access to the decryption oracle. At the end, $\mathcal{A}$ outputs a quantum state.

Game $G_{real}^{\mathsf{pqPA1\text{-}C_{dec}}}$ _____

$(\mathsf{pk}, \mathsf{sk}) \leftarrow \mathrm{KGen}(1^{\eta})$, $\rho_{\eta} \leftarrow \mathcal{A}^{\mathrm{Dec_{sk}}}(\mathsf{pk})$

Game $G_{fake}^{\mathsf{pqPA1\text{-}C_{dec}}}$. In this game, $\mathcal{A}$'s decryption queries will be responded by a plaintext-extractor algorithm $\mathcal{A}^{*}$. Here, $\mathcal{A}^{*}$ has access to pk and the internal register of $\mathcal{A}$. At the end, $\mathcal{A}$ outputs a quantum state.

Game $G_{fake}^{\mathsf{pqPA1\text{-}C_{dec}}}$ _____

$(\mathsf{pk}, \mathsf{sk}) \leftarrow \mathrm{KGen}(1^{\eta})$, $\rho_{\eta} \leftarrow \mathcal{A}^{\mathcal{A}^{*}(\mathsf{pk}, Q_{int})}(\mathsf{pk})$

Definition 6 (pqPA1-C$_{dec}$). *We say a public-key encryption scheme* Enc *is* pqPA1-C$_{dec}$ *plaintext-aware if for any* QPT *ciphertext-creator* $\mathcal{A}$, *there exists a* QPT *plaintext-extractor* $\mathcal{A}^{*}$ *such that for all* QPT *distinguishing algorithms* $\mathcal{D}$, *the advantage of* $\mathcal{D}$ *in distinguishing* $G_{real}^{\mathsf{pqPA1\text{-}C_{dec}}}$ *and* $G_{fake}^{\mathsf{pqPA1\text{-}C_{dec}}}$ *is negligible as a function of the security parameter:*

$$\mathbf{Adv}_{\mathcal{D},\,\mathcal{A}} = |\Pr[\mathcal{D}(\rho_{\eta}) = 1 : \rho_{\eta} \leftarrow G_{real}^{\mathsf{pqPA1\text{-}C_{dec}}}] -$$
$$\Pr[\mathcal{D}(\rho_{\eta}) = 1 : \rho_{\eta} \leftarrow G_{fake}^{\mathsf{pqPA1\text{-}C_{dec}}}]| \le neg(\eta),$$

where the output of $\mathcal{D}$ *is determined with the computational basis measurement.*

Definition 7 (pqPA0-C$_{dec}$). *This is defined similarly to* pqPA1-C$_{dec}$ *except the adversary* $\mathcal{A}$ *is allowed to make only one decryption query.*

Superposition Decryption Queries. In this subsection, we define plaintext-awareness definition when the adversary $\mathcal{A}$ has superposition access to the decryption oracle. Similar to the above definition, we define this notion using two games.

Game $G_{real}^{\mathsf{pqPA1\text{-}Q_{dec}}}$. In this game, the ciphertext-creator adversary $\mathcal{A}$ given pk has quantum access to the decryption oracle. At the end, $\mathcal{A}$ outputs a quantum state.

Game $G_{real}^{\mathsf{pqPA1\text{-}Q_{dec}}}$ _____

$(\mathsf{pk}, \mathsf{sk}) \leftarrow \mathrm{KGen}(1^{\eta})$, $\rho_{\eta} \leftarrow \mathcal{A}^{\mathbb{U}_{\mathrm{Dec_{sk}}}}(\mathsf{pk})$

Game $G_{fake}^{pqPA1\text{-}Q_{dec}}$. In this game, $\mathcal{A}$'s quantum decryption queries will be responded by a plaintext-extractor algorithm $\mathcal{A}^*$. Here, $\mathcal{A}^*$ has access to pk and the internal register of $\mathcal{A}$. At the end, $\mathcal{A}$ outputs a quantum state.

Game $G_{fake}^{pqPA1\text{-}Q_{dec}}$

$$(\mathsf{pk}, \mathsf{sk}) \leftarrow \mathrm{KGen}(1^\eta), \; \rho_\eta \leftarrow \mathcal{A}^{\mathcal{A}^*(\mathsf{pk}, Q_{int})}(\mathsf{pk})$$

Definition 8 (pqPA1-Q_{dec}). *We say a public-key encryption scheme* Enc *is* pqPA1-Q_{dec} *plaintext-aware if for any* QPT *ciphertext-creator* $\mathcal{A}$, *there exists a* QPT *plaintext-extractor* $\mathcal{A}^*$ *such that for all* QPT *distinguishing algorithms* $\mathcal{D}$, *the advantage of* $\mathcal{D}$ *in distinguishing* $G_{real}^{pqPA1\text{-}Q_{dec}}$ *and* $G_{fake}^{pqPA1\text{-}Q_{dec}}$ *is negligible as a function of the security parameter:*

$$\mathbf{Adv}_{\mathcal{D},\mathcal{A}} = |\Pr[\mathcal{D}(\rho_\eta) = 1 : \rho_\eta \leftarrow G_{real}^{pqPA1\text{-}Q_{dec}}] -$$
$$\Pr[\mathcal{D}(\rho_\eta) = 1 : \rho_\eta \leftarrow G_{fake}^{pqPA1\text{-}Q_{dec}}]| \leq neg(\eta),$$

where the output of $\mathcal{D}$ *is determined with the computational basis measurement.*

Definition 9 (pqPA0-Q_{dec}). *This is defined similarly to* pqPA1-Q_{dec} *except the adversary* $\mathcal{A}$ *is allowed to make only one decryption query.*

3.2   Post-quantum PA2

In pqPA0 and pqPA1 definitions, it has not been considered that the adversary may be able to eavesdrop some ciphertexts and use them to generate new ciphertexts without knowing their corresponding plaintexts. There are two scenarios for the eavesdropping:

– The adversary may eavesdrop some classical ciphertexts.
– The adversary may obtain some superposition of ciphertexts.

Note that in the post-quantum setting, the honest parties are using their classical devices to communicate. So the assumption that the adversary may be able to eavesdrop some superposition of ciphertexts seems too exotic and we do not analyse it in this paper. We provide a short discussion on the main obstacle in defining a plaintext-awareness definition with the superposition eavesdropping in Appendix B.

The possibility for eavesdropping is granted to the adversary by a randomized algorithm $\mathcal{P}$ (called the plaintext-creator). Here, $\mathcal{P}$ upon receiving a query from $\mathcal{A}$ outputs the encryption of a message of its choosing to $\mathcal{A}$. Additionally, $\mathcal{P}$ adds m and its corresponding ciphertext to a **List**.

Similar to pqPA0 and pqPA1, we consider two possible goals for the adversary $\mathcal{A}$: outputting a classical ciphertext without knowing its corresponding plaintext or a superposition of ciphertexts without knowing its corresponding superposition of plaintexts.

Recall that $\text{Dec}'_{(\text{sk},\textbf{List})}$ is defined as:

$$\text{Dec}'_{(\text{sk},\textbf{List})}(c) = \begin{cases} \perp & \text{if } \textbf{List} \text{ is defined and } c \in \textbf{List} \\ \text{Dec}_{\text{sk}}(c) & \text{otherwise} \end{cases}.$$

Classical Decryption Queries. In this subsection, we define plaintext-awareness when the adversary $\mathcal{A}$ has classical access to a plaintext creator algorithm $\mathcal{P}$ and the decryption oracle $\text{Dec}'_{(\text{sk},\textbf{List})}$. Similarly, we define the notion using two games.

Game $G_{real}^{\text{pqPA2-C}_{\text{dec}}}$. In this game, the ciphertext-creator adversary $\mathcal{A}$ given pk has oracle access to $\mathcal{P}$. It has classical access to the decryption oracle $\text{Dec}'_{(\text{sk},\textbf{List})}$. At the end, $\mathcal{A}$ outputs a quantum state.

Game $G_{real}^{\text{pqPA2-C}_{\text{dec}}}$

$(\text{pk}, \text{sk}) \leftarrow \text{KGen}(1^\eta), \ \rho_\eta \leftarrow \mathcal{A}^{\mathcal{P},\text{Dec}'_{(\text{sk},\textbf{List})}}(\text{pk})$

Game $G_{fake}^{\text{pqPA2-C}_{\text{dec}}}$. In this game, $\mathcal{A}$'s decryption queries will be responded by a plaintext-extractor algorithm $\mathcal{A}^*$. Here, $\mathcal{A}^*$ given pk has access to **List** and the internal register of $\mathcal{A}$. At the end, $\mathcal{A}$ outputs a quantum state.

Game $G_{fake}^{\text{pqPA2-C}_{\text{dec}}}$

$(\text{pk}, \text{sk}) \leftarrow \text{KGen}(1^\eta), \ \rho_\eta \leftarrow \mathcal{A}^{\mathcal{P},\mathcal{A}^*(\text{pk},\textbf{List},Q_{int})}(\text{pk})$

Definition 10 (pqPA2-C$_{\text{dec}}$). *We say a public-key encryption scheme* Enc *is* pqPA2-C$_{\text{dec}}$ *plaintext-aware if for any* QPT *ciphertext-creator* $\mathcal{A}$, *there exists a* QPT *plaintext-extractor* $\mathcal{A}^*$ *such that for any* QPT *plaintext-creator* $\mathcal{P}$ *and any* QPT *distinguishing algorithms* $\mathcal{D}$, *the advantage of* $\mathcal{D}$ *in distinguishing* $G_{real}^{\text{pqPA2-C}_{\text{dec}}}$ *and* $G_{fake}^{\text{pqPA2-C}_{\text{dec}}}$ *is negligible as a function of the security parameter:*

$$\textbf{Adv}_{\mathcal{D},\mathcal{A}} = |\Pr[\mathcal{D}(\rho_\eta) = 1 : \rho_\eta \leftarrow G_{real}^{\text{pqPA2-C}_{\text{dec}}}] -$$
$$\Pr[\mathcal{D}(\rho_\eta) = 1 : \rho_\eta \leftarrow G_{fake}^{\text{pqPA2-C}_{\text{dec}}}]| \leq neg(\eta),$$

where the output of $\mathcal{D}$ *is determined with the computational basis measurement.*

Superposition Decryption Queries. In this subsection, we define plaintext-awareness when the adversary $\mathcal{A}$ has classical access to a plaintext creator algorithm $\mathcal{P}$ and superposition access to the decryption oracle $\text{Dec}'_{(\text{sk},\textbf{List})}$. Similarly, we define the notion using two games.

Game $G_{real}^{\text{pqPA2-Q}_{\text{dec}}}$. In this game, the ciphertext-creator adversary $\mathcal{A}$ given pk has oracle access to $\mathcal{P}$ and superposition access to the decryption oracle. At the end, $\mathcal{A}$ outputs a quantum state.

Game $G_{real}^{pqPA2\text{-}Q_{dec}}$

$$(\mathsf{pk}, \mathsf{sk}) \leftarrow \mathrm{KGen}(1^\eta), \; \rho_\eta \leftarrow \mathcal{A}^{\mathcal{P}, \mathrm{U}_{\mathrm{Dec}'(\mathsf{sk}, \mathbf{List})}}(\mathsf{pk})$$

Game $G_{fake}^{pqPA2\text{-}Q_{dec}}$. In this game, $\mathcal{A}$'s decryption queries will be responded by a plaintext-extractor algorithm $\mathcal{A}^*$. Here, $\mathcal{A}^*$ given pk has access to **List** and the internal register of $\mathcal{A}$. At the end, $\mathcal{A}$ outputs a quantum state.

Game $G_{fake}^{pqPA2\text{-}Q_{dec}}$

$$(\mathsf{pk}, \mathsf{sk}) \leftarrow \mathrm{KGen}(1^\eta), \; \rho_\eta \leftarrow \mathcal{A}^{\mathcal{P}, \mathcal{A}^*(\mathsf{pk}, \mathbf{List}, Q_{int})}(\mathsf{pk})$$

Definition 11 (pqPA2-Q_{dec}). *We say a public-key encryption scheme* Enc *is* pqPA2-Q_{dec} *plaintext-aware if for any* QPT *ciphertext-creator* $\mathcal{A}$, *there exists a* QPT *plaintext-extractor* $\mathcal{A}^*$ *such that that for any* QPT *plaintext-extractor* $\mathcal{P}$ *and any* QPT *distinguishing algorithms* $\mathcal{D}$, *the advantage of* $\mathcal{D}$ *in distinguishing* $G_{real}^{pqPA2\text{-}Q_{dec}}$ *and* $G_{fake}^{pqPA2\text{-}Q_{dec}}$ *is negligible as a function of the security parameter:*

$$\mathbf{Adv}_{\mathcal{D}, \mathcal{A}} = |\Pr[\mathcal{D}(\rho_\eta) = 1 : \rho_\eta \leftarrow G_{real}^{pqPA2\text{-}Q_{dec}}] -$$
$$\Pr[\mathcal{D}(\rho_\eta) = 1 : \rho_\eta \leftarrow G_{fake}^{pqPA2\text{-}Q_{dec}}]| \le neg(\eta),$$

where the output of $\mathcal{D}$ *is determined with the computational basis measurement.*

4   Relationships Between Notions

In this section, we study the relations between different PA notions defined in this paper. In addition, we show that the pqPA2-Q_{dec} plaintext-awareness notion defined in this paper along with IND-qCPA security implies IND-qCCA security.

4.1   Relationships Between PA Notions

Implications. First we show implications between the notions. Clearly, pqPAi-Q_{dec} plaintext-awareness implies pqPAi-C_{dec} plaintext-awareness for $i = 0, 1, 2$. The reason is the existence of a plaintext-extractor algorithm $\mathcal{A}^*$ for an adversary $\mathcal{A}$ that makes superposition queries to the decryption oracle is enough to prove pqPAi-C_{dec} plaintext-awareness. In other words, the algorithm $\mathcal{A}^*$ is a plaintext extractor for an adversary attacking in the sense of pqPAi-C_{dec}.

Theorem 1. *For any* $i = 0, 1, 2$, *a public-key encryption scheme* Enc *that is* pqPAi-Q_{dec} *plaintext-aware, it is* pqPAi-C_{dec} *plaintext-aware.*

Below, we investigate the relations between PAi notions for different i.

Theorem 2. *If an encryption scheme is* pqPA2-Qu *aware then it is* pqPA1-Qu *aware when* $Qu \in \{C_{dec}, Q_{dec}\}$.

Proof. The proof is straightforward because an adversary $\mathcal{A}$ that breaks pqPA1-Qu awareness can be run to break pqPA2-Qu awareness. In more detail, the reduction adversary $\mathcal{B}$ runs $\mathcal{A}$ and simulates $\mathcal{A}$'s decryption queries using its decryption oracle. (Note that the reduction adversary $\mathcal{B}$ does not use the possibility of querying the plaintext-creator and breaks the pqPA2-Qu awareness notion.) □

Theorem 3. *If an encryption scheme is* pqPA1-Qu *aware then it is* pqPA0-Qu *aware when* $Qu \in \{\mathsf{C_{dec}}, \mathsf{Q_{dec}}\}$.

Proof. The proof is obvious since the only difference between $PA1$ and $PA0$ notions are the number of decryption queries, which is polynomially many queries and one query, respectively. □

Non-implications. The rest of this subsection shows non-implications (i.e. separations) between notions. Note that in order to exclude the trivial encryption schemes that are plaintext-aware with respect to all definitions (for instance, the identity encryption), we add a security requirement (one-wayness or IND-qCPA security) for encryption in the separation theorems.

Below, we show that pqPAi-$\mathsf{Q_{dec}}$ is strictly stronger than pqPAi-$\mathsf{C_{dec}}$ for $i = 1, 2$. The high-level idea is to take an encryption scheme that is pqPAi-$\mathsf{C_{dec}}$ plaintext-aware and modifies its decryption algorithm in a way that remains pqPAi-$\mathsf{C_{dec}}$ plaintext-aware but it leaks a valid ciphertext to the pqPAi-$\mathsf{Q_{dec}}$ adversary.

Theorem 4. *A one-way* pqPAi-$\mathsf{C_{dec}}$ *plaintext-aware public-key encryption scheme is not necessarily* pqPAi-$\mathsf{Q_{dec}}$ *plaintext-aware for* $i = 1, 2$.

Proof. Let $\Pi = (\mathsf{KGen}, \mathsf{Enc}, \mathsf{Dec})$ be a public-key encryption scheme that is pqPAi-$\mathsf{C_{dec}}$ plaintext-aware. Let $\{0, 1\}^n$ be the ciphertext space of Π. Let the ciphertext c_v be generated by choosing a random message m and a randomness r and computing $\mathsf{Enc}(m; r)$. We modify Π to a new encryption scheme $\Pi' = (\mathsf{KGen}', \mathsf{Enc}', \mathsf{Dec}')$. The algorithm KGen' runs KGen to get $(\mathsf{pk}, \mathsf{sk})$, it outputs a key pk_{com} for a computationally hiding and binding commitment scheme $(\mathsf{Com}, \mathsf{Ver})$, and it chooses a random periodic function f on c_v. (That is for any $x \in \{0, 1\}^n$, $f(x \oplus c_v) = f(x)$.) It returns the pair $(\mathsf{pk}', \mathsf{sk}') = ((\mathsf{pk}, \mathsf{pk}_{com}), (\mathsf{sk}, f))$ and the commitment value $c_{com} = \mathsf{Com}(\mathsf{pk}_{com}, c_v)$ with the corresponding opening ω. For any message m in the message-space of Π, $\mathsf{Enc}'_{\mathsf{pk}'}(m) = \mathsf{Enc}_{\mathsf{pk}}(m) \| \perp$. The new decryption algorithm $\mathsf{Dec}'_{(\mathsf{sk}, f)}$ takes as input a ciphertext from $(\{0, 1\}^n \cup \perp) \times (\{0, 1\}^n \cup \perp)$ and operates as the following:

$$\mathsf{Dec}'_{(\mathsf{sk}, f, r)}(c_1, c_2) = \begin{cases} \mathsf{Dec}_{\mathsf{sk}}(c_1) & \text{if } c_1 \neq \perp \text{ and } c_2 = \perp \\ \mathsf{Dec}_{\mathsf{sk}}(c_v) \| r \| \omega & \text{if } c_1 = \perp \text{ and } c_2 = c_v \\ \perp & \text{if } c_1 = \perp \text{ and } c_2 \neq c_v \\ f(c_2) & \text{otherwise} \end{cases}.$$

Since $\mathrm{Dec}'_{sk'}(\mathrm{Enc}'_{pk'}(m)) = \mathrm{Dec}_{sk}(\mathrm{Enc}_{pk}(m))$, Π' satisfies the correctness property. It is clear that Π' is one-way since Π is one-way. We show that Π' is pqPA1-C_{dec} plaintext-aware. Let $\mathcal{A}^*$ be the QPT plaintext-extractor algorithm for Π. We construct a QPT plaintext-extractor algorithm $\mathcal{A}'^*$ for Π'. Namely, $\mathcal{A}'^*$ chooses a random function f' with the same domain and co-domain as f and for any (c_1, c_2) operates as follows:

$$\mathcal{A}'^*(c_1, c_2) = \begin{cases} \mathcal{A}^*(c_1) & \text{if } c_1 \neq \perp \text{ and } c_2 = \perp \\ \perp & \text{if } c_1 = \perp \\ f'(c_2) & \text{otherwise} \end{cases}.$$

Note that an adversary with classical access to the decryption oracle is not able to get c_v. In addition, the commitment scheme is computationally hiding and c_{com} reveals c_v only with a negligible probability. Therefore, the decryption query $(\perp, c_v)$ will be submitted with a negligible probability. Since for a polynomial-time adversary with classical access to f and f', these two functions are indistinguishable, $\mathcal{A}'^*$ is a successful polynomial-time plaintext-extractor algorithm for Π'.

However, an adversary $\mathcal{A}$ with superposition access to Dec', can choose a random ciphertext c' from $\{0,1\}^n$ and queries $|c'\rangle \otimes \sum_{c \in \{0,1\}^n} \frac{1}{\sqrt{n}} |c\rangle$ to Dec'. Therefore, the adversary can employ the Simon's quantum algorithm [20] to obtain c_v and break pqPAi-Q_{dec} plaintext-awareness. In more detail, $\mathcal{A}$ submits $(\perp, c_v)$ as a decryption query. After getting a response $m'\|r'\|\omega'$, it checks if $c_v = \mathrm{Enc}(m'; r')$ and $\mathrm{Ver}(pk_{com}, c_{com}, c_v, \omega') = 1$. If both equalities hold, it returns 1, otherwise, it returns 0.

In the real case, the Dec' returns $\mathrm{Dec}_{sk}(c_v)\|r$ and $\mathcal{A}$ outputs 1 with a high probability, namely the probability of Simon's algorithm succeeding. However, in the fake game, since Enc is one-way and the commitment scheme is computationally binding, there is no QPT algorithm $\mathcal{A}^*$ that can simulate an answer to the decryption query $(\perp, c_v)$ such that both equalities above hold with a non-negligible probability. So $\mathcal{A}$ returns 1 with a negligible probability in this case. Consequently, a distinguisher that returns the output of $\mathcal{A}$ can distinguish between the real game and the fake game with a non-negligible probability.   □

We can use a similar trick to show that pqPA0-Q_{dec} is strictly stronger than pqPA0-C_{dec}. Since Simon's algorithm needs a polynomial number of queries to extract c_v but in the pqPA0-C_{dec} notion the adversary is only allowed to make a single query, we need to modify Dec' a bit further. Namely, we expand the ciphertext space and define Dec'' as the following:

$$\mathrm{Dec}''(c_1, c_2, \cdots, c_m) = \begin{cases} \mathrm{Dec}(c_1) & \text{if } c_1 \neq \perp \text{ and } c_2 = \cdots = c_m = \perp \\ \mathrm{Dec}_{sk}(c_v)\|r\|\omega & \text{if } c_1 = c_3 = \cdots = c_m = \perp \text{ and } c_2 = c_v \\ \perp & \text{if } c_1 = \perp \text{ and } c_2 \neq c_v \\ f(c_2)\|\cdots\|f(c_m) & \text{otherwise} \end{cases}.$$

The adversary queries

$$|c\rangle \otimes \sum_{c\in\{0,1\}^n} \frac{1}{\sqrt{n}} |c\rangle \otimes \cdots \otimes \sum_{c\in\{0,1\}^n} \frac{1}{\sqrt{n}} |c\rangle$$

to Dec'' to extract c_v. (Note that m is big enough that Simon's algorithm returns c_v with a high probability.)

Corollary 1. *A one-way* pqPA0-C$_{dec}$ *plaintext-aware public-key encryption scheme Enc is not necessarily* pqPA0-Q$_{dec}$ *plaintext-aware.*

Therefore, we can conclude that even the strongest plaintext-awareness notion with classical decryption queries will not imply the weakest plaintext-awareness notion with quantum decryption queries.

Corollary 2. *A one-way* pqPA2-C$_{dec}$ *plaintext-aware public-key encryption scheme Enc is not necessarily* pqPA0-Q$_{dec}$ *plaintext-aware.*

Proof. The proof is similar to the proof of Corollary 1.   □

In the theorem below, we show that an adversary with the ability to eavesdrop some ciphertexts is strictly stronger than an adversary without this ability. Namely, we show that an encryption scheme that is pqPA1-Q$_{dec}$ plaintext-aware, it is not necessarily pqPA2-C$_{dec}$ plaintext-aware. The high-level idea to show this claim is to design an encryption scheme that is malleable on the last bit, however, this malleability does not change the corresponding plaintext. In other words, if we flip the last bit of any ciphertext, we will get a valid ciphertext, but, without any change on the corresponding plaintext. A PA1 adversary is not able to use this malleability since this does not change the plaintext inside of the ciphertext. However, an PA2 adversary can obtain a valid ciphertext (c, b) by eavesdropping and change it to a new ciphertext $(c, b \oplus 1)$ where its corresponding plaintext is unknown to the adversary.

Theorem 5. *A public-key encryption scheme that is* pqPA1-Q$_{dec}$ *plaintext-aware and IND-qCPA secure, it is not necessarily* pqPA2-C$_{dec}$ *plaintext-aware.*

Proof. Let Π = (Enc, Dec, KGen) be a pqPA1-Q$_{dec}$ plaintext-aware. We construct the following encryption scheme Π':

- KGen$'$ = KGen
- Enc$'(m)$ = Enc$(m)\|0$
- Dec$'(c\|b)$ = Dec(c), where $b \in \{0, 1\}$

The IND-qCPA security of Π' is obtained easily by the IND-qCPA security of Π. We show that Π' is also pqPA1-Q$_{dec}$ plaintext-aware. Let $\mathcal{A}$ be an adversary that attacks Π' in the sense of pqPA1-Q$_{dec}$. We construct an adversary $\mathcal{B}$ that attacks Π. The adversary $\mathcal{B}$ runs $\mathcal{A}$ and answers its decryption queries as follows. Let Q_c, Q_b be the input quantum registers for c, b respectively. Let Q_{out} be the output quantum register. The adversary $\mathcal{B}$ upon receiving Q_c, Q_b, Q_{out} registers from $\mathcal{A}$, it forwards Q_c, Q_{out} registers to its decryption oracle. After getting back $\mathbb{U}_{Dec}(Q_c Q_{out})$ from its decryption oracle, it sends all three registers to $\mathcal{A}$. It is clear that the decryption queries are simulated perfectly for $\mathcal{A}$. Since Π is pqPA1-Q$_{dec}$ plaintext-aware, there exists a plaintext-extractor algorithm $\mathcal{B}^*$ for $\mathcal{B}$. Now from $\mathcal{B}^*$, one can construct an extractor $\mathcal{A}^*$ for $\mathcal{A}$. Namely, $\mathcal{A}^*(c\|b) := \mathcal{B}^*(c)$.

However, Π' is not pqPA2-C$_{dec}$ plaintext-aware. Let $\mathcal{A}$ be an adversary that sends two messages $m_0 := 0^n$ and $m_1 := 1^n$ as a query to its plaintext-creator $\mathcal{P}$. Upon receiving a ciphertext $(c\|0)$ from $\mathcal{P}$, it sends $(c\|1)$ as a decryption query. If the answer is 0^n, it returns 0, otherwise it returns 1. Consider a plaintext-creator algorithm $\mathcal{P}_b$ that upon receiving a query m_0, m_1, it sends m_b to Enc. Then, it forwards $(c_b\|0) := \text{Enc}(m_b)$ to the adversary. Let $\mathcal{D}$ be a distinguisher that returns the output of $\mathcal{A}$. Proof by contrary, let assume that Π' is pqPA2-C$_{dec}$ plaintext-aware. Then, there exists a plaintext-extractor algorithm $\mathcal{A}^*$ that works for $(\mathcal{A}, \mathcal{P}_0, \mathcal{D})$ and $(\mathcal{A}, \mathcal{P}_1, \mathcal{D})$. That is,

$$G_{real}^{\text{pqPA2-C}_{dec}}(\mathcal{A}, \mathbb{U}_{Dec'}, \mathcal{P}_0, \mathcal{D}) \cong G_{fake}^{\text{pqPA2-C}_{dec}}(\mathcal{A}, \mathcal{A}^*, \mathcal{P}_0, \mathcal{D})$$

and

$$G_{real}^{\text{pqPA2-C}_{dec}}(\mathcal{A}, \mathbb{U}_{Dec'}, \mathcal{P}_1, \mathcal{D}) \cong G_{fake}^{\text{pqPA2-C}_{dec}}(\mathcal{A}, \mathcal{A}^*, \mathcal{P}_1, \mathcal{D})$$

It is clear that in the real case, $\mathcal{D}$ returns 0 with the probability 1 when $\mathcal{A}$ interacts with $\mathcal{P}_0$ and it returns 1 with the probability 1 when $\mathcal{A}$ interacts with $\mathcal{P}_1$. So these two games are distinguishable. Consequently, in the fake game, $\mathcal{A}$'s interaction with $\mathcal{P}_0$ is distinguishable from its interaction with $\mathcal{P}_1$. And this is a contradiction to the IND-qCPA security of Π'. Namely, an adversary $\mathcal{B}$ that runs $\mathcal{A}$ and answers its decryption queries with $\mathcal{A}^*$ and its queries to a plaintext creator with Π''s challenger can break IND-qCPA security of Π'. $\square$

In the following theorem, we show that a one-way public-key encryption scheme that is plaintext-aware against adversaries that make a single quantum decryption query is not necessarily plaintext-aware against adversaries that make many classical decryption queries. The high-level idea is that the decryption oracle partially reveals a valid ciphertext in each query. In more details, we write a valid ciphertext c_v as XOR of two random values $c_v^{(1)}$ and $c_v^{(2)}$, that is $c_v = c_v^{(1)} \oplus c_v^{(2)}$. Then the decryption oracle reveals one of $c_v^{(1)}$ or $c_v^{(2)}$ randomly in each query. Obviously, the adversary with a single query is able to get one of $c_v^{(1)}$ or $c_v^{(2)}$ and that does not give any useful information. On other hand, the adversary with many decryption queries is able to obtain c_v.

Theorem 6. *A one-way* pqPA0-Q$_{dec}$ *plaintext-aware public-key encryption scheme is not necessarily* pqPA1-C$_{dec}$ *plaintext-aware.*

Proof. Let $\Pi = (\text{KGen}, \text{Enc}, \text{Dec})$ be a pqPA0-Q$_{dec}$ plaintext-aware encryption scheme. Let c_v be a ciphertext that is generated by choosing a random message m and a randomness r and computing $\text{Enc}(m; r)$. Let $c_v^{(1)}$ and $c_v^{(2)}$ be two random elements such that $c_v = c_v^{(1)} \oplus c_v^{(2)}$. We construct an encryption scheme

$\Pi' = (\text{KGen}', \text{Enc}', \text{Dec}')$. The algorithm KGen' runs KGen to get (pk, sk) and it outputs a key pk_{com} for a computationally hiding and binding commitment scheme (Com, Ver). That is, the outputs of KGen' are $((\text{pk}, \text{pk}_{com}), \text{sk})$ and the commitment value $c_{com} = \text{Com}(\text{pk}_{com}, c_v)$ with the corresponding opening ω. Note that a QPT adversary is not able to compute c_v from c_{com} with a non-negligible probability since the commitment scheme is computationally hiding. Let $\omega = \omega^{(1)} \oplus \omega^{(2)}$ for random values $\omega^{(1)}$ and $\omega^{(2)}$. For any message m, $\text{Enc}'(m) = \text{Enc}(m)\|0$. Dec' is a probabilistic algorithm and is defined as:

$$\text{Dec}'(c\|b) = \begin{cases} \text{Dec}(c) & \text{if } \text{Dec}(c) \neq \bot \text{ or } b = 0 \\ c_v^{(i)}\|r\|\omega^{(i)} \text{ for a random } i \in \{0,1\} & \text{if } b = 1 \text{ and } \text{Dec}(c) = \bot \end{cases}.$$

It is clear that $\text{Dec}'(\text{Enc}'(m)) = m$ with the probability 1. We make a convention that for any bit string x, $x \oplus \bot = x$. We show that Π' is $\text{pqPA0-Q}_{\text{dec}}$ plaintext-aware. Let $\mathcal{A}$ be an adversary that attacks Π' in the sense of $\text{pqPA0-Q}_{\text{dec}}$. From $\mathcal{A}$, we construct an adversary $\mathcal{B}$ that attacks Π in the sense of $\text{pqPA0-Q}_{\text{dec}}$. The adversary $\mathcal{B}$ runs $\mathcal{A}$ and answers to its decryption query as follows. Let Q_c, Q_b be the quantum input registers to store the c-part and the b-part of the ciphertext, respectively. Let Q_{out} be a register to store the output. The adversary $\mathcal{B}$ upon receiving these three registers Q_c, Q_b, Q_{out}, it forwards Q_c, Q_{out} to its decryption oracle. After getting $\mathbb{U}_{\text{Dec}}(Q_c Q_{out})$ back from its decryption oracle, it applies a control operator $\mathbb{U}_{cnt}$ on Q_c, Q_b, Q_{out}. The unitary $\mathbb{U}_{cnt}$ XORs a classical random value $c'\|r'\|\omega'$ to the Q_{out} register if $b = 1$ and $\text{Dec}(c) = \bot$. Otherwise, $\mathbb{U}_{cnt}$ is identity. It is clear that the decryption query is simulated perfectly. Since Π is $\text{pqPA0-Q}_{\text{dec}}$, there exists a successful plaintext-extractor $\mathcal{B}^*$ for $\mathcal{B}$. Now we construct a successful plaintext-extractor for $\mathcal{A}$. Namely,

$$\mathcal{A}^*(c\|b) = \begin{cases} \mathcal{B}^*(c) & \text{if } \mathcal{B}^*(c) \neq \bot \text{ or } b = 0 \\ c'\|r'\|\omega' & \text{if } b = 1 \text{ and } \mathcal{B}^*(c) = \bot \end{cases},$$

where c', r' and ω' are random values.

The encryption scheme Π' is not $\text{pqPA1-C}_{\text{dec}}$ aware since an adversary $\mathcal{A}$ is able to obtain c_v, ω, and the corresponding randomness r. It then sends c_v as a decryption query to get m'. Then it outputs 1 if $c_v = \text{Enc}(m'; r)$ and $\text{Ver}(\text{pk}_{com}, c_{com}, c_v, \omega) = 1$. Otherwise, it returns 0. It is clear that in the real case, $\mathcal{A}$ outputs 1 with the probability 1. However, in the fake game, $\mathcal{A}$ outputs 0 with a non-negligible probability since Π is one-way and the commitment scheme is computationally binding. $\square$

4.2   Relation with IND-qCCA

First we show that IND-qCPA security and $\text{pqPA2-C}_{\text{dec}}$ plaintext-awareness notions are not enough to conclude IND-qCCA security. The proof technique is similar to the proof of Theorem 4.

Theorem 7. *A public-key encryption scheme* Enc *that is* $\text{pqPA2-C}_{\text{dec}}$ *plaintext-aware and IND-qCPA secure is not necessarily IND-qCCA secure.*

Proof. Let Enc with the decryption algorithm Dec be a public-key encryption scheme that is pqPA2-C_{dec} plaintext-aware and IND-qCPA. Let $\{0,1\}^n$ is the ciphertext space of Enc. We modify Dec to a new decryption algorithm Dec$'$ in which it takes as input a ciphertext from $\{0,1\}^n \times \{0,1\}^n$ and operates as the following:

$$\text{Dec}'(c_1, c_2) = \begin{cases} \text{Dec}(c_1) || \perp & \text{if } \text{Dec}(c_1) \neq \perp \\ \perp || f(c_2) & \text{otherwise} \end{cases},$$

where f is a periodic function on the secret key sk. (That is for any $x \in \{0,1\}^n$, $f(x \oplus \text{sk}) = f(x)$.) It is clear that Enc remains pqPA1-C_{dec} plaintext-aware and IND-qCPA secure with this modification to Dec since exponential classical decryption queries are needed to recover sk. However, an adversary with superposition access to Dec$'$, can choose a random ciphertext c' from $\{0,1\}^n$ and queries $|c'\rangle \otimes \sum_{c \in \{0,1\}^n} \frac{1}{\sqrt{n}} |c\rangle$ to Dec$'$. Since Enc is pqPAi-C_{dec} plaintext-aware, with overwhelming probability $\text{Dec}(c') = \perp$. Therefore, the adversary can employ the Simon's quantum algorithm [20] to obtain sk and breaks IND-qCCA security. □

Since pqPA2-C_{dec} plaintext-awareness notion implies classical PA2 notion, we can conclude that PA2 + IND-qCPA notion does not imply IND-qCCA security.

Corollary 3. *A public-key encryption scheme* Enc *that is PA2 plaintext-aware and IND-qCPA secure is not necessarily IND-qCCA secure.*

In the theorem below, we show that a plaintext-awareness notion that allows quantum decryption queries, namely the pqPA2-Q_{dec} notion, along with the IND-qCPA notion is enough to imply IND-qCCA security.

Theorem 8. *Any public-key encryption scheme* Enc *that is* pqPA2-Q_{dec} *plaintext-aware and IND-qCPA secure is IND-qCCA secure.*

Proof. On a high level, we start with the IND-qCCA game when $b = 0$. Since Enc is plaintext-aware there is a ciphertext-extractor algorithm $\mathcal{A}^*$ that can simulate the decryption queries. We replace the decryption oracle with $\mathcal{A}^*$. Then, we switch to the IND-qCCA game with $b = 1$ by IND-qCPA security of Enc. And finally, we replace $\mathcal{A}^*$ with the actual decryption oracle. (See Appendix C for a detailed proof.) □

5   Achievability

In Appendix D, we argue that OAEP transform is pqPA1-Q_{dec} plaintext-aware using a recent result [10]. In addition, we lift any public-key encryption scheme that is PA2 plaintext-aware against a quantum adversary (a post-quantum secure public-key encryption scheme that is PA2) to a public-key encryption scheme that is pqPA2-Q_{dec} plaintext-aware. We use the hybrid framework. Namely to encrypt a message m, a fresh randomness r is encrypted using the public-key encryption scheme and m appended with a zero bitstring is encrypted with a strong PRP defined with the key r.

Acknowledgment. We would like to thank Peter Ryan, Peter Browne Rønne and Dimiter Ostrev for discussions about this work. Jeroen van Wier is supported by the Luxembourg National Research Fund (FNR), under the joint CORE project Q-CoDe (CORE17/IS/11689058/Q-CoDe/Ryan).

A   Preliminaries

A.1   Commitment Scheme

In the following, we define a commitment scheme.

Definition 12 (Commitment Scheme). *A commitment scheme consists of three polynomial algorithms* Gen, Com *and* Ver *described below.*

- *The key generating algorithm* Gen *that on the input of the security parameter* 1^n *returns a public-key* pk_{com}.
- *The commitment algorithm* Com *on the inputs* pk_{com} *and a message* m *chooses a randomness* r *and returns* $c := \mathrm{Com}(\mathsf{pk}_{com}, m; r)$ *and the corresponding opening information* ω.
- *The verification algorithm* Ver *on the inputs* pk_{com}, c, ω *and* m, *either accepts* $(b = 1)$ *or rejects* $(b = 0)$.

The scheme has the correctness property, that is, the verification algorithm returns 1 with the probability 1 if c, ω *are the output of* Com:

$$\Pr[b = 1 : \mathsf{pk}_{com} \leftarrow \mathrm{Gen}(1^n), (c, \omega) \leftarrow \mathrm{Com}(\mathsf{pk}_{com}, m), b \leftarrow \mathrm{Ver}(\mathsf{pk}_{com}, c, \omega, m)] = 1.$$

We define hiding and binding properties of a commitment scheme against a QPT adversary.

Definition 13. *We say a commitment scheme* $(\mathrm{Gen}(1^n), \mathrm{Com}, \mathrm{Ver})$ *is computationally hiding if for any* $\mathsf{pk}_{com} \leftarrow \mathrm{Gen}(1^n)$, *for any two messages* m_1, m_2 *and for any* QPT *distinguisher* $\mathcal{D}$

$$|\Pr[\mathcal{D}(\mathsf{pk}_{com}, c_1) = 1 : (c_1, \omega_1) \leftarrow \mathrm{Com}_{\mathsf{pk}_{com}}(m_1)] -$$
$$\Pr[\mathcal{D}(\mathsf{pk}_{com}, c_2) = 1 : (c_2, \omega_2) \leftarrow \mathrm{Com}_{\mathsf{pk}_{com}}(m_2)]| \leq \mathbf{neg}(n).$$

Definition 14. *A commitment scheme* $(\mathrm{Gen}(1^n), \mathrm{Com}, \mathrm{Ver})$ *is computationally binding if for any commitment* c, *and any* QPT *adversary* $\mathcal{A}$

$$|\Pr[\mathrm{Ver}(\mathsf{pk}_{com}, c, m_1, \omega_1) = 1 \wedge \mathrm{Ver}(\mathsf{pk}_{com}, c, m_2, \omega_2) = 1 \wedge m_1 \neq m_2 :$$
$$\mathsf{pk}_{com} \leftarrow \mathrm{Gen}(1^n), (m_1, \omega_1, m_2, \omega_2) \leftarrow \mathcal{A}(c, \mathsf{pk}_{com})]| \leq \mathbf{neg}(n).$$

Note that these properties are achievable, for instance, the commitment scheme in [14] fulfills these properties.

A.2   Basics of Quantum Computing

Here, we present some basics of quantum information and computation. For two vectors $|\Psi\rangle = (\psi_1, \psi_2, \cdots, \psi_n)$ and $|\Phi\rangle = (\phi_1, \phi_2, \cdots, \phi_n)$ in $\mathbb{C}^n$, the inner product is defined as $\langle \Psi, \Phi \rangle = \sum_i \psi_i^* \phi_i$ where ψ_i^* is the complex conjugate of ψ_i. Norm of $|\Phi\rangle$ is defined as $\| |\Phi\rangle \| = \sqrt{\langle \Phi, \Phi \rangle}$. The n-dimensional Hilbert space $\mathcal{H}$ is the complex vector space $\mathbb{C}^n$ with the inner product defined above. A quantum system is a Hilbert space $\mathcal{H}$ and a quantum state $|\psi\rangle$ is a vector $|\psi\rangle$ in $\mathcal{H}$ with norm 1. A unitary operation over $\mathcal{H}$ is a transformation $\mathbb{U}$ such that $\mathbb{U}\mathbb{U}^\dagger = \mathbb{U}^\dagger\mathbb{U} = \mathbb{I}$ where $\mathbb{U}^\dagger$ is the Hermitian transpose of $\mathbb{U}$ and $\mathbb{I}$ is the identity operator over $\mathcal{H}$. The computational basis for $\mathcal{H}$ consists of $\log n$ vectors $|b_i\rangle$ of length $\log n$ with 1 in the position i and 0 elsewhere. With this basis, the Hadamard unitary is defined as

$$\mathbb{H} : |b\rangle \rightarrow \frac{1}{\sqrt{2}}(|\bar{b}\rangle + (-1)^b |b\rangle),$$

for $b \in \{0, 1\}$ where $\bar{b} = 1 - b$. An orthogonal projection $\mathbb{P}$ over $\mathcal{H}$ is a linear transformation such that $\mathbb{P}^2 = \mathbb{P} = \mathbb{P}^\dagger$. A measurement on a Hilbert space is defined with a family of projectors that are pairwise orthogonal. An example of measurement is the computational basis measurement in which any projection is defined by a basis vector. The output of computational measurement on a state $|\Psi\rangle$ is i with probability $\| \langle b_i, \Psi \rangle \|^2$ and the post measurement state is $|b_i\rangle$. For a general measurement $\{\mathbb{P}_i\}_i$, the output of this measurement on a state $|\Psi\rangle$ is i with probability $\| \mathbb{P}_i |\Psi\rangle \|^2$ and the post measurement state is $\frac{\mathbb{P}_i |\Psi\rangle}{\|\mathbb{P}_i|\Psi\rangle\|}$.

For two quantum systems $\mathcal{H}_1$ and $\mathcal{H}_2$, the composition of them is defined by the tensor product and it is $\mathcal{H}_1 \otimes \mathcal{H}_2$. For two unitary $\mathbb{U}_1$ and $\mathbb{U}_2$ defined over $\mathcal{H}_1$ and $\mathcal{H}_2$ respectively, $(\mathbb{U}_1 \otimes \mathbb{U}_2)(\mathcal{H}_1 \otimes \mathcal{H}_2) = \mathbb{U}_1(\mathcal{H}_1) \otimes \mathbb{U}_2(\mathcal{H}_2)$.

B   Discussion on Quantum Eavesdropping

A possible plaintext-awareness definition that considers superposition eavesdropping may be difficult to define due to the no-cloning theorem. For instance, if we follow the above formalism, the plaintext-creator adversary $\mathcal{P}$ upon receiving the input and output registers Q_{inp} and Q_{out} from $\mathcal{A}$, can apply a random unitary to Q_{inp}, then applies the encryption unitary and sends both registers back to the adversary. But now it is not clear how one can handle decryption queries. More specifically, the superposition ciphertexts that have been created by calling $\mathcal{P}$ can not be recorded in general and if one of them is submitted as a decryption query, in the real game, the decryption oracle will return the corresponding superposition of messages but in the fake game, $\mathcal{A}^*$ is not able to return the corresponding superposition of messages without access to the internal register of $\mathcal{P}$. Note that if $\mathcal{A}^*$ is able to decrypt those queries without access to the internal register of $\mathcal{P}$ and the secret key, it renders the encryption scheme insecure.

C   Proof of Theorem 8

Proof. Let $\mathcal{X}$ be a QPT adversary that attacks the encryption scheme Enc in the sense of IND-qCCA. We start with IND-qCCA game with the challenge bit $b = 0$ (G_0^{qCCA}) and reach the IND-qCCA game with the challenge bit 1 (G_1^{qCCA}) by introducing intermediate games that are in a negligible distance.

Game 0: G_0^{qCCA}

$$(\mathsf{pk}, \mathsf{sk}) \leftarrow \mathrm{KGen}(1^\eta), \qquad m_0, m_1 \leftarrow \mathcal{X}^{\mathrm{U}_{\mathrm{Dec}'(\mathsf{sk}, \mathbf{List})}}(\mathsf{pk}),$$
$$\mathrm{Enc}(m_0; r_0) \leftarrow \mathrm{Challenger}(m_0, m_1), \, b \leftarrow \mathcal{X}^{\mathrm{U}_{\mathrm{Dec}'(\mathsf{sk}, \mathbf{List})}}(\mathsf{pk}, \mathrm{Enc}(m_0; r_0))$$

Let $\mathcal{P}_0$ be a plaintext-creator that upon receiving a query of type m_0, m_1 chooses a randomness r_0 and returns $\mathrm{Enc}(m_0, r_0)$. We replace the challenger in $G_{b=0}^{qCCA}$ with $\mathcal{P}_0$ to reach Game 1.

Game 1: $G_{real}^{\mathsf{pqPA2\text{-}Q_{dec}}}$ with $\mathcal{P}_0$

$$(\mathsf{pk}, \mathsf{sk}) \leftarrow \mathrm{KGen}(1^\eta), \qquad m_0, m_1 \leftarrow \mathcal{X}^{\mathrm{U}_{\mathrm{Dec}'(\mathsf{sk}, \mathbf{List})}}(\mathsf{pk}),$$
$$\mathrm{Enc}(m_0; r_0) \leftarrow \mathcal{P}_0(m_0, m_1), \, b \leftarrow \mathcal{X}^{\mathrm{U}_{\mathrm{Dec}'(\mathsf{sk}, \mathbf{List})}}(\mathsf{pk}, \mathrm{Enc}(m_0; r_0))$$

It is obvious that Game 0 and Game 1 are indistinguishable.

Since Enc is $\mathsf{pqPA2\text{-}Q_{dec}}$ aware there exists a successful ciphertext extractor $\mathcal{A}^*$ for $\mathcal{X}$. Let Q_{int} be the internal register of $\mathcal{X}$. In Game 2, we replace the decryption oracle with $\mathcal{A}^*$.

Game 2: $G_{fake}^{\mathsf{pqPA2\text{-}Q_{dec}}}$ with $\mathcal{P}_0$

$$(\mathsf{pk}, \mathsf{sk}) \leftarrow \mathrm{KGen}(1^\eta), \qquad m_0, m_1 \leftarrow \mathcal{X}^{\mathcal{A}^*(\mathsf{pk}, Q_{int})},$$
$$\mathrm{Enc}(m_0; r_0) \leftarrow \mathcal{P}_0, \quad b \leftarrow \mathcal{X}^{\mathcal{A}^*(\mathsf{pk}, \mathbf{List}, Q_{int})}(\mathsf{pk}, \mathrm{Enc}(m_0; r_0))$$

Since $\mathcal{A}^*$ is a successful ciphertext extractor for $\mathcal{X}$, Game 1 and Game 2 are indistinguishable.

Let $\mathcal{P}_1$ be a plaintext-creator algorithm that upon receiving a query of type m_0, m_1 chooses randomness r_1 and returns $\mathrm{Enc}(m_1; r_1)$. We replace $\mathcal{P}_0$ with $\mathcal{P}_1$ in Game 2 to reach Game 3.

Game 3: $G_{fake}^{\mathsf{pqPA2\text{-}Q_{dec}}}$ with $\mathcal{P}_1$

$$(\mathsf{pk}, \mathsf{sk}) \leftarrow \mathrm{KGen}(1^\eta), \qquad m_0, m_1 \leftarrow \mathcal{X}^{\mathcal{A}^*(\mathsf{pk}, Q_{int})},$$
$$\mathrm{Enc}(m_1; r_1) \leftarrow \mathcal{P}_1, \quad b \leftarrow \mathcal{X}^{\mathcal{A}^*(\mathsf{pk}, \mathbf{List}, Q_{int})}(\mathsf{pk}, \mathrm{Enc}(m_1; r_1))$$

Since Enc is IND-qCPA secure, Game 2 and Game 3 are indistinguishable. In more detail, let us assume there is a distinguisher $\mathcal{D}$ with a non-negligible advantage for these two games. Now $\mathcal{Y} = (\mathcal{X}, \mathcal{A}^*, \mathcal{D})$ is an adversary to break IND-qCPA security of Enc that is a contradiction.

In Game 4, we replace $\mathcal{A}^*$ with the decryption oracle.

Game 4

$$(\mathsf{pk}, \mathsf{sk}) \leftarrow \mathrm{KGen}(1^\eta), \qquad m_0, m_1 \leftarrow \mathcal{X}^{\mathrm{U}_{\mathrm{Dec}'(\mathsf{sk},\mathbf{List})}}(\mathsf{pk}),$$
$$\mathrm{Enc}(m_1; r_1) \leftarrow \mathcal{P}_1(m_0, m_1), \; b \leftarrow \mathcal{X}^{\mathrm{U}_{\mathrm{Dec}'(\mathsf{sk},\mathbf{List})}}(\mathsf{pk}, \mathrm{Enc}(m_1; r_1))$$

Since $\mathcal{A}^*$ is a successful plaintext-extractor for $\mathcal{X}$, these two games are indistinguishable.

Finally, we replace $\mathcal{P}_1$ with the challenger in Game 5 to reach G_1^{qCCA}.

Game 5: G_1^{qCCA}

$$(\mathsf{pk}, \mathsf{sk}) \leftarrow \mathrm{KGen}(1^\eta), \qquad m_0, m_1 \leftarrow \mathcal{X}^{\mathrm{U}_{\mathrm{Dec}'(\mathsf{sk},\mathbf{List})}}(\mathsf{pk}),$$
$$\mathrm{Enc}(m_1; r_1) \leftarrow \mathrm{Challenger}(m_0, m_1), \; b \leftarrow \mathcal{X}^{\mathrm{U}_{\mathrm{Dec}'(\mathsf{sk},\mathbf{List})}}(\mathsf{pk}, \mathrm{Enc}(m_1; r_1))$$

It is clear that Game 4 and Game 5 are indistinguishable. And this finishes the proof.   □

D   Achievability

In this section, we lift a public-key encryption scheme that is PA2 plaintext-aware against a quantum adversary (PA2 notion with classical decryption) to an encryption scheme that is $\mathsf{pqPA2}$-$\mathsf{Q}_{\mathsf{dec}}$.

Let $\Pi^{asy} = (\mathrm{KGen}^{asy}, \mathrm{Enc}^{asy}, \mathrm{Dec}^{asy})$ be a public-key encryption scheme that is PA2 plaintext-aware. We construct a public-key encryption scheme $\Pi^{hyb} = (\mathrm{KGen}^{hyb}, \mathrm{Enc}^{hyb}, \mathrm{Dec}^{hyb})$ and shows that it is $\mathsf{pqPA2}$-$\mathsf{Q}_{\mathsf{dec}}$. The encryption scheme Π^{hyb} is defined as :

- The algorithm KGen^{hyb} on input of the security parameter η runs $\mathrm{KGen}^{asy}(\eta)$ and returns its output $(\mathsf{pk}, \mathsf{sk})$.
- For any message $m \in \{0,1\}^n$, the algorithm Enc^{hyb} chooses a randomness r and returns $\mathrm{Enc}_{\mathsf{pk}}^{asy}(r) || qPRP_r(m||0^k)$ where $qPRP$ is a strong quantum-secure pseudo-random permutation and k depends on the security parameter η.
- For any ciphertext (c_1, c_2), Dec^{hyb} first decrypts c_1 using sk, if the output is $\bot$, it returns $\bot$. Otherwise, it uses the output as the key for $qPRP$ to decrypt c_2. If the k_1 least significant bits of the outcome is not 0, it returns $\bot$, otherwise it returns the n most significant bits of the outcome.

$$\mathrm{Dec}^{hyb}(c_1, c_2) = \begin{cases} \bot & \text{if } \mathrm{Dec}_{\mathsf{sk}}^{asy}(c_1) = \bot \\ \bot & \text{if } [qPRP_{\mathrm{Dec}_{\mathsf{sk}}^{asy}(c_1)}^{-1}(c_2)]_k \neq 0^k \\ [qPRP_{\mathrm{Dec}_{\mathsf{sk}}^{asy}(c_1)}^{-1}(c_2)]^n & \text{otherwise} \end{cases}.$$

Theorem 9. *Under the assumption of the existence of a quantum one-way function, the public-key encryption scheme* $\Pi^{hyb} = (\mathrm{KGen}^{hyb}, \mathrm{Enc}^{hyb}, \mathrm{Dec}^{hyb})$ *described above is* $\mathsf{pqPA2}$-$\mathsf{Q}_{\mathsf{dec}}$.

Proof. Let $\mathcal{A}$ be an adversary that attacks Π^{hyb} in the sense of pqPA2-Q_{dec}. We construct an adversary $\mathcal{B}$ that attacks Π^{asy} in the sense of PA2. Let $\mathcal{P}_B$ be a plaintext-creator adversary that upon receiving a query, chooses a randomness r and sends it to the encryption oracle Π^{asy} to receive $\text{Enc}_{pk}^{asy}(r)$. Then it sends $\text{Enc}_{pk}^{asy}(r)$ to the ciphertex-creator adversary. The adversary $\mathcal{B}$ runs $\mathcal{A}$ and answers to the decryption queries as follows. When $\mathcal{A}$ makes a decryption query $\sum_{c_2} \alpha_{c_2} |c_1\rangle |c_2\rangle$, the adversary $\mathcal{B}$ forwards only the first part of the ciphertext (c_1) to its oracle. (Note that c_1 is a classical value and it is not entangled with the rest of the query. So forwarding the c_1-part does not disturb the decryption query.) If its oracle on input c_1 returns $\perp$, $\mathcal{B}$ returns $\perp$. Otherwise, if its oracle on input c_1 returns r $(\neq\perp)$, $\mathcal{B}$ uses r as the key for $qPRP$ to decrypt the c_2-part. Note that if the k_1 least significant bits of $qPRP_r^{-1}(c_2)$ is not zero, the output of $\mathcal{B}$ will be $\perp$. Otherwise, the output will be the n most significant bits of $qPRP_r^{-1}(c_2)$. When $\mathcal{A}$ makes a query m to its plaintext-creator $\mathcal{P}_A$, $\mathcal{B}$ makes a query to $\mathcal{P}_B$ to receive the ciphertext c_1. Then it sends $(c_1, \pi(m\|0^k))$ to $\mathcal{A}$ where π is a random permutation. Since Π^{asy} is PA2, there exists a ciphertex extractor $\mathcal{B}^*$ for $\mathcal{B}$.

Now we consider the ciphertex extractor $\mathbb{U}_{\mathcal{A}_1^*}$ where for any (c_1, c_2),

$$
\mathcal{A}_1^*(c_1, c_2) = \begin{cases} \perp & \text{if } \mathcal{B}^*(c_1) = \perp \\ \perp & \text{if } [qPRP_{\mathcal{B}^*(c_1)}^{-1}(c_2)]_k \neq 0^k \ . \\ [qPRP_{\mathcal{B}^*(c_1)}^{-1}(c_2)]^n & \text{otherwise} \end{cases}
$$

We show that $\mathbb{U}_{\mathcal{A}_1^*}$ is a successful plaintext-extractor for $\mathcal{A}$ in the following.

Game 0: We start with $G_{real}^{\text{pqPA2-}Q_{dec}}$ that is run by a plaintext-creator $\mathcal{P}_A$ and a distinguisher $\mathcal{D}$.

Game 1: We change the plaintex creator $\mathcal{P}_A$ to a new plaintext-creator $\mathcal{P}_B'$ that upon receiving a query m runs $\mathcal{P}_B$ to obtain c_1, then it chooses a random permutation π and returns $(c_1, \pi(m\|0^k))$. We show that these two games are indistinguishable. An observation is that the first part of the $\mathcal{P}_A$'s output (c_1) is independent of $\mathcal{P}_A$ since it is the encryption of a random string that is chosen by the encryption algorithm. In other words, the c_1-part is generated exactly the same by $\mathcal{P}_A$ and $\mathcal{P}_B'$. The indistinguishability of the c_2-part holds as well since a quantum-secure pseudo-random permutation is indistinguishable from a random permutation.

Game 2: In this game, the decryption queries will be answered by $\mathbb{U}_{\mathcal{A}_1^*}$. An observation is that $\mathcal{A}_1^*$ is indistinguishable from Dec^{hyb} because $\mathcal{B}^*$ is indistinguishable from Dec_{sk}^{asy} (the rest of $\mathcal{A}_1^*$ and Dec^{hyb} are the same). Therefore, these two games remain indistinguishable. In other words, these two games are indistinguishable because $\mathcal{B}^*$ is a successful plaintext-extractor for $\mathcal{B}$.

Game 3: In the last game, we replace the plaintext-creator $\mathcal{P}_B'$ with $\mathcal{P}_A$. The same reasoning as Game 0,1 shows that Game 2 and Game 3 are indistinguishable and this finishes the proof. $\square$

D.1   OAEP transform

The main motivation to present the first definition for plaintext-awareness notion [4] was to show the security of Optimal Asymmetric Encryption Padding (OAEP). Even though our definitions for PA notions are in the standard model, we argue that these definitions apply to the random oracle model as well because queries to the random oracles is a part of the internal register of the adversary. We briefly explain why we think OAEP is pqPA1-Q_{dec} plaintext-aware. We take this from a recent work on the IND-qCCA security of OAEP transform [10]. There, Ebrahimi started with the actual decryption algorithm $\mathbb{U}_{Dec}$ and introduced a sequence of indistinguishable decryption algorithms to construct a decryption algorithm $\mathbb{U}_{Dec^{(4)}}$ that does not use the secret key. (Since the queries to the random oracles are quantum, Zhandry's compressed oracle technique [21] has been used in [10].) This decryption algorithm $\mathbb{U}_{Dec^{(4)}}$ can be invoked by a plaintext-extractor adversary $\mathcal{A}^*$ in the fake game. The indistinguishably of $\mathbb{U}_{Dec}$ and $\mathbb{U}_{Dec^{(4)}}$ gives us the pqPA1-Q_{dec} plaintext-awareness. However, whether OAEP is pqPA2-Q_{dec} plaintext-aware or not is an open question. The reason is the random oracle queries that are submitted by a plaintext-creator $\mathcal{P}$ are not accessible by $\mathcal{A}^*$. So $\mathbb{U}_{Dec^{(4)}}$ sketched above is not able to decrypt a ciphertext that is obtained by indirect (for instance by a malleability of a ciphertext obtained from $\mathcal{P}$) use of these random oracle queries.

References

1. Andreeva, E., Bogdanov, A., Luykx, A., Mennink, B., Mouha, N., Yasuda, K.: How to securely release unverified plaintext in authenticated encryption. In: Sarkar, P., Iwata, T. (eds.) ASIACRYPT 2014. LNCS, vol. 8873, pp. 105–125. Springer, Heidelberg (2014). https://doi.org/10.1007/978-3-662-45611-8_6
2. Bellare, M., Desai, A., Pointcheval, D., Rogaway, P.: Relations among notions of security for public-key encryption schemes. In: Krawczyk, H. (ed.) CRYPTO 1998. LNCS, vol. 1462, pp. 26–45. Springer, Heidelberg (1998). https://doi.org/10.1007/BFb0055718
3. Bellare, M., Palacio, A.: Towards plaintext-aware public-key encryption without random oracles. In: Lee, P.J. (ed.) ASIACRYPT 2004. LNCS, vol. 3329, pp. 48–62. Springer, Heidelberg (2004). https://doi.org/10.1007/978-3-540-30539-2_4
4. Bellare, M., Rogaway, P.: Optimal asymmetric encryption. In: De Santis, A. (ed.) EUROCRYPT 1994. LNCS, vol. 950, pp. 92–111. Springer, Heidelberg (1995). https://doi.org/10.1007/BFb0053428
5. Birkett, J., Dent, A.W.: Security models and proof strategies for plaintext-aware encryption. J. Cryptol. **27**(1), 139–180 (2014). https://doi.org/10.1007/s00145-012-9141-6
6. Boneh, D., Zhandry, M.: Secure signatures and chosen ciphertext security in a quantum computing world. In: Canetti, R., Garay, J.A. (eds.) CRYPTO 2013. LNCS, vol. 8043, pp. 361–379. Springer, Heidelberg (2013). https://doi.org/10.1007/978-3-642-40084-1_21
7. Carstens, T.V., Ebrahimi, E., Tabia, G.N., Unruh, D.: Relationships between quantum IND-CPA notions. In: Nissim, K., Waters, B. (eds.) TCC 2021. LNCS, vol. 13042, pp. 240–272. Springer, Cham (2021). https://doi.org/10.1007/978-3-030-90459-3_9

8. Chevalier, C., Ebrahimi, E., Vu, Q.H.: On the security notions for encryption in a quantum world. IACR Cryptol. **2020**, 237 (2020). ePrint Archive

9. Dent, A.W.: The cramer-shoup encryption scheme is plaintext aware in the standard model. In: Vaudenay, S. (ed.) EUROCRYPT 2006. LNCS, vol. 4004, pp. 289–307. Springer, Heidelberg (2006). https://doi.org/10.1007/11761679_18

10. Ebrahimi, E.: Post-quantum security of plain OAEP transform. In: PKC 2022, vol. 13177, pp. 34–51. Springer (2022). https://doi.org/10.1007/978-3-030-97121-2_2

11. Gagliardoni, T., Hülsing, A., Schaffner, C.: Semantic security and indistinguishability in the quantum world. In: Robshaw, M., Katz, J. (eds.) CRYPTO 2016. LNCS, vol. 9816, pp. 60–89. Springer, Heidelberg (2016). https://doi.org/10.1007/978-3-662-53015-3_3

12. Gagliardoni, T., Krämer, J., Struck, P.: Quantum indistinguishability for public key encryption. In: Cheon, J.H., Tillich, J.-P. (eds.) PQCrypto 2021 2021. LNCS, vol. 12841, pp. 463–482. Springer, Cham (2021). https://doi.org/10.1007/978-3-030-81293-5_24

13. Herzog, J., Liskov, M., Micali, S.: Plaintext awareness via key registration. In: Boneh, D. (ed.) CRYPTO 2003. LNCS, vol. 2729, pp. 548–564. Springer, Heidelberg (2003). https://doi.org/10.1007/978-3-540-45146-4_32

14. Jain, A., Krenn, S., Pietrzak, K., Tentes, A.: Commitments and efficient zero-knowledge proofs from learning parity with noise. In: Wang, X., Sako, K. (eds.) ASIACRYPT 2012. LNCS, vol. 7658, pp. 663–680. Springer, Heidelberg (2012). https://doi.org/10.1007/978-3-642-34961-4_40

15. Kashefi, E., Kent, A., Vedral, V., Banaszek, K.: Comparison of quantum oracles. Phys. Rev. A **65**, 050304 (2002)

16. Kawachi, A., Koshiba, T., Nishimura, H., Yamakami, T.: Computational indistinguishability between quantum states and its cryptographic application. In: Cramer, R. (ed.) EUROCRYPT 2005. LNCS, vol. 3494, pp. 268–284. Springer, Heidelberg (2005). https://doi.org/10.1007/11426639_16

17. McEliece, R.J.: A public-key cryptosystem based on algebraic. Coding Thv **4244**, 114–116 (1978)

18. Regev, O.: On lattices, learning with errors, random linear codes, and cryptography. In: ACM Symposium on Theory of Computing, vol. 2005, pp. 84–93. ACM (2005)

19. Shor, P.W.: Polynomial-time algorithms for prime factorization and discrete logarithms on a quantum computer. SIAM J. Comput. **26**(5), 1484–1509 (1997)

20. Simon, D.R.: On the power of quantum computation. SIAM J. Comput. **26**(5), 1474–1483 (1997)

21. Zhandry, M.: How to record quantum queries, and applications to quantum indifferentiability. In: Boldyreva, A., Micciancio, D. (eds.) CRYPTO 2019. LNCS, vol. 11693, pp. 239–268. Springer, Cham (2019). https://doi.org/10.1007/978-3-030-26951-7_9

On Quantum Ciphertext Indistinguishability, Recoverability, and OAEP

Juliane Krämer and Patrick Struck[✉]

Universität Regensburg, Regensburg, Germany
{juliane.kraemer,patrick.struck}@ur.de

Abstract. The qINDqCPA security notion for public-key encryption schemes by Gagliardoni et al. (PQCrypto'21) models security against adversaries which are able to obtain ciphertexts in superposition. Defining this security notion requires a special type of quantum operator. Known constructions differ in which keys are necessary to construct this operator, depending on properties of the encryption scheme.

We argue—for the typical setting of securing communication between Alice and Bob—that in order to apply the notion, the quantum operator should be realizable for challengers knowing only the public key. This is already known to be the case for a wide range of public-key encryption schemes, in particular, those exhibiting the so-called recoverability property which allows to recover the message from a ciphertext using the randomness instead of the secret key.

The open question is whether there are real-world public-key encryption schemes for which the notion is not applicable, considering the aforementioned observation on the keys known by the challenger. We answer this question in the affirmative by showing that applying the qINDqCPA security notion to the OAEP construction requires the challenger to know the secret key. We conclude that the qINDqCPA security notion might need to be refined to eventually yield a universally applicable PKE notion of quantum security with a quantum indistinguishability phase.

1 Introduction

In light of the threat posed by quantum algorithms such as Shor's [33], cryptographic primitives that are assumed to withstand attacks using quantum computing are mandatory to ensure security also in the future. Over the last decade, a lot of research focused on exactly this type of cryptographic primitives—commonly known as post-quantum cryptography.

Security against attackers with quantum computing power can be divided into two categories. The first, and arguably the one that will be realistic in the upcoming years, is post-quantum security. Here, the adversary has local quantum computing power, which allows to evaluate public primitives like hash functions in superposition, while keyed cryptographic primitives can be accessed only classically. The second, and more conservative setting, is quantum security,

J. H. Cheon and T. Johansson (Eds.): PQCrypto 2022, LNCS 13512, pp. 286–306, 2022.
https://doi.org/10.1007/978-3-031-17234-2_14

which grants the adversary superposition access also to keyed cryptographic primitives. The latter defines the scope of this work.

The research area of quantum security was initiated by Boneh and Zhandry, who gave the first quantum security notions for encryption schemes and signature schemes [8]. At the moment, quantum security is still at a point where definitional challenges have to be solved, e.g., it has to be understood how classically well-established concepts like "distinguishing two ciphertexts" and "forge a signature for a new message" can be translated to the quantum setting. For signatures, initial problems of the Boneh–Zhandry notion where identified in [20] and a potential solution was given in [1]. For public-key encryption schemes, there are two different approaches to avoid limitations when switching to a quantum challenge phase: a left-or-right approach given in [19] and a real-or-random approach given in [12]. While the latter can be defined for any public-key encryption scheme, this is not the case for the former. This is discussed in detail in the full version of [19] and stems from the fact that the security notion developed in [19] requires a special type of quantum operator. Simply speaking, the notion requires an in-place quantum operator that transforms a state $|x\rangle$ into $|\mathcal{F}(x)\rangle$ instead of the canonical xor operator that transforms $|x, y\rangle$ into $|x, y \oplus \mathcal{F}(x)\rangle$. The authors of [19] give two constructions for the required in-place operator, based on the properties of the encryption scheme. These two constructions, which we describe later, differ in the keys that are necessary: one construction requires merely the public key, the other construction requires both the secret key and the public key. While the latter seems artificial, we stress that [19] focuses on whether the operator required by their security notion can be constructed *at all*. In fact, the authors show, surprisingly, that most real-world public-key encryption schemes allow for the construction that requires just the public key.

1.1 Our Contribution

In this work, we study the quantum security notion from [19] regarding its applicability.

We first revisit the typical notion of ciphertext indistinguishability in the context of securing communication between two parties. We argue that, for this setting, challengers should only have access to the public key. Regarding the construction of the in-place quantum operator from the qINDqCPA security notion, this is known to be the case for most real-world public-key encryption schemes, namely, those exhibiting the recoverability property [19].

We then focus on the question whether there are public-key encryption schemes which do not have the recoverability property. The only known schemes are obtained by a generic transformation [19] which transforms a recoverable public-key encryption scheme into a non-recoverable one. We refine the classification by showing that there are not just recoverable and non-recoverable public key encryption schemes, but also what we call *equivalent recoverable*.

Finally, we investigate the OAEP construction. We show that this construction is non-recoverable, thereby giving the first real-world PKE scheme with this property. We then show that—for the OAEP construction—the in-place operator needed for the quantum security notion from [19] cannot be constructed using just the public key. Thereby we show that the quantum security notion qINDqCPA cannot be applied to all PKE schemes when imposing the restriction that the challenger only knows the public key.

1.2   Related Work

Quantum security notions were first considered by Boneh and Zhandry [8]. Since then, many works developed new quantum security notions or analyzed primitives with respect to existing notions, ranging from signature schemes and message authentication codes [1,7,20], to symmetric encryption [11,12,14,18,28,29], and to public-key encryption schemes [12,19].

A series of works [2,3,9,10,21–23,25–27,31] show that superposition attacks (which are modeled by quantum security notions) can have devastating effects on cryptographic primitives by providing attacks against primitives like Even-Mansour, the FX construction, Feistel networks, block ciphers, and HMAC.

The optimal asymmetric encryption padding (OAEP) was developed by Bellare and Rogaway [6]. The initial proof had a gap, as detected by Shoup [34], who provided a variant of OAEP with an alternative proof. Fujisaki et al. [17] provide a proof for OAEP avoiding the initial gap by strengthening the requirements of the underlying function. Security of OAEP against quantum attackers was first considered in [35] which required a slight modification to prove security. Recently, post-quantum security of the plain OAEP construction was shown [15].

1.3   Outline

In Sect. 2, we provide background on quantum security notions, quantum operators, and cryptography as necessary for this work. In Sect. 3, we refine the qINDqCPA security notion. In Sect. 4 we review the notion of recoverable PKE schemes. In Sect. 5, we analyze the OAEP construction with respect to the qINDqCPA security notion.

2   Preliminaries

2.1   Notation

For a set $\mathcal{X}$, we write $x \leftarrow_\$ \mathcal{X}$ to denote the process of picking an element from $\mathcal{X}$ at random and assigning it to x. By $\mathcal{P}$, $\mathcal{S}$, $\mathcal{M}$, $\mathcal{C}$, and $\mathcal{R}$, we denote the public key space, secret key space, message space, ciphertext space, and randomness space of a cryptographic scheme, respectively. For a deterministic algorithm $\mathcal{F}$, we write $y \leftarrow \mathcal{F}(x)$ to denote that y is the output of $\mathcal{F}$ on input x. For a probabilistic algorithm, $y \leftarrow \mathcal{F}(x; r)$ denotes that the output of $\mathcal{F}$ on input x with randomness r equals y. We write $y \leftarrow_\$ \mathcal{F}(x)$ to denote the process that the randomness r is chosen uniformly at random and y is the output of $\mathcal{F}$ on input x with randomness r.

2.2 Public-Key Cryptography

Public-key encryption schemes are defined below.

Definition 1. *A* public-key encryption (PKE) *scheme is a tuple* (KGen, Enc, Dec) *of three efficient algorithms such that:*

- KGen: $\mathbb{N} \times \mathcal{R} \to \mathcal{P} \times \mathcal{S}$ *is the key generation algorithm which takes a security parameter λ and a randomness r as input, and returns a keypair consisting of a public key pk and a secret key sk. If clear from the context, we will denote it by $(pk, sk) \leftarrow_\$ \text{KGen}()$. We will generally drop the security parameter.*
- Enc: $\mathcal{P} \times \mathcal{M} \times \mathcal{R} \to \mathcal{C}$ *is the encryption algorithm which takes a public key pk, a message m, and a randomness r as input, and returns a ciphertext c. It will be usually denoted by $c \leftarrow_\$ \text{Enc}(pk, m)$ or $c \leftarrow \text{Enc}(pk, m; r)$.*
- Dec: $\mathcal{S} \times \mathcal{C} \to \mathcal{M}$ *is the deterministic decryption algorithm which takes as input a secret key sk and a ciphertext c, and returns a message m. It will be usually denoted by $m \leftarrow \text{Dec}(sk, c)$.*

Next we define trapdoor permutations. The definition is tailored to permutations over the Cartesian product over two sets $\mathcal{X}_1$ and $\mathcal{X}_2$. This is without loss of generality but allows for a simple definition of the security notions required later.

Definition 2. *A* trapdoor permutation *is a tuple* $(\text{KGen}^{\mathcal{F}}, \mathcal{F}, \mathcal{F}^{-1})$ *of three efficient algorithms such that:*

- KGen: $\mathbb{N} \times \mathcal{R} \to \mathcal{P} \times \mathcal{S}$ *is the key generation algorithm which takes a security parameter λ and a randomness r as input, and returns a keypair consisting of a public key pk and a secret key sk.*
- $\mathcal{F}$: $\mathcal{P} \times \mathcal{X}_1 \times \mathcal{X}_2 \to \mathcal{X}_1 \times \mathcal{X}_2$ *is the permutation algorithm which takes a public key pk, permuting over the set $\mathcal{X}_1 \times \mathcal{X}_2$.*
- $\mathcal{F}^{-1}$: $\mathcal{S} \times \mathcal{X}_1 \times \mathcal{X}_2 \to \mathcal{X}_1 \times \mathcal{X}_2$ *is the inverse permutation which takes as input a secret key sk and permutes over the set $\mathcal{X}_1 \times \mathcal{X}_2$.*

Below we define two security notions for a trapdoor permutation $\Pi = (\text{KGen}^{\mathcal{F}}, \mathcal{F}, \mathcal{F}^{-1})$. One asks to find the preimage of a given output whereas the other only asks to find a partial preimage, i.e., a preimage with respect to $\mathcal{X}_1$.

Definition 3. *Let $\Pi = (\text{KGen}^{\mathcal{F}}, \mathcal{F}, \mathcal{F}^{-1})$ be a trapdoor permutation. Let further the games* OW *and* pdOW *be defined as in Fig. 1. For any adversary $\mathcal{A}$, we define its advantages as*

$$\mathbf{Adv}^{\mathsf{OW}}(\mathcal{A}) := \Pr[\mathsf{OW}^{\mathcal{A}} \to \text{true}]$$
$$\mathbf{Adv}^{\mathsf{pdOW}}(\mathcal{A}) := \Pr[\mathsf{pdOW}^{\mathcal{A}} \to \text{true}].$$

Game OW

$(pk, sk) \leftarrow_\$ \mathsf{KGen}()$
$(x_1, x_2) \leftarrow_\$ \mathcal{X}_1 \times \mathcal{X}_2$
$(z_1, z_2) \leftarrow \mathcal{F}(pk, (x_1, x_2))$
$(y_1, y_2) \leftarrow \mathcal{A}(pk, (z_1, z_2))$
return $(y_1, y_2) = (x_1, x_2)$

Game pdOW

$(pk, sk) \leftarrow_\$ \mathsf{KGen}()$
$(x_1, x_2) \leftarrow_\$ \mathcal{X}_1 \times \mathcal{X}_2$
$(z_1, z_2) \leftarrow \mathcal{F}(pk, (x_1, x_2))$
$y_1 \leftarrow \mathcal{A}(pk, (z_1, z_2))$
return $y_1 = x_1$

Fig. 1. Game OW (One-Wayness) and game pdOW (Partial-Domain One-Wayness) to define security of a trapdoor permutation $\mathcal{F}$.

2.3 Quantum Computing

We assume familiarity with quantum computing and refer to [30] for details. Implementing a function $\mathcal{F}: \mathcal{X} \to \mathcal{Y}$ on a quantum computer is typically done via the canonical construction. This is what we call an xor operator, which is defined as

$$U_{\mathcal{F}}^{\oplus}: \sum_{x,y} \alpha_{x,y} |x, y\rangle \mapsto \sum_{x,y} \alpha_{x,y} |x, y \oplus \mathcal{F}(x)\rangle .$$

This xor operator can be implemented efficiently whenever $\mathcal{F}$ is efficient [30]. If a function is invertible, there is another operator—besides the xor operator—with which the function can be realized. This operator is what we call an in-place operator, which is defined as

$$U_{\mathcal{F}}^{(ip)}: |x\rangle \mapsto |\mathcal{F}(x)\rangle .$$

Figure 2 illustrates the two operators for a function $\mathcal{F}$. Kashefi et al. [24] first introduced in-place operators giving them the name minimal oracles. They show that the two variants are not equivalent by showing that in-place operators are stronger than xor operators. The core observation is that inverting an in-place operator gate-by-gate gives an in-place operator for the inverse function. The same does not apply to the xor operator, as xor operators are self-inverse.

Fig. 2. Left: xor operator for $\mathcal{F}$. **Right:** in-place operator for $\mathcal{F}$.

In the following we recall two variants how xor and in-place operators (for invertible functions) can be constructed from one another. Figure 3 shows how an xor operator for $\mathcal{F}$ can be constructed from an in-place operator for $\mathcal{F}$. Likewise, Fig. 4 shows how an in-place operator for $\mathcal{F}$ can be constructed from xor operators for *both* $\mathcal{F}$ and $\mathcal{F}^{-1}$. Note here, that an xor operator for $\mathcal{F}$ does—in general—not allow to construct an xor operator for $\mathcal{F}^{-1}$. As an example, consider $\mathcal{F}$ to be some one-way function. The latter construction (cf. Fig. 4) is important for the qINDqCPA security notion.

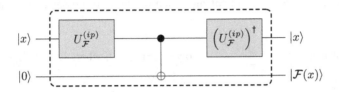

Fig. 3. Construction of an xor operator for a function $\mathcal{F}$ from an in-place operator for $\mathcal{F}$ and its inverse.

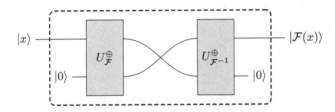

Fig. 4. Construction of an in-place operator for a function $\mathcal{F}$ from xor operators for $\mathcal{F}$ and $\mathcal{F}^{-1}$.

3   (Quantum) Ciphertext Indistinguishability

3.1   The qINDqCPA Security Notion

Ciphertext indistinguishability is a security notion for encryption schemes—both symmetric encryption and public-key encryption. It asks an adversary to distinguish between the encryption of two adversarial chosen messages. An encryption scheme that achieves ciphertext indistinguishability comes with the guarantee that an adversary cannot learn any information about the message underlying a ciphertext.

When considering quantum adversaries, one can distinguish between adversaries restricted to local quantum computing power—the setting that is widely known as post-quantum security—and adversaries that have full quantum access to all oracles—known as quantum security. The latter is the setting considered by Gagliardoni et al. [19] who develop the qINDqCPA security notion for public-key encryption schemes. This notion models security where the challenge ciphertexts by the adversary can be in superposition, hence it provides stronger security guarantees than post-quantum security.

The security game qINDqCPA is displayed in Fig. 5. The adversary receives a public key pk and gets access to an in-place operator for encryption.[1] The adversary then outputs two messages $|\varphi_0\rangle$ and $|\varphi_1\rangle$, possibly in superposition, one of which will be encrypted and then sent back to the adversary. The adversary continues to have access to the in-place operator for encryption and finally has to output its guess b', indicating which of the two messages was encrypted.

Game qINDqCPA	oracle $\mathsf{Enc}(|\varphi\rangle)$, where $|\varphi\rangle = \sum_m \alpha_m |m\rangle$
$b \leftarrow_\$ \{0,1\}$	$r \leftarrow_\$ \mathcal{R}$
$(pk, sk) \leftarrow_\$ \mathsf{KGen}()$	$|r\rangle |c\rangle \leftarrow U^{ip}_{\mathsf{Enc}} (|r\rangle |\varphi\rangle |0 \cdots 0\rangle)$
$|\varphi_0\rangle, |\varphi_1\rangle \leftarrow \mathcal{A}_1^{\mathsf{Enc}}(pk)$	trace out $|r\rangle$
trace out $|\varphi_{1-b}\rangle$	return $|c\rangle$
$r \leftarrow_\$ \mathcal{R}$	
$|r\rangle |c\rangle \leftarrow U^{ip}_{\mathsf{Enc}} (|r\rangle |\varphi_b\rangle |0 \cdots 0\rangle)$	
trace out $|r\rangle$	
$b' \leftarrow \mathcal{A}_2^{\mathsf{Enc}}(|c\rangle)$	
return $(b' = b)$	

Fig. 5. Security game qINDqCPA.

At the core of the qINDqCPA security notion[2] is the in-place operator U^{ip}_{Enc} of the form

$$U^{ip}_{\mathsf{Enc}}: |r, m, 0 \cdots 0\rangle \mapsto |r\rangle |\mathsf{Enc}(pk, m; r)\rangle, \tag{1}$$

where the extra qubits initialized with 0 are for the ciphertext expansion as, in general, we have $|\mathcal{C}| > |\mathcal{M}|$. In [19], the authors observe that this is the most general in-place operator for encryption. Keeping the randomness in an extra register deals with randomness collisions, i.e., different randomnesses that encrypt a message to the same ciphertext, which would thwart the mandatory reversibility. Note that the extra randomness register also prevents to construct a simple decryption operator by inverting the encryption operator gate-by-gate. It would only allow to decrypt if the randomness used to produce a ciphertext is known.

---

[1] Note that this oracle is important in case the adversary cannot locally implement this oracle. Without it, the standard simplification to a single challenge via a hybrid argument does not work.

[2] Note that there are other security notions [8,12,28] which only require an xor operator. However, the relation between these different approaches is not completely understood and requires more research.

The core part of [19] lies in the construction of the in-place operator for encryption. The authors show that for schemes which do not suffer from decryption failures, such in-place operators can be efficiently constructed. This construction consists of an xor operator for encryption and an xor operator for decryption. This part exploits that decryption is the inverse of encryption and essentially follows the idea of the construction in Fig. 4. They further show that in-place operators can also be constructed for schemes which are recoverable; a property they define and which was concurrently[3] and independently defined by Bellare et al. in the context of domain separation for random oracles [4]. This construction also consists of an xor operator for encryption, but instead of an xor operator for decryption, it uses an xor operator for the so-called recover algorithm (see Sect. 4 for details). Interestingly, realizations of the in-place operator for the two types of encryption schemes—those without decryption failures and those exhibiting the recoverable property—is quite different: while it can be realized solely from the public key for the latter, the former necessitates the secret key. For schemes which fall into neither category, they show that there are schemes for which the in-place operator can be realized, as well as schemes for which it simply cannot be realized. We illustrate the two constructions from [19] in Fig. 6.

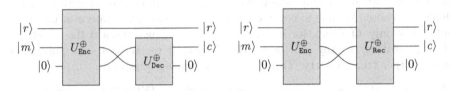

Fig. 6. Two constructions for an in-place encryption operator as given in [19].

3.2 Interpretation of Ciphertext Indistinguishability

Having discussed the qINDqCPA security notion and the relevance of the keys for constructing the required in-place operator, we now take a step back and focus on ciphertext indistinguishability in general.

Figure 7 displays the security game for ciphertext indistinguishability under chosen ciphertext attacks. Here, the adversary receives a public key and can query two oracles: First, an encryption oracle that takes two messages as input and encrypts one of the two, based on a secret bit chosen uniformly at random at the beginning of the game. Second, a decryption oracle which takes a ciphertext as input and returns the decryption of it.[4]

---

[3] The full version of both works appeared within a week.

[4] For simplicity we ignore how cheating adversaries, which forward a response from the encryption to the decryption oracle, are prevented. For a detailed discussion on this, we refer to [5].

In the security notion, there is only one challenger providing the adversary its input (the public key) and its oracles (encryption and decryption oracle). In particular, the challenger generates, and thus knows, both keys. Considering what the two oracles correspond to in the real-world, they are quite different. The encryption oracle represents the sender, sending a ciphertext, while the decryption oracle represents the recipient, receiving a ciphertext. In the typical setting of Alice sending an encrypted message to Bob, Alice is represented by the encryption oracle while Bob is represented by the decryption oracle. The main difference is that Alice only knows Bob's public key, whereas Bob knows both his public and secret key. In this sense, the encryption oracle should be realizable using only the public key. The decryption oracle can be realized from both the secret and the public key.[5]

We note that there are scenarios where the above observation does not apply, for instance when considering public-key encryption schemes used for commitment schemes. Here, Alice, holding both keys, would encrypt the message she wants to commit to and send the ciphertext to Bob. Later, when Alice wants to open the commitment, she reveals her secret key, more precisely the random coins used to generate it, to Bob. In this case, the encrypting party, Alice, knows both keys while the adversary still only knows the public key.

We conclude this section with the observation that in the qINDqCPA security notion—when modeling standard encrypted communication with it—, the challenger should be able to construct the in-place encryption operator using the public key only. One can, for instance, let the challenger discard the secret key after generating the key pair or let the challenger receive only the public key from another trusted party. This raises the following question:

Are there public-key encryption schemes for which qINDqCPA security cannot be defined for challengers knowing only the public key?

Using the results by Gagliardoni et al. [19], we know that the notion, when imposing the restriction that the challenger only knows the public key, can be defined for any recoverable public-key encryption scheme. For non-recoverable schemes, however, the answer is unclear. Gagliardoni et al. [19] show that it *can* be defined for challengers knowing both keys, but they do not discuss if it *can only* be defined if the challenger knows both keys. Hence, in Sect. 4 we will focus on non-recoverable public-key encryption schemes and recoverability in general. In Sect. 5 we return to the main question above by studying the OAEP construction.

4   Observations on Recoverability

The notion of recoverable PKE schemes has been introduced in [19]. In Sect. 3 we concluded that especially non-recoverable schemes have to be further studied

---

[5] When using the FO transformation [16], the public key is mandatory for the re-encrypting part. This dependence is often implicit, e.g., schemes such as Kyber [32] and Saber [13] specify the secret key to already include the public key.

Game INDCCA	oracle LR-Enc(m_0, m_1)	oracle Dec(c)
$b \leftarrow_\$ \{0,1\}$	$c \leftarrow \texttt{Enc}(pk, m_b)$	$m \leftarrow \texttt{Dec}(sk, c)$
$(pk, sk) \leftarrow_\$ \texttt{KGen}()$	**return** c	**return** m
$b' \leftarrow \mathcal{A}^{\text{LR-Enc,Dec}}(pk)$		
return $(b' = b)$		

Fig. 7. Security game INDCCA. For simplicity we drop the check that the decryption oracle checks whether a queried ciphertext was forwarded from the oracle LR-Enc.

to understand whether qINDqCPA security can be defined using solely the public key. Unfortunately, so far we are not aware of any real-world non-recoverable scheme. Instead of a concrete non-recoverable scheme, in [19] a generic transformation was introduced that transforms a recoverable scheme into a non-recoverable scheme. In this section, however, by introducing what we call equivalent recoverable schemes, we show that this transformation can also be defined inversely, which questions the meaningfulness of the transformation with respect to the existence of a non-recoverable scheme. By introducing equivalent recoverable schemes, we hence refine the classification introduced in [19], such that two kinds of schemes exist which are not recoverable: equivalent recoverable schemes and non-recoverable schemes. We conclude this section with the open question whether (real-world) non-recoverable PKE schemes exist at all.

We first repeat the notion of recoverability in Sect. 4.1 and then define equivalent recoverable schemes in Sect. 4.2.

4.1 Recoverability

Recoverability is a property of public-key encryption schemes that was defined by Gagliardoni et al. [19]. Simply speaking, a public-key encryption scheme is recoverable if one can recover the message from a ciphertext when knowing the randomness that was used to create said ciphertext—even without the secret key. Below we formally define recoverable public-key encryption schemes.

Definition 4 (Recoverable PKE Scheme [19, Definition 6]). *Let* $\Sigma = (\texttt{KGen}, \texttt{Enc}, \texttt{Dec})$ *be a PKE scheme. We call* Σ *a recoverable PKE scheme if there exists an efficient algorithm* $\texttt{Rec} \colon \mathcal{P} \times \mathcal{R} \times \mathcal{C} \to \mathcal{M}$ *such that, for any* $pk \in \mathcal{P}, r \in \mathcal{R}, m \in \mathcal{M}$, *it holds that*

$$\texttt{Rec}(pk, r, \texttt{Enc}(pk, m; r)) = m \,.$$

An important property of recoverable PKE schemes is that the recover algorithm $\texttt{Rec}$ allows to perfectly recover the message from a ciphertext; even if the scheme itself suffers from decryption failures as is the case for many candidate quantum-resistant cryptographic algorithms.

Based on the recoverability property, the following Fig. 8 classifies PKE schemes regarding the applicability of the qINDqCPA security notion.

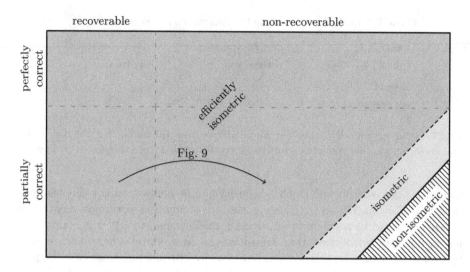

Fig. 8. Classification of PKE schemes as presented in the full version of [19]. (The terms (efficiently) isometric and non-isometric have been introduced in the full version of [19]. They are not relevant for the work at hand, but for better comprehensibility and comparability with the original work, we decided not to remove them from this figure.)

Remark 5. Concurrently and independent of [19], Bellare et al. [4] defined the same property, which they call *randomness-based decryption*. They show that some submissions to the NIST PQC standardization process instantiate the random oracles in a way, that an adversary can recover the randomness (that is used for encryption) from the ciphertext. Based on this, they then exploit the randomness-based decryption property (i.e., the recoverability) to extract the message, thereby breaking these submission. We note that this weakness is not due to the scheme but rather the specific choice of how the random oracles are instantiated from a single hash function.

Gagliardoni et al. [19] show that most real-world PKE schemes are indeed recoverable. In fact, they do not give a real-world PKE scheme that is non-recoverable. They provide, however, a generic transformation from a recoverable PKE scheme into a non-recoverable PKE scheme via a trapdoor permutation. The transformed scheme is displayed in Fig. 9. It first permutes the message using the trapdoor permutation and afterwards encrypts the permuted message using the encryption scheme. Decryption works in the obvious reversed way, i.e., first decrypting using the encryption scheme followed by inverting the trapdoor permutation. Gagliardoni et al. [19] observe that the trapdoor permutation prevents the transformed scheme from being recoverable.

In Theorem 6 we show that the transformed scheme as displayed in Fig. 9 indeed is non-recoverable.

$\mathsf{KGen}^{\Sigma'}()$	$\mathsf{Enc}^{\Sigma'}(pk, m; r)$	$\mathsf{Dec}^{\Sigma'}(sk, c)$
$(pk_\Sigma, sk_\Sigma) \leftarrow_\$ \mathsf{KGen}^\Sigma()$	**parse** pk **as** (pk_Σ, pk_Π)	**parse** sk **as** (sk_Σ, sk_Π)
$(pk_\Pi, sk_\Pi) \leftarrow_\$ \mathsf{KGen}^\mathcal{F}()$	$y \leftarrow \mathcal{F}(pk_\Pi, m)$	$y \leftarrow \mathsf{Dec}^\Sigma(sk_\Sigma, c)$
$pk \leftarrow (pk_\Sigma, pk_\Pi)$	$c \leftarrow \mathsf{Enc}^\Sigma(pk_\Sigma, y; r)$	$m \leftarrow \mathcal{F}^{-1}(sk_\Pi, y)$
$sk \leftarrow (sk_\Sigma, sk_\Pi)$	**return** c	**return** m
return (pk, sk)		

Fig. 9. Transformed scheme $\Sigma' = (\mathsf{KGen}^{\Sigma'}, \mathsf{Enc}^{\Sigma'}, \mathsf{Dec}^{\Sigma'})$ as presented in the full version of [19], where $\Sigma = (\mathsf{KGen}^\Sigma, \mathsf{Enc}^\Sigma, \mathsf{Dec}^\Sigma)$ is a public-key encryption scheme and $\Pi = (\mathsf{KGen}^\mathcal{F}, \mathcal{F}, \mathcal{F}^{-1})$ is a deterministic trapdoor permutation.

Theorem 6 ([19, adapted from the full version's Theorem 26]). *Let $\Pi = (\mathsf{KGen}^\mathcal{F}, \mathcal{F}, \mathcal{F}^{-1})$ be a deterministic trapdoor permutation and $\Sigma = (\mathsf{KGen}^\Sigma, \mathsf{Enc}^\Sigma, \mathsf{Dec}^\Sigma)$ be a PKE scheme. Let further $\Sigma' = (\mathsf{KGen}^{\Sigma'}, \mathsf{Enc}^{\Sigma'}, \mathsf{Dec}^{\Sigma'})$ be the PKE scheme constructed from Π and Σ according to the transformation depicted in Fig. 9. If Σ is recoverable, then Σ' is non-recoverable.*

Remark 7. In the full version of [19], the theorem comprises further requirements on Π and Σ, which achieve further properties for the transformed scheme. Since these are not relevant for the remainder of this section, we omit them.

4.2 Equivalent Recoverable PKE Schemes

We refine the classification shown in Fig. 8 by identifying a set of schemes which are not recoverable but for which it is possible to transform them into a recoverable PKE scheme. We call such schemes *equivalent recoverable*. Hence, equivalent recoverable schemes are not recoverable, but for them it still holds that after transformation it is possible to decrypt a ciphertext without knowledge of the secret key, but having access to the randomness used for the encryption instead. The transformation exploits that the secret key of an equivalent recoverable scheme consists of two parts, one of which is part of the public key after transformation. Note that equivalent recoverable schemes are neither recoverable nor non-recoverable (and, hence, not all schemes that are not recoverable are non-recoverable), but a third class of PKE schemes that are worth to be studied in the context of qINDqCPA security.

Definition 8 (Equivalent recoverable PKE Scheme). *Let $\Sigma' = (\mathsf{KGen}^{\Sigma'}, \mathsf{Enc}^{\Sigma'}, \mathsf{Dec}^{\Sigma'})$ be a PKE scheme with key pair $(pk_{\Sigma'}, sk_{\Sigma'})$, using internally a deterministic trapdoor permutation $\Pi = (\mathsf{KGen}^\mathcal{F}, \mathcal{F}, \mathcal{F}^{-1})$ and a PKE scheme $\Sigma = (\mathsf{KGen}^\Sigma, \mathsf{Enc}^\Sigma, \mathsf{Dec}^\Sigma)$ such that $pk_{\Sigma'} = (pk_\Pi, pk_\Sigma)$ and $sk_{\Sigma'} = (sk_\Pi, sk_\Sigma)$.*
Let $\Sigma^* = (\mathsf{KGen}^{\Sigma^*}, \mathsf{Enc}^{\Sigma^*}, \mathsf{Dec}^{\Sigma^*})$ be a transformed scheme which works identically as Σ' (thus, Σ^* and Σ' have the same plaintext, ciphertext, and randomness spaces $\mathcal{M}, \mathcal{C}$, and $\mathcal{R}$, respectively) except that the secret key sk_Π of Π is part of the scheme's public key, i.e., $pk_{\Sigma^*} = (pk_{\Sigma'}, sk_\Pi) = (pk_\Pi, pk_\Sigma, sk_\Pi)$ and $sk_{\Sigma^*} = sk_\Sigma$.

We call Σ' an equivalent recoverable PKE scheme *if Σ' is not recoverable but Σ^* is recoverable, i.e., if there exists an efficient algorithm* $\mathtt{Rec} : \mathcal{P}_{\Sigma^*} \times \mathcal{R} \times \mathcal{C} \to \mathcal{M}$ *such that, for any* $pk \in \mathcal{P}_{\Sigma^*}, r \in \mathcal{R}, m \in \mathcal{M}$, *it holds that*

$$\mathtt{Rec}(pk, r, \mathtt{Enc}^{\Sigma^*}(pk, m; r)) = m.$$

In particular, all schemes that are constructed from the transformation shown in Fig. 9 are equivalent recoverable, thus they are not really non-recoverable since the transformation can be inverted. In the following Fig. 10 we display an equivalent recoverable scheme after transformation.

$\mathtt{KGen}^{\Sigma^*}()$	$\mathtt{Enc}^{\Sigma^*}(pk, m; r)$	$\mathtt{Dec}^{\Sigma^*}(sk, c)$
$(pk_\Sigma, sk_\Sigma) \leftarrow_\$ \mathtt{KGen}^\Sigma()$	**parse** pk **as** $(pk_\Pi, pk_\Sigma, sk_\Pi)$	**parse** sk **as** (sk_Σ)
$(pk_\Pi, sk_\Pi) \leftarrow_\$ \mathtt{KGen}^{\mathcal{F}}()$	$y \leftarrow \mathcal{F}(pk_\Pi, m)$	$y \leftarrow \mathtt{Dec}^\Sigma(sk_\Sigma, c)$
$pk \leftarrow (pk_\Pi, pk_\Sigma, sk_\Pi)$	$c \leftarrow \mathtt{Enc}^\Sigma(pk_\Sigma, y; r)$	$m \leftarrow \mathcal{F}^{-1}(sk_\Pi, y)$
$sk \leftarrow (sk_\Sigma)$	**return** c	**return** m
return (pk, sk)		

Fig. 10. Transformed recoverable scheme $\Sigma^* = (\mathtt{KGen}^{\Sigma^*}, \mathtt{Enc}^{\Sigma^*}, \mathtt{Dec}^{\Sigma^*})$, where $\Sigma = (\mathtt{KGen}^\Sigma, \mathtt{Enc}^\Sigma, \mathtt{Dec}^\Sigma)$ and $\Pi = (\mathtt{KGen}^{\mathcal{F}}, \mathcal{F}, \mathcal{F}^{-1})$ are a PKE scheme and a deterministic trapdoor permutation, respectively, that are used internally within an equivalent recoverable PKE scheme Σ'.

Recoverability of the transformed scheme from Fig. 10 can be easily seen. First, the recover algorithm from the underlying PKE scheme is applied to recover y from the ciphertext c, subsequently, the trapdoor permutation is inverted which can be done as sk_Π is part of the public key.

Note that the above definition of equivalent recoverable schemes does not include a statement on the security of the involved schemes. In particular, we do not claim that all equivalent recoverable schemes are as secure after transformation as they are before. This of course depends on whether the security of the equivalent recoverable scheme depends on the trapdoor permutation or only on the underlying encryption scheme. What we claim instead is that all schemes that are constructed from the transformation shown in Fig. 9 are not helpful examples for non-recoverable schemes since in fact they are equivalent recoverable. For these schemes, we observe that their security depends entirely on the underlying encryption scheme, but not on the trapdoor permutation. Hence, after applying the transformation from Fig. 10, these schemes remain as secure as they are before.

We conclude this section with two findings: First, the transformation presented in [19] (cf. Fig. 9), that transforms a recoverable PKE scheme into a non-recoverable PKE scheme, in fact transforms the scheme into an equivalent recoverable PKE scheme, see Fig. 11. We are not aware of any transformation

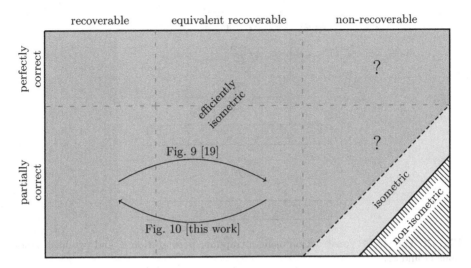

Fig. 11. Refined classification of PKE schemes. Compared to Fig. 8, equivalent recoverable schemes have been included. The transformation shown in Fig. 10 unveils that the existence of a non-recoverable PKE scheme is still unexplained.

that transforms a recoverable PKE scheme into a non-recoverable PKE scheme. Any such transformation would, if it was reversible, entail the extension of Definition 8, hence also transform the scheme into an equivalent recoverable PKE scheme. Second, the existence of real-world schemes that are non-recoverable (and not equivalent recoverable) remains unclear. We will provide an example of such a scheme in the following section by proving that the OAEP construction is non-recoverable, i.e., both not recoverable and not equivalent recoverable.

5 OAEP

The optimal asymmetric encryption padding (OAEP) is due to Bellare and Rogaway [6]. It constructs an encryption scheme from a trapdoor permutation $\Pi = (\texttt{KGen}^{\mathcal{F}}, \mathcal{F}, \mathcal{F}^{-1})$ and two hash functions G and H. The construction is illustrated in Fig. 12, the pseudocode is given in Fig. 13.[6] The OAEP construction takes a message m and randomness r and applies a two-round Feistel construction using G and H to it, yielding s and t. These values are then used as input to the trapdoor permutation $\mathcal{F}$ to compute the ciphertext c. The security of the construction is based on the trapdoor permutation being partial-domain one-way (cf. Definition 3), meaning it is infeasible to compute s from a ciphertext c.

---

[6] Note that we consider the CPA-secure variant of OAEP for simplicity. The CCA-secure variant pads the message with additional 0 s.

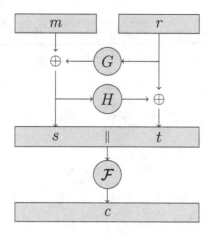

Fig. 12. The OAEP construction using a trapdoor permutation $\mathcal{F}$ and two hash functions G and H.

KGen()	Enc($pk, m; r$)	Dec(sk, c)
$(pk, sk) \leftarrow\!\!{}_{\$}\, \texttt{KGen}^{\mathcal{F}}()$	$s \leftarrow m \oplus G(r)$	$s \parallel t \leftarrow \mathcal{F}^{-1}(sk, c)$
return (pk, sk)	$t \leftarrow r \oplus H(s)$	$r \leftarrow H(s) \oplus t$
	$c \leftarrow \mathcal{F}(pk, s \parallel t)$	$m \leftarrow s \oplus G(r)$
	return c	**return** m

Fig. 13. Pseudocode of the OAEP construction using a trapdoor permutation $\Pi = (\texttt{KGen}^{\mathcal{F}}, \mathcal{F}, \mathcal{F}^{-1})$ and two hash functions G and H.

5.1   Recoverability of OAEP

Section 4 raises the question whether there are real-world public-key encryption scheme which are non-recoverable. In the following lemma, we answer this question in the affirmative by showing that the OAEP construction is non-recoverable, given that the trapdoor permutation is partial-domain one-way.

Lemma 9. *The OAEP construction is non-recoverable under the assumption that the trapdoor permutation is partial-domain one-way with respect to $\mathcal{X}_1$.*

Proof. We can view $G(r)$ as a one-time pad encryption of m with key s. From the randomness r, one can trivially compute $G(r)$. The ciphertext c does not reveal s due to the assumption of $\mathcal{F}$ being partial-domain one-way. Knowledge of the randomness r (corresponding to $H(s) \oplus t$) does not provide any additional information about s due to H being a random oracle, hence one-way.   □

It turns out that partial-domain one-wayness is crucial for the non-recoverability of the OAEP construction—just one-wayness is not sufficient. To show this, we consider the function

$$\mathcal{F}^*(s,t) := (s, \mathcal{F}(t)).$$

If the underlying function $\mathcal{F}$ is OW-secure, then $\mathcal{F}^*$ is OW-secure but not pdOW-secure. The adversary trivially finds s as it is part of its input. Based on this, it is straightforward to show that the OAEP construction instantiated with this function is recoverable. The adversary obtains the value s from the ciphertext (simply the first part of the ciphertext). From the randomness r, it computes $G(r)$ and xors it with s to get the message m.

5.2 Quantum Operators for OAEP

In the previous section we showed that the OAEP construction is non-recoverable. This precludes the construction of the public-key-based in-place encryption operator that Gagliardoni et al. [19] provide for recoverable public-key encryption schemes. The open question is whether the in-place operator can be constructed solely using the public key, which we answer negatively here. This also answers the main question from Sect. 3 by showing that there are PKE schemes for which the qINDqCPA security notion cannot be defined for challengers knowing only the public key.

We first introduce a variant of pdOW, which we denote pdOW*. The corresponding game is illustrated in Fig. 14. In this variant, the adversary receives some extra information, which corresponds to the randomness of the OAEP construction. As a first step, we show that the extra information does not help the adversary in breaking security (cf. Lemma 10). Subsequently, we show how an in-place operator for the OAEP construction can be transformed into one breaking security according to pdOW*, yielding a contradiction (cf. Theorem 11).

The following lemma shows that, for OAEP, the extra information from game pdOW* does not help the adversary in breaking security.

Lemma 10. *Let H be a random oracle and the games* pdOW *and* pdOW* *be as displayed in Fig. 1 and Fig. 14, respectively. Then for any adversary $\mathcal{A}$, there exists an adversary $\mathcal{B}$ such that*

$$\mathbf{Adv}_{OAEP}^{\mathsf{pdOW}^*}(\mathcal{A}) \le 2\,\mathbf{Adv}_{OAEP}^{\mathsf{pdOW}}(\mathcal{B}).$$

Proof. The proof essentially relies on the fact that r does not yield any additional information for $\mathcal{A}$. As a first step, we modify game pdOW* by picking r uniformly at random. To distinguish pdOW* from the modified game, $\mathcal{A}$ needs to query H on s. Hence, a distinguishing adversary can be transformed into an adversary winning pdOW. In the modified game, the value r is independent of anything else, hence a straightforward reduction allows to transform any adversary $\mathcal{A}$, playing pdOW*, into an adversary $\mathcal{B}$, playing pdOW, with the same winning probability. Adversary $\mathcal{B}$ simply runs $\mathcal{A}$ on its own challenge and a value r sampled uniformly at random. In addition, $\mathcal{B}$ simulates two random oracles G and H for $\mathcal{A}$.   □

Game pdOW*

$(pk, sk) \leftarrow_\$ \text{KGen}^{\mathcal{F}}()$

$(s, t) \leftarrow_\$ \mathcal{X}_1 \times \mathcal{X}_2$

$c \leftarrow \mathcal{F}(pk, (s, t))$

$r \leftarrow H(s) \oplus t$

$s' \leftarrow \mathcal{A}(pk, c, r)$

return $s' = s$

Fig. 14. Security game pdOW*. It is a variant of pdOW where the adversary addition-ally receives the xor of $H(s)$ and t as an input.

We finally show that an in-place encryption operator can be used to construct an xor operator for the inverse permutation $\mathcal{F}^{-1}$ underlying the OAEP construction. Hence, assuming that the in-place operator can be constructed using just the public key would yield an xor operator for the inverse permutation, contradicting its security as anyone could invert it using only the public key.

Theorem 11. *Assuming $\mathcal{F}$ to be partial-domain one-way, the in-place encryption operator for the OAEP construction instantiated with $\mathcal{F}$ cannot be constructed using solely the public key.*

Proof. For sake of contradiction, assume that the in-place encryption operator for the OAEP construction can be constructed solely using the public key. We show how to use this operator to construct an xor operator for the inverse trapdoor permutation which also only requires the public key, thus contradicting its security. The circuit is displayed in Fig. 15.

Constructing the in-place operator $U_{\text{Enc}}^{(ip)}$ allows to compute its inverse operator $\left(U_{\text{Enc}}^{(ip)}\right)^\dagger$. By definition of the operator, $\left(U_{\text{Enc}}^{(ip)}\right)^\dagger$ on input $|r\rangle$ and $|c\rangle$ yields $|r\rangle$, $|m\rangle$, and $|0\rangle$, such that encrypting m using randomness r equals c. In the next step, the registers $|r\rangle$ and $|m\rangle$ are xored to the two output registers initialized with $|0\rangle$. The first three registers are input to $U_{\text{Enc}}^{(ip)}$, yielding $|r\rangle$ and $|c\rangle$. The operator $U_G^\oplus$ is applied to the third and fourth register (the former being the input, the latter being the output), which yields $|r\rangle$ and $|m \oplus G(r)\rangle$. Then the operator $U_H^\oplus$ is applied to $|m \oplus G(r)\rangle$ (input register) and $|r\rangle$ (output register) which results in $|m \oplus G(r)\rangle$ and $|r \oplus H(m \oplus G(r))\rangle$.

By construction, it holds that the concatenation of register $|m \oplus G(r)\rangle$ and register $|r \oplus H(m \oplus G(r))\rangle$ equals the preimage of $|c\rangle$ under the function $\mathcal{F}$ (otherwise, the in-place operator would not correctly encrypt). This contradicts the security of $\mathcal{F}$ as we get an algorithm for inverting the trapdoor permutation $\mathcal{F}$ (using r as the extra information as specified in game pdOW) using only the public key. $\square$

The above theorem shows that there are PKE schemes for which the in-place encryption operator, required for the qINDqCPA security notion, cannot be constructed using only the public key. This answers the open question from Sect. 3 by showing that the qINDqCPA security notion is not always applicable for the scenario of confidential communication between two parties.

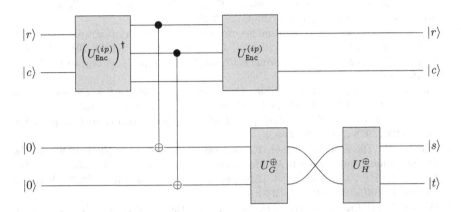

Fig. 15. Circuit for inverting $\mathcal{F}$ based on an in-place operator for $\mathtt{Enc}$ and xor operators for G and H.

Remark 12. The qINDqCPA security notion essentially provides the adversary a quantum channel transforming the message into a ciphertext, where the randomness is out of reach for the adversary. One might wonder whether ruling out the in-place quantum operator from above (cf. Eq. (1)) is sufficient to argue that the qINDqCPA security is not applicable to the OAEP construction. Theoretically, one can consider alternative ways of realizing the quantum channel. Consider, for instance, that the challenger itself has some quantum channel which it uses to realize the quantum channel for the adversary. In this case, the challenger might not know the secret key but its own quantum channel uses it; the quantum channel from the qINDqCPA security notion would then still depend on the secret key. From a cryptographic perspective, we do not believe this setting to be of relevance as the security notion corresponds to communication between the adversary and a challenger, where parts (i.e., the randomness) are beyond the access of the adversary. In this sense, we believe the quantum channel realized by the quantum operator from above to be the only relevant one, while we consider other realizations to be irrelevant from a cryptographic point of view.

Acknowledgements. We thank Nina Bindel for fruitful discussions on the OAEP construction. We also thank Mariami Gachechiladze for helpful discussions about quantum channels. This work was funded by the Deutsche Forschungsgemeinschaft (DFG) – SFB 1119 – 236615297.

References

1. Alagic, G., Majenz, C., Russell, A., Song, F.: Quantum-access-secure message authentication via blind-unforgeability. In: Canteaut, A., Ishai, Y. (eds.) EUROCRYPT 2020, Part III. LNCS, vol. 12107, pp. 788–817. Springer, Cham (2020). https://doi.org/10.1007/978-3-030-45727-3_27

2. Alagic, G., Russell, A.: Quantum-secure symmetric-key cryptography based on hidden shifts. In: Coron, J.-S., Nielsen, J.B. (eds.) EUROCRYPT 2017, Part III. LNCS, vol. 10212, pp. 65–93. Springer, Cham (2017). https://doi.org/10.1007/978-3-319-56617-7_3

3. Anand, M.V., Targhi, E.E., Tabia, G.N., Unruh, D.: Post-quantum security of the CBC, CFB, OFB, CTR, and XTS modes of operation. In: Takagi, T. (ed.) PQCrypto 2016. LNCS, vol. 9606, pp. 44–63. Springer, Cham (2016). https://doi.org/10.1007/978-3-319-29360-8_4

4. Bellare, M., Davis, H., Günther, F.: Separate your domains: NIST PQC KEMs, Oracle cloning and read-only indifferentiability. In: Canteaut, A., Ishai, Y. (eds.) EUROCRYPT 2020. LNCS, vol. 12106, pp. 3–32. Springer, Cham (2020). https://doi.org/10.1007/978-3-030-45724-2_1

5. Bellare, M., Hofheinz, D., Kiltz, E.: Subtleties in the definition of IND-CCA: when and how should challenge decryption be disallowed? J. Cryptol. **28**(1), 29–48 (2015)

6. Bellare, M., Rogaway, P.: Optimal asymmetric encryption. In: De Santis, A. (ed.) EUROCRYPT 1994. LNCS, vol. 950, pp. 92–111. Springer, Heidelberg (1995). https://doi.org/10.1007/BFb0053428

7. Boneh, D., Zhandry, M.: Quantum-secure message authentication codes. In: Johansson, T., Nguyen, P.Q. (eds.) EUROCRYPT 2013. LNCS, vol. 7881, pp. 592–608. Springer, Heidelberg (2013). https://doi.org/10.1007/978-3-642-38348-9_35

8. Boneh, D., Zhandry, M.: Secure signatures and chosen ciphertext security in a quantum computing world. In: Canetti, R., Garay, J.A. (eds.) CRYPTO 2013, Part II. LNCS, vol. 8043, pp. 361–379. Springer, Heidelberg (2013). https://doi.org/10.1007/978-3-642-40084-1_21

9. Bonnetain, X., Hosoyamada, A., Naya-Plasencia, M., Sasaki, Yu., Schrottenloher, A.: Quantum attacks without superposition queries: the offline Simon's algorithm. In: Galbraith, S.D., Moriai, S. (eds.) ASIACRYPT 2019, Part I. LNCS, vol. 11921, pp. 552–583. Springer, Cham (2019). https://doi.org/10.1007/978-3-030-34578-5_20

10. Bonnetain, X., Naya-Plasencia, M., Schrottenloher, A.: On quantum slide attacks. In: Paterson, K.G., Stebila, D. (eds.) SAC 2019. LNCS, vol. 11959, pp. 492–519. Springer, Cham (2020). https://doi.org/10.1007/978-3-030-38471-5_20

11. Carstens, T.V., Ebrahimi, E., Tabia, G.N., Unruh, D.: Relationships between quantum IND-CPA notions. In: Nissim, K., Waters, B. (eds.) TCC 2021. LNCS, vol. 13042, pp. 240–272. Springer, Cham (2021). https://doi.org/10.1007/978-3-030-90459-3_9

12. Chevalier, C., Ebrahimi, E., Vu, Q.-H.: On security notions for encryption in a quantum world. Cryptology ePrint Archive, Report 2020/237 (2020). https://eprint.iacr.org/2020/237

13. D'Anvers, J.-P., et al.: SABER. Technical report, National Institute of Standards and Technology (2020). https://csrc.nist.gov/projects/post-quantum-cryptography/round-3-submissions

14. Doosti, M., Delavar, M., Kashefi, E., Arapinis, M.: A unified framework for quantum unforgeability. CoRR, abs/2103.13994 (2021)
15. Ebrahimi, E.: Post-quantum security of plain OAEP transform. In: Hanaoka, G., Shikata, J., Watanabe, Y. (eds.) PKC 2022. LNCS, vol. 13177, pp. 34–51. Springer, Cham (2022). https://doi.org/10.1007/978-3-030-97121-2_2
16. Fujisaki, E., Okamoto, T.: Secure integration of asymmetric and symmetric encryption schemes. J. Cryptol. **26**(1), 80–101 (2013)
17. Fujisaki, E., Okamoto, T., Pointcheval, D., Stern, J.: RSA-OAEP is secure under the RSA assumption. J. Cryptol. **17**(2), 81–104 (2004)
18. Gagliardoni, T., Hülsing, A., Schaffner, C.: Semantic security and indistinguishability in the quantum world. In: Robshaw, M., Katz, J. (eds.) CRYPTO 2016, Part III. LNCS, vol. 9816, pp. 60–89. Springer, Heidelberg (2016). https://doi.org/10.1007/978-3-662-53015-3_3
19. Gagliardoni, T., Krämer, J., Struck, P.: Quantum indistinguishability for public key encryption. In: Cheon, J.H., Tillich, J.-P. (eds.) PQCrypto 2021 2021. LNCS, vol. 12841, pp. 463–482. Springer, Cham (2021). https://doi.org/10.1007/978-3-030-81293-5_24. Most of the content we refer to in this work is only included in the full version of the paper. For the full version, we refer to Cryptology ePrint Archive, Report 2020/266, https://eprint.iacr.org/2020/266
20. Garg, S., Yuen, H., Zhandry, M.: New security notions and feasibility results for authentication of quantum data. In: Katz, J., Shacham, H. (eds.) CRYPTO 2017, Part II. LNCS, vol. 10402, pp. 342–371. Springer, Cham (2017). https://doi.org/10.1007/978-3-319-63715-0_12
21. Hosoyamada, A., Sasaki, Yu.: Quantum Demiric-Selçuk meet-in-the-middle attacks: applications to 6-round generic feistel constructions. In: Catalano, D., De Prisco, R. (eds.) SCN 2018. LNCS, vol. 11035, pp. 386–403. Springer, Cham (2018). https://doi.org/10.1007/978-3-319-98113-0_21
22. Ito, G., Hosoyamada, A., Matsumoto, R., Sasaki, Yu., Iwata, T.: Quantum chosen-ciphertext attacks against feistel ciphers. In: Matsui, M. (ed.) CT-RSA 2019. LNCS, vol. 11405, pp. 391–411. Springer, Cham (2019). https://doi.org/10.1007/978-3-030-12612-4_20
23. Kaplan, M., Leurent, G., Leverrier, A., Naya-Plasencia, M.: Breaking symmetric cryptosystems using quantum period finding. In: Robshaw, M., Katz, J. (eds.) CRYPTO 2016, Part II. LNCS, vol. 9815, pp. 207–237. Springer, Heidelberg (2016). https://doi.org/10.1007/978-3-662-53008-5_8
24. Kashefi, E., Kent, A., Vedral, V., Banaszek, K.: Comparison of quantum oracles. Phys. Rev. A **65**, 050304 (2002)
25. Kuwakado, H., Morii, M.: Quantum distinguisher between the 3-round feistel cipher and the random permutation. In: IEEE International Symposium on Information Theory, ISIT 2010, 13–18 June 2010, Austin, Texas, USA, Proceedings, pp. 2682–2685 (2010)
26. Kuwakado, H., Morii, M.: Security on the quantum-type even-mansour cipher. In: Proceedings of the International Symposium on Information Theory and its Applications, ISITA 2012, Honolulu, HI, USA, 28–31 October 2012, pp. 312–316 (2012)
27. Leander, G., May, A.: Grover meets Simon – quantumly attacking the FX-construction. In: Takagi, T., Peyrin, T. (eds.) ASIACRYPT 2017, Part II. LNCS, vol. 10625, pp. 161–178. Springer, Cham (2017). https://doi.org/10.1007/978-3-319-70697-9_6

28. Mossayebi, S., Schack, R.: Concrete security against adversaries with quantum superposition access to encryption and decryption oracles. CoRR, abs/1609.03780 (2016)
29. Nemoz, T., Amblard, Z., Dupin, A.: Characterizing the qIND-qCPA (in)security of the CBC, CFB, OFB and CTR modes of operation. IACR Cryptol. ePrint Arch. 236 (2022)
30. Nielsen, M.A., Chuang, I.L.: Quantum Computation and Quantum Information, 10th Anniversary edn. Cambridge University Press (2016)
31. Rötteler, M., Steinwandt, R.: A note on quantum related-key attacks. Inf. Process. Lett. 115(1), 40–44 (2015)
32. Schwabe, P., et al.: CRYSTALS-KYBER. Technical report, National Institute of Standards and Technology (2020). https://csrc.nist.gov/projects/post-quantum-cryptography/round-3-submissions
33. Shor, P.W.: Algorithms for quantum computation: discrete logarithms and factoring. In: 35th FOCS, pp. 124–134. IEEE Computer Society Press, November 1994
34. Shoup, V.: OAEP reconsidered. In: Kilian, J. (ed.) CRYPTO 2001. LNCS, vol. 2139, pp. 239–259. Springer, Heidelberg (2001). https://doi.org/10.1007/3-540-44647-8_15
35. Targhi, E.E., Unruh, D.: Post-quantum security of the Fujisaki-Okamoto and OAEP transforms. In: Hirt, M., Smith, A. (eds.) TCC 2016, Part II. LNCS, vol. 9986, pp. 192–216. Springer, Heidelberg (2016). https://doi.org/10.1007/978-3-662-53644-5_8

Implementation and Side Channel Attacks

Efficiently Masking Polynomial Inversion at Arbitrary Order

Markus Krausz[1,2], Georg Land[1,2(✉)], Jan Richter-Brockmann[1], and Tim Güneysu[1,2]

[1] Horst Görtz Institute for IT Security, Ruhr University Bochum, Bochum, Germany
{markus.krausz,georg.land,tim.guneysu}@rub.de
[2] DFKI GmbH, Cyber-Physical Systems, Bremen, Germany

Abstract. Physical side-channel analysis poses a huge threat to post-quantum cryptographic schemes implemented on embedded devices. Still, secure implementations are missing for many schemes. In this paper, we present an efficient solution for masked polynomial inversion, a main component of the key generation of multiple post-quantum Key Encapsulation Mechanisms (KEMs). For this, we introduce a polynomial-multiplicative masking scheme with efficient arbitrary order conversions from and to additive masking. Furthermore, we show how to integrate polynomial inversion and multiplication into the masking schemes to reduce costs considerably. We demonstrate the performance of our algorithms for two different post-quantum cryptographic schemes on the Cortex-M4. For NTRU, we measure an overhead of 35% for the first-order masked inversion compared to the unmasked inversion while for BIKE the overhead is as little as 11%. Lastly, we verify the security of our algorithms for the first masking order by measuring and performing a TVLA based side-channel analysis.

Keywords: PQC · Masking · Polynomial inversion · Higher-order masking

1 Introduction

Our digital infrastructure relies and trusts Public-Key Cryptography (PKC) to establish secure communication channels. However, due to Shor's algorithm presented in 1999 [36], currently used schemes like RSA [33] and ECC [29] can be broken by quantum computers in polynomial time. Therefore, in 2017, the National Institute of Standards and Technology (NIST) announced a *Post-Quantum Cryptography Standardization Project* to find and standardize new cryptographic schemes that provide security against attacks mounted on classical and quantum computers. After three rounds, the NIST identified seven finalists and eight alternate candidates which are considered for standardization. Besides security, important metrics like costs, performance, and implementation characteristics on var-

---

M. Krausz, G. Land and J. Brockmann—These authors contributed equally to this work.

J. H. Cheon and T. Johansson (Eds.): PQCrypto 2022, LNCS 13512, pp. 309–326, 2022.
https://doi.org/10.1007/978-3-031-17234-2_15

ious platforms are considered in the selection process [2]. Driven by these criteria, the research community has proposed a plethora of highly efficient implementations for software and hardware. However, implementations of Post-Quantum Cryptography (PQC) schemes on embedded devices are faced with the same problems as traditional cryptographic algorithms, which includes physical attacks like Side-Channel Analysis (SCA) and Fault-Injection Analysis (FIA).

So far, most of the side-channel research with respect to the finalists in NIST's PQC standardization process focuses on schemes based on the Learning with Error (LWE) problem. Bos et al. presented the first higher-order masked implementation for the Cortex-M0+ and the Cortex-M4 for Kyber [8]. Just recently, Heinz et al. published a report on an optimized first-order protected Kyber implementation for the Cortex-M4 including practical measurements [19]. In 2021, Beirendonck et al. presented a first-order protected implementation of Saber for the Cortex-M4 [4]. An optimized implementation that also provides protection against higher-order attacks was afterwards proposed in [26].

Besides these studies that directly target the protection of specific algorithms, others [14,18] proposed optimizations and implementations which can be applied to both schemes. Coron et al.[14] concentrated their work on the improvements of higher-order masked comparisons by considering different approaches and techniques. As a case study, they applied their optimizations to Kyber and Saber. The work of Fritzmann et al.[18] explored different masked accelerators used as instruction set extensions for a RISC-V processor. They demonstrated their improvements on a hardware software co-design for Kyber and Saber. Eventually, D'Anvers et al. improved the work of Coron et al.[14] and presented an optimized higher-order masked comparison [15].

Summarizing, we can see that the side-channel security countermeasures for the LWE problem based schemes Kyber and Saber have already received some attention. However, masking NTRU-like [20,21] and code-based [3,28] systems is still an open research question and has so far only been sparsely investigated. In contrast, several side-channel attacks on these schemes were demonstrated. At CHES 2019, Sim et al. present a generic side-channel attack using conditional moves in implementations of PQC schemes based on Quasi-Cyclic Moderate-Density Parity-Check (QC-MDPC) codes [37]. Recently, a single-trace side-channel attack on the polynomial sampling of NTRU, NTRU Prime, and Dilithium has been proposed in [25]. In the work of Mujdei et al.[30] the authors present a powerful correlation power analysis on polynomial multiplications effecting all lattice-based PQC schemes.

An important operation in almost all NTRU-like and code-based systems is the polynomial inversion. It is required in the key generation of the finalists NTRU-HPS and NTRU-HRSS [10] as well as in the two alternate candidates Streamline NTRU Prime [5] and BIKE [3].

Contribution. To this end, we present the first efficient methodology for masking polynomial inversion by introducing polynomial-multiplicative masking (Sect. 3). As a foundation for our approach, we develop secure arbitrary-order conversions from polynomial-additive to polynomial-multiplicative masking (Sect. 3.1) and vice versa (Sect. 3.2). We show how to integrate a masked polynomial inversion into this conversion to reduce the number of unmasked inversions to one, independent of the masking order (Sect. 3.3). Additionally, we develop an algorithm to integrate a masked polynomial multiplication into the conversion to save costly unmasked multiplications (Sect. 3.4). Finally, we implement our algorithms for two use cases to demonstrate the performance benefits and we back our security claims for the first masking order by performing practical measurements on a Cortex-M4 microcontroller (Sect. 4).

2 Preliminaries

In this section we introduce important preliminaries that are necessary to adequately describe our approaches of masked arithmetic operations. Besides stating notations used throughout this work, we briefly recap masking. Eventually, we describe practical applications of masked polynomial inversions in the field of PQC.

2.1 Notation

Throughout this work, we denote polynomials by x. The i-th share of a shared polynomial x is denoted by x_i. A uniform random sampling of a polynomial r is denoted by $r \xleftarrow{\$} \mathcal{R}$ where $\mathcal{R}$ is the set of all valid polynomials. The set $\mathcal{R}^*$ denotes all uniform sampled polynomials from $\mathcal{R}$ that are invertible.

2.2 Masking

Masking is a common countermeasure to prevent SCA on embedded devices and is studied in the scientific community for more than twenty years [9]. The foundation of masking is *secret sharing* which splits a sensitive value x into multiple shares x_i with $0 \leq i \leq d$. For a correct sharing holds

$$x = x_0 \circ x_1 \circ \cdots \circ x_d \tag{1}$$

where $\circ$ defines the group operator of the applied masking scheme and d defines the security order based on the d-probing model proposed in [22]. As a consequence, a function f processing x needs to be transformed as well such that $f = f_0 \circ f_1 \circ \cdots \circ f_d$. When applying $\oplus$ as the group operator in Eq. 1, the secret sharing scheme is called *boolean masking*. The encoding is called *arithmetic masking* when $\circ$ is replaced by an addition or multiplication which we further categorize as *additive masking* or *multiplicative masking*, respectively.

2.3 Polynomial Inversion Applications

Polynomial inversion is a regular used operation in several PQC schemes [3,20,21]. Since it is such a critical operation, several works concentrated on efficient implementations of the polynomial inversion for software and hardware [11,17,31,32]. However, most approaches are based on Fermat's Little Theorem performed by the Itoh-Tsujii Algorithm (ITA) algorithm [23] or on the extGCD proposed by Bernstein and Yang [7]. In the following, we will briefly introduce the finalist NTRU, and the two alternate candidates streamlined NTRU Prime and Bit Flipping Key Encapsulation (BIKE) as examples of PQC schemes requiring polynomial inversions.

NTRU. The finalist NTRU is based on the original work by Hoffstein et al. [20] and on the work by Hülsing et al. [21]. NTRU is defined by three coprime positive integers (n, p, q), the sample spaces $\mathcal{L}_f, \mathcal{L}_g, \mathcal{L}_r, \mathcal{L}_m$, and an injection Lift : $\mathcal{L}_m \to \mathbb{Z}[\mathbf{X}]$. Furthermore, the authors of the NTRU submission recommend two families of parameter sets called NTRU-HPS and NTRU-HRSS [10]. NTRU-HPS uses a *fixed-weight* sampling space and allows several choices of q for each n which are based on [20] while NTRU-HRSS uses an *arbitrary weight* sampling space and fixed q as a function of n as suggested in [21].

The key generation requires to perform two polynomial inversions to generate the public and private key as shown in Algorithm 1. Note, for NTRU-HPS as well as for NTRU-HRSS the parameter p is always fixed to three. However, the two parameters (n, q) are different for the three security levels $\lambda \in \{1, 3, 5\}$ and are defined as $(509, 2048)$, $(677, 2048)$, and $(821, 4096)$, respectively.

Streamlined NTRU Prime. Streamlined NTRU Prime [5] is an alternate candidate in the NIST standardization process. NTRU Prime is also based on the original proposal by Hoffstein et al. [20] and defined by a prime number p, a prime number q, and a positive integer w [6]. One of the main differences to the classic NTRU cryptosystem is that NTRU Prime works over prime fields which avoids various attack vectors as claimed by the authors [5]. The key generation in NTRU Prime (see Algorithm 2) also contains two polynomial inversions. The first inversion inverts the randomly sampled polynomial g drawn from R while the second inversion inverts $3 \cdot f$ where f is a polynomial with coefficients $f_i \in \{-1, 0, 1\}$ with exactly w non-zero coefficients. Note, the first sampled polynomial g is not always invertible in R_3 while the second polynomial f is always invertible in R_q since it is a field.

For the three security levels $\lambda \in \{1, 3, 5\}$ the NTRU Prime parameters (p, q, w) are defined as $(653, 4621, 288)$, $(953, 6343, 396)$, and $(1277, 7879, 492)$, respectively.

Algorithm 1. KeyGen NTRU.	**Algorithm 2.** KeyGen sNTRUp.
Require: NTRU parameters n, p, q.	**Require:** sNTRUp parameter q.
Ensure: Priv. key (f, f_p, f_q), pub. key h.	**Ensure:** Priv. key (f, g_{inv}), pub. key h.
1: Generate $f \xleftarrow{\$} \mathcal{L}_f$	**repeat**
2: Generate $g \xleftarrow{\$} \mathcal{L}_g$	Generate $g \xleftarrow{\$} R$, g small
3: Compute $f_p \leftarrow 1/f$ in S_3	**until** g is invertible in R_3
4: Compute $f_q \leftarrow 1/f$ in S_q	Generate $f \xleftarrow{\$} Short$
5: Compute $g \leftarrow 3 \cdot g \cdot f_g$ in R_q	Compute $g_{inv} \leftarrow 1/g$ in R_3
6: Compute $h_q \leftarrow 1/h$ in S_q	Compute $h \leftarrow g/(3 \cdot f)$ in R_q
7: Return (f, f_p, f_q) and h.	Return (f, g_{inv}) and h.

BIKE. As well as Streamlined NTRU Prime, BIKE has been selected as an alternate candidate. In contrast to NTRU, BIKE is a code-based scheme relying on QC-MDPC codes [3]. The scheme originally consists of three different algorithms BIKE-1, BIKE-2, and BIKE-3 which, however, were reduced to just one single Key Encapsulation Mechanism (KEM) called BIKE. In BIKE, all polynomials are from the cyclic polynomial ring $\mathcal{R} := \mathbb{F}_2[X]/(X^r - 1)$ where r defines the size of the polynomials. The public key h is generated by sampling two private sparse polynomials (h_0, h_1) with $|h_0| = |h_1| = w/2$, inverting h_0, and multiplying the results with h_1. The entire key generation is formally described in Algorithm 3. For the three security levels $\lambda \in \{1, 3, 5\}$, the two parameters (r, w) are defined as $(12323, 141)$, $(24659, 206)$, and $(40973, 274)$, respectively. Since BIKE is suggested to be used with ephemeral keys, an efficient masked implementation of the polynomial inversion for side-channel protected designs is necessary.

In summary, it can be seen in Algorithm 1, Algorithm 2, and Algorithm 3 that the polynomial inversion is a major operation in the key generation of all three algorithms. Our measurements in Sect. 4.1 confirm that the polynomial inversion dominates the costs in terms of cycle counts. Hence, to construct protected designs against SCA, it is essential to find efficient algorithms for masked implementations. However, not only the inversion itself should be implemented efficiently but also preceding and subsequent operations must be masked without any expensive conversions between different masking techniques. Before we present our approach of an efficient higher-order masked polynomial inversion, we briefly discuss different cases of invertibility of random polynomials.

Invertibility of Random Polynomials. Among these three schemes, three different cases of invertibility occur. Since the target polynomials are sampled randomly but based on certain rules, we identify the following cases.

Algorithm 3. Key Generation of BIKE.

Require: BIKE parameters n, w, ℓ.
Ensure: Private key (h_0, h_1, σ) and public key h.
　Generate $(h_0, h_1) \xleftarrow{\$} \mathcal{R}^2$ both of odd weight $|h_0| = |h_1| = w/2$.
　Generate $\sigma \xleftarrow{\$} \{0,1\}^\ell$ uniformly at random.
　Compute $h \leftarrow h_1 h_0^{-1}$.
　Return (h_0, h_1, σ) and h.

---

1. All sampled polynomials (except the polynomial representing 0) are invertible. This case is trivial and no further exceptions need to be covered which is the case for NTRU.
2. Not all polynomials from the used ring are invertible but following some certain rules always allows to sample an invertible polynomial. For example, this is the case for BIKE where the polynomials requires to have an odd Hamming weight. Hence, applying the defined sampling procedure always generates an invertible polynomials such that the inversion cannot fail.
3. Not all polynomials from the underlying ring are invertible and they are not easily distinguishable. For example, this is the case for Streamlined NTRU Prime where the sampling procedure just sample uniformly random polynomials without applying dedicated rules. In case the sampled polynomial is not invertible, the inversion fails in the last step and a new polynomial needs to be sampled.

3   Masking Polynomial Inversion

Masking boolean operations in PQC schemes can efficiently be implemented with a boolean sharing, while arithmetic operations such as the addition and subtraction of polynomials or the multiplication with public values are implemented with additive sharing as the masked implementation for Kyber [8] demonstrates. An alternative sharing, that had already been proposed for AES in the year 2001 [1], is multiplicative sharing. The problem with multiplicative sharing that hinders its application, is that if one share is zero, the attacker already knows that the masked value is zero.

For polynomial inversion, that is used in multiple PQC schemes as shown in Sect. 2.3, we need a masking approach for which inversion is a linear operation. Given uniformly random polynomials $m_i \in \mathcal{R}$ such that $m = \prod_{i=0}^{d} m_i$, a valid polynomial-multiplicative sharing can be realized by

$$m^{-1} = \prod_{i=0}^{d} m_i^{-1}, \tag{2}$$

i.e., the inversion is applied to each share independently. As the zero polynomial is not invertible, it will not be given as an input to a masked inversion. With

$d + 1$ unmasked polynomial inversions, that is already an expensive operation on its own, this approach is very costly and asks for alternative solutions.

Obviously, multiplication of *two secret* polynomials is very efficient in the multiplicative domain as it requires only $d + 1$ unmasked multiplications compared to the additive domain where the number of unmasked multiplications is quadratic to the masking order in current solutions [35]. The cost to convert polynomials from and to the multiplicative domain determines, however, whether this approach is viable (cf. Section 3.4).

In the following, we present algorithms that efficiently transform additive shares of polynomials in a ring to multiplicative shares and vice versa. With the motivation to perform a more efficient polynomial inversion than shown in Eq. 2, we demonstrate how to integrate the inversion into the transformation, and how to perform a multiplication and back transformation in one joint operation.

3.1 Conversion from Additive to Multiplicative Sharing

Let a be a polynomial and a_i shares with $a = \sum_{i=0}^{d} a_i$, where all a_i are uniform random in the respective polynomial ring. To transform this sharing to a polynomial-multiplicative sharing in the same ring, we adapt the well-known technique of first appending a share in the new masking domain, enlarging the sharing in two domains (additive and multiplicative), and then to combine two old shares to remove one share.

We now introduce our algorithm by presenting an example for first-order masking. Given a polynomial a split into two additive shares a_0 and a_1, we start by sampling one invertible polynomial r and multiply each additive share with this polynomial, yielding ra_0 and ra_1. We set the inverted polynomial r^{-1} as a new multiplicative share, expanding the number of shares from two to three. To reduce our number of shares, we add corresponding two additive shares: $ra_0 + ra_1 = r(a_0 + a_1)$. By treating the sum as a multiplicative share, we are left with two correct multiplicative shares for a, since $r^{-1}r(a_0 + a_1) = a$.

The full algorithm for arbitrary orders can be summarized with the following steps:

1. Sample a uniform random and invertible polynomial r, observing that $a = r^{-1}ra$.
2. Compute $a_i' = ra_i$, we now have $d + 2$ shares, $d + 1$ additive shares and one multiplicative share.
3. To return to $d + 1$ shares, we combine two additive shares.
4. Repeat from start until there is only one additive share left, which now can be viewed as a multiplicative share.

The algorithm is shown in detail in Algorithm 4. Note that for this conversion, d polynomial inversions and $(d + 1)(d + 2)/2 - 1$ polynomial multiplications, as well as $d - 1$ polynomial additions are needed.

Algorithm 4. Additive to Polynomial-Multiplicative Masking Conversion (A2M)

Require: $a = \sum_{i=0}^{d} a_i$

Ensure: $m = \prod_{i=0}^{d} m_i = a$

    function A2M($a_0, \ldots, a_d$)

        for $i := d$ **downto** 1 **do**

            $r \xleftarrow{\$} \mathcal{R}^*$ ▷ sample from the set of invertible polynomials

            for $j := 0$ **to** i **do**

                $a_j := r a_j$

            end for

            $m_i := r^{-1}$ ▷ now we have $d + 2$ shares with $a = \left(\sum_{j=0}^{i} a_j \right) \prod_{j=i}^{d} m_j$

            $a_{i-1} := a_{i-1} + a_i$ ▷ combining two additive shares

        end for

        $m_0 := a_0$

    end function

3.2   Conversion from Multiplicative to Additive Sharing

For subsequent operations in the additive domain, a transformation from the multiplicative to the additive domain is necessary. Given a masked polynomial m split into two multiplicative shares m_0 and m_1 for our M2A conversion, we start by sampling one random polynomial r. The first step is to compute $m_0 + r$ before we multiply it with m_1 to get $(m_0 + r)m_1 = m_0 m_1 + r m_1$. Together with the product $-r m_1$ we have two additive shares that yield $m_0 m_1 + r m_1 - r m_1 = m_0 m_1 = m$.

    This method can be generalized to arbitrary masking orders by reapplying the core idea of adding a random polynomial before the multiplication with one of the multiplicative shares m_i. Our strategy is to compute $m = \prod_{i=0}^{d} m_i$ step by step in the first share, while protecting this sum with d random summands. Thus, iterating from $i = 1$ to d, we sample a uniform random additive sharing of $i + 1$ polynomials such that $\sum_{j=0}^{i} r_{ij} = 0$. We add these random polynomials to the first $i + 1$ shares before we multiply the shares with m_i. After d iterations, we get $a_0 = m + \sum_{i=1}^{d} (r_{i0} \prod_{j=i}^{d} m_j)$ as the first additive share for m together with d additive shares $a_k = \sum_{i=k}^{d} (r_{ik} \prod_{j=i}^{d} m_j)$ that cancel out the summands in a_0 except m.

    The algorithm can efficiently be implemented in situ as shown in Algorithm 5 and utilizes $d(d+1)/2 + d$ polynomial multiplications, $d(d+1) + d$ additions, $d(d+1)/2$ fresh random polynomials and no costly inversion.

3.3   Reducing the Number of Inversions

The main application of the polynomial-multiplicative masking is polynomial inversion. Naively, we would perform a polynomial inversion on each polynomial-multiplicative share individually to obtain a sharing of the inverted polynomial (cf. Equation 2). Together with the d inversions required for the A2M conversion,

---

Algorithm 5. Polynomial-Multiplicative to Additive Masking Conversion (M2A)

Require: $m = \prod_{i=0}^{d} m_i$
Ensure: $a = \sum_{i=0}^{d} a_i = m$
  function M2A$(m_0, \ldots, m_d)$
    for $i := 1$ **to** d **do**
      $r_i := 0$
      for $j := 0$ **to** $i - 1$ **do**
        $r \xleftarrow{\$} \mathcal{R}$
        $r_i := r_i + r$
        $m_j := m_j + r$ ▷ refreshing
        $m_j := m_j m_i$ ▷ combining two multiplicative shares
      end for
      $m_i := -r_i m_i$
    end for
    for $i := 0$ **to** d **do**
      $a_i := m_i$
    end for
  end function

---

this would lead to $2d + 1$ unmasked inversions for one masked inversion, given a polynomial shared in the additive domain.

However, we can adapt Algorithm 4 such that only one polynomial inversion is necessary, independent of the masking degree. This is shown in Algorithm 6. The idea is to not set the new multiplicative shares to the inverse, which we would invert again later, but to the original sample. Instead we only invert m_0 at the end to get an A2M conversion with implicit inversion. With this method we can drastically reduce the number of polynomial inversions that are the most expensive operations compared to polynomial multiplications and additions as we show in Sect. 4. We thus save two inversions for first order, four inversions for second and already six inversions for third order masking, compared to the naive approach.

3.4 Reducing the Number of Multiplications

Although a masked polynomial multiplication is cheaper in the multiplicative domain ($d + 1$ unmasked multiplications) compared to the additive domain where it is quadratic [35], the additional costs of the A2M and M2A conversions render this approach obsolete for polynomials that are not given in the multiplicative domain anyway. In particular the A2M conversion without inversion is too expensive with its d unmasked inversions.

We can, however, save unmasked multiplications when one factor is already in the multiplicative domain due to a prior inversion. Given a polynomial $a = \sum_{i=0}^{d} a_i$ in the additive domain and a polynomial $b = \prod_{i=0}^{d} b_i$ in the multiplicative domain, we observe that the masked product $c = \sum_{i=0}^{d} c_i = ab$

Algorithm 6. Additive to Polynomial-Multiplicative Masking Conversion with Implicit Polynomial Inversion (A2M$_{\text{INV}}$)

Require: $a = \sum_{i=0}^{d} a_i$
Ensure: $m = \prod_{i=0}^{d} m_i = a^{-1}$
   function A2M$_{\text{INV}}(a_0, \ldots, a_d)$
     for $i := d$ downto 1 **do**
       $r \xleftarrow{\$} \mathcal{R}^*$ ▷ sample from the set of invertible polynomials
       for $j := 0$ to i **do**
         $a_j := r a_j$
       end for
       $m_i := r$ ▷ note that we do not set this to the inverse
       $a_{i-1} := a_{i-1} + a_i$
     end for
     $m_0 := a_0^{-1}$ ▷ the only inverse we need to compute
   end function

---

can be computed with $c = ab = \sum_{i=0}^{d} a_i \prod_{j=0}^{d} b_j = \sum_{i=0}^{d}(a_i \prod_{j=0}^{d} b_j)$, where $c_i = a_i \prod_{j=0}^{d} b_j$ represents an additive share of the product c. The straightforward computation would leak the polynomial b, but by adding fresh random polynomials between the unmasked multiplications similar as in our M2A conversion, we can get a secure conversion from multiplicative domain to additive domain including a multiplication with an additive shared polynomial as shown in Algorithm 7.

The costs for this masked conversion with implicit multiplication are $(d+1)^2$ unmasked multiplications, $(d+1)2d$ additions and $(d+1)d$ fresh random polynomials. Compared to the naive approach of first converting a from the multiplicative to the additive domain and then performing the multiplication, we save about the amount of unmasked multiplications and additions required for the M2A conversion.

For the case where we want to securely invert a polynomial and multiply the result with another polynomial, which is often the case as we see in Sect. 2.3, we apply our A2M$_{\text{INV}}$ first, where the costs are dominated by the single unmasked inversion, resulting in an inverted polynomial in the multiplicative domain. As a second step, we apply our M2A$_{\text{MUL}}$, to transform the inverted polynomial back into the additive domain while simultaneously multiplying it with another additive shared polynomial, at the cost of a multiplication in the additive domain, so the back transformation is basically free. In Sect. 4 we present performance results by exemplary applying our approaches to NTRU and BIKE.

4   Implementation and Evaluation

To evaluate the performance and security of our algorithms, we implemented them for NTRU and BIKE on the STM32F4 discovery board, which is equipped with a 32-bit Cortex-M4 microcontroller, 192-KB SRAM and 1-MB flash memory and can be clocked up to 168 MHz.

Algorithm 7. Polynomial-Multiplicative to Additive Masking Conversion with Implicit Polynomial Multiplication (M2A$_{\text{MUL}}$)

Require: $a = \sum_{i=0}^{d} a_i$, $b = \prod_{i=0}^{d} b_i$
Ensure: $c = \sum_{i=0}^{d} c_i = ab$
  function M2A$_{\text{MUL}}(a_0, \ldots, a_d, b_0, \ldots, b_d)$
    for $j := 0$ **to** d **do**
      $c_j := a_j b_0$ ▷ implicit multiplication
    end for
    for $i := 1$ **to** d **do**
      $r_d := 0$
      for $j := 0$ **to** $d-1$ **do**
        $r \xleftarrow{\$} \mathcal{R}$
        $r_d := r_d + r$
        $c_j := c_j + r$ ▷ refreshing
        $c_j := c_j b_i$ ▷ combining two multiplicative shares
      end for
      $c_d := c_d - r_d$
      $c_d := c_d b_i$
    end for
  end function

We based our implementation on the respective ring operations of the state-of-the-art Cortex-M4 implementations of the schemes. For BIKE this is the work by Chen et al. [12], for NTRU this is the work by Chung et al. [13] with an improved inversion by Li et al. [27].

4.1 Implementation Results

As it is common [24], we measured cycle counts at 24 MHz to not have memory wait states. We compiled our code with the `arm-none-eabi-gcc-10.3.1` compiler with optimization-level `O3`. The stated cycle counts are averages of 100 runs.

We did not implement and measure the plain A2M conversion, because it is not interesting for our use cases with its high costs.

NTRU. We first measured the cycle counts for unmasked ring operations to have a baseline to compare our masked versions with. For NTRU in the parameter set `ntruhps2048677`, polynomials in the ring S_3 have 677 coefficients $\in \{0, 1, 2\}$. Unprotected polynomial inversion costs 1273864 clock cycles here, about six times the cycles for an unprotected polynomial multiplication that takes 201383 cycles. An unprotected addition is done in only 18340 cycles and is thus insignificant compared to inversions and multiplications.

The costs for the masked A2M$_{\text{INV}}$ in the first masking order are mainly determined by the unmasked inversion and two unmasked multiplications. The overhead compared to an unmasked inversion is therefore mostly the cost of two multiplications, resulting in about 35% overhead, which is an excellent result compared to other masked operations. This calculation excludes the cost of an M2A conversion, but as we argued in Sect. 3.4, this comes for free by using the M2A$_{MUL}$. Since the number of unmasked inversions required for one A2M$_{INV}$ is only one, independent of the masking order, the cycle counts of the A2M$_{INV}$ increase only slowly with the masking order. For the sixth order, which operates on seven shares, the cycle counts are less than six fold the ones of the unmasked as shown in Table 1.

For the M2A$_{MUL}$ we measured 885773 cycles in the first order, less than twice the cost of one M2A that costs 486165. This proportion stays with increasing masking order while the number of unmasked multiplications and additions grows quadratically for both algorithms.

Table 1. Cycle counts for our proposed masked A2M$_{INV}$, M2A$_{MUL}$, and M2A conversion for ntruhps2048677 on the Cortex-M4. Unprotected addition requires 18340 clock cycles, unprotected multiplication requires 201383 clock cycles and unprotected inversion 1273864 clock cycles.

Ord. d	A2M inversion			M2A mul.			M2A conversion		
	Cycles	MUL	INV	Cycles	MUL	ADD	Cycles	MUL	ADD
1	1723778	2	1	885773	4	4	486165	2	3
2	2372502	5	1	2090841	9	12	1230767	5	8
3	3211410	9	1	3802004	16	24	2238833	9	15
4	4260732	14	1	6057128	25	40	3503189	14	24
5	5524861	20	1	8848501	36	60	5049140	20	35
6	6991050	27	1	12097869	49	84	6859272	27	48

BIKE. For BIKE in the parameter set `bike1`, polynomials have 12323 coefficients $\in \{0,1\}$. As 32 coefficients are stored in one register and the addition of coefficients equates to a xor operation, the unmasked addition of polynomials is very cheap with 3534 clock cycles. Due to the higher polynomial degree, however, multiplications and inversions take longer, compared to the operations in NTRU. For one unmasked multiplication, we measured about one million cycles, and for one unmasked inversion 19182916 cycles.

With the increased gap between multiplication and inversion, compared to NTRU, the overhead of the A2M$_{INV}$ reduces. With 21317392 cycles for the first order A2M$_{INV}$, the overhead is as little as 11% compared to an unmasked inversion. Also the cost of M2A$_{MUL}$ and M2A become less significant compared a A2M$_{INV}$ in the lower masking orders, due to the order of magnitude difference in cycle counts between unmasked inversion and unmasked multiplication. In the first masking order we measure 4240017 cycles for one M2A$_{MUL}$ and 2131405 for one M2A as shown in Table 2. The gap between A2M$_{INV}$ and M2A or M2A$_{MUL}$

decreases in relative terms with increasing masking order due to the quadratic cost in unmasked multiplications.

Table 2. Cycle counts for our proposed masked A2M$_{INV}$, M2A$_{MUL}$, and M2A conversion for bikel1 on the Cortex-M4. Unprotected addition requires 3534 clock cycles, unprotected multiplication requires 1052253 clock cycles and unprotected inversion 19182916 clock cycles.

Ord. d	A2M inversion			M2A mul.			M2A conversion		
	Cycles	MUL	INV	Cycles	MUL	ADD	Cycles	MUL	ADD
1	21317392	2	1	4240017	4	4	2131405	2	3
2	24487146	5	1	9584999	9	12	5342630	5	8
3	28736397	9	1	17068753	16	24	9622491	9	15
4	34007250	14	1	26740596	25	40	14994627	14	24
5	40275530	20	1	38507790	36	60	21419851	20	35
6	47744390	27	1	52493255	49	84	28945019	27	48

4.2 Side-Channel Evaluation

To evaluate the security against power side-channel attacks, we performed measurements on the same STM32F4 discovery board with the Cortex-M4 microcontroller. The power consumption is indirectly measured via a 1 Ω shunt resistor placed in the supply path of the microcontroller (the board provides dedicated pads for such applications) and the signal is amplified by a ZFL-1000LN+ Low Noise Amplifier (LNA). We use an 8 bit oscilloscope from PicoScope sampling with 625 MS/s to acquire the power traces. During the measurements, the microcontroller operates with a 24 MHz clock, which results in roughly 26 sample points per clock cycle, and is powered by an external power supply to ensure a clean and stable supply voltage.

For the security evaluation, we use a common fixed vs. random univariate Test Vector Leakage Assessment (TVLA) evaluation procedure as detailed described in [34]. Commonly, the measured power traces of the fixed and random inputs are used for a Welsh t-test where the t-value is compared to a ± 4.5 threshold corresponding to a $\alpha = 0.0001$ confidence level. In case the threshold is exceeded, the implementation is assumed to leak sensitive information since the power consumption of the fixed and the random inputs can be distinguished. However, in 2017 Ding et al. demonstrated that the threshold of ± 4.5 needs to be adapted for measurements with many sample points to avoid false positives in the evaluation [16]. Since we measure operations that require up to 1.7e6 clock cycles (which are approximately $26 \cdot 1.7e6 = 44.2e6$ sample points with our setup), we applied their approach and adapted the corresponding threshold that still results in a confidence level of α.

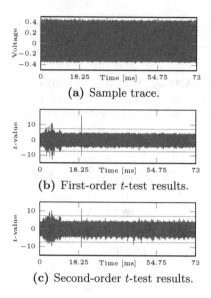

Fig. 1. Measurement results of A2M$_{INV}$ with no randomness (2000 traces).

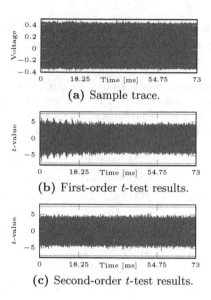

Fig. 2. Measurement results of A2M$_{INV}$ with randomness (100000 traces).

In the following, we present the measurement results for the first-order masked inversion A2M$_{INV}$ and the multiplicative to additive conversion M2A. We limit our evaluation to these two algorithms as they exemplary demonstrate the ideas of our proposals. Both, the A2M conversion and the M2A$_{MUL}$, are similar to the other two algorithms such that we only performed the time-consuming measurements for them.

Masked Inversion. Figure 1 shows the measurement results for the masked inversion presented in Algorithm 6 with disabled randomness to demonstrate the correct functionality of our measurement setup. As expected, the t-test reveals first- and second-order univariate leakage. Figure 2 presents the measurement results for the protected inversion with randomness enabled. We acquired 100000 power traces and could not detect any first-order univariate leakage. Interestingly, the second-order t-test also does not reveal any leakage which is may due to the univariate analysis technique applied in our evaluation. We expect that second-order leakage would be visible once an attacker utilizes multivariate analysis techniques, i.e., combines samples from multiple points in time. Another reason for this phenomena could be the applied masking technique. When we look at a single coefficient of a polynomial with multiplicative sharing, it can not be recreated by $d+1$ respective coefficients of the polynomial shares, but depends on other coefficients too. For the first masking order we combine one random coefficient of one polynomial with all random coefficients of another polynomial

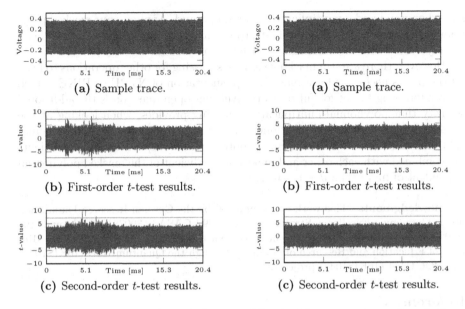

(a) Sample trace.

(a) Sample trace.

(b) First-order t-test results.

(b) First-order t-test results.

(c) Second-order t-test results.

(c) Second-order t-test results.

Fig. 3. Measurement results of the M2A conversion with no randomness (2000 traces).

Fig. 4. Measurement results of the M2A conversion with randomness (100000 traces).

which can be seen as some kind of higher-order masking. However, this artifact is out of scope of this work and we leave the investigation for future work.

Multiplicative to Additive Conversion. Besides the masked polynomial inversion, we additionally evaluate the multiplicative to additive conversion M2A from Algorithm 5. Again, we first measured the operation with disabled randomness (masks and fresh randomness are constant) which is visualized in Fig. 3. After 2000 traces, the t-test results for the first- and second-order clearly indicate leakage. However, in the next experiment we enable all randomness and perform 100000 measurements. The t-test does not reveal any leakage which is shown in Fig. 4. Again, no second-order leakage is visible due to the same argumentation as above.

5 Conclusion

In this work, we demonstrate that polynomial-multiplicative sharing is a viable solution to mask arithmetic operations of multiple PQC schemes. To this end, we propose an efficient higher-order masked polynomial inversion with implicit additive to multiplicative conversion, conversion algorithms used to switch between different sharings, and a novel masked multiplication that accepts an additive shared operand and a multiplicative shared operand. Applying our masked polynomial inversion to NTRU, the first-order masked design requires an overhead of only 35%, while the overhead for BIKE is only 11%.

However, there are still masking solutions missing for other operations to have all the pieces necessary for a masked implementation of NTRU or BIKE, which is an interesting target for future work. Another open question is the additional security that polynomial-multiplicative masking provides, when looking at the coefficient level. As already mentioned in Sect. 4.2, traditional masking schemes split one value into $d+1$ values. But in polynomial multiplication, all coefficients are combined with each other and make one coefficient of the masked polynomial dependent of more than $d + 1$ values.

Acknowledgments. This work was supported by the German Research Foundation under Germany's Excellence Strategy – EXC 2092 CASA – 390781972, through the H2020 project PROMETHEUS (grant agreement ID 780701), and by the Federal Ministry of Education and Research of Germany through the QuantumRISC (16KIS1038) and PQC4Med (16KIS1044) projects.

References

1. Akkar, M.-L., Giraud, C.: An implementation of DES and AES, secure against some attacks. In: Koç, Ç.K., Naccache, D., Paar, C. (eds.) CHES 2001. LNCS, vol. 2162, pp. 309–318. Springer, Heidelberg (2001). https://doi.org/10.1007/3-540-44709-1_26

2. Alagic, G., et al.: Status report on the first round of the NIST post-quantum cryptography standardization process. US Department of Commerce, National Institute of Standards and Technology (2019). https://tsapps.nist.gov/publication/get_pdf.cfm?pub_id=927303

3. Aragon, N., et al.: BIKE: bit flipping key encapsulation (2021). https://bikesuite.org/files/v4.2/BIKE_Spec.2021.07.26.1.pdf

4. Van Beirendonck, M., D'anvers, J.-P., Karmakar, A., Balasch, J., Verbauwhede, I.: A Side-channel Resistant Implementation of SABER. ACM J. Emerg. Technol. Comput. Syst. (JETC) **17**(2), 1–26 (2021)

5. Bernstein, D.J., Chuengsatiansup, C., Lange, T., van Vredendaal, C.: NTRU prime: reducing attack surface at low cost. In: Adams, C., Camenisch, J. (eds.) SAC 2017. LNCS, vol. 10719, pp. 235–260. Springer, Cham (2018). https://doi.org/10.1007/978-3-319-72565-9_12

6. Bernstein, D.J., Chuengsatiansup, C., Lange, T., van Vredendaal, C.: Ntru prime: round 3. Submission to the NIST PQC standardization process (2020). https://ntruprime.cr.yp.to

7. Bernstein, D.J., Yang, B.-Y.: Fast constant-time GCD computation and modular inversion. IACR Trans. Cryptogr. Hardw. Embed. Syst. **2019**(3), 340–398 (2019)

8. Bos, J.W., Gourjon, M., Renes, J., Schneider, T., van Vredendaal, C.: Masking kyber: first- and higher-order implementations. IACR Trans. Cryptogr. Hardw. Embed. Syst. **2021**(4), 173–214 (2021)

9. Chari, S., Jutla, C.S., Rao, J.R., Rohatgi, P.: Towards sound approaches to counteract power-analysis attacks. In: Wiener, M. (ed.) CRYPTO 1999. LNCS, vol. 1666, pp. 398–412. Springer, Heidelberg (1999). https://doi.org/10.1007/3-540-48405-1_26

10. Chen, C., et al.: NTRU - algorithm specifications and supporting documentation. Brown University and Onboard security company, Wilmington USA (2019)
11. Chen, M.-S., Chou, T.: Classic McEliece on the arm cortex-M4. IACR Trans. Cryptogr. Hardw. Embed. Syst. **2021**(3), 125–148 (2021)
12. Chen, M.S., Güneysu, T., Krausz, M., Thoma, J.P.: Carry-less to BIKE faster. In: Ateniese, G., Venturi, D. (eds.) Applied Cryptography and Network Security - 20th International Conference, ACNS 2022, Rome, Italy, 20–23 June 2022, Proceedings, vol. 13269 of Lecture Notes in Computer Science, pp. 833–852. Springer, Heidelebrg (2022). https://doi.org/10.1007/978-3-031-09234-3_41
13. Chung, C.M.M., Hwang, V., Kannwischer, M.J., Seiler, G., Shih, C.J., Yang, B.Y.: NTT multiplication for NTT-unfriendly rings new speed records for saber and NTRU on cortex-M4 and AVX2. IACR Trans. Cryptogr. Hardw. Embed. Syst. **2021**(2), 159–188 (2021)
14. Coron, J.S., Gérard, F., Montoya, S., Zeitoun, R.: High-order polynomial comparison and masking lattice-based encryption. Cryptology ePrint Archive (2021)
15. D'Anvers, J.P., Van Beirendonck, M., Verbauwhede, I.: Revisiting higher-order masked comparison for lattice-based cryptography: algorithms and bit-sliced implementations. IACR Cryptol. ePrint Arch., p. 110 (2022)
16. Ding, A.A., Zhang, L., Durvaux, F., Standaert, F.-X., Fei, Y.: Towards sound and optimal leakage detection procedure. In: Eisenbarth, T., Teglia, Y. (eds.) CARDIS 2017. LNCS, vol. 10728, pp. 105–122. Springer, Cham (2018). https://doi.org/10.1007/978-3-319-75208-2_7
17. Drucker, N., Gueron, S., Kostic, D.: Fast polynomial inversion for post quantum QC-MDPC cryptography. In: Dolev, S., Kolesnikov, V., Lodha, S., Weiss, G. (eds.) CSCML 2020. LNCS, vol. 12161, pp. 110–127. Springer, Cham (2020). https://doi.org/10.1007/978-3-030-49785-9_8
18. Fritzmann, T., et al.: Masked accelerators and instruction set extensions for post-quantum cryptography. IACR Trans. Cryptogr. Hardw. Embed. Syst. **2022**(1), 414–460 (2021)
19. Heinz, D., Kannwischer, M.J., Land, G., Pöppelmann, T., Schwabe, P., Sprenkels, D.: First-order masked kyber on ARM cortex-M4. Cryptology ePrint Archive, Report 2022/058 (2022). https://ia.cr/2022/058
20. Hoffstein, J., Pipher, J., Silverman, J.H.: NTRU: a ring-based public key cryptosystem. In: Buhler, J.P. (ed.) ANTS 1998. LNCS, vol. 1423, pp. 267–288. Springer, Heidelberg (1998). https://doi.org/10.1007/BFb0054868
21. Hülsing, A., Rijneveld, J., Schanck, J., Schwabe, P.: High-speed key encapsulation from NTRU. In: Fischer, W., Homma, N. (eds.) CHES 2017. LNCS, vol. 10529, pp. 232–252. Springer, Cham (2017). https://doi.org/10.1007/978-3-319-66787-4_12
22. Ishai, Y., Sahai, A., Wagner, D.: Private circuits: securing hardware against probing attacks. In: Boneh, D. (ed.) CRYPTO 2003. LNCS, vol. 2729, pp. 463–481. Springer, Heidelberg (2003). https://doi.org/10.1007/978-3-540-45146-4_27
23. Itoh, T., Tsujii, S.: A fast algorithm for computing multiplicative inverses in GF(2^m) using normal bases. Inf. Comput. **78**(3), 171–177 (1988)
24. Kannwischer, M.J., Rijneveld, J., Schwabe, P., Stoffelen, K.: PQM4: post-quantum crypto library for the ARM cortex-M4. https://github.com/mupq/pqm4
25. Karabulut, E., Alkim, E., Aysu, A.: Single-trace side-channel attacks on ω-small polynomial sampling: with applications to NTRU, NTRU prime, and crystals-dilithium. In: HOST, pp. 35–45. IEEE (2021)
26. Kundu, S., D'Anvers, J.P., Van Beirendonck, M., Karmakar, A., Verbauwhede, I.: Higher-order masked Saber. IACR Cryptol. ePrint Arch., 389 (2022)

27. Li, C.L.: Implementation of polynomial modular inversion in lattice based cryptography on ARM (2021)
28. Melchor, C.A., et al.: Hamming Quasi-Cyclic (HQC) - Third round version (2021)
29. Miller, V.S.: Use of elliptic curves in cryptography. In: Williams, H.C. (ed.) CRYPTO 1985. LNCS, vol. 218, pp. 417–426. Springer, Heidelberg (1986). https://doi.org/10.1007/3-540-39799-X_31
30. Mujdei, C., et al.: Side-channel analysis of lattice-based post-quantum cryptography: exploiting polynomial multiplication. IACR Cryptol. ePrint Arch., 474 (2022)
31. Richter-Brockmann, J., Chen, M.-S., Ghosh, S., Güneysu, T.: Racing BIKE: improved polynomial multiplication and inversion in hardware. IACR Trans. Cryptogr. Hardw. Embed. Syst. **2022**(1), 557–588 (2022)
32. Richter-Brockmann, J., Mono, J., Güneysu, T.: Folding BIKE: scalable hardware implementation for reconfigurable devices. IEEE Trans. Comput. **71**(5), 1204–1215 (2022)
33. Rivest, R.L., Shamir, A., Adleman, L.: A method for obtaining digital signatures and public-key cryptosystems. Commun. ACM **21**(2), 120–126 (1978)
34. Schneider, T., Moradi, A.: Leakage assessment methodology - a clear roadmap for side-channel evaluations. In: Güneysu, T., Handschuh, H. (eds.) CHES 2015. LNCS, vol. 9293, pp. 495–513. Springer, Heidelberg (2015). https://doi.org/10.1007/978-3-662-48324-4_25
35. Schneider, T., Paglialonga, C., Oder, T., Güneysu, T.: Efficiently masking binomial sampling at arbitrary orders for lattice-based crypto. In: Lin, D., Sako, K. (eds.) PKC 2019. LNCS, vol. 11443, pp. 534–564. Springer, Cham (2019). https://doi.org/10.1007/978-3-030-17259-6_18
36. Shor, P.W.: Polynomial-time algorithms for prime factorization and discrete logarithms on a quantum computer. SIAM Rev. **41**(2), 303–332 (1999)
37. Sim, B.Y., Kwon, J., Choi, K.Y., Cho, J., Park, A., Han, D.G.: Novel side-channel attacks on quasi-cyclic code-based cryptography. IACR Trans. Cryptogr. Hardw. Embed. Syst., 180–212 (2019)

A Power Side-Channel Attack
on the Reed-Muller Reed-Solomon
Version of the HQC Cryptosystem

Thomas Schamberger[✉], Lukas Holzbaur, Julian Renner,
Antonia Wachter-Zeh, and Georg Sigl

Technical University of Munich, Munich, Germany
{t.schamberger,lukas.holzbaur,julian.renner,
antonia.wachter-zeh,sigl}@tum.de

Abstract. The code-based post-quantum algorithm Hamming Quasi-Cyclic (HQC) is a fourth round candidate in the NIST standardization project. Since their third round version the authors utilize a new combination of error correcting codes, namely a combination of a Reed-Muller and a Reed-Solomon code, which requires an adaption of published attacks. We identify that the power side-channel attack by Uneo et al. from CHES 2021 does not work in practice as they miss the fact that the implemented Reed-Muller decoder does not have a fixed decoding boundary. In this work we provide a novel attack strategy that again allows for a successful attack. Our attack does not rely on simulation to verify its success but is proven with high probability for the HQC parameter sets. In contrast to the timing side-channel attack by Guo et al. we are able to reduce the required attack queries by a factor of 12 and are able to eliminate the inherent uncertainty of their used timing oracle. We show practical attack results utilizing a power side-channel of the used Reed-Solomon decoder on an ARM Cortex-M4 microcontroller. In addition, we provide a discussion on how or whether our attack strategy is usable with the side-channel targets of mentioned related work. Finally, we use information set decoding to evaluate the remaining attack complexity for partially retrieved secret keys. This work again emphasizes the need for a side-channel secure implementation of all relevant building blocks of HQC.

Keywords: Error correction · HQC · Post-quantum cryptography · Power analysis · Side-channel analysis

1 Introduction

The post-quantum cryptography (PQC) contest of NIST is currently in its fourth round with the goal of evaluating alternative candidates, which are based on other mathematical problems than the lattice-based algorithm CRYSTALS-KYBER that is already chosen for standardization. While the first two rounds

© The Author(s), under exclusive license to Springer Nature Switzerland AG 2022
J. H. Cheon and T. Johansson (Eds.): PQCrypto 2022, LNCS 13512, pp. 327–352, 2022.
https://doi.org/10.1007/978-3-031-17234-2_16

were dominated with research on possible performance improvements and optimized implementations the focus of the third round was mainly on the side-channel security of systems. Research in this direction is again encouraged by NIST in its final report of the third round [10]. This paper discusses a new side-channel attack against the code-based post-quantum cryptosystem Hamming Quasi Cyclic (HQC) [8], which is a candidate in the fourth round of the contest. HQC makes use of the concatenation of two error correcting codes in order to offer a good trade-off between error-correction capability and fast encryption and decryption. The authors changed the used codes in their third round submission from a repetition in combination with a BCH code to a concatenated Reed-Muller and Reed-Solomon code. As most works on side-channel attacks against HQC are based on the former combination, these attacks have to be revised.

Related Work. Attacks on the second-round version of HQC are mostly based on the observation that a side-channel leakage of the used BCH code can be used to construct a decoding oracle that allows to distinguish whether an error has to be corrected by the BCH decoder during decryption. There are timing side-channel attacks [11,16] against a non-constant time implementation of the BCH decoder as well as a power side-channel attack [13].

Attacks against the current version of the HQC cryptosystem, with a combination of a Reed-Muller and Reed-Solomon code, use parts of the implemented variant of the Fujisaki-Okamoto transformation to build a plaintext-checking oracle. This allows distinguishing if crafted ciphertexts decrypt to the same plaintext dependent on the secret key, again resulting in a possible attack on the whole key using multiple queries to the oracle. Xagawa et al. [17] use a fault injection to skip the ciphertext comparison setup of the transformation resulting in direct access to the plaintext, while Ueno et al. [15] attack the used pseudorandom number generator (PRG) required in the transformation through a power side-channel. Both use an adaption of an attack described in [2,5] to the third round version of HQC. Most recent Guo et al. [3] observed that the implemented fixed-weight sampler in combination with the pseudorandom function (PRF) provide a timing side-channel that can be used as a plaintext checking oracle. They claim a success rate of 87% in retrieving the whole key.

Contributions. With their choice of Reed-Muller codes in their third round version of the HQC algorithm the authors implicitly induce a different form of decoder, as for Reed-Muller codes the decoder is usually implemented as a maximum likelihood decoder. This decoder class, in contrast to a bounded-distance decoder, as used for the former repetition code, does not have a distinct decoding boundary. In other words the amount of correctable errors is dependent on the support of the error, which in some cases allows correcting more errors than the specified error correction capability of the code. This characteristic breaks the attack attempts by [2,5], which has been unfortunately missed in [15,17] and therefore described attacks do not work. In this paper we provide an attack strategy that again allows successful power side-channel attacks on the third round version of HQC. Our contributions are as follows:

- We show through simulation and with the use of a counterexample that attacks described in [15,17] are not successful. Thus, we develop a new attack strategy that again allows the retrieval of the secret key through a power side-channel attack.
- While the previous attacks had to rely on simulations or an attack on a few keys to verify the success of their attack strategy, we are able to prove sufficient conditions for the success of our approach. These conditions are fulfilled with very high probability for the parameters of HQC.
- We provide an evaluation of the remaining attack complexity for partially retrieved secret keys with the use of information set decoding.
- Finally, we discuss possible side-channel oracles and show an analysis of the power side-channel from [13] for the updated HQC version.

2 Preliminaries

2.1 Notation

Let $\mathbb{F}_q$ be the finite field of size q. Denote by $\mathbb{F}_2[x_1, \ldots, x_m] = \mathbb{F}_2[\boldsymbol{x}]$ the ring of polynomials in $\boldsymbol{x} = (x_1, \ldots, x_m)$ with coefficients in $\mathbb{F}_2$. For a polynomial $f(\boldsymbol{x}) \in \mathbb{F}_2[\boldsymbol{x}]$ and integer $s \geq 1$, define the evaluation map

$$\mathrm{ev}^{\times s}: \quad \mathbb{F}_2[\boldsymbol{x}] \mapsto \mathbb{F}_2^{s2^m}$$
$$\mathrm{ev}^{\times s}(f(\boldsymbol{x})) \mapsto (\underbrace{f(\boldsymbol{a}), f(\boldsymbol{a}), \ldots, f(\boldsymbol{a})}_{s \text{ times}})_{\boldsymbol{a} \in \mathbb{F}_2^m}.$$

Note that if the degree of each variable $x_1, \ldots, x_m$ is restricted to be at most 1, this is a bijective mapping, i.e., any vector in $\mathbb{F}_2^{2^m}$ can be uniquely associated to a polynomial $f(\boldsymbol{x}) \in \mathbb{F}_2[\boldsymbol{x}]$. For any ordering of the elements $\boldsymbol{a} \in \mathbb{F}_2^{2^m}$ we define the mapping $\chi(\boldsymbol{a})$ from $\mathbb{F}_2^m$ to the indices of the s positions in $\mathrm{ev}^{\times s}(f(\boldsymbol{x}))$ corresponding to $f(\boldsymbol{a})$. For ease of notation, we neglect the dependence of $f(\boldsymbol{x})$ on $\boldsymbol{x}$, if clear from context. By slight abuse of notation, we define the Hamming weight $\mathrm{HW}^{\times s}(f) := \mathrm{HW}^{\times s}(\mathrm{ev}^{\times s}(f))$ and Hamming distance $d^{\times s}(f, f') := d(\mathrm{ev}^{\times s}(f), \mathrm{ev}^{\times s}(f'))$ of polynomials via the respective evaluation map. The support of a polynomial is defined to be $\mathrm{supp}^{\times s}(f) := \{\chi(\boldsymbol{a}) \mid f(\boldsymbol{a}) \neq 0, \boldsymbol{a} \in \mathbb{F}_2^m\}$. If $s = 1$ we omit the $\times 1$ superscript from our notation.

We define $\mathbb{F}_2^{m \times n}$ to be the set of all $m \times n$ matrices over $\mathbb{F}_2$, $\mathbb{F}_2^n = \mathbb{F}_2^{1 \times n}$ for the set of all row vectors of length n over $\mathbb{F}_2$, and define the set of integers $[a, b] := \{i : a \leq i \leq b\}$. We index rows and columns of $m \times n$ matrices by $0, \ldots, m - 1$ and $0, \ldots, n - 1$, where the entry in the i-th row and j-th column of the matrix $\boldsymbol{A}$ is denoted by $A_{i,j}$.

The Hamming weight of a vector $\boldsymbol{a}$ is indicated by $\mathrm{HW}(\boldsymbol{a})$ and the Hamming support of $\boldsymbol{a}$ is denoted by $\mathrm{supp}(\boldsymbol{a}) := \{i \in \mathbb{Z} : a_i \neq 0\}$. Let $\mathcal{V}$ be a vector space of dimension n over $\mathbb{F}_2$. We define the product of $u, v \in V$ as $uv = u\,\mathrm{rot}(v)^\top = v\,\mathrm{rot}(u)^\top = vu$, where

$$\mathrm{rot}(v) := \begin{bmatrix} v_0 & v_{n-1} & \cdots & v_1 \\ v_1 & v_0 & \cdots & v_2 \\ \vdots & \vdots & \ddots & \vdots \\ v_{n-1} & v_{n-2} & \cdots & v_0 \end{bmatrix} \in \mathbb{F}_2^{n \times n}.$$

As a consequence of this definition, elements of V can be interpreted as polynomials in the ring $\mathcal{R} := \mathbb{F}_2[X]/(X^n - 1)$.

2.2   HQC

The HQC scheme consists of a public code $\mathcal{C} \subseteq \mathbb{F}_2^n$ of length n and dimension k, where it is assumed that both an efficient encoding algorithm **Encode** and an efficient decoding algorithm **Decode** are known publicly. In the following we describe the HQC algorithm as submitted to the third round of the NIST postquantum standardization contest with its specification last updated in June 2021. We start by introducing the PKE version of the algorithm as shown in Algorithms 1, 2 and 3. Within these algorithms several polynomials are uniformly sampled from $\mathcal{R}$, denoted as $\xleftarrow{\$}$ with the optional argument of specifying the Hamming weight w of the polynomial as well as the randomness θ used to initialize the sampler. The parameter sets of HQC are shown in Table 1.

Algorithm 1: Key-Gen	**Algorithm 2:** Encrypt	**Algorithm 3:** Decrypt
Input: param	**Input:** m, pk, θ	**Input:** $\mathrm{sk} = (x, y)$
Output: pk, sk	**Output:** c	$c = (u, v)$
1 $h \xleftarrow{\$} \mathcal{R}$	1 $e' \xleftarrow{\$(w_e, \theta)} \mathcal{R}$	**Output:** m
2 $(x, y) \xleftarrow{\$(w)} \mathcal{R}^2$	2 $(r_1, r_2) \xleftarrow{\$(w_r, \theta)} \mathcal{R}^2$	1 $v' \leftarrow v - uy$
3 $s \leftarrow x + hy$	3 $u \leftarrow r_1 + hr_2$	2 $m \leftarrow \mathbf{Decode}(v')$
4 $\mathrm{pk} = (h, s)$	4 $v \leftarrow \mathbf{Encode}(m) + sr_2 + e'$	3 **return** m
5 $\mathrm{sk} = (x, y)$	5 **return** $c = (u, v)$	
6 **return** pk, sk		

Table 1. Parameter sets of HQC [9]

	Shortened RS code $[n_1, k, d_{RS}]$	Duplicated RM code $[n_2, k_{RM}, d_{RM}, s]$	n	w	$w_r = w_e$
HQC-128	[46, 16, 31]	[384, 8, 192, 3]	17,669	66	75
HQC-192	[56, 24, 33]	[640, 8, 320, 5]	35,851	100	114
HQC-256	[90, 32, 49]	[640, 8, 320, 5]	57,637	131	149

The HQC authors use the PKE version of HQC to construct an IND-CCA2 secure KEM. Using this KEM, a random shared secret K can be exchanged where the sender applies encapsulation (Algorithm 4) and the receiver decapsulation (Algorithm 5). These algorithms use three different hash functions $\mathcal{G}, \mathcal{H}$, and $\mathcal{K}$, which are based on SHAKE256 with 512 bits of output. In order to counteract chosen-chipertext attacks, the decrypted message is re-encrypted and compared to the original ciphertext input. Only if both ciphertexts are equal K gets released otherwise the decapsulation is aborted. In order for the re-encryption to be possible the sampling of the random elements has to be deterministic, which is ensured by deriving a seed from the message which is used to initialize the sampler.

Algorithm 4: Encapsulate	**Algorithm 5:** Decapsulate
Input: pk	**Input:** sk, c, d
Output: $K, c = (u, v), d$	**Output:** K
1 $m \xleftarrow{\$} \mathbb{F}_2^k$	1 $m' \leftarrow$ Decrypt(sk, c)
2 $\theta \leftarrow \mathcal{G}(m)$	2 $\theta' \leftarrow \mathcal{G}(m')$
3 $c \leftarrow$ Encrypt(pk, m, θ)	3 $c' \leftarrow$ Encrypt(pk, m', θ')
4 $K \leftarrow \mathcal{K}(m, c)$	4 **if** $c \neq c'$ *and* $d \neq \mathcal{H}(m')$ **then**
5 $d \leftarrow \mathcal{H}(m)$	5 $\quad$ abort
	6 **else**
	7 $\quad K \leftarrow \mathcal{K}(m, c)$

2.3 Choice of Error Correcting Code $\mathcal{C}$

For the third round version of HQC the code $\mathcal{C}$ is instantiated as a concatenated code with a Reed-Muller (RM) code as the inner and a Reed-Solomon (RS) code as the outer code. The function **Encode** describes the encoding of a message $m \in \mathbb{F}_2^k$ into $\tilde{m} \in \mathbb{F}_2^{n_1 n_2}$ using the concatenated code. First the outer RS code is used to encode m into $m_1 \in \mathbb{F}_{2^8}^{n_1}$, followed by encoding each coordinate $m_{1,i}$ of m_1 into $\tilde{m}_{1,i} \in \mathbb{F}_2^{n_2}$ using the inner duplicated RM code. The duplicated encoding works in two phases. First, each $m_{1,i}$ is encoded with the underlying [128, 8, 64]-RM code to obtain $\bar{m}_{1,i}$, which is then duplicated based on the multiplicity s (see Table 1) resulting in $\tilde{m}_{1,i}$. In other words the final encoding result is constructed as $\tilde{m} = (\tilde{m}_{1,0}, \ldots, \tilde{m}_{1,n_1-1}) \in \mathbb{F}_2^{n_1 n_2}$.

The function **Decode** describes the decoding of an input in $\mathbb{F}_2^{n_1 n_2}$ to a message $m \in \mathbb{F}_2^k$. First the individual $\tilde{m}_{1,i}$ are decoded with the duplicated RM decoder ($\mathfrak{D}_{\mathcal{RM}}$), which results in the input to RS decoder ($\mathfrak{D}_{\mathcal{RS}}$) as an element in $\mathbb{F}_{2^8}^{n_1}$. Finally, the RS decoding results in the message $m \in \mathbb{F}_2^k$.

Definition 1 (First Order Reed-Muller Code). *Denote* $x = (x_1, \ldots, x_m)$. *Define the code* $\mathcal{RM}^{\times s}(m)$ *to be*

$$\mathcal{RM}^{\times s}(m) = \left\{ \mathrm{ev}^{\times s}(f(x)) \mid f(x) \in \mathbb{F}_2[x], \deg(f(x)) \leq 1 \right\}.$$

We refer to s as the multiplicity of the RM code. If $s = 1$ we omit the superscript and write $\mathcal{RM}(m)$.

For details on RM codes and their properties we refer the reader to [7, Chap. 13].

3   Novel Oracle-Based Side-Channel Attack

In this section we describe our chosen-ciphertext attack against the HQC cryptosystem which is able to retrieve the secret key polynomial y during decryption/decapsulation. We start by describing the support distribution of y, which is essential for the attack. In a second step we introduce the general idea of our attack and focus on the characteristics of RM codes that render some published attacks unsuccessful. As a third step we describe our attack strategy based on a close-to-zero oracle. We additionally provide attack results and compare the required oracle queries to related work. Finally, we show how to retrieve the secret key from partial attack results using information set decoding.

3.1   Support Distribution of y

With the proposed HQC parameter sets, y is sampled as a sparse polynomial with $\mathrm{HW}(y) = w$. As our attack targets each duplicated RM codeword of length n_2 individually, we split y into corresponding chunks $y_i^{(0)}$ with $0 \leq i \leq n_1$, as shown in Fig. 1. In order to prevent algebraic attacks, y is chosen to be of length n, which is the smallest primitive prime greater than $n_1 n_2$. Therefore, y contains a second part $y^{(1)}$ consisting of the remaining $n - n_1 n_2$ bits.

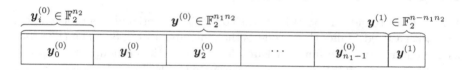

Fig. 1. Different parts of the secret key $y \in \mathbb{F}_2^n$.

Our proof of the attack is defined for a maximum Hamming weight of all $y_i^{(0)}$. For this we define $y_{w,max} = \max\{\mathrm{HW}(y_0^{(0)}), \ldots, \mathrm{HW}(y_{n_1-1}^{(0)})\}$ as the maximum Hamming weight of all chunks of $y^{(0)}$. We determine the probabilities of certain $y_{w,max}$ by simulating the weight distribution of 10 million samples of $y^{(0)}$ with the results shown in Table 2.

With our attack strategy we are able to attack $y^{(0)}$, as only this part acts as an input to the decoder. Nevertheless, we discuss methods to retrieve the whole y in Sect. 3.2. The probability that $\mathrm{HW}(y^{(1)}) > 0$ can be computed by $1 - \binom{n_1 \cdot n_2}{w} / \binom{n}{w}$. Considering the parameters of HQC-128, HQC-192, and HQC-256 we determine the respective probabilities to be 1.85%, 3.02%, and 8.07%. This means that in most cases it suffices to determine the $y^{(0)}$ because there are no ones in $y^{(1)}$.

Table 2. Probabilities that $y^{(0)}$ is generated such that the weight of $y_i^{(0)}$ for $i = 0, \ldots, n_1 - 1$ is at most $y_{w,max}$.

$y_{w,max}$	1	2	3	4	5	6	7	8	9
HQC-128	0%	≈0%	3.75%	48.77%	86.49%	97.44%	99.59%	99.94%	99.99%
HQC-192	0%	≈0%	0.01%	10.74%	57.96%	88.50%	97.57%	99.56%	99.93%
HQC-256	0%	≈0%	0.09%	20.83%	71.87%	93.94%	98.96%	99.84%	99.97%

3.2 General Attack Idea

With our chosen-ciphertext attack we are able to determine all parts of the secret key $y^{(0)}$ individually and in sequential manner. Within the Hamming Quasi-Cyclic (HQC) algorithm the only operation utilizing the secret key is the decoding of the vector $v' = v - uy$ during decryption (c.f. Algorithm 3). By setting $u = (1, 0 \ldots, 0) \in \mathbb{F}_2^n$ the decoder input results in $v' = v - y$. As v is part of the ciphertext $c = (u, v)$, it is controllable by the attacker. By setting it to a valid codeword $\in \mathcal{C}$, y can be seen as an error that has to be corrected by the decoder. Note that due to the sparseness of y it is sufficient to only retrieve its support.

Now the general idea of the attack is to choose v such that the decoding result depends on $y_i^{(0)}$, revealing its support. In the case of HQC an attacker requires access to the individual RM decoder results, as the respective input consists of $y_i^{(0)}$ subtracted from its corresponding part of v. It is not possible to directly attack the decapsulation of HQC (Algorithm 5), as it includes a check for the validity of the ciphertext that does not reveal information about m in case of failure. Nevertheless, a side-channel can be used in order to construct an oracle that again reveals information about the decoding result. We therefore construct an oracle that is able to determine whether the RM decoder decoded to the all-zero or a non-zero codeword in a given position. The oracle is formally defined in Definition 2. We discuss different side-channels, which can be used to construct this oracle, in Sect. 4.

Definition 2 (Close-to-zero Oracle). *Let $\mathcal{C}$ be an $\mathcal{RM}(m)$ code. Define $\mathfrak{D}_0^e : \mathbb{F}_q^n \mapsto \{\text{True}, \text{False}\}$ with $e \in \mathbb{F}_q^n$ to be the function given by*

$$\mathfrak{D}_0^e(r) = \begin{cases} \text{True}, & \text{if } \mathfrak{D}_{\mathcal{RM}}(r + e) = 0, \\ \text{False}, & \text{else}, \end{cases}$$

where $\mathfrak{D}_{\mathcal{RM}}$ denotes a decoder for the RM code.

By querying the oracle and therefore having access to the decoding result our attack strategy as well as the related work is based on two steps. First, an input has to be found (or set for some attacks) that, after the subtraction of the corresponding $y_i^{(0)}$, lies exactly at the decoding boundary of the RM decoder. An example is to find an input that lies exactly one error above the border meaning the input results in a decoding error, i.e. in the decoder not returning the all-zero codeword $\mathbf{0}$, and therefore the oracle returns False. This implies that if we set an additional bit in the input, which is in the support of $\mathbf{y}_i^{(0)}$, we reduce the error resulting in a successful decoding indicated by the oracle as True. Now in the second attack step we can query the oracle by successively inverting each bit of the input we found in the first step. In this process an oracle result of True, i.e., a successful decoding to the all-zero codeword, indicates that this position is in the support of $\mathbf{y}_i^{(0)}$. This allows to retrieve the whole support of the attacked secret key block. By repeating this approach for all n_1 RM blocks we can retrieve the complete $\mathbf{y}^{(0)}$.

Limitations of Previous Works. With the change of the used codes in the third round version of the HQC, the first attack step, namely finding an input that lies at the decoding border of the internal code, has to be changed due to the use of a different decoder type. This is the case as the decoder of the now used RM code is implemented as a maximum likelihood (ML) decoder, where ties are resolved in favor of the word of smaller lexicographical order. An ML decoder is formally defined as follows:

Definition 3 (Maximum likelihood (ML) decoder). *Let C be an $[n, k]_q$ code. Define $\mathfrak{D}_{\mathsf{ML}} : \mathbb{F}_q^n \mapsto C$ to be a function returning the codeword that maximizes the probability $P(\mathbf{r}|\mathbf{c})$, i.e.,*

$$\mathfrak{D}_{\mathsf{ML}}(\mathbf{r}) = \arg\max_{\mathbf{c} \in C} P(\mathbf{r}|\mathbf{c}).$$

If this choice is not unique, it returns the word that is smaller in lexicographical order.

In the Hamming metric and without considering soft information an ML decoder translates to a function returning the codeword of the smallest Hamming distance to the given vector, i.e., $\mathfrak{D}_{\mathsf{ML}}(\mathbf{r}) = \arg\min_{\mathbf{c} \in C} d(\mathbf{r}, \mathbf{c})$. Note that ML decoding is known to be very complex and therefore rarely used in practice. However, for a few code classes, such as first-order RM codes, efficient decoders are known, a fact that is exploited in this system. Most other systems based on algebraic codes, such as Classic McEliece [1], instead employ bounded-distance decoders, which decode *any* error up to a given weight and fail if no codeword is within this specified radius[1]. On the other hand, for a symmetric memoryless channel an ML decoder *always* returns (one of) the codeword(s) closest to the received word, regardless of its distance to the received word. Importantly, this

---

[1] The previous version of the HQC system employed repetition codes of odd length instead of RM codes. It is well-known that this class of codes is *perfect*, i.e., the unique decoding error balls centered on the codewords fill the entire space. In this specific case, a bounded-distance decoder with radius $(d-1)/2$ is equivalent to an ML decoder. Note that first-order RM codes are *not perfect*, so this special case does not apply here.

implies that the behavior of this decoder does not only depend on the *number of errors* but also on the *positions of these errors*. However, this independence of the error positions in a bounded-distance decoder is essential to some known attack strategies such as [2,5]. Hence, while the setup might look similar, these methods cannot be directly applied to a system employing an ML decoder instead of a bounded-distance decoder. For instance, the side-channel attack in [17, Sect. C.7][2] claims that the method for determining an additive error vector from oracle outputs, given in [2, Fig. 7], also applies the third round version of HQC. In Appendix A we show that this leads to incorrect outputs of the algorithm, which are caused by exactly this difference in behavior between an ML and a bounded-distance decoder, rendering their described attack unsuccessful.

Retrieval of $y^{(1)}$. If $y^{(0)}$ has been retrieved completely and error free, we can use the published linear algebraic approach shown in [13] to get the remaining part of the secret key defined as $y^{(1)}$. Assuming that $\mathrm{HW}(y^{(1)}) \leq 2$ the resulting work factor of this approach for HQC-128, HQC-192 and HQC-256 is $2^{19.02}$, $2^{24.08}$ and $2^{30.32}$, respectively. In the case that $y^{(0)}$ is only partially retrieved we have to use information set decoding, as described in Sect. 3.4, which directly retrieves the complete secret key y from the partial information.

3.3 Description of the Attack Strategy

In this section we introduce our attack strategy that considers the characteristics of the RM ML decoder and therefore again allows for the correct retrieval of $y^{(0)}$. It is based on two algorithms, where first the strategy to find an input word that lies at the decoder border is described as Algorithm 6 and then the strategy to retrieve the support of the error with the use of multiple of these words as Algorithm 7. We start by introducing the reasoning for our strategy leading to a formal proof to successfully retrieve $y^{(0)}$ if the Hamming weight of the respective RM block is smaller than $\frac{d_{\mathcal{RM}}}{4}$. Our simulation of $y_{w,max}$ (see Table 2) indicates that this condition holds for nearly all possible keys of HQC, as 99.9% of simulated keys show a $y_{w,max}$ of 9 with $d_{\mathcal{RM}}$ being 192 for HQC-128 and 320 for HQC-192/HQC-256 (c.f. Table 1), respectively. We conclude this section with a discussion of the required oracle calls of our strategy in comparison to related work.

---

[2] Note that the description of the attack in [15] is based on the same assumptions, as it directly refers to [17].

Algorithm 6: FindWordAtBorder	**Algorithm 7:** FindError
Input : Oracle function $\mathfrak{D}_0^e$ Sets $\hat{\mathcal{I}}, \check{\mathcal{I}} \subset [0, n_2 - 1]$	**Input** : Oracle function $\mathfrak{D}_0^e$ Sets $\mathcal{I}_1, \mathcal{I}_2 \subset [0, n_2 - 1]$
Output: Vector $r \in \mathbb{F}_2^{n_2}$	**Output:** Vector $\tilde{e} \in \mathbb{F}_2^{n_2}$
1 $r \leftarrow 0$	1 $\tilde{e} \leftarrow 0$
2 for $\xi \in \hat{\mathcal{I}} \cap \check{\mathcal{I}}$ do	2 for $\hat{\mathcal{I}} \in \{\mathcal{I}_1, [0, n_2 - 1] \setminus \mathcal{I}_1\}$ do
3 $\quad$ if $\mathfrak{D}_0^e(r) = $ True then	3 $\quad$ for $\check{\mathcal{I}} \in \{\mathcal{I}_2, [0, n_2 - 1] \setminus \mathcal{I}_2\}$ do
4 $\quad\quad$ $r_\xi \leftarrow 1$	4 $\quad\quad$ $r \leftarrow$
	$\quad\quad$ FindWordAtBorder($\mathfrak{D}_0^e, \hat{\mathcal{I}}, \check{\mathcal{I}}$)
5 $\quad$ else	5 $\quad\quad$ $\hat{e} \leftarrow r$
6 $\quad\quad$ return Vector $r \in \mathbb{F}_2^{n_2}$	6 $\quad\quad$ for $\xi \in \hat{\mathcal{I}} \cap \check{\mathcal{I}}$ do
7 for $\xi \in \hat{\mathcal{I}} \setminus \check{\mathcal{I}}$ do	7 $\quad\quad\quad$ $r_\xi \leftarrow r_\xi + 1$
8 $\quad$ if $\mathfrak{D}_0^e(r) = $ True then	8 $\quad\quad\quad$ if $\mathfrak{D}_0^e(r) = $ True then
9 $\quad\quad$ $r_\xi \leftarrow 1$	9 $\quad\quad\quad\quad$ $\hat{e}_\xi \leftarrow \hat{e}_\xi + 1$
10 $\quad$ else	10 $\quad\quad\quad$ $r_\xi \leftarrow r_\xi + 1$
11 $\quad\quad$ return Vector $r \in \mathbb{F}_2^{n_2}$	11 $\quad\quad$ $\tilde{e}_{\hat{\mathcal{I}} \cap \check{\mathcal{I}}} \leftarrow \hat{e}_{\hat{\mathcal{I}} \cap \check{\mathcal{I}}}$
	12 return Vector $\tilde{e} \in \mathbb{F}_2^{n_2}$

To begin, we show some general results on the intersection of the supports of $\mathcal{RM}(m)$ codewords. Note that there exists an extensive literature on RM codes and their supports are well understood. For completeness, we nevertheless include the following statement in the form required to prove the main results of this section. As the statements and proofs in the following heavily rely on the properties of the multivariate polynomials associated with each RM codeword, we denote all vectors in the following by the polynomial which results in the respective vector when evaluated in $\mathbb{F}_2^{2^m}$.

Lemma 1. *Consider two polynomials* $\hat{p}, \check{p} \in \mathbb{F}_2[x]$ *with* $\deg(\hat{p}) = \deg(\check{p}) = 1$ *and* $\check{p} \notin \{\hat{p}, \hat{p} + 1\}$. *Denote* $d = 2^{m-1}$. *Then, for any* $f \in \mathcal{RM}(m)$ *we have*

$$|\operatorname{supp}(f) \cap \operatorname{supp}(\hat{p}\check{p})| = \operatorname{HW}(f\hat{p}\check{p}) = \begin{cases} 0, & \text{if } f \in \{0, \hat{p}+1, \check{p}+1, \hat{p}+\check{p}\} \\ \frac{d}{2}, & \text{if } f \in \{1, \hat{p}, \check{p}, \hat{p}+\check{p}+1\} \\ \frac{d}{4}, & \text{else.} \end{cases}$$

Proof. The first case follows from observing that $f\hat{p}\check{p} = 0$ for these polynomials[3]. It is well-known that any codeword $p \in \mathcal{RM}(m)$, except the all-zero and the all-one word, i.e., any word with $\deg(p) = 1$, is of weight $d = 2^{m-1}$. Since $\deg(\hat{p}) = \deg(\check{p}) = 1$ and $\check{p} \notin \{\hat{p}, \hat{p}+1\}$ we have $\deg(\hat{p}+\check{p}) = 1$. Therefore, $\operatorname{HW}(\hat{p}+\check{p}) = d$ and we get

$$\operatorname{HW}(\hat{p}+\check{p}) = \operatorname{HW}(\hat{p}) + \operatorname{HW}(\check{p}) - 2\operatorname{HW}(\hat{p}\check{p})$$

---

[3] Note that $f^2 = f$ in $\mathbb{F}_2[x]$, so $(\hat{p}+1)\hat{p}\check{p} = \hat{p}^2\check{p} + \hat{p}\check{p} = 2\hat{p}\check{p} = 0$.

$$d = 2d - 2\mathrm{HW}(\hat{p}\check{p})$$
$$\frac{d}{2} = \mathrm{HW}(\hat{p}\check{p}).$$

The second case follows since we have $\mathrm{supp}(\hat{p}\check{p}) \subset \mathrm{supp}(f)$ for any $f \in \{1, \hat{p}, \check{p}, \hat{p}+\check{p}+1\}$. Now consider some $f \in \mathcal{RM}(m)\backslash\{0, \hat{p}+1, \check{p}+1, \hat{p}+\check{p}, 1, \hat{p}, \check{p}, \hat{p}+\check{p}+1\}$ and note that $\deg(f) = 1$. Observe that the supports of the polynomials $\{\hat{p}\check{p}, \hat{p}(\check{p} + 1), (\hat{p} + 1)\check{p}, (\hat{p} + 1)(\check{p} + 1)\}$ partition the 2^m codeword positions. Hence, by the pigeonhole principle, there exists some $\bar{p} \in \{\hat{p}(\check{p} + 1), (\hat{p} + 1)\check{p}, (\hat{p} + 1)(\check{p} + 1)\}$ with

$$\mathrm{HW}(\bar{p}f) \geq \left\lceil \frac{\mathrm{HW}(f) - \mathrm{HW}(\hat{p}\check{p}f)}{3} \right\rceil \geq \frac{d - \mathrm{HW}(\hat{p}\check{p}f)}{3}.$$

Further, it is easy to check that $\hat{p}\check{p} + \bar{p} \in \{\hat{p}, \check{p}, \hat{p}+\check{p}+1\}$, which implies $\deg(\hat{p}\check{p} + \bar{p}) = 1$ and $\mathrm{HW}(\hat{p}\check{p} + \bar{p}) = d$. Now, towards a contradiction, assume $\mathrm{HW}(f\hat{p}\check{p}) > \frac{d}{4}$. Then, we have

$$
\begin{aligned}
d(\hat{p}\check{p} + \bar{p}, f) &= \mathrm{HW}(\hat{p}\check{p} + \bar{p}) + \mathrm{HW}(f) - 2\mathrm{HW}((\hat{p}\check{p} + \bar{p})f) \\
&= 2d - 2(\mathrm{HW}(\hat{p}\check{p}f) + \mathrm{HW}(\bar{p}f)) \\
&\leq 2\left(d - \left(\mathrm{HW}(\hat{p}\check{p}f) + \frac{d - \mathrm{HW}(\hat{p}\check{p}f)}{3}\right)\right) \\
&\leq 2\left(d - \frac{d + 2\mathrm{HW}(\hat{p}\check{p}f)}{3}\right) \\
&< 2\left(d - \frac{d + 2\frac{d}{4}}{3}\right) = d.
\end{aligned}
$$

As both $\hat{p}\check{p} + \bar{p}$ and f are in $\mathcal{RM}(m)$, this can only be true if $\hat{p}\check{p} + \bar{p} = f$. However, we have $\hat{p}\check{p} + \bar{p} \in \{\hat{p}, \check{p}, \hat{p} + \check{p} + 1\}$ and therefore, by definition of f, a contradiction. Now assume there exists an $f' \in \mathcal{RM}(m)\backslash\{0, \hat{p} + 1, \check{p} + 1, \hat{p} + \check{p}, 1, \hat{p}, \check{p}, \hat{p} + \check{p} + 1\}$ with $\mathrm{HW}(f'\hat{p}\check{p}) < \frac{d}{4}$ and note that this set is closed under inversions, i.e., also contains $f' + 1$. Then, we have $\mathrm{HW}((f' + 1)\hat{p}\check{p}) > \frac{d}{4}$, which cannot be true, as shown above. $\square$

Using these results, we now show that the output of Algorithm 6 always results in a word that causes a specific ML decoding result, under certain non-restrictive assumptions.

Lemma 2. *Denote by $\hat{p}, \check{p} \in \mathbb{F}_2[x]$ two polynomials with $\deg(\hat{p}) = \deg(\check{p}) = 1$ and $\check{p} \notin \{\hat{p}, \hat{p} + 1\}$. Then, for $r = \mathsf{FindWordAtBorder}(\mathfrak{D}_0^e, \mathrm{supp}(\hat{p}), \mathrm{supp}(\check{p}))$ as in Algorithm 6 it holds that $\mathfrak{D}_{\mathcal{RM}}(r + e) \in \{\hat{p}, \check{p}, \hat{p} + \check{p} + 1\}$ and the decision is not the result of a tie in the distance with some other word $\mathcal{RM}(m)\backslash\mathcal{F}$.*

Proof. Denote $\mathcal{F} = \{\hat{p}, \check{p}, \hat{p} + \check{p} + 1\}$. First note that the algorithm always returns a word r such that $\mathfrak{D}_0^e(r) = \mathsf{False}$. Clearly, this statement would only be false if $\mathfrak{D}_0^e(r) = \mathsf{True}$ for all steps in the for loops of Lines 2 and 7. To see that this cannot be the case, consider the $\frac{d}{4}$-th iteration in the for-loop of Line 7. In this iteration we have $\mathrm{HW}(r) = \frac{3}{4}d$ and $\mathrm{supp}(r) \subset \hat{\mathcal{I}} = \mathrm{supp}(\hat{p})$, where $\hat{p} \in \mathcal{RM}(m)$ by definition. It follows that $r + e$ is in the unique decoding ball of $\hat{p}$, since

$$
\begin{aligned}
d(r + e, \hat{p}) &= \mathrm{HW}(\hat{p} + r + e) \\
&\leq \mathrm{HW}(\hat{p} + r) + \mathrm{HW}(e) \\
&= d - \mathrm{HW}(r) + \mathrm{HW}(e) < \frac{d}{2}.
\end{aligned}
$$

In this case, an ML decoder for the RM code would decide for $\hat{p}$, and it holds that $\mathfrak{D}_0^e(r) = \mathsf{False}$ and $\mathfrak{D}_{\mathcal{RM}}(r + e) = \hat{p} \in \{\hat{p}, \check{p}, \hat{p} + \check{p} + 1\}$. Note that this also implies $\mathrm{HW}(\hat{p}(\check{p} + 1)r) \leq \frac{d}{4}$ for any returned word r. Now consider the case that Algorithm 6 terminates in the for loop of Line 2, i.e., for an r with $\mathrm{supp}(r) \subseteq (\hat{\mathcal{I}} \cap \check{\mathcal{I}})$. For this case, we show a statement that is slightly stronger than required, namely, we prove that for any $f \in \mathcal{RM}(m) \backslash (\mathcal{F} \cup \{0\})$ we have $d(r + e, 0) < d(r + e, f)$, which implies that f cannot be the outcome of an ML decoder[4]. To begin, observe that $\mathfrak{D}_{\mathcal{RM}}(r + e) \neq 1$ since $\mathrm{HW}(r + e) \leq \mathrm{HW}(r) + \mathrm{HW}(e) < \frac{n}{4} + \frac{d}{4}$ and therefore $d(r + e, 0) = \mathrm{HW}(r + e) < n - \mathrm{HW}(r + e) = d(r + e, 1)$, so the ML decoder does not decode to the all-one word in this case. If $\mathrm{HW}(r) \leq \frac{d}{4}$, we get $\mathrm{HW}(r + e) < \frac{d}{2}$ and an ML decoder always decides for 0, i.e., $\mathfrak{D}_0^e = \mathsf{True}$, so we can assume that $\mathrm{HW}(r) > \frac{d}{4}$ when Algorithm 6 terminates. Denote $\bar{\mathcal{F}} = \mathcal{RM}(m) \backslash (\mathcal{F} \cup \{0, 1\})$. Now consider some $f \in \bar{\mathcal{F}}$ and note that $\mathrm{supp}(\hat{p}\check{p}) = \hat{\mathcal{I}} \cap \check{\mathcal{I}}$. Then, we have

$$
\begin{aligned}
d(r + e, f) &= \mathrm{HW}(f + r + e) \\
&\geq \mathrm{HW}(f + r) - \mathrm{HW}(e) \\
&= \mathrm{HW}(\hat{p}\check{p}(f + r)) + \mathrm{HW}((\hat{p}\check{p} + 1)(f + r)) - \mathrm{HW}(e) \\
&= \mathrm{HW}(\hat{p}\check{p}(f + r)) + \mathrm{HW}((\hat{p}\check{p} + 1)f) - \mathrm{HW}(e) \\
&\geq \mathrm{HW}(r) - \mathrm{HW}(\hat{p}\check{p}f) + \mathrm{HW}((\hat{p}\check{p} + 1)f) - \mathrm{HW}(e).
\end{aligned}
$$

Since $f \notin (\mathcal{F} \cup \{0, 1\})$ Lemma 1 gives $\mathrm{HW}(\hat{p}\check{p}f) \leq \frac{d}{4}$, so $-\mathrm{HW}(\hat{p}\check{p}f) + \mathrm{HW}((\hat{p}\check{p} + 1)f) \geq \frac{3}{4}d$. Therefore, we get $d(r + e, f) > \mathrm{HW}(r) + \frac{3}{4}d - \frac{1}{4}d = \mathrm{HW}(r) + \frac{1}{4}d$. On the other hand, the distance of $r + e$ to 0 is

$$
\begin{aligned}
d(r + e, 0) &= \mathrm{HW}(r + e) \\
&\leq \mathrm{HW}(r) + \mathrm{HW}(e) \\
&< \mathrm{HW}(r) + \frac{1}{4}d.
\end{aligned}
$$

Therefore, if Algorithm 6 terminates in the for-loop of Line 2, the outcome of the ML decoder cannot be a word of $\bar{\mathcal{F}} \cup \{1\}$, which implies that $\mathfrak{D}_{\mathcal{RM}}(r) \in \mathcal{F}$. Now consider the case where Algorithm 6 terminates in the for-loop of Line 7. Note that, by definition of the sets $\hat{\mathcal{I}}$ and $\check{\mathcal{I}}$, we have $\mathrm{supp}(r) \subset \mathrm{supp}(\hat{p})$ and,

---

[4] Note that this does *not* imply that the outcome is 0, since one of the words of $\mathcal{F}$ could still be closer to $r + e$ than 0.

since the for-loop of Line 2 is completed, it holds that $\mathrm{HW}(\hat{p}\check{p}r) = \frac{d}{2}$. To begin, observe that

$$d(r + e, \hat{p}) = \mathrm{HW}(\hat{p} + r + e)$$
$$\geq \mathrm{HW}(\hat{p} + r) + \mathrm{HW}(e)$$
$$\stackrel{\text{(a)}}{=} d - \mathrm{HW}(r) + \mathrm{HW}(e) < \frac{5}{4}d - \mathrm{HW}(r), \tag{1}$$

where (a) holds because $\mathrm{supp}(r) \subset \mathrm{supp}(\hat{p})$ and $\mathrm{HW}(\hat{p}) = d$. It follows immediately from Lemma 1 that an $\mathcal{RM}(m)$ code can be partitioned by

$$\mathcal{RM}(m) = \{0\} \cup \{1\} \cup \{\hat{p} + 1\} \cup \mathcal{F} \cup \{f \mid \mathrm{HW}(\hat{p}\check{p}f) = 0, \mathrm{HW}(\hat{p}(\check{p} + 1)f) = \frac{d}{2}\}$$
$$\cup \{f \mid \mathrm{HW}(\hat{p}\check{p}f) = \frac{d}{4}, \mathrm{HW}(\hat{p}(\check{p} + 1)f) = \frac{d}{4}\}.$$

The statement holds if the distance to the words in all subsets except $\{0\}$ and $\mathcal{F}$ is larger than Eq. 1. We consider each subset separately:

- For $f = 1$ we have

$$d(r + e, f) = \mathrm{HW}(f + r + e)$$
$$\geq \mathrm{HW}(f) - \mathrm{HW}(r) - \mathrm{HW}(e)$$
$$> 2d - \mathrm{HW}(r) - \frac{d}{4}$$
$$> \frac{7}{4}d - \mathrm{HW}(r) > d(r + e, \hat{p}).$$

- For $f = \hat{p} + 1$ we have

$$d(r + e, f) = \mathrm{HW}(f + r + e)$$
$$\geq \mathrm{HW}(f + r) - \mathrm{HW}(e)$$
$$= \mathrm{HW}(\hat{p}(f + r)) + \mathrm{HW}((\hat{p} + 1)(f + r)) - \mathrm{HW}(e)$$
$$= \mathrm{HW}(\hat{p}r) + \mathrm{HW}((\hat{p} + 1)f) - \mathrm{HW}(e)$$
$$= \mathrm{HW}(r) + \mathrm{HW}(f) - \mathrm{HW}(e)$$
$$= 2\mathrm{HW}(r) + d - \mathrm{HW}(r) - \mathrm{HW}(e)$$
$$\stackrel{\text{(a)}}{\geq} 2d - \mathrm{HW}(r) - \mathrm{HW}(e)$$
$$> \frac{7}{4}d - \mathrm{HW}(r) > d(r + e, \hat{p}),$$

where (a) holds because $\mathrm{HW}(r) \geq \mathrm{HW}(\hat{p}\check{p}r) = \frac{d}{2}$, as noted above.

- For any $f \in \mathcal{RM}(m)$ with $\mathrm{HW}(\hat{p}\check{p}f) = 0$ and $\mathrm{HW}(\hat{p}(\check{p} + 1)f) \geq \frac{d}{4}$ we have

$$d(r + e, f) = \mathrm{HW}(f + r + e)$$

$$\geq \mathrm{HW}(f+r) - \mathrm{HW}(e)$$
$$= \mathrm{HW}(\hat{p}\breve{p}(f+r)) + \mathrm{HW}((\hat{p}\breve{p}+1)(f+r)) - \mathrm{HW}(e)$$
$$\geq \mathrm{HW}(\hat{p}\breve{p}r) + \underbrace{\mathrm{HW}((\hat{p}\breve{p}+1)f)}_{=\mathrm{HW}(f)=d} - \mathrm{HW}((\hat{p}\breve{p}+1)r) - \mathrm{HW}(e)$$
$$= d + \mathrm{HW}(\hat{p}\breve{p}r) - \mathrm{HW}((\hat{p}\breve{p}+1)r) - \mathrm{HW}(e)$$
$$= d + \underbrace{2\mathrm{HW}(\hat{p}\breve{p}r)}_{=d} - (\mathrm{HW}(\hat{p}\breve{p}r) + \mathrm{HW}((\hat{p}\breve{p}+1)r)) - \mathrm{HW}(e)$$
$$= 2d - \mathrm{HW}(r) - \mathrm{HW}(e)$$
$$> \frac{7}{4}d - \mathrm{HW}(r) > d(r+e,\hat{p}).$$

- For any $f \in \mathcal{RM}(m)$ with $\mathrm{HW}(\hat{p}\breve{p}f) = \mathrm{HW}(\hat{p}(\breve{p}+1)f) = \frac{d}{4}$ we have

$$d(r+e,f) = \mathrm{HW}(f+r+e)$$
$$\geq \mathrm{HW}(f+r) - \mathrm{HW}(e)$$
$$= \mathrm{HW}(\hat{p}\breve{p}(f+r)) + \mathrm{HW}(\hat{p}(\breve{p}+1)(f+r)) + \mathrm{HW}((p_1+1)(f+r))$$
$$\quad - \mathrm{HW}(e)$$
$$= \mathrm{HW}(\hat{p}\breve{p}(f+r)) + \mathrm{HW}(\hat{p}(\breve{p}+1)f) - \mathrm{HW}(\hat{p}(\breve{p}+1)r)$$
$$\quad + \underbrace{\mathrm{HW}((p_1+1)f)}_{=\frac{d}{2}} - \mathrm{HW}(e)$$
$$= \frac{d}{4} + \frac{d}{4} - \mathrm{HW}(\hat{p}(\breve{p}+1)r) + \frac{d}{2} - \mathrm{HW}(e)$$
$$= d + \mathrm{HW}(\hat{p}\breve{p}r) - (\mathrm{HW}(\hat{p}\breve{p}r) + \mathrm{HW}(\hat{p}(\breve{p}+1)r)) - \mathrm{HW}(e)$$
$$= \frac{3}{2}d - \mathrm{HW}(r) - \mathrm{HW}(e)$$
$$> \frac{5}{4}d - \mathrm{HW}(r) > d(r+e,\hat{p}).$$

We conclude that for any $f \in \mathcal{RM} \backslash (\mathcal{F} \cup \{0\})$ a word of $\mathcal{F}$ (specifically $\hat{p}$) is closer[5] to $r+e$ than f, and it follows that $\mathfrak{D}_{\mathcal{RM}}(r+e) \in \mathcal{F}$. Since the distance to the word of $\mathcal{F}$ was truly smaller in each of the discussed cases, i.e., not a tie, the decision is not the result of a tie in the distance with some other word $\mathcal{RM}(m) \backslash \mathcal{F}$. □

Due to the specific structure of the words in the set $\mathcal{F}$, i.e., the possible outputs of an ML decoder for the considered input, we are now able to make a statement on the behavior of the oracle when a single bit of this input is flipped.

Lemma 3. *Denote by* $\hat{p}, \breve{p} \in \mathbb{F}_2[x]$ *two polynomials with* $\deg(\hat{p}) = \deg(\breve{p}) = 1$ *and* $\breve{p} \notin \{\hat{p}, \hat{p}+1\}$. *Then, for* $r = \mathsf{FindWordAtBorder}(\mathfrak{D}_0^e, \mathrm{supp}(\hat{p}), \mathrm{supp}(\breve{p}))$ *as in*

---

[5] Similarly to the previous case, this does not mean that the ML decoding result is necessarily $\hat{p}$, since the proof does not hold for $\breve{p}$ and $\hat{p}+\breve{p}+1$.

Algorithm 6 and any $\xi \in \mathrm{supp}(\hat{p}\check{p})$ it holds that

$$\mathfrak{D}_0^e(r + u^{(\xi)}) = \begin{cases} \text{True,} & \text{if } r_\xi + e_\xi = 1 \\ \text{False,} & \text{else,} \end{cases}$$

where $u^{(\xi)} \in \mathbb{F}_2^{2^m}$ denotes (polynomial corresponding to) the ξ-th unit vector.

Proof. Denote $\mathcal{F} = \{\hat{p}, \check{p}, \hat{p} + \check{p} + 1\}$. By Lemma 2, we have $\mathfrak{D}_{\mathcal{RM}}(r + e) =: \tilde{p} \in \mathcal{F}$ for the word r returned at Step 4 of Algorithm 7. By definition of $\mathcal{F}$, this implies that $(\hat{\mathcal{I}} \cap \check{\mathcal{I}}) \subset \mathrm{supp}(\tilde{p})$, i.e., the positions $\hat{\mathcal{I}} \cap \check{\mathcal{I}}$ of $\tilde{p}$ are all one. Therefore, if a position in $\hat{\mathcal{I}} \cap \check{\mathcal{I}}$ of $r + e$ is changed from 0 to 1, the distance to $\tilde{p}$ *always* decreases by 1 and the ML decoder output does not change. On the other hand, if a position in $\hat{\mathcal{I}} \cap \check{\mathcal{I}}$ of $r + e$ is changed from 1 to 0, the distance to any polynomial of $\mathcal{F}$ *always* increases by 1, the distance to 0 decreases by 1, and the distance to any other word in $\mathcal{RM}(m) \backslash (\mathcal{F} \cup \{0\})$ decreases by at most 1. Hence, the ML decoding result changes from $\tilde{p}$ to 0 and the oracle returns True.   □

Finally, we show that Algorithm 7 is always successful in recovering the correct vector e, given that some non-restrictive assumptions are fulfilled.

Theorem 1. *Let $\mathfrak{D}_0^e$ be a oracle for the code $\mathcal{RM}^{\times s}(m) \subset \mathbb{F}_2^{s2^m}$ of minimum distance $d = s2^{m-1}$, where $e \in \mathbb{F}_2^{s2^m}$ with $\mathrm{HW}(e) < \frac{d}{4}$. Consider two polynomials $p_1, p_2 \in \mathbb{F}_2[x]$ with $\deg(p_1) = \deg(p_2) = 1$ and $p_2 \notin \{p_1, p_1 + 1\}$. Then, the output of Algorithm 7 is $\mathrm{FindError}(\mathfrak{D}_0^e, \mathrm{supp}^{\times s}(p_1), \mathrm{supp}^{\times s}(p_2)) = e$.*

Proof. For sake of readability and ease of notation, we focus on the case of multiplicity $s = 1$ in this proof. It is easy to verify that all statements also hold for $s > 1$ by essentially multiplying every weight/distance by s. Note that both Algorithms 6 and 7 are independent of s. Consider some choice of $\hat{\mathcal{I}}$ and $\check{\mathcal{I}}$ in Steps 2 and 3 of Algorithm 7. Note that there exist corresponding polynomials $\hat{p} \in \{p_1, p_1 + 1\}$ and $\check{p} \in \{p_2, p_2 + 1\}$ with $\mathrm{supp}(\hat{p}) = \hat{\mathcal{I}}$ and $\mathrm{supp}(\check{p}) = \check{\mathcal{I}}$ and we have $\deg(\hat{p}) = \deg(\check{p}) = 1$ and $\check{p} \notin \{\hat{p}, \hat{p} + 1\}$ for any such choice. Step 6 iterates over all positions of r in $\hat{\mathcal{I}} \cap \check{\mathcal{I}}$ and queries the oracle with this bit flipped. If this changes the oracle output to True, the corresponding bit is flipped in $\hat{e}$, with the goal of obtaining $\hat{e}_{\hat{\mathcal{I}} \cap \check{\mathcal{I}}} = e_{\hat{\mathcal{I}} \cap \check{\mathcal{I}}}$ at the end of the loop. We consider the four different possible combinations of e_ξ and r_ξ:

- $e_\xi = 0, r_\xi = 0$ or $e_\xi = 1, r_\xi = 1$: Flipping positions r_ξ corresponds to setting a 0 in $r + e$ to 1. By Lemma 3, this does not change the ML decoding result, i.e., the oracle still returns False. The bit $\hat{e}_\xi$ is not flipped, i.e., we have $\hat{e}_\xi = r_\xi$, and we correctly obtain $\hat{e}_\xi = e_\xi$.
- $e_\xi = 0, r_\xi = 1$ or $e_\xi = 1, r_\xi = 0$: Flipping positions r_ξ corresponds to setting a 1 in $r + e$ to 0. By Lemma 3, this does change the ML decoding result to all-zero, i.e., the oracle now returns True. The bit $\hat{e}_\xi$ is flipped, i.e., we have $\hat{e}_\xi = r_\xi + 1$, and we correctly obtain $\hat{e}_\xi = e_\xi$.

We conclude that $\tilde{e}_{\hat{\mathcal{I}} \cap \check{\mathcal{I}}} = \hat{e}_{\hat{\mathcal{I}} \cap \check{\mathcal{I}}} = e_{\hat{\mathcal{I}} \cap \check{\mathcal{I}}}$. This holds for any choice of $\hat{\mathcal{I}}$ and $\check{\mathcal{I}}$. The lemma statement follows from observing that the corresponding sets $\hat{\mathcal{I}} \cap \check{\mathcal{I}}$ partition the set of all positions $[0, q^m - 1]$.   □

Required Oracle Calls. Our strategy as described in Algorithm 7 requires at most $4 \cdot \left(\frac{2 \cdot n_2}{4} + \frac{n_2}{4} \right)$ oracle calls dependent on the length of the RM code. Note that the algorithm has to be repeated for all n_1 blocks of $\boldsymbol{y}^{(0)}$ introducing an additional factor of n_1. We compare the required oracle calls with the timing attack by Guo et al. [3] in Table 3. In addition to some disadvantages of the exploited timing side-channel (see Sect. 4 for a detailed discussion) this approach shows a largely increased number of required oracle calls. In essence their attack works by randomly increasing the Hamming weight of an input to the RM decoder until they reach the decoding boundary. Then the oracle can be queried with the individual bits of the input flipped. From the now found error positions only those that are not self introduced in the first step are counted as a valid part of the support of $\boldsymbol{y}_i^{(0)}$. Therefore, the attack steps have to be repeated until each position is evaluated and optionally a certain threshold for each position is reached. This makes the attack non-deterministic and therefore the authors report the amount of required ideal timing oracle calls as the median of 6096 attacks. For HQC-128 our attack strategy reduces the required oracle queries by a factor of 16.34.

We additionally observed that the attack strategy shown by Guo et al. [3] is also useable with our close-to-zero oracle. We implemented their strategy targeting a single $\boldsymbol{y}_i^{(0)}$ block and simulated the required oracle calls[6] for 400,000 attacks with $y_{w,max}$ in the range $1 \le y_{w,max} \le 10$ given a threshold of one (each position has to be evaluated once). The resulting median of the required oracle calls is shown in the third column of Table 3. We report these numbers in the paper to ensure a fair comparison that is not influenced by the different types of oracles. To summarize, our attack strategy in comparison to [3] requires by a factor of 11.44 (HQC-128) and 12.07 (HQC-192/256) less oracle queries when using the proposed close-to-zero oracle. In addition, it is proven to be successful for $\mathrm{HW}(\boldsymbol{y}_i^{(0)}) < \frac{d_{\mathcal{RM}}}{4}$, where $d_{\mathcal{RM}} = s \cdot 2^{m-1}$.

Table 3. Comparison of required oracle queries for the different attack strategies.

	This work	Timing attack [3]	Strategy of [3] using $\mathfrak{D}_0^e$
HQC-128	1152 * 46	18829 * 46[a]	13174 * 46
HQC-192	1920 * 56	–[b]	23170 * 56
HQC-256[c]	1920 * 90	–[b]	23170 * 90

a) The authors report a median of 866,143 oracle calls to retrieve the whole $\boldsymbol{y}^{(0)}$. To provide comparable numbers we report the required calls per block.
b) Numbers not given in [3].
c) Same simulation results as for HQC-192, since both use the same RM code.

---

[6] The simulation integrates the C reference implementation of the RM decoder and directly uses the decoding result to build the required oracle.

3.4 Retrieval of y from Partial Information with Information Set Decoding

In the case that $y^{(0)}$ is only partially retrieved we can still use this partial information to mount an attack through information set decoding. For a general approach on how to incorporate partial side-channel information into information set decoding we refer the reader to [4]. There are two main reasons for the information to be limited. Either there is a limit on the amount of possible oracle calls due to the amount of decryptions that can be observed by the attacker or the side-channel used to create the oracle does not result in perfect oracle answers. In Appendix B we describe a modified variant of Stern's algorithm [14] that is able to incorporate correct information about the support of the individual $y_i^{(0)}$ to lower the complexity of information set decoding. The resulting work factor $\mathcal{W}_{\text{ModSt}}$ given the knowledge of τ elements of the support of $y^{(0)}$ is shown in Fig. 2. Note that our algorithm also uses the information whether a full block $y_i^{(0)}$ has been retrieved, and we therefore assume the support of $y^{(0)}$ is evenly distributed between the different blocks of $y_i^{(0)}$ in Fig. 2.

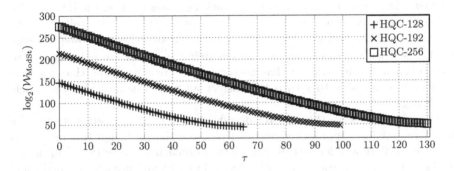

Fig. 2. Resulting work factor of Algorithm 8 for all HQC parameter sets given the knowledge of τ elements of the support of $y^{(0)}$.

4 Side-Channel Targets to Build the Required Oracle

There are several possible side-channels that can be used to construct our close-to-zero oracle as given in Definition 2. In this section we describe our results of directly attacking the implemented RS decoder of the HQC round 3 reference implementation using our power side-channel described in [13]. In addition, we discuss the approaches in related work and show how or whether these side-channels can be adapted to build our oracle. An overview of the different side-channel targets of the HQC decapsulation is shown in Fig. 3. Note that we consider a discussion of the fault-attack of Xagawa et al. [17] out of scope for this work.

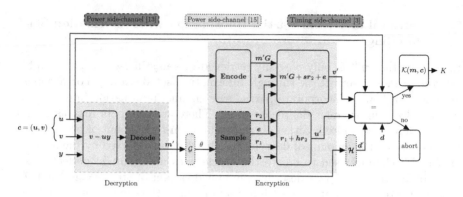

Fig. 3. Building blocks of the HQC decapsulation (c.f. Algorithm 5) with the side-channel attack targets used in related work.

4.1 Power Side-Channel of the RS Decoder

It is possible to construct our required oracle from the decoding result of the RS decoder. First we have to recall that our oracle indicates whether the RM decoder is able to correctly decode to the all-zero codeword or the decoding fails, and any other codeword is returned. Transferring this behavior to be observable through the RS decoder requires to set all the remaining $y_i^{(0)}$ that are not attacked to zero. Then if the RS decoder has to correct an error we know that the RM decoder was not able to return the correct all-zero codeword and the oracle result is True.

In order to observe that the RS decoder has to correct an error we use the template matching approach shown in [13]. Note that although this method is targeting a BCH decoder we can still use the approach in our setting. This is due to the fact that BCH codes are subcodes of RS codes and usually decoded using the same procedure as RS codes[7]. Therefore, steps during the decoding of these codes are essentially the same. The attack target for building the templates is the computation of the error-locator polynomial, as it showed the highest amount of exploitable leakage. As the input can be directly controlled by an attacker, templates for both classes can be constructed through the power side-channel. Then for each oracle call the constructed input is fed into the decapsulation and the respective power trace is compared to the templates through the use of a sum-of-squared-difference metric. As a result the class with the smallest metric is chosen as the oracle result.

---

[7] A (linear) subcode consists of a subset of codewords of the original code, usually in the form of a linear subspace. It is easy to see that any decoder for the original code can also be applied to the subcode, since it contains any codeword of the subcode. For more details on the relation between RS and BCH codes, the reader is referred to [7, Chap. 12].

Attack Results. We evaluated the oracle with our power side-channel setup consisting of a STM32F415RGT6 ARM Cortex-M4 microcontroller mounted on a Chipwhisperer CW308 UFO board running at 10 MHz. The power consumption is measured through the integrated shunt resistor with a PicoScope 6402D USB-oscilloscope running at a sampling rate of 156.25 MHz. As an attack target we use the latest version of the HQC-128 reference implementation. With our setup a total amount of 1000 template traces is used for the initialization of the oracle using a t-test threshold of 100 for point of interest detection (see Appendix C for the t-test result). Using the initialized oracle we are able to correctly classify 100,000 attack traces. As this number is above the required number of oracle calls for a complete key recovery we consider an attack on the complete secret key successful.

4.2 Power Side-Channel of the Used Hash Functions $\mathcal{G}, \mathcal{H}$

In [15] the authors show how to create a plaintext-checking oracle for HQC by observing a power side-channel of the used hash functions SHAKE256-512. With their oracle they are able to distinguish if a certain input results in a fixed message m' or if the result is different to this fixed message. As m' is directly used as an input to $\mathcal{G}$ and $\mathcal{H}$ the authors identify these hash functions as an attack target. In order to instantiate their oracle they use a machine learning classifier based on a convolutional neural network (CNN). They evaluate their CNN on the SHAKE software implementation of pqm4 [6] with the same side-channel platform and microcontroller as we described in the previous section. Using 30,000 training traces they achieve an accuracy of 0.998 when classifying 10,000 test traces, which can be further increased through the combination of multiple classifications.

This oracle can not be directly used with our proposed attack strategy as the resulting message after decryption is always zero. It can nevertheless be adapted to work as our close-to-zero oracle (Definition 2) by setting the resulting input to **Decode** such that the input to the RS decoder is set to its decoding boundary. This can be done by setting $(d_{\mathcal{RS}} - 1)/2$ blocks of $y^{(0)}$, that are not currently attacked, to be decoded as a non-zero value and therefore acting as an error for the all-zero RS codeword. Then the RM decoding result of the attacked $y_i^{(0)}$ determines if the resulting message is zero (True) or unequal to zero (False), which is observable through their oracle.

4.3 Timing Side-Channel of the Used Sampler

Guo et al. [3] showed a timing side-channel in the implementation of the sampler of the HQC reference implementation that is used to generate the random fixed-weight vectors e, r_1, and r_2. This is the case as the sampler implements rejection sampling, which requires a varying amount of calls to the PRNG in order to generate potential required additional randomness. As the seed θ for the PRNG is derived from the message m, the amount of additional required PRNG calls is dependent on m and therefore also the execution time of the decapsulation. This timing side-channel allows to build a plaintext-checking oracle for which the authors show an attack strategy. In order for two different messages to be distinguishable through their oracle the initial message is chosen such that it requires at least three additional calls to the PRNG which has a low probability of 0.58% for all possible messages. Due to the inherent uncertainty of timing side-channels and this probability still leaving room for ambiguity the authors introduce a majority threshold for the classification of each bit. Their empirical results show a classification success rate of 87% with a majority threshold of five.

Their oracle can not be used with our attack strategy as its resulting message m is always zero. This message unfortunately does not require multiple calls to the PRNG, and therefore it is not easily distinguishable through this timing side-channel. In contrast, our developed attack strategy allows the usage of both described power side-channels, which show a better classification result and eliminate the inherent uncertainty of timing side-channels removing the need for a majority decision.

5   Conclusion

In this paper we showed a novel proven side-channel attack strategy that again allows for a successful power side-channel attack against the updated round three version of the HQC cryptosystem. Published attacks against the former HQC version are not valid anymore, as the authors updated their used error correcting codes for their third round submission. We identified that the published power side-channel attack on the updated HQC version by Uneo et al. [15] is not valid in practice, as the authors miss a crucial property of the implemented Reed-Muller decoder that renders their attack unsuccessful. In contrast to the attack strategy by Guo et al. [3], that exploits a timing side-channel in the implemented polynomial sampler, our attack shows a by a factor of 12 reduced amount of required side-channel oracle calls. Our attack strategy allows the use of two power side-channel targets, namely the Reed-Solomon decoder as shown in [13] and the used SHAKE256 hash function as described in [15], to build the required oracle for our attack. We show practical attack results for the latest Reed-Solomon decoder of the latest HQC-128 implementation on an ARM Cortex-M4 microcontroller. Finally, we provided an estimation of the remaining attack complexity for partial attack results with the use of information set decoding.

Acknowledgment. This work was supported by the German Research Foundation (Deutsche Forschungsgemeinschaft, DFG) under Grant No. SE2989/1-1 as well as WA3907/4-1 and the European Research Council (ERC) under the European Union's Horizon 2020 research and innovation programme (grant agreement No 801434). We would like to thank Christoph Frisch for his helpful feedback.

A   Counterexample to the Attack Strategy in [15, 17]

The work [2, Fig. 7] presents a learning algorithm which allows for determining an additive error given access to a decode-to-zero oracle for a bounded-distance decoder. In [2, Theorem 11] it is shown that this algorithm succeeds with probability 1 in the considered setting. Given the vectors r and e, the oracle is defined as

$$\mathsf{BOO}(r) = \begin{cases} \mathsf{True}, & \text{if } \mathrm{HW}(r+e) \leq \tau, \\ \mathsf{False}, & \text{else.} \end{cases}$$

In other words, the oracle provides the information whether the sum of the input r and the error e would be corrected to zero by a bounded-distance decoder of radius τ. Note that $\mathsf{BOO}(r)$ is similar to the oracle $\mathfrak{D}_0^e(r)$ in our work, as given in Definition 2, except that it assumes a bounded-distance decoder, i.e., a fixed decoding threshold, instead of an ML decoder. In [17, Sect. C.7][8] it is claimed that this algorithm can be applied to the round three version of HQC system, which employs an ML decoder. However, the fixed decoding threshold of the bounded-distance decoder is essential to the algorithm of [2, Fig. 7] and in this section we show that replacing the $\mathsf{BOO}(r)$ oracle with the $\mathfrak{D}_0^e(r)$ oracle, i.e., considering an ML decoder instead of a bounded-distance decoder, causes this algorithm to return incorrect error vectors. Note that this choice of decoder is inherent to the system and cannot be influenced by the attacker, so the oracle $\mathfrak{D}_0^e(r)$ is the appropriate oracle to use for this system. In addition to this counterexample we implemented the attack strategy and performed a simulated attack by directly accessing the RM decoder results of the HQC reference implementation. We were not able to correctly retrieve the support $y_i^{(0)}$ with our simulations.

The algorithm of [2, Fig. 7] is based on constructing a vector, such that the sum of this vector and the error is at the decoding threshold. For a bounded-distance decoder, the result of the BOO oracle, when queried with a single bit of this input flipped, then determines the corresponding position of the error vector. However, this only applies if the result of input x plus error e is at the decoding threshold *for every position*. We give an example of a vector for which this is only the case for a subset of positions, which leads to an incorrect output, even in the case of a single error. We follow the steps of the algorithm of [2, Fig. 7] and fix the error vector to be the first unit vector $e = e^{(1)}$.

Initialize

x $(0,0,0,0,0,0,0,0,0,0,0,0,0,0,0,0)$

y $(1,1,1,1,1,1,1,1,1,1,1,1,1,1,1,1)$

First while loop iteration

u $(1,1,1,1,1,1,1,1,0,0,0,0,0,0,0,0)$

v $(0,0,0,0,0,0,0,0,1,1,1,1,1,1,1,1)$

$\mathfrak{D}_0^e(x+u) = \mathsf{False}$

$y \leftarrow u$ $(1,1,1,1,1,1,1,1,0,0,0,0,0,0,0,0)$

---

[8] The authors of [15] directly cite [17] for their attack description.

Second while loop iteration

$$u \quad (0,1,1,1,1,0,0,0,0,0,0,0,0,0,0,0)$$
$$v \quad (1,0,0,0,0,1,1,1,0,0,0,0,0,0,0,0)$$
$$\mathfrak{D}_0^e(x+u) = \mathsf{False}$$
$$y \leftarrow u \quad (0,1,1,1,1,0,0,0,0,0,0,0,0,0,0,0)$$

Third while loop iteration

$$u \quad (0,1,1,0,0,0,0,0,0,0,0,0,0,0,0,0)$$
$$v \quad (0,0,0,1,1,0,0,0,0,0,0,0,0,0,0,0)$$
$$\mathfrak{D}_0^e(x+u) = \mathsf{True}$$
$$x \leftarrow x+u \quad (0,1,1,0,0,0,0,0,0,0,0,0,0,0,0,0)$$
$$y \leftarrow v \quad (0,0,0,1,1,0,0,0,0,0,0,0,0,0,0,0)$$

Fourth while loop iteration

$$u \quad (0,0,0,0,1,0,0,0,0,0,0,0,0,0,0,0)$$
$$v \quad (0,0,0,1,0,0,0,0,0,0,0,0,0,0,0,0)$$
$$\mathfrak{D}_0^e(x+u) = \mathsf{True}$$
$$x \leftarrow x+u \quad (0,1,1,0,1,0,0,0,0,0,0,0,0,0,0,0)$$
$$y \leftarrow v \quad (0,0,0,1,0,0,0,0,0,0,0,0,0,0,0,0)$$
$$\|y\| = 1 \text{ Terminate while loop.}$$

As claimed, we now have a word $x + e$ that is at the threshold of decoding, i.e., if a position inside its support is flipped, we decode to zero, i.e., $\mathfrak{D}_0^e(x) = \mathsf{True}$. The last for-loop of the algorithm iterates over all positions, checking if flipping each bit alters the decoding result. Initialize z to

$$z \leftarrow x \quad (0,1,1,0,1,0,0,0,0,0,0,0,0,0,0,0).$$

So, e.g., for the error position we have

$$x + e^{(1)} \quad (1,1,1,0,1,0,0,0,0,0,0,0,0,0,0,0)$$
$$x + e^{(1)} + e \quad (0,1,1,0,1,0,0,0,0,0,0,0,0,0,0,0)$$

and therefore $\mathfrak{D}_0^e(x + e^{(1)}) = \mathsf{True}$. Hence, the first bit in the vector z is flipped to obtain

$$z \leftarrow z + e^{(1)} \quad (1,1,1,0,1,0,0,0,0,0,0,0,0,0,0,0).$$

Similarly, for any other position in the support, such as, e.g., $i = 2$, we have

$$x + e^{(2)} \quad (1,0,1,0,1,0,0,0,0,0,0,0,0,0,0,0)$$
$$x + e^{(2)} + e \quad (0,0,1,0,1,0,0,0,0,0,0,0,0,0,0,0)$$

and therefore $\mathfrak{D}_0^e(x + e^{(2)}) = \mathsf{True}$, so the second bit of z is flipped to obtain

$$z \leftarrow z + e^{(2)} \quad (0,0,1,0,1,0,0,0,0,0,0,0,0,0,0,0).$$

After the first 8 positions we have

$$z \leftarrow z + e^{(1)} \quad (1,0,0,0,0,0,0,0,0,0,0,0,0,0,0,0) \, .$$

However, take for example $i = 9$. Then,

$$\begin{aligned} x + e^{(9)} \quad & (0,1,1,0,1,0,0,0,1,0,0,0,0,0,0,0) \\ x + e^{(9)} + e \quad & (1,1,1,0,1,0,0,0,1,0,0,0,0,0,0,0) \end{aligned} \, .$$

At this point the difference between a bounded-distance decoder and an ML decoder affects the decoding decision. While this word does have weight more than $d/2$, it is easy to check that an ML decoder still decides for the all-zero word, so $\mathfrak{D}_0^e(x + e^{(9)}) = \mathsf{True}$ and we get

$$z \leftarrow z + e^{(1)} \quad (1,0,0,0,0,0,0,0,1,0,0,0,0,0,0,0) \, .$$

This holds for all positions in the second part of the word, so at the end of the algorithm the "approximated error vector" is given by

$$z \leftarrow z + e^{(1)} \quad (1,0,0,0,0,0,0,0,1,1,1,1,1,1,1,1) \, .$$

Hence, even in this simple case of a single error, the strategy does not return the correct error vector.

B   Modified Variant of Stern's Algorithm

Let $\mathcal{J} := \{j_0, \ldots, j_{\tau-1}\} \subseteq \mathrm{supp}(y) \subseteq [0 : n-1]$ be the subset of the support of y that we retrieved, and let $\mathcal{L} := \{l_0, \ldots, l_{\iota-1}\} \subseteq [0 : n-1] \backslash \mathrm{supp}(y)$ denote the indices of the zero entries in y that we determined. Then, we us obtain the secret vectors x and y using the modified variant of Stern's algorithm [14] that is shown in Algorithm 8.

Theorem 2. *Let n and w be parameters chosen according to Table 1. Let (x, y) and (h, s) be a private and public key pair generated by Algorithm 1 for the chosen parameters. Let $\mathcal{J} := \{j_0, \ldots, j_{\tau-1}\}$ be a subset of the support of y, let $\mathcal{L} = \{l_0, \ldots, l_{\iota-1}\}$ denote a set of indices of zero entries in y, and let $n' = n - \iota$ and $w' = w - \tau$. Furthermore, let k_1, p_{St}, $\nu_{\mathrm{St},1}$, and $\nu_{\mathrm{St},2}$ be non-negative integers such that $k_1 \leq n'$, $p_{\mathrm{St}} \leq w + w'$, $\nu_{\mathrm{St},1} \leq n - k_1$, and $\nu_{\mathrm{St},2} \leq n - n' + k_1$.*
Then, given $H = [1, \mathrm{rot}(h)] \in \mathbb{F}_2^{n \times 2n}$, w, $s \in \mathbb{F}_2^n$, k_1, p_{St}, $\nu_{\mathrm{St},1}$, $\nu_{\mathrm{St},2}$, $\mathcal{J}$, and $\mathcal{L}$, Algorithm 8 outputs the vector $[x, y]$ with, on average, approximately

$$\mathcal{W}_{\mathrm{ModSt}} := \frac{\mathcal{W}_{\mathrm{St,Iter}}}{P_{\mathrm{St}}}$$

operations in $\mathbb{F}_2$, where

$$\mathcal{W}_{\mathrm{St,Iter}} := (n + n')^3 + (\nu_{\mathrm{St},1} + \nu_{\mathrm{St},2}) \left(\sum_{i=1}^{p_{\mathrm{St}}} \binom{M_1}{i} + \sum_{i=1}^{p_{\mathrm{St}}} \binom{M_2}{i} - n' + \binom{M_2}{p_{\mathrm{St}}} \right)$$

$$+ 2^{1-\nu_{\text{St},1}-\nu_{\text{St},2}} \binom{M_1}{p_{\text{St}}} \binom{M_2}{p_{\text{St}}} (w + w' - 2p_{\text{St}} + 1)(2p_{\text{St}} + 1),$$

the quantities $M_1 = \lfloor k_1/2 \rfloor + \lfloor (n' - k_1)/2 \rfloor$ and $M_2 = \lceil k_1/2 \rceil + \lceil (n' - k_1)/2 \rceil$, and

$$P_{\text{St}} := \sum_{\substack{a \in \mathbb{N}_0^2 \\ a_1 \leq w \\ a_2 \leq w' \\ a_1 + a_2 = p_{\text{St}}}} \sum_{\substack{b \in \mathbb{N}_0^2 \\ b_1 \leq w - a_1 \\ b_2 \leq w' - a_2 \\ b_1 + b_2 = p_{\text{St}}}} \frac{\binom{\lfloor k_1/2 \rfloor}{a_1} \binom{\lceil k_1/2 \rceil}{b_1} \binom{n - k_1 - \nu_{\text{St},1}}{w - a_1 - b_1}}{\binom{n}{w}} \frac{\binom{\lfloor (n'-k_1)/2 \rfloor}{a_2} \binom{\lceil (n'-k_1)/2 \rceil}{b_2} \binom{k_1 - \nu_{\text{St},2}}{w' - a_2 - b_2}}{\binom{n'}{w'}}.$$

Proof. In Line 1, the algorithm uses $\mathcal{J}$ to transform the syndrome decoding instance $(\boldsymbol{H}, \boldsymbol{s}, [\boldsymbol{x}, \boldsymbol{y}])$ of length $2n$, dimension n and error weight $2w$ into the syndrome decoding instance $(\boldsymbol{H}, \tilde{\boldsymbol{s}}, [\boldsymbol{x}, \tilde{\boldsymbol{y}}])$ of length $2n$, dimension n and error weight $w + w'$, where $\text{HW}(\tilde{\boldsymbol{y}}) = w'$ and $\text{supp}(\tilde{\boldsymbol{y}}) \cup \mathcal{J} = \text{supp}(\boldsymbol{y})$. The remaining steps are equal to the modification of Stern's algorithm presented in [4] and [12, Alg. 17] except that the set $\mathcal{X}_2$ always contains $\mathcal{L}_1 = \{l_0, \ldots, l_{\lceil \iota/2 \rceil - 1}\}$ and the set $\mathcal{Y}_2$ always contains $\mathcal{L}_2 = \{l_{\lceil \iota/2 \rceil}, \ldots, l_{\iota-1}\}$. By this choice of $\mathcal{X}_2$ and $\mathcal{Y}_2$, the syndrome decoding instance $(\boldsymbol{H}, \tilde{\boldsymbol{s}}, [\boldsymbol{x}, \tilde{\boldsymbol{y}}])$ is transformed into the $(\bar{\boldsymbol{H}}, \bar{\boldsymbol{s}}, [\boldsymbol{x}, \bar{\boldsymbol{y}}])$ instance of length $n + n'$, dimension n' and error weight $w + w'$, where $\bar{\boldsymbol{H}} \in \mathbb{F}_2^{n' \times (n+n')}$, $\bar{\boldsymbol{s}} \in \mathbb{F}_2^{n+n'}$, and $\bar{\boldsymbol{y}} \in \mathbb{F}_2^{n'}$.

Such that an iteration of Stern's algorithm can solve the $(\bar{\boldsymbol{H}}, \bar{\boldsymbol{s}}, [\boldsymbol{x}, \bar{\boldsymbol{y}}])$ syndrome decoding instance, there must be exactly p_{St} error positions in both $\mathcal{X}_1 \cup \mathcal{X}_2$ and $\mathcal{Y}_1 \cup \mathcal{Y}_2$ and no error positions in $\mathcal{Z}_1$ and $\mathcal{Z}_2$. The probability that this event occurs is equal to P_{St}, cf. [4] and [12, Thm. 4.9]. This implies that, on average, Lines 5 to 12 need to be executed $1/P_{\text{St}}$, where each iteration has a complexity of $\mathcal{W}_{\text{St,Iter}}$. $\qquad\square$

C   T-Test Result: Power Side-Channel of the RS Decoder

The t-test results used for identifying points of interest for building our oracle with the power side-channel of the RS decoder (Sect. 4.1) is shown in Fig. 4. The high t-values clearly indicate that both classes can be distinguished through this power side-channel. The shown samples correspond to the complete execution time of the error-locator polynomial computation implemented in the HQC-128 reference implementation.

Algorithm 8: Modified Stern Algorithm

Input : Parity-check matrix $\boldsymbol{H} \in \mathbb{F}_2^{n \times 2n}$

      Non-negative integer w

      Syndrome vector $\boldsymbol{s} \in \mathbb{F}_2^n$

      Non-negative integers k_1, p_{St}, $\nu_{\mathrm{St},1}$, $\nu_{\mathrm{St},2}$

      Subset of the support $\mathcal{J} := \{j_0, \ldots, j_{\tau-1}\} \subseteq \mathrm{supp}(\boldsymbol{y})$

      Subset of zero entries $\mathcal{L} = \{l_0, \ldots, l_{\iota-1}\} \subseteq [0{:}n-1] \backslash \mathrm{supp}(\boldsymbol{y})$

Output: Vector $[\boldsymbol{x}, \boldsymbol{y}] \in \mathbb{F}_2^{2n}$

1   $\tilde{\boldsymbol{s}} \leftarrow \boldsymbol{s} + \boldsymbol{h}_{n+j_0}^{\top} + \ldots + \boldsymbol{h}_{n+j_{\tau-1}}^{\top} \in \mathbb{F}_2^n$, where $\boldsymbol{h}_\ell$ is the ℓ-th column of $\boldsymbol{H}$

2   $\mathcal{L}_1 \leftarrow \{l_0, \ldots, l_{\lceil \iota/2 \rceil - 1}\}$

3   $\mathcal{L}_2 \leftarrow \{l_{\lceil \iota/2 \rceil}, \ldots, l_{\iota-1}\}$

4   $\boldsymbol{e}' \leftarrow \boldsymbol{0} \in \mathbb{F}_2^{2n}$

5   **while** $\mathrm{HW}(\boldsymbol{e}') > 2w - \tau \vee \tilde{\boldsymbol{s}} \neq \boldsymbol{e}'\boldsymbol{H}^{\top}$ **do**

6      $\mathcal{X}_1 \xleftarrow{\$} \{\mathcal{S} \subseteq [0{:}n-1] : |\mathcal{S}| = \lfloor k_1/2 \rfloor\}$

7      $\mathcal{Y}_1 \xleftarrow{\$} \{\mathcal{S} \subseteq [0{:}n-1] \backslash \mathcal{X}_1 : |\mathcal{S}| = \lceil k_1/2 \rceil\}$

8      $\mathcal{Z}_1 \xleftarrow{\$} \{\mathcal{S} \subseteq [0{:}n-1] \backslash (\mathcal{X}_1 \cup \mathcal{Y}_1) : |\mathcal{S}| = \nu_{\mathrm{St},1}\}$

9      $\mathcal{X}_2 \xleftarrow{\$} \{\mathcal{S} \cup \mathcal{L}_1 \subseteq [n{:}2n-1] \backslash \mathcal{L}_2 : |\mathcal{S} \cup \mathcal{L}_1| = \lfloor (n-k_1)/2 \rfloor\}$

10     $\mathcal{Y}_2 \xleftarrow{\$} \{\mathcal{S} \cup \mathcal{L}_2 \subseteq [n{:}2n-1] \backslash \mathcal{X}_2 : |\mathcal{S} \cup \mathcal{L}_2| = \lceil (n-k_1)/2 \rceil\}$

11     $\mathcal{Z}_2 \xleftarrow{\$} \{\mathcal{S} \subseteq [n{:}2n-1] \backslash (\mathcal{X}_2 \cup \mathcal{Y}_2) : |\mathcal{S}| = \nu_{\mathrm{St},2}\}$

12     $\boldsymbol{e}' \leftarrow$ Iteration of original Stern algorithm w.r.t. the syndrome $\tilde{\boldsymbol{s}}$, the sets

        $\mathcal{X}_1 \cup \mathcal{X}_2$, $\mathcal{Y}_1 \cup \mathcal{Y}_2$, $\mathcal{Z}_1 \cup \mathcal{Z}_2$ and the parameters p_{St} and $\nu_{\mathrm{St}} = \nu_{\mathrm{St},1} + \nu_{\mathrm{St},2}$

13 **return** $\boldsymbol{e} \in \mathbb{F}_2^{2n}$ *with support* $\mathrm{supp}\, \boldsymbol{e}' \cup \mathcal{J}$

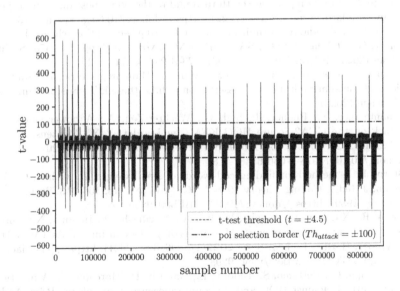

Fig. 4. Resulting t-values used for identifying points of interest using the side-channel described in Sect. 4.1. The marked Th_{attack} is used as a threshold for the actual attack.

References

1. Albrecht, M.R., et al.: NIST post-quantum cryptography standardization round 3 submission: classic McEliece. https://classic.mceliece.org
2. Bâetu, C., Durak, F.B., Huguenin-Dumittan, L., Talayhan, A., Vaudenay, S.: Misuse attacks on post-quantum cryptosystems. In: Ishai, Y., Rijmen, V. (eds.) EUROCRYPT 2019. LNCS, vol. 11477, pp. 747–776. Springer, Cham (2019). https://doi.org/10.1007/978-3-030-17656-3_26
3. Guo, Q., Hlauschek, C., Johansson, T., Lahr, N., Nilsson, A., Schröder, R.L.: Don't reject this: Key-recovery timing attacks due to rejection-sampling in HQC and BIKE. IACR Trans. Cryptogr. Hardw. Embed. Syst. **2022**(3), 223–263 (2022)
4. Horlemann, A.L., Puchinger, S., Renner, J., Schamberger, T., Wachter-Zeh, A.: Information-set decoding with hints. In: Wachter-Zeh, A., Bartz, H., Liva, G. (eds.) CBCrypto 2021. LNCS, vol. 13150, pp. 60–83. Springer, Cham (2022). https://doi.org/10.1007/978-3-030-98365-9_4
5. Huguenin-Dumittan, L., Vaudenay, S.: Classical misuse attacks on NIST round 2 PQC: the power of rank-based schemes. In: Conti, M., Zhou, J., Casalicchio, E., Spognardi, A. (eds.) ACNS 2020. LNCS, vol. 12146, pp. 208–227. Springer, Cham (2020). https://doi.org/10.1007/978-3-030-57808-4_11
6. Kannwischer, M.J., Rijneveld, J., Schwabe, P., Stoffelen, K.: PQM4: post-quantum crypto library for the ARM Cortex-M4. https://github.com/mupq/pqm4
7. MacWilliams, F.J., Sloane, N.J.A.: The Theory of Error Correcting Codes, vol. 16. Elsevier, Amsterdam (1977)
8. Melchor, C.A., et al.: NIST post-quantum cryptography standardization round 2 submission: hamming Quasi-Cyclic (HQC). http://pqc-hqc.org/
9. Melchor, C.A., et al.: NIST post-quantum cryptography standardization round 3 submission: hamming Quasi-Cyclic (HQC). http://pqc-hqc.org/
10. Moody, D.: Status report on the third round of the NIST post-quantum cryptography standardization process (2022). https://doi.org/10.6028/nist.ir.8413
11. Paiva, T.B., Terada, R.: A timing attack on the HQC encryption scheme. In: Paterson, K.G., Stebila, D. (eds.) SAC 2019. LNCS, vol. 11959, pp. 551–573. Springer, Cham (2020). https://doi.org/10.1007/978-3-030-38471-5_22
12. Renner, J.: Post-quantum cryptography in the Hamming metric, the rank metric, and the sum-rank metric. Dissertation (Ph.D. thesis), Technische Universität München (2022)
13. Schamberger, T., Renner, J., Sigl, G., Wachter-Zeh, A.: A power side-channel attack on the CCA2-Secure HQC KEM. In: Liardet, P.-Y., Mentens, N. (eds.) CARDIS 2020. LNCS, vol. 12609, pp. 119–134. Springer, Cham (2021). https://doi.org/10.1007/978-3-030-68487-7_8
14. Stern, J.: A method for finding codewords of small weight. In: Cohen, G., Wolfmann, J. (eds.) Coding Theory 1988. LNCS, vol. 388, pp. 106–113. Springer, Heidelberg (1989). https://doi.org/10.1007/BFb0019850
15. Ueno, R., Xagawa, K., Tanaka, Y., Ito, A., Takahashi, J., Homma, N.: Curse of re-encryption: a generic power/EM analysis on post-quantum KEMs. IACR Trans. Cryptogr. Hardw. Embed. Syst. **2022**(1), 296–322 (2021). https://tches.iacr.org/index.php/TCHES/article/view/9298
16. Wafo-Tapa, G., Bettaieb, S., Bidoux, L., Gaborit, P., Marcatel, E.: A practicable timing attack against HQC and its countermeasure. Cryptology ePrint Archive, Report 2019/909 (2019). https://eprint.iacr.org/2019/909
17. Xagawa, K., Ito, A., Ueno, R., Takahashi, J., Homma, N.: Fault-injection attacks against NIST's post-quantum cryptography round 3 KEM candidates. Cryptology ePrint Archive, Report 2021/840 (2021). https://ia.cr/2021/840

A New Key Recovery Side-Channel Attack on HQC with Chosen Ciphertext

Guillaume Goy[1,2](✉), Antoine Loiseau[1](✉), and Philippe Gaborit[2](✉)

[1] Univ. Grenoble Alpes, CEA, Leti, MINATEC Campus, 38054 Grenoble, France
{guillaume.goy,antoine.loiseau}@cea.fr
[2] XLIM, University of Limoges, Limoges, France
gaborit@unilim.fr

Abstract. Hamming Quasi-Cyclic (HQC) is a code-based candidate of NIST post-quantum standardization procedure. The decoding steps of code-based cryptosystems are known to be vulnerable to side-channel attacks and HQC is no exception to this rule. In this paper, we present a new key recovery side-channel attack on HQC with chosen ciphertext. Our attack takes advantage of the reuse of a static secret key on a micro-controller with a physical access. The goal is to retrieve the static secret key by targeting the Reed-Muller decoding step of the decapsulation and more precisely the Hadamard transform. This function is known for its diffusion property, a property that we exploit through side-channel analysis. The side-channel information is used to build an Oracle that distinguishes between several decoding patterns of the Reed-Muller codes. We show how to query the Oracle such that the responses give a full information about the static secret key. Experiments show that less than 20.000 electromagnetic attack traces are sufficient to retrieve the whole static secret key used for the decapsulation. Finally, we present a masking-based countermeasure to thwart our attack.

Keywords: HQC · Reed-Muller codes · Chosen ciphertext attack · Side-channel attack · Post-quantum cryptography

1 Introduction

The interest for Post-Quantum Cryptography (PQC) increased with the quantum computers threat to classic cryptography schemes like RSA [20]. The research is promoted by the National Institute of Standards and Technology (NIST) who launched a call for proposal [16] in 2016 with the aim to standardize new signature and Key Encapsulation Mechanism (KEM) schemes. NIST moves closer to making standardization decisions and aims to precisely measuring the security of the schemes, including Side-Channel Attacks (SCA) and their countermeasures. Thus, the security against SCA and the cost and performance of side-channel protection could be criteria for standards selection [3].

Hamming Quasi-Cyclic (HQC) [1,2,4] is a promising candidate of the fourth round of the PQC NIST contest. Unlike the McEliece construction [15] and

© The Author(s), under exclusive license to Springer Nature Switzerland AG 2022
J. H. Cheon and T. Johansson (Eds.): PQCrypto 2022, LNCS 13512, pp. 353–371, 2022.
https://doi.org/10.1007/978-3-031-17234-2_17

derivates, the security of HQC is not related to hiding the structure of an error correcting code. In HQC, the structure of the decoding codes is publicly known and the security can be reduced to the Quasi-Cyclic version of the well know Syndrome Decoding (SD) problem [2,5,24].

Nowadays cryptographic schemes are assessed to be theoretically secure, for HQC, the security comes from two sides. On the one hand, the IND-CCA2 security is provided by the transformation of a IND-CPA scheme with a Fujisaki-Okamoto like transform [7,8,11]. This point guarantees the security against malicious adversaries who would make a diverted use of the scheme. On the other hand, finding the secret key is impossible given the reduction of security to a known NP-hard problem [5]. However, implementation of a secure scheme in constrained devices, such as micro-controller, can still be vulnerable to physical attacks.

Side-Channel Attacks (SCA) [12,13], introduced by P. Kocher in 1996, are non-invasive physical attacks with aim to exploit side-channel leakage (timing, power consumption, electromagnetic radiation, execution time, heat, sound ...). Since their introduction, SCA have a long history of success in extracting secret information (such as secret key or message) of cryptographic algorithms [6,19, 26]. The leakage is statistically dependent on the intermediate variables that are processed and this side-channel information can be exploited to extract secret information.

Related Works. SCA already targeted the HQC scheme in various ways. In 2019 and 2020, the first version of HQC based on BCH codes was attacked by Timing attacks (TA). These TA [17,25] use a correlation between the weight of the decoded error and the computation time of the decoder. As a result, HQC authors' team proposed a constant time implementation for decoding BCH codes to mitigate these TA.

In 2021, a novel TA [10,23] targeted the RMRS version of HQC. This TA uses the rejection sampling construction to attack both HQC and BIKE. Indeed, the sampling of a vector of small Hamming weight ω is performed by randomly choosing its support. ω locations are sampled and sometimes collisions occur at these locations which, leads to rejecting the vector and sampling another one from the beginning. However, all the randomness is generated with a seed (see Algorithm 4) which is derived from the exchanged message used to compute the shared key. This observation leads to a relation between the run-time of the rejection sampling and the exchanged message. This relation is strong enough to extract information about the secret key in HQC with a chosen ciphertext strategy.

In 2022, an horizontal SCA [9] used the Decryption Failure Rate (DFR) of HQC by targeting Reed-Solomon (RS) decoding. Indeed, the low DFR implies that the Reed-Muller decoder almost always decodes all the errors. This leads to an error-free codeword decoding by the RS decoder. By studying the behaviour of the RS decoder and using a better decoder for the RS codes in order to correct side-channel induced errors, authors are able to recover the exchanged message in a single trace.

In 2020 and 2022, Schamberger et al. [21,22] proposed two chosen ciphertext attacks (CCA) based on a side-channel Oracle able to determine whenever an error is corrected by the HQC decoder through a supervised approach. These attacks are possible despite the IND-CCA2 security because the side-channel distinguisher is performed before the re-encryption phase, during the decoding part. The first attack [22] targets the BCH version of HQC, they chose the ciphertext in order to create a single error for the BCH decoder, which can be seen by the Oracle. They are able to recover a large part of the possible keys in HQC with a secret key support (non-zero locations) research. By a complex chosen ciphertext attack, they are able to deduce information about the support of the secret key which is used during the decapsulation. Authors adapted their power side-channel attack to the Reed-Muller Reed-Solomon version of HQC [21], leading to a complex but functional attack on the new version of HQC. These attacks are a serious threat to the HQC security and no countermeasure have been proposed to thwart these attacks neither in the first paper, nor in the second. In this context, finding a new distinguisher on the HQC decoding procedure allows to build the same kind of attacks.

Our Contributions. In this paper, we propose a simpler key recovery side-channel attack with a chosen ciphertext strategy targeting the new RMRS version of HQC. We are able to retrieve a static secret key of HQC by building a chosen ciphertext attack with a less complex queries selection process. The main idea is to build queries in order to create collisions with the secret key support, changing the decoding behaviour. We show how to construct a new simple Oracle on the RM decoding step that is able to determine the number of corrected errors. This Oracle is based on a supervised side-channel approach with the used of a Linear Discriminant Analysis. The knowledge of the secret key is not required for the Oracle's training stage, allowing a training phase on a clone device and reducing the number of attack measurements. We build an Oracle of 120.000 training traces and use 50 attack traces per bit to create an attack with 100% accuracy. A divide and conquer strategy allows at recovering the whole decoding static secret key with less than 20.000 attack traces. Our attack can be avoided by a masking-based countermeasure applied on the Oracle target function.

Paper Organization. The paper is organized as follows: In Sect. 2, we recall the HQC framework and the main algorithms useful for the understanding of the attack. Section 3 is devoted to the description of our chosen ciphertext attack, showing how to build the queries in order to recover the secret key using a decoding Oracle. In Sect. 4, we describe the construction and evaluation of the Oracle based on side-channel measurements. Then we present our results and give the attack complexity. We present a simple masking based countermeasure in Sect. 5 to thwart our attack before concluding.

2   Hamming Quasi-Cyclic (HQC)

2.1   HQC Overview

HQC [2] is a code-based post-quantum resistant Key Encapsulation Mechanism (KEM). Unlike other code-based cryptosystems, the security of HQC does not rely on hiding the structure of an error correcting code. The security is guaranteed by a random double circulant code with a reduction to the well-studied Quasi-Cyclic Syndrome Decoding Problem (QCSD) [2,5,24]. HQC uses another code $\mathcal{C}$ with an efficient decoder $\mathcal{C}.\mathsf{Decode}$ that is publicly known. Neither the security of the scheme nor the decryption capability depend on the knowledge of $\mathcal{C}.\mathsf{Decode}$. A classic construction is to turn a Public Key Encryption (PKE) scheme into a KEM. HQC-PKE is fully described by three algorithms (see Algorithms 1,2 and 3 in Fig. 1). Considering $\mathcal{R} = \mathbb{F}_2[X]/(X^n - 1)$ the ambient space with n a primitive prime given as parameter and $\mathcal{R}_\omega$ the space restriction to words of Hamming weight ω.

Algorithm 1 Keygen	**Algorithm 2** Encrypt	
Input: param	**Input:** $(\mathsf{pk}, \mathbf{m})$, param	
Output: $(\mathsf{pk}, \mathsf{sk})$	**Output:** ciphertext $\mathbf{c}$	**Algorithm 3** Decrypt
1: $\mathbf{h} \xleftarrow{\$} \mathcal{R}$	1: $\mathbf{e} \xleftarrow{\$} \mathcal{R}$, $\mathrm{wt}(\mathbf{e}) = \omega_e$	**Input:** $(\mathsf{sk}, \mathbf{c})$
2: $(\mathbf{x}, \mathbf{y}) \xleftarrow{\$} \mathcal{R}_\omega^2$	2: $(\mathbf{r}_1, \mathbf{r}_2) \xleftarrow{\$} \mathcal{R}_{\omega_r}^2$	**Output:** $\mathbf{m}$
3: $\mathbf{s} = \mathbf{x} + \mathbf{h}\mathbf{y}$	3: $\mathbf{u} = \mathbf{r}_1 + \mathbf{h}\mathbf{r}_2$	1: $\mathbf{m} = \mathcal{C}.\mathsf{Decode}(\mathbf{v} - \mathbf{u}\mathbf{y})$
4: $\mathsf{pk} = (\mathbf{h}, \mathbf{s})$	4: $\mathbf{v} = \mathbf{m}G + \mathbf{s}\mathbf{r}_2 + \mathbf{e}$	
5: $\mathsf{sk} = (\mathbf{x}, \mathbf{y})$	5: $\mathbf{c} = (\mathbf{u}, \mathbf{v})$	

Fig. 1. HQC-PKE algorithms [1,2]

A quantum adapted Fujisaki-Okamoto transformation [7,8] called the Hofheinz-Hövelmanns-Kiltz (HHK) transformation [11] turns the PKE into a KEM and allows HQC-KEM scheme to reach IND-CCA2 security. The main idea of such a construction is the re-encryption during the decapsulation that prevent from chosen ciphertext attack (CCA). The KEM IND-CCA2 property is guaranteed given that the PKE has been proved IND-CPA (see HQC specifications [2] for details). HQC KEM algorithms [1] are described with Algorithms 4 and 5 in Fig. 2.

As mentioned earlier, the formal security of HQC does not rely on the chosen publicly known code. Therefore, this code can be chosen at the convenience of the developer. Authors of HQC propose the use of a concatenated code with a duplicated Reed-Muller (RM) code for internal code and a Reed-Solomon (RS) code for the external one. Formally, the internal code is a $[n_1, k_1, d_1]$ code over $\mathbb{F}_q$ and an external code a $[n_2, k_2, d_2]$ code, with $q = 2^{k_2}$. To encode with a concatenated construction, we first encode a message of length k_1 with the external code to obtain an intermediate codeword of length n_1 over $\mathbb{F}_q = \mathbb{F}_{2^{k_2}}$.

Algorithm 4 Encaps
Input: pk = (**h**, **s**)
Output: (**c**, **d**)
1: $\mathbf{m} \xleftarrow{\$} \mathbb{F}_2^k$
2: $\theta = \mathcal{G}(\mathbf{m})$ ▷ seed
3: $\mathbf{c} = \mathsf{Encrypt}(\mathbf{m}, \mathsf{pk}, \theta)$
4: $K = \mathcal{K}(\mathbf{m}, \mathbf{c})$
5: $\mathbf{d} = \mathcal{H}(\mathbf{m})$
6: **return** (**c**, **d**)

Algorithm 5 Decaps
Input: c, d, sk, pk
Output: shared key K or $\perp$
1: $\mathbf{m'} = \mathsf{Decrypt}(\mathbf{c}, \mathsf{sk})$
2: $\theta' = \mathcal{G}(\mathbf{m'})$ ▷ seed
3: $\mathbf{c'} = \mathsf{Encrypt}(\mathbf{m'}, \mathsf{pk}, \Theta')$ ▷ re-encrypt
4: **if** $\mathbf{c} \neq \mathbf{c}$ or $\mathbf{d} \neq \mathcal{H}(\mathbf{m'})$ **then**
5:      **return** $\perp$
6: **else**
7:      **return** $K = \mathcal{K}(\mathbf{m}, \mathbf{c})$
8: **end if**

Fig. 2. HQC-KEM algorithms [1,2]. (Same key gen. as PKE version, see Fig. 1)

The internal code can be independently applied on each of the n_1 elements of $\mathbb{F}_q$, leading to encode n_1 times with the internal code, obtaining a final codeword of length $n_1 n_2$ (see Fig. 3).

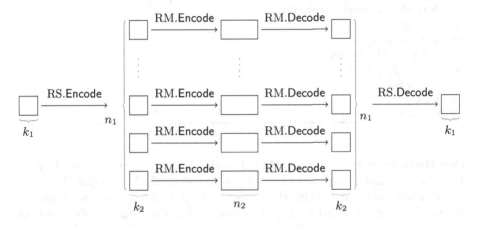

Fig. 3. Simplified HQC concatenated RMRS codes framework

The decoder is then a double decoder that decodes the internal code first and then the external. The decoding procedure is the same as the encoder and the first operation is to decode a $n_1 n_2$ sized codeword with n_1 independent decoding steps applied on blocs of size n_2. Our attack only targets these RM decoding steps and, for the sake of clarity, we will only describe the RM construction in this paper.

2.2 Decoding Reed-Muller Codes

HQC uses the same RM code RM(1, 7), which is a [128, 8, 64] code over $\mathbb{F}_2$, regardless of the chosen security level. Furthermore, each bit is duplicated 3 or

5 times (see Fig. 2), adding multiplicity to the codewords, to obtain codes of parameters $[384, 8, 192]$ or $[640, 8, 320]$. These RM codes of order 1 are seen as Hadamard codes and can be decoded using a Fast Hadamard Transform (FHT). The decoding procedure is always the same, composed of three main algorithms in the June 2020 HQC reference implementation [1]. The procedure is composed by the following main steps:

1. Removing the multiplicity of codewords with the expand and sum function (see Algorithm 6).
2. Apply the Fast Hadamard Transform (FHT) (see Algorithm 7).
3. Recover the message with the find peaks function (see Algorithm 8).

The first step goal is to remove the multiplicity of the codeword by adding in $\mathbb{N}$ bit to bit each repetition (see Algorithm 6). The result is an expanded codeword of length 128 leaving in $[\![0, 3]\!]$ or $[\![0, 5]\!]$ depending on the value of the multiplicity mul.

Algorithm 6. Expand and sum

    Input: codeword $\mathbf{c}$ and the multiplicity mul.
    Output: expanded codeword $\mathbf{c}'$
1: $\mathbf{c}' = \mathbf{0} \in \mathbb{N}^{128}$
2: **for** $i \in [\![0, \text{mul}]\!]$ **do**
3:     **for** $j \in [\![0, 128]\!]$ **do**
4:         $\mathbf{c}'[j] \mathrel{+}= \mathbf{c}[128 \times i + j]$
5:     **end for**
6: **end for**
7: **return** c'

Fast Hadamard Transform (FHT). The FHT is a generalized discrete Fourier Transform applied to expand codeword (see Algorithm 7). In practice, this function is equivalent to multiplying the expand codeword with an Hadamard matrix. Indeed, MacWilliams and Sloane [14] showed that the weight distribution of the cosets can be determined by the application of an Hadamard transform. This allows to decode with a maximum likelihood strategy, finding the distance between a received message and every codewords. For a RM$(1, m)$ code, the Hadamard matrix to choose is H_{2^m} which can be described recursively (see Eq. (1)).

$$H_{2m} = \begin{pmatrix} H_m & H_m \\ H_m & -H_m \end{pmatrix}, \; H_1 = 1 \tag{1}$$

Applying such a vector matrix multiplication would require $2^m \times 2^m$ additions and subtractions. Fortunately, H_{2^m} can be written as a product of m $2^m \times 2^m$ sparse matrices with only two non-zeros elements per column (see Eq. 2). This observation allows to change the vector matrix multiplication by m vector and sparse matrix multiplication.

$$H_{2^m} = M_{2^m}^{(1)} M_{2^m}^{(2)} \cdots M_{2^m}^{(m)}, \; M_{2^m}^{(i)} = I_{2^{m-i}} \otimes H_2 \otimes I_{2^{i-1}}, \; 1 \leq i \leq m \tag{2}$$

with I_n the identity matrix of size $n \times n$ and $\otimes$ the Kronecker product. That is the reason why the Algorithm 7 is composed of a for loop with argument $m = 7$.

Algorithm 7. Fast Hadamard Transform (FHT)

Input: expanded codeword $\mathbf{c}$ and the multiplicity mul.
Output: expanded codeword transformed structure $\mathbf{c}$
1: **for** $pass \in [\![0, 6]\!]$ **do**
2:     **for** $i \in [\![0, 63]\!]$ **do**
3:         $\mathbf{d}[i] = \mathbf{c}[2i] + \mathbf{c}[2i + 1]$
4:         $\mathbf{d}[i + 64] = \mathbf{c}[2i] - \mathbf{c}[2i + 1]$
5:     **end for**
6:     swap($\mathbf{d}, \mathbf{c}$)   ▷ copy $\mathbf{d}$ in $\mathbf{c}$ and $\mathbf{c}$ in $\mathbf{d}$
7: **end for**
8: $\mathbf{c}'[0] \mathrel{-}= 64 * \mathsf{mul}$
9: **return** $\mathbf{c}$

In our $\mathrm{RM}(1, 7)$ case, this transformation returns a vector of length 128. The last function Find Peaks permits to finish the decoding. Among this vector, the argument of the absolute maximum gives the 7 least significant bits of the decoded message. The most significant bit is given by the sign of this maximum (see Algorithm 8).

Algorithm 8. Find Peaks

Input: expanded codeword transformed structure $\mathbf{c}$
Output: message $\mathbf{m}$
1: (peak_value, peak_abs_value, peak_pos) = $(0, 0, 0)$
2: **for** $i \in [\![0, 123]\!]$ **do**
3:     $(t, t_{\mathrm{abs}}) = (\mathbf{c}[i], \mathsf{absolute}(\mathbf{c}[i]))$
4:     **if** $t_{\mathrm{abs}} >$ peak_abs_value **then**
5:         (peak_value, peak_abs_value, peak_pos) = (t, t_{abs}, i)
6:     **end if**
7: **end for**
8: peak_pos += $128 * ($peak_value $> 0)$ ▷ Setting the msb
9: **return** peak_pos

---

3   Theoretical Combined Chosen Ciphertext and Side-Channel Attacks

In this section, we present a new attack to recover the secret key $\mathbf{y} \in \mathbb{F}_2^n$. The main operation during the decapsulation part of HQC is decoding the erroneous codeword $\mathbf{v} - \mathbf{uy}$. Then the knowledge of the $\mathbf{y}$ part of the secret key is enough to decapsulate.

Attack Scenario. We consider a physical access to a device performing the HQC decapsulation with a static secret key. We assume that we can submit any ciphertext to the device. Our goal is to retrieve this key and then be able to decapsulate any message encapsulated by the associated public key. Our attack exploits the side-channel leakage to create an Oracle that is able to distinguish between several decoding patterns. We use the chosen ciphertext attack construction to send appropriate ciphertexts to the static secret key decapsulation chip. The electromagnetic measurements during the decapsulation constitute queries we can give to the Oracle.

We show how to build queries that allows to fully recover $\mathbf{y}$. First of all, notice that choosing the special ciphertext $(\mathbf{u}, \mathbf{v}) = (\mathbf{1}, \mathbf{0})$ leads to decode the secret key $\mathbf{y}$. Vector $\mathbf{y}$ is a sparse vector, with a small Hamming weight $\mathrm{wt}(\mathbf{y}) = \omega$. As a result, the RM decoder manipulates almost only zeros which is decoding into $\mathbf{0}$. This ciphertext is rejected by the re-encryption phase and the decapsulation returns a random vector as shared key for the IND-CCA2 security. This security could prevent our attack, however this is not an issue, given that our distinguisher does not depend on the output of the decapsulation but on the SCA leakage. Indeed, before the re-encryption, this ciphertext is manipulated by HQC decryption algorithms, among which the RM decoder, which give us all the necessary information to recover the secret key.

The RM decoder is independently applied on n_1 codewords blocs of size n_2 (see Fig. 3), individually retrieving each of the n_1 bloc of $\mathbf{y}$ leads at recovering $\mathbf{y}$. Our Oracle allows to recognize the number of errors corrected in each bloc. The idea is to vary the number of corrected errors by choosing the value of $\mathbf{v}$. The goal is to find $\mathbf{v} = \mathbf{y}$ which leads to decode $\mathbf{v} - \mathbf{y} = \mathbf{0}$. We show a strategy to effectively achieve this result.

The Oracle behaviour depends on the Hamming weight of the bloc to be decoded. Then, we study the support distribution of $\mathbf{y}$ among its different blocs.

3.1 Support Distribution of y

The support $\mathsf{Supp}(\mathbf{x})$ of a vector $\mathbf{x} = (x_0, \cdots, x_n)$ is the location of its non-zero coordinates (see Eq. (3)). If $\mathbf{x}$ is seen as a binary vector, its support is exactly the locations of the ones and the knowledge of the support is equivalent to the knowledge of the vector.

$$\mathsf{Supp}(\mathbf{x}) = \{i \in \mathbb{Z} \,|\, x_i \neq 0\} \tag{3}$$

The vector $\mathbf{y}$ has a length of n bits which is the smallest primitive prime number greater than $n_1 n_2$. The primitive prime n is used for the ambient space in order to thwart structural attacks. However, only the $n_1 n_2$ first bits, corresponding to the length of the concatenated code, are used during the decoding code, making the last $l = n - n_1 n_2$ truncated bits useless. Then, $\mathbf{y} \in \mathbb{F}_2^n$ can be seen as the concatenation of two vectors $\mathbf{y} = (\mathbf{y}', \mathbf{y}'')$ with $\mathbf{y}' \in \mathbb{F}_2^{n_1 n_2}$ and $\mathbf{y}'' \in \mathbb{F}_2^l$. This particularity prevents us for recovering any information about $\mathsf{Supp}(\mathbf{y}'')$. Fortunately, these bits are not relevant for the decoding step, and setting them to $\mathbf{0}$ is sufficient for a successful decoding. Furthermore, in almost all cases, $\mathrm{wt}(\mathbf{y}'') = 0$ (see Fig. 1) and in other cases, $\mathrm{wt}(\mathbf{y}'')$ is close too zero with a high probability. The probability $\mathbb{P}\left(\mathrm{wt}(\mathbf{y}'') = k\right)$ can be approximated by:

$$Q_k := \mathbb{P}\left(\mathrm{wt}(\mathbf{y}'') = k\right) \cong \binom{\omega}{k} p^k (1-p)^{\omega-k} \tag{4}$$

where $\omega = \mathrm{wt}(\mathbf{y})$ and p the probability to draw with replacement a bit in $\mathbf{y}'$ which is equal to $p = \dfrac{|\mathbf{y}'|}{|\mathbf{y}|}$.

Table 1. A few parameters of HQC and Support Probability Distribution (For each line, the sum is not equal to one because of the chosen approximation) between $\mathbf{y}'$ and $\mathbf{y}''$ following Eq. (4)

λ	n	$n_1 n_2$	ω	Q_0	Q_1	Q_2	$Q_{\geq 2}$
128	17.669	17.664	66	98,15%	1,83%	0,02%	$\leq 10^{-3}\%$
192	35.851	35.840	100	96,98%	2,98%	0,05%	$\leq 10^{-3}\%$
256	57.637	57.600	131	91,93%	7,73%	0,32%	$\leq 10^{-2}\%$

Recovering $\mathbf{y}'$ is enough to call the attack successful. Nevertheless, strategies exist to deduce the last l bits, for a complete recovery of $\mathbf{y}$. This low Hamming weight distribution allows to build an exhaustive research for the last $l = n - n_1 n_2$ bits of $\mathbf{y}$. Alternatively, Schamberger et al. [22], proposes a method in Sect. 3.3 of their paper to recover $\mathsf{Supp}(\mathbf{y}'')$ given the knowledge of $\mathsf{Supp}(\mathbf{y}')$ in polynomial time.

Support Distribution of $\mathbf{y}'$. The vector $\mathbf{y}'$ lives in $\mathbb{F}_2^{n_1 n_2}$ and the external decoder manipulates the codeword by bloc of size n_1, we can rewrite:

$$\mathbf{y}' = (\mathbf{y}_0', \mathbf{y}_1', \cdots, \mathbf{y}_{n_1-1}') \text{ and for all } i, \ \mathbf{y}_i' \in \mathbb{F}_2^{n_2} \tag{5}$$

For our attack, the worst case is when $\mathbf{y}'$ is full weight, i.e. $\mathrm{wt}(\mathbf{y}') = \mathrm{wt}(\mathbf{y})$ which happens when $\mathrm{wt}(\mathbf{y}'') = 0$ with a high probability (see Fig. 1). Indeed, this case increases the probability of having blocs with high Hamming weight. Later we will see that our distinguisher can only distinguish blocs with Hamming weight up to τ. Since the support distribution of $\mathbf{y}$ is almost always in this unfavorable case, we will only consider it for the following.

The Reed-Muller decoder manipulates each bloc $\mathbf{y}_i'$ independently, we calculate the probability P_k such as a randomly sampled bloc $\mathbf{y}_i'$ has an Hamming weight of k (see Eq. (6) and Fig. 2).

$$P_k := \mathbb{P}\left(\mathrm{wt}(\mathbf{y}_i') = k \ \middle| \ \mathbf{y} \xleftarrow{\$} \mathcal{R}_\omega, \ i \xleftarrow{\$} [\![0, n_1 - 1]\!]\right) \tag{6}$$

From Fig. 2, we observe that the small Hamming weight blocs are mostly represented. Furthermore, it is relatively rare to sample blocs of weight greater than or equal to 5. For the following, as an approximation, we consider all blocs of weight 5 or more in the same class.

Table 2. A few parameters of HQC and Support Probability Distribution (For each line, the sum is not equal to one because of the chosen approximation) among the blocs of $\mathbf{y'}$ following Eq. (6).

λ	mul.	n_1	n_2	ω	P_0	P_1	P_2	P_3	P_4	$P_{\geq 5}$
128	3	46	384	66	23,44%	34,38%	24,83%	11,77%	4,12%	1,45%
192	5	56	640	100	16,50%	30,00%	27,00%	16,04%	7,07%	3.40%
256	5	90	640	131	23,14%	34,06%	24,87%	12,02%	4,32%	1,59%

Higher Magnitude Error (HME). Expand And Sum is the first decoding function and realises a classic addition over $\mathbb{N}$. Then, the expanded codeword lives in $[\![0, \mathsf{mul}]\!]$. Applied to $\mathbf{y}$, in most cases, the result is in $[\![0, 1]\!]$ but it happens that two errors share the same location modulo 128 in a bloc ($\mathbf{y'}_i$). This gives an error of magnitude 2. These errors induce a slightly different behavior of the FHT within the same class, affecting the behavior of our Oracle. Fortunately, these higher magnitude errors happen with a low probability. Equation (7) gives the probability of having an error of magnitude at least 2.

$$
\begin{aligned}
\mathbb{P}\left(\text{HME}\right) &= \sum_{k=0}^{n_2} \mathbb{P}\left(\text{wt}(\mathbf{y'}_i) = k\right) \times \mathbb{P}\left(\text{HME} \mid \text{wt}(\mathbf{y'}_i) = k\right) \\
&= \sum_{k=0}^{n_2} P_k \times \left(1 - \mathbb{P}\left(\overline{\text{HME}} \mid \text{wt}(\mathbf{y'}_i) = k\right)\right) \\
&= \sum_{k=0}^{n_2} P_k \times \left(1 - \prod_{i=0}^{k} \frac{n_2 - (\mathsf{mul} - 1) \times i}{n_2}\right)
\end{aligned}
\tag{7}
$$

An HME happens in vector $\mathbf{y'}$ with probabilities $0,53\%$, $0,97\%$ and $0,65\%$ for respectively HQC-128, HQC-192 and HQC-256.

3.2 Chosen Ciphertext Attack with Oracle

We use a RM decoding Oracle $\mathcal{O}_{i,b}^{\text{RM}}$ which takes as input an HQC ciphertext $(\mathbf{u}, \mathbf{v})$. $\mathcal{O}_{i,b}^{\text{RM}}$ is able to determine the number of errors corrected by the RM decoder in the ith bloc $\mathbf{y'}_i$ for $i \in [\![0, n_1 - 1]\!]$. Our oracle works in a given range and correctly determine the number of corrected errors if it does not exceed a given threshold τ. The Oracle can be queried for different inputs and returns $b \in [\![0, \tau]\!]$. Notice that in the case of decoding $\mathbf{y}$, the number of decoded errors in a bloc $\mathbf{y'}_i$ is almost always the Hamming weight $\text{wt}(\mathbf{y'}_i)$. We describe how to construct this Oracle $\mathcal{O}_{i,b}^{\text{RM}}$ from side-channel leakage in Sect. 4.

Attack Description. Let us focus on a single chosen bloc $\mathbf{y'}_j$, the attack is identical for other blocs of $\mathbf{y}$. In a first step, the Oracle $\mathcal{O}_{j,b}^{\text{RM}}$ is queried to known the number of errors to correct in $\mathbf{y'}_j$ which gives a reference value for the next steps. Second, the main idea of the attack is to recursively select $\mathbf{v}_j$ of Hamming weight 1 in order to find a collision with the support of $\mathbf{y}'_j$. Finding a collision implies to modify the number of errors decoded compared to the reference value and then recover an information about $\mathsf{Supp}(\mathbf{y}'_j)$. In fact, for a chosen $\mathbf{v}_j$ there are two cases we can distinguish with the Oracle:

1. $\mathsf{Supp}(\mathbf{y}'_j) \cap \mathsf{Supp}(\mathbf{v}_j) = \mathsf{Supp}(\mathbf{v}_j)$. Then $\mathrm{wt}(\mathbf{v}_j - \mathbf{y}'_j) = \mathrm{wt}(\mathbf{y}'_j) - 1$, the decoder will correct one error less than the reference decoding of $\mathbf{y}'_j$.

$$O_{j,b}^{\mathrm{RM}}(\mathbf{v} - \mathbf{y}) = O_{j,b}^{\mathrm{RM}}(\mathbf{y}) - 1$$

2. $\mathsf{Supp}(\mathbf{y}'_j) \cap \mathsf{Supp}(\mathbf{v}_j) = \varnothing$. Then $\mathrm{wt}(\mathbf{v}_j - \mathbf{y}_j) = \mathrm{wt}(\mathbf{y}_j) + 1$, the decoder will correct one error more than the reference decoding of $\mathbf{y}$.

$$O_{j,b}^{\mathrm{RM}}(\mathbf{v} - \mathbf{y}) = O_{j,b}^{\mathrm{RM}}(\mathbf{y}) + 1$$

These observations allow to determine the support of $\mathbf{y}'_j$ by choosing $\mathbf{v}_j$ successively equal to all vectors of Hamming weight 1. By remembering the locations for which the Oracle outputs 1 less than the reference value $O_{j,b}^{\mathrm{RM}}(\mathbf{y})$, we are able to determine the entire support $\mathsf{Supp}(\mathbf{y}'_j)$. Applying this strategy to all blocs of $\mathbf{y}'$ aims at recovering the entire support $\mathsf{Supp}(\mathbf{y}')$.

Divide and Conquer Strategy. As described, the attack requires as many queries as the number of bits in $\mathbf{y}'$, i.e. $n_1 n_2$ bits, in order to test all elements of Hamming weight one. However, given that the RM blocs decoding are independent, the attack can be performed in parallel on each bloc. We query the n_1 Oracles $O_{i,b}^{\mathrm{RM}}$ at the same time, leading to a single query. Then, the minimal number of query needed to recover $\mathbf{y}'$ is reduced to the number of bits in a single bloc, i.e. n_2 bits. As a result, targeting HQC-128 (resp. HQC-192 and HQC-256) requires 384 queries (resp. 640). To know the total number of attack traces needed, this value is multiplied by the number of attack traces necessary to determine a single bit.

4   Building Decoding Oracle with a Side-Channel

In this section, we build a RM decoding Oracle that allows to identify the number of decoded errors. This Oracle is constructed from side-channel leakages and enables to retrieve the secret key $\mathbf{y}'$, as explained in Sect. 3. We first present our practical set-up which allows traces measurements. Then we describe our Oracle and conduct a leakage assessment with Welch t-test. Finally we evaluate the strength of our Oracle with a different number of training traces and give the cost and performance of the practical attack.

Side-Channel Attack Set-up. We realise our measurements on a ARM Cortex M4 micro-controller with a clock frequency of 168 MHz. We record the side-channel leakage from electromagnetic emanations (EM) with a LANGER EMV-Technik near field microprobe ICR HH 100-6. Measurements are registered with a 750M sampling rate oscilloscope ROHDE & SCHWARZ RTO2014. During acquisitions, the communication between the micro-controller and the computer is performed through an UART connection. During the acquisitions, we used an external clock to mitigate the jitter effects among the traces. We extract the Hadamard transform algorithm from the reference implementation of HQC [1] of June 2021. We set a dedicated GPIO pin just before the FHT function to trigger the oscilloscope and reset it after, we will call trace the resulting EM measurement.

4.1   Building the Oracle

We build the Oracle according to the 6 main classes identified with the support probability distribution (see Fig. 2). Each of these classes corresponds to a different Hamming weight for $\mathbf{y}'_i$ a bloc of $\mathbf{y}$. Each element of class k is created by randomly sampling its supports, corresponding to k random locations for the ones. Then, among these classes, the proportion of HME vectors is the same as in a HQC instance, following Eq. (7). The randomness is provided by the random generator of the micro-controller. We acquired a set of 10.000 traces per class used to evaluate the Oracle. These acquisitions were performed in a random order.

Leakage Assesment. We use a Welch t-test to conduct a leakage assessment for the Oracle. The t-value between two sets S_0 and S_1 with their respective cardinality n_0 and n_1, mean of μ_0 and μ_1 and variance of σ_0 and σ_1 is computed with the formula from Eq. (8). Usually, a threshold $|t| = 4.5$ is defined, admitting a significant statistical difference with a high degree of confidence when this threshold is exceeded.

$$t = \frac{\mu_0 - \mu_1}{\sqrt{\left(\frac{\sigma_0^2}{n_0} + \frac{\sigma_1^2}{n_1}\right)}} \tag{8}$$

We compute the t-values for each class pair in order to characterize the distinction between them. Results are presented in Fig. 4. For each sub-figure, we observe the 7 occurrences of the for loop during the FHT (see Algorithm 7). This test indicates a good level of distinguishability, which could allow to build a classifier.

Regions of Interest. In the way of the Points of Interest (PoI) selection, the leakage assessment allows us to select Regions of Interest (RoI). This selection allows to keep only relevant parts of the traces and to reduce the computation

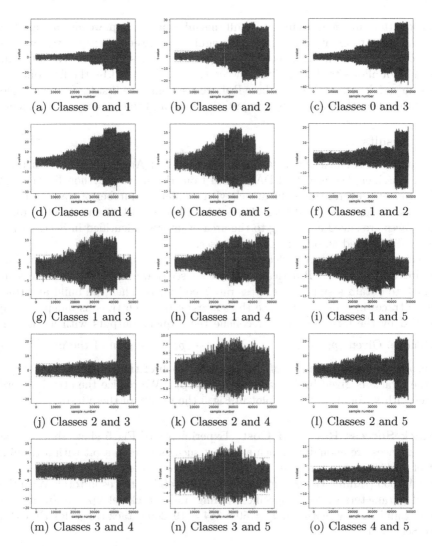

Fig. 4. Welch *t*-test results between each classes using 10,000 traces of randomly sampled inputs within the classe. The trace correspond to the FHT. $-4, 5$ and $4, 5$ are plotted with dashed red lines. (Color figure online)

time of our classifier. As we can see, among the seven occurrences of the for loop, the last one (approx. samples 41,000 to 48,000) seems to be very informative (see Fig. 4a, c, f, h, j, l, m, o). This part of the traces is the first considered RoI for further studies.

However, this RoI does not seem sufficient to build a complete distinguisher, indeed, some results show no leakage in the last occurrence (see Figs. 4e, g, i, n). In practice, using only trace segments in this RoI is not enough to mount an attack with a sufficient accuracy. To fill this information gap, we also use another RoI. In order to create a complete distinguisher between every classes, we also extract a RoI from the fifth occurrence (approx. samples $27,300$ to $34,200$). This second RoI allows to distinguish between cases not covered by the first one (see Figs. 4e, g, i, k, n). For both of these RoI, we keep only the first thousand samples which significantly reduces the computation time and the memory requirements.

4.2   Results

We build a distinguisher with a Linear Discriminant Analysis (LDA) which is a linear classifier. We use the LDA version from the sklearn python library [18]. We carry out several times the attack with a different number of training traces per class, respectively $1,000$, $2,500$, $5,000$, $10,000$, $20,000$ and $40,000$ traces. The traces are sliced according to the area of interest identified in Sect. 4.1 and evenly distributed among the target classes.

Theoretically, with a perfect Oracle, recovering a single bit in a given bloc requires only one trace. Practically, we quickly see that a single attack trace is not enough to obtain a sufficient success rate (see Fig. 5). Then, we build an attack with s traces in order to increase the success rate. Each trace is independently handled by the Oracle and we reconcile the s query outputs with a soft-max technique. Given $(p_1, \cdots, p_\tau) = \sum_{i=1}^{s} (p_{1,i}, \cdots, p_{\tau,i})$ the sum of the probabilities returning by the s instances of the attack for each of the τ classes. The output of the Oracle is given by $b = \mathsf{argmax}(p_1, \cdots, p_\tau)$. We realize the attack several times with s from 0 to 60, we plot in Fig. 5 the results of these tests.

Attack Success Rate and Cost. Experiments of Fig. 5 show that $s = 50$ attack traces are enough to reach a perfect success rate on a bit with a training set of $40,000$ traces per class. We build the attack on our set of measurements with $40,000$ training traces per class, $240,000$ training traces in total. With this set of parameters and our specific training and attack set-up, we are able to recover all bits of $\mathbf{y}'$ with $s \times n_2 = 50 \times 384 = 19,200$ attack traces for HQC-128 (see Sect. 3.2).

5   Countermeasure

A direct countermeasure against RM decoding distinguisher is the used of a mask. The idea is to hide the sensitive data by dividing its knowledge in several part. Indeed, if the input $\mathbf{c}$ of the FHT satisfies the relation 9,

$$\mathbf{c} = \sum_{i=0}^{n} \mathbf{c}_i \qquad (9)$$

by the linearity of the Hadamard transform, the result is given by Eq. (10).

$$\mathsf{FHT}(\mathbf{c}) = \sum_{i=0}^{n} \mathsf{FHT}(\mathbf{c}_i) \qquad (10)$$

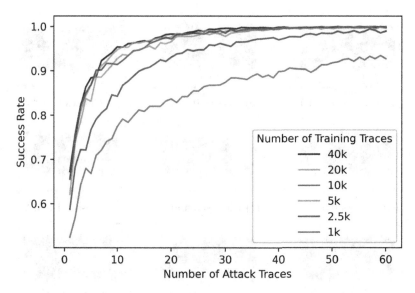

Fig. 5. Single bit success rate recovery depending on the number of attack traces s. Comparison of the success rate between attacks with a different number of training traces per class.

To create a secure masking scheme, the $n - 1$ first c_i must be sampled uniformly at random and the last element c_n is chosen to satisfy the relation (9). The n order mask countermeasure requires to compute $n + 1$ times the FHT. We give the first order masking Hadamard transform in Algorithm 9.

Algorithm 9. Hadamard Transform with first order mask

    Input: expanded codeword $\mathbf{c}$ and the multiplicity mul.
    Output: expanded codeword transformed structure $\mathbf{c}$
1: $\mathbf{c}_0 \xleftarrow{\$}$ expanded codeword
2: $\mathbf{c}_1 = c - c_0$
3: $\mathbf{c}_0 = \mathsf{FHT}(\mathbf{c}_0)$
4: $\mathbf{c}_1 = \mathsf{FHT}(\mathbf{c}_1)$
5: $\mathbf{c} = \mathbf{c}_0 + \mathbf{c}_1$
6: **return c**

Countermeasure Evaluation. An attacker who would like to target the masked version of the Hadamard transform would have to target the n shares in order to retrieve the whole information. Our attack scenario cannot be applied directly against the shares given that the expanded codewords $\mathbf{c}_i$ are randomly sampled. This implies that the shares do not respect the Hamming weight restrictions imposed by our Oracle.

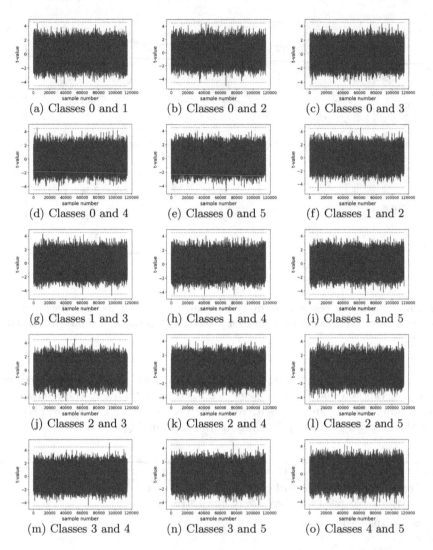

Fig. 6. Welch t-test results between each classes using $10,000$ traces of randomly sampled inputs within the classe. The trace correspond to the FHT with the countermeasure. $-4, 5$ and $4, 5$ are plotted with dashed red lines. (Color figure online)

In spite of this, we evaluate the strength of the counter-measure by repeating the experiment as in the Sect. 4. We compute the FHT with the first order mask (see Algorithm 9) on $60,000$ expanded codewords evenly distributed among the classes. Then, we compute the t-values for each class peer, leading to the results presented in Fig. 6. We assume that the significant reduction in the number of observed statistical differences with the Welch t-test ensures that the counter-measure is effective against our attack.

6   Conclusion and Future Work

In this paper we present a new side-channel attack on the RMRS version of HQC which aims at recovering a static secret key. We show that by choosing a certain ciphertext, a part of the secret key is given as input of the decoding algorithm. We build a chosen ciphertext attack from this point by slightly modifying the ciphertext in order to find collision with the secret key. In the paper, we show a strategy, a query sequence, that allows to find collisions and then recover the entire secret key.

Our attack is based on a side-channel Oracle that is able to distinguish between several decoding patterns. We evaluate our Oracle with electromagnetic side-channel measurements from our Cortex M4 micro-controller set-up and show that it is easy to build and reliable. Indeed, the best performances of our Oracle were observed with a trade-off of 40,000 training traces per classes, and 50 attack trace to recover a bit on a bloc with a success rate of 1 on our test set measurements. The independence of the decoding among the different blocs allows to parallelize the attack and recover all bits of the secret key with 19,200 attacks traces.

Our attack is a threat to the security of HQC and contributes to the need of an efficient countermeasure to mitigate such attacks. We propose a simple masking-based countermeasure in order to thwart our attack that doubles the run-time of the target function. As a perspective, the number of attack traces could be reduce by finding more efficient query sequence. For the same purpose, other functions of HQC could play the role of distinguisher, allowing to improve the performance or even to build new attacks.

Acknowledgements. This work was supported by the French National Agency in the framework of the *"Investissements d'avenir"* (future-oriented investments) program (ANR-10-AIRT-05) and by the defense innovation agency (AID) from the french ministry of armed forces.

References

1. Aguilar-Melchor, C., et al.: HQC reference implementation. https://pqc-hqc.org/implementation.html
2. Aguilar-Melchor, C., et al.: Hamming Quasi-Cyclic (HQC) (2017)
3. Alagic, G., et al.: Status report on the second round of the NIST post-quantum cryptography standardization process. US Department of Commerce, NIST (2020)
4. Aragon, N., Gaborit, P., Zémor, G.: HQC-RMRS, an instantiation of the HQC encryption framework with a more efficient auxiliary error-correcting code. arXiv preprint arXiv:2005.10741 (2020)
5. Berlekamp, E., McEliece, R., van Tilborg, H.: On the inherent intractability of certain coding problems (corresp.). IEEE Trans. Inf. Theory **24**(3), 384–386 (1978). https://doi.org/10.1109/TIT.1978.1055873
6. Brier, E., Clavier, C., Olivier, F.: Correlation power analysis with a leakage model. In: Joye, M., Quisquater, J.-J. (eds.) CHES 2004. LNCS, vol. 3156, pp. 16–29. Springer, Heidelberg (2004). https://doi.org/10.1007/978-3-540-28632-5_2

7. Fujisaki, E., Okamoto, T.: Secure integration of asymmetric and symmetric encryption schemes. In: Wiener, M. (ed.) CRYPTO 1999. LNCS, vol. 1666, pp. 537–554. Springer, Heidelberg (1999). https://doi.org/10.1007/3-540-48405-1_34

8. Fujisaki, E., Okamoto, T.: Secure integration of asymmetric and symmetric encryption schemes. J. Cryptol. **26**(1), 80–101 (2013)

9. Goy, G., Loiseau, A., Gaborit, P.: Estimating the strength of horizontal correlation attacks in the hamming weight leakage model: a side-channel analysis on HQC KEM (2022)

10. Guo, Q., Hlauschek, C., Johansson, T., Lahr, N., Nilsson, A., Schröder, R.L.: Don't reject this: key-recovery timing attacks due to rejection-sampling in HQC and bike. Cryptology ePrint Archive (2021)

11. Hofheinz, D., Hövelmanns, K., Kiltz, E.: A modular analysis of the Fujisaki-Okamoto transformation. In: Kalai, Y., Reyzin, L. (eds.) TCC 2017. LNCS, vol. 10677, pp. 341–371. Springer, Cham (2017). https://doi.org/10.1007/978-3-319-70500-2_12

12. Kocher, P., Jaffe, J., Jun, B.: Differential power analysis. In: Wiener, M. (ed.) CRYPTO 1999. LNCS, vol. 1666, pp. 388–397. Springer, Heidelberg (1999). https://doi.org/10.1007/3-540-48405-1_25

13. Kocher, P.C.: Timing attacks on implementations of Diffie-Hellman, RSA, DSS, and other systems. In: Koblitz, N. (ed.) CRYPTO 1996. LNCS, vol. 1109, pp. 104–113. Springer, Heidelberg (1996). https://doi.org/10.1007/3-540-68697-5_9

14. MacWilliams, F.J., Sloane, N.J.A.: The Theory of Error Correcting Codes, vol. 16. Elsevier (1977)

15. McEliece, R.J.: A public-key cryptosystem based on algebraic. Coding Thv **4244**, 114–116 (1978)

16. NIST: Submission requirements and evaluation criteria for the post-quantum cryptography standardization process (2016)

17. Paiva, T.B., Terada, R.: A timing attack on the HQC encryption scheme. In: Paterson, K.G., Stebila, D. (eds.) SAC 2019. LNCS, vol. 11959, pp. 551–573. Springer, Cham (2020). https://doi.org/10.1007/978-3-030-38471-5_22

18. Pedregosa, F., et al.: Scikit-learn: machine learning in Python. J. Mach. Learn. Res. **12**, 2825–2830 (2011)

19. Petrvalsky, M., Richmond, T., Drutarovsky, M., Cayrel, P.L., Fischer, V.: Differential power analysis attack on the secure bit permutation in the mceliece cryptosystem. In: 2016 26th International Conference Radioelektronika (RADIOELEKTRONIKA), pp. 132–137. IEEE (2016)

20. Rivest, R.L., Shamir, A., Adleman, L.: A method for obtaining digital signatures and public-key cryptosystems. Commun. ACM **21**(2), 120–126 (1978)

21. Schamberger, T., Holzbaur, L., Renner, J., Wachter-Zeh, A., Sigl, G.: A power side-channel attack on the reed-muller reed-solomon version of the HQC cryptosystem. Cryptology ePrint Archive (2022)

22. Schamberger, T., Renner, J., Sigl, G., Wachter-Zeh, A.: A power side-channel attack on the CCA2-secure HQC KEM. In: 19th Smart Card Research and Advanced Application Conference (CARDIS2020) (2020)

23. Schröder, L.: A novel timing side-channel assisted key-recovery attack against HQC. Ph.D. thesis, Wien (2022)

24. Sendrier, N.: Decoding one out of many. In: Yang, B.-Y. (ed.) PQCrypto 2011. LNCS, vol. 7071, pp. 51–67. Springer, Heidelberg (2011). https://doi.org/10.1007/978-3-642-25405-5_4

25. Wafo-Tapa, G., Bettaieb, S., Bidoux, L., Gaborit, P., Marcatel, E.: A practicable timing attack against HQC and its countermeasure. In: Advances in Mathematics of Communications (2020)
26. Walter, C.D.: Sliding windows succumbs to big mac attack. In: Koç, Ç.K., Naccache, D., Paar, C. (eds.) CHES 2001. LNCS, vol. 2162, pp. 286–299. Springer, Heidelberg (2001). https://doi.org/10.1007/3-540-44709-1_24

Isogeny

On Actively Secure Fine-Grained Access Structures from Isogeny Assumptions

Fabio Campos[1,2($\boxtimes$)] and Philipp Muth[3]

[1] RheinMain University of Applied Sciences, Wiesbaden, Germany
[2] Radboud University, Nijmegen, The Netherlands
campos@sopmac.de
[3] Technische Universität Darmstadt, Darmstadt, Germany
philipp.muth@tu-darmstadt.de

Abstract. We present an actively secure threshold scheme in the setting of Hard Homogeneous Spaces (HHS) which allows fine-grained access structures. More precisely, we elevate a passively secure isogeny-based threshold scheme to an actively secure setting. We prove the active security and simulatability of our advanced schemes. By characterising the necessary properties, we open our schemes to a significantly wider field of applicable secret sharing schemes. Furthermore, we show that Shamir's scheme has our generalised properties, and thereby our approach truly represents a less restrictive generalisation.

Keywords: Post-quantum cryptography · Isogeny-based cryptography · Threshold cryptography

1 Introduction

The principal motivation for a secret sharing scheme is to split private information into fragments and securely distribute these shares among a set of shareholders. Then, any collaborating set with a sufficient number of participants is able to reconstruct the shared private information, while the secret remains confidential to any unauthorised, that is not sufficiently large, subset of shareholders.

Since their introduction in the 1970s s by Blakley [4] and Shamir [15], the field of secret sharing schemes, information theoretic and computational, has been studied extensively. In previous years, due to applications in blockchain and other scenarios, the interest in new developments and applications for secret sharing schemes has increased.

Post-quantum schemes have, however, only received little attention with respect to secret sharing. Recently, De Feo and Meyer [11] proposed a key exchange mechanism and a signature scheme making use of isogeny based public key cryptography for which the secret key is stored in a Shamir shared way. Their

---

Author list in alphabetical order; see https://www.ams.org/profession/leaders/culture/CultureStatement04.pdf.

© The Author(s), under exclusive license to Springer Nature Switzerland AG 2022
J. H. Cheon and T. Johansson (Eds.): PQCrypto 2022, LNCS 13512, pp. 375–398, 2022.
https://doi.org/10.1007/978-3-031-17234-2_18

approach enables decapsulation for the key exchange mechanism and signing for the signature scheme in a round-robin way without reconstructing the secret key in clear for any sufficiently large set of shareholders. Yet in applying Shamir's secret sharing scheme they restrict themselves to simple threshold access structures. Furthermore, their protocols are only passively secure, in that while a misbehaving shareholder cannot obtain information on the secret key shares of other shareholders participating in a decapsulation or a signing execution via maliciously formed inputs, his deviation from the protocol cannot be detected.

We aim to tackle both caveats by proposing an actively secure isogeny based key exchange mechanism, for which the secret key is secret shared by a trusted dealer. We further transform the key exchange mechanism into an actively secure signature scheme with shared secret key.

Our Contribution. Our contribution is manifold. First, we transfer the active security measures outlined in [2] from their setting of full engagement protocols to a setting of threshold secret sharing. We thereby open the active security measures to a wider field of application and improve upon their efficiency significantly. Second, we apply the adapted active security measures to propose an actively secure key exchange mechanism with secret shared secret key. Third, we present an actively secure signature scheme by applying a Fiat-Shamir transform to our key exchange mechanism. And fourth, we expand our key encapsulation mechanism and our signature scheme to a wider field of secret sharing schemes. For that we characterise the necessary properties for a secret sharing scheme and give several examples of compatible schemes.

Related Work. Secret sharing schemes were first introduced by Blakley [4] and Shamir [15]. In both their approaches, secrets from the secret space $\mathbb{Z}_p := \mathbb{Z} \bmod p$ for prime p are shared by distributing interpolation points of randomly sampled polynomials. Damgård and Thorbek [9] presented a secret sharing scheme with secret space $\mathbb{Z}$. Thorbek [18] later improved their scheme. Yet their scheme is only computationally confidential, compared to the information theoretical confidentiality of Shamir and Blakley's schemes. Tassa [17] opened Shamir's scheme to a more general application by utilising the derivatives of the sharing polynomial to construct a hierarchical access structure,. These basic secret sharing schemes rely on the dealer providing honestly generated shares to the shareholders. Verifiable secret sharing schemes eliminate this drawback by providing the shareholders with the means to verify the correctness of the received shares with varying overhead. Examples of these are [1,13,16]. With minor efficiency losses, Herranz and Sáez [12] were able to achieve verifiable secret sharing for generalised access structures. Traverso et al. [19] proposed an approach for evaluating arithmetic circuits on secret shared in Tassa's scheme, that also enabled auditing the results. Cozzo and Smart [7] investigated the possibility of constructing shared secret schemes based on the Round 2 candidate signature schemes in the NIST standardization process[1]. Based on CSI-FiSh [3], De Feo and Meyer [11] introduced threshold variants of passively secure encryption and signature schemes in the Hard Homogeneous Spaces (HHS) setting. Cozzo and Smart [8] presented the first actively secure but not robust distributed signature scheme based on isogeny assumptions. In [2], the authors presented CSI-RAShi, a robust and actively secure distributed key generation protocol based on Shamir's secret sharing in the setting of HHS, which necessitates all shareholders to participate.

Outline. In Sect. 2 the terminology, primitives and security notions relevant for this work are introduced. Section 3 presents an actively secure threshold key exchange mechanism and proves our scheme's active security and simulatability. The actively secure signature scheme resulting from applying the Fiat-Shamir-transform to our key exchange mechanism is discussed in Sect. 4. Finally, the necessary properties for a secret sharing scheme to be compatible with our key exchange mechanism and signature scheme are characterised in Sect. 5 in order to enable applying a more general class of secret sharing schemes.

2 Preliminaries

Notation. Throughout this work we use a security parameter $\lambda \in \mathbb{N}$. It is implicitly handed to a protocol whenever needed, that is protocols with computational security. Information theoretic schemes and protocols such as secret sharing schemes used in this work do not require a security parameter.

For an indexed set $X = \{x_i\}_{i \in I}$, we denote the projection onto a subset $I' \subset I$ by $X_{I'} = \{x_i \in X : i \in I'\}$. The same holds for indexed tuples $(x_i)_{i \in I}$.

2.1 Secret Sharing Schemes

A secret sharing scheme is a cryptographic primitive that allows a dealer to share a secret among a set of shareholders. An instance is thus defined by a secret space G, a set of shareholders S and an access structure Γ_S. A set $S' \in \Gamma_S$ is called *authorised* and can from their respective shares reconstruct a shared secret. If the instance S is clear from the context, we omit the index in the access structure Γ. In this work, we consider monotone access structures, that is for any $A \subset B \subset S$ with $A \in \Gamma$, we also have $B \in \Gamma$.

A secret sharing instance S provides two algorithms: Share and Rec. A dealer executes $S.\mathsf{Share}(s)$ to generate shares $s_1, \ldots, s_k$ of a secret s. A share s_i is assigned to a shareholder $P_{\phi(i)}$ via a surjective map $\phi : \{1, \ldots, k\} \to \{1, \ldots, n\}$ induced by Γ_S. A set of shareholders $S' \in \Gamma_S$ executes

$$S.\mathsf{Rec}\Big(\{s_i\}_{P_{\phi(i)} \in S'}\Big)$$

---

[1] https://csrc.nist.gov/Projects/post-quantum-cryptography/Post-Quantum-Cryptography-Standardization.

on their respective shares to retrieve a previously shared secret.

Definition 1 (Superauthorised sets). *For a secret sharing instance $\mathcal{S} = (G, S, \Gamma_{\mathcal{S}})$, we call a set $S' \subset S$ superauthorised, if for any $P \in S'$, we have $S' \setminus \{P\} \in \Gamma_{\mathcal{S}}$. We denote the set of superauthorised sets of shareholders by $\Gamma_{\mathcal{S}}^{+}$.*

Any superauthorised set is also authorised.

Example 1 (Shamir's secret sharing). An instance of Shamir's famous secret sharing scheme consists of a set of $n > 0$ shareholders, a secret space $\mathbb{Z}$ mod p, where p is a prime larger than n, and an access structure $\Gamma = \{S' \subset S : \#S' \geq t\}$ for a threshold $t \leq n$. A secret $s \in \mathbb{Z}$ mod p is shared by handing each shareholder P_i an interpolation point of a randomly sampled polynomial of degree $t-1$ with constant term s. Reconstruction is achieved via Lagrange interpolation, that is

$$s = \sum_{P_i \in S'} L_{i,S'} s_i = \sum_{P_i \in S'} \prod_{\substack{P_j \in S' \\ j \neq i}} \frac{j}{j-i} f(i)$$

for some $S' \in \Gamma$ and Lagrange interpolation coefficients $L_{i,S'}$. The set of superauthorised sets of shareholders is

$$\Gamma^{+} = \{S^{+} \subset S : \#S^{+} \geq t + 1\}.$$

2.2   Hard Homogeneous Spaces

We present our key exchange mechanism and signature scheme in the context of *hard homogeneous spaces* (HHS). HHS were first discussed by Couveignes [6] in 2006. He defines a HHS $(\mathcal{E}, \mathcal{G})$ as a set $\mathcal{E}$ and a group $(\mathcal{G}, \odot)$ equipped with a transitive action $* : \mathcal{G} \times \mathcal{E} \to \mathcal{E}$. This action has the following properties:

- Compatibility: For any $g, g' \in \mathcal{G}$ and any $E \in \mathcal{E}$, we have $g * (g' * E) = (g \odot g') * E$.
- Identity: For any $E \in \mathcal{E}$, $i * E = E$ if and only if $i \in \mathcal{G}$ is the identity element.
- Transitivity: For any $E, E' \in \mathcal{E}$, there exists exactly one $g \in \mathcal{G}$ such that $g * E = E'$.

Definition 2 (Notation). *For a HHS $(\mathcal{E}, \mathcal{G})$ with a fixed $g \in \mathcal{G}$, let $p|\#\mathcal{G}$ be a fixed prime. We denote $[s] E := g^s * E$ for all $s \in \mathbb{Z}_p$ and all $E \in \mathcal{E}$.*

The following problems are assumed to be efficiently computable in a HHS $(\mathcal{E}, \mathcal{G})$, i.e., there exist polynomial time algorithms to solve them:

- Group operations on $\mathcal{G}$ (membership, inverting elements, evaluating $\odot$).
- Sampling elements of $\mathcal{E}$ and $\mathcal{G}$.
- Testing the membership of $\mathcal{E}$.
- Computing the transitive action $*$: given $g \in \mathcal{G}$ and $E \in \mathcal{E}$ as input, compute $g * E$.

Whereas the subsequent problems are assumed to be hard in a HHS $(\mathcal{E}, \mathcal{G})$.

Problem 1 (Group Action Inverse Problem (GAIP)). Given two elements $E, E' \in \mathcal{E}$ as input, the challenge is to provide $g \in \mathcal{G}$ with $E' = g * E$. Due to the transitivity property of HHS given instance of the GAIP has a solution.

Problem 2 (Parallelisation Problem). An instance of the *Parallelisation Problem* is defined by a triple $(E, E', F) \in \mathcal{E}^3$ with $E' = g * E$. The challenge is to provide F' with $F' = g * F$.

The intuitive decisional continuation of this problem is as follows.

Problem 3 (Decisional Parallelisation Problem). An instance of the *Decisional Parallelisation Problem* is defined by a base element $E \in \mathcal{E}$ and a triple (E_a, E_b, E_c) with $E_a = [a]E$, $E_b = [b]E$ and $E_c = [c]E$. The challenge is to distinguish whether $c = a + b$ or $c \leftarrow_\$ \mathbb{Z}_p$ was randomly sampled.

Remark 1. It is obvious that the decisional parallelisation problem reduces to the parallelisation problem, which reduces to the group action inverse problem.

2.3   Threshold Group Action

Let s be a Shamir shared secret among shareholders $P_1, \ldots, P_n$, that is each P_i holds a share s_i of s, $i = 1, \ldots, n$. To compute $E' = [s]E$ for an arbitrary but fixed $E \in \mathcal{E}$ without reconstructing s, we have an authorised set of shareholders execute Algorithm 5. If it is executed successfully, we have by the compatibility property of $*$ and the repeated application of $E^k \leftarrow [L_{i,S'} s_i] E^{k-1}$ the result

$$E^{\#S'} = \left[\sum_{P_i \in S'} L_{i,S'} s_i \right] E = [s] E.$$

2.4   Piecewise Verifiable Proofs

A piecewise verifiable proof (PVP) is a cryptographic primitive in the context of hard homogeneous spaces and was first introduced in [2]. It is a compact non-interactive zero-knowledge proof of knowledge of a witness $f \in \mathbb{Z}_q[X]$ for a statement

$$x = ((E_0, E_1), s_1, \ldots, s_n), \tag{2.1}$$

with statement pieces $s_i = f(i)$ for $i = 0, \ldots, n$ and $E_1 = [s_0] E_0 \in \mathcal{E}$. A PVP provides a proving protocol PVP.P, which takes a statement x of the form (2.1) and a witness f and outputs a proof $(\pi, \{\pi_i\}_{i=0,\ldots,n})$, where (π, π_i) is a proof piece for s_i, $i = 0, \ldots, n$. The PVP also provides a verifying protocol PVP.V, which takes an index $i \in \{0, \ldots, n\}$, a statement piece s_i and a proof piece (π, π_i) and outputs true or false. Let $\mathcal{R} = \{(x, f)\}$, where f is a witness for the statement x. The projection R_I for some $I \subset \{0, \ldots, n\}$ denotes (x_I, f).

Definition 3 (Completeness). *We call a PVP complete, if, for any* $(x, f) \in \mathcal{R}$ *and*

$$(\pi, \{\pi_i\}_{i=0,\ldots,n}) \leftarrow \mathsf{PVP}.P(f, x),$$

the verification succeeds, that is

$$\forall j \in \{0, \ldots, n\} \colon \Pr\left[\mathsf{PVP}.V(j, x_j, (\pi, \pi_j)) = \mathsf{true}\right] = 1.$$

Definition 4 (Soundness). *A PVP is called* sound *if, for any adversary* $\mathcal{A}$, *any* $I \subset \{0, \ldots, n\}$ *and any* x *for which there exists no* f *with* $(x_I, f) \in \mathcal{R}_I$,

$$\Pr\left[\mathsf{PVP}.V(j, x_j, (\pi, \pi_j)) = \mathsf{true}\right]$$

is negligible in the security parameter λ *for all* $j \in I$, *where* $(\pi, \{\pi_i\}_{i \in I}) \leftarrow \mathcal{A}(1^\lambda)$.

Definition 5 (Zero-knowledge). *A PVP is* zero-knowledge, *if for any* $I \subset \{1, \ldots, n\}$ *and any* $(x, f) \in \mathcal{R}$, *there exists a simulator* Sim *such that for any polynomial-time distinguisher* $\mathcal{A}$ *the advantage*

$$\left| \Pr\left[\mathcal{A}^{\mathsf{Sim}(x_I)}(1^\lambda) = 1 \right] - \Pr\left[\mathcal{A}^{P(x,f)}(1^\lambda) = 1 \right] \right|$$

is negligible in the security parameter λ, *where* P *is an oracle that upon input* (x, f) *returns* $(\pi, \{\pi_j\}_{j \in I})$ *with* $(\pi, \{\pi_j\}_{j=0,\ldots,n}) \leftarrow \mathsf{PVP}.P(f, x)$.

We refer to [2] for the precise proving and verifying protocols and the security thereof. In combination they state a complete, sound and zero-knowledge non-interactive PVP. A prover can hence show knowledge of a sharing polynomial f to a secret $s_0 = f(0)$ with shares $s_i = f(i)$. In Sect. 3, we adjust [2]'s proving protocol to our setting of threshold schemes, so that knowledge of a subset of interpolation points is proven instead of all interpolation points.

2.5   Zero-Knowledge Proofs for the GAIP

We give a non-interactive zero-knowledge proof protocol for an element $s \in \mathbb{Z}_p$ with respect to the group action inverse problem. That is, a prover shows the knowledge of s so that $E'_i = [s] E_i$, for $E_i, E'_i \in \mathcal{E}$ and $i = 1, \ldots, m$, simultaneously, without revealing s.

The prover samples $b_j \in \mathbb{Z}_p$ and computes $\hat{E}_{i,j} \leftarrow [b_j] E_i$ for $i = 1, \ldots, m$ and $j = 1, \ldots, \lambda$. He then derives challenge bits

$$(c_1, \ldots, c_\lambda) \leftarrow \mathcal{H}\left(E_1, E'_1, \ldots, E_m, E'_m, \hat{E}_{1,1} \ldots, \hat{E}_{m,\lambda}\right)$$

via a hash function $\mathcal{H} : \mathcal{E}^{(2+\lambda)m} \rightarrow \{0, 1\}^\lambda$ and prepares the answers $r_j \leftarrow b_j - c_j s$, $j = 1, \ldots, \lambda$. The proof $\pi = (c_1, \ldots, c_\lambda, r_1, \ldots, r_\lambda)$ is then published.

The verification protocol is straight forward: given a statement $(E_i, E'_i)_{i=1,\ldots,m}$ and a proof $\pi = (c_1, \ldots, c_\lambda, r_1, \ldots, r_\lambda)$, the verifier computes $\tilde{E}_{i,j} \leftarrow [r_j] E_i$ if $c_j = 0$ and $\tilde{E}_{i,j} \leftarrow [r_j] E'_i$ otherwise, for $i = 1, \ldots, m$ and $j = 1, \ldots, \lambda$. He then generates verification bits $(\tilde{c}_1, \ldots \tilde{c}_\lambda) \leftarrow \mathcal{H}\left(E_1, E_1', \ldots, E_m, E_m', \tilde{E}_{1,1} \ldots, \tilde{E}_{m,\lambda}\right)$ and accepts the proof if $(c_1, \ldots, c_\lambda) = (\tilde{c}_1, \ldots, \tilde{c}_\lambda)$.

We sketch the proving and verifying protocols in Algorithm 6 and Algorithm 7, respectively. Again, we refer to [3] for the proof of completeness, soundness and zero-knowledge with respect to the security parameter λ.

2.6   The Adversary

We consider a static and active adversary. At the beginning of a protocol execution, the adversary corrupts a set of shareholders. The adversary is able to see their inputs and control their outputs. The set of corrupted shareholders cannot be changed throughout the execution of the protocol.

The adversary's aim is two-fold. On the one hand it wants to obtain information on the uncorrupted parties' inputs, on the other hand it wants to manipulate the execution of our protocol towards an incorrect output without detection.

2.7   Communication Channels

Both our schemes assume the existence of a trusted dealer in the secret sharing instance. The shareholders' communication occurs in the execution of the decapsulation protocol of our key exchange mechanism and the signing protocol of our signature scheme.

The communication from the dealer to a shareholder must not be eavesdropped upon or tampered with, we hence assume secure private channels between the dealer and each shareholder. However, the communication between shareholders need not be kept private, thus we assume a simple broadcast channel between the shareholders. The means of how to establish secure private channels and immutable broadcast channels are out of scope of this work.

3   Key Exchange Mechanism

A key exchange mechanism is a cryptographic public key scheme that provides three protocols: KeyGen, Encaps and Decaps. These enable a party to establish an ephemeral key between the holder of the secret key. We present our actively secure key exchange mechanism with private key that is secret shared among a set of shareholders. An authorised subset can execute the Decaps protocol without reconstructing the secret key.

3.1   Public Parameters

We fix the following publically known parameters.

- A secret sharing instance $\mathcal{S}$ with shareholders $S = \{P_1, \ldots, P_n\}$, secret space $\mathbb{Z}_p$ and access structure Γ.

- A hard homogeneous space $(\mathcal{E}, \mathcal{G})$ with a fixed starting point $E_0 \in \mathcal{E}$.
- A fixed element $g \in \mathcal{G}$ with $\mathrm{ord} g = p$ for the mapping $[\cdot] \cdot : \mathbb{Z}_p \times \mathcal{E} \to \mathcal{E}; s \mapsto g^s E$.

We give our key exchange mechanism in the context of Shamir's secret sharing scheme and elaborate possible extensions to other, more general secret sharing schemes in Sect. 5.

3.2 Key Generation

A public and secret key pair is established by a trusted dealer (even an untrusted dealer is feasible by employing verifiable secret sharing schemes) executing Algorithm 1. For that he samples a secret key s and publishes the public key $\mathsf{pk} \leftarrow [s]E_0$. The secret key s is then shared among the $\{P_1, \ldots, P_n\}$ via $\mathcal{S}.\mathsf{Share}(s)$. The dealer shares each share s_i, $i = 1, \ldots, n$, once more. Each shareholder P_i, $i = 1, \ldots, n$, eventually receives s_i, $\{s_{ji}, s_{ij}\}_{j=1,\ldots,n}$, that is his share s_i of s, the sharing of s_i and a share of other s_j, $j \neq i$.

Algorithm 1: Key generation

Input: $\mathcal{S}$

$s \leftarrow_\$ \mathbb{Z}_p$

$\mathsf{pk} \leftarrow [s] E_0$

$\{s_1, \ldots, s_n\} \leftarrow \mathcal{S}.\mathsf{Share}(s)$

for $i = 1, \ldots, n$ **do**
$\quad \lfloor \ \{s_{i1}, \ldots, s_{in}\} \leftarrow \mathcal{S}.\mathsf{Share}(s_i)$

publish pk

for $i = 1, \ldots, n$ **do**
$\quad \lfloor$ send $\{s_i, \{s_{ij}\}_{j=1,\ldots,n}, \{s_{ki}\}_{k=1,\ldots,n}\}$ to P_i

---

This key generation protocol can be regarded as a "two-level sharing", where each share of the secret key is itself shared again among the shareholders. While this is not necessary for De Feo and Meyer's passively secure protocol, we require the two-level sharing in ensuring the active security of our key encapsulation mechanism.

3.3 Encapsulation

With a public key $\mathsf{pk} \in \mathcal{E}$ as input, the encapsulation protocol returns an ephemeral key $\mathcal{K} \in \mathcal{E}$ and a ciphertext $c \in \mathcal{E}$. Our encapsulation protocol is identical to the protocol of [11], thus we just give a short sketch and refer to De Feo's and Meyer's work for the respective proofs of security.

Algorithm 2: Encapsulation

> **Input:** pk
> $b \leftarrow_\$ \mathcal{G}$
> $\mathcal{K} \leftarrow b * \mathsf{pk}$
> $c \leftarrow b * E_0$
> **return** $(\mathcal{K}, c)$

3.4 Decapsulation

A decapsulation protocol takes a ciphertext c and outputs a key $\mathcal{K}$. De Feo and Meyer [11] applied the threshold group action (Algorithm 5) so that an authorised set $S' \in \Gamma$ decapsulates a ciphertext c and produces an ephemeral key $[s] c = [s] (b * E_0) = b * ([s] E_0)$. For that, the shareholders agree on an arbitrary order of turns. With $E^0 := c$, the kth shareholder P_i outputs $E^k = [L_{i,S'} s_i] E^{k-1}$ for $k = 1, \ldots, \#S'$. The last shareholder outputs the decapsulated ciphertext $E^{\#S'} = [s] c$. Their approach is simulatable. It does not leak any information on the shares s_i, yet it is only passively secure. Thus, a malicious shareholder can provide malformed input to the protocol and thereby manipulate the output of the computation towards incorrect results without the other parties recognising this deviation from the protocol. We extend their approach to enable the detection of misbehaving shareholders in a decapsulation. For that we maintain the threshold group action and apply the PVP and zero-knowledge proof for the group action inverse problem as layed out in Sect. 2.

3.5 Amending the PVP

In the PVP protocol sketched in Sect. 2, a prover produces a proof of knowledge for a witness polynomial f of the statement $((E_0, E_1), s_1, \ldots, s_n)$, where $E_0 \leftarrow_\$ \mathcal{E}$, $E_1 = [s_0] E_0$ and $s_i = f(i)$ for $i = 0, \ldots, n$. He thereby proves knowledge of the sharing polynomial f of $s_0 = f(0)$.

This approach does not agree with the threshold group action, for which a shareholder P_i's output in the round-robin approach is $E^k \leftarrow [L_{i,S'} s_i] E^{k-1}$ rather than $E^k \leftarrow [s_i] E^{k-1}$, where E^{k-1} denotes the previous shareholder's output. Futhermore, authorised sets need not contain all shareholders. Example 2 illustrates a further conflict with of the PVP with the threshold group action.

Example 2. Let sk be a secret key generated and shared by KeyGen. That is each shareholder P_i holds

$$\{s_i, f_i, \{f_j(i)\}_{P_j \in S}\}.$$

Also let $S' \in \Gamma$ be a minimally authorised set executing Algorithm 5, i.e., for any $P_i \in S'$, $S' \backslash \{P_i\}$ is unauthorised. Thus, for any arbitrary but fixed $s'_i \in \mathbb{Z}_p$, there exists a polynomial $f'_i \in \mathbb{Z}_p[X]_{k-1}$ so that $f'_i(j) = L_{i,S'} f_i(j)$ and $R' = [f'_i(0)] R$ for any $R, R' \in \mathcal{E}$ and all $P_j \in S' \backslash \{P_i\}$. Therefore, P_i can publish

$$\left(\pi, \{\pi_j\}_{P_j \in S}\right) \leftarrow \mathsf{PVP.P}\left(\left((R, R'), (L_{i,S'} f_i(*) j)_{P_j \in S}\right), f'_i\right)$$

which is indistinguishable from

$$\mathsf{PVP}.P\left(\left((E_0, E_1), (L_{i,S'} f_i (*) j)_{P_j \in S}\right), L_{i,S'} f_i\right)$$

to $S' \setminus \{P_i\}$ with $E_0 \leftarrow_\$ \mathcal{E}$ and $E_1 = [L_{i,S'} s_i] E_0$. Thus, for a minimally authorised set S', the soundness of the PVP does not hold with respect to $P_i \in S'$ and f_i.

We resolve the conflicts by amending [2]'s PVP protocol, so that a shareholder $P_i \in S^*$ proves knowledge of a witness polynomial $L_{i,S^*} f_i$ for a statement

$$\left((R, R'), (f_i (j))_{P_j \in S^*}\right),$$

to a superauthorised set S^*, where $R \leftarrow_\$ \mathcal{E}$, $R' = [L_{i,S^*} f_i (0)] R = [L_{i,S^*} s_i] R$. The inputs of our amended proving protocol are the proving shareholder's index i, the witness polynomial f_i, the superauthorised set $S^* \in \Gamma^+$ and the statement $\left((R, R'), (f_i (j))_{P_j \in S^*}\right)$. The protocol can be found in Algorithm 8, in which $\mathcal{C}$ denotes a commitment scheme. The verifying protocol in turn has the prover's and the verifier's indices i and j, respectively, a set $S^* \in \Gamma^+$, a statement piece x_j and a proof piece (π, π_j) as input, where $x_j = (R, R') \in \mathcal{E}^2$ if $j = 0$ and $x_j \in \mathbb{Z}_p$ otherwise. The verifying protocol is given in Algorithm 9.

It is here, that the two-level sharing we introduced in Sect. 3.2 comes into play. We will have each shareholder P_i engaged in an execution of Decaps provide a PVP with respect to its share s_i of the secret key sk, that is then verified by each other participating shareholder with its respective share of s_i.

The definitions of soundness and zero-knowledge for a threshold PVP scheme carry over from the non-threshold setting in Sect. 2 intuitively, yet we restate the completeness definition for the threshold setting.

Definition 6 (Completeness in the threshold setting). *We call a threshold PVP scheme complete if, for any $S' \in \Gamma$, any $(x, f) \in \mathcal{R}$, any $P_i \in S'$ and $\left(\pi, \{\pi_j\}_{P_j \in S'}\right) \leftarrow \mathsf{PVP}.P (i, f, S', x_{S'})$, we have*

$$\Pr\left[\mathsf{PVP}.V (i, j, S', x_j, (\pi, \pi_j)) = \mathsf{true}\right] = 1 \text{ for all } P_j \in S'.$$

The proofs for soundness, correctness and zero-knowledge for Beullens et al.'s [2] approach are easily transferred to our amended protocols, thus we do not restate them here.

We arrive at our decapsulation protocol, executed by a superauthorised set S^*: The partaking shareholders fix a turn order. A shareholder P_i's turn consists of the following steps.

1. If the previous shareholder's output E^{k-1} is not in $\mathcal{E}$, P_i outputs $\bot$ and aborts. The first shareholder's input E^0 is the protocol's input ciphertext c.
2. Otherwise P_i samples $R_k \leftarrow_\$ \mathcal{E}$ and computes $R'_k \leftarrow [L_{i,S^*} s_i] R_k$.
3. P_i computes and publishes

$$\left(\pi^k, \{\pi_j^k\}_{P_j \in S^*}\right) \leftarrow \mathsf{PVP}.P \left(i, f_i, S^*, \left((R_k, R'_k), (f_i (j))_{P_j \in S^*}\right)\right).$$

4. P_i computes $E^k \leftarrow [L_{i,S^*} s_i] E^{k-1}$ and the zero-knowledge proof

$$zk \leftarrow \mathsf{ZK}.P\left((R_k, R'_k), (E^{k-1}, E^k), L_{i,S^*} s_i\right).$$

He publishes both.
5. Each shareholder $P_j \in S^* \setminus \{P_i\}$ verifies

$$\mathsf{PVP}.V\left(i, j, S^*, f_i(j), (\pi^k, \pi_j^k)\right) \wedge \mathsf{PVP}.V\left(i, 0, S^*, (R_k, R'_k), (\pi^k, \pi_0^k)\right) \quad (3.1)$$

and

$$\mathsf{ZK}.V\left((R_k, R'_k), (E^{k-1}, E^k), zk\right). \quad (3.2)$$

If (3.1) fails, P_j issues a complaint against P_i. If P_i is convicted of cheating by more than $\#S^*/2$ shareholders, decapsulation is restarted with an $S^{*'} \in \Gamma^+$, so that $P_i \notin S^{*'}$. If (3.2) fails, the decapsulation is restarted outright with $S^{*'} \in \Gamma^+$, so that $P_i \notin S^{*'}$.
6. Otherwise, P_i outputs E^k and finalises its turn.
7. The protocol terminates with the last shareholder's $E^{\#S^*}$ as output.

The combination of the PVP and the zero-knowledge proof in steps 3 and 4 ensure, that P_i has knowledge of the sharing polynomial $L_{i,S^*} f_i$ and also inputs $L_{i,S^*} f_i(0)$ to compute E^k. We give the precise protocol in Algorithm 3.

Definition 7. *A key exchange mechanism with secret shared private key is correct, if for any authorised set S', any public key* pk *and any* $(\mathcal{K}, c) \leftarrow$ Encaps (pk), *we have* $\mathcal{K} = \mathcal{K}' \leftarrow$ Decaps (c, S').

The correctness of our key exchange mechanism presented in Algorithm 1, Algorithm 2 and Algorithm 3 follows from the correctness of the threshold group action (Algorithm 5). Let sk be a secret key and pk $= [\mathsf{sk}] E_0$ be the respective public key, that have been generated by KeyGen, thus each shareholder P_i holds a share s_i of sk, $i = 1, \ldots, n$. For an authorised set S' we therefore have

$$\mathsf{sk} = \sum_{P_i \in S'} L_{i,S'} s_i.$$

Furthermore, let $(\mathcal{K}, c) \leftarrow$ Encaps (pk). To show correctness, $\mathcal{K}' = \mathcal{K}$ has to hold, where $\mathcal{K}' \leftarrow$ Decaps (c, S'). Now, after executing Decaps (c, S'), we have $\mathcal{K}' = E^{\#S'}$ emerging as the result of the threshold group action applied to c. This gives us

$$\mathcal{K}' = \left[\sum_{P_i \in S'} L_{i,S'} s_i\right] c = [\mathsf{sk}] (b * E_0) = b * \mathsf{pk} = \mathcal{K}.$$

The decapsulation is executed by superauthorised sets $S^* \in \Gamma^+ \subset \Gamma$. This shows that our key exchange mechanism is correct.

Algorithm 3: Decapsulation

Input: c, S^*

$E^0 \leftarrow c$

$k \leftarrow 0$

for $P_i \in S^*$ **do**

    if $E^k \notin \mathcal{E}$ **then**

        P_i outputs $\perp$ and aborts.

    $k \leftarrow k + 1$

    $R_k \leftarrow_\$ \mathcal{E}$

    $R'_k \leftarrow [L_{i,S^*} s_i] R_k$

    $\left(\pi^k, \{\pi_j^k\}_{P_j \in S^*}\right) \leftarrow \mathsf{PVP}.P\left(i, f_i, S^*, ((R_k, R'_k), (f_i(j))_{P_j \in S^*})\right)$

    P_i publishes (R_k, R'_k) and $\left(\pi^k, \{\pi_j^k\}_{P_j \in S^*}\right)$

    $E^k \leftarrow [L_{i,S^*} s_i] E^{k-1}$

    $zk^k \leftarrow \mathsf{ZK}.P\left((R_k, R'_k), (E^{k-1}, E^k), L_{i,S^*} s_i\right)$

    P_i publishes $\left(E^k, zk^k\right)$

    for $P_j \in S^* \setminus \{P_i\}$ **do**

        if $\mathsf{ZK}.V\left((R_k, R'_k), (E^{k-1}, E^k), zk^k\right) = \mathsf{false}$ **then**

            return Decapsulation $\left(c, S^{*\prime}\right)$ *with* $S^{*\prime} \in \Gamma \wedge P_i \notin S^{*\prime}$

        if $\mathsf{PVP}.V\left(i, j, S^*, f_i(j), (\pi^k, \pi_j^k)\right) = \mathsf{false} \vee$

        $\mathsf{PVP}.V\left(i, 0, S^*, (R_k, R'_k), (\pi^k, \pi_0^k)\right) = \mathsf{false}$ **then**

            P_j publishes $f_i(j)$

            if P_i *is convicted* **then**

                return Decapsulation $\left(c, S^{*\prime}\right)$ *with* $S^{*\prime} \in \Gamma \wedge P_i \notin S^{*\prime}$

return $\mathcal{K} \leftarrow E^k$

3.6 Security

There are two aspects of security to consider:

- Active security: A malicious shareholder cannot generate his contribution to the decapsulation protocol dishonestly without being detected. We prove this by showing that an adversary that can provide malformed inputs without detection can break the PVP or the zero-knowledge proof of knowledge.
- Simulatability: An adversary that corrupts an unauthorised set of shareholders cannot learn any information about the uncorrupted shareholders' inputs from an execution of the decapsulation protocol. We show this by proving the simulatability of Decaps.

Active Security

Theorem 1. *Let* $S^* \in \Gamma^+$ *and let* $(\mathsf{pk}, \mathsf{sk}) \leftarrow \mathsf{KeyGen}$ *be a public/secret key pair, where* sk *has been shared. Also let* $(\mathcal{K}, c) \leftarrow \mathsf{Encaps}(\mathsf{pk})$. *Denote the transcript of* Decaps (c, S^*) *by*

$$\left(E^k, (R_k, R'_k), \left(\pi^k, \{\pi_j^k\}_{P_j \in S^*}\right), zk^k\right)_{k=1,\ldots,\#S^*}.$$

Let $P_i \in S^*$ be an arbitrary but fixed shareholder. If Decaps (c, S^*) *terminated successfully and $P_{i'}$'s output was generated dishonestly, then there exists an algorithm that breaks the soundness property of* PVP *or* ZK.

Proof. Let $P_{i'}$ be the malicious shareholder and let k' be the index of $P_{i'}$'s output in the transcript. Since Decaps (c, S^*) terminated successfully, we have

$$\mathsf{PVP}.V\left(i', j, S^*, f_{i'}(j), \left(\pi^{k'}, \pi_j^{k'}\right)\right) = \text{true} \tag{3.3}$$

$$\mathsf{PVP}.V\left(i', 0, S^*, (R_{k'}, R'_{k'}), \left(\pi^{k'}, \pi_0^{k'}\right)\right) = \text{true} \tag{3.4}$$

$$\mathsf{ZK}.V\left(\left(E^{k'-1}, E^{k'}\right), (R_{k'}, R'_{k'}), zk^{k'}\right) = \text{true} \tag{3.5}$$

for all $P_j \in S^* \setminus \{P_{i'}\}$. $E^{k'}$ was generated dishonestly, thus we have

$$E^{k'} = [\alpha] E^{k'-1}, \text{ for some } \alpha \neq L_{i', S^*} s_{i'}.$$

We distinguish two cases: $R'_{k'} \neq [\alpha] R_{k'}$ and $R'_{k'} = [\alpha] R_{k'}$.

In the first case, $P_{i'}$ published a zero-knowledge proof $zk^{k'}$ so that (3.5) holds, where $E^{k'} = [\alpha] E^{k'-1}$ yet $R'_{k'} \neq [\alpha] R_{k'}$. $P_{i'}$ thus broke the soundness property of the zero-knowledge proof.

In the second case, $P_{i'}$ published $\left(\pi^{k'}, \{\pi_j^{k'}\}_{P_j \in S^*}\right)$ so that (3.3) and (3.4) hold for all $P_j \in S^* \setminus \{P_{i'}\}$ and for $j = 0$. Thus, $P_{i'}$ proved knowledge of a witness polynomial f' with

$$f'(j) = L_{i', S^*} f_{i'}(j) \tag{3.6}$$

for all $P_j \in S^* \setminus \{P_{i'}\}$ and $R'_{k'} = [f'(0)] R_{k'}$, that is $f'(0) = \alpha$. Since f' has degree at most $k - 1$, it is well-defined from (3.6). Thus, we have $f' \equiv L_{i', S^*} f_{i'}$, where $f_{i'}$ is the polynomial with which $s_{i'}$ was shared, i.e., $f_{i'}(0) = s_{i'}$. This gives us $\alpha = f'(0) = L_{i', S^*} f_{i'}(0) = L_{i', S^*} s_{i'}$. We arrive at a contradiction, assuming the soundness of the PVP.

Simulatability. We show that an adversary who corrupts an unauthorised subset of shareholder does not learn any additional information from an execution of the decapsulation protocol.

Definition 8 (Simulatability). *We call a key exchange mechanism simulatable, if for any HHS $(\mathcal{E}, \mathcal{G})$ with security parameter λ and any compatible secret sharing instance $\mathcal{S}$, there exists a polynomial-time algorithm* Sim *so that, for any polynomial-time adversary $\mathcal{A}$ the advantage*

$$\mathsf{Adv}_{\mathcal{A}, \mathsf{Sim}}^{dist-transcript}\left((\mathcal{E}, \mathcal{G}), \mathcal{S}\right) := \left| \Pr\left[\mathsf{Exp}_{\mathcal{A}, \mathsf{Sim}}^{dist-transcript}(\mathcal{S})\right] - \frac{1}{2} \right|$$

in the security game $\mathsf{Exp}_{\mathcal{A}, \mathsf{Sim}}^{dist-transcript}(\mathcal{S})$ (Algorithm 10) is negligible in λ.

Theorem 2. *If the* PVP *protocol and the* GAIP ZK *protocol employed are zero-knowledge, then the decapsulation protocol (Algorithm 3) is simulatable.*

Proof. We give a finite series of simulators, the first of which simulates the behaviour of the uncorrupted parties faithfully and the last of which fulfills the secrecy requirements. This series is inspired by the simulators, that [2] gave for the secrecy proof of their key generation algorithm, yet differs in some significant aspects. The outputs of the respective simulators will be proven indistinguishable, hence resulting in the indistinguishability of the first and last one. As a slight misuse of the notation, we denote the set of corrupted shareholders by $\mathcal{A}$, where $\mathcal{A}$ is the adversary corrupting an unauthorised set of shareholders. This means P_i is corrupted iff $P_i \in \mathcal{A}$.

The input for each simulator is a ciphertext c, a derived key $\mathcal{K}$ and the adversary's knowledge after KeyGen was successfully executed, that is

$$\{s_i, f_i, \{f_j(i)\}_{P_j \in S^* \setminus \mathcal{A}}\}_{P_i \in \mathcal{A}}.$$

1. The adversary corrupted an unauthorised set $\mathcal{A}$, hence each share of the secret key is uniformly distributed from his view. Sim^1 samples a polynomial $f_i' \in \mathbb{Z}_p[X]_{k-1}$ with

$$\forall P_j \in \mathcal{A} : f_i'(j) = f_i(j)$$

   uniformly at random for each $P_i \in S^* \setminus \mathcal{A}$. Since $\mathcal{A}$ is unauthorised, f_i' exists. Sim^1 then proceeds by honestly producing the output of each $P_i \in S^* \setminus \mathcal{A}$ according to the decapsulation protocol, i.e., it samples $R_k \leftarrow_\$ \mathcal{E}$, computes $R_k' \leftarrow [L_{i,S^*} f_i'(0)] R_k$ and outputs

$$\mathsf{PVP}.P\left(i, f_i', S^*, \left((R_k, R_k'), (f_i'(j))_{P_j \in S^*}\right)\right),$$

$$E^k \leftarrow [L_{i,S^*} f_i'(0)] E^{k-1}$$

   and

$$\mathsf{ZK}.P\left((R_k, R_k'), (E^{k-1}, E^k), L_{i,S^*} f_i'(*) 0\right),$$

   where k is the index of P_i's output in the transcript. Since, for all $P_i \in S^* \setminus \mathcal{A}$, the real share $s_i = f_i(0)$ of P_i is information theoretically hidden to the adversary, the resulting transcript is identically distributed to a real transcript.

2. Let i' denote the index of the last honest party in the execution of the decapsulation protocol and k' the index of its output. Sim^2 behaves exactly as Sim^1 with the exception, that it does not compute the PVP itself but calls the simulator $\mathsf{Sim}^{\mathsf{PVP}}$ for the PVP to generate the proof $\left(\pi^{k'}, \{\pi_j^{k'}\}\right)$ for the statement $\left((R_{k'}, R_{k'}'), (f_{i'}(j))_{P_j \in S^*}\right)$. Since the PVP is zero-knowledge, Sim^2's output is indistinguishable from that of Sim^1.

3. Sim^3 behaves identical to Sim^2 apart from not generating the zero-knowledge proof for $P_{i'}$ itself, but outsourcing it to the simulator for the zero-knowledge

proof. That is Sim^3 hands tuples $(R_{k'}, R'_{k'})$ and $\left(E^{k'-1}, E^{k'}\right)$ to $\mathsf{Sim}^{\mathsf{ZK}}$ and publishes its answer as the zero-knowledge proof. With ZK being zero-knowledge, the output of Sim^3 is indistinguishable from that of Sim^2.

4. The final simulator Sim^4 enforces the correct decapsulation output, that is $E^{\#S^*} = \mathcal{K}$. Since, for $P_j \in \mathcal{A}$, s_j was provided as input and $P_{i'}$ is the last honest shareholder in the order of decapsulation execution, Sim^4 computes

$$\sum_{P_j \in S'} L_{j,S^*} s_j,$$

where S' contains the shareholders, whose turn is after $P_{i'}$'s. To achieve the correct output of the decapsulation E, Sim^4 thus sets

$$E^{k'} \leftarrow \left[-\sum_{P_j \in S'} L_{j,S^*} s_j\right] E$$

instead of $E^{k'} \leftarrow [L_{i',S^*} s'_{i'}] E^{k'-1}$. Assuming the soundness of the PVP as well as of the zero-knowledge proof, this guarantees the result to be $E^{\#S^*} = E$, since

$$E^{\#S^*} = \left[\sum_{P_j \in S'} L_{j,S^*} s_j\right] E^{k'} = E$$

holds. It remains to show, that the output of Sim^4 cannot be distinguished from that of Sim^3. The following reasoning is similar to that of [2], yet for completeness we give a reduction $\mathcal{B}'$, that uses a distinguisher $\mathcal{A}'$, that distinguishes Sim^3 from Sim^4, to break the decisional parallelisation problem. We highlight the necessary modifications.

Let (E_a, E_b, E_c) be an instance of the decisional parallelisation problem with base element c. $\mathcal{B}'$ computes

$$E^{k'} \leftarrow \left[\sum_{P_j \in S^* \setminus (S' \cup \{P_{i'}\})} L_{j,S^*} s_j\right] E_a.$$

With $s_{i'}$ looking uniformly distributed from $\mathcal{A}$'s view, this choice of $E^{k'}$ is indistinguishable from $E^{k'} = [L_{i',S^*} s'_{i'}] E^{k'-1}$. $\mathcal{B}'$ furthermore does not sample $R_{k'} \leftarrow_\$ \mathcal{E}$ but puts $R_{k'} \leftarrow E_b$ and $R'_{k'} \leftarrow E_c$. The resulting transcript is handed to $\mathcal{A}'$ and $\mathcal{B}'$ outputs whatever $\mathcal{A}'$ outputs.

Comparing the distributions, we see that

$$E^{k'} = [a] E^{k'-1} = [a]\left(\left[\sum_{P_j \in S^* \setminus (S' \cup \{P_{i'}\})} L_{j,S^*} s_j\right] c\right)$$

if and only if $E_a = [a]c$, where $s_j := s'_j$ for $P_j \notin \mathcal{A}$. Furthermore, $R'_{k'} = [a]R_{k'}$ is equivalent to $E_c = [a]E_b$. In the case of $E_a = [a]c$ and $E_c = [a]E_b$, the transcript handed to $\mathcal{A}'$ is identically distributed to Sim^3's output. If, on the other hand, (E_a, E_b, E_c) is a random triple, then the transcript follows the same distribution as Sim^4's output. $\mathcal{B}'$ thus breaks the DPP with the same advantage as $\mathcal{A}'$ distinguishes Sim^3 from Sim^4.

Sim^4 outputs a transcript of the decapsulation protocol with input c and output $\mathcal{K}$ that cannot be distinguished from the output of Sim^1, which is indistinguishable from a real execution protocol.

3.7   Efficiency

Each shareholder engaged in an execution of the decapsulation protocol has one round of messages to send. The messages of the k-th shareholder consist of the tuple (R_k, R'_k), a PVP proof $\left(\pi^k, \{\pi_j^k\}_{P_j \in S^*}\right)$, the output E^k and the zero-knowledge proof zk. Thus, the total size of a shareholder's messages is

$$2x + 2c + \lambda k \log p + 2\lambda(\#S^*) + x + \lambda k \log p + \lambda$$
$$= 3x + 2c + \lambda\left(1 + 2(\#S^*) + 2k \log p\right)$$

where x is the size of the bit representation of an element of $\mathcal{E}$ and c is the size of a commitment produced in $\mathsf{PVP}.P$. Assuming x, c and the secret sharing parameters k and p to be constant, the message size is thus linear in the security parameter λ with moderate cofactor.

4   Actively Secure Secret Shared Signature Protocols

We convert the key exchange mechanism in Algorithm 1, Algorithm 2 and Algorithm 3 into an actively secure signature scheme with secret shared signing key.

A signature scheme consists of three protocols: key generation, signing and verifying. We transfer the unmodified key generation protocol from the key exchange mechnism in Sect. 3 to our signature scheme. The signing protocol is derived from the decapsulation protocol (Algorithm 3) by applying the Fiat-Shamir-transformation, the verifying protocol follows straightforward. The protocols are given in Algorithm 4 and Algorithm 11.

We concede, that applying active security measures to a signature scheme to ensure the correctness of the resulting signature is counter-intuitive, since the correctness of a signature can easily be checked through the verifying protocol. Yet verification returning false only shows that the signature is incorrect, a misbehaving shareholder cannot be identified this way. An actively secure signature scheme achieves just that. An identified cheating shareholder can hence be excluded from future runs of the signing protocol.

Similar to [3], the results from [10] on Fiat-Shamir in the QROM can be applied to our setting as follows. First, in the case without hashing, since the sigma protocol has special soundness [3] and in our case perfect unique reponses, [10] shows that the protocol is a quantum proof of knowledge. Further, in the case with hashing, the collapsingness property implies that the protocol has unique responses in a quantum scenario.

Algorithm 4: Secret Shared Signing Algorithm

Input: m, S^*

$\left(E_1^0, \ldots, E_\lambda^0\right) \leftarrow (E_0, \ldots, E_0)$

$k \leftarrow 0$

for $P_i \in S^*$ **do**

  $k \leftarrow k + 1$

  for $l \in 1, \ldots, \lambda$ **do**

    P_i samples $b_{il} \leftarrow\!\!\text{\$}\ \mathbb{Z}_q\left[X\right]_{\leq k-1}$

    P_i publishes $R_{il}^k \leftarrow\!\!\text{\$}\ \mathcal{E}$

    P_i publishes ${R'_{il}}^k \leftarrow [b_{il}(0)] R_{il}^k$

    P_i publishes $\left(\pi, \{\pi_j\}_{P_j \in S^*}\right) \leftarrow$

    $\mathsf{PVP}.P\left(i, b_{il}, S^*, \left(\left(R_{il}^k, {R'_{il}}^k\right), (b_{il}(*)\,l)_{P_j \in S^*}\right)\right)$

    P_i outputs $E_l^k \leftarrow [b_{il}(0)]\, E_l^{k-1}$

    P_i publishes $zk \leftarrow \mathsf{ZK}.P\left(\left(R_{il}^k, {R'_{il}}^k\right), \left(E_l^{k-1}, E_l^k\right), b_{il}(0)\right)$

    if $\mathsf{ZK}.V\left(\left(R_{il}^k, {R'_{il}}^k\right), \left(E_l^{k-1}, E_l^k\right), zk\right) = \mathsf{false}$ **then**

      restart without P_i

$(c_1, \ldots, c_\lambda) \leftarrow \mathcal{H}\left(E_1^{\#S^*}, \ldots, E_\lambda^{\#S^*}, m\right)$

for $P_i \in S^*$ **do**

  for $l \in 1, \ldots, \lambda$ **do**

    P_i outputs $z_{il} = b_{il} - c_l \cdot L_{i,S^*} \cdot s_i$

    for $P_j \in S^*$ **do**

      P_j computes $b'_{il}(j) \leftarrow z_{il}(j) + c_l L_{i,S^*} f_i(j)$

      and verifies

      $\mathsf{PVP}.V\left(i, j, S^*, b'_{il}(*)\,j, \pi, \pi_j\right) \wedge \mathsf{PVP}.V\left(i, 0, S^*, \left(R_{il}^k, {R'_{il}}^k\right), \pi, \pi_0\right)$

      if P_i *is convicted of cheating* **then**

        restart without P_i

for $l \in 1, \ldots, \lambda$ **do**

  $z_j \leftarrow \sum_{P_i \in S^*} z_{ij}$

return $\left((c_1, \ldots, c_\lambda), (z_1, \ldots, z_\lambda)\right)$

4.1 Instantiations

As a practical instantiation, we propose the available parameter set for CSIDH-512 HHS from [3]. Currently no other instantiation of the presented schemes seems feasible in a practical sense. Furthermore, according to recent works [5,14] CSIDH-512 may not reach the initially estimated security level.

5   Generalising the Secret Sharing Schemes

We constructed the protocols above in the context of Shamir's secret sharing protocol [15]. The key exchange mechanism in Sect. 3 as well as the signature scheme in Sect. 4 can be extended to more general secret sharing schemes. In the following, we characterise the requirements that a secret sharing scheme has to meet in order to successfully implement the key exchange mechanism and the signature scheme.

5.1   Compatibility Requirements

Definition 9 (Independent Reconstruction). *We say a secret sharing instance $\mathcal{S} = (S, \Gamma, G)$ is independently reconstructible, if, for any shared secret $s \in G$, any $S' \in \Gamma$ and any shareholder $P_i \in S'$, P_i's input to reconstructing s is independent of the share of each other engaged shareholder $P_j \in S'$.*

A secret sharing scheme compatible with our key exchange mechanism and signature scheme has to be independently reconstructible, since each shareholder's input into the threshold group action is hidden from every other party by virtue of the GAIP.

Definition 10 (Self-contained reconstruction). *An instance $\mathcal{S} = (S, \Gamma, G)$ of a secret sharing scheme is called self-contained, if, for any authorised set S', the input of any shareholder $P_i \in S'$ in an execution of Rec is an element of G.*

It is necessary, that $G = \mathbb{Z}_p$ for some prime p holds to enable the mapping $\cdot \mapsto [\cdot]$. This requirement may be loosened by replacing $\cdot \mapsto [\cdot]$ appropriately. To enable two-level sharing, it has to hold that for a share $s_i \in \mathcal{S}.\mathsf{Share}\,(s)$ of a secret s, $s_i \in G$ holds. The secret sharing scheme also has to allow for a PVP scheme, that is compatible with a zero-knowledge proof for the GAIP.

5.2   Examples of Secret Sharing Schemes

- It is evident, that Shamir's approach fulfills all aforementioned requirements. In fact, the two-level sharing and the PVP have been tailored to Shamir's polynomial based secret sharing approach.
- Tassa [17] extended Shamir's approach of threshold secret sharing to a hierarchical access structure. To share a secret $s \in \mathbb{Z}_p$ with prime p, a polynomial f with constant term s is sampled. Shareholders of the top level of the hierarchy are assigned interpolation points of f as in Shamir's scheme. The k-th level of the hierarchy receives interpolation points of the $k - 1$st derivative of f. The shares in Tassa's scheme are elements of $\mathbb{Z}_p$ themselves. The key generation (Algorithm 1) can easily be transferred to this setting, as each shareholder receives a description of the polynomial utilised in sharing his share. Hence all derivatives and their respective interpolation points can easily be computed. Reconstructing a shared secret is achieved via Birkhoff interpolation, the execution of which is independent and self-contained. The zero-knowledge proof

(Algorithm 6 and Algorithm 7) as well as the piecewise verifiable proof (Algorithm 8 and Algorithm 9) thus directly transfer to Tassa's approach utilising the appropriate derivatives in the verifying protocols. The decapsulation and the signing protocols hence can be executed with adjustments only to the verifying steps.

– In 2006, Damgard and Thorbek proposed a linear integer secret sharing scheme [9] with secret space $\mathbb{Z}$. Given an access structure Γ, a matrix M is generated in which each shareholder is assigned a column so that iff $S' \in \Gamma$, the submatrix $M_{S'}$ has full rank. A secret s is shared by multiplying a random vector v with first entry s with M and sending the resulting vector entries to the respective shareholders. Reconstruction follows intuitively. Their scheme hence further generalises Tassa's with respect to secret space and feasible access structures. With the secret space $\mathbb{Z}$ their approach is not compatible with the mapping $\cdot \mapsto [\cdot]$ and our PVP scheme. Thus, neither our key exchange mechanism nor our signature scheme can in its current form be instantiated with Damgard's and Thorbek's scheme.

6 Conclusion

In this work, we presented an actively secure key exchange mechanism based on Shamir's secret sharing scheme and derived a signature scheme from it. The active security measures consist of a piecewise verifiable proof and a zero-knowledge proof for the GAIP, that in combination prove the knowledge of the correct share of the secret key and ensure its use in the protocol. For that we reworked the piecewise verifiable proof and zero-knowledge proof introduced in [2] to fit the threshold setting of Shamir's secret sharing and applied it to the threshold group action of [11]. Active security and simulatability were proven under the assumption of hardness of the decisional parallelisation problem.

Furthermore, we characterised the properties necessary for a secret sharing scheme in order for our key exchange mechanism and signature scheme to be based on it. We gave examples and counter-examples of secret sharing schemes compatible with our approach to demonstrate its limits. We thereby demonstrated that cryptographic schemes with secret shared private key in the HHS setting are not limited to threshold schemes, but applicable to more general access structures.

Acknowledgements. We thank Lena Ries, Luca De Feo, and Michael Meyer for inspiring discussions. Philipp Muth was funded by the Deutsche Forschungsgemeinschaft (DFG) – SFB 1119 – 236615297.

Appendix A   Algorithms

Algorithm 5: Threshold group action

Input: E, S'
$E^0 \leftarrow E$
$k \leftarrow 0$
for $P_i \in S'$ **do**
  if $E^k \notin \mathcal{E}$ **then**
    P_i outputs $\perp$ and aborts.
  else
    $k \leftarrow k + 1$
    P_i outputs $E^k \leftarrow [L_{i,S'} s_i] E^{k-1}$

return E^k

Algorithm 6: The ZK proving protocol for the GAIP

Input: $s, (E_i, E_i')_{i=1,\ldots,m}$
for $j = 1, \ldots, \lambda$ **do**
  $b_j \leftarrow_\$ \mathbb{Z}_p$
  for $i = 1, \ldots, m$ **do**
    $\hat{E}_{ij} \leftarrow [b_j] E_i$
$(c_1, \ldots, c_\lambda) \leftarrow \mathcal{H}\left(E_1, E_1', \ldots, E_m, E_m', \hat{E}_{1,1}, \ldots, \hat{E}_{m,\lambda} \right)$
for $j = 1, \ldots, m$ **do**
  $r_j \leftarrow b_j - c_j s$
return $\pi \leftarrow (c_1, \ldots, c_\lambda, r_1, \ldots, r_\lambda)$

Algorithm 7: The ZK verifying protocol for the GAIP

Input: $\pi, (E_i, E_i')_{i=1,\ldots,m}$
Parse $(c_1, \ldots, c_\lambda, r_1, \ldots, r_\lambda) \leftarrow \pi$
for $i = 1, \ldots, m$ and $j = 1, \ldots, \lambda$ **do**
  if $c_j == 0$ **then**
    $\tilde{E}_{i,j} \leftarrow [r_j] E_i$
  else
    $\tilde{E}_{i,j} \leftarrow [r_j] E_i'$
$(c_1', \ldots, c_\lambda') \leftarrow \mathcal{H}\left(E_1, E_1', \ldots, E_m, E_m', \tilde{E}_{1,1}, \ldots, \tilde{E}_{m,\lambda} \right)$
return $(c_1, \ldots, c_\lambda) == (c_1', \ldots, c_\lambda')$

Algorithm 8: Proving protocol of the threshold PVP

Input: $i, f, S^*, \left((E_0, E_1), (f_i(j))_{P_j \in S^*} \right)$

for $l \in 1, \ldots, \lambda$ **do**
    $b_l \leftarrow_\$ \mathbb{Z}_N[x]_{\leq k-1}$
    $\hat{E}_l \leftarrow [b_l(0)] E_0$

$y_0, y_0' \leftarrow_\$ \{0,1\}^\lambda$
$C_0 \leftarrow \mathcal{C} \left(\hat{E}_1 \| \ldots \| \hat{E}_\lambda, y_0 \right)$
$C_0' \leftarrow \mathcal{C} (E_0 \| E_1, y_0')$
for $P_j \in S^*$ **do**
    $y_j, y_j' \leftarrow_\$ \{0,1\}^\lambda$
    $C_j \leftarrow \mathcal{C} (b_1(*) j \| \ldots \| b_\lambda(*) j, y_j)$
    $C_j' \leftarrow \mathcal{C} (L_{i,S^*} \cdot f_i(j), y_j')$

$C \leftarrow (C_j)_{P_j \in S^*}$
$C' \leftarrow (C_j')_{P_j \in S^*}$
$c_1, \ldots, c_\lambda \leftarrow \mathcal{H}(C, C')$
for $l \in 1, \ldots, \lambda$ **do**
    $r_l \leftarrow b_l - c_l \cdot L_{i,S^*} \cdot f$

$\mathbf{r} \leftarrow (r_1, \ldots, r_\lambda)$
$\left(\pi, \{\pi_j\}_{P_j \in S^*} \right) \leftarrow \left((C, C', \mathbf{r}), \{(y_j, y_j')\}_{P_j \in S^*} \right)$
return $\left(\pi, \{\pi_j\}_{P_j \in S^*} \right)$

Algorithm 9: Verifying protocol of the threshold PVP

Input: $i, j, S^*, x_j, (\pi, \pi_j)$
parse $(C, C', \mathbf{r}) \leftarrow \pi$
parse $(y_j, y_j') \leftarrow \pi_j$
$c_1, \ldots, c_\lambda \leftarrow \mathcal{H}(C, C')$
if $j == 0$ **then**
    if $C_j' \neq \mathcal{C}(x_j, y_j')$ **then**
        return false
    for $l \in 1, \ldots, \lambda$ **do**
        $\tilde{E}_l \leftarrow [r_l(0)] E_{c_l}$
    return $C_0 == \mathcal{C} \left(\tilde{E}_1 \| \ldots \| \tilde{E}_\lambda, y_0 \right)$
else
    if $C_j' \neq \mathcal{C}(L_{i,S^*} x_j, y_j')$ **then**
        return false
    return $C_j == \mathcal{C}(r_1(*) j + c_1 \cdot L_{i,S^*} \cdot x_j \| \ldots \| r_\lambda(*) j + c_\lambda \cdot L_{i,S^*} \cdot x_j, y_j)$

Algorithm 10: The security game $\mathsf{Exp}_{\mathcal{A},\mathsf{Sim}}^{\text{dist-transcript}}(S)$

Input: $\mathcal{S}$

$b \leftarrow_\$ \{0,1\}$

$S^* \leftarrow_\$ \Gamma^+$

$S' \leftarrow_\$ 2^{S^*} \setminus \Gamma$

$(\{s_i, f_i, f_j(i)\}_{P_i, P_j \in S}, \mathsf{pk}) \leftarrow \mathsf{KeyGen}(\mathcal{S})$

$(\mathcal{K}, c) \leftarrow \mathsf{Encaps}(\mathsf{pk})$

$t_0 \leftarrow \mathsf{Sim}\left(\mathcal{K}, c, \{s_i, f_i, f_j(i)\}_{P_i \in S', P_j \in S}\right)$

$E^0 \leftarrow E_0, \ k \leftarrow 0$

for $P_i \in S^*$ **do**

$\quad k \leftarrow k+1$

$\quad E^k \leftarrow [L_{i,S^*} s_i] E^{k-1}$

$\quad R_k \leftarrow_\$ \mathcal{E}$

$\quad R'_k \leftarrow [L_{i,S^*} s_i] R_k$

$\quad \left(\pi^k, \{\pi_j^k\}_{P_j \in S^*}\right) \leftarrow \mathsf{PVP}.P\left(i, f_i, S^*, \left((R_k, R'_k), (L_{i,S^*} f_i(j))_{P_j \in S^*}\right)\right)$

$\quad zk^k \leftarrow \mathsf{ZK}.P\left((R_k, R'_k), (E^{k-1}, E^k), L_{i,S^*} s_i\right)$

$t_1 \leftarrow \left(E^k, \left(\pi^k, \{\pi_j^k\}_{P_j \in S^*}\right), zk^k\right)_{k=1,\dots,\#S^*}$

$b' \leftarrow \mathcal{A}(t_b)$

return $b == b'$

Algorithm 11: Signature verification protocol

Input: m, s, pk

parse $(c_1, \dots, c_\lambda, z_1, \dots, z_\lambda) \leftarrow s$

for $j = 1, \dots, \lambda$ **do**

$\quad$ **if** $c_j == 0$ **then**

$\quad\quad E'_j \leftarrow [z_j] E_0 = \left[\sum_{P_i \in S^*} b_{ij}\right] E_0$

$\quad$ **else**

$\quad\quad E'_j \leftarrow [z_j] \mathsf{pk} = \left[\sum_{P_i \in S^*} b_{ij} - L_{i,S^*} s_i + s\right] E_0$

$(c'_1, \dots, c'_\lambda) \leftarrow \mathcal{H}(E'_1, \dots, E'_\lambda, m)$

return $(c_1, \dots, c_\lambda) == (c'_1, \dots, c'_\lambda)$

References

1. Beth, T., Knobloch, H., Otten, M.: Verifiable secret sharing for monotone access structures. In: Denning, D.E., Pyle, R., Ganesan, R., Sandhu, R.S., Ashby, V. (eds.) CCS '93, Proceedings of the 1st ACM Conference on Computer and Communications Security, Fairfax, Virginia, USA, 3–5 November 1993, pp. 189–194. ACM (1993). https://doi.org/10.1145/168588.168612

2. Beullens, W., Disson, L., Pedersen, R., Vercauteren, F.: CSI-RAShi: distributed key generation for CSIDH. In: Cheon, J.H., Tillich, J.-P. (eds.) PQCrypto 2021 2021. LNCS, vol. 12841, pp. 257–276. Springer, Cham (2021). https://doi.org/10.1007/978-3-030-81293-5_14

3. Beullens, W., Kleinjung, T., Vercauteren, F.: CSI-FiSh: efficient isogeny based signatures through class group computations. In: Galbraith, S.D., Moriai, S. (eds.) ASIACRYPT 2019. LNCS, vol. 11921, pp. 227–247. Springer, Cham (2019). https://doi.org/10.1007/978-3-030-34578-5_9

4. Blakley, G.R.: Safeguarding cryptographic keys. In: Merwin, R.E., Zanca, J.T., Smith, M. (eds.) 1979 National Computer Conference: AFIPS Conference proceedings, New York, New York, 4–7 June 1979, vol. 48, pp. 313–317. AFIPS Press, pub-AFIPS:adr (1979)

5. Bonnetain, X., Schrottenloher, A.: Quantum security analysis of CSIDH. In: Canteaut, A., Ishai, Y. (eds.) EUROCRYPT 2020. LNCS, vol. 12106, pp. 493–522. Springer, Cham (2020). https://doi.org/10.1007/978-3-030-45724-2_17

6. Couveignes, J.M.: Hard homogeneous spaces. IACR Cryptol. ePrint Arch., 291 (2006). http://eprint.iacr.org/2006/291

7. Cozzo, D., Smart, N.P.: Sharing the LUOV: threshold post-quantum signatures. In: Albrecht, M. (ed.) IMACC 2019. LNCS, vol. 11929, pp. 128–153. Springer, Cham (2019). https://doi.org/10.1007/978-3-030-35199-1_7

8. Cozzo, D., Smart, N.P.: Sashimi: cutting up CSI-FiSh secret keys to produce an actively secure distributed signing protocol. In: Ding, J., Tillich, J.-P. (eds.) PQCrypto 2020. LNCS, vol. 12100, pp. 169–186. Springer, Cham (2020). https://doi.org/10.1007/978-3-030-44223-1_10

9. Damgård, I., Thorbek, R.: Linear integer secret sharing and distributed exponentiation. In: Yung, M., Dodis, Y., Kiayias, A., Malkin, T. (eds.) PKC 2006. LNCS, vol. 3958, pp. 75–90. Springer, Heidelberg (2006). https://doi.org/10.1007/11745853_6

10. Don, J., Fehr, S., Majenz, C., Schaffner, C.: Security of the fiat-shamir transformation in the quantum random-oracle model. In: Boldyreva, A., Micciancio, D. (eds.) CRYPTO 2019. LNCS, vol. 11693, pp. 356–383. Springer, Cham (2019). https://doi.org/10.1007/978-3-030-26951-7_13

11. De Feo, L., Meyer, M.: Threshold schemes from isogeny assumptions. In: Kiayias, A., Kohlweiss, M., Wallden, P., Zikas, V. (eds.) PKC 2020. LNCS, vol. 12111, pp. 187–212. Springer, Cham (2020). https://doi.org/10.1007/978-3-030-45388-6_7

12. Herranz, J., Sáez, G.: Verifiable secret sharing for general access structures, with application to fully distributed proxy signatures. In: Wright, R.N. (ed.) FC 2003. LNCS, vol. 2742, pp. 286–302. Springer, Heidelberg (2003). https://doi.org/10.1007/978-3-540-45126-6_21

13. Pedersen, T.P.: Non-interactive and information-theoretic secure verifiable secret sharing. In: Feigenbaum, J. (ed.) CRYPTO 1991. LNCS, vol. 576, pp. 129–140. Springer, Heidelberg (1992). https://doi.org/10.1007/3-540-46766-1_9

14. Peikert, C.: He gives c-sieves on the CSIDH. In: Canteaut, A., Ishai, Y. (eds.) EUROCRYPT 2020. LNCS, vol. 12106, pp. 463–492. Springer, Cham (2020). https://doi.org/10.1007/978-3-030-45724-2_16

15. Shamir, A.: How to share a secret. Commun. ACM **22**(11), 612–613 (1979). http://doi.acm.org/10.1145/359168.359176

16. Stadler, M.: Publicly verifiable secret sharing. In: Maurer, U. (ed.) EUROCRYPT 1996. LNCS, vol. 1070, pp. 190–199. Springer, Heidelberg (1996). https://doi.org/10.1007/3-540-68339-9_17

17. Tassa, T.: Hierarchical threshold secret sharing. In: Naor, M. (ed.) TCC 2004. LNCS, vol. 2951, pp. 473–490. Springer, Heidelberg (2004). https://doi.org/10.1007/978-3-540-24638-1_26

18. Thorbek, R.: Proactive linear integer secret sharing. IACR Cryptol. ePrint Arch., p. 183 (2009). http://eprint.iacr.org/2009/183

19. Traverso, G., Demirel, D., Buchmann, J.: Performing computations on hierarchically shared secrets. In: Joux, A., Nitaj, A., Rachidi, T. (eds.) AFRICACRYPT 2018. LNCS, vol. 10831, pp. 141–161. Springer, Cham (2018). https://doi.org/10.1007/978-3-319-89339-6_9

Attack on SHealS and HealS: The Second Wave of GPST

Steven D. Galbraith⬤ and Yi-Fu Lai(✉)⬤

University of Auckland, Auckland, New Zealand
s.galbraith@auckland.ac.nz, ylai276@aucklanduni.ac.nz

Abstract. We cryptanalyse the isogeny-based public key encryption schemes SHealS and HealS, and the key exchange scheme HealSIDH of Fouotsa and Petit from Asiacrypt 2021.

1 Introduction

An important problem is to have an efficient and secure static-static key exchange protocol or public key encryption (PKE) from isogenies. A static-static protocol enables participants to execute the desired primitives without changing the public keys from time to time. This is possible and natural using CSIDH [CLM+18], which has been used to construct several competitive isogeny-based cryptographic primitives [BKV19, MOT20, EKP20, LGd21, BDK+22] while the counterparts are missing in the SIDH-based constructions. However due to subexponential attacks on CSIDH based on the Kuperberg algorithm [Kup05, Pei20], SIDH-related assumptions [JD11] might provide a more robust foundation[1]. Hence, an efficient protocol with a robust underlying assumption from isogenies is still an open problem.

The main bottleneck for SIDH-family schemes to achieve the static-static property boils down to the adaptive GPST attack [GPST16]. The attack enables malicious Bob to extract Alice's secret key bit by bit from each handshake and vice versa. The known countermeasures against the attack are to embed a zero-knowledge proof [UJ20] or to utilize the k-SIDH method [AJL17]. However, these countermeasures also inevitably incur multiple parallel isogeny computations so that the deduced schemes are not practical. To resolve this, Fouotsa and Petit [FP21] (Asiacrypt'21) presented a variant of SIDH with a novel key validation mechanism by using the commutativity of the isogeny diagram [Leo20]. The scheme requires fewer isogeny computations than SIKE [ACC+17] with the prime number doubled in length which still is far more efficient than the other known abovementioned solutions. In [FP21], it is claimed that the work gives the static-static key exchange and PKE solutions from isogenies which are immune to any adaptive attacks.

---

[1] We remark that the confidence of the SIDH-based protocols is still under debate due to the recent advance given by Castryck and Decru [CD22].

© The Author(s), under exclusive license to Springer Nature Switzerland AG 2022
J. H. Cheon and T. Johansson (Eds.): PQCrypto 2022, LNCS 13512, pp. 399–421, 2022.
https://doi.org/10.1007/978-3-031-17234-2_19

In this work we refute the claim by presenting an adaptive attack against the protocols presented in [FP21]. Our attack builds on the flaw in the key validation mechanism, which is the core result [FP21] to construct SHealS, HealS, and HealSIDH. The attack can be viewed as a simple tweak of the GPST attack and, surprisingly, it takes the same number of oracle queries as the GPST attack against SIDH to adaptively recover a secret key. In other words, the additional key validation mechanism not only slows down the protocol with respect to the original SIDH scheme but also gives no advantage to the scheme in preventing adaptive attacks.

1.1   Concurrent Works

An exciting advance in isogeny cryptanalysis given by Castryck and Decru [CD22] gives a polynomial time key-recovery attack against the original SIDH [JD11] by exploiting the torsion points and the known endomorphism ring of E_0. The current version of the attack does not run in polynomial time against SHealS and HealS where the endomorphism ring is assumed to be unknown, as a potential patch suggested in [CD22] using a trusted set-up for the public curve. Whether the Castryck-Decru attack can be extended to the unknown endomorphism and run in polynomial time, of course, is worthwhile to be investigated further before jumping to conclusions.

1.2   Technical Overview

The cornerstone of our attack is the flaw originating in the proof of the main theorems for the key validation mechanism (Theorems 1 and 2 in [FP21]). The main idea of the mechanism exploits the nontrivial commutativity of the SIDH diagram [Leo20] (i.e. $\phi'_A \phi_B = \phi'_B \phi_A$ when Alice and Bob both behave honestly). For a given curve E_0, a natural number b and a basis $\{P_2, Q_2\}$ for $E_0[4^a]$ from the public parameter, the key validation mechanism checks the validity of three following relations:

$$
\begin{aligned}
e_{4^a}(R_a, S_a) &= e_{4^a}(P_2, Q_2)^{3^b}, \\
\phi'_A(R_a) &= [e_1]R_{ab} + [f_1]S_{ab} \in E_{AB}, \\
\phi'_A(S_a) &= [e_2]R_{ab} + [f_2]S_{ab} \in E_{AB},
\end{aligned}
$$

where ϕ'_A is an isogeny from E_B with kernel $\langle [2^a]R_a + [\alpha 2^a]S_a \rangle \subset E_B$, $\{R_a, S_a\}$ and $\{R_{ab}, S_{ab}\}$ are bases for $E_B[4^a]$ and $E_{AB}[4^a]$ respectively, $(R_a, S_a, R_{ab}, S_{ab}, E_B, E_{AB})$ is the input given by Bob, and $(\alpha, e_1, f_1, e_2, f_2)$ is Alice's secret key. The first equation comes from the relations between isogenies and the Weil pairing. The last two equations are derived from the commutativity of the SIDH diagram [Leo20].

These relations will be satisfied when Bob produces the input honestly. In the security analysis in [FP21], to make another valid input, which is not obtained by taking negations of the curve points, is equivalent to solve four linear equations with four unknown variables (e_1, f_1, e_2, f_2) over the ring $\mathbb{Z}/4^a\mathbb{Z}$. Furthermore, Bob's input also has the restriction that $e_{4^a}(R_a, S_a) = e_{4^a}(P_2, Q_2)^{3^b}$ and ϕ'_A might vary with the choice of R_a and S_a. Therefore, it is deduced that Bob, without knowing Alice's secret, is not able to produce another valid input, which is not obtained by taking negations of the original input. In this way, since Bob, restricted by the mechanism, behaves honestly, the cryptosystem will be secure based on the hardness assumption.

However, for an adaptive attack, what malicious Bob wants to exploit is that Alice's behaviour is dependent on the secret. The proof in [FP21] neglects the spirit of the adaptive attack where malicious Bob can learn the desired information adaptively. For example, write $\mathbf{M} = \begin{pmatrix} e_1 & f_1 \\ e_2 & f_2 \end{pmatrix} \in M_{2\times2}(\mathbb{Z}/4^a\mathbb{Z}), \mathbf{u} = (R_a \ S_a)^T$ and $\mathbf{v} = (R_{ab} \ S_{ab})^T$. We may therefore abuse the notation by writing $\phi'_A\mathbf{u} = \mathbf{Mv}$. As we will show in Sect. 3, by considering matrices $\mathbf{P}_1 = \begin{pmatrix} 1 & 0 \\ 2^{2a-1} & 1 \end{pmatrix}$ and $\mathbf{P}_2 = \mathbf{I}_2$, the relation $\mathbf{P}_1\mathbf{M} = \mathbf{M}\mathbf{P}_2$ holds if and only if $e_1 = f_1 = 0$ mod 2. Hence, on input $(R'_a, S'_a, R'_{ab}, S'_{ab}, E_B, E_{AB})$ where $(R'_a \ S'_a)^T = \mathbf{P}_1\mathbf{u}$ and $(R'_{ab} \ S'_{ab})^T = \mathbf{P}_2\mathbf{v}$ the key validation mechanism will pass if and only if $\phi'_A\mathbf{P}_1\mathbf{u} = \mathbf{M}\mathbf{P}_2\mathbf{v}$ if and only if $e_1 = f_1 = 0$ mod 2. Note that because $\det(\mathbf{P}_1) = 1$ and $(2^a \ 2^a)\mathbf{P}_1 = (c \ c)$ for some $c \in \mathbb{Z}_{2^a}$, the Weil pairing check will also pass and the isogeny used by the mechanism is still ϕ'_A. In this way, Bob learns one bit information of e_1 and f_1. Moreover, as we will show in Sect. 3, this is enough to recover the least significant bit of α.

On top of that, Bob can utilize the GPST attack in a "reciprocal" sense to extract further information further. If the least significant bit of α, denoted by α_0, is 1, the secret α is invertible over the ring $\mathbb{Z}/2^a\mathbb{Z}$. By further replacing R_a with $R'_a = R_a + [2^{2a-2}]R_a - [2^{2a-2}\alpha_0]S_a$, the validity of the second relation in the mechanism depends on the second least significant bit of α. However, $e_{4^a}(R'_a, S_a)$ will never satisfy the first relation. To overcome this, Bob will replace S_a with $[\alpha_0^{-1}2^{2a-2}]R_a + [1 - 2^{2a-2}]S_a$ which can be used to extract the second least significant bit of α^{-1}, because the equality of the third equation depends on the second least significant bit of α^{-1}. Remark that, the isogeny used in the key validation mechanism is not necessarily the same ϕ'_A if the kernel is not $\langle [2^a]R_a + [\alpha 2^a]S_a \rangle$. In Sect. 4, we present the attack in details including the case where α is even.

Structure of this Paper. We begin in Sect. 2 with some preliminary background on elliptic curves, isogenies, a brief outline the fundamental scheme of [FP21], together with a few immediate properties of the scheme. We then introduce the method of using commutativity of matrices to extract the least significant bit of Alice's secret in Sect. 3. Based on the least significant bit information, a tweak of the GPST attack to recursively and adaptively recover Alice's secret is then deduced in Sect. 4. A brief summary is made in Sect. 5. We also provide in Appendix A a generalized attack against mechanism using commutativity of isogenies.

2   Preliminaries

Notations. We begin by introducing some notations that will be used through-out the paper. Let $\mathbf{O}$ represent the point at infinity of an elliptic curve, $\mathbb{N}$ be the set of natural numbers, and $\mathbb{Z}$ be the set of integers. For $n \in \mathbb{N}$, let $\mathbb{Z}_n$ defined to be $\mathbb{Z}/n\mathbb{Z}$ and $\mathbb{F}_n$ be the finite field of order n. For convenience, when we write $u \in \mathbb{Z}_n$, we consider u is a representative taken from $\{0, \cdots, n-1\} \subset \mathbb{Z}$. Similarly, when we write $u \mod n$, we consider the unique representative taken from $\{0, \cdots, n-1\} \subset \mathbb{Z}$. Also, for $n \in \mathbb{N}$, $e_n(\cdot, \cdot)$ represents the Weil e_n-pairing.

2.1   Elliptic Curves and Isogenies

An elliptic curve is a rational nonsingular curve of genus one with a distinguished point at infinity denoted by $\mathbf{O}$. An elliptic curve with $\mathbf{O}$ forms an additive commutative group. Let p be an odd prime number and q be a power of p. If E is an elliptic curve defined over $\mathbb{F}_q$, then $E(\mathbb{F}_q)$, collecting $\mathbb{F}_q$-rational points of E and $\mathbf{O}$, is a finite subgroup of E. Moreover, E is said to be supersingular if the endomorphism ring of E is a maximal order in a quaternion algebra. For $n \in \mathbb{N}$ coprime with p, the n-torsion subgroup $E[n]$, collecting points of order dividing n, is isomorphic to $\mathbb{Z}_n \oplus \mathbb{Z}_n$. The Weil e_n-pairing $e_n(\cdot, \cdot)$ is bilinear, alternating and nondegenerate.

An isogeny is a morphism between elliptic curves preserving the point at infinity. The kernel of an isogeny is always finite and defines the isogeny up to a power of the Frobenius map. We restrict our attention to separable isogenies (which induce separable extensions of function fields over $\mathbb{F}_q$) between supersingular elliptic curves defined over $\mathbb{F}_q$. Given a finite subgroup S of E, there exists a unique separable isogeny with kernel S from E to the codomain denoted by E/S which can be computed via Vélu's formulas. We refer to [Sil09] to get more exposed to the elliptic curve theory.

2.2   Brief Outline of HealSIDH Key Exchange

Both SHealS and HealS, introduced in [FP21], are PKE schemes building on the key exchange scheme HealSIDH with a key validation mechanism. Concretely, SHealS is a PKE scheme using the padding to encrypt the message where the padding is the hash value of the shared curve (j-invariant) obtained from Heal-SIDH. HealS is a variant of SHealS by changing the parameters. In other words, our adaptive attack on HealSIDH is applicable to both SHealS and HealS.

We briefly introduce HealSIDH with the key validation mechanism as shown in Fig. 1. The public parameter $\mathsf{pp} = (E_0, P_2, Q_2, P_3, Q_3, p, a, b)$ contains a super-singular curve E_0 defined over $\mathbb{F}_{p^2}$ with an unknown endomorphism ring and $(p, a, b) \in \mathbb{N}^3$ where p is a prime of the form $2^{2a}3^{2b}f - 1$ such that $2^a \approx 3^b$. The requirement of the unknown endomorphism prevents the torsion-point attack [dQKL+21] (and also [CD22]). The sets $\{P_2, Q_2\}$, $\{P_3, Q_3\}$ are bases for $E_0[4^a]$ and $E_0[9^b]$ respectively and $P_A = [2^a]P_2, Q_A = [2^a]Q_2, P_B = [3^b]P_3$, and

$Q_B = [3^b]Q_3$. Alice and Bob sample α and β uniformly at random from $\mathbb{Z}_{2^a}$ and $\mathbb{Z}_{3^b}$ respectively. Also, Alice and Bob compute $\phi_A : E_0 \rightarrow E_A = E_0/\langle P_A + [\alpha]Q_A \rangle$ and $\phi_B : E_0 \rightarrow E_B = E_0/\langle P_B + [\beta]Q_B \rangle$, respectively. Alice and Bob compute $(\phi_A(P_2), \phi_A(Q_2), \phi_A(P_3), \phi_A(Q_3))$ and $(\phi_B(P_3), \phi_B(Q_3), \phi_B(P_2), \phi_B(Q_2))$ respectively. Alice's and Bob's public keys are $(E_A, \phi_A(P_3), \phi_A(Q_3))$ and $(E_B, \phi_B(P_2), \phi_B(Q_2))$ respectively. Alice computes the canonical basis $\{R_A, S_A\}$ for $E_A[4^a]$ and represents $\phi_A(P_2) = [e_1]R_A + [f_1]S_A$ and $\phi_A(Q_2) = [e_2]R_A + [f_2]S_A$. Bob computes the canonical basis $\{R_B, S_B\}$ for $E_B[9^a]$ and represents $\phi_B(P_3) = [g_1]R_B + [h_1]S_B$ and $\phi_B(Q_3) = [g_2]R_B + [h_2]S_B$. Alice's and Bob's secret keys are $\mathsf{sk}_A = (\alpha, e_1, f_1, e_2, f_2)$ and $\mathsf{sk}_B = (\beta, g_1, h_1, g_2, h_2)$ respectively.

To establish a shared secret with Alice, Bob collects Alice's public key, denoted by (E_A, R_b, S_b), and computes $\phi_B' : E_A \rightarrow E_{AB} = E_A/\langle [3^b]R_b + [\beta 3^b]S_b \rangle$ together with $(\phi_B'(R_A), \phi_B'(S_A), \phi_B'(R_b), \phi_B'(S_b))$. He sends $(R_{ab} = \phi_B'(R_A), S_{ab} = \phi_B'(S_A))$ to Alice.

Upon receiving (R_{ab}, S_{ab}) from Bob, Alice collects Bob's public key (E_B, R_a, S_a). She computes $\phi_A' : E_B \rightarrow E_{BA} = E_B/\langle [2^a]R_a + [\alpha 2^a]S_a \rangle$ together with $(\phi_A'(R_B), \phi_A'(S_B), \phi_A'(R_a), \phi_A'(S_a))$. If $e_{4^a}(R_a, S_a) \neq e_{4^a}(P_2, Q_2)^{3^b}$, $\phi_A'(R_a) \neq [e_1]R_{ab} + [f_1]S_{ab}$, or $\phi_A'(S_a) \neq [e_2]R_{ab} + [f_2]S_{ab}$, then Alice aborts (the session). Otherwise, she sends $(R_{ba} = \phi_A'(R_B), S_{ba} = \phi_A'(S_B))$ to Bob and keeps the j-invariant j_{BA} of E_{BA} as the shared secret.

Similarly, upon receiving (R_{ba}, S_{ba}), Bob aborts if $e_{9^b}(R_b, S_b) \neq e_{9^b}(P_3, Q_3)^{2^a}$, $\phi_B'(R_b) \neq [g_1]R_{ba} + [h_1]S_{ba}$, or $\phi_B'(S_b) \neq [g_2]R_{ba} + [h_2]S_{ba}$, If not he takes the j-invariant of E_{AB} as the shared secret.

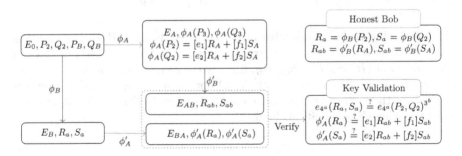

Fig. 1. The outline of HealSIDH with the key validation mechanism. The upper right box shows the points honest Bob will compute. The lower right box is the key validation process used by Alice to verify the public key given by Bob. The evaluations of $\phi_A(P_2), \phi_A(Q_2)$ are secretly computed by Alice and the coefficients e_1, f_1, e_2, f_2 are included in her secret key.

Remark 1. In the real protocol, instead of giveing R_{ab}, S_{ab} directly, Bob will give the coordinates of them with respect to the canonical basis of $E_{AB}[4^a]$. Otherwise, the secretly shared curve E_{AB} can be reconstructed by an eavesdropper by computing its Montgomery coefficient $A_{E_{AB}} = (y(R_{ab})^2 - x(R_{ab})^3 -$

$x(R_{ab}))/x(R_{ab})^2$. For simplicity we ignore this detail and pretend Bob does send the points R_{ab} and S_{ab} to Alice. Hence, for the convenience, we may assume Bob sends the entire points R_{ab}, S_{ab} to Alice.

We have the following two immediate results.

Proposition 2. *If Bob honestly generates* $R_a = \phi_B(P_2)$, $S_a = \phi_B(Q_2)$, $R_{ab} = \phi'_B(R_A)$ *and* $S_{ab} = \phi'_B(S_A)$, *then* $\{R_{ab}, S_{ab}\}$ *is a basis of* $E_{AB}[4^a]$ *and* $\{R_a, S_a\}$ *is a basis of* $E_B[4^a]$.

Proof. Since $[4^a]R_a = \phi_B([4^a]P_2) = \mathbf{O}$ and $[4^a]S_a = \phi_B([4^a]Q_2) = \mathbf{O}$, both R_a and S_a are in $E_B[4^a]$. Due to $e_{4^a}(R_a, S_a) = e_{4^a}(P_2, Q_2)^{3^b}$, we know $e_{4^a}(R_a, S_a)$ is a primitive 4^a-th root of unity. Similarly, since $[4^a]R_{ab} = \phi'_B([4^a]R_A) = \mathbf{O}$ and $[4^a]S_{ab} = \phi'_B([4^a]S_A) = \mathbf{O}$, both R_{ab} and S_{ab} are in $E_{AB}[4^a]$. Due to $e_{4^a}(R_{ab}, S_{ab}) = e_{4^a}(R_A, S_A)^{3^b}$, we know $e_{4^a}(R_{ab}, S_{ab})$ is a primitive 4^a-th root of unity. Therefore, the result follows.

Lemma 3. *Let* e_1, e_2, f_1, f_2 *be defined as above and* $\alpha \in \mathbb{Z}_{2^a}$ *be Alice's secret key i.e.* $\ker(\phi_A) = \langle [2^a]P_2 + [\alpha 2^a]Q_2 \rangle$. *If Alice follows the protocol specification, then* $e_1 + \alpha e_2 = f_1 + \alpha f_2 = 0 \mod 2^a$.

Proof. Given $\phi_A(P_2) = [e_1]R_A + [f_1]S_A$ and $\phi_A(Q_2) = [e_2]R_A + [f_2]S_A$, we have $\mathbf{O} = \phi_A([2^a]P_2 + [\alpha 2^a]Q_2) = [2^a e_1 + \alpha 2^a e_2]R_A + [2^a f_1 + \alpha 2^a f_2]S_A = [e_1 + \alpha e_2]([2^a]R_a) + [f_1 + \alpha f_2]([2^a]S_A)$.

Note that $\{[2^a]R_A, [2^a]S_A\}$ is a basis for $E_A[2^a]$ due to $\{R_A, S_A\}$ being a basis for $E_A[4^a]$. Therefore, $e_1 + \alpha e_2 = f_1 + \alpha f_2 = 0 \mod 2^a$.

Modeling. We consider adaptive attacks against HealSIDH throughout this paper. Bob, as a malicious adversary, is given access to an oracle $\mathcal{O}_{\mathsf{sk}_A} \to 0/1$ taking as input $(R_a, S_a, R_{ab}, S_{ab}, E_B, E_{AB})$ with the relations specified as above. For simplicity, we denote the oracle by $\mathcal{O}$ and omit curves E_B, E_{AB} from the input when they are clear from the context. The oracle $\mathcal{O}$ returns 1 if and only if the following three equations hold:

$$e_{4^a}(R_a, S_a) = e_{4^a}(P_2, Q_2)^{3^b}, \tag{1}$$

$$\phi'_A(R_a) = [e_1]R_{ab} + [f_1]S_{ab}, \tag{2}$$

$$\phi'_A(S_a) = [e_2]R_{ab} + [f_2]S_{ab}, \tag{3}$$

where ϕ'_A is an isogeny from E_B with kernel $\langle [2^a]R_a + [\alpha 2^a]S_a \rangle \in E_B$.

When Bob follows the protocol specification, the three equations hold naturally. The goal of malicious Bob in our attack is to recover Alice's core secret α by adaptively manipulating his input.

The flaw of the claim in [FP21] comes from the main theorem (Theorem 2) for the key validation mechanism. Theorem 2 of [FP21] states that if on input $(\widetilde{R_a}, \widetilde{S_a}, \widetilde{R_{ab}}, \widetilde{S_{ab}})$ the oracle returns 1, then there are only 16 forms of $(\widetilde{R_a}, \widetilde{S_a}, \widetilde{R_{ab}}, \widetilde{S_{ab}})$ as follows:

$$(\widetilde{R_a}, \widetilde{S_a}, \widetilde{R_{ab}}, \widetilde{S_{ab}}) = ([\pm 1]\phi_B(P_2), [\pm 1]\phi_B(Q_2), [\pm 1]\phi'_B(R_A), [\pm 1]\phi'_B(S_A)),$$

where ϕ_B, ϕ'_B are the isogenies computed by Bob following the protocol specification. We will immediately show this is not true in the next section.

3   Parity Recovering

In this section, we consider the least significant bits of e_1, e_2, f_1, f_2 and α. We can recover the least significant bit of α with one oracle query by relying the relations given by Lemma 3.

Say Bob computes ϕ_B, ϕ'_B honestly. The attack presented in this section and the next section relies on following facts:

- $\{P_2, Q_2\}$, is a basis for $E_0[4^a]$.
- $\{R_{ab}, S_{ab}\} = \{\phi'_B(R_A), \phi'_B(S_A)\}$ is a basis of $E_{AB}[4^a]$ (Proposition 2).
- $\{R_a, S_a\} = \{\phi_B(P_2), \phi_B(Q_2)\}$ is a basis of $E_B[4^a]$ (Proposition 2).
- $e_1 + \alpha e_2 = f_1 + \alpha f_2 = 0 \mod 2^a$ (Lemma 3).

The high-level idea in this section is simple. Assume Alice and Bob follows the protocol specification. Write $\mathbf{M} = \begin{pmatrix} e_1 & f_1 \\ e_2 & f_2 \end{pmatrix} \in M_{2\times 2}(\mathbb{Z}_{4^a})$, $\mathbf{u} = (R_a\ S_a)^T$ and $\mathbf{v} = (R_{ab}\ S_{ab})^T$. Recall that $\phi'_A(R_a) = [e_1]R_{ab} + [f_1]S_{ab}$, $\phi'_A(S_a) = [e_2]R_{ab} + [f_2]S_{ab}$ where R_a, S_a, R_{ab}, S_{ab} are honestly generated by Bob. We may abuse the notation by writing $\phi'_A \mathbf{u} = \mathbf{M}\mathbf{v}$ based on Eqs. (2) and (3). The idea is to find a pair of particular square matrices $\mathbf{P}_1, \mathbf{P}_2 \in M_{2\times 2}(\mathbb{Z}_{4^a})$ where $\mathbf{P}_1$ is of determinant 1 such that the commutativity of $\mathbf{P}_1\mathbf{M} = \mathbf{M}\mathbf{P}_2$ is conditioned on the information (parity for instance) to be extracted from $\mathbf{M}$. Let $(R'_a\ S'_a)^T = \mathbf{P}_1\mathbf{u}$ and $(R'_{ab}\ S'_{ab})^T = \mathbf{P}_2\mathbf{v}$. On input $(R'_a, S'_a, R'_{ab}, S'_{ab})$ the oracle returns 1 if $\mathbf{M}$ satisfies the commutativity condition $\mathbf{P}_1\mathbf{M} = \mathbf{M}\mathbf{P}_2$, because $\mathbf{P}_1\phi'_A\mathbf{u} = \phi'_A\mathbf{P}_1\mathbf{u} = \mathbf{P}_1\mathbf{M}\mathbf{v} = \mathbf{M}\mathbf{P}_2\mathbf{v}$ holds. Remark that the determinant 1 of $\mathbf{P}_1$ ensures the new pair $(R'_a\ S'_a)$ will satisfy the Weil pairing verification Eq. (1). Futhermore, we require $(2^a\ \alpha 2^a)\mathbf{P}_1 = (c\ c)$ for some $c \in \mathbb{Z}_{2^a}$ so that the isogeny used by the oracle is still the one with the kernel $\langle [2^a]R_a + [\alpha 2^a]S_a \rangle$.

Though there are 2^4 combinations of the least significant bits of e_1, e_2, f_1, f_2. The following lemma shows that when Alice generates them honestly, there are only six patterns.

Lemma 4. *If Alice produces $\phi_A(P_2)$ and $\phi_A(Q_2)$ honestly, then there are only 6 possible patterns of parities of e_1, e_2, f_1, f_2:*

1. $f_2 = 1 \mod 2$ and $e_2 = e_1 = f_1 = 0 \mod 2$,
2. $e_2 = 1 \mod 2$ and $e_1 = f_1 = f_2 = 0 \mod 2$,
3. $e_2 = f_2 = 1 \mod 2$ and $e_1 = f_1 = 0 \mod 2$,
4. $f_1 = f_2 = 1 \mod 2$ and $e_1 = e_2 = 0 \mod 2$,

5. $e_1 = e_2 = 1 \mod 2$ *and* $f_1 = f_2 = 0 \mod 2$,

6. $e_1 = e_2 = f_1 = f_2 = 1 \mod 2$.

Proof. Recall $e_{4^a}(\phi_A(P_2), \phi_A(Q_2)) = e_{4^a}(P_2, Q_2)^{2^a} = e_{4^a}(R_A, S_A)^{e_1 f_2 - e_2 f_1}$. Since both $\{P_2, Q_2\}$ and $\{R_A, S_A\}$ are bases for $E_0[4^a], E_A[4^a]$ respectively, both $e_{4^a}(P_2, Q_2)$ and $e_{4^a}(R_A, S_A)$ are primitive 4^a-th roots of unity. Given

$$e_{4^a}(R_A, S_A)^{2^a(e_1 f_2 - e_2 f_1)} = 1,$$

we have $e_1 f_2 - e_2 f_1 = 0 \mod 2^a$.

Furthermore, e_2, f_2 cannot be both even. Recall $\phi(Q_2) = e_2 R_A + f_2 S_A$. Suppose for the purpose of contradiction that both e_2 and f_2 are even. Then, $[2^{2a-1}]\phi_A(Q_2) = \mathbf{O}$, which implies $\ker(\phi_A) = \langle P_2 + [\alpha]Q_2 \rangle$ contains $[2^{2a-1}]Q_2$. That is, $[k]P_2 + [k\alpha]Q_2 = [2^{2a-1}]Q_2$ for some $k \in \mathbb{Z}_{2^a}$, so $k = 0$. This contradicts the fact that $\{P_2, Q_2\}$ is a basis for $E_0[4^a]$. The result follows.

We order the six cases according to the lemma above. The following lemmata indicate that we can divide the overall cases into two partitions: $\{Case\,1, Case\,2, Case\,3\}$ and $\{Case\,4, Case\,5, Case\,6\}$ with 1 oracle query.

Lemma 5. *Assume Bob honestly generates* $R_a, S_a, R_{ab}, S_{ab}, E_B, E_{AB}$. *On input* $(\widetilde{R_a}, \widetilde{S_a}, R_{ab}, S_{ab})$, *where* $\widetilde{R_a} = R_a$ *and* $\widetilde{S_a} = [2^{2a-1}]R_a + S_a$ *the oracle returns* 1 *only for Cases 1 to 3.*

Proof. Firstly, the isogeny ϕ'_A computed by the oracle is the same one used by Alice in the honest execution. This is because both kernels are the same:

$$\langle [2^a]R_a + [\alpha 2^a]S_a \rangle = \langle [2^a]\widetilde{R_a} + [\alpha 2^a]\widetilde{S_a} \rangle.$$

Therefore, since R_a, S_a, R_{ab}, S_{ab} are honestly generated, we may assume $e_{4^a}(R_a, S_a) = e_{4^a}(P_2, Q_2)^{3^b}$, $\phi'_A(R_a) = [e_1]R_{ab} + [f_1]S_{ab}$, and $\phi'_A(S_a) = [e_2]R_{ab} + [f_2]S_{ab}$.

For Eq. (1), since $e_{4^a}(R_a, S_a) = e_{4^a}(P_2, Q_2)^{3^b}$, we have

$$e_{4^a}(\widetilde{R_a}, \widetilde{S_a}) = e_{4^a}(R_a, S_a) = e_{4^a}(P_2, Q_2)^{3^b}.$$

Given $\phi'_A(R_a) = [e_1]R_{ab} + [f_1]S_{ab}$, $\phi'_A(S_a) = [e_2]R_{ab} + [f_2]S_{ab}$ and $R_{ab}, S_{ab} \in E_{AB}[2^a]$, we have

$$\phi'_A(\widetilde{R_a}) - [e_1]R_{ab} - [f_1]S_{ab} = \mathbf{O},$$
$$\phi'_A(\widetilde{S_a}) - [e_2]R_{ab} - [f_2]S_{ab} = [2^{2a-1}e_1]R_{ab} + [2^{2a-1}f_1]S_{ab}.$$

Recall that $\{R_{ab}, S_{ab}\}$ is a basis. Therefore, the oracle returns 1 if and only if $[2^{2a-1}e_1]R_{ab} + [2^{2a-1}f_1]S_{ab} = \mathbf{O}$ or, equivalently, $e_1 = f_1 = 0 \mod 2$. The result follows.

Lemma 6. *Assume Bob honestly generates* $R_a, S_a, R_{ab}, S_{ab}, E_B, E_{AB}$. *On input* $(\widetilde{R_a}, \widetilde{S_a}, R_{ab}, S_{ab})$, *where* $\widetilde{R_a} = [1 + 2^{2a-1}]R_a - [2^{2a-1}]S_a$ *and* $\widetilde{S_a} = [2^{2a-1}]R_a + [1 - 2^{2a-1}]S_a$ *the oracle returns* 1 *only for Cases 4 to 6.*

Proof. Firstly, the isogeny ϕ'_A computed by the oracle is the same one used by Alice in the honest execution. This is because both kernels are the same:

$$\langle [2^a]R_a + [\alpha 2^a]S_a \rangle = \langle [2^a]\widetilde{R_a} + [\alpha 2^a]\widetilde{S_a} \rangle.$$

Therefore, since R_a, S_a, R_{ab}, S_{ab} are honestly generated, we may assume $e_{4^a}(R_a, S_a) = e_{4^a}(P_2, Q_2)^{3^b}$, $\phi'_A(R_a) = [e_1]R_{ab} + [f_1]S_{ab}$, and $\phi'_A(S_a) = [e_2]R_{ab} + [f_2]S_{ab}$.

For Eq. (1), since $e_{4^a}(R_a, S_a) = e_{4^a}(P_2, Q_2)^{3^b}$, we have

$$e_{4^a}(\widetilde{R_a}, \widetilde{S_a})$$
$$= e_{4^a}([1 + 2^{a-1}]R_a - [2^{a-1}]S_a, [2^{a-1}]R_a + [1 - 2^{a-1}]S_a)$$
$$= e_{4^a}(R_a, S_a)^{1 - 2^{2a-2} + 2^{2a-2}}$$
$$= e_{4^a}(P_2, Q_2)^{3^b}.$$

Given $\phi'_A(R_a) = [e_1]R_{ab} + [f_1]S_{ab}$, $\phi'_A(S_a) = [e_2]R_{ab} + [f_2]S_{ab}$ and $R_{ab}, S_{ab} \in E_{AB}[2^a]$, we have

$$\phi'_A(\widetilde{R_a}) - [e_1]R_{ab} - [f_1]S_{ab} = [2^{2a-1}]([e_1]R_{ab} + [f_1]S_{ab} + [e_2]R_{ab} + [f_2]S_{ab}),$$
$$\phi'_A(\widetilde{S_a}) - [e_2]R_{ab} - [f_2]S_{ab} = [2^{2a-1}]([e_1]R_{ab} + [f_1]S_{ab} + [e_2]R_{ab} + [f_2]S_{ab}).$$

Recall that $\{R_{ab}, S_{ab}\}$ is a basis of $E_{AB}[2^a]$. Therefore, the oracle returns 1 if and only if $e_1 = e_2 \mod 2$ and $f_1 = f_2 \mod 2$. The result follows.

The cases $\{Case\,1,\ Case\,2,\ Case\,3\}$ occur if and only if the least significant bit of α is 0 by Lemma 4. In fact, by choosing particular matrices $\mathbf{P}_1$ and $\mathbf{P}_2$, one can precisely recover all parities of e_1, e_2, f_1 and f_2. However, by Lemma 4, we do not bother to find them all since the information given in Lemma 5 already is sufficient to recover the least significant bit of α. In the next section, we will present a variant of the GPST attack. We start with the least significant bit of α to recover each higher bit with one oracle query for each.

4   Recover the Secret

In this section, we present a variant of the GPST attack to recover the secret α based on the knowledge extracted from the previous section. The high-level idea is to use the GPST attack in a "reciprocal" manner. Recall that Bob has two following equations when he generates the points $(R_a, S_a, R_{ab}, S_{ab})$ honestly:

$$\phi'_A(R_a) = [e_1]R_{ab} + [f_1]S_{ab},$$
$$\phi'_A(S_a) = [e_2]R_{ab} + [f_2]S_{ab},$$

where $\ker(\phi'_A) = \langle [2^a]R_a + [2^a\alpha]S_a \rangle$.

To extract the second least significant bit of $-\alpha$, denoted by α_1, based on the least bit α_0, we consider $\phi'_A(R_a + [2^{2a-2}]R_a - [2^{2a-2}\alpha_0]S_a) = [e_1]R_{ab} + [f_1]S_{ab} + ([2^{2a-2}e_1 - 2^{2a-2}\alpha_0 e_2]R_{ab} + [2^{2a-2}f_1 - 2^{2a-2}\alpha_0 f_2]S_{ab})$ where the purpose of

$[2^{2a-2}\alpha_0]S_a$ is to eliminate the lower bit. Note that $([2^{2a-2}e_1 - 2^{2a-2}\alpha_0 e_2]R_{ab} + [2^{2a-2}f_1 - 2^{2a-2}\alpha_0 f_2]S_{ab}) = ([\alpha_1 2^{2a-1}][e_2]R_{ab} + [\alpha_1 2^{2a-1}][f_2]S_{ab})$ because $e_1 + \alpha e_2 = f_1 + \alpha f_2 = 0 \mod 2^a$ and $\{R_a, S_a\}$ is a basis for $E_B[4^a]$ (Lemma 3 and Proposition 2). By Lemma 4, since e_2 and f_2 cannot be both even, at least one of $[2^{2a-1}e_2]R_{ab}$ and $[2^{2a-1}f_2]S_{ab}$ is of order 2. It follows that the equation

$$\phi'_A(R_a + [2^{2a-2}]R_a - [2^{2a-2}\alpha_0]S_a) = [e_1]R_{ab} + [f_1]S_{ab}$$

holds if and only if $\alpha_1 = 0$.

Unfortunately, querying the oracle on input $(R_a + [2^{2a-2}]R_a - [2^{2a-2}\alpha_0]S_a, S_a, R_{ab}, S_{ab})$ will always return 0 so that Bob cannot obtain any useful information. This is because $e_{4^a}(R_a + [2^{2a-2}]R_a - [2^{2a-2}\alpha_0]S_a, S_a)$ never equals $e_{4^a}(P_2, Q_2)^{3^b}$. In other words, if Bob does so, he will always get $\perp$ from Alice. To resolve this, we use the idea of "reciprocal". Assume α is invertible modulo 2^a. Bob will craft a point replacing S_a for *recovering* $\alpha^{-1} \mod 2^a$ *at the same time*. Concretely, Bob computes $\hat{\alpha} = \alpha_0^{-1} \mod 4$. For the same reasoning as above, the equation

$$\phi'_A(\hat{\alpha}[2^{2a-2}]R_a + [1 - 2^{2a-2}]S_a) = [e_2]R_{ab} + [f_2]S_{ab}$$

holds if and only if $\alpha^{-1} = \hat{\alpha} \mod 4$ if and only if $\alpha_1 = 0$.

Moreover, $e_{4^a}(R_a + [2^{2a-2}]R_a - [2^{2a-2}\alpha_0]S_a, \hat{\alpha}[2^{2a-2}]R_a + [1 - 2^{2a-2}]S_a) = e_{4^a}(R_a, S_a)$. Therefore, by sending $(R_a + [2^{2a-2}]R_a - [2^{2a-2}\alpha_0]S_a, \hat{\alpha}[2^{2a-2}]R_a + [1 - 2^{2a-2}]S_a, R_{ab}, S_{ab})$ to Alice, Bob can know whether $\alpha_1 = 0$. However, α is not necessarily odd. We have to use unbalanced powers of 2 on each query and introduce the concept of *quasi-inverse* elements.

Remark 7. On input $(R_a + [2^{2a-2}]R_a - [2^{2a-2}\alpha_0]S_a, \hat{\alpha}[2^{2a-2}]R_a + [1 - 2^{2a-2}]S_a, R_{ab}, S_{ab})$, honest Alice will use the same isogeny ϕ'_A because $\langle [2^a](R_a + [2^{2a-2}]R_a - [2^{2a-2}\alpha_0]S_a) + [\alpha 2^a](\hat{\alpha}[2^{2a-2}]R_a + [1 - 2^{2a-2}]S_a)\rangle = \langle [2^a]R_a + [\alpha 2^a]S_a\rangle$. The same kernel will therefore derive the same isogeny ϕ'_A.

4.1   Quasi-Inverse Element

Definition 8. *Let p be a prime and $a \in \mathbb{N}$. For an element $u \in \mathbb{Z}$, a p^a-quasi-inverse element of u is a non-zero element $v \in \mathbb{Z}_{p^a}$ such that $uv = p'$ mod p^a where p' is the maximal power of p dividing u.*

When $a = 1$, every element obviously has a *p-quasi-inverse element* by taking either its inverse over $\mathbb{Z}_p$ or 1. Unlike the inverse over a ring, a quasi-inverse is not necessarily unique. For instance, $1, 9, 17$ and 25 are 2^5-quasi-inverse elements of 4 over $\mathbb{Z}_{32}$. Also, if $u = 0$, any non-zero element can be its quasi-inverse.

A non-zero element being not a unit of $\mathbb{Z}_{p^a}$ can still have a p^a-quasi-inverse element. However, a non-zero element v in $\mathbb{Z}_{p^a}$ being a p^a-quasi-inverse element for a non-zero integer in $\mathbb{Z}_{p^a}$ implies v is a unit of $\mathbb{Z}_{p^a}$.

Proposition 9. *Let p be a prime and $a \in \mathbb{N}$. For $u \in \mathbb{Z}$, a non-zero element over $\mathbb{Z}_{p^a}$, any p^a-quasi-inverse element of u is a unit of $\mathbb{Z}_{p^a}$.*

Proof. Write $u = u'p^j$ where $u', j \in \mathbb{Z}$ and u' is not divisible by p and $j < a$. Say there exists $v \in \mathbb{Z}_{p^a}$ such that $uv = p^j \mod p^a$. Since u is a non-zero element over $\mathbb{Z}_{p^a}$, we know $a > j$ so that $(u/p^j)v = 1 \mod p^{j-a}$. It follows that v is not divided by p, so v is a unit of $\mathbb{Z}_{p^a}$.

In fact, for any $u \in \mathbb{Z}_{p^a}$ where $p^j \mid u$ and $p^{j+1} \nmid u$ for some non-negative integer j, one can always find a p^a-quasi-inverse by taking $v = (u/p^j)^{-1} \in \mathbb{Z}_{p^{a-j}}$ and naturally lifting v to $\mathbb{Z}_{p^a}$ Therefore, we may let $\mathsf{Quasilnv}(u, p, i)$ be an efficient algorithm outputting a p^i-quasi-inverse element of u and restrict it to output 1 when $p^i \mid u$.

Remark 10. Looking ahead, in our attack, we need to compute 2^{i+1}-quasi-inverse elements for either α_l or $\alpha_l + 2^i$ in the i-th iteration, where $\alpha_l = \alpha \mod 2^i$ has been extracted in the previous iterations. In a more general case where the prime 2 is replaced by $q \in \mathbb{N}$, the attack enumerates q^{i+1}-quasi-inverse elements for $\alpha_l + tq^i$ for every $t \in \{0, \cdots, q-1\}$, which corresponds to guess whether the next digit is t or not. See Appendix A for more details.

4.2 Attack on HealS and SHealS

The algorithm in Fig. 2 together with Theorem 12 provides an iterative approach for recovering α. It requires one oracle query to recover each bit of α in each iteration. We need the following lemma to prove the main theorem.

Lemma 11. *Let $(\alpha, e_1, f_1, e_2, f_2)$ denote Alice's HealSIDH secret key as Sect. 2.2. For any $i \in \{1, \ldots, a-1\}$, write $-\alpha = \alpha_l + 2^i \alpha_i \pmod{2^{i+1}}$ where $\alpha_l \in \mathbb{Z}_{2^i}$ and $\alpha_i \in \mathbb{Z}_2$. Let $\hat{\alpha}_l$ be a 2^{i+1}-quasi-inverse element of α_l such that $\hat{\alpha}_l \alpha_l = 2^j \mod 2^{i+1}$. Then, $\alpha_i = 0$ if and only if each of the following two equations is true:*

$$e_1 - \alpha_l e_2 = f_1 - \alpha_l f_2 = 0 \mod 2^{i+1} \tag{4}$$

$$\hat{\alpha}_l e_1 - 2^j e_2 = \hat{\alpha}_l f_1 - 2^j f_2 = 0 \mod 2^{i+1} \tag{5}$$

Proof. By Lemma 3, we have $e_1 - \alpha_l e_2 = -\alpha e_2 - \alpha_l e_2 \mod 2^{i+1}$ and $f_1 - \alpha_l f_2 = -\alpha f_2 - \alpha_l f_2 \mod 2^{i+1}$. By Lemma 4, not both e_2 and f_2 are divisible by 2. Therefore, the first equation is zero if and only if $\alpha_i = 0$.

Similarly, by Lemma 3, we have $\hat{\alpha}_l e_1 - 2^j e_2 = \hat{\alpha}_l \alpha e_2 - 2^j e_2 = \hat{\alpha}(\alpha_l + \alpha_i 2^i) e_2 - 2^j e_2 = \hat{\alpha} \alpha_i e_2 2^i \mod 2^{i+1}$. Also, $\hat{\alpha}_l f_1 - 2^j f_2 = \hat{\alpha} \alpha_i f_2 2^i \mod 2^{i+1}$. By Lemma 4 and Proposition 9, not both $e_2 \hat{\alpha}$ and $f_2 \hat{\alpha}$ are divisible by 2. Therefore, the second equation is zero if and only if $\alpha_i = 0$.

Theorem 12. *Assume Alice follows the protocol specification. The algorithm in Fig. 2 returns α in Alice's secret key.*

Proof. We are going to prove the theorem by induction on i for the i-th bit of α where $i < a$. Write $-\alpha = \alpha_l + 2^i \alpha_i \in \mathbb{Z}_{2^{i+1}}$ for some $i \in \{1, \ldots, a-1\}$ where

---

Algorithm: Recover($\mathsf{pp}, \mathsf{sk}_B, \alpha_0$)
Input: pp public parameter of the protocol, sk_B the secret key of Bob,
$\qquad \alpha_0 = \alpha \mod 2$
Given: access to an oracle $\mathcal{O}(R_a, S_a, R_{ab}, S_{ab}; E_B, E_{AB}) \to 0/1$ returns 1 iff
$\qquad$ the following equations hold:
$$e_{4^a}(R_a, S_a) = e_{4^a}(P_2, Q_2),$$
$$\phi'_A(R_a) = [e_1]R_{ab} + [f_1]S_{ab},$$
$$\phi'_A(S_a) = [e_2]R_{ab} + [f_2]S_{ab},$$
$\qquad$ where ϕ'_A is an isogeny from E_B with kernel $\langle [2^a]R_a + [\alpha 2^a]S_a \rangle \in E_B$.
Ensure: Alice's secret key α

1: Compute $(R_a, S_a, R_{ab}, S_{ab}) \leftarrow (\phi_B(P_2), \phi_B(Q_2), \phi'_B(R_A), \phi'_B(S_A))$ by follow-
$\quad$ ing the protocol specification using sk_B.
2: Obtain a from pp.
3: Obtain $\alpha_l \leftarrow \alpha_0$.
4: $i = 1$
5: $j = \bot$ $\qquad\qquad\qquad\qquad$ $\triangleright$ j will indicate the maximal power of 2 dividing α.
6: **if** $\alpha_l = 1$ **then** $j \leftarrow 0$
7: **while** $i < a$ **do**
8: $\quad$ **if** $\alpha_l = 0$ **then**
9: $\qquad$ $(\widetilde{R}_a, \widetilde{S}_a) \leftarrow ([1 + 2^{2a-1}]R_a, [2^{2a-i-1}]R_a + [1 - 2^{2a-1}]S_a)$
10: $\qquad$ $c \leftarrow \mathcal{O}(\widetilde{R}_a, \widetilde{S}_a, R_{ab}, S_{ab})$
11: $\qquad$ $c \leftarrow 1 - c$
12: $\qquad$ **if** $c = 0$ **then** $j \leftarrow i$ $\triangleright$ Assert 2^j is the maximal power of 2 dividing α.
13: $\quad$ **else**
14: $\qquad$ $\hat{\alpha}_l \leftarrow \mathsf{Quasilnv}(\alpha_l, 2, i+1)$ $\qquad\qquad$ $\triangleright$ $\hat{\alpha}_l(\alpha_l) = 0$ or $2^j \mod 2^{i+1}$
15: $\qquad$ $\widetilde{R}_a \leftarrow [1 + 2^{2a-i+j-1}]R_a - [\alpha_l 2^{2a-i+j-1}]S_a$
16: $\qquad$ $\widetilde{S}_a \leftarrow [\hat{\alpha}_l 2^{2a-i-1}]R_a + [1 - 2^{2a-i+j-1}]S_a$
17: $\qquad$ $c \leftarrow \mathcal{O}(\widetilde{R}_a, \widetilde{S}_a, R_{ab}, S_{ab})$
18: $\qquad$ **if** $c \neq 1$ **then** $\qquad\qquad\qquad\qquad$ $\triangleright$ Assert i-th bit of α is 1.
19: $\qquad\qquad$ $\alpha_l \leftarrow \alpha_l + 2^i$
20: **return** $-\alpha_l$

Fig. 2. An algorithm to recover the secret α in $\mathsf{sk}_A = (\alpha, e_1, f_1, e_2, f_2)$.

$\alpha_l \in \mathbb{Z}_{2^i}$ and $\alpha_i \in \mathbb{Z}_2$ represent the bits that have been recovered and the next bit to be recovered respectively. Since we have assumed the correctness of the given least significant bit of α, it suffices to show that given α_l the extraction of α_i, the i-th bit of α, is correct in each iteration of the while-loop of Fig. 2.

Firstly, within each query, the isogeny ϕ'_A computed by the oracle is the same because the kernels are all identical:

$$\langle [2^a]R_a + [\alpha 2^a]S_a \rangle = \langle [2^a]([1 + 2^{2a-1}]R_a - [t2^{2a-i-1}]S_a)$$
$$+ [\alpha 2^a]([t' 2^{2a-i-1}]R_a + [1 - 2^{2a-1}]S_a)\rangle$$
$$= \langle [2^a]([1 + 2^{2a-i+j-1}]R_a - [t2^{2a-i+j-1}]S_a)$$
$$+ [\alpha 2^a]([t' 2^{2a-i-1}]R_a + [1 - 2^{2a-i+j-1}]S_a)\rangle,$$

for any $t, t' \in \mathbb{Z}_{2^a}$ where $i, j \in \mathbb{Z}_a$. Therefore, since R_a, S_a, R_{ab}, S_{ab} are honestly generated, we may assume $e_{4^a}(R_a, S_a) = e_{4^a}(P_2, Q_2)^{3^b}$, $\phi'_A(R_a) = [e_1]R_{ab} + [f_1]S_{ab}$, and $\phi'_A(S_a) = [e_2]R_{ab} + [f_2]S_{ab}$.

Also, every input satisfies Eq. (1). Since $e_{4^a}(R_a, S_a) = e_{4^a}(P_2, Q_2)^{3^b}$, we have for any $\hat{\alpha}_l \in \mathbb{Z}_{2^a}$, and $i, j \in \mathbb{Z}_a$,

$$e_{4^a}([1 + 2^{2a-1}]R_a - [\alpha_l 2^{2a-i-1}]S_a, [\hat{\alpha}_l 2^{2a-i-1}]R_a + [1 - 2^{2a-1}]S_a)$$
$$= e_{4^a}([1 + 2^{2a-i+j-1}]R_a - [\alpha_l 2^{2a-i+j-1}]S_a, [\hat{\alpha}_l 2^{2a-i-1}]R_a + [1 - 2^{2a-i+j-1}]S_a)$$
$$= e_{4^a}(R_a, S_a)$$
$$= e_{4^a}(P_2, Q_2)^{3^b}.$$

To prove the correctness of the extraction of α_i, we claim that Eqs. (2) and (3) are both satisfied if and only if α_i is 1 in the if-loop of $\alpha_l = 0$ or is 0 in the if-loop of $\alpha_l \neq 0$. We therefore consider these two cases.

Case 1: the if-loop of $\alpha_l = 0$. Being in this loop in the i-th iteration means $\alpha = 0 \mod 2^i$. The oracle takes $(\widetilde{R_a}, \widetilde{S_a}, R_{ab}, S_{ab})$ as input where $(\widetilde{R_a}, \widetilde{S_a}) = ([1 + 2^{2a-1}]R_a, [2^{2a-i-1}]R_a + [1 - 2^{2a-1}]S_a)$. Recall $\phi'_A(R_a) = [e_1]R_{ab} + [f_1]S_{ab}$, and $\phi'_A(S_a) = [e_2]R_{ab} + [f_2]S_{ab}$. For Eq. (2), we have

$$\phi'_A(\widetilde{R_a}) - [e_1]R_{ab} - [f_1]S_{ab}$$
$$= [(1 + 2^{2a-1})e_1]R_{ab} + [(1 + 2^{2a-1})f_1]S_{ab} - [e_1]R_{ab} - [f_1]S_{ab}$$
$$= [2^{2a-1}e_1]R_{ab} + [2^{2a-1}f_1]S_{ab}$$
$$= [-\alpha 2^{2a-1}e_2]R_{ab} + [-\alpha 2^{2a-1}f_2]S_{ab}$$
$$= \mathbf{O}.$$

That is, Eq. (2) will always hold. Remark the third equation comes from Lemma 3 and the fact that i is less than a. The fourth equation comes from the fact that $\alpha = 0 \mod 2^i$ and $i \geq 1$ and $\{R_{ab}, S_{ab}\}$ is a basis for $E_{AB}[4^a]$.

Also, since $\alpha_l = 0$, $\hat{\alpha}_l$ is 1 by the specification of Quasilnv. Recall $\phi'_A(R_a) = [e_1]R_{ab} + [f_1]S_{ab}$, and $\phi'_A(S_a) = [e_2]R_{ab} + [f_2]S_{ab}$. For Eq. (3), we have

$$\phi'_A(\widetilde{S_a}) - [e_2]R_{ab} - [f_2]S_{ab}$$
$$= [2^{2a-i-1}e_1 - 2^{2a-1}e_2]R_{ab} + [2^{2a-i-1}f_1 - 2^{2a-1}f_2]S_{ab}$$
$$= [-\alpha 2^{2a-i-1}e_2 - 2^{2a-1}e_2]R_{ab} + [-\alpha 2^{2a-i-1}f_2 - 2^{2a-1}f_2]S_{ab}$$
$$= [\alpha_i 2^{2a-1} - 2^{2a-1}][e_2]R_{ab} + [\alpha_i 2^{2a-1} - 2^{2a-1}][f_2]S_{ab}.$$

Similarly, the third equation comes from Lemma 3 and the fact that i is less than a. The fourth equation comes from the fact that $\alpha = 0 \mod 2^i$ and $\{R_{ab}, S_{ab}\}$ is a basis for $E_{AB}[4^a]$. By Lemma 4, e_2 and f_2 cannot be both even so that at least one of $[2^{2a-1}e_2]R_{ab}$ and $[2^{2a-1}f_2]S_{ab}$ is of order 2. Equation (3) holds if and only if α_i is 1.

Therefore, by combining conditions of Eqs. (1) to (3), in the if-loop of $\alpha_l = 0$, the oracle outputs $c = 1$ if and only if $\alpha_i = 1$.

Case2: the if-loop of $\alpha_l \neq 0$. The condition is equivalent to 2^j is the maximal power of 2 dividing α. The oracle takes $(\widetilde{R_a}, \widetilde{S_a}, R_{ab}, S_{ab})$ as input where $(\widetilde{R_a}, \widetilde{S_a})$ $= ([1 + 2^{2a-i+j-1}]R_a - [\alpha_l 2^{2a-i+j-1}]S_a, [\hat{\alpha}_l 2^{2a-i-1}]R_a + [1 - 2^{2a-i+j-1}]S_a)$.

Recall $\phi'_A(R_a) = [e_1]R_{ab} + [f_1]S_{ab}$, and $\phi'_A(S_a) = [e_2]R_{ab} + [f_2]S_{ab}$. For Eq. (2), we have

$$\phi'_A(\widetilde{R_a}) - [e_1]R_{ab} - [f_1]S_{ab}$$
$$= [(2^{2a-i+j-1})e_1 - \alpha_l 2^{2a-i+j-1}e_2]R_{ab} + [(2^{2a-i+j-1})f_1 - \alpha_l 2^{2a-i+j-1}f_2]S_{ab}$$

Recall that $\{R_{ab}, S_{ab}\}$ is a basis for $E_{AB}[4^a] \simeq \mathbb{Z}_{4^a} \times \mathbb{Z}_{4^a}$. By Lemma 11 (Eq. (4)), we know $\phi'_A(\widetilde{R_a}) - [e_1]R_{ab} - [f_1]S_{ab} = \mathbf{O}$ if and only if $\alpha_i 2^j = 0 \mod 2$.

Also, for Eq. (3), we have $\hat{\alpha}$

$$\phi'_A(\widetilde{S_a}) - [e_2]R_{ab} - [f_2]S_{ab}$$
$$= [\hat{\alpha}_l 2^{2a-i-1}e_1 + (-2^{2a-i+j-1})e_2]R_{ab} + [\hat{\alpha}_l 2^{2a-i-1}f_1 + (-2^{2a-i+j-1})f_2]S_{ab}$$

Recall that $\{R_{ab}, S_{ab}\}$ is a basis for $E_{AB}[4^a] \simeq \mathbb{Z}_{4^a} \times \mathbb{Z}_{4^a}$. By Lemma 11 (Eq. (5)), we know $\phi'_A(\widetilde{S_a}) - [e_2]R_{ab} - [f_2]S_{ab} = \mathbf{O}$ if and only if $\alpha_i = 0$.

Therefore, by combining conditions of Eqs. (1) to (3), in the if-loop of $j \neq \perp$, the oracle outputs $c = 1$ if and only if $\alpha_i = 0$.

Remark 13. It seems that in our attack, both the satisfaction of Eq. (1) and the identical kernels of ϕ'_A used by the oracle the proof of Theorem 12 are derived from the fact that the kernel is of the form $\langle [2^a]P_2 + [2^a\alpha]Q_2 \rangle$. Hence, one may guess that relaxing the kernel to be $\langle [2^i]P_2 + [2^i\alpha]Q_2 \rangle$ for some $i \in \{0, \cdots, a-1\}$ can give a variant secure against the attack we presented. However, in the appendix, we consider a more generic situation for HealSIDH covering the concern, and the prime 2 can be replaced by any small natural number q. The algorithm takes $2a(q-1)$ oracle queries to fully recover Alice's secret key $\alpha \in \mathbb{Z}_{q^{2a}}$.

5   Summary

This work presents an adaptive attack on the isogeny-based key exchange and PKE schemes in [FP21], which were claimed to have the static-static property against any adaptive attack. Our attack is based on the subtle flaws in the main theorems (Theorems 1 and 2) in [FP21] for the key validation mechanism used in each scheme, which states that Bob can pass the key validation mechanism only if his input is correctly formed. We not only show that multiple non-trivial solutions can pass the check but also derive a concrete and efficient adaptive attack against the static-static proposals by tweaking the GPST attack. Furthermore, we provide a generalized attack in the appendix on any immediate repairs to the mechanism exploiting the commutativity of the SIDH evaluations.

Hence, our result points out that having an efficient static-static key exchange or PKE from a robust isogeny assumption remains an open problem. We look forward to future work in the community to resolve this problem.

Acknowledgement. This project is supported by the Ministry for Business, Innovation and Employment in New Zealand. We thank Shuichi Katsumata and Federico Pintore (alphabetically ordered) for pointing out errors in the previous version and helpful comments to improve clarity. Also, we thank anonymous reviewers from PQCrypto2022 for their detailed comments and suggestions.

A   A Generalized Attack

This section presents a generalized result. We consider a more generic condition where Alice uses q^n torsion subgroup for some natural numbers n, q to replace 2^{2a}. Furthermore, we do not restrict the secret kernel to be of the form $\langle [q^{n/2}]P_q + [\alpha][q^{n/2}]Q_q \rangle$ where $\{P_q, Q_q\}$ is a basis of $E_0[q^n]$ and $\alpha \in \mathbb{Z}_{q^a}$. Instead, we permit α to be drawn arbitrarily from $\mathbb{Z}_{q^a}$ and the kernel to be $\langle [q^{n-a}](P_q + [\alpha]Q_q) \rangle$. When n is even and $q = 2$, taking $a = n/2$ is the case considered in Sect. 2.2. The generalization captures any straightforward modification of the HealSIDH cryptosystem. The final algorithm takes $a(q - 1)$ oracle queries to fully recover Alice's secret key $\alpha \in \mathbb{Z}_{q^a}$. Therefore, as long as q is small, the HealSIDH cryptosystem and the key validation algorithm are vulnerable to our new variant of GPST attack.

To be more specific, the public parameter $\mathsf{pp} = (E_0, P_q, Q_q, P_{q'}, Q_{q'}, p, q, q')$ where $q, q' \in \mathbb{N}$ are coprime, $p = fq^n q'^{n'} - 1$ is prime, $q^n \approx q'^{n'}$, and $\{P_q, Q_q\}$ and $\{P_{q'}, Q_{q'}\}$ are bases for $E_0[q^n]$ and $E_0[q'^{n'}]$, resp. Alice samples a secret α uniformly at random from $\mathbb{Z}_{q^a}$, computes $\phi_A : E_0 \to E_A = E_0/\langle [q^{n-a}](P_q + [\alpha]Q_q) \rangle$ and representing $\phi_A(P_q) = [e_1]R_A + [f_1]S_A$ and $\phi_A(Q_q) = [e_2]R_A + [f_2]S_A$ where $\{R_A, S_A\}$ is a canonical basis for $E_A[q^a]$. Alice's secret key is $\mathsf{sk}_A = (\alpha, e_1, f_1, e_2, f_2)$ and public key is $(E_A, \phi_A(P_{q'}), \phi_A(Q_{q'}))$.

The high-level idea of the generalized attack is similar. Different from the "reciprocal" GPST attack presented in Sect. 4, one can view the generalized attack as the "triple" GPTS attack. Similarly, we use the equalities of Eq. (2) and Eq. (3) to extract the information of α and a quasi-inverse of α simultaneously. Additionally, on input $(R'_a, S'_a, R'_{ab}, S'_{ab})$, the oracle computes the isogeny with kernel $\langle R'_a + \alpha S'_a \rangle$. We will use the equality between $\langle R'_a + \alpha S'_a \rangle$ and $\langle \phi_B(P_q) + \alpha\phi_B(Q_q) \rangle$ to extract α again (see Lemma 18). We will show three equalities hold if and only if the extraction of a digit of α is correct.

Heuristic Assumption. We assume that the oracle will return 0 with an overwhelming probability if the input does not induce the same kernel as the honest input. Since we do not restrict the secret kernel to be of the form $\langle [q^{n/2}]P_q + [\alpha][q^{n/2}]Q_q \rangle$, the isogeny used by the oracle might therefore vary with each query[2]. We thereby require this assumption. Given the randomness of isogeny evaluation, the assumption is reasonable. Assume a new induced isogeny used by the oracle mapping R_a and S_a uniformly at random over $\mathbb{F}_p^2$. Then both equations (Eqs. (2) and (3)) are satisfied with probability around $1/p^2$ even if we only focus on the x-coordinate.

We start with following three simple facts similar to Proposition 2 and Lemmas 3 and 4.

Proposition 14. *If Bob honestly generates R_a, S_a, R_{ab}, S_{ab} by $R_a = \phi_B(P_q)$, $S_a = \phi_B(Q_q)$, $R_{ab} = \phi'_B(R_A)$ and $S_{ab} = \phi'_B(S_A)$, then $\{R_{ab}, S_{ab}\}$ is a basis of $E_{AB}[q^n]$ and $\{R_a, S_a\}$ is a basis of $E_B[q^n]$.*

Proof. Since $[q^n]R_a = \phi_B([q^n]P_q) = \mathbf{O}$ and $[q^n]S_a = \phi_B([q^n]Q_q) = \mathbf{O}$, both R_a and S_a are in $E_B[q^n]$. Due to $e_{q^n}(R_a, S_a) = e_{q^n}(P_q, Q_q)^{q'^{n'}}$, we know $e_{q^n}(R_a, S_a)$ is a primitive q^n-th root of unity. Similarly, Since $[q^n]R_{ab} = \phi'_B([q^n]R_A) = \mathbf{O}$ and $[q^n]S_{ab} = \phi'_B([q^n]S_A) = \mathbf{O}$, both R_{ab} and S_{ab} are in $E_{AB}[q^n]$. Due to $e_{q^n}(R_{ab}, S_{ab}) = e_{q^n}(R_A, S_A)^{q'^{n'}}$, we know $e_{q^n}(R_{ab}, S_{ab})$ is a primitive q^n-th root of unity. Therefore, the result follows.

Lemma 15. *Let e_1, e_2, f_1, f_2 defined as above and $\alpha \in \mathbb{Z}_{q^a}$ be the secret key of Alice such that $\ker(\phi_A) = \langle [q^{n-a}](P_q + [\alpha]Q_q) \rangle$. If Alice follows the protocol specification, then $e_1 + \alpha e_2 = f_1 + \alpha f_2 = 0 \mod q^a$.*

Proof. Given $\phi_A(P_2) = [e_1]R_A + [f_1]S_A$ and $\phi_A(Q_2) = [e_2]R_A + [f_2]S_A$, we have $\mathbf{O} = \phi_A([q^{n-a}](P_q + [\alpha]Q_q)) = [q^{n-a}][e_1 + \alpha e_2]R_A + [q^{n-a}][f_1 + \alpha f_2]S_A = [e_1 + \alpha e_2]R_A + [f_1 + \alpha f_2]S_A$. Recall that $\{[q^{n-a}]R_A, [q^{n-a}]S_A\}$ is a basis of $E_A[q^a]$. Therefore, $e_1 + \alpha e_2 = f_1 + \alpha f_2 = 0 \mod q^a$.

Lemma 16. *If Alice produces $\phi_A(P_q)$ and $\phi_A(Q_q)$ honestly, then e_2 and f_2 cannot be both divisible by q.*

Proof. Suppose for the purpose of contradiction that both e_2 and f_2 are divisible by q. Then, $[q^{n-1}]\phi_A(Q_q) = \mathbf{O}$, which implies $\ker(\phi_A) = \langle [q^{n-a}](P_q + [\alpha]Q_q) \rangle$ contains $[q^{n-1}]Q_q$. That is, $[kq^{n-a}]P_q + [kq^{n-a}\alpha]Q_q = [q^{2a-1}]Q_q$ for some $k \in \mathbb{Z}_{q^a}$, so $k = 0$. This contradicts the fact that $\{P_q, Q_q\}$ is a basis for $E_0[q^n]$. The result follows.

The algorithm in Fig. 3 together with Theorem 17 provides an iterative approach for recovering α. It requires $q - 1$ oracle queries to recover each digit of α in each iteration.

Theorem 17. *Assume Alice follows the protocol specification. The algorithm in Fig. 3 returns α in Alice's secret key.*

---

[2] For instance, on input $(R_a, [2^{a-1}]R_a + S_a, R_{ab}, S_{ab})$ as Lemma 5 for $q = 2$ and $n = a$, the isogeny used by the oracle is with kernel $\langle R_a + [\alpha]S_a + [\alpha 2^{2a-1}]R_a \rangle$. The kernel is the same if and only if α is divisible by 2.

Proof. We are going to prove the theorem by induction on i for the i-th digit of α where $i < a$. Write $-\alpha = \alpha_l + q^i \alpha_i \mod q^{i+1}$ for some $i \in \{0, \ldots, a-1\}$ where $\alpha_l \in \mathbb{Z}_{q^i}$ and $\alpha_i \in \mathbb{Z}_q$ represent the digits that have been recovered and the next digit to be recovered respectively.

First of all, we will show that within each query in each loop with respect to i, the isogeny ϕ'_A computed by the oracle is of the kernel $\langle R_a + \alpha S_a \rangle$ if $t = \alpha_i$.

Lemma 18 *(Kernel analysis). For each query made in Fig. 3 in each loop with respect to i, the kernel used by the oracle internally is identical to $\langle [q^{n-a}](P_q + [\alpha]Q_q) \rangle$ if $t = \alpha_i$.*

Proof. **Case1: the if-loop of $i = 0$.** For the queries in the if-loop of $i = 0$, if $t = \alpha_i$, we have

$$\langle [q^{n-a}](([1 + q^{n-1}]R_a - [tq^{n-1}]S_a) + [\alpha]([\hat{\alpha}_{tl}q^{n-1}]R_a + [1 - q^{n-1}]S_a))\rangle$$
$$= \langle [q^{n-a}](P_q + [\alpha]Q_q) \rangle$$

Remark that here $\alpha_i = \alpha_0$ and the quasi-inverse $\hat{\alpha}_{tl} = t^{-1} \mod q$ for $t \neq 0$. Therefore, $1 + \alpha\hat{\alpha}_{tl} = 0 \mod q$ and $-\alpha_0 - \alpha = 0 \mod q$, and the second equation follows.

Case2: the if-loop of $\alpha_l = 0$. For the queries in the while-loop of $\alpha_l = 0$, we have

$$\langle [q^{n-a}](([1 + q^{n-1}]R_a) + [\alpha]([\hat{\alpha}_{tl}q^{n-i-1}]R_a + [1 - q^{n-1}]S_a))\rangle$$
$$= \langle [q^{n-a}](P_q + [\alpha]Q_q) \rangle$$

Remark that being in the if-loop of $\alpha_l = 0$ implies $i \geq 1$ and $q^i \mid \alpha$. Hence, in this case the kernel computed by the oracle is always $\langle [q^{n-a}](P_q + [\alpha]Q_q) \rangle$.

Case3: the if-loop of $\alpha_l \neq 0$. For the queries in the while-loop of $\alpha_l \neq 0$, if $t = \alpha_i$, we have

$$\langle [q^{n-a}](([1 + q^{n-i+j-1}]R_a - [(\alpha_l + tq^i)q^{n-i+j-1}]S_a)$$
$$+ [\alpha]([\hat{\alpha}_{tl}q^{n-i-1}]R_a + [1 - q^{n-i+j-1}]S_a))\rangle$$
$$= \langle [q^{n-a}](P_q + [\alpha]Q_q) \rangle$$

Remark that we have $\hat{\alpha}_{tl}(\alpha_l + tq^i) = q^j \mod q^n$ and $-\alpha = \alpha_l + q^i\alpha_i \mod q^{i+1}$ where $i > j$. Therefore, when $t = \alpha_i$, we have $q^j + \alpha\hat{\alpha}_{tl} = 0 \mod q^{i+1}$ and $(\alpha_l + tq^i) + \alpha = 0 \mod q^{i+1}$. The second equation follows.

Similarly, we analyze the satisfaction of Eq. (1) (the Weil pairing check) for the oracle input. The following lemma shows that all oracle inputs will satisfy Eq. (1).

Lemma 19 *(Eq. (1) analysis). Each query made in Fig. 3 in each loop satisfies Eq. (1).*

Proof. Recall that we have $e_{q^a}(R_a, S_a) = e_{q^a}(P_2, Q_2)^{q'^b 3}$.

Case1: the if-loop of $i = 0$. For the queries in the if-loop of $i = 0$, we always have

$$
e_{q^a}([1 + q^{n-1}]R_a - [tq^{n-1}]S_a, [\hat{\alpha}_{tl}q^{n-1}]R_a + [1 - q^{n-1}]S_a)
$$
$$
= e_{q^a}(R_a, S_a)
$$
$$
= e_{q^a}(P_q, Q_q)^{q'^b}.
$$

Case2: the if-loop of $j = \perp$. For the queries in the while-loop of $j = \perp$, we always have

$$
e_{q^a}([1 + q^{n-1}]R_a, [\hat{\alpha}_{tl}q^{n-i-1}]R_a + [1 - q^{n-1}]S_a)
$$
$$
= e_{q^a}(R_a, S_a)
$$
$$
= e_{q^a}(P_q, Q_q)^{q'^b}.
$$

Case3: the if-loop of $j \neq \perp$. For the queries in the while-loop of $j \neq \perp$, we always have

$$
e_{q^a}(R_a, S_a)^{1 - q^{2n-2i+2j-2} + \hat{\alpha}_{tl}(\alpha_l + tq^i)q^{2n-2i+j-2}}
$$
$$
= e_{q^a}(R_a, S_a)
$$
$$
= e_{q^a}(P_q, Q_q)^{q'^b}.
$$

Note that since $\hat{\alpha}_{tl}(\alpha_l + tq^i) = q^j \mod q^n$, we have

$$
1 - q^{2n-2i+2j-2} + \hat{\alpha}_{tl}(\alpha_l + tq^i)q^{2n-2i+j-2} = 1 \mod q^n.
$$

Therefore, all oracle queries made in Fig. 3 satisfy Eq. (1).

For the case $i = 0$ of induction, we have to show the correctness of the extraction of α_0, the least significant digit of $-\alpha$. We restrict our attention to the if-loop of the condition $i = 0$. Recall $\phi'_A(R_a) = [e_1]R_{ab} + [f_1]S_{ab}$, and $\phi'_A(S_a) = [e_2]R_{ab} + [f_2]S_{ab}$. For Eq. (2) $t \in \mathbb{Z}_q$, we have

$$
\phi'_A([1 + q^{n-1}]R_a - [tq^{n-1}]S_a) - [e_1]R_{ab} - [f_1]S_{ab}
$$
$$
= [(1 + q^{n-1})e_1 - tq^{n-1}e_2]R_{ab} + [(1 + q^{n-1})f_1 - tq^{n-1}f_2]S_{ab} - [e_1]R_{ab} - [f_1]S_{ab}
$$
$$
= [q^{n-1}e_1 - tq^{n-1}e_2]R_{ab} + [q^{n-1}f_1 - tq^{n-1}f_2]S_{ab}
$$
$$
= [-\alpha q^{n-1}e_2 - tq^{n-1}e_2]R_{ab} + [-\alpha q^{n-1}f_2 - tq^{n-1}f_2]S_{ab}
$$
$$
= [\alpha_0 q^{n-1}e_2 - tq^{n-1}e_2]R_{ab} + [\alpha_0 q^{n-1}f_2 - tq^{n-1}f_2]S_{ab}
$$

That is, Eq. (2) will always hold. Remark the third equation comes from Lemma 15. Therefore, the condition of Eq. (2) is satisfied if and only if $t = \alpha_0$.

---

[3] Since we allow to use q^a- and q'^b-isogenies here, the exponent thereby is q'^b here.

Similarly, for Eq. (3), we have

$$\phi'_A([\hat{\alpha}_{tl}q^{n-i-1}]R_a + [1 - q^{n-1}]S_a) - [e_2]R_{ab} - [f_2]S_{ab}$$
$$= [\hat{\alpha}_{tl}q^{n-1}e_1 - q^{n-1}e_2]R_{ab} + [\hat{\alpha}_{tl}q^{n-1}f_1 - q^{n-1}f_2]S_{ab}$$
$$= [-\alpha\hat{\alpha}_{tl}q^{n-1}e_2 - q^{n-1}e_2]R_{ab} + [-\alpha\hat{\alpha}_{tl}q^{n-1}f_2 - q^{n-1}f_2]S_{ab}$$
$$= [\alpha_0\hat{\alpha}_{tl}q^{n-1} - q^{n-1}][e_2]R_{ab} + [\alpha_0\hat{\alpha}_{tl}q^{n-1} - q^{n-1}][f_2]S_{ab}.$$

That is, Eq. (3) will always hold. Remark the third equation comes from Lemma 15. Therefore, the condition of Eq. (3) is satisfied if and only if $\alpha_0\hat{\alpha}_{tl} = 1$ mod q. Equivalently, $t = \alpha_0$, because $t\hat{\alpha}_{tl} = 1$ mod q. If $\alpha_0\hat{\alpha}_{tl} \neq 1$ mod q for all $t \in \{1, \cdots, q-1\}$, then $\alpha_0 = 0$. Therefore, by combining conditions of Eqs. (1) to (3), the extraction of α_0 is correct.

It suffices to show that given α_l the extraction of α_i, the i-th digit of $-\alpha$ mod q^a for $i \geq 1$, is correct in each iteration of the while-loop of Fig. 3. To prove the correctness of the extraction of α_i, in either the if-loop of $\alpha_l = 0$ or the else-loop ($\alpha_l \neq 0$), we claim that Eqs. (2) and (3) are both satisfied if and only if the output of the oracle is $c = 1$ for $t \in \{1, \cdots, q-1\}$ used in the loop if and only if $\alpha_i = t$ for some $t \in \{1, \cdots, q-1\}$. We therefore consider two cases.

Case1: the if-loop of $\alpha_l = 0$. The condition is equivalent to $\alpha_l = 0$ which means $-\alpha = 0$ mod q^i. We require the following to show the result.

Lemma 20. *Assume $\alpha_i \neq 0$. Then, both of the following two equations are true if and only if $\alpha_i = t$ for some $t \in \{1, \cdots, a-1\}$:*

$$q^{n-1}e_1 = q^{n-1}f_1 = 0 \quad \mod q^n \tag{6}$$
$$\hat{\alpha}_{tl}e_1 - q^i e_2 = \hat{\alpha}_{tl}f_1 - q^i f_2 = 0 \quad \mod q^{i+1} \tag{7}$$

Proof. By Lemma 15, we have $q^{n-1}e_1 = -\alpha q^{n-1}e_2$ mod q^n. Also, $q^{n-1}f_1 = -\alpha q^{n-1}f_2$ mod q^n. The execution of this loop implies α is divisible by q. Therefore, the first equation always holds.

By Lemma 15, we have $\hat{\alpha}_{tl}e_1 - q^i e_2 = -\hat{\alpha}_{tl}\alpha e_2 - q^i e_2$ mod q^{i+1}. Since $(\alpha_l + tq^i)\hat{\alpha}_{tl} = q^i$ mod q^{i+1}, we have $-\hat{\alpha}_{tl}\alpha e_2 - q^i e_2 = (\alpha_i - t)q^i\hat{\alpha}_{tl}e_2$ mod q^{i+1}. Similarly, we have $\hat{\alpha}_{tl}f_1 - q^i f_2 = (\alpha_i - t)q^i\hat{\alpha}_{tl}f_2$ mod q^{i+1}. By Lemma 16 and Proposition 9, $e_2\hat{\alpha}_{tl}$ and $f_2\hat{\alpha}_{tl}$ cannot both be divisible by q. Therefore, the second equation is zero if and only if $\alpha_i = t$.

Hence, both of the following two equations are true if and only if $\alpha_i = t$.

Recall $\phi'_A(R_a) = [e_1]R_{ab} + [f_1]S_{ab}$, and $\phi'_A(S_a) = [e_2]R_{ab} + [f_2]S_{ab}$. For Eq. (2), we have

$$\phi'_A([1 + q^{n-1}]R_a) - [e_1]R_{ab} - [f_1]S_{ab}$$
$$= [q^{n-1}e_1]R_{ab} + [q^{n-1}f_1]S_{ab}$$

Recall that $\{R_{ab}, S_{ab}\}$ is a basis for $E_{AB}[q^n] \simeq \mathbb{Z}_{q^n} \times \mathbb{Z}_{q^n}$. By using Lemma 20 (Eq. (6)), this condition always holds.

Also, for Eq. (3), we have

$$\phi'_A([\hat{\alpha}_{tl}q^{n-i-1}]R_a + [1 - q^{n-1}]S_a) - [e_2]R_{ab} - [f_2]S_{ab}$$
$$= [\hat{\alpha}_{tl}q^{n-i-1}e_1 - q^{n-1}e_2]R_{ab} + [\hat{\alpha}_{tl}q^{n-i-1}f_1 - q^{n-1}f_2]S_{ab}$$

Recall that $\{R_{ab}, S_{ab}\}$ is a basis for $E_{AB}[q^n] \simeq \mathbb{Z}_{q^n} \times \mathbb{Z}_{q^n}$. By using Lemma 20 (Eq. (7)), this condition holds if and only if $\alpha_i = t$ for some $t \in \{1, \cdots, a-1\}$.

Therefore, by combining conditions of Eqs. (1) to (3), in the if-loop of $\alpha_l = 0$, the oracle outputs $c = 1$ for $t \in \{1, q - 1\}$ used in the loop if and only if $\alpha_i = t$. Moreover, if all outputs of the oracle in the loop are 0, then $\alpha_i = 0$. The extraction of α_i is correct in this case.

Case2: the if-loop of $\alpha_l \neq 0$. The condition is equivalent to q^j is the maximal power of q dividing α.

Lemma 21. *Let notation be as above. Both of the following two equations are true if and only if $\alpha_i = t$:*

$$e_1 - (\alpha_l + tq^i)e_2 = f_1 - (\alpha_l + tq^i)f_2 = 0 \mod q^{i-j+1} \tag{8}$$
$$\hat{\alpha}_{tl}e_1 - q^j e_2 = \hat{\alpha}_{tl}f_1 - q^j f_2 = 0 \mod q^{i+1} \tag{9}$$

Proof. By Lemma 15, we have $e_1 - (\alpha_l + tq^i)e_2 = -\alpha e_2 - (\alpha_l + tq^i)e_2 = (\alpha_i - t)q^i e_2$ mod q^{i-j+1} and $f_1 - (\alpha_l + tq^i)f_2 = -\alpha f_2 - (\alpha_l + tq^i)f_2 = (\alpha_i - t)q^i f_2 \mod q^{i-j+1}$. By Lemma 16, not both e_2 and f_2 are divisible by q. Therefore, the first equation is zero if and only if $\alpha_i = t$ or $j \geq 1$.

Similarly, by Lemma 15, we have $\hat{\alpha}_{tl}e_1 - q^j e_2 = -\alpha\hat{\alpha}_{tl}e_2 - q^j e_2 \mod q^{i+1}$. Since $(\alpha_l + tq^i)\hat{\alpha}_{tl} = q^j \mod q^{i+1}$, we have $-\alpha\hat{\alpha}_{tl}e_2 - q^j e_2 = (\alpha_i - t)q^i\hat{\alpha}_{tl}e_2$ mod q^{i+1}. Similarly, we have $\hat{\alpha}_{tl}f_1 - q^j f_2 = (\alpha_i - t)q^i\hat{\alpha}_{tl}f_2 \mod q^{i+1}$. By Lemma 16 and Proposition 9, not both $e_2\hat{\alpha}_{tl}$ and $f_2\hat{\alpha}_{tl}$ are divisible by q. Therefore, the second equation is zero if and only if $\alpha_i = t$.

Hence, both of the following two equations are true if and only if $\alpha_i = t$.

Recall $\phi'_A(R_a) = [e_1]R_{ab} + [f_1]S_{ab}$, and $\phi'_A(S_a) = [e_2]R_{ab} + [f_2]S_{ab}$. For Eq. (2), we have

$$\phi'_A([1 + q^{n-i+j-1}]R_a - [(\alpha_l + tq^i)q^{n-i+j-1}]S_a) - [e_1]R_{ab} - [f_1]S_{ab}$$
$$= [(q^{n-i+j-1})e_1 - (\alpha_l + tq^i)q^{n-i+j-1}e_2]R_{ab}$$
$$+ [(q^{n-i+j-1})f_1 - (\alpha_l + tq^i)q^{n-i+j-1}f_2]S_{ab}$$

For Eq. (3), we have $\hat{\alpha}$

$$\phi'_A([\hat{\alpha}_{tl}q^{n-i-1}]R_a + [1 - q^{n-i+j-1}]S_a) - [e_2]R_{ab} - [f_2]S_{ab}$$
$$= [\hat{\alpha}_{tl}q^{n-i-1}e_1 + (-q^{n-i+j-1})e_2]R_{ab} + [\hat{\alpha}_{tl}q^{n-i-1}f_1 + (-q^{n-i+j-1})f_2]S_{ab}$$

Recall that $\{R_{ab}, S_{ab}\}$ is a basis for $E_{AB}[q^n] \simeq \mathbb{Z}_{q^n} \times \mathbb{Z}_{q^n}$. By Lemma 21, we know both conditions (Eqs. (2) to (3)) hold if and only if $\alpha_i = t$.

Algorithm: Recover(pp, sk$_B$)

Input: pp public parameter of the protocol, sk$_B$ the secret key of Bob,

Given: an oracle $\mathcal{O}_\alpha(R_a, S_a, R_{ab}, S_{ab}; E_B, E_{AB}) \to 0/1$ returns 1 if and only if the following equations hold:

$$e_{q^n}(R_a, S_a) = e_{q^n}(P_q, Q_q),$$
$$\phi'_A(R_a) = [e_1]R_{ab} + [f_1]S_{ab},$$
$$\phi'_A(S_a) = [e_2]R_{ab} + [f_2]S_{ab},$$

where ϕ'_A is an isogeny from E_B with kernel $\langle [q^{n-a}](P_q + [\alpha]Q_q) \rangle \in E_B$.

Ensure: Alice's secret key α

1: Obtain $(R_a, S_a, R_{ab}, S_{ab}) \leftarrow (\phi_B(P_q), \phi_B(Q_q), \phi'_B(R_A), \phi'_B(S_A))$ by following the protocol specification using sk$_B$.

2: Obtain a from pp.

3: $i = 0$

4: $j = \perp$

5: $\alpha_l = 0$

6: **while** $i < a$ **do**

7:     $c = 0$

8:     $t = q$

9:     **for** $t \in \{0, \cdots, q-1\}$ **do**

10:         $\hat{\alpha}_{tl} \leftarrow$ Quasilnv$(\alpha_l + tq^i, q, n)$

11:         **if** $i = 0$ **then**   ▷ Extract α_0.

12:             **while** $c = 0$ or $t > 0$ **do**

13:                 $t -= 1$

14:                 $\widetilde{R_a}, \widetilde{S_a} \leftarrow [1 + q^{n-1}]R_a - [tq^{n-1}]S_a, [\hat{\alpha}_{tl}q^{n-1}]R_a + [1 - q^{n-1}]S_a$

15:                 $c \leftarrow \mathcal{O}(\widetilde{R_a}, \widetilde{S_a}, R_{ab}, S_{ab})$

16:             $\alpha_l \leftarrow t$

17:             $i += 1$

18:             **if** $t \neq 0$ **then** $j \leftarrow i$ ▷ Assert q is the maximal power of q dividing α.

19:             **Continue**

20:         **if** $\alpha_l = 0$ **then**   ▷ Assert $\hat{\alpha}_{tl}t = 1$ or $0 \mod q$.

21:             **while** $c = 0$ or $t > 0$ **do**

22:                 $t -= 1$

23:                 $\widetilde{R_a}, \widetilde{S_a} \leftarrow [1 + q^{n-1}]R_a, [\hat{\alpha}_{tl}q^{n-i-1}]R_a + [1 - q^{n-1}]S_a$

24:                 $c \leftarrow \mathcal{O}(\widetilde{R_a}, \widetilde{S_a}, R_{ab}, S_{ab})$

25:             $\alpha_l \leftarrow \alpha_l + tq^i$ ▷ Assert i-th digit of $-\alpha$ is t.

26:             **if** $t \neq 0$ **then** $j \leftarrow i$ ▷ Assert q^j is the maximal power of q dividing α.

27:         **else**   ▷ Assert $\hat{\alpha}_{tl}(\alpha_l + tq^i) = q^j \mod q^n$.

28:             **while** $c = 0$ or $t > 0$ **do**

29:                 $t -= 1$

30:                 $\widetilde{R_a} \leftarrow [1 + q^{n-i+j-1}]R_a - [(\alpha_l + tq^i)q^{n-i+j-1}]S_a$

31:                 $\widetilde{S_a} \leftarrow [\hat{\alpha}_{tl}q^{n-i-1}]R_a + [1 - q^{n-i+j-1}]S_a$

32:                 $c \leftarrow \mathcal{O}(\widetilde{R_a}, \widetilde{S_a}, R_{ab}, S_{ab})$

33:             $\alpha_l \leftarrow \alpha_l + tq^i$ ▷ Assert i-th digit of $-\alpha$ is t.

34:     $i += 1$

35: **return** $-\alpha_l \mod q^a$

Fig. 3. A general algorithm to recover the secret α.

Therefore, by combining conditions of Eqs. (1) to (3), in the else-loop, the oracle outputs $c = 1$ for $t \in \{1, \cdots, q-1\}$ used in the loop if and only if $\alpha_i = t$. If all outputs of the oracle in the loop is 0, then $\alpha_i = 0$. The extraction in this case is correct. Hence, the algorithm in Fig. 3 successfully extracts Alices's secret key.

References

[ACC+17] Azarderakhsh, R., et al.: Supersingular isogeny key encapsulation. Submission NIST Post-Quantum Standard. Proj. **152**, 154–155 (2017)

[AJL17] Azarderakhsh, R., Jao, D., Leonardi, C.: Post-quantum static-static key agreement using multiple protocol instances. In: Adams, C., Camenisch, J. (eds.) SAC 2017. LNCS, vol. 10719, pp. 45–63. Springer, Cham (2018). https://doi.org/10.1007/978-3-319-72565-9_3

[BDK+22] Beullens, W., Dobson, S., Katsumata, S., Lai, Y.F., Pintore, F.: Group signatures and more from isogenies and lattices: generic, simple, and efficient. In: Dunkelman, O., Dziembowski, S. (eds.) EUROCRYPT 2022, Part II. LNCS, vol. 13276, pp. 95–126. Springer, Cham (2022). https://doi.org/10.1007/978-3-031-07085-3_4

[BKV19] Beullens, W., Kleinjung, T., Vercauteren, F.: CSI-FiSh: efficient isogeny based signatures through class group computations. In: Galbraith, S.D., Moriai, S. (eds.) ASIACRYPT 2019, Part I. LNCS, vol. 11921, pp. 227–247. Springer, Cham (2019). https://doi.org/10.1007/978-3-030-34578-5_9

[CD22] Castryck, W., Decru, T.: An efficient key recovery attack on SIDH (preliminary version). Cryptology ePrint Archive, Paper 2022/975 (2022). https://eprint.iacr.org/2022/975

[CLM+18] Castryck, W., Lange, T., Martindale, C., Panny, L., Renes, J.: CSIDH: an efficient post-quantum commutative group action. In: Peyrin, T., Galbraith, S. (eds.) ASIACRYPT 2018, Part III. LNCS, vol. 11274, pp. 395–427. Springer, Cham (2018). https://doi.org/10.1007/978-3-030-03332-3_15

[dQKL+21] de Quehen, V., et al.: Improved torsion-point attacks on SIDH variants. In: Malkin, T., Peikert, C. (eds.) CRYPTO 2021, Part III. LNCS, vol. 12827, pp. 432–470. Springer, Cham (2021). https://doi.org/10.1007/978-3-030-84252-9_15

[EKP20] El Kaafarani, A., Katsumata, S., Pintore, F.: Lossy CSI-FiSh: efficient signature scheme with tight reduction to decisional CSIDH-512. In: Kiayias, A., Kohlweiss, M., Wallden, P., Zikas, V. (eds.) PKC 2020, Part II. LNCS, vol. 12111, pp. 157–186. Springer, Cham (2020). https://doi.org/10.1007/978-3-030-45388-6_6

[FP21] Fouotsa, T.B., Petit, C.: SHealS and HealS: isogeny-Based PKEs from a key validation method for SIDH. In: Tibouchi, M., Wang, H. (eds.) ASIACRYPT 2021, Part IV. LNCS, vol. 13093, pp. 279–307. Springer, Cham (2021). https://doi.org/10.1007/978-3-030-92068-5_10

[GPST16] Galbraith, S.D., Petit, C., Shani, B., Ti, Y.B.: On the security of supersingular isogeny cryptosystems. In: Cheon, J.H., Takagi, T. (eds.) ASIACRYPT 2016, Part I. LNCS, vol. 10031, pp. 63–91. Springer, Heidelberg (2016). https://doi.org/10.1007/978-3-662-53887-6_3

[JD11] Jao, D., De Feo, L.: Towards quantum-resistant cryptosystems from super-singular elliptic curve isogenies. In: Yang, B.-Y. (ed.) PQCrypto 2011. LNCS, vol. 7071, pp. 19–34. Springer, Heidelberg (2011). https://doi.org/10.1007/978-3-642-25405-5_2

[Kup05] Kuperberg, G.: A subexponential-time quantum algorithm for the dihedral hidden subgroup problem. SIAM J. Comput. **35**(1), 170–188 (2005)

[Leo20] Leonardi, C.: A note on the ending elliptic curve in SIDH. Cryptology ePrint Archive, Report 2020/262 (2020). https://eprint.iacr.org/2020/262

[LGd21] Lai, Y.-F., Galbraith, S.D., Delpech de Saint Guilhem, C.: Compact, efficient and UC-secure isogeny-based oblivious transfer. In: Canteaut, A., Standaert, F.-X. (eds.) EUROCRYPT 2021, Part I. LNCS, vol. 12696, pp. 213–241. Springer, Cham (2021). https://doi.org/10.1007/978-3-030-77870-5_8

[MOT20] Moriya, T., Onuki, H., Takagi, T.: SiGamal: a supersingular isogeny-based PKE and its application to a PRF. In: Moriai, S., Wang, H. (eds.) ASIACRYPT 2020, Part II. LNCS, vol. 12492, pp. 551–580. Springer, Cham (2020). https://doi.org/10.1007/978-3-030-64834-3_19

[Pei20] Peikert, C.: He gives C-sieves on the CSIDH. In: Canteaut, A., Ishai, Y. (eds.) EUROCRYPT 2020, Part II. LNCS, vol. 12106, pp. 463–492. Springer, Cham (2020). https://doi.org/10.1007/978-3-030-45724-2_16

[Sil09] Silverman, J.H.: The Arithmetic of Elliptic Curves, vol. 106. Springer, Heidelberg (2009). https://doi.org/10.1007/978-0-387-09494-6

[UJ20] Urbanik, D., Jao, D.: New techniques for SIDH-based NIKE. J. Math. Cryptol. **14**(1), 120–128 (2020)

Post-Quantum Signal Key Agreement from SIDH

Samuel Dobson$^{(\boxtimes)}$ and Steven D. Galbraith

Mathematics Department, University of Auckland, Auckland, New Zealand
`samuel.dobson.nz@gmail.com`, `s.galbraith@auckland.ac.nz`

Abstract. In the effort to transition cryptographic primitives and protocols to quantum-resistant alternatives, an interesting and useful challenge is found in the Signal protocol. The initial key agreement component of this protocol, called X3DH, has so far proved more subtle to replace—in part due to the unclear security model and properties the original protocol is designed for. This paper defines a formal security model for the original Signal protocol, in the context of the standard eCK and CK+ type models, which we call the Signal-adapted-CK model. We then propose a replacement for the Signal X3DH key exchange protocol based on SIDH, and provide a proof of security in the Signal-adapted-CK model, showing our protocol satisfies all security properties of the original Signal X3DH. We call this new protocol SI-X3DH. Our protocol shows that SIDH can be used to construct a secure X3DH replacement despite the existence of adaptive attacks against it. Unlike the generic constructions proposed in the literature, our protocol achieves deniability without expensive machinery such as post-quantum ring signatures. It also benefits from the small key sizes of SIDH, and its efficiency as a key-exchange protocol compared to other isogeny-based protocols such as CSIDH.

1 Introduction

Signal is a widely-used secure messaging protocol with implementations in its namesake app (Signal Private Messenger), as well as others including WhatsApp, Facebook Messenger and more. Due to its popularity, it is an interesting problem to design a post-quantum secure variant of the protocol. However, some difficulty arises due to the lack of a formally-defined security model or properties for the original protocol itself.

The Signal protocol consists of two general stages: the first is the initial key agreement, which is then followed by the double ratchet protocol [MP16a]. The initial key agreement is currently done via a protocol known as Extended Triple Diffie–Hellman (X3DH) [MP16b]. While Alwen, Coretti, and Dodis [ACD19] construct a version of the double ratchet component using key encapsulation mechanisms (KEMs), which can be made post-quantum secure, the X3DH stage has proven to be more subtle and challenging to replace in an efficient way with post-quantum solutions. Recent work by Brendel, Fischlin, Günther, Janson, and

© The Author(s), under exclusive license to Springer Nature Switzerland AG 2022
J. H. Cheon and T. Johansson (Eds.): PQCrypto 2022, LNCS 13512, pp. 422–450, 2022.
https://doi.org/10.1007/978-3-031-17234-2_20

Stebila [BFG+20] examines some of these challenges and suggests that SIDH cannot be used to make X3DH post-quantum secure due to its vulnerability to adaptive attacks when static keys are used.[1]

Specifically, [BFG+20] is referring to an adaptive attack on SIDH given by Galbraith, Petit, Shani, and Ti [GPST16] (henceforth referred to as the GPST attack), which uses specially crafted points in a user's public key to extract bits of information about the isogeny path (and thus the secret key) of the other participant. The Signal X3DH protocol is an authenticated key exchange (AKE) protocol, requiring keys from both parties involved. Without a secure method of validating the correctness of the other party's keys, it would be insecure to perform a naive SIDH key exchange with them. For example, the initiator of a key exchange could adaptively modify the ephemeral public keys they use, in order to learn the receiver's long-term identity private key via this GPST attack.

Known methods of validation used to prevent adaptive attacks in SIDH are not well-suited to solving this issue in the Signal X3DH context. One proposed method of overcoming the GPST attack, known as k-SIDH [AJL17], has both parties use k different SIDH public keys, and runs k^2 instances of SIDH in parallel with pairwise combinations of these keys, combining all the shared secrets using a hash function in the final step of the protocol. The GPST attack was extended to k-SIDH in [DGL+20] and shown to be feasible for small k (an attack on $k = 2$ is demonstrated concretely). Due to the possibility of attacking k-SIDH for small k, it has been suggested that k of at least 92 would be required to achieve security against quantum adversaries. Unfortunately, this makes the protocol very inefficient. An alternative which is commonly used, as in SIKE [CCH+19], is to convert the key exchange into a key encapsulation mechanism (KEM) using the Fujisaki–Okamoto (FO) transform or its variants [HHK17], and verify that the public key is well-formed and honestly generated [Pei14, KLM+15]. The idea of the FO-transform is that the initiator, A, of the key exchange can encrypt the randomness they used in the exchange (for example, to generate their secret key) under the symmetric shared key K they derived, and send it to their partner B. If the encryption method is one-time secure, then because only A and B know K, only they can decrypt this randomness. B can then check that A performed the exchange protocol correctly, and in particular, that the public key they generated is indeed derived from the randomness they provided, to prove that A's public key is well-formed. Because B learns the secret key of A in every exchange, A can only do this with ephemeral keys. Hence, while extremely useful, the FO-transform does not provide a solution in cases where both parties use static keys. We cannot exclude the possibility that participants use their long-term (static) keys as part of an attack: a dedicated or well-resourced attacker could certainly

---

[1] Since this paper was submitted for publication, new attacks on SIDH have been announced [CD22, MM22, Rob22]. This paper assumes that a variant of SIDH can be developed which is still secure. However, if SIDH is broken entirely, techniques from this paper may be of independent interest—for example, the Signal security model and use of the Honest and Verifiable CDH problems to avoid relying on Gap-DH assumptions.

register many new accounts whose identity keys are maliciously crafted, and initiate exchanges with an unsuspecting user (perhaps by masquerading as their friends or colleagues) to learn their secret key. For these reasons, [BFG+20] disregards SIDH as a contender and suggest using CSIDH [CLM+18] for an isogeny-based variant of Signal. However, this primitive is much less efficient than SIDH—in part due to sub-exponential quantum attacks that lead to much larger parameters.

One of the primary goals of this paper is to show that SIDH can indeed be used to construct a post-quantum X3DH replacement that satisfies the same security model as the original X3DH protocol—despite the existence of these adaptive attacks. In order to design good post-quantum replacements for the Signal protocol, a clear security model is required. This is an area of difficulty because the original Signal protocol did not define a security model—it appears to be designed empirically. There have since been a few efforts to formalise the security properties of the Signal protocol and X3DH. Notably, the work by Cohn-Gordon, Cremers, Dowling, Garratt, and Stebila [CGCD+20] was the first to propose a security model and prove the security of Signal in it. The recent work of Hashimoto, Katsumata, Kwiatkowski, and Prest [HKKP21] also proposes a generic security model for the Signal initial key agreement (specifically, for what they call Signal-conforming AKEs), and gives a generic construction from KEMs and signature schemes (as mentioned above, KEMs do not allow static–static key exchange, so a signature scheme is required to provide explicit authentication of the initiating party). From these analyses of the protocol, the following security properties have been identified as important, which any post-quantum replacement should therefore also satisfy:

1. Correctness: If Alice and Bob complete an exchange together, they should derive the same shared secret key.
2. Secrecy (also known as key-indistinguishability): Under the corruption of various combinations of the participants' secret keys, the shared secret for the session should not be recoverable, or even distinguishable from a random key. The combinations are defined by the specific security model used, for example, the CK model [CK01] or the model in [CGCD+20]. This is, of course, a basic requirement for any secure key exchange.
3. (Implicit) authentication: Both participants should know who they are talking to, and be able to verify their partner's identity.
4. Perfect forward secrecy (PFS): Past communication should remain secure and unreadable by adversaries even if the participants' long-term keys are compromised in the future.
5. Asynchronicity: The protocol can be made non-interactive by hosting participants' public keys on a third-party server, which is untrusted. In the security model, the only possible malicious ability the server should have is that it could deny Alice the retrieval of Bob's keys (or, say, not give out his one-time keys). This property is also called *receiver obliviousness* in [HKKP21].
6. (Offline) deniability [VGIK20], also known as identity-hiding: The transcript of an exchange session should not reveal the participants of the exchange (in a non-repudiable way).

We propose a new post-quantum key exchange protocol using SIDH, modelled after X3DH, which we call SI-X3DH. This new protocol solves the problem of adaptive attacks by using a variant of the FO transformation to prove that the initiator's ephemeral key is honestly generated, and a Proof of Knowledge to ensure the long term public keys are well-formed. We prove security of the SI-X3DH protocol formally in the random oracle model (ROM) using a new key-indistinguishability model we call the Signal-adapted-CK model. We show the security of SI-X3DH reduces to the hardness of the supersingular isogeny CDH (SI-CDH) assumption in the ROM.

SIDH has small key sizes compared to other post-quantum proposals (e.g. lattice-based key exchange), and is much faster than using CSIDH—as was suggested in [BFG+20]—because CSIDH uses larger-prime degree isogenies while SIDH commonly uses only isogenies of degree (a power of) two and three. During the online phase of an exchange (i.e., ignoring the initial setup with the proof of knowledge), our scheme only requires three or four SIDH instances (unlike k-SIDH) and one small FO-proof, and achieves deniability without using a ring signature (as [HKKP21] does). There are some structural differences between SI-X3DH and X3DH—for example, SI-X3DH performs an SIDH exchange between the two parties' identity keys (IK_A and IK_B), while X3DH used IK_A and SK_B (Bob's semi-static key) instead; also, due to the asymmetry between the degrees of the isogenies the two parties in SIDH use, SI-X3DH requires different keys for receiving and sending. Despite these differences, the structure of our protocol more closely resembles X3DH than any of the other post-quantum proposals presented to date. For example, SI-X3DH allows Bob the balance between one-time keys and medium-term (semi-static) keys—where the former may be exhausted, leading to denial of service, while the latter provide less security in some attack scenarios. These semi-static receiver keys are a feature that no other post-quantum proposal has captured. These factors make our protocol viable for use in post-quantum Signal initial key agreement.

There are two primary drawbacks of our scheme. The first is that it relies on proving knowledge of the secret long-term identity keys, by using the SIDH Proof of Knowledge from [DDGZ21] for example. This only needs to be done once per contact (or could be offloaded to the keyserver, if we trusted it—we shall not delve deeper into the discussion on Signal's trust model here), but for users who add many new contacts regularly, this may create an unacceptable overhead. The efficiency of our scheme is discussed more in Sect. 6. The second, as discussed in Sect. 5, is that SI-X3DH suffers from the possibility of more permanent key compromise impersonation (KCI) than the original Signal X3DH protocol does. Technically, neither Signal X3DH nor SI-X3DH satisfy the KCI resistance requirement of the eCK and CK+ security models, but there is a practical difference between the schemes. Impersonation was possible with the compromise of the semi-static key in Signal X3DH, whereas in SI-X3DH, impersonation is possible with compromise of the long-term identity key. Thus, cycling the semi-static key is no longer sufficient to prevent long-term impersonation.

1.1 Related Work

[BFG+20] proposed a new model for post-quantum X3DH replacements using a primitive they call split-KEMs. Their construction is a theoretical work, as they leave it an open question whether post-quantum primitives such as CSIDH satisfy the security definitions of their split-KEM. Recently, [HKKP21] presented their Signal-Conforming AKE (SC-AKE) construction, also using post-quantum KEMs to construct a generic Signal X3DH replacement. To achieve deniability, their scheme requires a post-quantum ring signature scheme. Independently, but following a very similar approach to [HKKP21], [BFG+22] also proposed a deniable AKE using post-quantum KEMs (which they call "Signal in a Post-Quantum Regime" (SPQR)) and a designated verifier signature (DVS) scheme. As they mention, little work has been done to date in constructing DVS schemes from post-quantum assumptions (an isogeny-based scheme was proposed in [STW12], but is broken by the GPST attack), so [BFG+22] also propose using a two-party post-quantum ring signature scheme for the same purpose. We briefly outline the differences between these works and that presented in this paper using Table 1, with the original Signal X3DH protocol included as a reference.

The original Signal X3DH scheme requires Bob to sign his semi-static keys (using XEdDSA [Per16] with his identity key), to prevent a malicious keyserver from providing its own keys and compromising the perfect forward secrecy guarantee of the scheme. This requirement must still hold in any post-quantum replacement too, otherwise MITM attacks can break the PFS of the scheme. Because there are no efficient post-quantum constructions with a public key that can be used in both a signature scheme and a key exchange, requiring a separate signature scheme (and verification key K_σ) seems unavoidable for any post-quantum X3DH replacement. In general, these X3DH replacements (including SI-X3DH) are agnostic to the signature scheme used for this purpose, so any efficient post-quantum signature scheme may be used alongside them—there is no restriction to use an isogeny-based signature scheme with SI-X3DH.

For deniability, SC-AKE requires the initiator of the key exchange to sign the session ID. This signature creates non-repudiable evidence of the initiator's involvement in the exchange. [HKKP21] and [BFG+22] suggest using a ring signature to attain deniability. Specifically, a signature under a two-party ring involving just the sender and receiver is sufficient to authenticate the other party in the exchange (since one party knows the signatures that they themselves generated), but to a third party, the signature could have been generated by either participant. Unfortunately, however, a post-quantum ring signature scheme is a much more expensive construction than a standard signature. In both [HKKP21] and [BFG+22], one of these signatures is required in every exchange session. Deniability of the split-KEM construction is not discussed in [BFG+20], and would appear to depend on how the split-KEM is instantiated. Our scheme attains deniability without using a ring signature.

Finally, it is important to note that the SC-AKE protocol does not use a semi-static key—only long-term and ephemeral keys. This means that unlike in

Table 1. Comparison of post-quantum Signal X3DH replacements. *Long-term data* refers to the size of the initial registration cost for each user (the "offline" data). *Exchanged data* gives the amount of ephemeral data sent in a single exchange (by both parties combined), that is, the size of the "online" transcript.

Scheme	PQ-secure	Deniable	Requires sig	Long-term data	Exchanged data
Original Signal X3DH protocol	✗	✓	✓	K	3 keys
Split-KEM based X3DH [BFG+20]	✓	?	✓	K, K_σ	3 keys, 4 ciphertexts
Signal-Conforming AKE [HKKP21]	✓	*with PQ ring signature	✓ (×2)	K, K_σ, K_σ^*	1 key, 3 ciphertexts
SPQR [BFG+22]	✓	*with PQ ring signature or DVS	✓ (×2)	K, K_σ, K_σ^*	2 keys, 4 ciphertexts
SI-X3DH (this work)	✓	✓	✓	K_2, K_3, K_σ + PoK	3 keys, 1 ciphertext

Signal X3DH, if a receiver is offline for an extended period of time, it is possible for all the ephemeral keys they uploaded to the server to be exhausted (either due to popularity or a malicious attempt to do so). This creates an opportunity for denial of service which is not present when semi-static keys are used and the ephemeral component is optional. Our scheme, and the scheme in [BFG+22], address this by using both semi-static and ephemeral keys if available, as in Signal's X3DH.

Other works on post-quantum key exchange, for example for TLS, are not suitable for use in the Signal X3DH setting because these schemes are interactive over multiple rounds (failing the asynchronicity requirement above), and often do not authenticate the initiator (or client).

We begin in Sect. 2 by reviewing the existing X3DH protocol used as Signal's initial key agreement. We then review the supersingular isogeny Diffie–Hellman key exchange (SIDH) in Sect. 3. In Sect. 4 we discuss the security properties of an appropriate Signal key agreement protocol in more detail and define a security model to be used. This is followed by our construction of a new protocol in Sect. 5 using SIDH, which we propose as a post-quantum replacement for X3DH. Section 6 discusses the efficiency of our protocol and the key differences between our proposal and the original X3DH scheme.

2 The Signal X3DH Protocol

The basic process of the X3DH protocol is given in Fig. 1, where Alice is the initiator and Bob is the responder. Let $\mathrm{DH}_{\mathsf{pp}}(g^a, g^b) = g^{ab}$ denote the result of a Diffie–Hellman key exchange between keys A and B (at least one of the private keys is needed to compute this, but the result is unambiguous), with public parameters pp including g. Because we assume fixed public parameters, we will usually omit the subscript. Throughout this paper, we will use ⌜dashed boxes⌟ to denote optional parameters which may be omitted.

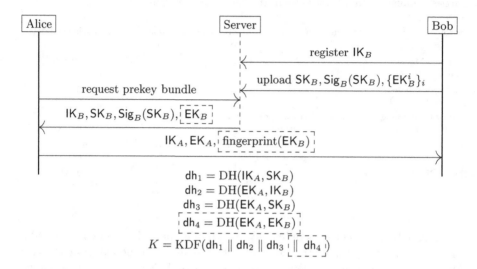

Fig. 1. The X3DH protocol [MP16b]. dh_4 is optional on the basis of one-time key availability.

Because the X3DH protocol is designed to work when the recipient (Bob) is offline, Alice obtains his public key information from a server. IK_A and IK_B are the fixed long-term identity keys of Alice and Bob respectively. Bob additionally uploads a semi-static public key SK_B signed by him to the server, which he rotates semi-regularly. He also uploads a number of one-time keys EK_B, but the use of these is optional as the supply on the server may run out.

After Alice has received Bob's identity, semi-static, and (optional) one-time keys from the server, she performs a three- or four-part key exchange with her own identity key and ephemeral key. These three or four shared keys are specified in the figure (denoted by dh_i), and are combined using some sort of secure hash or key derivation function (KDF). We shall assume they are simply concatenated and hashed with a cryptographic hash function. This results in the master shared secret for the exchange, which is then used in subsequent protocols such as Signal's Double Ratchet protocol.

Finally, Alice sends to Bob identifiers of which of his semi-static and one-time public keys she used (for example, short fingerprint), as well as her own identity and ephemeral keys. This allows Bob to also compute the same shared master secret.

Verification of the long-term identity keys is out-of-scope for the protocol, and may be done either by trusting a third party (e.g. the server) as a PKI, or verifying the keys in-person or out-of-band in some other way.

3   SIDH

We briefly recall the Supersingular Isogeny Diffie–Hellman (SIDH) key exchange protocol[2] [JD11] by Jao and De Feo. Let $p = \ell_1^{e_1} \ell_2^{e_2} f \pm 1$ be prime, with ℓ_1, ℓ_2 distinct small primes, f an integer cofactor, and $\ell_1^{e_1} \approx \ell_2^{e_2}$. We work over the finite field $\mathbb{F}_{p^2}$. Fix a supersingular elliptic curve E_0 and a basis $\{P_i, Q_i\}$ for both the ℓ_1 and ℓ_2 torsion subgroups of $E_0(\mathbb{F}_{p^2})$ (such that $E_0[\ell_i^{e_i}] = \langle P_i, Q_i \rangle$). Typically $\ell_1 = 2$ and $\ell_2 = 3$, and this will be assumed from here forward in this paper. We will use both the index 1 and the subscript A to represent Alice's information, while $B \simeq 2$ will be used interchangeably for Bob's, for clarity in various situations and for consistency with existing literature.

Alice's secret key is an isogeny $\phi_A : E(\mathbb{F}_{p^2}) \to E_A(\mathbb{F}_{p^2})$ of degree 2^{e_1} (Bob's is analogous, with degree 3^{e_2}). It is well known that knowledge of an isogeny (up to equivalence, i.e., post-composition with an isomorphism) and knowledge of its kernel are equivalent via Vélu's formulae [Vél71], so both the kernel and the isogeny will be referred to as "the secret key". Alice's public key is the tuple $(E_A, \phi_A(P_B), \phi_A(Q_B))$. The image of the 3^{e_2} basis under ϕ_A allows Bob to "transport" his isogeny to E_A and make the diagram commute: if the kernel of ϕ_B on E_0 is generated by $P_B + [\beta]Q_B$, then Bob defines the corresponding kernel $\langle \phi_A(P_B) + [\beta]\phi_A(Q_B) \rangle$ on E_A. Both Alice's and Bob's transported isogenies will have isomorphic codomain curves $E_{AB} \simeq E_{BA}$, and their j-invariant $j(E_{AB}) = j(E_{BA})$ can be used as a shared secret. Figure 2 depicts the commutative diagram making up the SIDH key exchange.

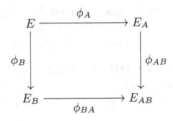

Fig. 2. Commutative diagram of SIDH, where $\ker(\phi_{BA}) = \phi_B(\ker(\phi_A))$ and $\ker(\phi_{AB}) = \phi_A(\ker(\phi_B))$.

Throughout this paper, we will use the function $\mathrm{SIDH}_{pp}(\cdot, \cdot)$ to represent this protocol with respect to public parameters pp, outputting the final j-invariant. Generally, the public parameters will be clear from context, so they may be omitted for ease of notation. The arguments to SIDH will be the two public keys of the participants (first the degree-3^{e_2} isogeny key, second the degree-2^{e_1} isogeny key), because clearly the result is independent of which participant computed the value (using their secret key). Specifically, if $\langle P_B + [\beta]Q_B \rangle$ is

---

[2] Since publication, attacks have been proposed on the variant of SIDH described here [CD22, MM22, Rob22].

the secret kernel corresponding to the public key $K_B = (E_B, P'_A, Q'_A)$, then $SIDH_{pp}((E_A, P'_B, Q'_B), K_B) = j(E_A/\langle P'_B + [\beta]Q'_B\rangle)$.

Definition 1 (Computational Supersingular Isogeny Diffie–Hellman (SI-CDH) problem). *Let* $pp = (p, \ell_1, \ell_2, e_1, e_2, E_0, P_1, Q_1, P_2, Q_2)$ *be SIDH public parameters, and*

$$K_1 = (E_1, \phi_1(P_2), \phi_1(Q_2)),$$
$$K_2 = (E_2, \phi_2(P_1), \phi_2(Q_1)),$$

be two SIDH public keys, where $\phi_i : E_0 \to E_i$ *has degree* $\ell_i^{e_i}$. *The SI-CDH problem is, given* pp, K_1, *and* K_2, *to compute the j-invariant* $j = SIDH_{pp}(K_2, K_1)$.

We define the advantage of a probabilistic polynomial-time (PPT) adversary $\mathcal{A}$ solving the SI-CDH problem as

$$\mathsf{Adv}^{\text{si-cdh}}(\mathcal{A}) = \Pr\left[j' = SIDH_{pp}(K_2, K_1) \mid j' \leftarrow \mathcal{A}(pp, K_1, K_2)\right].$$

3.1   New SI-CDH-Based Assumptions

We now introduce two new computational assumptions, both of which SI-CDH (Definition 1) can be reduced to in the random oracle model. These two assumptions are merely tools to simplify the proof of security of our new SI-X3DH protocol. For ease of notation, let $\mathcal{K}_i$ (the i-keyspace) be the set of possible isogenies of degree $\ell_i^{e_i}$ from the fixed SIDH base curve E_0 (up to equivalence). Let $H_1 : \{0,1\}^* \to \mathcal{K}_2$ be a pseudorandom generator (PRG) whose codomain is the second of these secret isogeny keyspaces. PubkeyFromSecret is a function taking a secret isogeny or kernel generator and outputting the SIDH public key corresponding to that isogeny (or the isogeny with that kernel, via Vélu's formulae).

Definition 2 (Verifiable SI-CDH (VCDH) problem).
Let pp *be SIDH public parameters, and* K_1 *and* K_2 *be two SIDH public keys (whose secret isogenies have coprime degrees specified by* pp*). Let* $\mathcal{O}_{K_1,K_2}$ *be an oracle defined as*

$$\mathcal{O}_{K_1,K_2}(j') = \begin{cases} 1 & \text{if } j' = SIDH_{pp}(K_2, K_1), \\ 0 & \text{otherwise.} \end{cases}$$

Note that K_1, K_2 *are fixed in the definition of* $\mathcal{O}$.
     The Verifiable SI-CDH problem is to compute the j-invariant $j = SIDH_{pp}(K_2, K_1)$, *given* pp, K_1, K_2, *and* $\mathcal{O}_{K_1,K_2}$.

On all except one j-invariant, the oracle $\mathcal{O}_{K_1,K_2}$ will return 0. Because K_1 and K_2 are fixed, the oracle $\mathcal{O}$ is much weaker than an SI-DDH oracle (which takes keys as input parameters). Thus, intuitively, in polynomially-many queries, the likelihood of guessing the correct j-invariant is negligible (as in the SI-CDH problem). The second problem models an SI-CDH instance with an additional FO-like proof that the second key in the instance, K_2, was honestly generated.

Definition 3 (Honest SI-CDH (HCDH) problem).
Let pp *be SIDH public parameters, and* $s \leftarrow \{0,1\}^n$ *be a random seed, where* n *is the security parameter. Then, let* $K_2 = \mathsf{PubkeyFromSecret}(H_1(s))$ *be a public key derived from* s, *where* $H_1(s)$ *is an isogeny of degree* $\ell_2^{e_2}$. *Let* K_1 *be a second public key (corresponding to an isogeny of degree* $\ell_1^{e_1}$*). Finally, let* π *be an FO-proof of the form*

$$\pi = s \oplus H_2(\mathrm{SIDH}_{\mathsf{pp}}(K_2, K_1)),$$

where $H_2 : \{0,1\}^* \rightarrow \{0,1\}^n$ *is a PRG.*
   The Verifiable SI-CDH problem is, given pp, K_1, K_2, *and* π, *to compute the* j-*invariant* $j = \mathrm{SIDH}_{\mathsf{pp}}(K_2, K_1)$.

Reductions from SI-CDH to both of these problems can be found in Appendix A.

4 Security Model

In the field of Authenticated Key Exchange (AKE), the eCK and CK+ models are generally viewed as the strongest and most desirable security models, as they capture attacks which are outside the scope of the earlier CK model [CK01]: weak perfect forward secrecy (wPFS), key compromise impersonation (KCI), and maximal exposure (MEX). All of these properties relate to certain combinations of long-term and ephemeral keys being compromised by an adversary. A protocol is secure in these models if an adversary cannot distinguish the true session key from a random one, even when given these abilities to compromise keys.

   Unfortunately, Signal X3DH does not meet the definition of security required by these models. This was observed in [CGCD+20]. Precisely, this is because some combinations of keys from Alice and Bob are not used for Diffie–Hellman exchanges in the protocol—for example, there is no DH exchange between Alice's identity key and Bob's identity or ephemeral keys. Our benchmark for security is that a replacement protocol should meet at least the same security definition as that of the original protocol, so we must observe where exactly the original protocol breaks down in the eCK and CK+ models. This allows us to propose a slightly weaker model, though still stronger than the CK model, that successfully represents the security goals of Signal X3DH. This gives a formal security model with a more standard presentation than the model used in [CGCD+20] to prove security of the original Signal X3DH protocol—allowing much easier comparison with other works. We call our new security model the Signal-adapted-CK model. One difference of note is that standard security models generally define keys to be either long-term or ephemeral. As a recipient in the Signal protocol uses up to three keys, including a semi-static (medium-term) key, it is not at first obvious how to integrate this semi-static key into such two-key models. We choose to consider it as both long-term and ephemeral in different situations. This is discussed further in Remark 1.

   [HKKP21] provides a similar security model, for what they call a Signal-conforming AKE protocol. Their security model differs from ours in the fact that it does not take semi-static keys into account (their proposed construction does not use semi-static keys). Their model is stronger than the Signal-adapted-CK model—in fact, the original Signal X3DH protocol would not satisfy their model even if the semi-static keys were somehow included (it requires security against the two events E_4 and E_8 in Table 3, discussed further below). However, our goal is to propose a model that exactly captures the security properties of the original Signal X3DH protocol, which was not the goal of their model. In other words, we wish to analyse Signal, not some stronger protocol.

4.1   Key Indistinguishability Experiment

Due to space requirements, standard definitions for the key indistinguishability experiment can be found in Appendix C. We focus on our non-standard definition of **freshness**, which differentiates the Signal-adapted-CK model from the standard eCK and CK+ models.

Definition 4 (Freshness).   *A session Π_i^j, with $\Pi_i^j.\text{peer\_id} = k$, is **fresh** if none of the following hold:*

- $\Pi_i^j.\text{status} \neq \texttt{accept}$.
- *The* session_key *of Π_i^j, or any matching session, is revealed.*
- *If $\Pi_i^j.\text{role} = \texttt{init}$:*
  - *Both **RevealIK**(i) and **RevealEK**(i,j) are issued.*
  - *Π_i^j has a partner Π_k^ℓ for some ℓ, **RevealIK**(k) is issued, and either **RevealSK**$(k, \Pi_i^j.\text{peer\_sk\_id})$ $(\star)$ or **RevealEK**(k, ℓ) are issued. See Remark 1.*
- *If $\Pi_i^j.\text{role} = \texttt{resp}$:*
  - *Π_i^j has a partner Π_k^ℓ for some ℓ and both **RevealIK**(k) and **RevealEK**(k, ℓ) are issued.*
  - ***RevealIK**(i) and either **RevealSK**$(i, \Pi_i^j.\text{sk\_id})$ $(\star)$ or **RevealEK**(i, j) are issued. See Remark 1.*
- *Π_i^j has no partner session and **RevealIK**$(\Pi_i^j.\text{peer\_id})$ is issued.*

We emphasise that Table 2 and our definition of freshness in Definition 4 are strictly weaker than the standard eCK/CK+ cases and definitions—specifically, we have removed the adversary's ability to perform two specific cases of KCI attack. Both of these removed cases are given in Table 3, and correspond to the extra restrictions on freshness marked with a $(\star)$ in Definition 4. These are the cases that weaken the eCK/CK+ models to our Signal-adapted-CK model.

The KCI attack on the original protocol is as follows: if Bob's semi-static key SK_B is compromised, an adversary can impersonate anyone to Bob. This is because Alice is only authenticated through dh_1 (the exchange with SK_B), so an adversary can claim the use of any other public key IK_E and calculate the correct Diffie–Hellman value with SK_B. As SK_B is periodically replaced by Bob, the impersonation to Bob can last only as long as he accepts exchanges with that particular SK_B. However, we consider this a failure of the KCI property because SK_B is not ephemeral. This is discussed further in Remark 1.

Table 2. Behaviour of the adversary in our model, corresponding to the various freshness conditions in Definition 4. $\mathcal{I}$ and $\mathcal{R}$ denote whether the key belongs to the initiator or responder respectively. "✓" means the corresponding secret key is revealed or corrupted, "x" means it is not revealed, and "-" means it does not exist or is provided by the adversary. *Discussed further in Remark 1.

Event	Matching session exists	$IK_{\mathcal{I}}$	$EK_{\mathcal{I}}$	$IK_{\mathcal{R}}$	$SK_{\mathcal{R}}$	$EK_{\mathcal{R}}$	Attack
E_1	No	✓	x	x	✓	-	KCI
E_2	No	x	✓	x	x *	-	MEX
E_3	No	x	-	x	x *	✓	MEX
E_5	Yes	✓	x	✓	x	x	wPFS
E_6	Yes	x	✓	x	x *	✓	MEX
E_7	Yes	✓	x	x	✓	✓	KCI

Table 3. The two cases of the eCK/CK+ model which are NOT satisfied by Signal's X3DH, and so are not included in our model. This lack of KCI is exactly where these protocols break down.

Event	Matching session exists	$IK_{\mathcal{I}}$	$EK_{\mathcal{I}}$	$IK_{\mathcal{R}}$	$SK_{\mathcal{R}}$	$EK_{\mathcal{R}}$	Attack
E_4	No	x	-	✓	✓	x	KCI
E_8	Yes	x	✓	✓	✓	x	KCI

Remark 1. In the original Signal X3DH protocol, the semi-static keys SK_B are used to strike a balance between perfect forward secrecy and key-exhaustion denial of service. To correctly model the purpose of this key, we assume it is "ephemeral enough" to have been replaced some time before a PFS attack (event E_5 in Table 2) takes place—this is generally a longer-term attack and the cycling of the semi-static key is designed to prevent precisely this. However, the semi-static key is not truly ephemeral, so we allow it to be revealed as both ephemeral and long-term in the KCI attacks of Table 2. This properly captures the various forms of key-leakage that could lead to a KCI attack and strengthens the security model. Finally, in the MEX cases, we observe that the original Signal X3DH protocol is not secure if the semi-static key can be revealed in cases E_2, E_3, and E_6. They are set to x in Table 2 due to our goal of accurately capturing the security of this original Signal protocol. In the spirit of the MEX property, the protocol would ideally be secure even when these three cases allowed SK to be revealed—there is no reason to treat the semi-static key as long-term in these cases. As we will show later, our new protocol (SI-X3DH) is secure even if these three cases marked by asterisks are changed to ✓.

4.2 Further Security Properties

It is claimed in [MP16b] that X3DH can be considered to have (full) perfect forward secrecy (PFS), as opposed to just weak PFS which is proved in the model above. The situation is identical in our scheme, so will not be discussed further in this paper.

Another very important property of X3DH, which is not captured by the above security model (or in general by the eCK or CK+ models), is that of *deniability*. Deniability has two flavours: offline and online deniability. A protocol is offline-deniable if an adversary can gain no non-repudiable evidence of message authorship from a transcript even if the long-term keys involved are compromised. On the other hand, online deniability means that even by interacting with the target (or colluding with another user with whom the target interacts), the adversary cannot gain any such evidence. A protocol satisfying both offline and online deniability is known as strongly-deniable. Unfortunately, the Signal protocol fails to achieve online-deniability, as shown by Unger and Goldberg [UG18]—although this notion is very difficult to obtain and arguably less important that offline-deniability. The first formal proof that offline-deniability is indeed achieved by Signal was given by [VGIK20].

The proof of offline-deniability for Signal carries over to our protocol in an essentially identical manner, because of how similar the two protocols are. The proof reduces to the Knowledge of DH (KDH) assumption and its variants (K2DH and EKDH) which informally state that it should be infeasible for an adversary, given as input public keys for which the secret keys are unknown, to output DH values and other public keys they do not know the secret key to, yet still satisfy relationships of the form $\mathsf{dh} = \mathrm{DH}(K_1, K_2)$ (where K_1, K_2 are public keys). We will not formally define the assumptions here, but refer the reader to [VGIK20]. We give a brief, informal outline of this proof in Appendix B.4.

5 Using SIDH for Post-quantum X3DH

We now briefly outline the design process of our SI-X3DH scheme. The obvious starting point is to naively drop in SIDH as a replacement for DH in Fig. 1. Due to adaptive attacks, we then require both parties to prove that their keys are honestly generated whenever they are used in exchanges with non-ephemeral keys from their partner. In the case of EK_A, this can easily be done through an FO-like transformation [HHK17], as was done in the SIKE [CCH+19] KEM.

Unfortunately this approach cannot be used to prove the honest generation of non-ephemeral keys. For example, Bob's semi-static key could be used to adaptively attack Alice's identity key if not proven to be well-formed, but he may be offline at the time of exchange, and the semi-static key may be reused across multiple sessions of the protocol with different users, so he cannot reveal the secret key to Alice. It is undesirable to use the other known methods of proving honest generation of SK_B, due to their inefficiency and the fact that regular rotation of SK_B mean such proofs need to be regenerated and reverified every time. Instead, we modify the original X3DH protocol somewhat, replacing

dh_1 between IK_A and SK_B with one between IK_A and IK_B. Then, SK_B is only used in exchanges with ephemeral key EK_A, removing the need to prove its honesty. The other components, dh_2, dh_3, and dh_4, all involve only Alice's provably honest ephemeral key, so neither party can learn anything in these exchanges.

Finally, we require proof that IK_A and IK_B are honestly generated, to ensure an adaptive attack cannot be performed by registering multiple fake users with adaptive public identity keys to attack a target's private identity key. Because identity keys are fixed (and only need to be verified once per new contact), we do not encounter the efficiency degradation of using a more expensive proof to prove knowledge of the corresponding secret keys. The Signal X3DH protocol already assumes that participants will verify each other's identity public key for authentication, so verifying honest key generation can be done at the same time. One method of proving SIDH public keys are honestly generated is via a non-interactive zero-knowledge (NIZK) Proof of Knowledge (PoK) of the corresponding secret key. De Feo, Dobson, Galbraith, and Zobernig [DDGZ21] present such a proof protocol and show that using it as part of a non-interactive key exchange is asymptotically more efficient than resorting to other protocols such as k-SIDH (in terms of isogeny computations). Thus, this SIDH PoK is perfectly suitable for our situation.

One disadvantage of this modification is that it impacts the KCI resistance of the scheme. If an adversary corrupted IK_B, they could pretend to Bob to be Alice by choosing any ephemeral key they like, and calculating dh_1 using the known secret key, so Bob would accept it as coming from Alice herself. This was the case with the original Signal X3DH if SK_B was corrupted, as discussed above. However, there is a practical difference to consider—the impersonation can persist for longer than in X3DH, since corruption is no longer repaired by the regular replacement of SK_B. We suspect that medium-term impersonation would be just as damaging as long-term, and corruption of an identity key is a severe break in security anyway. Because neither scheme can claim to have KCI resistance, we still assert that SI-X3DH satisfies the same security requirements as Signal X3DH, but this difference may be worthy of consideration.

Unlike traditional Diffie–Hellman, where both participants' keys are of the form g^x, in SIDH we have an asymmetric setup—one user uses a degree-$\ell_1^{e_1}$ isogeny, while the other uses a degree-$\ell_2^{e_2}$ isogeny. In order to make this work in X3DH where users can be both initiators and receivers, we require that all "initiating" keys (IK_A and EK_A) have degree 3^{e_2}, and all "receiving" keys (IK_B, SK_B, and optionally EK_B) have degree 2^{e_1}. This arrangement is chosen so that the sender has a slightly higher computational burden than the receiver, for DOS reasons. This does mean that all users will require two identity keys—a receiving and an initiating key. All other aspects of the SI-X3DH protocol follow the original Signal X3DH closely, including Bob's signatures on his semi-static keys (already discussed in Sect. 1.1), for which any suitable post-quantum signature scheme (for example, a hash-based signature) can be used.

We remark that Galbraith [Gal18, A.3] briefly suggests that using an ephemeral key in an exchange introduces enough randomness to prevent information about the long-term secret being leaked, however in CK-type models the adversary can make reveal queries against the private key of EK_A, providing a concrete attack. We also remark that in the Signal protocol, there is a natural asymmetry between sender and receiver in the exchange, so we avoid interleaving attacks like the one by Blake-Wilson, Johnson, and Menezes [BWJM97, Protocol 3]).

Our **SI-X3DH** (Supersingular Isogeny X3DH) protocol is given in Fig. 3. In each instance of the protocol, Alice obtains a key package from the server including Bob's signature verification key VK_B, which is used to validate the signature on his semi-static key SK_B. Alice will then generate a random seed s and use a preimage resistant hash function H_1 to compute an ephemeral secret key $\phi_e \leftarrow H_1(s)$. Let the corresponding public key be EK_A. She will then compute the pre-shared key PSK, and an FO-proof π as follows:

$$
\begin{aligned}
dh_1 &= SIDH(IK_A, IK_B), \\
dh_2 &= SIDH(EK_A, IK_B), \\
dh_3 &= SIDH(EK_A, SK_B), \\
dh_4 &= SIDH(EK_A, EK_B), \\
PSK &= KDF(dh_1 \parallel dh_2 \parallel dh_3 \parallel dh_4), \\
\pi &= s \oplus H_2(dh_1) \oplus H_2(dh_2) \oplus H_2(dh_3) \oplus H_2(dh_4).
\end{aligned}
\tag{1}
$$

H_1 and H_2 are the same PRGs used in Sect. 3.1. The reason π takes this form will be clear from the security proof we present in Appendix B. Alice then sends (EK_A, π) to Bob, along with an identifier for herself, and information about which of his ephemeral keys she used in the exchange (if any). Bob can check π is valid and honest by using IK_A and EK_A to compute the values $H_2(dh_j)$ (for $j = 1, 2, 3$, and if used, 4), XORing these with π to compute s', then recomputing $\phi_e' \leftarrow H_1(s')$, and checking that the corresponding public key is equal to EK_A. He computes PSK as in Eq. 1. If the verification of π succeeds, both Alice and Bob can compute the shared secret $K = KDF(s \parallel EK_A \parallel PSK)$. However, if verification fails, Bob should instead choose a (or, to avoid timing leakage, use a pre-chosen) random $r \leftarrow \{0,1\}^n$ and compute $K = KDF(r \parallel EK_A \parallel PSK)$. This way, his key will not match the one Alice derives with overwhelming probability, and the exchange fails, with Alice learning no information about the cause of failure (or about Bob's secret keys).

Theorem 1. *The SI-X3DH protocol presented in Sect. 5 is secure (correct and sound) in the Signal-adapted-CK model of Definition 5, in the random oracle model (where H_1, H_2 and KDF are modelled as random oracles), assuming the SI-CDH problem is hard.*

The proof of Theorem 1 can be found in Appendix B. Furthermore, as mentioned in Sect. 4.2, the proof of offline-deniability of SI-X3DH is almost identical to that of the original Signal X3DH protocol (given in [VGIK20]), due to the

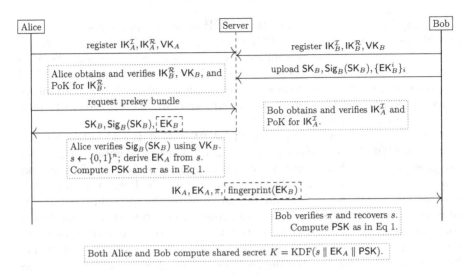

Fig. 3. The SI-X3DH protocol.

similarity between the schemes. We give a brief informal outline of that proof in Appendix B.4.

6   Efficiency

An SI-X3DH session requires sharing a total of four or five keys between Alice and Bob, along with a small n-bit FO-proof π, and the unavoidable signature from Bob on SK_B. Because SIDH has some of the shortest public key sizes of any of the post-quantum contenders, the total transcript size of an SI-X3DH exchange is competitive (albeit still larger than the original X3DH protocol transcripts). One minor drawback of the SI-X3DH protocol is that it requires registering two identity keys rather than one on the server—a receiving key and a sending key (note that this does not apply to the semi-static key, which is always of degree 2^{e_1}). Because of the short key sizes, and the fact that only one of the peer's keys is ever required per session (e.g. a peer's sending key is not needed if they are the responder), we believe this is of little practical impact. Duits [Dui19] examined the efficiency of using SIDH in the Signal protocol (though note that the implementation is not SI-X3DH, but the naive implementation, vulnerable to adaptive attacks), and also concluded that the speed was practical.

In particular, our protocol is more efficient in terms of computation at exchange-time than the Split-KEM based X3DH protocol in [BFG+20] using CSIDH (assuming CSIDH does even satisfy the security properties needed for their split-KEM scheme, which they leave as an open problem). Based on NIST security level 1, we compare the fast, constant-time CTIDH [BBC+21] implementation of CSIDH-512 with the SIKEp434 parameter set. According to

[BBC+21], the cost of computing the CSIDH action is approximately 125 million Skylake clock cycles, while [COR21] states that SIKEp434 key generation and agreement takes around 5 million Skylake clock cycles—roughly 25 times faster. The split-KEM protocol proposed in [BFG+20] would require two CSIDH actions for each of the four encapsulations and decapsulations. SI-X3DH on the other hand, ignoring the PoK, requires only four SIDH exchanges so in total would be around 50 times faster.

The main efficiency drawback of SI-X3DH is that the identity keys also require an SIDH Proof of Knowledge or proof of honest generation, such as the one given by [DDGZ21]. Because identity keys are retrieved and verified once per contact, in advance of key establishment taking place, the PoK has no impact on exchange-time efficiency—it essentially just increases the bandwidth required to retrieve the identity keys, and can be discarded after verification. As mentioned earlier, depending on the amount of trust users wish to place in the server, verification of these proofs can be offloaded to the server at registration time. The best case is that a user verifies the proof for a contact once and then continues creating sessions with that same contact over a long period of time. However, if users regularly add new contacts, this could create a large overhead by requiring verification of such a proof for each. In the worst case, if a proof is required on nearly every new key exchange session, the overhead would be very large, and our scheme would no longer be competitive, though still more efficient than k-SIDH. On the plus side, SI-X3DH does not require an expensive ring or DVS signature to attain deniability as the generic schemes in [HKKP21] and [BFG+22] do. If these schemes were instantiated with the ring signature schemes of Beullens, Katsumata, and Pintore [BKP20], then choosing the lattice-based instantiation (Falafl) to optimise for speed (rather than signature and key size) would require around 78 million clock cycles for signing—already four times slower than the full SI-X3DH key exchange—and such a signature would be around 30 KB in size. The smaller isogeny-based instantiation (Calamari), whose signatures are around 3.6 KB, would take on the order of 10^{11} clock cycles—many orders of magnitude slower.

7   Conclusion

An SIDH key exchange is still safe for use if we have sufficient guarantee by both parties that their keys are honestly generated. This important observation allows us to use SIDH in a secure post-quantum replacement for Signal's X3DH protocol, despite concerns around the adaptive attacks against SIDH [BFG+20]. While a naive drop-in use of SIDH into X3DH would be insecure as [BFG+20] claims, by tweaking the protocol to use a novel FO-like transform and a proof of knowledge for identity keys, we can make SIDH safe for use in the Signal X3DH protocol. Our new protocol, SI-X3DH, provides an efficient, post-quantum secure replacement for X3DH which closely resembles the original protocol.

Acknowledgements. We thank the anonymous reviewers for their helpful comments and feedback. We also thank Jason LeGrow for his feedback and advice. This research was partially funded by MBIE catalyst grant UOAX1933.

A   Proofs of VCDH and HCDH Reductions

Theorem 2. *Let $\mathcal{B}$ be an adversary solving the VCDH problem with advantage ϵ after making q queries to the oracle $\mathcal{O}_{K_1,K_2}$. Then $\mathcal{B}$ can be used to solve the SI-CDH problem with probability at least $\epsilon/2q$.*

Proof. Without loss of generality, we assume all q queries are made with distinct inputs. Let (K_1, K_2) be an SI-CDH challenge instance. We define two different oracles $\mathcal{O}^0$ and $\mathcal{O}^1$. Oracle $\mathcal{O}^0$ will return 0 regardless of the query made. To define oracle $\mathcal{O}^1$, we select a random index $0 \le \ell < q$ and let $\mathcal{O}^2$ return 1 on the ℓ-th unique query (and 0 on all other queries). We run the adversary $\mathcal{B}$ in two settings, giving instance $(K_1, K_2, \mathcal{O}^i)$ to $\mathcal{B}$ in setting $i \in \{0, 1\}$. Define found to be the event that $\mathcal{B}$ makes a query to the oracle $\mathcal{O}$ it is given with the correct j-invariant (the solution to the SI-CDH instance). We can consider the probability of $\mathcal{B}$ succeeding against the VCDH problem as

$$\epsilon = \Pr[\,\mathcal{B}\text{ wins} \mid \text{found occurs}\,] \cdot \Pr[\,\text{found occurs}\,]$$
$$+ \; \Pr[\,\mathcal{B}\text{ wins} \mid \text{found does not occur}\,] \cdot \Pr[\,\text{found does not occur}\,].$$

If found does not occur, then $\mathcal{B}$ running in setting 0 (where oracle $\mathcal{O}^0$ always returns 0) will be unable to distinguish the simulated oracle from the true one, and will win with advantage ϵ. Hence,

$$\Pr[\,\mathcal{B}\text{ wins in setting } 0\,] \ge \Pr[\,\mathcal{B}\text{ wins} \mid \text{found does not occur}\,].$$

On the other hand, if found occurs, then we correctly simulated the oracle in setting 1 with probability $1/q$ (the probability that we guessed ℓ correctly). Therefore,

$$\Pr[\,\mathcal{B}\text{ wins in setting } 1\,] \ge \frac{1}{q}\Pr[\,\mathcal{B}\text{ wins} \mid \text{found occurs}\,].$$

We uniformly sample $b \leftarrow \{0, 1\}$ and return the solution from $\mathcal{B}$ running in setting b to the SI-CDH challenger. Because $0 \le \Pr[\,\text{found occurs}\,] \le 1$, we solve the SI-CDH instance with overall probability

$$\frac{1}{2}\Pr[\,\mathcal{B}\text{ wins in setting } 0\,] + \frac{1}{2}\Pr[\,\mathcal{B}\text{ wins in setting } 1\,]$$

$$\ge \frac{1}{2}\Pr[\,\mathcal{B}\text{ wins} \mid \text{found does not occur}\,] + \frac{1}{2q}\Pr[\,\mathcal{B}\text{ wins} \mid \text{found occurs}\,]$$

$$\ge \frac{1}{2q}\left(\Pr[\,\mathcal{B}\text{ wins} \mid \text{found does not occur}\,] + \Pr[\,\mathcal{B}\text{ wins} \mid \text{found occurs}\,]\right)$$

$$\ge \frac{1}{2q}\epsilon,$$

which is non-negligible if ϵ is (since q must be polynomially-sized).

Theorem 3. *Let $\mathcal{B}$ be an adversary solving the HCDH problem with advantage ϵ after making q queries to H_2, modelled as a random oracle. Then $\mathcal{B}$ can be used to solve the SI-CDH problem with probability at least $\min(1/q, \epsilon)/2$.*

Proof. We argue that the FO-like proof leaks no information because we obviously assume that $\mathrm{SIDH}_{pp}(K_2, K_1)$ is unknown (since it is the answer to the SI-CDH problem) and s is random. Thus, if the SI-CDH problem is hard, then so too is this problem. We sketch a reduction in the random oracle model. Treat H_2 as a random oracle. Let $\mathcal{B}$ be an adversary making q queries to H_2 and winning with advantage ϵ against the HCDH problem. Obtain an SI-CDH challenge (K_1, K_2). Choose π to be a random binary string, and provide (K_1, K_2, π) to $\mathcal{B}$.

In order to distinguish the simulated π from an honest FO-proof, $\mathcal{B}$ must query $H_2(j)$ for the correct j-invariant solution of the SI-CDH instance. Call this even found, as above. If found occurs, we can return one of the q queries made to H_2 and win with probability $1/q$. Otherwise, the output of $\mathcal{B}$ wins with advantage ϵ despite π being uniformly random, by a simple hybrid argument. Thus, the reduction can simply return one of the q queries to H_2 or the output of $\mathcal{B}$ to the SI-CDH challenger with equal probability. We then have that $\mathcal{B}$'s advantage against the CDH problem is at least:

$$\frac{1}{2q}\Pr[\text{found occurs}] + \frac{\epsilon}{2}\Pr[\text{found does not occur}]$$

$$\geq \min\left(\frac{1}{2q}, \frac{\epsilon}{2}\right).$$

which is non-negligible if ϵ is, since q is polynomially-sized.

B   Proof of Theorem 1

Proof Sketch. We briefly outline the proof methodology. The proof is similar to the one given by [CGCD+20], refitted to our Signal-adapted-CK model and using the Verifiable and Honest SI-CDH assumptions from Sect. 3.1 instead of the standard DDH oracle in the gap assumption. Cases E_2, E_3, and E_6 require IK_A and IK_B not to be revealed, so we use that as the basis for security in those cases. Similarly, cases E_1 and E_7 will use the fact that EK_A and IK_B are not revealed, and case E_5 relies on EK_A and SK_B not being revealed. Informally, the proof begins by forming a game in which the challenger guesses in advance which session will be tested, as well as the peer ID of that session. The challenger then simulates the game and inserts a VCDH or HCDH challenge into that predicted session, showing that an adversary winning the game can be used to successfully solve the respective hard problem. Once the cases are combined, this gives a proof of soundness of the SI-X3DH protocol.

Proof. It is clear that two parties following the protocol honestly will become partners. It is also clear that they will both successfully derive the same session key and enter an `accept` state, as an SIDH protocol has no failure probability if both parties are faithful. Thus the SI-X3DH protocol is *correct*.

To prove soundness, we will use a series of game hops. The proof will require splitting into cases following Table 2. Games 0 to 3 are common to all cases; we then break into a case-by-case proof. Without loss of generality, we assume participant A is the initiator and B is the responder—the test query is handled in the same way by the simulator regardless of whether it is called on the initiator or responder.

Game 0. This game equals the security experiment in Sect. 4.1. The advantage of the adversary in this game is Adv_0. All queries to the random oracles (H_1, H_2, KDF) are simulated in an on-the-fly manner, and a table of (query, result) pairs is stored.

Game 1. We ensure all honestly generated SIDH keys are unique, or in other words, that there are no key collisions. If a key is generated that collides with any previously generated key, the challenger aborts and the adversary loses the game. With at most n parties, S sessions per party, m medium-term (semi-static) keys per party, we have at most $n + nm + nS$ receiving (2^{e_1}-isogeny) keys, and at most $n + nS$ sending (3^{e_2}-isogeny) keys. A collision among these keys is an instance of the generalised birthday problem, which we now briefly recall.

If M is the size of the domain from which $N \leq M$ objects are uniformly drawn, the generalised birthday problem shows that the probability of a collision between two objects is

$$p(N; M) = 1 - \prod_{k=1}^{N-1} \left(1 - \frac{k}{M}\right). \tag{2}$$

So,
$$\mathsf{Adv}_0 \leq p(n + nm + nS; |\mathcal{K}_2|) + p(n + nS; |\mathcal{K}_3|) + \mathsf{Adv}_1.$$

To be explicit, the size of an ℓ^e-isogeny keyspace is

$$(\ell + 1) \cdot \ell^{e-1}, \tag{3}$$

so $|\mathcal{K}_2| = 3 \cdot 2^{e_1 - 1}$ and $|\mathcal{K}_3| = 4 \cdot 3^{e_2 - 1}$. Note that the difference between Adv_0 and Adv_1 is therefore negligible, since the numerator in the collision probability is polynomially-sized while the denominator is exponential.

Game 2. We guess in advance which session Π_u^i the adversary will call the Test query against, and abort if this guess is incorrect. Note that we abort with high probability—there is only a $1/nS$ chance of success—but the advantages still only differ by a polynomial factor.

$$\mathsf{Adv}_1 = nS\mathsf{Adv}_2.$$

Game 3. In this game, we guess in advance the index of the peer of the test session Π_u^i—we guess a $v \in \{1, \ldots, n\}$ and abort if $\Pi_u^i.\mathsf{peer\_id} \neq v$. The probability of guessing v correctly is $1/n$, so

$$\mathsf{Adv}_2 \leq n\mathsf{Adv}_3.$$

We now split into cases based on Table 2. The cases will be grouped by the approach we take to reduce each case to the VCDH and HCDH hard problems. Specifically, in each scenario, we consider which of the (three or four) SIDH exchanges is *not* compromised by any reveal queries (i.e., neither key involved is compromised), and embed the hard problem into that pair of keys. Firstly, we address the MEX events, where neither IK_A nor IK_B are revealed—cases E_2, E_3, and E_6. We then treat the KCI events, cases E_1 and E_7, where EK_A and IK_B remain unrevealed. Finally, we come to the wPFS event, E_5, in which the adversary does not reveal either EK_A or SK_B. We shall have, overall, that

$$\mathsf{Adv}_3 = \mathsf{Adv}_3^{2,3,6} + \mathsf{Adv}_3^{1,7} + \mathsf{Adv}_3^5.$$

B.1   Cases E_2, E_3, E_6 (MEX)

As mentioned above, the three cases E_2, E_3, and E_6 all rely on IK_A and IK_B not being revealed—the adversary should thus be unable to compute $\mathrm{SIDH}(\mathsf{IK}_A, \mathsf{IK}_B)$. This is the basis for the following part of the security proof.

Game 4. In this game, we abort if the adversary queries $\mathsf{dh}_1 = \mathrm{SIDH}(\mathsf{IK}_A, \mathsf{IK}_B)$ as the first component of a call to the KDF oracle. We call this event abort_4.

Whenever abort_4 occurs, we show that we can construct an algorithm $\mathcal{B}$ that can solve the Verifiable SI-CDH problem (VCDH) in Definition 2. As per that problem, $\mathcal{B}$ receives a triple $(K_1, K_2, \mathcal{O})$. $\mathcal{B}$ will simulate Game 3, except that it replaces IK_u with K_2 and IK_v with K_1. It is guaranteed by freshness that $\mathcal{B}$ will never have to output the corresponding (unknown) secret keys. However, these two keys may be used in other sessions, so $\mathcal{B}$ must be able to behave in a consistent manner even when these keys are involved. Specifically, there are only two cases in which $\mathcal{B}$ is unable to compute the session key:

1. A non-tested session between the same users u, v where u is the initiator and v is the responder.
2. A non-tested session between any user other than u, and v, where v is the responder.

In the first of these two cases, the simulator does not know $\mathrm{SIDH}(K_2, K_1)$, which is needed for two reasons: $\mathcal{B}$ needs it to compute the session key, but it is also the solution to the VCDH challenge. In the second case, the simulator does not know $\mathrm{SIDH}(\mathsf{EK}_E, K_1)$ for potentially malicious ephemeral key EK_E, whose secret key is unknown to $\mathcal{B}$. In all other situations, $\mathcal{B}$ will know at least one of the secret keys involved in each SIDH exchange because they were all generated by the challenger.

We begin with the first case. If a session key or ephemeral key reveal query is made on such a session, $\mathcal{B}$ returns a random key. $\mathcal{B}$ also maintains a list of these random keys it generated, and correspondingly the public keys which *should* have been used to compute each one. Then, to ensure that other KDF queries made are consistent with these replaced keys, we do the following on receipt of a query $\mathrm{KDF}(\mathsf{dh}_1 \| \mathsf{dh}_2 \| \mathsf{dh}_3)$: $\mathcal{B}$ will query $\mathcal{O}(\mathsf{dh}_1)$, and if 1 is returned, this is exactly the case where abort_4 occurs—then $\mathcal{B}$ can return dh_1 as the answer to the VCDH challenge. Otherwise, $\mathcal{B}$ samples a new random key to return as the KDF response, and updates its list accordingly.

In the second case, we involve the FO-proof π_E also sent as part of the key exchange—a proof of honest generation for EK_E. In such a session, $\mathcal{B}$ will check through the output table of queries $\mathcal{A}$ has made to oracle H_2 (which can only have polynomially-many entries). Let IK_w be the identity key of the initiator. For each pair of entries (h, h'), we check whether $H_1(\pi_E \oplus h \oplus h' \oplus H_2(\mathrm{SIDH}(\mathsf{IK}_w, K_1)))$ is the secret key of EK_E. The simulator can always compute $\mathrm{SIDH}(\mathsf{IK}_w, K_1)$ when $w \neq u$ because it knows the private key for IK_w. In order for π_E to be valid, it must have the form

$$\pi_E = s_E \oplus H_2(\mathrm{SIDH}(\mathsf{IK}_w, K_1)) \oplus H_2(\mathsf{dh}_2) \oplus H_2(\mathsf{dh}_3)$$

so the only way for the adversary to have honestly generated π_E is for it to have queried H_2 on inputs $\mathsf{dh}_2, \mathsf{dh}_3$. Therefore, searching through all pairs (h, h') of queries will always result in recovery of s_E if π_E is valid, and if no such pair exists, the receiver would reject the FO-proof and fail the exchange. If such a pair is found, we can use the computed secret key s_E to also compute $\mathrm{SIDH}(\mathsf{EK}_E, K_1)$. $\mathcal{B}$ can now use this j-invariant in a query to KDF to compute a consistent session key. Thus, $\mathsf{Adv}(\mathsf{abort}_4) = \mathsf{Adv}^{\mathrm{vcdh}}(\mathcal{B})$ and

$$\mathsf{Adv}_3^{2,3,6} \leq \mathsf{Adv}^{\mathrm{vcdh}}(\mathcal{B}) + \mathsf{Adv}_4.$$

Game 5. In this game, we replace the session key of the test session with a uniformly random key. Because Game 4 aborts whenever a KDF oracle query is made involving dh_1, we know in this game that the adversary never queried KDF to get the true session key. Hence, the advantage of winning this game is

$$\mathsf{Adv}_4 = \mathsf{Adv}_5 = 0.$$

Therefore, we have

$$\mathsf{Adv}_3^{2,3,6} \leq \mathsf{Adv}_{\mathrm{vcdh}}(\mathcal{B}).$$

B.2 Cases E_1, E_7

These two cases rely on EK_A and IK_B not being revealed. Then $\mathsf{dh}_2 = \mathrm{SIDH}(\mathsf{EK}_A, \mathsf{IK}_B)$ should be unknown to the adversary. The proof is very similar to the first cases above, but now relies on the Honest SI-CDH assumption from Definition 3. The main difference is that now, we must guess which of the signed semi-static keys will be used in the test session because we will need to modify the FO proof provided in the Honest SI-CDH assumption to get a correct FO proof for the SI-X3DH protocol.

Game 4'. In this game, the challenger guesses the index $j \in \{1, \ldots, m\}$, such that signed semi-static key SK_v^j is used in the test session, and aborts if this guess is wrong. Consequently,

$$\mathsf{Adv}_3^{1,7} \leq m\mathsf{Adv}_{4'}.$$

Game 5′ and 6′. In Game 5′, we abort if the adversary queries the KDF oracle with second component dh_2, equal to the test session's dh_2 component (derived from EK_u and IK_v). Once again, $\mathcal{B}$ will simulate Game 4′. After receiving an HCDH instance triple (K_1, K_2, π), $\mathcal{B}$ will replace the ephemeral key of the test session with K_2, and IK_v with K_1. $\mathcal{B}$ will then also replace the test session FO-proof with $\pi_T := \pi \oplus H_2(SIDH(K_2, SK_v^j)) \oplus H_2(SIDH(IK_u, K_1))$. Recall from the definition of the HCDH problem, that π already includes the component $H_2(SIDH(K_2, K_1))$, as required, so π_T has the correct form.

There are two cases in which $\mathcal{B}$ will not be able to compute valid session keys for non-tested sessions. The first is for a session where any user initiates with $EK_E \neq EK_u$, and v is the responder. This is because $SIDH(EK_E, K_1)$ is unknown when the secret key of EK_E is unknown. The second case is a special case of the first, when EK_u is reused in an exchange with v as the responder. As above, at least one secret key is known in all other situations, so these are the only two SIDH exchanges unable to be computed by $\mathcal{B}$.

In the first case, $\mathcal{B}$ will look up all pairs (h, h') in the polynomial-length output table of queries $\mathcal{A}$ has made to H_2. Suppose IK_w is the identity key of the initiator, and π_E is the FO-proof sent along with the ephemeral key EK_E. $\mathcal{B}$ will check whether $H_1(\pi_E \oplus h \oplus h' \oplus H_2(SIDH(IK_w, K_1)))$ is the secret key of EK_E. As above, $SIDH(IK_w, K_1)$ is known to $\mathcal{B}$ since the secret key of IK_w is. Also as above, the only way for the adversary to have generated a valid proof π_E is if they had made queries $H_2(dh_2)$ and $H_2(dh_3)$—otherwise, even if the adversary guessed the outputs of H_2 correctly (with negligible probability), they would not be able to verify that the π_E they created was actually correct without making the required queries to H_2 anyway. Hence, the only case the proof π_E is accepted is when a valid pair (h, h') exists in the query list of H_2, and if such a pair is found, we can use the secret key to compute the needed j-invariant $SIDH(EK_E, K_1)$. $\mathcal{B}$ can now use this j-invariant in a query to KDF to compute a consistent session key. If no pair is found, the receiver would reject the FO-proof and fail the exchange.

In the second case, we cannot compute the output of KDF because $dh_2 = SIDH(K_2, K_1)$ is unknown. So $\mathcal{B}$ will return a random key and keep a table for consistency as in the previous cases. Whenever the adversary makes a query to the KDF oracle, we check if $H_1(\pi \oplus H_2(dh_2))$ corresponds to the secret key of K_2, and if it does, $\mathcal{B}$ has learned dh_2 as the SI-CDH value of K_1 and K_2, this is also the case in which the game aborts. Note that the π used here is the one from the HCDH challenge, not from the exchange (π_E) or the test session (π_T). There is a negligible probability $1/2^n$ that the adversary guessed the correct output of H_2 without making a query of the form $H_2(dh_2)$ (leading to an abort without recovering the answer to the HCDH challenge).

Game 6′ is identical to Game 5 in the previous section. We therefore have

$$\text{Adv}_3^{1,7} \leq m(\text{Adv}^{\text{hcdh}}(\mathcal{B}) + 1/2^n).$$

B.3   Case E_5 (wPFS)

This case relies on EK_A and SK_B not being revealed (wPFS assumes that, in the future, these secrets are unrecoverable). Alternatively, this proof could be reduced to EK_A and EK_B which are both purely ephemeral. However, because EK_B is optional in the Signal protocol (to avoid key exhaustion DoS), we reduce to the former scenario. In this case, we must again guess which of the signed semi-static keys will be used in the test session.

Game 4''. In this game, the challenger guesses the index $j \in \{1, \ldots, m\}$, such that signed semi-static key SK_v^j is used in the test session. The game aborts if this guess is wrong. Hence,

$$\mathsf{Adv}_3^5 \leq n_m \mathsf{Adv}_{4''}.$$

Game 5'' and 6''. These proceed exactly as in Games 5' and 6' of cases E_1 and E_7 above, but with the HCDH challenge keys inserted into EK_u and SK_v^j. Furthermore, exactly as in the previous subsections, $\mathcal{B}$ knows the secret keys needed to compute the SIDH values of all exchanges except in two cases: an exchange with v as the responder using semi-static key SK_v^j (because EK_E is unknown and potentially maliciously chosen), and the specific subcase where $\mathsf{EK}_E = \mathsf{EK}_u$. This is essentially identical to cases E_1 and E_7. We conclude that

$$\mathsf{Adv}_3^5 \leq m(\mathsf{Adv}^{\mathrm{hcdh}}(\mathcal{B}) + 1/2^n).$$

Finally, bringing all the game hops and cases together, we have

$$
\begin{aligned}
\mathsf{Adv}_{n,m,S}^{\mathrm{kie}} \leq\ & p(n + nm + nS; |\mathcal{K}_2|) \\
& + p(n + nS; |\mathcal{K}_3|) \\
& + n^2 S \left[\mathsf{Adv}^{\mathrm{vcdh}} + 2m\mathsf{Adv}^{\mathrm{hcdh}} + m/2^{n-1} \right],
\end{aligned}
\tag{4}
$$

where n is the number of participants, m is the number of semi-static keys per participant, and S is the maximum number of sessions run per party.

Because the VCDH and HCDH problems are hard if the SI-CDH problem is (shown in Sect. 3.1), it directly follows that SI-X3DH is secure if the standard SI-CDH problem is hard.

B.4   Deniability Proof Sketch

We now briefly sketch a proof of the offline deniability of SI-X3DH, in an identical manner to [VGIK20]. Intuitively, for Bob to prove Alice's involvement, he would have to provide a Diffie–Hellman value $\mathrm{DH}(A, \cdot)$ which he could not possibly have generated himself—it must therefore have been generated by Alice. Because no DH values are exchanged between Alice and Bob in X3DH or SI-X3DH, and because the KDH, K2DH and/or EKDH assumptions hold, this is impossible. On top of this, because neither protocol uses a signature on session-specific information (unlike [HKKP21]), there is no loss of deniability there either. Proof of offline-deniability proceeds as an argument about simulatability, which we shall now sketch.

In the case of deniability for the initiator, given Alice's public key IK_A, the simulator Sim will generate $x \leftarrow \mathcal{K}_3$ and compute EK_A. Sim will then send this to Bob, who outputs keys $\mathsf{IK}_B, \mathsf{SK}_B, \mathsf{EK}_B$. The simulator can compute $\mathsf{dh}_2 = \mathrm{SIDH}(\mathsf{EK}_A, \mathsf{IK}_B)$, $\mathsf{dh}_3 = \mathrm{SIDH}(\mathsf{EK}_A, \mathsf{SK}_B)$, and $\mathsf{dh}_4 = \mathrm{SIDH}(\mathsf{EK}_A, \mathsf{EK}_B)$ because x is known, but cannot compute $\mathrm{SIDH}(\mathsf{IK}_A, \mathsf{IK}_B)$. Under the KDH-type assumptions, there must be an extractor $\hat{\mathcal{B}}$ for Bob's key IK_B—let us call it $\hat{\mathcal{B}}$. If $\hat{\mathcal{B}}$ outputs $\hat{Z}$ then the shared key is $\mathrm{KDF}(\hat{Z} \parallel \mathsf{dh}_2 \parallel \mathsf{dh}_3 \parallel \mathsf{dh}_4)$—the real shared key. On the other hand, if $\hat{\mathcal{B}}$ outputs $\bot$, then Sim chooses a session key at random. In either case, Sim also computes the FO-proof π using the session key it computed. In the second case, no PPT algorithm can compute $\mathrm{SIDH}(\mathsf{IK}_A, \mathsf{IK}_B)$ without knowing IK_B, so the random key is indistinguishable from the real key.

We come now to the case of deniability for the responder, given Bob's public key IK_B, and also a signed semi-static key $\mathsf{SK}_B, \mathrm{Sig}_B(\mathsf{SK}_B)$. The simulator will send these two public keys to Alice, who outputs a key EK_A. Under the KDH-type assumptions, there exists an extractor $\hat{\mathcal{A}}$ for Alice which will either output the required SIDH values needed to compute the real key or will fail to output, in which case a random key will be indistinguishable from the real one as above. Thus, either way, assuming the KDH, K2DH and EKDH assumptions hold in the SIDH setting (which we claim they do), our SI-X3DH protocol is offline-deniable.

C   Standard Key Indistinguishability Definitions

Let $\mathcal{K}$ denote the space of all possible session keys that could be derived in an exchange between two parties. We model n parties $P_1, \ldots, P_n$ through oracles Π_i^j, denoting the j-th session run by participant P_i. We limit the number of sessions per party by $1 \leq j \leq S$. Each oracle has access to the secret key of the corresponding party P_i's fixed long-term identity key IK_i, as well as the secrets for each of the m semi-static keys $\mathsf{SK}_i^1, \ldots, \mathsf{SK}_i^m$. Each oracle also has the following local variables:

- $\Pi_i^j.\mathsf{rand}$: The fixed randomness of oracle i for its j-th session (where Π_i^j is deterministic based on this randomness).
- $\Pi_i^j.\mathsf{role} \in \{\bot, \texttt{init}, \texttt{resp}\}$: The role of participant i in their j-th exchange.
- $\Pi_i^j.\mathsf{sk\_id}$: The index ℓ of the semi-static key SK_i^ℓ that participant i uses in their exchange j.
- $\Pi_i^j.\mathsf{peer\_id}$: The index k of the alleged peer P_k in the j-th exchange of oracle i.
- $\Pi_i^j.\mathsf{peer\_sk\_id}$: The index ℓ of the alleged peer's semi-static key $\mathsf{SK}_{\mathsf{peer\_id}}^\ell$ used in the exchange.
- $\Pi_i^j.\mathsf{sid}$: The session ID, explained further below.
- $\Pi_i^j.\mathsf{status} \in \{\bot, \texttt{accept}, \texttt{reject}\}$: Indicates whether the oracle has completed this session of the key exchange protocol and computed a session key from the exchange.
- $\Pi_i^j.\mathsf{session\_key} \in \mathcal{K}$: The computed session key.

These values are all initialised to $\perp$ at the start of the security experiment, except rand, which is initialised with random coins for each oracle. The oracle status is set to accept or reject on the computation of session_key.

The session ID is a feature of the security experiment, not the real protocol. We define the session ID to be a tuple $(\Pi, \mathsf{IK}_\mathcal{I}, \mathsf{IK}_\mathcal{R}, \mathsf{SK}_\mathcal{R}, \mathsf{EK}_\mathcal{I}, \overline{\mathsf{EK}_\mathcal{R}})$ where $\mathcal{I}, \mathcal{R}$ denote the initiator and responder respectively, Π is a protocol identifier, and $\mathsf{EK}_\mathcal{R}$ is optional (so may be null). We say two sessions with the same sid are *matching*. This is done to restrict the adversary from making queries against any session matching the test session for the game—to avoid trivialising security. For a session Π_i^j we also define a *partner* session to be any session Π_k^ℓ for which Π_i^j.peer_id $= k$ and Π_k^ℓ.peer_id $= i$, Π_i^j.role $\neq \Pi_k^\ell$.role, and Π_i^j.sid $= \Pi_k^\ell$.sid. We say any two such sessions are *partners*. Note that if two sessions are partners, they are also, by definition, matching.

Setup. The security game is played between challenger $\mathcal{C}$ and a probabilistic polynomial-time (PPT) adversary $\mathcal{A}$. $\mathcal{C}$ will generate identity keys for the n participants, $\mathsf{IK}_1, \ldots, \mathsf{IK}_n$, and for each participant i, generate m semi-static keys $\mathsf{SK}_i^1, \ldots, \mathsf{SK}_i^m$. $\mathcal{C}$ will finally choose a uniformly random secret bit $b \leftarrow \{0,1\}$, and provide $\mathcal{A}$ with access to the oracles Π_i^j.

Game. Adversary $\mathcal{A}$ can adaptively make the following queries in the game:

- **Send**(i,j,μ): Send an arbitrary message μ to oracle Π_i^j. The oracle will behave according to the key exchange protocol and update its status appropriately.
- **RevealIK**(i): Return the secret long-term key(s) of participant i. After this, participant i is *corrupted*. See Remark 2.
- **RevealSK**(i, ℓ): Return the ℓ-th secret semi-static key of participant i. After this, SK_i^ℓ is said to be *revealed*.
- **RevealEK**(i, j): Return the ephemeral key (i.e., the random coins) of the j-th session of participant i. After this, EK_i^j and Π_i^j.rand are said to be *revealed*.
- **RevealSessionKey**(i,j): Return Π_i^j.session_key. After this, session Π_i^j is said to be *revealed*.

Test. At some point in the game, $\mathcal{A}$ will issue a special **Test**(i,j) query exactly once. $\mathcal{C}$ will return K_b to the adversary, where $K_0 := \Pi_i^j$.session_key and $K_1 \leftarrow \mathcal{K}$ (a random key from the keyspace). After this query is made, session Π_i^j is said to be *tested*. $\mathcal{A}$ can continue to adaptively make queries to the above game functions after the Test query has been issued. Finally, $\mathcal{A}$ outputs a bit $b^* \in \{0,1\}$ as their guess. At this point, the tested session Π_i^j must be *fresh*. Freshness is defined in Definition 4, and the cases for freshness are also summarised in Table 2 for clarity. Let **fresh**(session) return true if session is fresh, and false otherwise.

Definition 5 (Security). *Let $\mathcal{A}$ be a PPT adversary. We define the advantage of $\mathcal{A}$ in winning the above key indistinguishability experiment kie with n parties, m semi-static keys per party, and S sessions per party, as*

$$\mathsf{Adv}_{n,m,S}^{\mathrm{kie}}(\mathcal{A}) = \left| \Pr\left[b = b^* \wedge \mathbf{fresh}(\text{test\_session}) \right] - \frac{1}{2} \right|.$$

An authenticated key exchange protocol Π is secure in the Signal-adapted-CK model if it is:

- **Correct:** *Any two parties following the protocol honestly derive the same* sid, session_key, *and both arrive at an* accept *state.*
- **Sound:** *The advantage of any PPT adversary* $\mathcal{A}$ *is* $\mathsf{Adv}^{\mathsf{kie}}_{n,m,S}(\mathcal{A}) \leq \mathsf{negl}$.

Remark 2. Note that, in SI-X3DH, each participant has two identity keys (a receiving key and a sending key). We assume both are revealed to the adversary when a **RevealIK** query is made.

References

[ACD19] Alwen, J., Coretti, S., Dodis, Y.: The double ratchet: security notions, proofs, and modularization for the Signal protocol. In: Ishai, Y., Rijmen, V. (eds.) EUROCRYPT 2019. LNCS, vol. 11476, pp. 129–158. Springer, Cham (2019). https://doi.org/10.1007/978-3-030-17653-2_5

[AJL17] Azarderakhsh, R., Jao, D., Leonardi, C.: Post-quantum static-static key agreement using multiple protocol instances. In: Adams, C., Camenisch, J. (eds.) SAC 2017. LNCS, vol. 10719, pp. 45–63. Springer, Cham (2018). https://doi.org/10.1007/978-3-319-72565-9_3

[BBC+21] Banegas, G., et al.: CTIDH: faster constant-time CSIDH. IACR Trans. Cryptogr. Hardw. Embed. Syst. **2021**(4), 351–387 (2021)

[BFG+20] Brendel, J., Fischlin, M., Günther, F., Janson, C., Stebila, D.: Towards post-quantum security for Signal's X3DH handshake. In: Dunkelman, O., Jacobson, Jr., M.J., O'Flynn, C. (eds.) SAC 2020. LNCS, vol. 12804, pp. 404–430. Springer, Cham (2021). https://doi.org/10.1007/978-3-030-81652-0_16

[BFG+22] Brendel, J., Fiedler, R., Günther, F., Janson, C., Stebila, D.: Post-quantum asynchronous deniable key exchange and the Signal handshake. In: Hanaoka, G., Shikata, J., Watanabe, Y. (eds.) PKC 2022. LNCS, vol. 13178, pp. 3–34. Springer, Cham (2022). https://doi.org/10.1007/978-3-030-97131-1_1

[BKP20] Beullens, W., Katsumata, S., Pintore, F.: Calamari and Falafl: logarithmic (linkable) ring signatures from isogenies and lattices. In: Moriai, S., Wang, H. (eds.) ASIACRYPT 2020. LNCS, vol. 12492, pp. 464–492. Springer, Cham (2020). https://doi.org/10.1007/978-3-030-64834-3_16

[BWJM97] Blake-Wilson, S., Johnson, D., Menezes, A.: Key agreement protocols and their security analysis. In: Darnell, M. (ed.) Cryptography and Coding 1997. LNCS, vol. 1355, pp. 30–45. Springer, Heidelberg (1997). https://doi.org/10.1007/BFb0024447

[CCH+19] Campagna, M., et al.: Supersingular isogeny key encapsulation (2019). https://sike.org/

[CD22] Castryck, W., Decru, T.: An efficient key recovery attack on SIDH (preliminary version). Cryptology ePrint Archive, Paper 2022/975 (2022). https://ia.cr/2022/975

[CGCD+20] Cohn-Gordon, K., Cremers, C., Dowling, B., Garratt, L., Stebila, D.: A formal security analysis of the Signal messaging protocol. J. Cryptol. **33**(4), 1914–1983 (2020)

[CK01]   Canetti, R., Krawczyk, H.: Analysis of key-exchange protocols and their use for building secure channels. In: Pfitzmann, B. (ed.) EUROCRYPT 2001. LNCS, vol. 2045, pp. 453–474. Springer, Heidelberg (2001). https://doi.org/10.1007/3-540-44987-6_28

[CLM+18] Castryck, W., Lange, T., Martindale, C., Panny, L., Renes, J.: CSIDH: an efficient post-quantum commutative group action. In: Peyrin, T., Galbraith, S. (eds.) ASIACRYPT 2018. LNCS, vol. 11274, pp. 395–427. Springer, Cham (2018). https://doi.org/10.1007/978-3-030-03332-3_15

[COR21] Cervantes-Vázquez, D., Ochoa-Jiménez, E., Rodríguez-Henríquez, F.: Extended supersingular isogeny Diffie-Hellman key exchange protocol: revenge of the SIDH. IET Inf. Secur. **15**(5), 364–374 (2021)

[DDGZ21] De Feo, L., Dobson, S., Galbraith, S.D., Zobernig, L.: SIDH proof of knowledge. Cryptology ePrint Archive, Paper 2021/1023 (2021). https://ia.cr/2021/1023

[DGL+20] Dobson, S., Galbraith, S.D., LeGrow, J., Ti, Y.B., Zobernig, L.: An adaptive attack on 2-SIDH. Int. J. Comput. Math. Comput. Syst. Theory **5**(4), 282–299 (2020)

[Dui19] Duits, I.: The post-quantum Signal protocol: secure chat in a quantum world. Master's thesis, University of Twente (2019). https://essay.utwente.nl/77239/

[Gal18] Galbraith, S.D.: Authenticated key exchange for SIDH. Cryptology ePrint Archive, Paper 2018/266 (2018). https://ia.cr/2018/266

[GPST16] Galbraith, S.D., Petit, C., Shani, B., Ti, Y.B.: On the security of supersingular isogeny cryptosystems. In: Cheon, J.H., Takagi, T. (eds.) ASIACRYPT 2016. LNCS, vol. 10031, pp. 63–91. Springer, Heidelberg (2016). https://doi.org/10.1007/978-3-662-53887-6_3

[HHK17] Hofheinz, D., Hövelmanns, K., Kiltz, E.: A modular analysis of the Fujisaki-Okamoto transformation. In: Kalai, Y., Reyzin, L. (eds.) TCC 2017. LNCS, vol. 10677, pp. 341–371. Springer, Cham (2017). https://doi.org/10.1007/978-3-319-70500-2_12

[HKKP21] Hashimoto, K., Katsumata, S., Kwiatkowski, K., Prest, T.: An efficient and generic construction for Signal's handshake (X3DH): post-quantum, state leakage secure, and deniable. In: Garay, J.A. (ed.) PKC 2021. LNCS, vol. 12711, pp. 410–440. Springer, Cham (2021). https://doi.org/10.1007/978-3-030-75248-4_15

[JD11]   Jao, D., De Feo, L.: Towards quantum-resistant cryptosystems from supersingular elliptic curve isogenies. In: Yang, B.-Y. (ed.) PQCrypto 2011. LNCS, vol. 7071, pp. 19–34. Springer, Heidelberg (2011). https://doi.org/10.1007/978-3-642-25405-5_2

[KLM+15] Kirkwood, D., Lackey, B.C., McVey, J., Motley, M., Solinas, J.A., Tuller, D.: Failure is not an option: standardization issues for post-quantum key agreement. In: Workshop on Cybersecurity in a Post-Quantum World (2015)

[MM22]   Maino, L., Martindale, C.: An attack on SIDH with arbitrary starting curve. Cryptology ePrint Archive, Paper 2022/1026 (2022). https://ia.cr/2022/1026

[MP16a] Marlinspike, M., Perrin, T.: The double ratchet algorithm (2016). https://signal.org/docs/specifications/doubleratchet/. Accessed 20 Nov 2016

[MP16b] Marlinspike, M., Perrin, T.: The X3DH key agreement protocol 2016. https://signal.org/docs/specifications/x3dh/. Accessed 04 Nov 2016

[Pei14] Peikert, C.: Lattice cryptography for the internet. In: Mosca, M. (ed.) PQCrypto 2014. LNCS, vol. 8772, pp. 197–219. Springer, Cham (2014). https://doi.org/10.1007/978-3-319-11659-4_12

[Per16] Perrin, T.: The XEdDSA and VXEdDSA signature schemes 2016. https://signal.org/docs/specifications/xeddsa/. Accessed 20 Oct 2016

[Rob22] Robert, D.: Breaking SIDH in polynomial time. Cryptology ePrint Archive, Paper 2022/1038 (2022). https://ia.cr/2022/1038

[STW12] Sun, X., Tian, H., Wang, Y.: Toward quantum-resistant strong designated verifier signature from isogenies. In: INCoS 2012, pp. 292–296. IEEE (2012)

[UG18] Unger, N., Goldberg, I.: Improved strongly deniable authenticated key exchanges for secure messaging. Proc. Priv. Enh. Technol. **2018**(1), 21–66 (2018)

[Vél71] Vélu, J.: Isogénies entre courbes elliptiques. C. R. Acad. Sci. Paris Sér. A-B **273**, A238–A241 (1971)

[VGIK20] Vatandas, N., Gennaro, R., Ithurburn, B., Krawczyk, H.: On the cryptographic deniability of the Signal protocol. In: Conti, M., Zhou, J., Casalicchio, E., Spognardi, A. (eds.) ACNS 2020. LNCS, vol. 12147, pp. 188–209. Springer, Cham (2020). https://doi.org/10.1007/978-3-030-57878-7_10

Lattice-Based Cryptography

Forward-Secure Revocable Secret Handshakes from Lattices

Zhiyuan An[1,2], Jing Pan[3], Yamin Wen[2,4], and Fangguo Zhang[1,2(⊠)]

[1] School of Computer Science and Engineering,
Sun Yat-sen University, Guangzhou 510006, China
anzhy@mail2.sysu.edu.cn, isszhfg@mail.sysu.edu.cn
[2] Guangdong Province Key Laboratory of Information Security Technology,
Guangzhou 510006, China
[3] State Key Laboratory of Integrated Service Networks, Xidian University,
Xi'an 710071, China
jinglap@aliyun.com
[4] School of Statistics and Mathematics, Guangdong University of Finance
and Economics, Guangzhou 510320, China
wenyamin@gdufe.edu.cn

Abstract. Secret handshake (SH), as a fundamental privacy-preserving primitive, allows members from the same organization to anonymously authenticate each other. Since its proposal by Balfanz et al., numerous constructions have been proposed, among which only the ones separately designed by Zhang et al. over coding and An et al. over lattice are secure against quantum attacks. However, none of known schemes consider the issue of key exposure, which is a common threat to cryptosystem implementations. To guarantee users' privacy against the key exposure attack, forward-secure mechanism is believed to be a promising countermeasure, where secret keys are periodically evolved in such a one-way manner that, past transactions of users are protected even if a break-in happens.

In this work we formalize the model of forward-secure secret handshake and present the first lattice-based instantiation, where ABB HIBE is applied to handle key evolution process through regarding time periods as hierarchies. In particular, dynamic revocability is captured by upgrading the static verifier-local revocation techniques into updatable ones. To achieve anonymous handshake with ease, we present a generic way of transforming zero-knowledge argument systems termed as Fiat-Shamir with abort, into mutual authentication protocols. Our scheme is proved secure under the Short Integer Solution (SIS) and Learning With Errors (LWE) assumptions in the random oracle model.

Keywords: Secret handshake · Lattice cryptography · Forward security · User revocation · Zero-knowledge

1 Introduction

SECRET HANDSHAKE, introduced by Balfanz et al. [7], is a fundamental anonymity primitive, where potential members form different groups and

J. H. Cheon and T. Johansson (Eds.): PQCrypto 2022, LNCS 13512, pp. 453–479, 2022.
https://doi.org/10.1007/978-3-031-17234-2_21

conduct an interactive protocol to authenticate each other. The mutual hand-shake is successful if and only if both parties belong to the same organization. Except for the affiliations, no extra information (including the identities) about the involved members will be leaked. Therefore, secret handshakes provide all-sided privacy-preserving property for enrolled members. To date, many practical applications of secret handshakes in social networks have been explored, such as online dating, mobile access [30] and e-healthcare [39], etc.

Unfortunately, most online infrastructures offering authentication interface run in the unprotected environment, where key exposure can be one of the most fatal damages as it thoroughly destroys the expected security [36]. Forward-secure mechanism [8,21], is a promising method to address the above problem, which preserves the validity of users' past actions. Its core design is a key evolving technique that proceeds as follows. The lifetime of the related scheme is divided into discrete periods. Upon each new period advancing, a subsequent secret key is evolved from the current one via a one-way key update algorithm. Then the current key is erased from the user's records. Due to the one-wayness of the evolving method, the security of past periods' keys is preserved after a break-in at some group member. By leveraging this technique, numerous cryptographic primitives supporting forward security have been constructed, such as digital signature [1,12,32] and public-key encryption [10,15].

Compared with the cases of ordinary signatures or authentication protocols, key exposure can be more damaging to SH systems. Once an adversary obtains the exposed credential of some legitimate user, it can impersonate that user to authenticate any others from the same group, such that a successful handshake no longer ensures a valid authentication. Besides, due to the anonymity of inter-actions, key exposure essentially undermines the whole group as it invalidates all previously completed handshakes within that group, regardless of who the par-ticipants were. Moreover, malicious users, who communicated with honest ones (after authenticating each other) and got their handshakes opened, may defend themselves by giving away their credentials over the Internet and claiming that some hacker conducted the behaviors. Albeit the potential threats of credentials being compromised, no previous SH schemes considered this issue, except the construction of Wen et al. [38], where users are provided with a series of random credentials corresponding to discrete time periods. However, this countermea-sure obviously brings huge storage cost and falls short of being succinct. On the other side, to conceptually explore the security against key exposure in SH, it would be better to first formalize the related generic model.

OUR CONTRIBUTIONS. This work exploits the field of forward-secure secret hand-shakes. Our contributions are summarized in the following.

- By carefully reforming the desired functionalities and security notations, we adapt the basic model of SH to the forward-secure setting.
- Under the above model, we present a lattice-based SH scheme. In particular,
  - We upgrade the static verifier-local revocation method into time-advanced updatable one, and prove that the iterative process works exactly in a zero-knowledge manner.

– We show how to transform a special type of zero-knowledge system into an anonymous mutual authentication protocol, in a generic manner.

OTHER RELATED WORKS. Following Balfanz et al.'s pioneering work [7], early SH constructions [17,22,43] employed one-time pseudonyms, which bears huge storage cost. One more efficient method is to apply reusable credentials. Xu and Yung [40] first designed a such scheme with weaker unlinkability. Ateniese et al. [6] proposed an efficient unlinkable secret handshake scheme in the standard model. Subsequently, Jarecki and Liu [23] proposed a framework for unlinkable secret handshake scheme that supports both traceability and revocation. From then on, various SH schemes offering different functionalities were proposed [20, 37,39]. However, these schemes are designed over number-theoretic assumptions and are vulnerable to quantum attacks. As all we know, only the ones separately proposed by Zhang et al. over coding theory [42] and An et al. [5] over lattice are secure against quantum computations.

Note that none of existing SH schemes has formally considered the issue of key exposure, let alone propose available schemes over post-quantum candidates.

ORGANIZATION. In Sect. 2, we recall some necessary background and techniques. Model and security requirements of forward-secure secret handshakes are provided in Sect. 3. Section 4 describes the supporting zero-knowledge argument system, which is further modified to support mutual authentication in a handshake. In Sect. 5, we present our lattice-based secret handshake scheme, followed by the analysis of efficiency and security.

2   Preliminaries

Vectors will be denoted in bold lower-case letters and matrices will be denoted in bold upper-case letters. Let $\|\cdot\|$ and $\|\cdot\|_\infty$ denote the Euclidean norm (ℓ_2) and infinity norm (ℓ_∞), respectively. The Euclidean norm of matrix $\mathbf{B} \in \mathbb{R}^{m \times n}$ with columns $(\mathbf{b}_i)_{i \le n}$ is denoted by $\|\mathbf{B}\| = \max_{i \le n} \|\mathbf{b}_i\|$. If $\mathbf{B}$ is full column-rank, let $\widetilde{\mathbf{B}}$ denote its Gram-Schmidt orthogonalization. The concatenation of matrices $\mathbf{A} \in \mathbb{R}^{n \times m}$ and $\mathbf{B} \in \mathbb{R}^{n \times k}$ is denoted by $[\mathbf{A}|\mathbf{B}]$. For positive integer n, let $[n]$ denote the set $\{1, \ldots, n\}$. If S is a finite set, denote by $U(S)$ the uniform distribution over S and by $x \hookleftarrow D$ sampling x according to the distribution D.

2.1   Background on Lattices

Classic Lattices and Gaussian Distribution. Let $n, m, q \in \mathbb{Z}^+$ with $q > 2$. For $\mathbf{A} \in \mathbb{Z}_q^{n \times m}$, define two lattices as $\Lambda^\perp(\mathbf{A}) = \{\mathbf{x} \in \mathbb{Z}^m \mid \mathbf{A} \cdot \mathbf{x} = \mathbf{0} \mod q\}$ and $\Lambda^\mathbf{u}(\mathbf{A}) = \{\mathbf{x} \in \mathbb{Z}^m \mid \mathbf{A} \cdot \mathbf{x} = \mathbf{u} \mod q\}$. For a real $\sigma > 0$, a vector $\mathbf{c} \in \mathbb{R}^n$ and n-dimensional lattice L, define the function $\rho_{\sigma,\mathbf{c}}(\mathbf{x}) = \exp(-\pi \|\mathbf{x} - \mathbf{c}\|^2 / \sigma^2)$. The discrete Gaussian distribution over L with parameter σ and center $\mathbf{c}$ is defined as $D_{L,\sigma,\mathbf{c}}(\mathbf{x}) = \frac{\rho_{\sigma,\mathbf{c}}(\mathbf{x})}{\rho_{\sigma,\mathbf{c}}(L)}$ (write $D_{L,\sigma}(\mathbf{x})$ for short when $\mathbf{c} = 0$).

Lemma 1 ([19,29]). *Given integers n, $q \geq 2$, and $\sigma \geq \omega(\sqrt{\log n})$. we have $\Pr_{\mathbf{x} \hookleftarrow D_{\mathbb{Z}^n, \sigma}}[\|\mathbf{x}\|_\infty \geq \sigma \cdot \log n]$ is negligible.*

Lattice Algorithms. The following facts describe the algorithms for trapdoor generation, Gaussian sampling, lattice basis randomization and delegations.

Lemma 2 ([4]). *Given integers $n > 0$, $m = O(n \log n)$, $q \geq 2$, this PPT algorithm $\mathsf{TrapGen}(n, m, q)$ returns a matrix pair $(\mathbf{A}, \mathbf{T_A})$ satisfies that i) $\mathbf{A} \in \mathbb{Z}_q^{n \times m}$ is within negligible statistical distance from uniform. ii) $\mathbf{T_A}$ is a basis of $\Lambda^\perp(\mathbf{A})$ and $\|\widetilde{\mathbf{T_A}}\| \leq \mathcal{O}(\sqrt{n \log q})$.*

Lemma 3 ([19]). *Given matrices $\mathbf{A} \in \mathbb{Z}^{n \times m}$, $\mathbf{T_A} \in \mathbb{Z}^{m \times m}$ as a basis of $\Lambda^\perp(\mathbf{A})$, vector $\mathbf{u} \in \mathbb{Z}_q^n$ and gaussian parameter $\sigma \geq \omega(\sqrt{\log n}) \cdot \|\widetilde{\mathbf{T_A}}\|$, this PPT algorithm $\mathsf{SamplePre}(\mathbf{A}, \mathbf{T_A}, \mathbf{u}, \sigma)$ returns a vector $\mathbf{v} \in \Lambda^\mathbf{u}(\mathbf{A})$ sampled from a distribution statistically close to $D_{\Lambda^\mathbf{u}(\mathbf{A}), \sigma}$.*

Lemma 4 ([16]). *Given matrix $\mathbf{T_A}$ be a basis of lattice $\Lambda^\perp(\mathbf{A})$ and gaussian parameter $\sigma \geq \|\widetilde{\mathbf{T_A}}\| \cdot \omega\sqrt{\log n}$, this PPT algorithm $\mathsf{RandBasis}(\mathbf{T_A}, \sigma)$ outputs a new a basis $\mathbf{T'_A}$ of $\Lambda^\perp(\mathbf{A})$ such that $\|\mathbf{T'_A}\| \leq \sigma \cdot \sqrt{m}$ and the distribution of $\mathbf{T'_A}$ does not depend on $\mathbf{T_A}$ up to a statistical distance.*

Besides, the following depicts that lattice basis can be efficiently delegated and simulated, which will be used in the user key update and security proof.

Lemma 5 ([2,16]). *Set $\sigma_R = \sqrt{n \log q} \cdot \omega(\sqrt{\log m})$, let $\mathcal{D}_{m \times m}$ denote the distribution of matrices in $\mathbb{Z}^{m \times m}$ defined as $(D_{\mathbb{Z}^m, \sigma_R})^m$ conditioned on the sampled matrix being "$\mathbb{Z}_q$-invertible". Given matrices $\mathbf{A} \in \mathbb{Z}^{n \times m}$, $\mathbf{T_A} \in \mathbb{Z}^{m \times m}$ as a basis of $\Lambda^\perp(\mathbf{A})$, $\mathbf{R} \in \mathbb{Z}_q^{m \times m}$ as a product of ℓ matrices sampled from $\mathcal{D}_{m \times m}$. Then:*

1. *Let $\mathbf{A'} \in \mathbb{Z}^{n \times m'}$ be any matrix containing $\mathbf{A}$ as a submatrix. This deterministic polynomial-time algorithm $\mathsf{ExtBasis}(\mathbf{T_A}, \mathbf{A'})$ outputs a basis $\mathbf{T_{A'}}$ of $\Lambda^\perp(\mathbf{A'})$ with $\|\widetilde{\mathbf{T_{A'}}}\| = \|\widetilde{\mathbf{T_A}}\|$.*
2. *This PPT algorithm $\mathsf{SampleR}(1^m)$ outputs a matrix $\mathbf{R} \in \mathbb{Z}^{m \times m}$ from a distribution that is statistically close to $\mathcal{D}_{m \times m}$.*
3. *Let Gaussian parameter $\sigma \geq \|\widetilde{\mathbf{T_A}}\| \cdot (\sigma_R \sqrt{m} \omega(\log^{1/2} m))^\ell \cdot \omega(\log m)$. This PPT algorithm $\mathsf{BasisDel}(\mathbf{A}, \mathbf{R}, \mathbf{T_A}, \sigma)$ outputs a basis $\mathbf{T_B}$ of $\Lambda^\perp(\mathbf{A R^{-1}})$ distributed statistically close to the distribution $\mathsf{RandBasis}(\mathbf{T}, \sigma)$, where $\mathbf{T}$ is an arbitrary basis of $\Lambda^\perp(\mathbf{A R^{-1}})$ satisfying $\|\widetilde{\mathbf{T}}\| < \sigma/\omega(\sqrt{\log m})$.*
4. *This PPT algorithm $\mathsf{SampleRwithBasis}(\mathbf{A})$ outputs a matrix $\mathbf{R}$ sampled from a distribution statistically close to $\mathcal{D}_{m \times m}$ and a basis $\mathbf{T_B}$ of $\Lambda^\perp(\mathbf{A R^{-1}})$ having $\|\widetilde{\mathbf{T_B}}\| \leq \sigma_R/\omega(\sqrt{\log m})$.*

Computational Lattice Problems. We recall the definitions and hardness results of SIS, ISIS and LWE, on which the security of our scheme provably relies.

Definition 1 ([3,19]). *Given parameters m, q, β the functions of n, uniformly random vector $\mathbf{u} \in \mathbb{Z}_q^n$ and matrix $\mathbf{A} \in \mathbb{Z}_q^{n \times m}$, $\mathsf{SIS}_{n,m,q,\beta}$ (resp., $\mathsf{ISIS}_{n,m,q,\beta}$) demands to find a non-zero vector $\mathbf{x} \in \Lambda^{\perp}(\mathbf{A})$ (resp., $\Lambda^{\mathbf{u}}(\mathbf{A})$) such that $\|\mathbf{x}\| \leq \beta$.*

For any $q \geq \beta \cdot \omega(\sqrt{n \log n})$, hardness of $\mathsf{SIS}_{n,m,q,\beta}$ and $\mathsf{ISIS}_{n,m,q,\beta}$ is given by a worst-case to average-case reduction from SIVP_{γ} for some $\gamma = \beta \cdot \widetilde{\mathcal{O}}(\sqrt{nm})$.

Definition 2 ([35]). *Let $n, m \geq 1, q \geq 2$, and Let χ be a probability distribution over $\mathbb{Z}$. For $\mathbf{s} \in \mathbb{Z}_q^n$, let $A_{\mathbf{s}, \chi}$ be the distribution obtained by sampling $\mathbf{a} \xleftarrow{\$} \mathbb{Z}_q^n$ and $e \hookleftarrow \chi$, and outputting the pair $(\mathbf{a}, \mathbf{a}^{\top} \cdot \mathbf{s} + e) \in \mathbb{Z}_q^n \times \mathbb{Z}_q$. Decision-$\mathsf{LWE}_{n,q,\chi}$ problem is to distinguish m samples from $A_{\mathbf{s}, \chi}$ (let $\mathbf{s} \leftarrow U(\mathbb{Z}_q^n)$) and m samples chosen according to the uniform distribution over $\mathbb{Z}_q^n \times \mathbb{Z}_q$. Search-$\mathsf{LWE}_{n,q,\chi}$ problem is to find the uniformly random $\mathbf{s}$ given m samples from $A_{\mathbf{s}, \chi}$.*

For prime power q, $\beta \geq \sqrt{n} \mathcal{O}(\log n)$, $\gamma = \widetilde{\mathcal{O}}(nq/\beta)$, and a β-bounded distribution χ, *decision*-$\mathsf{LWE}_{n,q,\chi}$ problem is as least as hard as SIVP_{γ}. Also, *decision*-LWE is proved to be equivalent to *search*-LWE up to some polynomial increase of the sample number m (see [33]). In this work, for a discrete Gaussian distribution χ (i.e., $\chi = D_{\mathbb{Z}^m, \sigma}$), we write *decision*-$\mathsf{LWE}_{n,q,\chi}$ as $\mathsf{LWE}_{n,q,\sigma}$ for short.

2.2 Efficient Signature Scheme from Lattices

Libert *et al.* in [24] proposed a signature scheme (extended from the Böhl *et al.*'s signature [9]) with efficient protocols, of which a variant will serve for the joining phase in our scheme. The scheme utilizes the following parameters: security parameter λ; integers $\ell = \mathsf{poly}(\lambda)$, $n = \mathcal{O}(\lambda)$, $q = \widetilde{\mathcal{O}}(n^4)$ and $m = 2n\lceil \log q \rceil$; Gaussian parameter $\sigma = \Omega(\sqrt{n \log q})$; public key $\mathsf{pk} := (\mathbf{G}, \mathbf{G}_0, \mathbf{G}_1, \mathbf{D}, \mathbf{D}_0, \mathbf{D}_1, \mathbf{u})$ and private key $\mathsf{sk} := \mathbf{T}_{\mathbf{G}}$, where $(\mathbf{G}, \mathbf{T}_{\mathbf{G}}) \leftarrow \mathsf{TrapGen}(n, m, q)$, $\mathbf{D} \hookleftarrow U(\mathbb{Z}_q^{n \times m/2})$, $\mathbf{G}_i, \mathbf{D}_i \hookleftarrow U(\mathbb{Z}_q^{n \times m})$ for $i \in \{0, 1\}$ and $\mathbf{u} \hookleftarrow U(\mathbb{Z}_q^n)$.

To make a signature on $\mathbf{m} \in \{0,1\}^m$, one first chooses $i \hookleftarrow [2^{\ell}]$ and builds the encoding matrix $\mathbf{G}_i = [\mathbf{G}|\mathbf{G}_0 + i\mathbf{G}_1]$ with its delegated basis $\mathbf{T}_i$, then computes the chameleon hash of $\mathbf{m}$ as $\mathbf{c}_M = \mathbf{D}_0 \cdot \mathbf{r} + \mathbf{D}_1 \cdot \mathbf{m}$ with vector $\mathbf{r} \hookleftarrow D_{\mathbb{Z}^m, \sigma}$, which is used to define $\mathbf{u}_M = \mathbf{u} + \mathbf{D} \cdot \mathsf{vdec}_{n,q-1}(\mathbf{c}_M)$. The resulted signature is $sig = (i, \mathbf{d}, \mathbf{r})$ where $\mathbf{d} \in \mathbb{Z}_q^{2m}$ is a short vector in $D_{\Lambda^{\mathbf{u}_M}(\mathbf{G}_i), \sigma}$. The verification step is conducted via checking if $\mathbf{G}_i \cdot \mathbf{d} = \mathbf{u} + \mathbf{D} \cdot \mathsf{vdec}_{n,q-1}(\mathbf{D}_0 \cdot \mathbf{r} + \mathbf{D}_1 \cdot \mathbf{m})$, $\|\mathbf{d}\| < \sigma\sqrt{2m}$ and $\|\mathbf{r}\| < \sigma\sqrt{m}$. It was proved in [24] that the signature above is secure under chosen-message attacks under the SIS assumption.

2.3 Zero-Knowledge Argument Systems

In a zero-knowledge argument of knowledge (ZKAoK) system [13], a prover proves the possession of some witness for an NP relation to a verifier, without revealing any additional information. Generally, a secure ZKAoK must satisfy 3 requirements: *completeness, proof of knowledge* and *(honest verifier) zero knowledge.*

Yang et al. [41] have proposed an efficient lattice-based ZKAoK for relation:

$$\mathcal{R} = \{(M, y, \mathcal{L}), (x) : M \cdot x = y \wedge \forall (i, j, k) \in \mathcal{L}, x[i] = x[j] \cdot x[k]\},$$

where $x \in \mathbb{Z}_q^n$ is the secret witness and set $\mathcal{L}$ defines quadratic constraints over x. The protocol can be further transformed into an NIZKAoK consisting of two algorithms Prove and Verify via Fiat-Shamir heuristic. Prove produces commitments $cmt = (cmt_s, cmt_r)$, a challenge $ch = \mathcal{G}(cmt, \cdot)$ where $\mathcal{G}$ is a random oracle, and some responses rsp related to ch and cmt. Then (cmt_s, ch, rsp) is sent to a verifier, on input which Verify recovers reserved commitment cmt_r and computes ch' by assembling cmt, it finally checks $ch' \stackrel{?}{=} ch$ to verify the ZK proof. In this paper, we will adapt the NIZKAoK to an anonymous mutual authentication protocol.

Theorem 1. *The scheme described in Fig. 2 of [41] is a secure NIZKAoK with negligible completeness and soundness error, under the hardness assumptions of SIS and LWE, and has well-designed simulator and knowledge extractor.*

2.4 LWE-Based Key Exchange

Derived from the design in [18,34] describes an LWE-based key exchange using reconciliation mechanism, which yields keys indistinguishable from random. Let χ be a probability distribution over $\mathbb{Z}_q$, integer θ be the number of bits for key extraction and K is a public matrix. The following protocol is utilized to produce a communication key in our scheme.

- *Alice* samples a secret matrix $S_a \hookleftarrow \chi(\mathbb{Z}_q^{n \times m})$ and a small noise $E_a \hookleftarrow \chi(\mathbb{Z}_q^{n \times m})$. Then, she computes $C_a = K \cdot S_a + E_a$ and sends it to *Bob*.
- Receiving C_a, *Bob* chooses his secret matrix $S_b \hookleftarrow \chi(\mathbb{Z}_q^{m \times n})$ and computes $C_b = K \cdot S_b + E_b$, where $E_b \hookleftarrow \chi(\mathbb{Z}_q^{m \times n})$. Then he samples a noise $E_b' \hookleftarrow \chi(\mathbb{Z}_q^{m \times m})$ and sets $V_b = S_b \cdot C_a + E_b'$. Such that he extracts the shared secret key $K_b = \mathsf{Extract}(V_b)$, namely, $K_b[i, j] = \mathrm{round}((2^\theta/q_1) \cdot V_b[i, j])$ mod 2^θ.. *Bob* also produces a check matrix $M = \mathsf{Check}(V_b)$ as $M[i, j] = \mathrm{floor}((2^{\theta+1}/q_1) \cdot V_b[i, j])$ mod 2. Finally, *Bob* sends (C_b, M) to Alice.
- With (C_b, M), *Alice* computes $V_a = C_b \cdot S_a$ and obtains $K_a = \mathsf{Recon}(V_a, M)$ via $K_a[i, j] = \mathrm{round}((2^\theta/q_1) \cdot V_a[i, j] + \frac{1}{4} \cdot (2M[i, j] - 1))$ mod 2^θ.

Theorem 2. ([18]). *The key exchange above produces the same shared key, i.e., $K_a = K_b$, with overwhelming probability via applying suitable parameters.*

3 Model of Forward-Secure Secret Handshakes

As its analogues of group signature [26,32], we consider SH schemes having lifetime divided into discrete time periods, at the beginning of which group members autonomously update the secret keys for forward security. Let time period $t = 0$ be the moment that an SH system is activated, and assume that a handshake always finishes during the period at which it starts. The syntax of forward secure secret handshake (FSSH) is formalized as follows.

- Setup. Given a security parameter $\lambda \in \mathbb{N}$, this algorithm, possibly run by a trusted party or decentralized setting, generates public parameter par.
- CreateGroup. Given par, group authority (GA) invokes this algorithm to create a group. It publishes the group public key gpk and retains secret key gsk.
- AddMember. This protocol is run between a potential user U and GA to enroll the user into a chosen group. At time period t, U generates individual key pair $(\mathsf{upk}, \mathsf{usk}_t)$ and sends upk to GA. If it terminates successfully, GA issues a group credential cred_0 (including a unique group identity ID) to U and adds cred_0 to user's registration table Reg.
- Update$_U$. On input user's private pair $(\mathsf{cred}_{t-1}, \mathsf{usk}_{t-1})$ at the beginning of time period t, this one-way algorithm evolves it into $(\mathsf{cred}_t, \mathsf{usk}_t)$.
- Handshake. This is a mutual authentication protocol between two participants (A, B). It outputs 1 and produces a session key for both active parties at the current time period t if and only if they belong to the same group.
- TraceMember. Given a handshake transcript, GA runs this algorithm to trace the involved users, or outputs $\perp$ to indicate a failure.
- RemoveMember. This algorithm is invoked by GA to revoke an active member. GA also publishes some updated group information of that group for current time period, such that users can conduct revocation check.

Based on the considerations in [7, 26], we reform the security requirements an FSSH must satisfy as *Completeness, Forward impersonator resistance, Detector resistance* and *Backward unlinkability*, all of which are defined via the corresponding experiments. Hereafter we use CU and CG to denote the corruption list of users and groups, respectively.

Completeness demands that Handshake outputs 1 with overwhelming probability if both participants are active with updated secret keys and belong to the same group. Moreover, TraceMember can always identify the involved users. For plain description, we define an auxiliary polynomial-time algorithm IsActive(ID, t) : outputs 1 if ID is active at current time period t and 0 otherwise.

Definition 3. *The completeness is achieved if the following experiment returns 1 with negligible probability.*
  Experiment: $\mathbf{Exp}_{\mathcal{A}}^{\mathsf{COM}}(\lambda)$

---

par $\leftarrow$ Setup(λ), (gpk, gsk) $\leftarrow$ CreateGroup(par).
$\{(\mathsf{ID}_0, \mathsf{cred}_{0\|\bar{t}}, \mathsf{usk}_{0\|\bar{t}}), (\mathsf{ID}_1, \mathsf{cred}_{1\|\bar{t}}, \mathsf{usk}_{1\|\bar{t}})\} \leftarrow$ AddMember(gpk, gsk, $\bar{t}$)
IsActive(ID_b, t) = 1 $\wedge$ $\mathsf{usk}_{b\|t} \leftarrow$ Update$_U$($\mathsf{cred}_b, \mathsf{usk}_{b\|t-1}$) for $b \in \{0, 1\}$.
  If Handshake($\mathsf{ID}_0, \mathsf{ID}_1, t$) = 0 with transcript T or TraceMember(T) $\notin$ $\{\mathsf{ID}_0, \mathsf{ID}_1\}$,
  then return 1 else retun 0.

Forward impersonator resistance requires that it is infeasible for any PPT adversary $\mathcal{A}$ to impersonate an uncorrupted user, or some corrupted user at the period preceding the one where she was broken into, even if it can corrupt all the users and groups (except the chosen group) via accessing the following oracles.
  Below are oracles that entitle $\mathcal{A}$ to obtain exterior information of an FSSH.

- KeyP(par) simulates to create a new group and returns gpk to $\mathcal{A}$.
- HS(U, V) simulates a two-party handshake by generating the transcripts during the interaction.
- Trace(T) returns the participant of transcript T. Hereafter we require that T is not generated from the challenging oracles.
- Remove(U) simulates to revoke user U from her G, it also updates the corresponding group information at current period t.

The other oracles below enable $\mathcal{A}$ to break into the internal of an FSSH.

- CorU(U, G) is a user corruption oracle. It returns user's cred and usk of U in group G to $\mathcal{A}$ at period t, then it adds (ID_U, G, t) to CU.
- AddU(U, G) enrolls a user U whose key pair is chosen by $\mathcal{A}$ to G at period t. It also adds (ID_U, G, t) to CU. Compared with CorU, AddU endows $\mathcal{A}$ with more power to create dummy users or perform injection attacks.
- KeyG(par) returns msk of some group G to $\mathcal{A}$ and adds G to CG, meaning that G is under the control of $\mathcal{A}$.

Now we describe the challenge game of *forward impersonator resistance*.

- Chal$^{\text{F-IR}}$(ID, G, t) simulates ID of group G and executes a handshake with $\mathcal{A}$ using the updated secret key of ID at period t. It returns 1 if the protocol outputs 1 and 0 otherwise.

Hereafter we denote the transcript of $\mathcal{A}$ during the challenge game as T.

Definition 4. *Forward impersonator resistance is achieved if, for any $\mathcal{A}$, the following experiment returns 1 with negligible probability.*
Experiment: $\mathbf{Exp}_{\mathcal{A}}^{\text{F-IR}}(\lambda)$

---

par $\leftarrow$ Setup(λ), CG, CU := $\emptyset$.
(ID^*, G^*, t^*) $\leftarrow \mathcal{A}^{\text{KeyP,HS,Trace,Remove,CorU,AddU,KeyG}(\neg G^*)}$(par).
If Chal$^{F\text{-}IR}$(ID^*, G^*, t^*) = 0, return 0. Else if for $ID' \leftarrow$ TraceMember(T) :
($ID', \cdot, \cdot$) $\notin$ CU or $t^* < t$ for ($ID', \cdot, t$) $\in$ CU, return 1. Else return 0.

Detector resistance makes sure that $\mathcal{A}$ cannot succeed when he activates a handshake with an honest and active user to identify her affiliation at the chosen time period, even if it can corrupt all the users and groups (except the chosen group). The related challenge game is described as follows.

- Chal$_b^{\text{DR}}$(ID, G, t) chooses a random bit $b \in \{0,1\}$. For $b = 0$, it simulates ID from G to handshake with $\mathcal{A}$. For $b = 1$, it simulates an arbitrary (active) user ID_r to handshake with $\mathcal{A}$. Then $\mathcal{A}$ guesses the value of b as b^*.

Definition 5. *Detector resistance is achieved if, for any $\mathcal{A}$, the absolute difference of probability of outputting 1 between $\mathbf{Exp}_{\mathcal{A}}^{\text{DR}-1}$ and $\mathbf{Exp}_{\mathcal{A}}^{\text{DR}-0}$ is negligible.*

Experiment: $\mathbf{Exp}_{\mathcal{A}}^{DR-b}(\lambda)$

---

par $\leftarrow$ Setup(λ), CG, CU $:= \emptyset$.
$(ID^*, G^*, t^*) \leftarrow \mathcal{A}^{\mathsf{KeyP,HS,Trace,Remove,CorU,AddU,KeyG}(\neg G^*)}(\mathsf{par})$, $\mathsf{Chal}_b^{DR}(ID^*, G^*, t^*)$,
holding that for $ID' \leftarrow$ TraceMember(T), $(ID', \cdot, \cdot) \notin$ CU or IsActive$(ID', t^*) = 0$.
Return $b^* \leftarrow \mathcal{A}^{\mathsf{KeyP,HS,Trace,Remove,CorU,AddU,KeyG}(\neg G^*)}(\mathsf{par})$.

Backward Unlinkability ensures that no adversary can distinguish whether two handshakes (executed during two distinct periods) involve the same honest user, even if it can corrupt any user and any group (except the chosen pair), and that user is later revoked. Below is the related challenge game.

- $\mathsf{Chal}_b^{B\text{-}Unlink}(ID_0, G_0, ID_1, G_1, t)$ first picks a random bit $b \in \{0,1\}$, then it successively simulates ID_0 and ID_b to handshake with $\mathcal{A}$ using evolved secret. Finally $\mathcal{A}$ guesses the value of b as b^*.

Definition 6. *Backward unlinkability is achieved if, for any $\mathcal{A}$, the absolute difference of probability of outputting 1 between $\mathbf{Exp}_{\mathcal{A}}^{B\text{-}Unlink-1}$ and $\mathbf{Exp}_{\mathcal{A}}^{B\text{-}Unlink-0}$ is negligible.*
Experiment: $\mathbf{Exp}_{\mathcal{A}}^{B\text{-}Unlink-b}(\lambda)$

---

par $\leftarrow$ Setup(λ), CoG, CoU $:= \emptyset$.
$(ID_0, G_0, ID_1, G_1, t) \leftarrow \mathcal{A}^{\mathsf{KeyP,HS,Trace,Remove,CorU,AddU,KeyG}(\neg G^*)}(\mathsf{par})$,
holding that $G_i \notin$ CG $\wedge$ $(ID_i, G_i, \cdot) \notin$ CU for $i \in \{0,1\}$.
$b^* \leftarrow \mathcal{A}^{\mathsf{Chal}_b^{B\text{-}Unlink}(ID_0, G_0, ID_1, G_1, t)}(\mathsf{par})$. Return b^*.

Note that if $\mathcal{A}$ has corrupted some user of G_i for $i \in \{0,1\}$, then he is only allowed to choose target users within that group, i.e., $G_0 = G_1$.

4   The Supporting Zero-Knowledge Layer

In this section, we first construct a system that allows obtaining ZKAoK for some relations, which are linear equations within users' credential and secret key of our FSSH scheme. Then we clarify why ZK argument cannot be directly used in a handshake procedure, for this reason we further present a generic way of transforming ZK systems termed as Fiat-Shamir with abort into mutual authentication protocols, where participants can "handshake" with each other and negotiate a session key.

Below we extensively use the decomposition techniques in [24,27]. Namely, for any integer $\beta > 0$, let $\delta_\beta = \lceil \log(\beta+1) \rceil$ and $\beta_j = \lfloor \frac{\beta+2^{j-1}}{2^j} \rfloor \forall j \in [1, \delta_\beta]$. Then any $i \in [0, \beta]$ can be decomposed as $i = \mathbf{h}_\beta \cdot \mathsf{idec}_\beta(i)$, where $\mathbf{h}_\beta = (\beta_1, \ldots, \beta_{\delta_\beta})$ and idec_β is a binary function. Further, [25] build two more functions for decomposing vectors and matrices: $\mathsf{vdec}_{m,\beta} : [0, \beta]^m \to \{0,1\}^{m\delta_\beta}$; $\mathsf{mdec}_{n,m,q} : \mathbb{Z}_q^{m \times n} \to \{0,1\}^{nm\delta_{q-1}}$. (see [25] or the full version of this paper for detailed definitions.)

4.1   ZKAoK System for Proving a Valid User

Now we describe the system that produces ZK arguments for users' secret. Given the same situation as that of Handshake in Sect. 5 with extra setting: $\mathbf{H}_{m,\beta} = \mathbf{I}_m \otimes \mathbf{h}_\beta$, $t_i = t_{add} + i$ for $i \in [t^*]$, $\mathbf{h}_N = (N_1, \ldots, N_\ell)$, $\mathbf{a}' = (\mathbf{a}_1'^\top \ldots \mathbf{a}_n'^\top)^\top = \mathsf{mdec}_{n,m,q}(\mathbf{A}^\top)$, $\mathbf{b} = \mathsf{vdec}_{2n,q-1}(\mathbf{h})$, $\mathbf{w} = (\mathbf{w}_1^\top \ldots \mathbf{w}_n^\top)^\top = \mathsf{mdec}_{n,m,q}(\mathbf{A}_t^\top)$ and $\mathbf{z} = \mathsf{vdec}_{n,q-1}(\mathbf{D}_0 \cdot \mathbf{r} + \mathbf{D}_1 \cdot \mathbf{b})$, the desired system is summarized as follows.

Public Input: Matrices $\mathbf{G}, \mathbf{G}_0, \mathbf{G}_1, \mathbf{D}, \mathbf{D}_0, \mathbf{D}_1, \mathbf{B}, \mathbf{P}, \mathbf{W}$; Vectors $\mathbf{u}, \mathbf{t}, \mathbf{w}, \mathbf{k}$; Integer t^*. System public parameter par.

Prover's Witness: Vectors and Matrices which satisfy the following constraints

$$\begin{cases} \mathsf{ID} = \mathbf{i} \in \{0,1\}^\ell, \mathsf{urt}_t = \mathbf{q} \in \mathbb{Z}_q^n, \mathbf{d} = (\mathbf{d}_1^\top \ \mathbf{d}_2^\top)^\top \in \{-\beta, \beta\}^{2m}, \\ \mathbf{r} \in \{-\beta, \beta\}^m, \mathbf{a}' \in \{0,1\}^{nmk}, \mathbf{b} \in \{0,1\}^{2nk}, \mathbf{v} \in \{-\beta_d, \beta_d\}^m, \\ \mathbf{e} \in \{-B, B\}^m, \mathbf{s} \in \{-B, B\}^n, \mathbf{e}_1 \in \{-B, B\}^m, \mathbf{e}_2 \in \{-B, B\}^\ell, \\ \mathbf{A} = [\mathbf{a}_1 | \ldots | \mathbf{a}_n] \in \mathbb{Z}_q^{n \times m}, \mathbf{A}_t^\top = [\mathbf{a}_{t,1} | \ldots | \mathbf{a}_{t,n}] \in \mathbb{Z}_q^{m \times n}. \end{cases} \quad (1)$$

Prover's Goal: Convince the verifier in zero-knowledge that the following set of modular linear equations holds[1] (under the same modulus q):

$$\begin{cases} \mathbf{F} \cdot \mathbf{a} - \mathbf{H}_{2n,q-1} \cdot \mathbf{b} = \mathbf{0}, \\ \mathbf{D}_0 \cdot \mathbf{r} + \mathbf{D}_1 \cdot \mathbf{b} - \mathbf{H}_{n,q-1} \cdot \mathbf{z} = \mathbf{0}, \\ [\mathbf{G}|\mathbf{G}_0|N_1\mathbf{G}_1| \ldots |N_\ell\mathbf{G}_1] \cdot (\mathbf{d}_1, \mathbf{d}_2, \mathbf{i}[1]\mathbf{d}_2, \ldots, \mathbf{i}[\ell]\mathbf{d}_2)^\top - \mathbf{D} \cdot \mathbf{z} = \mathbf{u}, \\ \mathbf{A} \, (\mathbf{R}_1^{\mathbf{t}[1]})^{-1} \, (\mathbf{R}_2^{\mathbf{t}[2]})^{-1} \ldots (\mathbf{R}_d^{\mathbf{t}[d]})^{-1} - \mathbf{A}_t = \mathbf{0}, \\ \mathbf{A}_t \cdot \mathbf{v} = \mathbf{u}, \\ \mathbf{a}_1 - \mathbf{H}_{n,q-1} \cdot \mathbf{q}' = \mathbf{0}, \\ \mathbf{Q}_1 \cdot \mathbf{q}' + \mathbf{Q}_2 \cdot t_{add} - \mathbf{q}_0 = \mathbf{0}, \quad \mathbf{q}_{t^*} = \mathbf{q}, \\ \forall i \in [t^*] : (\mathbf{q}_{i-1} - \mathbf{H}_{n,q-1} \cdot \mathbf{q}'_{i-1}, \mathbf{Q}_1 \cdot \mathbf{q}'_{i-1} + \mathbf{Q}_2 \cdot t_i - \mathbf{q}_i) = (\mathbf{0},\mathbf{0}), \\ \mathbf{W} \cdot \mathbf{q} + \mathbf{e} = \mathbf{w}, \\ \mathbf{B}^\top \cdot \mathbf{s} + \mathbf{e}_1 = \mathbf{c}_1, \\ \mathbf{P}^\top \cdot \mathbf{s} + \mathbf{e}_2 + \lfloor \frac{q}{2} \rfloor \cdot \mathbf{i} = \mathbf{c}_2. \end{cases} \quad (2)$$

Since Set 2 is somewhat complicated, we first design two sub-systems: Π_1 arguing that user's credential is issued via making a signature on her public key, and her secret key is updated rightly with time advances.; Π_2 evidencing that 1) her updatable revocation token is rightly derived from the public key and embedded in an LWE function; 2) her identity is correctly encrypted with ciphertexts $(\mathbf{c}_1, \mathbf{c}_2)$. Then we establish Π_{hs} by combining Π_1 and Π_2.

Build System Π_1. This system covers the first five equations of Set 2. Our goal is to integrate these linear equations into a uniform relation

$$\mathcal{R}_1 = \{(\mathbf{M}_1, \mathbf{y}_1, \mathcal{L}_1), (\mathbf{x}_1) : \mathbf{M}_1 \cdot \mathbf{x}_1 = \mathbf{y}_1 \wedge \mathbf{x}_1 \in \mathsf{cons}_1\}.$$

Let $\boldsymbol{\beta} = (\beta \ldots \beta)^\top, \boldsymbol{\beta}_d = (\beta_d \ldots \beta_d)^\top \in \mathbb{Z}_q^m$. First perform the following steps.

---

[1] We refer readers to Sect. 5 for more information of these equations.

1. Set $\mathbf{r}' = \mathbf{r} + \beta \in [0, 2\beta]^m$, $\mathbf{d}_j'^\top = \mathbf{d}_j + \beta \in [0, 2\beta]^m$ for each $j \in \{1, 2\}$ and $\mathbf{v}' = \mathbf{v} + \beta_d \in [0, 2\beta_d]^m$. Decompose $\mathbf{r}', \mathbf{d}_j', \mathbf{v}'$ such that $\mathbf{r}' = \mathbf{H}_{m,2\beta} \cdot \mathbf{r}''$, $\mathbf{d}_j' = \mathbf{H}_{m,2\beta} \cdot \mathbf{d}_j''$ for $j \in \{1, 2\}$ and $\mathbf{v}' = \mathbf{H}_{m,2\beta_d} \cdot \mathbf{v}''$, respectively.

2. Set matrices $\mathbf{G}' = \mathbf{G} \cdot \mathbf{H}_{m,2\beta}$, $\mathbf{G}_0' = \mathbf{G}_0 \cdot \mathbf{H}_{m,2\beta}$, $\mathbf{D}_0' = \mathbf{D}_0 \cdot \mathbf{H}_{m,2\beta}$ and $\mathbf{G}_j' = N_j \mathbf{G}_1 \cdot \mathbf{H}_{m,2\beta}$ for each $j \in [\ell]$. Assemble auxiliary matrices $\mathbf{G}_j'' = -N_j \mathbf{G}_1 \cdot \beta$ for each $j \in [\ell]$, and vectors $\mathbf{u}' = \mathbf{u} + (\mathbf{G} + \mathbf{G}_0) \cdot \beta$, $\mathbf{u}_1 = \mathbf{D} \cdot \beta$.

3. Denote $[\mathbf{G}'|\mathbf{G}_0'|\mathbf{G}_1'|\ldots|\mathbf{G}_\ell']$ and $[\mathbf{G}_1''|\ldots|\mathbf{G}_\ell'']$ as $\bar{\mathbf{G}}'$ and $\bar{\mathbf{G}}''$, respectively.

4. Denote transpose of product $(\mathbf{R}_1^{t[d]})^{-1} \ldots (\mathbf{R}_d^{t[1]})^{-1}$ as $\mathbf{R}^{(t)}$. Define $\mathbf{N} = \mathbf{R}^{(t)} \cdot \mathbf{H}_{m,q-1}$, and build the extension matrix $\mathbf{L}_1 = \mathbf{I}_m \otimes \mathbf{N}$, $\mathbf{L}_2 = \mathbf{I}_n \otimes \mathbf{1}^m$.

5. Let $\mathbf{c} = (\mathbf{a}_{t,1}[1]\mathbf{v}[1] \ldots \mathbf{a}_{t,1}[m]\mathbf{v}[m] \ldots \mathbf{a}_{t,n}[1]\mathbf{v}[1] \ldots \mathbf{a}_{t,n}[m]\mathbf{v}[m]) \in \mathbf{Z}_q^{mn}$.

Through the above settings, we can change the target part of Set 2 into:

$$\begin{cases} \mathbf{F} \cdot \mathbf{a} - \mathbf{H}_{2n,q-1} \cdot \mathbf{b} = 0, \\ \mathbf{D}_0' \cdot \mathbf{r}'' + \mathbf{D}_1 \cdot \mathbf{b} - \mathbf{H}_{n,q-1} \cdot \mathbf{z} = \mathbf{u}_1, \\ \bar{\mathbf{G}}' \cdot (\mathbf{d}_1'', \mathbf{d}_2'', \mathbf{i}[1]\mathbf{d}_2'', \ldots, \mathbf{i}[\ell]\mathbf{d}_2'')^\top + \bar{\mathbf{G}}'' \cdot \mathbf{i} - \mathbf{D} \cdot \mathbf{z} = \mathbf{u}', \\ \mathbf{L}_1 \cdot [\mathbf{a}_1'|\ldots|\mathbf{a}_n'] - [\mathbf{a}_{t,1}|\ldots|\mathbf{a}_{t,n}] = 0, \\ (\mathbf{a}_{t,1}^\top \mathbf{v} \ldots \mathbf{a}_{t,n}^\top \mathbf{v})^\top = \mathbf{u}, \\ \mathbf{H}_{m,2\beta_d} \cdot \mathbf{v}'' - \mathbf{v} - \beta_d = 0. \end{cases} \quad (3)$$

After the above preparations, we can obtain the desired variables as follows:

1. Denote $-\mathbf{H}_{n,q-1}$, $-\mathbf{H}_{2n,q-1}$ and $\mathbf{H}_{m,2\beta_d}$ by $\mathbf{H}_1$, $\mathbf{H}_2$ and $\mathbf{H}_3$, respectively. Build the public matrix $\mathbf{M}_1$ and vector $\mathbf{y}_1$ as

$$\left(\begin{array}{ccccccccccccccc} \mathbf{F} & \mathbf{H}_2 & 0 & 0 & 0 & 0 & 0 & 0 & \ldots & 0 & 0 & 0 & 0 & 0 \\ 0 & \mathbf{D}_1 & \mathbf{D}_0' & \mathbf{H}_1 & 0 & 0 & 0 & 0 & \ldots & 0 & 0 & 0 & 0 & 0 \\ 0 & 0 & 0 & -\mathbf{D} & \bar{\mathbf{G}}'' & \mathbf{G}' & \mathbf{G}_0' & \mathbf{G}_1' & \ldots & \mathbf{G}_\ell' & 0 & 0 & 0 & 0 \\ \mathbf{L}_1 & 0 & 0 & 0 & 0 & 0 & 0 & 0 & \ldots & 0 & \mathbf{I}_{nm} & 0 & 0 & 0 \\ 0 & 0 & 0 & 0 & 0 & 0 & 0 & 0 & \ldots & 0 & 0 & \mathbf{L}_2 & 0 & 0 \\ 0 & 0 & 0 & 0 & 0 & 0 & 0 & 0 & \ldots & 0 & 0 & 0 & \mathbf{H}_3 & -\mathbf{I}_m \end{array} \right), \left(\begin{array}{c} 0 \\ \mathbf{u}_1 \\ \mathbf{u}' \\ 0 \\ \mathbf{u} \\ \beta_d \end{array} \right).$$

2. The private witness $\mathbf{x}$ can be build as

$$(\mathbf{a}'^\top \; \mathbf{b}^\top \; \mathbf{r}''^\top \; \mathbf{z}^\top \; \mathbf{i}^\top \; \mathbf{d}_1''^\top \; \mathbf{d}_2''^\top \; \mathbf{i}[1]\mathbf{d}_2''^\top \ldots \mathbf{i}[\ell]\mathbf{d}_2''^\top \; \mathbf{a}_{t,1}^\top \ldots \mathbf{a}_{t,n}^\top \; \mathbf{c}^\top \; \mathbf{v}''^\top \; \mathbf{v}^\top)^\top.$$

3. Then set $\mathsf{cons}_1 = \mathcal{L}_{1,1} \cup \mathcal{L}_{1,2} \cup \mathcal{L}_{1,3}$ where

$$\begin{cases} \mathcal{L}_{1,1} = \{(i,i,i)\}, \; i \in [1, (m+3)nk + \ell + 3m\delta_{2\beta}]; \\ \mathcal{L}_{1,2} = \{((m+3)nk + \ell + (3m+\ell)\delta_{2\beta} + mn + (u-1)m + v, \\ \qquad (m+3)nk + \ell + (3m+\ell)\delta_{2\beta} + (u-1)m + v, \\ \qquad (m+3)nk + \ell + (3m+\ell)\delta_{2\beta} + 2mn + 2m\delta_{\beta_d} + v)\}, \\ \qquad u \in [n], v \in [m]; \\ \mathcal{L}_{1,3} = \{(i,i,i)\}, \; i \in [(m+3)nk + \ell + (3m+\ell)\delta_{2\beta} + 2mn + 1, \\ \qquad (m+3)nk + \ell + (3m+\ell)\delta_{2\beta} + 2mn + 2m\delta_{\beta_d}], \end{cases}$$

where $\mathcal{L}_{1,1}$ indicates that $\mathbf{a}', \mathbf{b}, \mathbf{r}'', \mathbf{z}, \mathbf{i}, \mathbf{d}_1''$ and $\mathbf{d}_2''$ are all binary vectors, $\mathcal{L}_{1,2}$ ensures that $\mathbf{c}[(u-1)m+v] = \mathbf{a}_{t,u}[v] \cdot \mathbf{v}[v]$ for $(u,v) \in [n] \times [m]$, and $\mathcal{L}_{1,3}$ ensures that $\mathbf{v}''$ is binary.

Build System Π_2. This system also covers the rest part by a unified relation

$$\mathcal{R}_2 = \{(\mathbf{M}_2, \mathbf{y}_2, \mathcal{L}_2), (\mathbf{x}_2) : \mathbf{M}_2 \cdot \mathbf{x}_2 = \mathbf{y}_2 \wedge \mathbf{x}_2 \in \mathsf{cons}_2\},$$

which evidences the correct embedding of user's revocation token and identity. The concrete construction of Π_2 is much like that of Π_1 and we also take some preprocessing.

1. Let $\mathbf{b}_1 = (B \ \dots \ B)^\top \in \mathbf{Z}_q^m$, $\mathbf{b}_2 = (B \ \dots \ B)^\top \in \mathbf{Z}_q^n$ and $\mathbf{b}_3 = (B \ \dots \ B)^\top \in \mathbf{Z}_q^\ell$.
2. Set $\mathbf{e}' = \mathbf{e} + \mathbf{b}_1$, $\mathbf{s}' = \mathbf{s} + \mathbf{b}_2$, $\mathbf{e}_1' = \mathbf{e}_1 + \mathbf{b}_1$ and $\mathbf{e}_2' = \mathbf{e}_2 + \mathbf{b}_3$. Decompose them via functions vdec and mdec to get vectors $\mathbf{e}'', \mathbf{s}'', \mathbf{e}_1'', \mathbf{e}_2''$.
3. Compute time-binding vectors $\mathbf{t}_0' = \mathbf{Q}_2 \cdot \mathbf{t}_{add}$ and $\mathbf{t}_i' = \mathbf{Q}_2 \cdot \mathbf{t}_i$ for $i \in [t^*]$, set $\mathbf{t}' = (\mathbf{t}_0'^\top \ \mathbf{t}_1'^\top \ \dots \ \mathbf{t}_{t^*}'^\top)^\top$. Assemble quasi-diagonal matrices $\mathbf{L}_3$ and $\mathbf{L}_4$ as

$$\mathbf{L}_3 = \begin{pmatrix} -\mathbf{H}_1 & & \\ & \ddots & \\ & & -\mathbf{H}_1 \end{pmatrix}, \quad \mathbf{L}_4 = \begin{pmatrix} -\mathbf{Q}_1 & & \\ & \ddots & \\ & & -\mathbf{Q}_1 \end{pmatrix} \in \mathbb{Z}^{(t^*+1)n \times (t^*+1)(nk)}.$$

4. Set $\mathbf{B}' = \mathbf{B}^\top \cdot \mathbf{H}_{n,2B}$, $\mathbf{P}' = \mathbf{P}^\top \cdot \mathbf{H}_{n,2B}$, $\mathbf{I}' = \lfloor \frac{q}{2} \rfloor \cdot \mathbf{I}_\ell$, $\mathbf{w}' = \mathbf{w} + \mathbf{b}_1$, $\mathbf{c}_1' = \mathbf{c}_1 + \mathbf{b}_1 + \mathbf{B}^\top \cdot \mathbf{b}_2$ and $\mathbf{c}_2' = \mathbf{c}_2 + \mathbf{b}_3 + \mathbf{B}^\top \cdot \mathbf{b}_2$.

Use $\mathbf{H}_4$ and $\mathbf{H}_5$ to denote $\mathbf{H}_{m,2B}$ and $\mathbf{H}_{\ell,2B}$, respectively. Then we can construct the target variables as follows:

1. Build the public matrix $\mathbf{M}_2$ and vector $\mathbf{y}_2$ as

$$\begin{pmatrix} [\mathbf{I}_{(t^*+1)n}|\mathbf{0}] & \mathbf{L}_3 & \mathbf{0} & \mathbf{0} & \mathbf{0} & \mathbf{0} & \mathbf{0} \\ [\mathbf{0}|\mathbf{I}_{(t^*+1)n}] & \mathbf{L}_4 & \mathbf{0} & \mathbf{0} & \mathbf{0} & \mathbf{0} & \mathbf{0} \\ [\mathbf{0} \ \dots \ \mathbf{W}] & \mathbf{0} & \mathbf{H}_4 & \mathbf{0} & \mathbf{0} & \mathbf{0} & \mathbf{0} \\ \mathbf{0} \ \dots \ \mathbf{0} & \mathbf{0} & \mathbf{0} & \mathbf{B}' & \mathbf{H}_4 & \mathbf{0} & \mathbf{0} \\ \mathbf{0} \ \dots \ \mathbf{0} & \mathbf{0} & \mathbf{0} & \mathbf{P}' & \mathbf{0} & \mathbf{H}_5 & \mathbf{I}' \end{pmatrix}, \begin{pmatrix} \mathbf{0} \\ \mathbf{t}' \\ \mathbf{w}' \\ \mathbf{c}_1' \\ \mathbf{c}_2' \end{pmatrix}.$$

2. Set $\mathbf{x}_2 = (\mathbf{a}_1^\top \ \mathbf{q}_0^\top \ \dots \ \mathbf{q}_{t^*}^\top \ \mathbf{q}'^\top \ \mathbf{q}_0'^\top \ \dots \ \mathbf{q}_{t^*-1}'^\top \ \mathbf{e}''^\top \ \mathbf{s}''^\top \ \mathbf{e}_1''^\top \ \mathbf{e}_2''^\top \ \mathbf{i})^\top$, which has length $\mathfrak{n}_2 = (t^*+2)n + (t^*+1)nk + (2m+n+\ell)\delta_{2B} + \ell$.
3. The constraints over $\mathbf{x}_2$ is $\mathsf{cons}_2 = \{(i,i,i)\}$, $i \in [(t^*+2)n+1, (t^*+2)n+(t^*+1)nk+(2m+n+\ell)\delta_{2B}+\ell]$, indicating that $\mathbf{q}', \mathbf{q}_0', \dots, \mathbf{q}_{t^*-1}', \mathbf{e}'', \mathbf{s}'', \mathbf{e}_1'', \mathbf{e}_2''$ and $\mathbf{i}$ are all binary.

Build System Π_{hs}. We obtain the desired system Π_{hs} by instantiating the framework in Sect. 2.3 with Π_1 and Π_2. Namely, for the final relation

$$\mathcal{R}_{hs} = \{(\mathbf{M}, \mathbf{y}, \mathcal{L}), (\mathbf{x}) : \mathbf{M} \cdot \mathbf{x} = \mathbf{y} \wedge \mathbf{x} \in \mathsf{cons}\},$$

set $\mathbf{M} = \begin{pmatrix} \mathbf{M}_1 & \mathbf{0} \\ \mathbf{0} & \mathbf{M}_2 \end{pmatrix}$, $\mathbf{x} = \begin{pmatrix} \mathbf{x}_1 \\ \mathbf{x}_2 \end{pmatrix}$, $\mathbf{y} = \begin{pmatrix} \mathbf{y}_1 \\ \mathbf{y}_2 \end{pmatrix}$ and $\mathsf{cons} = \mathsf{cons}_1 \cup \mathsf{cons}_2' \cup \mathsf{cons}_3'$,
where cons_2' is simply performing right shift in cons_2 by the size of $\mathbf{x}_1$, and
$\mathsf{cons}_3' = (i, j, j)$ ensures that vector i in two sub-systems is the same one.

4.2 Transformation to Anonymous Mutual Authentication

Although users in our FSSH scheme can invoke $\varPi_{hs}$ to obtain ZK proof for their
group secrets, they cannot directly send the proof in Handshake. The reason is
that the other participant receiving that proof can unilaterally verify its validity,
so as to verify the legality of the sender without any further interactions, which
obviously violates the demand for mutual authentication.

To fill the gap, below we show how to adapt the Fiat-Shamir-type framework
[41], by transforming one-side identification into mutual authentication.

- Prove_{hs} : On input public parameter and secret witness, produce commitments $cmt = (cmt_s, cmt_r)$ and $ch = \mathcal{G}(cmt, \cdot)$ the same as the original algorithm. Then additionally compute a mixed challenge $\widetilde{ch} = ch \oplus \mathbf{C}$ where $\mathbf{C}$ is interim matrix in a KE, and generate rsp using $(cmt, \widetilde{ch})$. Finally output $\pi = (cmt_s, \widetilde{ch}, rsp)$.

- Verify_{hs} : Recover cmt_r via rsp and $\widetilde{ch}$ as Verify does, then get the original challenge $ch' = \mathcal{G}(cmt, \cdot)$ by assembling $cmt = (cmt_s, cmt_r)$, so as to retrieve the hidden message $\mathbf{C} = ch' \oplus \widetilde{ch}$.

Here the key point is that a receiver can no longer check the validity of the
proof by checking $ch' \overset{?}{=} ch$, since he only receives $\widetilde{ch}$. On the other side, a KE
element can be recovered to negotiate a communication key for both participants, whose hash value is further dispatched to conduct authentication. This
strategy can be seen as a generic way of transforming ZK systems termed as Fiat-
Shamir with abort into anonymous mutual authentication, for which a concrete
instantiation is detailed in Handshake of our main scheme.

5 FSSH with Revocability from Lattices

In this section, by devising updatable VLR method and adaptively applying the
building blocks recalled in Sect. 2, we present the first FSSH with revocability
from lattice. To clarify the roadmap on how to make all things work, below we
first give some key points of our construction.

When enrolling in a group, potential user first samples her initial public/secret key pair $(\mathbf{A}, \mathbf{T})$ via Trapdoor and sends $\mathbf{A}$ to GA, on which GA produces
an unforgeable signature [24] as her credential. Since users retain the secret keys,
even a malicious GA can not frame a legal user. To enable periodical key updating, we combine the binary-tree representation technique and ABB HIBE [2].
Namely, each node of the tree is assigned a short-norm invertible matrix $\mathbf{R}_i^b$ for
$i \in [d]$ and $b \in \{0, 1\}$, and successive periods are associated with leaves of the

binary tree in the LTR order. At the joining period $\mathbf{t} = (\mathbf{t}[1], \ldots, \mathbf{t}[d])$, users extract the corresponding key (trapdoor) $\mathbf{T}_t$ at this leaf for $\mathbf{A}(\mathbf{R}_d^{\mathbf{t}[d]} \ldots \mathbf{R}_1^{\mathbf{t}[1]})^{-1}$ by use of BasisDel. Observe that users can generate possible trapdoors of any leaves from the root key $\mathbf{T}$. Thus, one trivial method of key update is to precompute all possible $\mathbf{T}_t$ and then delete the previous one upon new period advancing. However, as noted in [28], this will bring key size undesirable dependency on T. Considering the level structure of a binary-tree, it suffices to only record the keys for sub-set $\mathsf{Evolve}_{(t \to T-1)}$ [12,26], which contains exactly one ancestor of each leaf between $[t, T-1]$ and has size at most $\log T$. Under this setting, users can update usk_t into usk_{t+1} (consisting of trapdoors for elements in $\mathsf{Evolve}_{(t+1 \to T-1)}$), by repeatedly invoking BasisDel within $\mathsf{Evolve}_{(t \to T-1)}$.

Now we demonstrate how to achieve revocability by applying VLR mechanism [11], where a revocation token urt is issued to a user and will be published when she is revoked. Similar to the case of key exposure, it is worthwhile to protect user's anonymity of previous behaviors even if her token is revealed (known as backward unlinkability [31]). We tackle this problem by subtly devising an updatable VLR algorithm: $\mathsf{urt}_t = \mathbf{Q} \cdot (\mathsf{vdec}(\mathsf{urt}_{t-1}), \mathbf{t})^\top \in \mathbb{Z}_q^n$. Choosing uniformly random $\mathbf{Q}$, this equation is linked to an ISIS instance, so as to achieve one-wayness of updating. Besides, we embed the time tag into the token to enable synchronous revocation check, such that expired tokens cannot be reused. Finally, to bind urt_t to user's secret, we set the initial token as $\mathbf{Q} \cdot (\mathsf{vdec}(\mathbf{a}_0), \mathbf{t})^\top$, where $\mathbf{a}_0$ is the first column of $\mathbf{A}$. When executing a handshake, users need to demonstrate in zero-knowledge the possession of a valid secret. This task is done by reducing the overall linear relations set to system Π_{hs} designed in Sect. 4.1. In particular, to argue the current urt_t and usk_t are correctly derived from the previous ones and are compatible with each other, we unify a time-advancing chain of iterative equations into a universal matrix-vector formula, which can be seen as a generic way of proving updatable VLR in zero-knowledge.

Finally, by combining the modified ZK system in Sect. 4.2 with a KE protocol [18], we obtain the desired algorithm Handshake, where participants can anonymously authenticate each other and negotiate a session key.

5.1 Description of the Scheme

As in [12,26,28], we imagine a binary tree of depth $d = \log T$ where the root has tag ϵ. For a node at depth $\leq d$ with tag w, its left and right children have tags $w0$ and $w1$, respectively. Lifetime of our scheme is divided into $T = 2^d$ discrete periods, such that successive periods $t \in [T]$ are associated with leaves of the binary tree in the LTR order. To derive keys from previous periods, let $\mathsf{Evolve}_{(t \to T-1)}$ be the set containing exactly one ancestor of each leaf or the leaf itself between period t and $T-1$. This set can be determined by function sibling in [12] or algorithm NodeSelect in [26]. Our FSSH scheme is described as follows.

- Setup. Given a security parameter $\lambda \in \mathbb{N}$, this algorithm specifies the following:
    - Maximum member size of a group $N = 2^\ell$, time period bound $T = 2^d$.

- Integer $n = \mathcal{O}(\lambda)$, prime modulus $q = \tilde{\mathcal{O}}(n^2) > T$, $k = \lceil \log q \rceil$ and dimension $m = 2nk, \overline{m} = nk$. B-bounded distribution χ over $\mathbb{Z}$ with $B = \sqrt{n}\omega(\log n)$.
- Discrete Gaussian distribution $D_{\mathbb{Z},\sigma}$ with parameter $\sigma = \Omega(\sqrt{n \log q} \log n)$. Let $\beta = \lceil \sigma \cdot \log n \rceil$ be the upper bound of samples from $D_{\mathbb{Z},\sigma}$.
- Guassian parameters $\overline{\sigma}_i = m^{\frac{3}{2}i+\frac{1}{2}} \cdot \omega(\log^{2k} n)$ for $i \in [d]$, and $\sigma_d = \overline{\sigma}_d \sqrt{m}\omega(\sqrt{\log m})$. Integer bound $\beta_d = \lceil \sigma_d \cdot \log n \rceil$.
- Uniformly random vector $\mathbf{u}_0 \in \mathbb{Z}_q^n$ and matrices $\mathbf{R}_i^b \leftarrow \mathsf{SampleR}(1^m)$ for all $i \in [d]$ and $b \in \{0,1\}$, $\mathbf{Q} = [\mathbf{Q}_1|\mathbf{Q}_2] \in \mathbb{Z}_q^{n \times (nk+d)}$, $\mathbf{F} \in \mathbb{Z}_q^{2n \times nmk}$, $\mathbf{K} \in \mathbb{Z}_{q_1}^{n_1 \times n_1}$.
- Matrix dimensions $n_1 = \mathsf{poly}(\lambda), m_1 = \mathcal{O}(n_1)$, integer modulus $q_1 = 2^{\mathcal{O}(n_3)}$, and integer $\theta \geq \frac{2\lambda}{n_1 m_1}$ for session key exchange.
- Discrete Gaussian distribution χ_1 over $\mathbb{Z}$ with deviation $\sigma_1 > \sqrt{\frac{2n_1}{\pi}}$.
- Injective mapping $F : \mathbb{Z}_{q_1}^{n_1 \times m_1} \rightarrow [-p,p]^t$ and its inverse F^{-1}, where p, t are defined in [41]. Random oracle $\mathcal{H}_0 : \{0,1\}^* \rightarrow \mathbb{Z}_q^{m \times n}$ and collision resistant hash function $\mathcal{H}_1 : \{0,1\}^* \rightarrow \mathbb{Z}_q^*$.

Outputs global public parameter

$$\mathsf{par} = \{N, \ell, T, d, n, q, k, m, \overline{m}, \chi, B, \sigma, \beta, \{\overline{\sigma}_k\}_{k=1}^d, \sigma_d, \beta_d, \mathbf{R}_1^0, \mathbf{R}_1^1, \ldots, \mathbf{R}_d^0, \mathbf{R}_d^1,$$

$$\mathbf{Q}, \mathbf{F}, n_1, m_1, q_1, \theta, \chi_1, \sigma_1, \mathbf{u}_0, \mathbf{K}, F, F^{-1}, \mathcal{H}_0, \mathcal{H}_1, \mathcal{H}_2\}.$$

- **CreateGroup.** On input par, GA performs the following to establish a new group.
  1. Run $\mathsf{TrapGen}(n, m, q)$ to get a tuple $(\mathbf{G}, \mathbf{T_G})$, then sample matrices $\mathbf{G}_0, \mathbf{G}_1, \mathbf{D}_0, \mathbf{D}_1 \leftarrow U(\mathbb{Z}_q^{n \times m})$, $\mathbf{D} \leftarrow U(\mathbb{Z}_q^{n \times \overline{m}})$ and vector $\mathbf{u} \leftarrow U(\mathbb{Z}_q^n)$.
  2. Run $\mathsf{TrapGen}(n, m, q)$ to generate a tracing key pair $(\mathbf{B}, \mathbf{S})$ (assume all groups share the same tracing keys).
  3. Set registration table $\mathsf{reg} = \emptyset$ and secret key $\mathsf{gsk} = (\mathbf{T_G}, \mathbf{S})$; Publish group public key $\mathsf{gpk} = (\mathbf{G}, \mathbf{G}_0, \mathbf{G}_1, \mathbf{D}, \mathbf{D}_0, \mathbf{D}_1, \mathbf{B}, \mathbf{u})$ and revocation list $\mathsf{RL} = \emptyset$.

- **AddMember.** At time period t, one prospective user U_i and GA interact in the following protocol to enroll her in group G. Denote $\mathbf{t} = (\mathbf{t}[1], \ldots, \mathbf{t}[d])$ as the binary representation of t with length d hereunder.
  1. U_i runs $\mathsf{TrapGen}(n, m, q)$ to generate a pair $(\mathbf{A}_i, \mathbf{T}_i)$, and builds the set $\mathsf{Evolve}_{(t \rightarrow T-1)}$. For $\mathbf{s} \in \mathsf{Evolve}_{(t \rightarrow T-1)}$, if $\mathbf{s} = \perp$, set $\mathsf{usk}_{i\|t}[\mathbf{s}] = \perp$. Otherwise, denote $d_{\mathbf{s}}$ as the length of $\mathbf{s}$ holding $d_{\mathbf{s}} \leq d$, set matrix $\mathbf{R}^{(\mathbf{s})} = (\mathbf{R}_1^{\mathbf{s}[1]})^{-1} (\mathbf{R}_2^{\mathbf{s}[2]})^{-1} \ldots (\mathbf{R}_{d_s}^{\mathbf{s}[d_s]})^{-1} \in \mathbb{Z}_q^{n \times m}$, and proceed as follows:
     a) If $d_{\mathbf{s}} = d$, compute a short vector $\mathbf{v}_{i\|\mathbf{s}}$ via $\mathsf{SamplePre}(\mathbf{A}_i \mathbf{R}^{(\mathbf{s})}, \mathsf{BasisDel}(\mathbf{A}_i, (\mathbf{R}^{(\mathbf{s})})^{-1}, \mathbf{T}_i, \overline{\sigma}_d), \mathbf{u}, \sigma_d)$. Set $\mathsf{usk}_{i\|t}[\mathbf{s}] = \mathbf{v}_{i\|\mathbf{s}}$.
     b) Else, evaluate $\mathsf{BasisDel}(\mathbf{A}_i, (\mathbf{R}^{(\mathbf{s})})^{-1}, \mathbf{T}_i, \overline{\sigma}_{d_s})$ to obtain a short basis $\mathbf{T}_{i\|\mathbf{s}}$ for $\Lambda_q^{\perp}(\mathbf{A}_i \mathbf{R}^{(\mathbf{s})})$, and set $\mathsf{usk}_{i\|t}[\mathbf{s}] = \mathbf{T}_{i\|\mathbf{s}}$.

     Now let $\mathsf{upk}_i = \mathbf{A}_i$ be the long-term public key and $\mathsf{usk}_{i\|t} = \{\mathsf{usk}_{i\|t}[\mathbf{s}] \mid \mathbf{s} \in \mathsf{Evolve}_{(t \rightarrow T-1)}\}$ be the initial secret key of U_i. Finally, U_i samples a proof vector $\mathbf{v}_i \leftarrow \mathsf{SamplePre}(\mathbf{A}_i, \mathbf{T}_i, \mathbf{u}_0, \sigma_d)$ and sends $(\mathbf{A}_i, \mathbf{v}_i)$ to GA. She discards the original $\mathbf{T}_i$ for forward security.

2. Upon receiving the request from U_i, GA first checks: (i) whether there is a collision between $\mathbf{A}_i$ and the previous records of users' public keys; (ii) whether $\mathbf{A}_i$ is valid w.r.t. $\mathbf{v}_i$ by verifying $\mathbf{A}_i\mathbf{v}_i = \mathbf{u}_0$ and $\|\mathbf{v}_i\|_\infty \le \beta_d$. If either case occurs, GA outputs $\perp$ and aborts. Otherwise, GA performs the following steps to issue a credential to U_i.

   a) To generate user's revocation token, set $\mathsf{urt}_{i\|t} = \mathbf{Q}_1 \cdot \mathsf{vdec}_{n,q-1}(\mathbf{a}_{i,0}) + \mathbf{Q}_2 \cdot \mathbf{t} \in \mathbb{Z}_q^n$, where $\mathbf{a}_{i,0}$ is the first column of $\mathbf{A}_i$ and we assume that it is a non-zero vector. In the long term, the current time period is embedded in the corresponding token, such that no adversary can deploy a previous token to conduct a handshake.

   b) Choose a random spare $\mathbf{i} \in \{0,1\}^\ell$ for user's identity ID_i having decimal value i. Then hash U_i's public key as $\mathbf{h}_i = \mathbf{F} \cdot \mathsf{mdec}_{n,m,q}(\mathbf{A}_i^\top) \in \mathbb{Z}_q^{2n}$.

   c) Encode the identity through building the compressed matrix $\mathbf{G}^{(i)} = [\mathbf{G}|\mathbf{G}_0 + i \cdot \mathbf{G}_1]$. Runs $\mathsf{ExtBasis}(\mathbf{G}^{(i)}, \mathbf{T_G})$ to get a basis $\mathbf{T}_{\mathbf{G}}^{(i)}$ for $\mathbf{G}^{(i)}$.

   d) Sample $\mathbf{r}_i \hookleftarrow D_{\mathbb{Z}^m,\sigma}$, and compute the chameleon hash of $\mathbf{h}_i$ as $\mathbf{c}_i = \mathbf{D}_0 \cdot \mathbf{r}_i + \mathbf{D}_1 \cdot \mathsf{vdec}_{2n,q-1}(\mathbf{h}_i)$.

   e) Invoke $\mathsf{SamplePre}(\mathbf{G}^{(i)}, \mathbf{T}_{\mathbf{G}}^{(i)}, \mathbf{u} + \mathbf{D} \cdot \mathsf{vdec}_{n,q-1}(\mathbf{c}_i), \sigma)$ to obtain a short vector $\mathbf{d}_i \in \mathbb{Z}^{2m}$ satisfying that

$$\mathbf{G}^{(i)}\mathbf{d}_i = \mathbf{u} + \mathbf{D} \cdot \mathsf{vdec}_{n,q-1}(\mathbf{c}_i) \mod q, \qquad (4)$$

   then return the credential $\mathsf{cred}_i = (\mathsf{upk}_i, \mathsf{ID}_i, \mathsf{urt}_{i\|t}, \mathbf{d}_i, \mathbf{r}_i)$ to U_i and adds cred_i to table reg.

3. U_i verifies that cred_i is consistent with Eq. 4 and $\mathbf{d}_i \in [-\beta,\beta]^{2m}$, $\mathbf{r}_i \in [-\beta,\beta]^m$. She aborts if it is not the case. To avoid confusion, use $t_{i,add} = t$ to denote the time period at which U_i has been registered.

- Update_U. At the beginning of time period t, member U_i conducts the following procedures to update her secret pair $(\mathsf{cred}_{i\|t-1}, \mathsf{usk}_{i\|t-1})$.

  For revocation token update, compute $\mathsf{urt}_{i\|t} = \mathbf{Q}_1 \cdot \mathsf{vdec}_{n,q-1}(\mathsf{urt}_{i\|t-1}) + \mathbf{Q}_2 \cdot \mathbf{t} \in \mathbb{Z}_q^n$. W.L.O.G, we assume that there is no all-zero token or two identical tokens. (Otherwise, the user would find a solution to $\mathsf{SIS}_{n,q,\sqrt{nk+d}}$ problem associated with matrix $\mathbf{Q}$, which is of negligible probability.)

  For the secret key derivation, first specify the node set $\mathsf{Evolve}_{(t \to T-1)}$. Then for $\mathbf{s} \in \mathsf{Evolve}_{(t \to T-1)}$, if $\mathbf{s} = \perp$, set $\mathsf{usk}_{i\|t}[\mathbf{s}] = \perp$, otherwise, there exists exactly one $\mathbf{s}' \in \mathsf{Evolve}_{(t-1 \to T-1)}$ as the prefix of $\mathbf{s}$, i.e., $\mathbf{s} = \mathbf{s}'\|\mathbf{x}$ for some binary string $\mathbf{x}$. Consider two cases:

1. If $\mathbf{s} = \mathbf{s}'$, set $\mathsf{usk}_{i\|t}[\mathbf{s}] = \mathsf{usk}_{i\|t-1}[\mathbf{s}']$.

2. Else, it holds that $\mathbf{x}$ is not empty and $\mathsf{usk}_{i\|t-1}[\mathbf{s}'] = \mathbf{T}_{i\|\mathbf{s}'}$ is a short basis. Compute matrix $\mathbf{R}^{(\mathbf{x})} = (\mathbf{R}_{1+d_{\mathbf{s}'}}^{\mathbf{x}[1]})^{-1} (\mathbf{R}_{2+d_{\mathbf{s}'}}^{\mathbf{x}[2]})^{-1} \ldots (\mathbf{R}_{d_{\mathbf{s}}}^{\mathbf{x}[d_{\mathbf{x}}]})^{-1}$, then consider the following two sub-cases:

   a) If $d_{\mathbf{s}} = d$, generate a short vector $\mathbf{v}_{i\|\mathbf{s}}$ by running $\mathsf{SamplePre}(\mathbf{A}_i\mathbf{R}^{(\mathbf{s}')}\mathbf{R}^{(\mathbf{x})}, \mathsf{BasisDel}(\mathbf{A}_i\mathbf{R}^{(\mathbf{s}')}, (\mathbf{R}^{(\mathbf{x})})^{-1}, \mathbf{T}_{i\|\mathbf{s}'}, \overline{\sigma}_{d_{\mathbf{s}}}), \mathbf{u}, \sigma_d)$. Set $\mathsf{usk}_{i\|t}[\mathbf{s}] = \mathbf{v}_{i\|\mathbf{s}}$.

    b) If $d_{\mathbf{s}} < d$, run $\mathsf{BasisDel}(\mathbf{A}_i \mathbf{R}^{(\mathbf{s}')}, (\mathbf{R}^{(\mathbf{x})})^{-1}, \mathbf{T}_{i\|\mathbf{s}'}, \overline{\sigma}_{d_{\mathbf{s}}})$ to obtain a short basis $\mathbf{T}_{i\|\mathbf{s}}$, and set $\mathsf{usk}_{i\|t}[\mathbf{s}] = \mathbf{T}_{i\|\mathbf{s}}$.

Set $\mathsf{usk}_{i\|t} = \{\mathsf{usk}_{i\|t}[\mathbf{s}] \mid \mathbf{s} \in \mathsf{Evolve}_{(t \to T-1)}\}$ and erases the previous one.

- **Handshake.** At time period t, suppose a member A from group G_a with $\mathsf{gpk}_a = (\mathbf{G}^{(a)}, \mathbf{G}_0^{(a)}, \mathbf{G}_1^{(a)}, \mathbf{D}^{(a)}, \mathbf{D}_0^{(a)}, \mathbf{D}_1^{(a)}, \mathbf{B}, \mathbf{u}_a)$, $\mathsf{cred}_a = (\mathsf{upk}_a, \mathsf{ID}_a, \mathsf{urt}_{a\|t}, \mathbf{d}_a, \mathbf{r}_a)$, revocation list RL_a, $\mathsf{usk}_{a\|t} = \{\mathsf{usk}_{a\|t}[\mathbf{s}] \mid \mathbf{s} \in \mathsf{Evolve}_{t \to T-1}\}$, and another member B from group G_b having $(\mathsf{gpk}_b, \mathsf{cred}_b, \mathsf{RL}_b, \mathsf{usk}_{b\|t})$ of same structure, aim to execute a handshake. They proceed the following two-round protocol.

1. $A \to B : (\mathsf{PROOF}_a)$
   a) A samples a small private key $\mathbf{S}_a \hookleftarrow \chi_1(\mathbb{Z}_{q_1}^{n_1 \times m_1})$ and a small noise $\mathbf{E}_a \hookleftarrow \chi_1(\mathbb{Z}_{q_1}^{n_1 \times m_1})$. Then she computes $\mathbf{C}_a = \mathbf{K} \cdot \mathbf{S}_a + \mathbf{E}_a \in \mathbb{Z}_{q_1}^{n_1 \times m_1}$.
   b) Parse $\mathsf{upk}_a = \mathbf{A}_a$, A fetches the secret key for string $\mathbf{t}$ from $\mathsf{usk}_{a\|t}$ as $\mathbf{v}_{a\|t}$ and assembles the corresponding matrix $\mathbf{A}_{a\|t}$ as

$$\mathbf{A}_{a\|t} = \mathbf{A}_a \, (\mathbf{R}_1^{t[1]})^{-1} \, (\mathbf{R}_2^{t[2]})^{-1} \dots (\mathbf{R}_d^{t[d]})^{-1} \in \mathbb{Z}_q^{n \times m}. \quad (5)$$

   c) A samples $\rho_a \overset{\$}{\leftarrow} \{0,1\}^n$ and let $\mathbf{W}_a = \mathcal{H}_0(\mathsf{gpk}_a, \rho_a)$. Next, she computes $\mathbf{w}_a = \mathbf{W}_a \cdot \mathsf{urt}_{a\|t} + \mathbf{e}_a \mod q$ where $\mathbf{e}_a \hookleftarrow \chi^m$.
   d) A samples $\mathbf{P}_a \hookleftarrow U(\mathbb{Z}_q^{n \times \ell})$, $\mathbf{s}^{(a)} \hookleftarrow \chi^n$, $\mathbf{e}_1^{(a)} \hookleftarrow \chi^m$, $\mathbf{e}_2^{(a)} \hookleftarrow \chi^\ell$, so that produces the ciphertext $(\mathbf{c}_1^{(a)}, \mathbf{c}_2^{(a)})$ as

$$(\mathbf{c}_1^{(a)} = \mathbf{B}^\top \cdot \mathbf{s}^{(a)} + \mathbf{e}_1^{(a)}, \mathbf{c}_2^{(a)} = \mathbf{P}_a^\top \cdot \mathbf{s}^{(a)} + \mathbf{e}_2^{(a)} + \lfloor \tfrac{q}{2} \rfloor \cdot \mathsf{ID}_a). \quad (6)$$

   e) With public input $\mathsf{pp}_a = (\mathsf{par}, \mathsf{gpk}_a, \mathbf{c}_1^{(a)}, \mathbf{c}_2^{(a)}, t_a)$ where $t_a = t - t_{a,add}$, A runs $\mathsf{Prove}_{\mathsf{hs}}$ designed in Sect. 4.2 to generate a proof π_a for $\xi_a = (\mathsf{ID}_a, \mathsf{urt}_{a\|t}, \mathbf{d}_a, \mathbf{r}_a, \mathbf{A}_a, \mathbf{v}_{a\|t}, \mathbf{e}_a, \mathbf{s}^{(a)}, \mathbf{e}_1^{(a)}, \mathbf{e}_2^{(a)})$, satisfying that:
      - $\mathsf{urt}_{a\|t}$ is correctly derived from $\mathbf{A}_a$ after t_a times of updates.
      - $(\mathsf{ID}_a, \mathbf{d}_a, \mathbf{r}_a)$ satisfies Eq. 4 with the specific form in AddMember.
      - $\mathbf{W}_a \cdot \mathsf{rt}_a + \mathbf{e}_a = \mathbf{w}_a$ and $\|\mathbf{e}_a\|_\infty \le B$.
      - Eq. 5 holds with $\mathbf{A}_{a\|t} \cdot \mathbf{v}_{a\|t} = \mathbf{u}_a \mod q$ and $\|\mathbf{v}_{a\|t}\|_\infty \le \beta_d$.
      - Eq. 6 holds with $\|\mathbf{s}^{(a)}\|_\infty \le B$, $\|\mathbf{e}_1^{(a)}\|_\infty \le B$, and $\|\mathbf{e}_2^{(a)}\|_\infty \le B$.
      Note that the challenge part of π_a is modified as $\widetilde{ch}_a := ch_a \oplus F(\mathbf{C}_a)$.
   f) A finally sends $\mathsf{PROOF}_a = (\rho_a, \mathbf{w}_a, \mathbf{P}_a, \mathbf{c}_1^{(a)}, \mathbf{c}_2^{(a)}, t_a, \pi_a)$ to B.

2. $B \to A : (\mathsf{PROOF}_b, V_b)$
   a) B computes $\mathbf{W}_a' = \mathcal{H}_0(\mathsf{gpk}_b, \rho_a)$. Then he checks if there exists an index i such that $\mathbf{e}_i' = \mathbf{w}_a - \mathbf{W}_a' \cdot \mathbf{v}_i$ and $\|\mathbf{e}_i'\|_\infty \le B$ for $\mathbf{v}_i \in \mathsf{RL}_b$. If so, B sends A a random pair (PROOF_b, V_b) and aborts. Otherwise, he continues to perform the following steps.
   b) B runs $\mathsf{Verify}_{\mathsf{hs}}(\mathsf{pp}_a', \pi_a)$ where $\mathsf{pp}_a' = (\mathsf{par}, \mathsf{gpk}_b, \mathbf{c}_1^{(a)}, \mathbf{c}_2^{(a)}, t_a)$, to recover the hidden message of A as $\mathbf{C}_a' = F^{-1}(ch_a' \oplus \widetilde{ch}_a)$.
   c) B samples his ephemeral private key $\mathbf{S}_b \hookleftarrow \chi_1(\mathbb{Z}_{q_1}^{n_1 \times m_1})$ and a small noise $\mathbf{E}_b \hookleftarrow \chi_1(\mathbb{Z}_{q_1}^{n_1 \times m_1})$. Then B computes $\mathbf{C}_b = \mathbf{K} \cdot \mathbf{S}_b + \mathbf{E}_b$.

d) Similarly, B computes the LWE function of his revocation token as $\mathbf{w}_b = \mathbf{W}_b \cdot \mathsf{urt}_{b\|t} + \mathbf{e}_b$, and encrypts his identity as $(\mathbf{c}_1^{(b)}, \mathbf{c}_2^{(b)})$.

e) With analogous public input pp_b, B runs $\mathtt{Prove_{hs}}$ to generate an argument π_b for his secret tuple ξ_b, of which each element meets the similar constraints as that of ξ_a. Remark $\widetilde{ch}_b := ch_b \oplus F(\mathbf{C}_b^\top)$.

f) Upon obtaining $\mathbf{C}_a'$, B generates the check matrix $\mathbf{M}$ and the communication key $\mathbf{K}_b$ as depicted in Sect. 2.4. Then B computes the authentication code $\mathsf{V}_b = \mathcal{H}_1(\mathbf{K}_b\|\mathbf{C}_b\|0)$.

g) B dispatches $\mathtt{PROOF}_b = (\rho_b, \mathbf{w}_b, \mathbf{P}_b, \mathbf{c}_1^{(b)}, \mathbf{c}_2^{(b)}, t_b, \pi_b, \mathbf{M})$ and V_b to A.

3. $A \rightarrow B : (\mathsf{V}_a)$

a) A computes $\mathbf{W}_b' = \mathcal{H}_0(\mathsf{gpk}_a, \rho_b)$ and also checks if there exists an index j such that $\mathbf{e}_j' = \mathbf{w}_b - \mathbf{W}_b' \cdot \mathbf{v}_j$ and $\|\mathbf{e}_j'\|_\infty \leq B$ for $\mathbf{v}_j \in \mathsf{RL}_a$. If so, A responds a random value $\mathsf{V}_a \leftarrow U(\{0,1\}^{q_1})$, outputs 0 and aborts. Otherwise, A moves to execute the following steps.

b) A also runs $\mathtt{Verify_{hs}}(\mathsf{pp}_b', \pi_b)$ to retrieve $\mathbf{C}_b'^\top = F^{-1}(\widetilde{ch}_b \oplus ch_b')$.

c) A extracts the shared key $\mathbf{K}_a$ following the steps in Sect. 2.4. Then A verifies that $\mathsf{V}_b \stackrel{?}{=} \mathcal{H}_1(\mathbf{K}_a\|\mathbf{C}_b'\|0)$. If so, A outputs 1 and sends $\mathsf{V}_a = \mathcal{H}(\mathbf{K}_a\|\mathbf{C}_a\|1)$ to B. Else, A outputs 0 and responds a random V_a.

d) B verifies V_a via a similar equation $\mathsf{V}_a \stackrel{?}{=} \mathcal{H}_1(\mathbf{K}_b\|\mathbf{C}_a'\|1)$. B outputs 1 if the equation holds, else he outputs 0.

- TraceMember. With transcript $(\mathtt{PROOF}, \mathsf{V})$ of a handshake executed at time period t, TA performs the following steps to trace the involved group member:
  1. Parse $\mathtt{PROOF} = (\rho, \mathbf{w}, \mathbf{P}, \mathbf{c}_1, \mathbf{c}_2, t^*, \pi)$ where $\mathbf{P} = [\mathbf{p}_1|\ldots|\mathbf{p}_\ell] \in \mathbb{Z}_q^{n \times \ell}$. Then for all $i \in [\ell]$, invoke $\mathsf{SamplePre}(\mathbf{B}, \mathbf{S}, \mathbf{p}_i, \sigma)$ to obtain a small vector $\mathbf{f}_i$. Set $\mathbf{F} = [\mathbf{f}_1|\ldots|\mathbf{f}_\ell]$ such that $\mathbf{B} \cdot \mathbf{F} = \mathbf{P} \mod q$.
  2. Decrypt $(\mathbf{c}_1, \mathbf{c}_2)$ by computing $\mathsf{ID} = \lfloor \mathbf{c}_2 - \mathbf{F}^\top \cdot \mathbf{c}_1 / \lfloor q/2 \rfloor \rceil \in \{0,1\}^\ell$.
  3. If there exists an elements $\mathsf{ID}_i = \mathsf{ID}$, return ID_i. Otherwise, output $\perp$.

- RemoveMember. To remove ID_i from group G at the beginning of period t, GA gets the initial revocation token $\mathsf{urt}_{i\|t_{i,add}}$ of ID_i from table Reg, and adds it to public list RL. Since the current token can be computed from the initial one, for simplicity we assume the elements of RL are all the updated ones.

5.2   Analysis of the Scheme

Completeness. We demonstrate that our scheme is complete with overwhelming probability if A and B belong to the same group ($\mathsf{gpk}_1 = \mathsf{gpk}_2$) with unrevoked and updated group secret, and they both follow the specified protocol.

First, by *completeness* of system Π_{hs}, both A and B can produce a valid proof (π_a, π_b) at the first round of a handshake, which means that the receiver can always rightly recover the original challenge $ch' = ch$, such that they can retrieve the hidden message $\mathbf{C}' = \mathbf{C}$. It follows that $\mathbf{K}_a \neq \mathbf{K}_b$ with negligible probability from Theorem 2. Therefore, the two members can verify the corresponding equations successfully, i.e., the message authentication code V_a (V_b)

is correct. Consequently, the handshake protocol will output 1 for both participants.

Next, we show that TraceMember always outputs ID_a (ID_b). Observe that, the decryption procedure computes $\mathbf{c}_2 - \mathbf{F}^\top \cdot \mathbf{c}_1 = \mathbf{P}^\top \cdot \mathbf{s} + \mathbf{e}_2 + \lfloor \frac{q}{2} \rfloor \cdot \mathsf{ID} - \mathbf{F}^\top \cdot (\mathbf{B}^\top \cdot \mathbf{s} + \mathbf{e}_1)$, which can be further simplified into $\mathbf{e}_2 - \mathbf{F}^\top \cdot \mathbf{e}_1 + \lfloor \frac{q}{2} \rfloor \cdot \mathsf{ID}$, where $\|\mathbf{e}_1\|_\infty \le B$, $\|\mathbf{e}_2\|_\infty \le B$, and $\|\mathbf{f}_i\|_\infty \le \lceil \sigma \cdot \log m \rceil$ implied by Lemma 1. Recall that $q = \widetilde{\mathcal{O}}(n^2)$, $m = 2n \log q$ and $B = \sqrt{n}\omega(\log n)$. Hence we always have $\|\mathbf{e}_2 - \mathbf{F}^\top \cdot \mathbf{e}_1\|_\infty \le B + m \cdot B \cdot \lceil \sigma \cdot \log m \rceil < q/5$, inducing that the $\mathsf{ID} = \mathsf{ID}_a$.

Security. Now we give security analysis for our scheme, proof of the following theorem is deferred to Appendix A.

Theorem 3. *In the random oracle model, our scheme satisfies the forward impersonator resistance, detector resistance and backward unlinkability under the* SIS, ISIS *and* LWE *assumptions.*

Efficiency. Finally we analyze the complexity of our scheme, with respect to security parameter λ, two system parameters $\ell = \log N$ and $d = \log T$.

- Group public key contains several matrices and a vector with bit-size $\widetilde{\mathcal{O}}(\lambda^2)$.
- Group credential consists of 4 vectors and has bit-size $\widetilde{\mathcal{O}}(\lambda + \ell)$.
- User secret key has one vector from SamplePre and at most d trapdoor matrices from BasisDel, all of which have bit-size $\widetilde{\mathcal{O}}(\lambda^2 d^3)$.
- The communication cost of a handshake protocol can be viewed as four parts: $(\rho, \mathbf{w}, \mathbf{P}, t)$ for revocation check; Modified ZK argument π_{hs}, whose bit-size largely relies on the length of witness $\mathbf{x}$ and can be quantized as $\widetilde{\mathcal{O}}(\lambda^2 + d \cdot \lambda + \ell^2)$; Two IBE ciphertexts and one authentication code. Overall, the dispatched data has bit-size $\widetilde{\mathcal{O}}(\lambda^2 + (d + \ell) \cdot \lambda + \ell^2)$.
- Dynamic revocation list has bit-size $\widetilde{\mathcal{O}}(N \cdot \lambda)$.

Table 1. Comparison between scheme [5] and ours.

Scheme	gpk	cred	usk	Handshake cost	RL	FS
[5]	$\widetilde{\mathcal{O}}(\lambda^2)$	$\widetilde{\mathcal{O}}(\ell \cdot \lambda)$	$\widetilde{\mathcal{O}}(\ell \cdot \lambda)$	$\widetilde{\mathcal{O}}(\ell \cdot \lambda)$	$\widetilde{\mathcal{O}}(N \cdot \lambda)$	✗
Ours	$\widetilde{\mathcal{O}}(\lambda^2)$	$\widetilde{\mathcal{O}}(\lambda + \ell)$	$\widetilde{\mathcal{O}}(\lambda^2 d^3)$	$\widetilde{\mathcal{O}}(\lambda^2 + (d + \ell) \cdot \lambda + \ell^2)$	$\widetilde{\mathcal{O}}(N \cdot \lambda)$	✓

In Table 1, we give a detailed comparison of our scheme with the only known lattice-based one [5], in terms of efficiency and functionality. Note that forward security is achieved with a reasonable increase in communication cost, thanks to the more efficient ZK system [41]. Besides, our scheme allows dynamic user enrollment. In other words, users autonomously generate their secret keys rather than being issued by GA, which prevents malicious GA from framing honest users.

Acknowledgements. This work is supported by Guangdong Major Project of Basic and Applied Basic Research (2019B030302008) and the National Natural Science Foundation of China (No. 61972429) and Guangdong Basic and Applied Basic Research Foundation (No. 2019A1515011797) and the Opening Project of Guangdong Provincial Key Laboratory of Information Security Technology (2020B1212060078-09).

A   Deferred Proof of Theorem 3

Proof. We prove Theorem 3 by separately proving that our scheme satisfies the 3 required properties defined in Sect. 3.

Forward Impersonator Resistance. We prove this property by contradiction. Suppose that a PPT adversary $\mathcal{A}$ succeeds in experiment $\mathbf{Exp}_{\mathcal{A}}^{\mathsf{F\text{-}IR}}$ with non-negligible advantage ϵ. Then we can build a PPT algorithm $\mathcal{B}$ that solves $\mathsf{SIS}_{n,m,q,2\sqrt{m}\beta_d}$ problem with non-negligible probability.

   Given an SIS instance $\mathbf{A} \in \mathbb{Z}_q^{n \times m}$, the goal of $\mathcal{B}$ is to find a non-zero vector $\mathbf{z} \in \mathbb{Z}_q^m$ such that $\mathbf{A} \cdot \mathbf{z} = \mathbf{0} \mod q$ and $\|\mathbf{z}\| \leq \sqrt{m}\beta$. Towards this goal, $\mathcal{B}$ first prepares a simulated attack environment for $\mathcal{A}$ as follows:

- Randomly guess the target user's identity $\mathsf{ID}^* : \mathbf{i}^* \in \{0,1\}^\ell$ and forgery time period $t^* \in [0, T-1]$.
- Sample random matrices $\mathbf{R}_1^{t^*[1]}, \mathbf{R}_2^{t^*[2]}, \ldots, \mathbf{R}_d^{t^*[d]} \in \mathbb{Z}^{m \times m}$ from the distribution $\mathcal{D}_{m \times m}$. Set $\mathbf{A}_{i^*} = \mathbf{A}\, \mathbf{R}_d^{t^*[d]} \cdots \mathbf{R}_2^{t^*[2]}\, \mathbf{R}_1^{t^*[1]} \in \mathbb{Z}_q^{n \times m}$, which is the public key of target user ID^*.
- Sample $\mathbf{v} \hookleftarrow D_{\mathbb{Z}^m, \sigma_d}$. If $\|\mathbf{v}\|_\infty > \beta_d$, then repeat the sampling. Compute $\mathbf{u}^* = \mathbf{A} \cdot \mathbf{v} \mod q$.
- Assemble d matrices $\mathbf{F}_j = \mathbf{A}_{i^*}\, (\mathbf{R}_1^{t^*[1]})^{-1} \ldots (\mathbf{R}_j^{t^*[j]})^{-1}$ for $j \in [0, d-1]$ ($\mathbf{F}_0 = \mathbf{A}_{i^*}$). For each $\mathbf{F}_j$, invoke $\mathsf{SampleRwithBasis}(\mathbf{F}_j)$ to obtain a matrix $\mathbf{R}_{j+1}^{1-t^*[j+1]}$, along with a short basis $\mathbf{T}_{j+1}$ for $\Lambda^\perp(\mathbf{F}_{j+1}')$ where $\mathbf{F}_{j+1}' = \mathbf{F}_j\, (\mathbf{R}_{j+1}^{1-t^*[j+1]})^{-1}$. As the simulation in [2], $\mathcal{B}$ can use these bases to generate ID^*'s secret key for every period $t' > t^*$.
- Generate other elements of $(\mathsf{gpk}^*, \mathsf{gsk}^*)$ for group G^* that ID^* belongs to.
- Operates as GA in algorithm $\mathsf{AddMember}$ to determine the target user's credential $\mathsf{cred}_{\mathsf{ID}^* \| t^*}$ at period t^*.

Note that, by construction, the distribution of $(\mathsf{par}^*, \mathsf{gpk}^*, \mathsf{gsk}^*, \mathsf{cred}_{\mathsf{ID}^* \| t^*})$ is statistically close to that of the real scheme, and the choice of (ID^*, t^*) is hidden from the adversary.

   $\mathcal{B}$ responds to $\mathcal{A}$'s queries of $\{\mathsf{KeyP}, \mathsf{Trace}, \mathsf{Remove}, \mathsf{AddU}, \mathsf{KeyG}\}$ exactly the same as the real scheme. For other queries at current period t, $\mathcal{B}$ interacts with $\mathcal{A}$ as follows.

- When $\mathcal{A}$ queries random oracles $\mathcal{H}_0$ or $\mathcal{G}$, $\mathcal{B}$ replies with uniformly random strings and records the inputs/outputs of these queries.
- For queries of oracle CorU, if the requested user has been already corrupted, i.e., $(\mathsf{ID}, \cdot, \cdot,) \in \mathsf{CU}$, $\mathcal{B}$ aborts. Otherwise, consider two cases:

i) The chosen user's identity is ID^*. If $t \leq t^*$, $\mathcal{B}$ aborts. Otherwise, for each node $\mathbf{s} \in \mathsf{Evolve}_{t \to T-1}$, denote the length of $\mathbf{s}$ as $d_\mathbf{s}$, $\mathcal{B}$ first computes the smallest index $j_\mathbf{s}$ such that $1 \leq j_\mathbf{s} \leq d_\mathbf{s}$ and $\mathbf{s}[j_\mathbf{s}] \neq \mathbf{t}^*[j_\mathbf{s}]$. After setting delegation matrix $\mathbf{R}^{(\mathbf{s})} = (\mathbf{R}_{j_\mathbf{s}+1}^{\mathbf{s}[j_\mathbf{s}+1]})^{-1} \cdots (\mathbf{R}_{d_\mathbf{s}}^{\mathbf{s}[d_\mathbf{s}]})^{-1}$, $\mathcal{B}$ computes $\mathsf{usk}_{i^* \| t}[\mathbf{s}]$ via $\mathsf{SamplePre}(\mathbf{F}'_{j_\mathbf{s}} \mathbf{R}^{(\mathbf{s})}, \mathsf{BasisDel}(\mathbf{F}'_{j_\mathbf{s}}, (\mathbf{R}^{(\mathbf{s})})^{-1}, \mathbf{T}_{j_\mathbf{s}}, \overline{\sigma}_{d_\mathbf{s}}), \mathbf{u}, \sigma_d)$ if $d_\mathbf{s} = d$, or via $\mathsf{BasisDel}(\mathbf{F}'_{j_\mathbf{s}}, (\mathbf{R}^{(\mathbf{s})})^{-1}, \mathbf{T}_{j_\mathbf{s}}, \overline{\sigma}_{d_\mathbf{s}})$ if $d_\mathbf{s} < d$. Next, $\mathcal{B}$ builds $\mathsf{usk}_{i^* \| t}$ and derives $\mathsf{cred}_{i^* \| t}$ as in our main scheme. Finally $\mathcal{B}$ returns the secret pair to $\mathcal{A}$ and adds (ID^*, G^*, t) to CU. Note that $\mathcal{A}$ can not obtain the target user's secret until period $t^* + 1$.

ii) $\mathsf{ID} \neq \mathsf{ID}^*$, then $\mathcal{B}$ can perfectly answer the query as it stores the initial secret key (a short basis $\mathbf{T}$) when ID was enrolled in group G. In other words, $\mathcal{B}$ performs as that in $\mathsf{Update}_\mathsf{U}$ to derive user's secret pair $(\mathsf{cred}_{\mathsf{ID}\|t}, \mathsf{usk}_{\mathsf{ID}\|t})$ and returns it to $\mathcal{A}$. Finally, it adds (ID, G, t) to CU.

- For queries of oracle HS with input ID, if $(\mathsf{ID}, \cdot, \cdot) \in \mathsf{CU}$, $\mathcal{B}$ aborts. Otherwise, if $\mathsf{ID} \neq \mathsf{ID}^*$ or $t > t^*$, $\mathcal{B}$ acts as in algorithm Handshake using the corresponding secrets. Else, $\mathcal{B}$ has to answer without using the user's secret key. To do so, $\mathcal{B}$ also performs the same as in Handshake, except that in the second flow $\mathcal{B}$ generates a simulated proof π' by utilizing the well-designed simulator of applied NIZKAoK [41].

We claim that $\mathcal{A}$ cannot distinguish whether it interacts with a real challenger or with $\mathcal{B}$. First, the secret pair of ID^* given to $\mathcal{A}$ after period t^* is indistinguishable from the real one, due to the facts that

i) the revocation token is uniform over $\mathbb{Z}_q^n$ and other elements of $\mathsf{cred}_{\mathsf{ID}^*\|t}$ are produced in the same way as that in AddMember;

ii) the outputs of BasisDel are uniformly random by Lemma 5. Second, the handshake queries make no difference to the view of $\mathcal{A}$, implied by the *zero knowledge* property of the underlying NIZKAoK.

After $\mathcal{A}$ halts with her output $\mathsf{PROOF}^* = (\rho^*, \mathbf{w}^*, \mathbf{P}^*, \mathbf{c}_1^*, \mathbf{c}_2^*, \hat{t}, \pi^*)$ at period t', $\mathcal{B}$ checks if $t' = t^*$. If not, the guess of the impersonator period t^* fails and $\mathcal{B}$ aborts. Else, parse $\pi^* = (cmt_s^*, \widetilde{ch}^*, rsp^*)$, since $\mathcal{A}$ wins, we argue that by *completeness* of our scheme, $\mathcal{A}$ must have queried the related random oracle $\mathcal{G}$ via Fiat-Shamir heuristic on input $\eta^* = (cmt^*, \mathsf{pp}^*)$. Otherwise, guessing correctly this value occurs only with negligible probability $\epsilon' = \left(\frac{1}{2p+1}\right)^t$. Therefore, with probability at least $\epsilon - \epsilon'$, the tuple η^* has been an input of one hash query, denoted as $\kappa^* \leq q_\mathcal{G}$, where $q_\mathcal{G}$ is the total number of queries to $\mathcal{G}$ made by $\mathcal{A}$.

Next, $\mathcal{B}$ picks κ^* as the target forking point and replays $\mathcal{A}$ polynomial time. For each new run, $\mathcal{B}$ starts with the same random tape and input as in the original execution, but from the κ^*-th query onwards, $\mathcal{B}$ will reply to $\mathcal{A}$ with fresh and independent hash values. Moreover, $\mathcal{B}$ always replies as in the original run for queries of $\mathcal{H}_0$. Note that the input of κ^* hash query must be η^*. The Forking Lemma in [14] implies that, with probability larger than $1/2$, $\mathcal{B}$ can obtain 3 forks involving the same tuple η^*, but with pairwise distinct challenges

$$\widetilde{ch}_1^*, \ \widetilde{ch}_2^*, \ \widetilde{ch}_3^* \in [-p, p]^t.$$

Moreover, by the binding property of used commitment scheme, $\mathcal{B}$ can obtain 3 valid tuples from the output of $\mathcal{A}$ as

$$\{(ch_1^*, cmt^*, rsp_1^*), (ch_2^*, cmt^*, rsp_2^*), ch_3^*, cmt^*, rsp_3^*\},$$

by first recovering the unsent cmt_r^* and then the original ch^*. Then by *proof of knowledge* of system Π_{hs}, $\mathcal{B}$ can extract the witness

$$\xi^* = (\mathsf{ID}', \mathsf{urt}_{\mathsf{ID}'\|t^*}^*, \mathbf{d}^*, \mathbf{r}^*, \mathbf{A}_{i^*}, \mathsf{v}_{\mathsf{ID}'\|t^*}, \mathbf{e}^*, \mathbf{s}^*, \mathbf{e}_1^*, \mathbf{e}_2^*),$$

which satisfies that

- $\mathsf{urt}_{\mathsf{ID}'\|t^*}^*$ is correctly derived from $\mathbf{A}_{i^*}$ after $\hat{t}$ times of updates.
- Triple $(\mathsf{ID}', \mathbf{d}^*, \mathbf{r}^*)$ has the specific form as that in algorithm AddMember and satisfies Eq. 4.
- $\mathbf{W}^* \cdot \mathsf{urt}_{\mathsf{ID}'\|t^*}^* + \mathbf{e}^* = \mathbf{w}^*$ and $\|\mathbf{e}^*\|_\infty \leq B$, where $\mathbf{W}^* = \mathcal{H}_1(\mathsf{gpk}^*, \rho^*)$.
- $\mathbf{A}_{\mathsf{ID}'\|t^*} = \mathbf{A}_{i^*} (\mathbf{R}_1^{t^*[1]})^{-1} (\mathbf{R}_2^{t^*[2]})^{-1} \dots (\mathbf{R}_d^{t^*[d]})^{-1}$.
- $\mathbf{A}_{\mathsf{ID}'\|t^*} \cdot \mathsf{v}_{\mathsf{ID}'\|t^*} = \mathbf{u}^*$ mod q and $\|\mathsf{v}_{\mathsf{ID}'\|t^*}\|_\infty \leq \beta_d$.
- $\mathbf{c}_1^* = \mathbf{B}^{*\top} \cdot \mathbf{s}^* + \mathbf{e}_1^*, \mathbf{c}_2^* = \mathbf{P}^{*\top} \cdot \mathbf{s}^* + \mathbf{e}_2^* + \lfloor \frac{q}{2} \rfloor \cdot \mathsf{ID}'$, where $\|\mathbf{s}^*\|_\infty \leq B$, $\|\mathbf{e}_1^*\|_\infty \leq B$, and $\|\mathbf{e}_2^*\|_\infty \leq B$.

Now consider the following cases:

a. There is no element in table reg that contains ID'. This implies that the pair $(\mathbf{A}^*, (\mathsf{ID}', \mathbf{d}^*, \mathbf{r}^*))$ forms a forgery for the SIS-based signature of Sect. 2.2.

b. $\mathsf{ID}' \neq \mathsf{ID}^*$, indicating the guess of the impersonator user fails, then $\mathcal{B}$ aborts.

c. Conditioned on guessing correctly t^* and ID^*, we have that $\mathbf{A}_{\mathsf{ID}'\|t^*} \cdot \mathsf{v}_{\mathsf{ID}'\|t^*} = \mathbf{A} \cdot \mathsf{v}_{\mathsf{ID}'\|t^*} = \mathbf{u}^*$ mod q, recall that $\mathbf{A}_{i^*} = \mathbf{A} \, \mathbf{R}_d^{t^*[d]} \dots \mathbf{R}_2^{t^*[2]} \, \mathbf{R}_1^{t^*[1]}$. Besides, with the fact that $\mathcal{A}$ either queried the secret key of ID^* after period t^* or never requested it at all, it is clear that $\mathbf{v}$ is not known to $\mathcal{A}$. In this sense, because $\mathbf{v}$ has large min-entropy given $\mathbf{u}^*$, we argue that $\mathsf{v}_{\mathsf{ID}'\|t^*} \neq \mathbf{v}$ with overwhelming probability. Now let $\mathbf{z} = \mathsf{v}_{\mathsf{ID}'\|t^*} - \mathbf{v} \in \mathbb{Z}_q^m$, it holds that i) $\mathbf{z} \neq \mathbf{0}$; ii) $\mathbf{A} \cdot \mathbf{z} = \mathbf{0}$ mod q; iii) $\|\mathbf{z}\| \leq \sqrt{m} \cdot \|\mathbf{z}\|_\infty \leq \sqrt{m} \cdot (\|\mathsf{v}_{\mathsf{ID}'\|t^*}\|_\infty + \|\mathbf{v}\|_\infty) \leq 2\sqrt{m}\beta_d$. $\mathcal{B}$ finally outputs $\mathbf{z}$, which is a valid solution of the given $\mathsf{SIS}_{n,m,q,2\sqrt{m}\beta_d}$ instance.

We observe that the probability that $\mathcal{B}$ does not abort is at least $\frac{1}{q_G \cdot N \cdot T}$, and conditioned on not aborting, it can solve the $\mathsf{SIS}_{n,m,q,2\sqrt{m}\beta_d}$ problem with probability larger than $1/2$.

Detector Resistance. We define a sequence of hybrid games G_i^b for $i \in [0, 5]$ and G_6, such that game G_0^b, for $b \in \{0, 1\}$, is the original experiment $\mathbf{Exp}_{\mathcal{A}}^{\mathsf{DR}-b}$. We then prove that any two consecutive games are indistinguishable. *Detector resistance* follows from the fact that game G_6 is independent of the bit b. For consistency, use ID_b to denote the involved user ($\mathsf{ID}_b = \mathsf{ID}^*$ or ID_r for $b = 0$ or 1, respectively).

Game G_0^b: This is exactly the original game $\mathbf{Exp}_{\mathcal{A}}^{\mathsf{DR}-b}$, where $\mathcal{B}$ relies with random strings for oracle queries of $\mathcal{H}_0$ and $\mathcal{G}$.

Game G_1^b: This game is the same as Game G_0^b with only one modification: at the challenge query $\mathsf{Chal}_b^{\mathsf{DR}}$, we utilize the well-designed simulator in [41], so as to produce a simulated proof $\widetilde{\pi}^*$, which is computationally indistinguishable from the real one due to *zero knowledge* of the underlying system.

Game G_2^b: There is one change in Game G_2^b: for the token embedding step in the challenge query, compute the LWE function of revocation token using a random nonce $\mathbf{s}$ instead of the real value $\mathsf{urt}_{\mathsf{ID}_b\|t^*}$, namely, $\mathbf{w}^* = \mathbf{W}\cdot\mathbf{s}+\mathbf{e}^* \mod q$ where $\mathbf{s} \leftarrow U(\mathbb{Z}_q^n)$. Recall that the current token $\mathsf{urt}_{\mathsf{ID}_b\|t^*} = \mathbf{Q}_1\cdot\mathsf{vdec}_{n,q-1}(\mathsf{urt}_{\mathsf{ID}_b\|t^*-1})+\mathbf{Q}_2 \cdot \mathbf{t}^*$ is statistically close to uniform over $\mathbb{Z}_q^n$. Thus, Game G_2^b and G_1^b are statistically indistinguishable.

Game G_3^b: This game follows Game G_2^b with one difference: sample $\mathbf{w}^*$ uniformly from $\mathbb{Z}_q^m$. Note that in the previous game, $\mathbf{W}$ is uniformly random over $\mathbb{Z}_q^{m\times n}$, so the pair $(\mathbf{W}, \mathbf{w}^*)$ is a valid $\mathsf{LWE}_{n,q,\chi}$ instance and its distribution is computationally close to the uniform distribution over $\mathbb{Z}_q^{m\times n} \times \mathbb{Z}_q^m$. Thus, the two games are computationally indistinguishable.

Game G_4^b: This game conducts the same as that in Game G_3^b, except that it uses matrix $\mathbf{B}' \leftarrow U(\mathbb{Z}_q^{n\times m})$ to encrypt users' identity. From Lemma 2, we know that the original matrix $\mathbf{B}$ is statistically close to uniform over $\mathbb{Z}_q^{n\times m}$. Hence, the two games are statistically indistinguishable.

Game G_5^b: This game encrypts the identity with random samples, namely, it generates ciphertexts $\mathbf{c}_1' = \mathbf{z}_1$ and $\mathbf{c}_2' = \mathbf{z}_2 + \lfloor\frac{q}{2}\rfloor \cdot \mathsf{ID}_b$ where $\mathbf{z}_1 \leftarrow U(\mathbb{Z}_q^m)$, $\mathbf{z}_2 \leftarrow U(\mathbb{Z}_q^\ell)$. Based on the hardness of *decision*-LWE, we have that Game G_5^b and G_4^b are computationally indistinguishable.

Game G_6: This game is the same as Game G_5^b except that it replaces the ciphertexts with random vectors, i.e., $\mathbf{c}_1'' = \mathbf{z}_1'$ and $\mathbf{c}_2'' = \mathbf{z}_2'$ where $\mathbf{z}_1' \leftarrow U(\mathbb{Z}_q^m)$, $\mathbf{z}_2' \leftarrow U(\mathbb{Z}_q^\ell)$. Since users' identity is an unknown random string in the view of $\mathcal{A}$, it is clear that Game G_6 and G_5^b are statistically indistinguishable.

Combine the whole analysis above, we have that

$$G_0^0 \overset{c}{\approx} G_1^0 \overset{s}{\approx} G_2^0 \overset{c}{\approx} G_3^0 \overset{s}{\approx} G_4^0 \overset{c}{\approx} G_5^0 \overset{s}{\approx} G_6, \ G_6 \overset{s}{\approx} G_5^1 \overset{c}{\approx} G_4^1 \overset{s}{\approx} G_3^1 \overset{c}{\approx} G_2^1 \overset{s}{\approx} G_1^1 \overset{c}{\approx} G_0^1,$$

it then follows that $|\Pr[\mathbf{Exp}_{\mathcal{A}}^{\mathsf{DR}-1} = 1] - \Pr[\mathbf{Exp}_{\mathcal{A}}^{\mathsf{DR}-0} = 1]| = \mathsf{negl}(\lambda)$. This concludes the proof.

Backward Unlinkability. Experiment $\mathbf{Exp}_{\mathcal{A}}^{\mathsf{B-Unlink}-b}$ is much similar to $\mathbf{Exp}_{\mathcal{A}}^{\mathsf{DR}-b}$, in the sense that the challenger also picks one out of two users to simulate a handshake with $\mathcal{A}$ twice, except now the arbitrary user is predetermined as ID_1. Therefore we can also build a sequence of hybrid games to prove this property as the above constructions, with the only difference that we need to additionally argue the anonymity of revoked users (attribute "backward"). To this effect, it suffices to prove that the publicity of revocation tokens at period t' brings no advantage for $\mathcal{A}$ at period t holding $t < t'$. We tackle this issue in two steps:

First we demonstrate that the update algorithm for revocation token is one-way, i.e., it is impossible to recover a previous token from the current one, the claimed fact is as follows.

Lemma 6. *The update function of revocation token defined in algorithm* Update$_{\mathsf{U}}$ *is one-way, assuming the hardness of* $\mathsf{ISIS}_{n,q,\sqrt{nk}}$ *problem.*

Proof. Let $\mathbf{u} = \mathsf{urt}_{i\|t} - \mathbf{Q}_2 \cdot \mathbf{t} \in \mathbb{Z}_q^n$, if one can recover the previous token $\mathsf{urt}_{i\|t-1} := \mathbf{v} \in \mathbb{Z}_q^n$ from the current one, satisfying that $\mathsf{urt}_{i\|t} = \mathbf{Q}_1 \cdot \mathsf{vdec}_{n,q-1}(\mathbf{v}) + \mathbf{Q}_2 \cdot \mathbf{t} \bmod q$, then one can obtain a non-zero vector $\mathbf{z} = \mathsf{vdec}_{n,q-1}(\mathbf{v}) \in \{0,1\}^{nk}$ such that $\mathbf{Q}_1 \cdot \mathbf{z} = \mathbf{u} \bmod q$. In other words, $\mathbf{z}$ is a valid solution to the $\mathsf{ISIS}_{n,q,\sqrt{nk}}$ problem associated with matrix $\mathbf{Q}_1$ and vector $\mathbf{u}$.

Next we show that $\mathcal{A}$ gains no extra advantage after knowing later revocation tokens (e.g., $\mathsf{urt}_{i\|t+1}$). It suffices to prove that $\mathcal{A}$ still can not distinguish the LWE instance $(\mathbf{W}, \mathbf{w}^*)$ in Game G_2^b from real random samples.

Suppose that now Game G_2^b and G_3^b are distinguishable with a non-negligible advantage, which directly implies that $\mathcal{A}$ solves *decision*-LWE with non-negligible probability. It then follows that $\mathcal{A}$ can also solve *search*-LWE with non-negligible probability and a larger sample number $m' = \mathsf{poly}(m)$, implying $\mathcal{A}$ can find the secret token $\mathsf{urt}_{i\|t}$ at current period t by use of $\mathsf{urt}_{i\|t+1}$. In this way, $\mathcal{A}$ will break the one-way property of the update function stated in Lemma 6.

References

1. Abdalla, M., Reyzin, L.: A new forward-secure digital signature scheme. In: Okamoto, T. (ed.) ASIACRYPT 2000. LNCS, vol. 1976, pp. 116–129. Springer, Heidelberg (2000). https://doi.org/10.1007/3-540-44448-3_10
2. Agrawal, S., Boneh, D., Boyen, X.: Lattice basis delegation in fixed dimension and shorter-ciphertext hierarchical IBE. In: Rabin, T. (ed.) CRYPTO 2010. LNCS, vol. 6223, pp. 98–115. Springer, Heidelberg (2010). https://doi.org/10.1007/978-3-642-14623-7_6
3. Ajtai, M.: Generating hard instances of lattice problems (extended abstract). In: Miller, G.L. (ed.) STOC 1996, pp. 99–108. ACM (1996). https://doi.org/10.1145/237814.237838
4. Alwen, J., Peikert, C.: Generating shorter bases for hard random lattices. Theory Comput. Syst. **48**(3), 535–553 (2011). https://doi.org/10.1007/s00224-010-9278-3
5. An, Z., Zhang, Z., Wen, Y., Zhang, F.: Lattice-based secret handshakes with reusable credentials. In: Gao, D., Li, Q., Guan, X., Liao, X. (eds.) ICICS 2021. LNCS, vol. 12919, pp. 231–248. Springer, Cham (2021). https://doi.org/10.1007/978-3-030-88052-1_14
6. Ateniese, G., Kirsch, J., Blanton, M.: Secret handshakes with dynamic and fuzzy matching. In: NDSS 2007. The Internet Society (2007). https://www.ndss-symposium.org/ndss2007/secret-handshakes-dynamic-and-fuzzy-matching/
7. Balfanz, D., Durfee, G., Shankar, N., Smetters, D.K., Staddon, J., Wong, H.: Secret handshakes from pairing-based key agreements. In: S&P 2003, pp. 180–196. IEEE Computer Society (2003). https://doi.org/10.1109/SECPRI.2003.1199336

8. Bellare, M., Miner, S.K.: A forward-secure digital signature scheme. In: Wiener, M. (ed.) CRYPTO 1999. LNCS, vol. 1666, pp. 431–448. Springer, Heidelberg (1999). https://doi.org/10.1007/3-540-48405-1_28

9. Böhl, F., Hofheinz, D., Jager, T., Koch, J., Striecks, C.: Confined guessing: new signatures from standard assumptions. J. Cryptol. **28**(1), 176–208 (2015). https://doi.org/10.1007/s00145-014-9183-z

10. Boneh, D., Boyen, X., Goh, E.-J.: Hierarchical identity based encryption with constant size ciphertext. In: Cramer, R. (ed.) EUROCRYPT 2005. LNCS, vol. 3494, pp. 440–456. Springer, Heidelberg (2005). https://doi.org/10.1007/11426639_26

11. Boneh, D., Shacham, H.: Group signatures with verifier-local revocation. In: Atluri, V., Pfitzmann, B., McDaniel, P.D. (eds.) CCS 2004, pp. 168–177. ACM (2004). https://doi.org/10.1145/1030083.1030106

12. Boyen, X., Shacham, H., Shen, E., Waters, B.: Forward-secure signatures with untrusted update. In: Juels, A., Wright, R.N., di Vimercati, S.D.C. (eds.) CCS 2006, pp. 191–200. ACM (2006). https://doi.org/10.1145/1180405.1180430

13. Brassard, G., Chaum, D., Crépeau, C.: Minimum disclosure proofs of knowledge. J. Comput. Syst. Sci. **37**(2), 156–189 (1988). https://doi.org/10.1016/0022-0000(88)90005-0

14. Brickell, E., Pointcheval, D., Vaudenay, S., Yung, M.: Design validations for discrete logarithm based signature schemes. In: Imai, H., Zheng, Y. (eds.) PKC 2000. LNCS, vol. 1751, pp. 276–292. Springer, Heidelberg (2000). https://doi.org/10.1007/978-3-540-46588-1_19

15. Canetti, R., Halevi, S., Katz, J.: A forward-secure public-key encryption scheme. In: Biham, E. (ed.) EUROCRYPT 2003. LNCS, vol. 2656, pp. 255–271. Springer, Heidelberg (2003). https://doi.org/10.1007/3-540-39200-9_16

16. Cash, D., Hofheinz, D., Kiltz, E., Peikert, C.: Bonsai trees, or how to delegate a lattice basis. In: Gilbert, H. (ed.) EUROCRYPT 2010. LNCS, vol. 6110, pp. 523–552. Springer, Heidelberg (2010). https://doi.org/10.1007/978-3-642-13190-5_27

17. Castelluccia, C., Jarecki, S., Tsudik, G.: Secret handshakes from CA-oblivious encryption. In: Lee, P.J. (ed.) ASIACRYPT 2004. LNCS, vol. 3329, pp. 293–307. Springer, Heidelberg (2004). https://doi.org/10.1007/978-3-540-30539-2_21

18. ETSI: ETSI TR 103 570: CYBER; Quantum-Safe Key Exchange, 1.1.1 edn (2017)

19. Gentry, C., Peikert, C., Vaikuntanathan, V.: Trapdoors for hard lattices and new cryptographic constructions. In: Dwork, C. (ed.) STOC 2008, pp. 197–206. ACM (2008). https://doi.org/10.1145/1374376.1374407

20. Hou, L., Lai, J., Liu, L.: Secret handshakes with dynamic expressive matching policy. In: Liu, J.K., Steinfeld, R. (eds.) ACISP 2016. LNCS, vol. 9722, pp. 461–476. Springer, Cham (2016). https://doi.org/10.1007/978-3-319-40253-6_28

21. Itkis, G., Reyzin, L.: Forward-secure signatures with optimal signing and verifying. In: Kilian, J. (ed.) CRYPTO 2001. LNCS, vol. 2139, pp. 332–354. Springer, Heidelberg (2001). https://doi.org/10.1007/3-540-44647-8_20

22. Jarecki, S., Kim, J., Tsudik, G.: Group secret handshakes or affiliation-hiding authenticated group key agreement. In: Abe, M. (ed.) CT-RSA 2007. LNCS, vol. 4377, pp. 287–308. Springer, Heidelberg (2006). https://doi.org/10.1007/11967668_19

23. Jarecki, S., Liu, X.: Private mutual authentication and conditional oblivious transfer. In: Halevi, S. (ed.) CRYPTO 2009. LNCS, vol. 5677, pp. 90–107. Springer, Heidelberg (2009). https://doi.org/10.1007/978-3-642-03356-8_6

24. Libert, B., Ling, S., Mouhartem, F., Nguyen, K., Wang, H.: Signature schemes with efficient protocols and dynamic group signatures from lattice assumptions.

In: Cheon, J.H., Takagi, T. (eds.) ASIACRYPT 2016. LNCS, vol. 10032, pp. 373–403. Springer, Heidelberg (2016). https://doi.org/10.1007/978-3-662-53890-6_13

25. Libert, B., Ling, S., Mouhartem, F., Nguyen, K., Wang, H.: Zero-knowledge arguments for matrix-vector relations and lattice-based group encryption. In: Cheon, J.H., Takagi, T. (eds.) ASIACRYPT 2016. LNCS, vol. 10032, pp. 101–131. Springer, Heidelberg (2016). https://doi.org/10.1007/978-3-662-53890-6_4

26. Libert, B., Yung, M.: Dynamic fully forward-secure group signatures. In: Feng, D., Basin, D.A., Liu, P. (eds.) ASIACCS 2010, pp. 70–81. ACM (2010). https://doi.org/10.1145/1755688.1755698

27. Ling, S., Nguyen, K., Stehlé, D., Wang, H.: Improved zero-knowledge proofs of knowledge for the ISIS problem, and applications. In: Kurosawa, K., Hanaoka, G. (eds.) PKC 2013. LNCS, vol. 7778, pp. 107–124. Springer, Heidelberg (2013). https://doi.org/10.1007/978-3-642-36362-7_8

28. Ling, S., Nguyen, K., Wang, H., Xu, Y.: Forward-secure group signatures from lattices. In: Ding, J., Steinwandt, R. (eds.) PQCrypto 2019. LNCS, vol. 11505, pp. 44–64. Springer, Cham (2019). https://doi.org/10.1007/978-3-030-25510-7_3

29. Micciancio, D., Regev, O.: Worst-case to average-case reductions based on gaussian measures. SIAM J. Comput. **37**(1), 267–302 (2007). https://doi.org/10.1137/S0097539705447360

30. Michalevsky, Y., Nath, S., Liu, J.: Mashable: mobile applications of secret handshakes over bluetooth LE. In: Chen, Y., Gruteser, M., Hu, Y.C., Sundaresan, K. (eds.) MobiCom 2016, pp. 387–400. ACM (2016). https://doi.org/10.1145/2973750.2973778

31. Nakanishi, T., Funabiki, N.: Verifier-local revocation group signature schemes with backward unlinkability from bilinear maps. In: Roy, B. (ed.) ASIACRYPT 2005. LNCS, vol. 3788, pp. 533–548. Springer, Heidelberg (2005). https://doi.org/10.1007/11593447_29

32. Nakanishi, T., Hira, Y., Funabiki, N.: Forward-secure group signatures from pairings. In: Shacham, H., Waters, B. (eds.) Pairing 2009. LNCS, vol. 5671, pp. 171–186. Springer, Heidelberg (2009). https://doi.org/10.1007/978-3-642-03298-1_12

33. Peikert, C.: Public-key cryptosystems from the worst-case shortest vector problem: extended abstract. In: Mitzenmacher, M. (ed.) STOC 2009, pp. 333–342. ACM (2009). https://doi.org/10.1145/1536414.1536461

34. Peikert, C.: Lattice cryptography for the internet. In: Mosca, M. (ed.) PQCrypto 2014. LNCS, vol. 8772, pp. 197–219. Springer, Cham (2014). https://doi.org/10.1007/978-3-319-11659-4_12

35. Regev, O.: On lattices, learning with errors, random linear codes, and cryptography. In: Gabow, H.N., Fagin, R. (eds.) STOC 2005, pp. 84–93. ACM (2005). https://doi.org/10.1145/1060590.1060603

36. Song, D.X.: Practical forward secure group signature schemes. In: Reiter, M.K., Samarati, P. (eds.) CCS 2001, pp. 225–234. ACM (2001). https://doi.org/10.1145/501983.502015

37. Tian, Y., Li, Y., Zhang, Y., Li, N., Yang, G., Yu, Y.: DSH: deniable secret handshake framework. In: Su, C., Kikuchi, H. (eds.) ISPEC 2018. LNCS, vol. 11125, pp. 341–353. Springer, Cham (2018). https://doi.org/10.1007/978-3-319-99807-7_21

38. Wen, Y., Zhang, F.: A new revocable secret handshake scheme with backward unlinkability. In: Camenisch, J., Lambrinoudakis, C. (eds.) EuroPKI 2010. LNCS, vol. 6711, pp. 17–30. Springer, Heidelberg (2011). https://doi.org/10.1007/978-3-642-22633-5_2

39. Wen, Y., Zhang, F., Wang, H., Gong, Z., Miao, Y., Deng, Y.: A new secret hand-shake scheme with multi-symptom intersection for mobile healthcare social networks. Inf. Sci. **520**, 142–154 (2020)
40. Xu, S., Yung, M.: k-anonymous secret handshakes with reusable credentials. In: Atluri, V., Pfitzmann, B., McDaniel, P.D. (eds.) CCS 2004, pp. 158–167. ACM (2004). https://doi.org/10.1145/1030083.1030105
41. Yang, R., Au, M.H., Zhang, Z., Xu, Q., Yu, Z., Whyte, W.: Efficient lattice-based zero-knowledge arguments with standard soundness: construction and applications. In: Boldyreva, A., Micciancio, D. (eds.) CRYPTO 2019. LNCS, vol. 11692, pp. 147–175. Springer, Cham (2019). https://doi.org/10.1007/978-3-030-26948-7_6
42. Zhang, Z., Zhang, F., Tian, H.: CSH: a post-quantum secret handshake scheme from coding theory. In: Chen, L., Li, N., Liang, K., Schneider, S. (eds.) ESORICS 2020. LNCS, vol. 12309, pp. 317–335. Springer, Cham (2020). https://doi.org/10.1007/978-3-030-59013-0_16
43. Zhou, L., Susilo, W., Mu, Y.: Three-round secret handshakes based on ElGamal and DSA. In: Chen, K., Deng, R., Lai, X., Zhou, J. (eds.) ISPEC 2006. LNCS, vol. 3903, pp. 332–342. Springer, Heidelberg (2006). https://doi.org/10.1007/11689522_31

Estimating the Hidden Overheads in the BDGL Lattice Sieving Algorithm

Léo Ducas[1,2(✉)]

[1] Cryptology Group, CWI, Amsterdam, The Netherlands
ducas@cwi.nl
[2] Mathematical Institute, Leiden University, Leiden, The Netherlands

Abstract. The lattice sieving algorithm based on list-decoding of Becker-Ducas-Gama-Laarhoven (SODA 2016) is currently at the center of cryptanalysis cost estimates of candidate lattice schemes for post-quantum standardization.

Yet, only an idealized version of this algorithm has been carefully modelled, i.e. given an efficient list-decoding oracle for a perfectly random spherical code. In this work, we propose an experimental analysis of the actual algorithm. The difficulty lies in estimating the probabilistic defect with respect to perfectly random spherical codes for the task at hand. While it should be in principle infeasible to run the algorithm in cryptographically relevant dimensions, a few tricks allow to nevertheless measure experimentally the relevant quantity.

Concretely, we conclude on an overhead factor of about 2^6 on the number of gates in the RAM model compared to the idealized model for dimensions around 380 after an appropriate re-parametrization. Part of this overhead can be traded for extra memory, at a costly rate. We also clarify that these overheads apply to an internal routine, and discuss how they can be partially mitigated in the whole attack.

Keywords: Concrete cryptanalysis · Lattice · Sieving

1 Introduction

1.1 Context

Sieving refers to a class of algorithm for finding the shortest vector in a Euclidean lattice; it proceeds by continuously searching within a list L of lattice vectors for pairs $\mathbf{u}, \mathbf{v} \in L$ such that $\mathbf{u} - \mathbf{v}$ is shorter than either of the original vectors. Assuming that all the vectors have roughly the same length (say, length 1), this is equivalent to searching for reducing pairs of vectors, i.e. pairs with angle less than $\pi/3$.

While proving that sieving does indeed succeed requires convoluted and costly tricks [AKS01], such a simple algorithm works well in practice [NV08] when working with a list of size roughly $N \approx (4/3)^{n/2}$ in dimension n. A naive implementation of this strategy therefore leads to finding the shortest vector in time

© The Author(s), under exclusive license to Springer Nature Switzerland AG 2022
J. H. Cheon and T. Johansson (Eds.): PQCrypto 2022, LNCS 13512, pp. 480–497, 2022.
https://doi.org/10.1007/978-3-031-17234-2_22

roughly $n^{O(1)} \cdot N^2$, for a complexity of $2^{.415n+o(n)}$. A line of work initiated by Laarhoven [Laa15a, Laa15b, LW15] has led to lower complexity, by the introduction of the Near Neighbour Search formalism (NNS), using Locality Sensitive Hashing. This approach allows one to find (most of) the reducing pairs in a time L^c for some constant $c \in [1, 2]$.

Among many variants [Laa15b, LW15, BGJ15, Laa15a], the asymptotically fastest is that of Becker-Ducas-Gama-Laarhoven [BDGL16], with a time complexity of $(3/2)^{n/2+o(n)} = 2^{.292n+o(n)}$. It is based on efficient list-decoding of well chosen spherical codes. It also underlies the current fastest implementation on CPUs [ADH+19, DSvW21], though the cross-over point with the simpler sieve of [BGJ15] has not yet been reached on GPUs [DSvW21].

This algorithm has also been the object of precise gate cost estimation in large dimensions [AGPS20], or more specifically its internal near-neighbors search (NNS) routine. These estimates are used in the documentation of several NIST post-quantum standardization candidates. In particular, the Kyber documentation [ABD+21, Sec. 5.3] gives a list of eight open question about various approximations and foreseeable improvements that may affect these estimates, both upward and downward.

1.2   This Work

This work aims to resolve the open question Q2 of [ABD+21, Sec. 5.3] regarding the idealized model for the near neighbors search procedure of [BDGL16]. In the idealized model, the spherical code is assumed to be perfectly random, and to be efficiently list-decodable. The instantiated NNS procedure instead resorts to a product of random codes, which induces overheads. More specifically, there is a trade-off between three overheads when instantiating the [BDGL16] framework with product codes:

- a computation overhead $\mathsf{CO}^\times$, to list-decode the spherical code,
- a memory overhead $\mathsf{MO}^\times$, to store pointers to vectors in buckets,
- a probability overhead $\mathsf{PO}^\times$, accounting for the randomness defect of product codes

The computation and probability overhead both contribute to the gate count of the algorithm, defining a time overhead $\mathsf{TO}^\times = \mathsf{CO}^\times \cdot \mathsf{PO}^\times$. It is known from [BDGL16] that all three overheads can be made subexponential, and that either the memory overhead or the computation overhead can be made negligible.

While the computation overhead $\mathsf{CO}^\times$ and memory overhead $\mathsf{MO}^\times$ are easy to calculate concretely, the probability overhead $\mathsf{PO}^\times$ seems harder to model precisely and rigorously, and naive measurements would not be feasible for cryptographically relevant parameters. The main technical contribution of this work resides in the design of feasible experiments to measure this overhead (Sect. 3).

Implementing this experiment leads to concrete conclusions on these overheads and their trade-off (Sect. 4). In dimension $n = 384$ (roughly what is needed to break lattice candidates at level NIST 1) the idealized NNS procedure is costed by [AGPS20] at $2^{134.1}$ gates and $2^{97.6}$ bits of memory. We conclude on a 2^6 slowdown factor on time for small memory overhead. A partial trade-off is possible, but costly, and even with a factor 2^{12} increase in memory consumption, a slowdown factor of $2^{2.5}$ remains.

We also discuss how these overheads of the internal NNS routine can be somewhat mitigated inside a complete lattice attacks (Sect. 5), and propose further open problems (Sect. 6).

Source Code. The artifact associated with this work are available at https://github.com/lducas/BDGL_overhead.

2   Preliminaries

Complexity. Time and memory complexity are given in the RAM model, and for readability are given in terms of elementary operations during most of this paper; constant factors will be gracefully ignored. Only in Sect. 4.3 do we quantify costs more precisely in terms of binary gates.

Independent Small Probability Events. We will silently abuse the approximation $1 - (1 - \mathcal{W})^M \approx \mathcal{W} \cdot M$ to our best convenience.

Euclidean Vector Space. In all this work, bold lowercase $(\mathbf{u}, \mathbf{v}, \mathbf{w}, \dots)$ letters denotes row vectors of the real vector space $\mathbb{R}^n$ endowed with its canonical Euclidean inner product: $\langle \mathbf{x}, \mathbf{y} \rangle := \sum x_i y_i$, and associated Euclidean metric $\|\mathbf{x}\| = \sqrt{\langle \mathbf{x}, \mathbf{x} \rangle}$.

Spheres, Caps and Wedges. We define the following bodies in dimension $\mathbb{R}^n$:

- The unit sphere : $\mathcal{S}^n := \{\mathbf{x} \in \mathbb{R}^n \mid \|x\| = 1\}$
- The halfspace : $\mathcal{H}^n_{\mathbf{v},a} := \{\mathbf{x} \in \mathbb{R}^n \mid \langle \mathbf{x}, \mathbf{v} \rangle \geq a\}$
- The spherical cap : $\mathcal{C}^n_{\mathbf{v},a} := \mathcal{S}^n \cap \mathcal{H}_{\mathbf{v},a}$
- The (symmetric) spherical wedge:[1] $\mathcal{W}^n_{\mathbf{v},\mathbf{w},a} := \mathcal{C}_{\mathbf{v},a} \cap \mathcal{C}_{\mathbf{w},a}$

where $\mathbf{v}, \mathbf{w} \in \mathcal{S}^n$ and $a \in [0, 1]$. Furthermore, we define the relative volume of caps and wedges as follows.

- $\mathcal{C}^n(a) := \mathrm{Vol}(\mathcal{C}_{\mathbf{v},a}) / \mathrm{Vol}(\mathcal{S}^n)$ for any $\mathbf{v} \in \mathcal{S}^n$
- $\mathcal{W}^n(a, c) := \mathrm{Vol}(\mathcal{W}_{\mathbf{v},\mathbf{w},a}) / \mathrm{Vol}(\mathcal{S}^n)$ for any $\mathbf{v}, \mathbf{w} \in \mathcal{S}^n$ such that $\langle \mathbf{v}, \mathbf{w} \rangle = c$.

The dimension n being generally clear from context, the exponent n might be omitted in the rest of this document. For asymptotic analysis, we have the following lemma.

---

[1] The literature usually defines asymmetric spherical wedge with two different bounds a, b for the halfspace in directions $\mathbf{v}$ and $\mathbf{w}$. However the best choice appears to be $a = b$ [BDGL16, AGPS20].

Lemma 1 ([BDGL16]). *For any fixed $a \in [0,1]$ and growing n,*

- $\mathcal{C}^n(a) = \left(1 - a^2\right)^{n/2} \cdot n^{O(1)}$
- $\mathcal{W}^n(a,c) = \left(1 - \frac{2a^2}{1+c}\right)^{n/2} \cdot n^{O(1)}$.

These quantities $\mathcal{C}^n(a)$ and $\mathcal{W}^n(a,c)$ can be efficiently computed precisely [AGPS20]; in particular $\mathcal{C}(a)$ directly relates to the incomplete beta function.

2.1 List-Decoding Sieve, Idealized

The idealized version of [BDGL16] proceeds by assuming that one is given random yet efficiently list decodable spherical code $F \subset \mathcal{S}^n$ of size M. More precisely, it is assumed that one can compute the set of codewords falling in a given spherical cap $F(\mathbf{v},a) := F \cap \mathcal{C}_{\mathbf{v},a}$, and this efficiently, that is in time, say, $\#F(\mathbf{v},a) + \mathsf{LDO}^+$ where $\mathsf{LDO}^+ = 2^{o(n)}$ denotes a sub-exponential additive overhead for list decoding. In the idealized model, this factor is assumed to be $\mathsf{LDO}^+ = 1$.

Given such a set and such an oracle, one proceeds with the search for reducing pairs as follows:

1. Compute $F(\mathbf{v},a)$ for each $\mathbf{v} \in L$, and store $\mathbf{v}$ in buckets labelled by each $\mathbf{f} \in F(\mathbf{v},a)$
2. For each $\mathbf{f} \in F$, and for each pair $\mathbf{v},\mathbf{w}$ in the bucket labelled by $\mathbf{f}$, check whether $\langle \mathbf{v}, \mathbf{w} \rangle \leq 1/2$.

Assuming that each codeword $\mathbf{f} \in F$ and each lattice vector of the list $\mathbf{v} \in L$ is uniform and independent over the sphere, one expects each $\mathbf{v}$ to fall in $M \cdot \mathcal{C}(a)$ buckets, and each bucket to contain $N \cdot \mathcal{C}(a)$ vectors, leading to a time complexity of

$$N \cdot (n \cdot M \cdot \mathcal{C}(a) + \mathsf{LDO}^+) + n \cdot M \cdot (N \cdot \mathcal{C}(a))^2$$
$$\approx 2nM \quad \text{when } a = 1/2$$

and a memory complexity of $N \cdot M \cdot \mathcal{C}(a)$ for the procedure.

A reducing pair will be detected if and only if there is a codeword falling in the wedge $\mathcal{W}_{\mathbf{v},\mathbf{w},a} = \mathcal{C}_{\mathbf{v},a} \cap \mathcal{C}_{\mathbf{w},a}$. Given that $\mathbf{f} \in F$ are uniform and independent, this happens with probability $1 - (1 - \mathcal{W}(a,1/2))^M \approx M \cdot \mathcal{W}(a,1/2)$. One should therefore choose $M \approx 1/\mathcal{W}(a,1/2)$ to find essentially all reducing pairs.

Recalling that $N \approx 1/\mathcal{C}(1/2) = (4/3)^{n/2} \cdot n^{O(1)}$, one finds that the optimal asymptotic time complexity of $\mathsf{T} = 1/\mathcal{W}(1/2,1/2) = (3/2)^{n/2} \cdot n^{O(1)}$ is reached at $a = 1/2$, and with a similar memory complexity $\mathsf{M} = (3/2)^{n/2} \cdot n^{O(1)}$. In practice [BDGL16], a slightly smaller value of $a < 1/2$ seems preferable. However we note that after the update of [AGPS20] including the model correction of [MAT22] for BDGL cost, a slightly larger $a > 1/2$ now gives optimal gate count.

Low Memory Variant. Following an original remark of [BGJ15, BDGL16] also propose a variant where the memory cost is dominated by that of the list of vectors, rather than by the buckets. One can simply choose a smaller value of $M = 1/\mathcal{C}(a)$, and to repeat the whole procedure with a fresh spherical code $R = M/\mathcal{W}(a, 1/2) = (9/8)^{n/2} \cdot n^{O(1)}$ many times. The new time complexity is now

$$RN \cdot (nM \cdot \mathcal{C}(a) + \mathsf{LDO}^+) + nRM \cdot (N \cdot \mathcal{C}(a))^2$$
$$\approx nRM(2 + \mathsf{LDO}^+) \quad \text{when } a = 1/2$$

which is similar to the above, up to an extra sub-exponential factor LDO^+. That is, we have traded an exponential factor $(9/8)^{n/2} \cdot n^{O(1)}$ on memory for a sub-exponential factor on time. Intermediate choices are also possible, ranging from $M_{\min} = 1/\mathcal{C}(a)$ to $M_{\max} = 1/\mathcal{W}(a, 1/2)$.

2.2   List-Decoding Sieve, Instantiated

It remains to replace the random spherical code by one that is structured enough to allow efficient list-decoding, while not affecting the success probability of detecting reducing pairs too much. This is an issue of independence. Indeed, consider for a second a code of size $M = 1/\mathcal{W}(a, 1/2)$, whose codewords would all be concentrated in a small region. The average number of codewords in a random wedge $\mathcal{W}^n_{\mathbf{v}, \mathbf{w}, a}$ would still be 1, yet most of the time a wedge will contain no codewords at all, while the remaining rare case is a wedge containing almost all of the M codewords. The desired situation is one there is always about 1 codeword in such a random wedge.

To do so, it is proposed in [BDGL16] to use a product of random codes in smaller dimensions. That is, F is constructed as the Cartesian product of m random spherical codes in dimension n/m, each of size $B = M^{1/m}$. For such a code, a decoding algorithm is devised [BDGL16, Sec. 5], running in time essentially

$$nB + mB \log B + m \cdot \#F(\mathbf{v}, a).$$

We will not describe the algorithm in detail (see [BDGL16, Sec. 5]), but briefly explain the three terms:

1. nB corresponds to the cost of computing B inner products in dimension n/m for each of the m subcode.
2. $mB \log B$ corresponds to sorting the m lists of inner products.
3. $m \cdot \#F(\mathbf{v}, a)$ corresponds to a tree enumeration without any backtracking, in a tree of depth m with $\#F(\mathbf{v}, a)$ leaves.

In practice, these costs can be tackled further [MLB17, DSvW21, MAT22], as will be discussed in Sect. 4.3, and a more optimistic model would be

$$mB + \#F(\mathbf{v}, a).$$

For now, one may simply consider that the additive overhead of the list decoder is $\mathsf{LDO}^+ = nB = nM^{1/m}$. Furthermore, it is proved [BDGL16, Theorem 5.1] that such random product codes are not that far off perfectly random codes when $m = \log n$; more precisely, the success probability for detecting a reducing pair is only a sub-exponential factor $\mathsf{PO}^\times = 2^{\tilde{O}(\sqrt{n})}$ away of the idealized model:

$$\mathbb{P}_W[\#(F \cap W) \geq 1] = M \cdot \mathcal{W}(a, c)/\mathsf{PO}^\times$$

where W is a random wedge with parameter (a, c). This multiplicative probability overhead must be compensated for by repeating the algorithm $\mathsf{PO}^\times$ many times.

Low Memory Variant. For the low memory variant, one can ensure independence across the R repetitions by applying a fresh random rotation to the input of each repetition. This ensures that the overall probability overhead is the same as the individual ones.

3   Analyzing the List-Decoding Sieve Instantiation

3.1   Overheads and Trade-Offs

We have identified three overheads between the idealized and the instantiated list-decoding sieving algorithm [BDGL16]: a cost overhead on the procedure $\mathsf{CO}^\times$ induced by the non-trivial cost of list-decoding, a memory overhead $\mathsf{MO}^\times$ for storing pointers to vectors in buckets, and a probabilistic overhead $\mathsf{PO}^\times$ induced by the independence defect of random product codes. The overall time overhead is given by $\mathsf{TO}^\times = \mathsf{CO}^\times \cdot \mathsf{PO}^\times$, and one may also consider the time-memory overhead $\mathsf{TMO}^\times = \mathsf{TO}^\times \cdot \mathsf{MO}^\times$.

The first two overheads $\mathsf{CO}^\times$ and $\mathsf{MO}^\times$ can be calculated from the algorithm parameter, though the exact formula might be bulky and hard to parse. For illustration, in a simple model ignoring constants, and assuming $a = 1/2$ and $N = 1/\mathcal{C}(1/2)$, we have:

$$\mathsf{TO}^\times \approx 1 + \frac{\mathsf{LDO}^+}{nM\mathcal{C}(a)} \approx 1 + \frac{M_{\min}}{M} \cdot M^{1/m} \text{ and } \mathsf{MO}^\times \approx 1 + \frac{M}{M_{\min}}.$$

The overhead $\mathsf{PO}^\times$ is however more problematic, and the author admits to having no clue on how to approach it analytically. In this position, one would be tempted to just ignore $\mathsf{PO}^\times$, and focus on the above; however such an analysis would result in essentially the same result as the idealized model: setting $M = M_{\min}$ and $m = \log_2(M) = \Theta(n)$ gives constants overheads $\mathsf{TO}^\times$ and $\mathsf{MO}^\times$. In such an extreme regime, the BDGL algorithm starts resembling the hyperplane-LSH algorithm of Laarhoven [Laa15b], whose complexity is supposed to be exponentially worse, that is, we'd expect $\mathsf{PO}^\times = 2^{\Theta(n)}$.

In conclusion, to refine the cost analysis of [BDGL16] one has no choice but to estimate $\mathsf{PO}^\times$ some way or another. Before we explore how to experimentally measure such a quantity, let us briefly recapitulate how the parameters affect each overhead:

1. The parameter M can range from $M_{min} = 1/\mathcal{C}(a)$ to $M_{max} = 1/\mathcal{W}(a, 1/2)$. Straightforwardly, increasing M decreases memory overhead and increases time overhead. One may also guess that $PO^{\times}$ grows with M; indeed, a larger value of $R = M_{max}/M$ improves independence of the success events bringing us closer to the idealized model. This trend is confirmed by the experiments of Sect. 4.2.
2. The parameter m is a positive integer, and time overhead decrease with it; however we expect $PO^{\times}$ to grow with m. This will also be confirmed by experiments of Sect. 4.2.
3. The parameter a may also affect both the base-line performance and the probabilistic overhead $PO^{\times}$. Though it is not clear a-priori in which direction. Experiments of Sect. 4.2 will show that for a fixed M, $PO^{\times}$ increases as a decrease.

3.2   Measuring $PO^{\times}$, Naively

In this section, we discuss how to experimentally measure $PO^{\times}$, hopefully up to cryptographically relevant dimension. By definition, running the full sieve algorithm is not an option. When giving explicit complexity, we tacitly assume $a = 1/2$.

The Naive Approach. The naive approach consists in generating random reducing pair on the sphere $\mathbf{v}, \mathbf{w}$ such that $\langle \mathbf{v}, \mathbf{w} \rangle = 1/2$, and simply testing whether $F(\mathbf{v}, a) \cap F(\mathbf{w}, a)$ is non-empty.

Lemma 2. *There is a polynomial time algorithm that, given $a \in [0, 1]$ samples a uniform pair $\mathbf{v}, \mathbf{w} \in \mathcal{S}^n$ conditioned on $\langle \mathbf{v}, \mathbf{w} \rangle = a$.*

Proof. The algorithm follows:

1. Sample $\mathbf{v}$ uniformly on $\mathcal{S}$
2. Sample $\mathbf{x}$ uniformly on $\mathcal{S} \cap \mathbf{v}^{\perp}$, by sampling uniformly on $\mathcal{S}$, projecting orthogonally to $\mathbf{v}$, and renormalizing.
3. Set $\mathbf{w} = \sqrt{1 - a^2} \cdot \mathbf{x} + a \cdot \mathbf{v}$.   □

Testing whether this pair is detected costs time $LDO^{+} + M/M_{min}$ per trial, and memory M/M_{min}. However, the success probability is only $M/(M_{max}PO^{\times})$, so the experiments must be repeated $(M_{max}PO^{\times})/M$ leading to a complexity of $(M_{max}PO^{\times})/M_{min} = (9/8)^{n/2+o(n)} = 2^{.085n+o(n)}$ to get a single success. And we may want to record up to a 1000 success for a decent estimate of the success probability.

3.3 Measuring PO$^\times$, a First Speed-Up

Because in this experimental set up we know in advance the reducing pair $\mathbf{v}, \mathbf{w}$ that the list-decoding is searching for, we can use this information to narrow down the search. In particular, consider the following lemma.

Lemma 3. *For any $a, c \in [0, 1]$, and $\mathbf{v}, \mathbf{w} \in \mathcal{S}^n$ such that $\langle \mathbf{v}, \mathbf{w} \rangle = c$, we have the inclusion*

$$\mathcal{W}^n_{\mathbf{v}, \mathbf{w}, a} \subset \mathcal{C}^n_{\mathbf{z}, 2 \cdot a / \sqrt{2 + 2c}}$$

where $\mathbf{z} = \frac{\mathbf{v} + \mathbf{w}}{\|\mathbf{v} + \mathbf{w}\|}$ is the midpoint of $\mathbf{v}, \mathbf{w}$ on the sphere $\mathcal{S}^n$.

Proof. Let $\mathbf{x}$ be in the wedge $\mathcal{W}^n_{\mathbf{v}, \mathbf{w}, a}$; by definition we have $\langle \mathbf{v}, \mathbf{x} \rangle \geq a$ and $\langle \mathbf{w}, \mathbf{x} \rangle \geq a$. Thus, it holds that $\langle \mathbf{v} + \mathbf{w}, \mathbf{x} \rangle \geq 2 \cdot a$, or equivalently that $\langle \mathbf{z}, \mathbf{x} \rangle \geq 2 \cdot a / \|\mathbf{v} + \mathbf{w}\|$. We conclude noting that $\|\mathbf{v} + \mathbf{w}\|^2 = \|\mathbf{v}\|^2 + \|\mathbf{w}\|^2 + 2 \langle \mathbf{v}, \mathbf{w} \rangle = 2 + 2c$. $\square$

Further, we note that this inclusion $\mathcal{C}^n_{\mathbf{z}, 2 \cdot a / \sqrt{2 + 2c}} \supset \mathcal{W}^n_{\mathbf{v}, \mathbf{w}, a}$ is rather a good over-approximation: the ratio $\mathsf{CW}(a, c) := \mathcal{C}(2a / \sqrt{2 + 2c}) / \mathcal{W}(a, c)$ is not too large.

Lemma 4 ([BDGL16], **App. A**). *For any $a, c \in [0, 1)$, $\mathsf{CW}(a, c) = O(\sqrt{n})$.*

In our case, this implies that $F(\mathbf{v}, a) \cap F(\mathbf{w}, a)$ is included in $F(\mathbf{z}, 2a / \sqrt{3})$; one can now test for each $\mathbf{f} \in F(\mathbf{z}, 2a / \sqrt{3})$ whether $\langle \mathbf{f}, \mathbf{v} \rangle \leq a$ and $\langle \mathbf{f}, \mathbf{w} \rangle \leq a$. This gives significant savings when $M / M_{\min} > \mathsf{LDO}^+$; in particular for $M = M_{\max}$ the time and memory complexity drop down to sub-exponential ($\mathsf{LDO}^+ + \mathsf{CW}) \cdot \mathsf{PO}^\times = 2^{o(n)}$ per successful sample.

3.4 Measuring PO$^\times$, a Second Speed-Up

While the previous speed-up is appreciable in the high-memory regime, it is not very effective in the low memory regime, the main issue being that it inherently takes $(M_{\max} \mathsf{PO}^\times) / M$ trials to get a success. And we are indeed most interested in the case where M is close to $M_{\min}$. To tackle it, we need not improve the algorithm, but instead design a different experiment.

Consider the following distribution $\mathcal{D} : \#(F(\mathbf{v}, a) \cap F(\mathbf{w}, a))$ where $\mathbf{v}, \mathbf{w}$ are uniform over the sphere conditioned on $\langle \mathbf{v}, \mathbf{w} \rangle = 1/2$. In other word, the distribution of the size of $W \cap F$ for a random $(a, 1/2)$-wedge. Let us call $d_i := \mathbb{P}_{j \leftarrow \mathcal{D}}[j = i]$ its density at i.

We know that the average size of $W \cap F$ is $M \cdot \mathcal{W}(a, 1/2)$, that is $\sum_{i \geq 0} d_i \cdot i = M \cdot \mathcal{W}(a, 1/2)$ is essentially equal to the success probability of when F is perfectly random. We are interested in the probability of success S, that $i \geq 1$ for $i \leftarrow \mathcal{D}$, i.e. $S = \sum_{i \geq 1} d_i$. An idea would be to design an experiment that focuses on the cases $i \geq 1$, *i.e.* an experiment that is conditioned on successful detection.

Conditioned Sampling. We start with a sampling procedure for generating pairs that are successfully detected by a given filter $\mathbf{f}$.

Lemma 5. *There is a polynomial time algorithm that, given $a, c \in [0,1]$ and $\mathbf{f} \in S^n$ samples a uniform pair $\mathbf{v}, \mathbf{w} \in S^n$ conditioned on $\langle \mathbf{v}, \mathbf{w} \rangle = c$ and $\mathcal{W}_{\mathbf{v}, \mathbf{w}, a} \ni \mathbf{f}$.*

Proof. Setting $\mathbf{z} = \frac{\mathbf{v}+\mathbf{w}}{\|\mathbf{v}+\mathbf{w}\|}$, we know by the previous lemma that $\mathbf{f} \in \mathcal{W}_{\mathbf{v},\mathbf{w},a}$ implies $\mathbf{f} \in C_{\mathbf{z}, 2\cdot a/\sqrt{2+2c}}$, which is equivalent to $\mathbf{z} \in C_{\mathbf{f}, 2\cdot a/\sqrt{2+2c}}$. Our strategy is therefore to

1. Sample $\mathbf{z}$ uniformly in $C_{\mathbf{f}, 2\cdot a/\sqrt{2+2c}}$
2. Sample $\mathbf{v}, \mathbf{w}$ such that $\mathbf{z}$ is their midpoint, and $\langle \mathbf{v}, \mathbf{w} \rangle = c$
3. Return $(\mathbf{v}, \mathbf{w})$ if $\mathbf{f} \in \mathcal{W}_{\mathbf{v},\mathbf{w},a}$, otherwise restart.

For the first step, note that $r := \langle \mathbf{f}, \mathbf{z} \rangle$ is not determined, but constrained to $r \in [b := \frac{2\cdot a}{\sqrt{2+2c}}, 1]$. Defining $\beta = \cos^{-1}(b)$, $\rho = \cos^{-1}(r)$, we sample ρ uniformly in $[0, \beta]$ and use rejection sampling with acceptance probability $(\sin(\rho)/\sin(\beta))^{n-2}$. Finally, we choose $\mathbf{z} \in S$ under the constraint $\langle \mathbf{f}, \mathbf{z} \rangle = r$.

The second step is easy, by first choosing $\mathbf{v}$ conditioned an inner product of $\frac{1+c}{\sqrt{2+2c}}$ with $\mathbf{z}$, and then setting $\mathbf{w}$ to be its reflection against the axis $\mathbf{z}$.

Regarding last step, we note that the accepting probability is $1/\mathsf{CW}(a,c) = 1/O(\sqrt{n})$ by Lemma 4. $\qquad\square$

An Auxiliary Distribution. We can now consider the following distribution $\mathcal{D}'$ of $\#(F(\mathbf{v}, a) \cap F(\mathbf{w}, a))$, where $\mathbf{f}$ is chosen uniformly from F, and $\mathbf{v}, \mathbf{w}$ chosen uniformly conditioned on $\langle \mathbf{v}, \mathbf{w} \rangle = 1/2$ and on $\mathcal{W}_{\mathbf{v},\mathbf{w},a} \ni \mathbf{f}$. By construction, it always holds that $i \geq 1$ for $i \leftarrow \mathcal{D}'$. In fact, the density at i is proportional to id_i, because there are i many ways to get to that same pair $(\mathbf{v}, \mathbf{w})$; that is, the density of $\mathcal{D}'$ is given by $d_i' = id_i / \sum_j j d_j$.

Conclusion. Now consider the expectation of $1/i$ for $i \leftarrow \mathcal{D}'$:

$$\mathbb{E}[1/i] = \frac{\sum_{i \geq 1} id_i/i}{\sum_j j d_j} = \frac{\sum_{i \geq 1} d_i}{\sum_j j d_j} = \frac{S}{M \cdot \mathcal{W}(a, 1/2)} = \frac{1}{\mathsf{PO}^\times}.$$

This means we can estimate $\mathsf{PO}^\times$ simply as the average of $\mathbb{E}[1/i]$ where $i \leftarrow \mathcal{D}'$.

The remaining question is how many sample do we need to get a precise estimate? The variance of the empirical average grows as $\Theta(\mathbb{V}/k)$ using k samples and where $\mathbb{V}$ denotes the variance of individual samples; drawing $k = \Theta(\mathbb{V}/\mathbb{E}^2)$ samples one therefore reaches a relative error of $\sqrt{\mathbb{V}}/\mathbb{E} = O(1)$. Because the $1/i$ is supported by $[0, 1]$, it holds that $\mathbb{V} \leq \mathbb{E}$, and we get $k \leq \Theta(1/\mathbb{E}) = O(\mathsf{PO}^\times)$.

We therefore only need a sub-exponential amount $O(\mathsf{PO}^\times)$ of sample in any regime, to be compared to $(M_{\max}\mathsf{PO}^\times)/M$, a quantity as large as $(9/8)^{n/2+o(n)}$ in the low memory regime.

4   Implementation and Experiments

We implemented BDGL list-decoder in `python`, with the library `numpy` for vector operation, which makes most of the operation reasonably fast. The experiments to measure $PO^{\times}$ are proudly parallel[2] over the many samples they require.

Only the tree enumeration is implemented without `numpy` acceleration, however this is reasonably mitigated by our first speed-up: the tree should be small on average for the regime we are interested in. We nevertheless experienced that a few instances had unreasonably large tree (enough to fill gigabytes worth of leaves); we therefore implemented a cap on the number of leaves at which the tree enumeration is halted, with a default value of 10^7. This might lead to underestimating $PO^{\times}$ in the experiments of Sect. 3.4, but no significantly unless $PO^{\times}$ itself reaches similar order of magnitude. In particular, this is not significant in the regime of our experiments.

We also depend on the software of [AGPS20] for computing $\mathcal{C}$ and $\mathcal{W}$ exactly, as well as for computing baseline cost, that is the cost of idealized near neighbor search.

4.1   Consistency Checks

In `consistency_check.py`, we implement some consistency checks for both speed-ups described in Sect. 3.3 and 3.4. For the first speed-up, we check that it is indeed the case that $F(\mathbf{v}, a) \cap F(\mathbf{w}, a)$ is included in $F(\mathbf{z}, 2a/\sqrt{3})$ where $\mathbf{z}$ is the spherical midpoint of $\mathbf{v}$ and $\mathbf{w}$.

For the second speed-up, we simply measure $PO^{\times}$ using both methods, using 2^{16} samples, and check that both results are equal up to a 20% relative error.

4.2   Trends

We plot the variation of $PO^{\times}$ as a function of various parameters in Fig. 1. These plots confirm that $PO^{\times}$ indeed increases with m and M. Interestingly, for fixed m and either $M = M_{\min}$ or $M = M_{\max}$, $PO^{\times}$ appears to be converging as n grows. We also note that $PO^{\times}$ decrease with a for a fixed M.

4.3   Concrete Estimate in Dimension 384

In this section, we will be more precise about costs, giving an gate count for time and a bit count for memory.

The [AGPS20] Estimates. The original version of the software associated with [AGPS20] was costing list-decoding in the idealized model, that is, the

---

[2] The terminology was communicated to us by M. Albrecht, and is meant as a synonym of embarrassingly parallel.

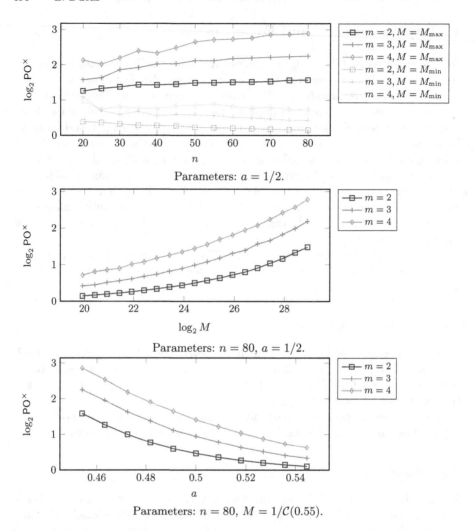

Fig. 1. Variations of $\mathsf{PO}^\times$ as a function of various parameters. Measured over 2^{14} samples per datapoint.

cost of bucketing a vector was proportional to the number of buckets it falls into, following the formula[3]:

$$m \cdot M \cdot \mathcal{C}(a) \cdot \mathsf{C}_{\mathsf{ip}}(n) \qquad (1)$$

choosing $m = \log_2(n)$ and where $\mathsf{C}_{\mathsf{ip}}(n) = 2^{10} \cdot n$ denotes the cost of an inner product in dimension n in gates (computed at 32 bit precision). Not withstanding the idealization of ignoring the additive overhead LDO^+, this formula does

---

[3] https://github.com/jschanck/eprint-2019-1161/blob/09d72d2125e75fdd35e49e54c3 5663a1affa212a/cost.py#L783.

not adequately reflects the cost stated in the original [BDGL16] paper; this was pointed out in [MAT22]. Indeed, in [BDGL16] the inner products are pre-computed and reused through the tree enumeration, reducing the $C_{ip}(n)$ factor[4] to a $C_{add} = 160$ factor, the cost of a single 32 bit addition. Furthermore, the work of [MAT22] propose a variation on the tree enumeration order to tackle the m factor[5].

Following this report and further discussion on the NIST forum[6], this cost has been revised to[7]

$$\underbrace{m \cdot B \cdot C_{ip}(n/m) + mB \log_2 B(C_{cp} + \log_2 B)}_{LDO^+} + M \cdot \mathcal{C}(a) \cdot (C_{add} + \log_2 B) \quad (2)$$

where $C_{cp} = 32$ is the cost of a comparison (for sorting), and the additive terms $\log_2(B)$ are meant to account for moving and addressing pointers[8].

The addition of the LDO^+ term is in fact negligible, because the whole algorithm is costed in its *high-memory regime* $M = M_{max}$, $R = 1$. Though, the memory consumption is not reported upon by the software, nor by other report using this software, nor in the reports of [AGPS20, GJ21, MAT22]. In the Kyber documentation (Round 3 version) [ABD+21], a memory cost of $2^{93.8}$ bits for sieving dimension 375, which corresponds to storing $N = 1/C(1/2)$ vectors of dimension n at 8-bit precision. That is, the memory was costed following the *low-memory regime*.

Costing time in the high memory regime, while costing memory in the low memory regime, all while ignoring the probabilistic overhead essentially corresponds to the idealized model for [BDGL16].

Further Improvement on LDO^+. There has been some further improvement on implementing [BDGL16], in particular improving the LDO^+ term. In personal communication about [MLB17], Laarhoven mentioned that partial inner products need not be entirely sorted as only the top fraction is visited during the tree enumeration. In the low memory regime, one would expect that the tree visit about a single branch on average, so this sorting may be reduced down to finding a single maximum. We will therefore ignore this cost which is dominated by the other LDO^+ term.

A second improvement comes from the implementation of [DSvW21], which replace explicit inner products with random vectors, by a sequence of implicit

---

[4] Even without this precomputation, this cost should have been $C_{ip}(n/m)$.

[5] Though in the original [BDGL16] this factor comes from a *worst-case* analysis on the tree shape, and one would expect this factor to also vanish to 1 for large random trees without tweaking the tree enumeration.

[6] https://groups.google.com/a/list.nist.gov/g/pqc-forum/c/Fm4cDfsx65s/m/m1vVrpoAAgAJ.

[7] https://github.com/jschanck/eprint-2019-1161/blob/a4d3a53fe1f428fe3b4402bd63e e164ba6cc571c/cost.py#L801.

[8] We believe the last term should be $\log_2(M)$ rather than $\log(B)$ since there are M buckets to point to.

inner products using permutations and Hadamard matrices. This allows to decrease the cost from $m \cdot B \cdot C_{ip}(n/m)$ to essentially

$$m \cdot \log_2 n/m \cdot B \cdot C_{add} \qquad (3)$$

where the additions are computed at 16-bit precision ($C_{add} = 80$).

First Overhead Estimation. Having now costed the overheads following the state of the art [MLB17, DSvW21], and being equipped with an efficient method to measure the probability overhead, we may now provide an analysis of the previously neglected overheads. We fix parameters according to the optimization provided by the (revised) software of [AGPS20]:

- Dimension is $n = 384$
- Xor-popcount parameters [FBB+14, Duc18, ADH+19] are done over 511 bits, with a threshold at 170, giving an positive detection rate of $\eta = 0.456$
- The number of vectors for the sieve is set to $N = 2/((1 - \eta)C(1/2)) = 2^{86.0}$,
- The filter parameter is optimized at $a = 0.512$ by the revised script of [AGPS20], giving $M_{min} = 2^{89.0}$ and $M_{max} = 2^{127.6}$.

The revised script of [AGPS20] concludes on a cost of $T_{ideal} = 2^{134.1}$ gates, while we need at least $M_{ideal} = 8nN = 2^{97.6}$ bits of memory for storing all the sieve vectors. In Fig. 2a we report on the time and memory overheads ($TO^\times, MO^\times$) for various values of m and M.

For each value of m, we first see time decrease as we increase the memory overhead, until a certain point, after which is starts increasing again. In other words, and perhaps surprisingly, the minimal time is not reached at the high-memory regime $M = M_{max}$, but somewhere halfway $M_{min} < M < M_{max}$. A breakdown of the time overhead $TO^\times = CO^\times \cdot PO^\times$ explains the phenomenon (Fig. 2b): while $CO^\times$ tends to 0, $PO^\times$ increases at a steady rate; once $CO^\times$ approaches 0, the decay of $CO^\times$ gets lower than the increase of $PO^\times$.

The plot shows that whatever the parametrization, the overhead on time-memory is $TO^\times \cdot MO^\times \geq 2^8$; furthermore, even for very large memory overhead the time overhead remains non-negligible.

One can also note that the number of vectors per bucket is $NC(a) \approx 1/8$, which is surprisingly low; only one bucket in 64 will actually have a pair to attempt reduction. This is understandable in the idealized model, because the cost of bucketing $C_{add} + \log_2 B$ is significantly lower than a xor-popcount on 511 bits (costed at 3072 gates by [AGPS20]). But this could be sub-optimal when considering overheads. That is, to conclude, we first need to re-optimize the value of a with the overhead in the equation.

Reparametrizing, with Overheads. We now have three parameters to optimize over, m, M, and a, so we need to be mindful of the search space for the experiment to be feasible. We explore M by multiplicative increment of 2, and for each M, we use the previous curve to determine the relevant range for a.

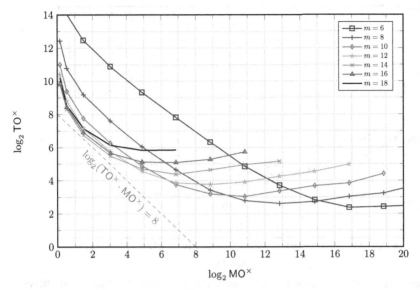

(a) Overall Time Overhead $\mathsf{TO}^\times$ as a function of the Memory Overhead $\mathsf{MO}^\times$.

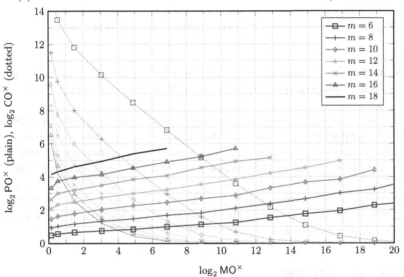

(b) Breakdown of Time Overhead $\mathsf{TO}^\times = \mathsf{CO}^\times \cdot \mathsf{TO}^\times$ as a function of the Memory Overhead $\mathsf{MO}^\times$.

Each measure of $\mathsf{PO}^\times$ was done over 2^{12} samples. The computation took about 20 core-days.

Fig. 2. Overheads in dimension 384 for $a = 0.512$.

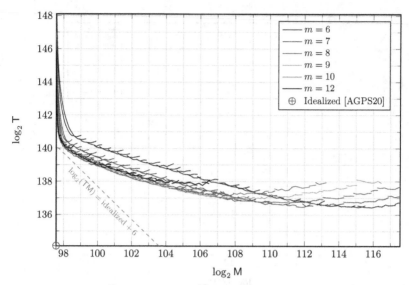

Each measure of $PO^\times$ was done over 2^{13} samples. The computation took about 40 core-days.

Fig. 3. Cost in dimension 384 when optimizing a with overheads.

This explain the "hairy" appearance of our plot in Fig. 3: each "thread" (for a fixed m) is in fact a union of curves for a fixed M and a small range of relevant a.

Qualitatively, the conclusion remain similar to that of the previous experiments, but quantitatively, the gap with the idealized cost is now a bit smaller near the low-memory regime (from 2^8 down to 2^6). Numerically, we can for example parametrize the algorithm to have time and memory complexity about $(T = 2^{140.1}, M = 2^{98})$, against a baseline of $(T_{\text{ideal}} = 2^{134.1}, T_{\text{ideal}} = 2^{97.6})$. The time-memory trade-off is however costly: from this point, decreasing the time by a factor 2^{-2} costs an extra factor of $2^{4.5}$ on memory, and gets worse as the curve flatten to minimal time around $(T = 2^{136.5}, M = 2^{112})$.

5   Impact on Attacks

We clarify that the cost given all along this paper corresponds to the NNS task of finding all reducing pairs once inside sieving, and not that of the whole attack. In particular, we *can not* conclude that all attacks using sieving have their time-memory cost increased by a 2^6 factor. The most advanced attacks [GJ21, MAT22] have several stages, and reparametrizing them adequately should partially mitigate these overheads.

We also recall that there remain several known unknown in precisely modeling and costing lattice attacks, summarized in [ABD+21, Sec. 5.3]. This works resolves question Q2 (Idealized Near-Neighbors Search) of [ABD+21, Sec. 5.3]. We note that question Q7 (Refined BKZ Strategies) is now accounted for in the recent estimator of Albrecht [Alb22] under the label bdd.

We also warn against regressions on the accuracy of lattice attack estimates [GJ21,MAT22], such as the use of the Geometric-Series Assumption instead of a (progressive) BKZ simulator [CN11,DSDGR20,Alb22].

5.1   Mitigation Inside Progressive-Sieve and Progressive-BKZ

Even in the simplest attack whose cost comes essentially from sieving, the overhead can also be mitigated. The reason is that the routine at hand is not only ran in the final sieving dimension (say $n = 384$) but also in dimension below it; for those calls in smaller dimension we can move on the time-memory curve.

More specifically, the simplest primal BKZ attack[9] makes about $d(i+1)$ calls in dimension $n - i$ where d is the total lattice dimension; these calls accumulates over progressive-sieving for each SVP oracle call [Duc18,ADH+19], and over progressive-BKZ tours. In the idealized model, this adds an extra dC^2 factor on time where $C = \sum_{i=0}^{\infty} 2^{-.292i} \approx 5.46$ stands for the progressivity overhead.

To correct the progressivity overhead using this strategy, we rely on the data collected at $n = 384$, and make the working assumption[10] that for small $i < 30$, the time-memory curve of Fig. 3 is simply shifted by $(T = 2^{-.292i}, M = 2^{-.2075i})$. We aim to make optimal use of $M = 2^{98}$ bits of memory throughout all calls to the inner routine in dimension $384 - i$.

For each i, we collect the minimal time T_i such that $M_i < 2^{98}$, and finally compute $\sum(i + 1)T_i/T_0 \approx 15.6$. This is to be compared with the idealized progressivity overhead squared $C^2 \approx 29.6$. That is, this strategy should mitigate the 2^6 overhead of the inner routine by a factor $2^{-0.9}$ on the whole primal BKZ attack, lowering the overhead down to $2^{5.1}$. Given the concavity of the curve, one would expect this mitigation works best in the low memory regime; for example, at $M = 2^{100}$ we get $\sum(i + 1)T_i/T_0 \approx 20.0$, i.e. a mitigation factor of $2^{-0.6}$.

For a single progressive sieve, we can also compare $\sum T_i/T_0 \approx 3.78$ to $C \approx 5.46$, and conclude on a mitigation factor of $2^{-0.5}$ at $M = 2^{98}$.

6   Open Problems

The analysis of the overheads of the algorithm of [BDGL16] presented in this work is based on instantiating it is random product codes. While this is the only proposed instantiation so far, the framework of [BDGL16] can also work with other efficiently list-decodable spherical codes. A natural open problem would

---

[9] The BKZ blocksize β is here slightly larger than n thanks to the dimensions for free of [Duc18].

[10] Collecting all those curves would be rather costly, about 40 core-days per curve. Furthermore, the software of [AGPS20] which we rely on is only set for n a multiple of 8.

therefore be to design spherical codes giving better trade-offs between $PO^\times$, $CO^\times$ and $MO^\times$.

Another natural problem would be to find a theoretical model for the probabilistic overhead $PO^\times$ as a function of the various parameters. We hope that the experimental data provided by the method of this work can be helpful for conjecturing or validating such a theoretical analysis.

Acknowledgments. The author wishes to thank Martin Albrecht, Vlad Gheorghiu, and Eamonn Postlethwaite, John Schanck for open-sourcing and maintaining various research artefacts making this research possible. The author was supported by the ERC-StG-ARTICULATE project (no. 947821).

References

[ABD+21] Avanzi, R., et al.: Crystals-kyber, algorithm specifications and supporting documentation (2021). Version 3.02. https://pq-crystals.org/kyber/data/kyber-specification-round3-20210804.pdf

[ADH+19] Albrecht, M.R., Ducas, L., Herold, G., Kirshanova, E., Postlethwaite, E.W., Stevens, M.: The general sieve kernel and new records in lattice reduction. In: Ishai, Y., Rijmen, V. (eds.) EUROCRYPT 2019. LNCS, vol. 11477, pp. 717–746. Springer, Cham (2019). https://doi.org/10.1007/978-3-030-17656-3_25

[AGPS20] Albrecht, M.R., Gheorghiu, V., Postlethwaite, E.W., Schanck, J.M.: Estimating quantum speedups for lattice sieves. In: Moriai, S., Wang, H. (eds.) ASIACRYPT 2020. LNCS, vol. 12492, pp. 583–613. Springer, Cham (2020). https://doi.org/10.1007/978-3-030-64834-3_20

[AKS01] Ajtai, M., Kumar, R., Sivakumar, D.: A sieve algorithm for the shortest lattice vector problem. In: Proceedings of the Thirty-Third Annual ACM Symposium on Theory of Computing, pp. 601–610. ACM (2001)

[Alb22] Albrecht, M.: Security estimates for lattice problems (2022). https://github.com/malb/lattice-estimator

[BDGL16] Becker, A., Ducas, L., Gama, N., Laarhoven, T.: New directions in nearest neighbor searching with applications to lattice sieving. In: Proceedings of the Twenty-Seventh Annual ACM-SIAM Symposium on Discrete Algorithms, pp. 10–24. SIAM (2016)

[BGJ15] Becker, A., Gama, N., Joux, A.: Speeding-up lattice sieving without increasing the memory, using sub-quadratic nearest neighbor search. Cryptology ePrint Archive (2015)

[CN11] Chen, Y., Nguyen, P.Q.: BKZ 2.0: better lattice security estimates. In: Lee, D.H., Wang, X. (eds.) ASIACRYPT 2011. LNCS, vol. 7073, pp. 1–20. Springer, Heidelberg (2011). https://doi.org/10.1007/978-3-642-25385-0_1

[DSDGR20] Dachman-Soled, D., Ducas, L., Gong, H., Rossi, M.: LWE with side information: attacks and concrete security estimation. In: Micciancio, D., Ristenpart, T. (eds.) CRYPTO 2020. LNCS, vol. 12171, pp. 329–358. Springer, Cham (2020). https://doi.org/10.1007/978-3-030-56880-1_12

[DSvW21] Ducas, L., Stevens, M., van Woerden, W.: Advanced lattice sieving on GPUs, with tensor cores. In: Canteaut, A., Standaert, F.-X. (eds.) EUROCRYPT 2021. LNCS, vol. 12697, pp. 249–279. Springer, Cham (2021). https://doi.org/10.1007/978-3-030-77886-6_9

[Duc18]   Ducas, L.: Shortest vector from lattice sieving: a few dimensions for free. In: Nielsen, J.B., Rijmen, V. (eds.) EUROCRYPT 2018. LNCS, vol. 10820, pp. 125–145. Springer, Cham (2018). https://doi.org/10.1007/978-3-319-78381-9_5

[FBB+14] Fitzpatrick, R., Bischof, C., Buchmann, J., Dagdelen, Ö., Göpfert, F., Mariano, A., Yang, B.-Y.: Tuning GaussSieve for speed. In: Aranha, D.F., Menezes, A. (eds.) LATINCRYPT 2014. LNCS, vol. 8895, pp. 288–305. Springer, Cham (2015). https://doi.org/10.1007/978-3-319-16295-9_16

[GJ21]   Guo, Q., Johansson, T.: Faster dual lattice attacks for solving LWE with applications to CRYSTALS. In: Tibouchi, M., Wang, H. (eds.) ASIACRYPT 2021. LNCS, vol. 13093, pp. 33–62. Springer, Cham (2021). https://doi.org/10.1007/978-3-030-92068-5_2

[Laa15a] Laarhoven, T.: Search problems in cryptography (2015). https://thijs.com/docs/phd-final.pdf

[Laa15b] Laarhoven, T.: Sieving for shortest vectors in lattices using angular locality-sensitive hashing. In: Gennaro, R., Robshaw, M. (eds.) CRYPTO 2015. LNCS, vol. 9215, pp. 3–22. Springer, Heidelberg (2015). https://doi.org/10.1007/978-3-662-47989-6_1

[LW15]   Laarhoven, T., de Weger, B.: Faster sieving for shortest lattice vectors using spherical locality-sensitive hashing. In: Lauter, K., Rodríguez-Henríquez, F. (eds.) LATINCRYPT 2015. LNCS, vol. 9230, pp. 101–118. Springer, Cham (2015). https://doi.org/10.1007/978-3-319-22174-8_6

[MAT22]   MATZOF. Report on the security of LWE: improved dual lattice attack (2022). https://zenodo.org/record/6412487

[MLB17]   Mariano, A., Laarhoven, T., Bischof, C.: A parallel variant of LDSieve for the SVP on lattices. In: 2017 25th Euromicro International Conference on Parallel, Distributed and Network-based Processing (PDP), pp. 23–30. IEEE (2017)

[NV08]   Nguyen, P.Q., Vidick, T.: Sieve algorithms for the shortest vector problem are practical. J. Math. Cryptol. $\mathbf{2}$(2), 181–207 (2008)

Cryptanalysis

Breaking Category Five
SPHINCS+ with SHA-256

Ray Perlner[1(✉)], John Kelsey[1,2], and David Cooper[1]

[1] National Institute of Standards and Technology, Gaithersburg, MD 20899, USA
ray.perlner@nist.gov
[2] COSIC/KU Leuven, Leuven, Belgium

Abstract. SPHINCS+ is a stateless hash-based signature scheme that has been selected for standardization as part of the NIST post-quantum cryptography (PQC) standardization process. Its security proof relies on the distinct-function multi-target second-preimage resistance (DM-SPR) of the underlying keyed hash function. The SPHINCS+ submission offered several instantiations of this keyed hash function, including one based on SHA-256. A recent observation by Sydney Antonov on the PQC mailing list demonstrated that the construction based on SHA-256 did not have DM-SPR at NIST category five, for several of the parameter sets submitted to NIST; however, it remained an open question whether this observation leads to a forgery attack. We answer this question in the affirmative by giving a complete forgery attack that reduces the concrete classical security of these parameter sets by approximately 40 bits of security.

Our attack works by applying Antonov's technique to the WOTS+ public keys in SPHINCS+, leading to a new one-time key that can sign a very limited set of hash values. From that key, we construct a slightly altered version of the original hypertree with which we can sign arbitrary messages, yielding signatures that appear valid.

Keywords: Hash-based signatures · Post-quantum cryptography · SPHINCS+

1 Introduction

SPHINCS+ [2] is a stateless hash-based signature scheme that has been selected for standardization as part of the NIST post-quantum cryptography standardization process [16]. Much of the underlying technology for SPHINCS+ goes back to the very earliest days of academic cryptography [13–15]. Its security is based entirely on the security of symmetric cryptographic primitives.

Because of the age of the underlying technology and the lack of additional hardness assumptions (most other post-quantum algorithms depend on the difficulty of problems such as finding short vectors in a lattice or solving systems of multivariate quadratic equations), SPHINCS+ appears to provide extremely

© The Author(s), under exclusive license to Springer Nature Switzerland AG 2022
J. H. Cheon and T. Johansson (Eds.): PQCrypto 2022, LNCS 13512, pp. 501–522, 2022.
https://doi.org/10.1007/978-3-031-17234-2_23

reliable security, albeit at the cost of larger and slower signatures than most other post-quantum signature schemes.

Recently, however, Sydney Antonov described a failure of a particular property (the DM-SPR property[1]) claimed by the SPHINCS+ designers when SHA-256 is the hash function used [1]. It was not clear, however, whether this observation led to an attack on the full SPHINCS+ signature scheme.

In this paper, we describe such an attack. Specifically, we extend Antonov's observation to a forgery attack on both of the recommended parameter sets for SPHINCS+ that claim category five [17] security (256 bits of classical security) and use the SHA-256 hash function. Our attack becomes even more powerful for other choices of SPHINCS+ parameters that use SHA-256 while claiming category five security, specifically for smaller values of w than are used in the recommended parameter sets.

Our attack allows forgery of an unlimited number of signatures of the attacker's choice. While our attack is far too expensive to pose a real-world security threat, it demonstrates a failure of SPHINCS+ to meet its claimed security goals for the category five parameter set. Table 1 gives the results of our attack for the two category five parameter sets in [2], assuming a SPHINCS+ key that has been used to sign its maximum allowed number of signatures (2^{64}).

Table 1. Summary of our results on SPHINCS+ category five parameters

Parameter set	Cost				Reference
	Herd	Link	Signable	Total	
SPHINCS+-256f	$2^{214.8}$	$2^{216.4}$	$2^{215.7}$	$\approx 2^{217.4}$	Section 4.3
SPHINCS+-256s	$2^{214.8}$	$2^{216.4}$	$2^{215.7}$	$\approx 2^{217.4}$	Section 4.3

Both Antonov's approach and our extension of it are partly based on properties of Merkle-Damgård hash functions first described in [9,11,12] (notably, these attacks would not work if the hash function were replaced with a random oracle), but also incorporate details of the internal structure of SPHINCS+. Earlier [19], another security issue with SPHINCS+ level five parameters was noted, again due to the use of SHA-256 to provide 256 bits of security.

These results do not seem to us to indicate any fundamental weakness in SPHINCS+. Instead, they demonstrate that using a 256-bit Merkle-Damgård hash like SHA-256 to get more than 128 bits of security is quite difficult. If SHA-512 were used in place of SHA-256 for category five security in SPHINCS+, all of these observations and attacks would be entirely blocked. Similarly, when SPHINCS+ uses SHAKE256 to get category five security, none of these attacks are possible. Very recently [7], the SPHINCS+ team has proposed a tweak which appears to block these attacks. A discussion of the proposed tweaks appears in Sect. 6.

---

[1] For a formal definition of this property, see Sect. 3.2.

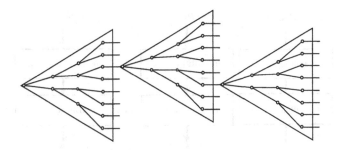

Fig. 1. The SPHINCS$^+$ hypertree.

The rest of the paper is organized as follows: We begin by describing SPHINCS$^+$ (Sect. 2). We then introduce some tools, concepts, and notation that will be used in the rest of the paper (Sect. 3). We then describe our attack (Sect. 4). Next, we justify the costs we assigned to each step of our attack, and some possible optimizations (Sect. 5). Finally, we conclude the paper with a discussion of what can be done to prevent this kind of attack, and where else the attack or variants of it may apply (Sect. 6).

2   The SPHINCS$^+$ Signature Scheme

The SPHINCS$^+$ signature scheme consists of a few components: a one-time signature scheme, WOTS$^+$ (a specific variant of Winternitz signatures defined in [8]); a few-time signature scheme, FORS (Forest of Random Subsets); and Merkle trees [14]. SPHINCS$^+$ forms the WOTS$^+$ public keys into a hypertree, or tree of trees (see Fig. 1). Each tree is a Merkle tree in which the leaves are WOTS$^+$ public keys. The root of each tree is signed by a WOTS$^+$ key from a tree at the next level up, and the root of the top-level tree is the SPHINCS$^+$ public key. The WOTS$^+$ keys from the lowest-level tree are used to sign FORS public keys, and the FORS keys are in turn used to sign messages.

SPHINCS$^+$ uses randomized hashing. When a message is to be signed, a random bit string, R, is generated and is hashed along with the message. Some bits from the hash value are then used to select a FORS key (which selects a path through the hypertree); the rest are signed using that FORS key. A SPHINCS$^+$ signature then consists of R, the signature created using the selected FORS key, the sequence of WOTS$^+$ signatures in the hypertree leading from the top-level tree to the FORS public key used to sign the message, and the authentication paths corresponding to each WOTS$^+$ signature needed to compute the roots of each of the Merkle trees.

In this paper, we apply a multi-target preimage attack (described in Sect. 3) to the WOTS$^+$ public keys that are used to sign the roots of Merkle trees and FORS public keys. The WOTS$^+$ public keys are computed as shown in Fig. 2. For the parameter sets in [2] that target category five security, which use a hash function with a 256-bit output and a Winternitz parameter, w, of 16, the

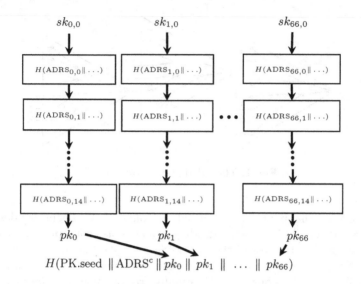

Fig. 2. A WOTS$^+$ public key.

public key is the hash of a public seed, PK.seed, which is padded to 64 bytes, a 22-byte compressed address, and 67 public values. Computing the public key hash requires 35 iterations of the SHA-256 compression function, as shown in Fig. 7. Each public value is computed by generating a hash chain, which involves iterating a different secret value through the hash function 15 times. Each call to the hash function includes an unique address as input, which identifies the tree layer in which the WOTS$^+$ key appears along with the key's index within that layer. For the computations of the public values, the address also identifies which of the 67 public values is being computed as well as the iteration of the hash function. It is these addresses that were intended to prevent multi-target attacks.

A WOTS$^+$ signature consists of one entry from each of the 67 hash chains of the WOTS$^+$ one-time key.[2] The 256-bit hash of the value to be signed is written as 64 hexadecimal digits, and each is signed using a different hash chain. For example, if the first hexadecimal digit is 0, then $sk_{0,0}$ is the signature for the first digit. If the second digit is f, then pk_1 is the signature for that digit. If the third digit is 3, then the signature value for the third digit is $sk_{2,3}$ – the result of iterating $sk_{2,0}$ through the hash function three times.

A WOTS$^+$ signature is verified by completing the computation of each of the hash chains. In the example from the previous paragraph, the signature on the first digit (0) is checked by iterating the signature value through the hash function 15 times and comparing the result to pk_0. The second digit (f)

---

[2] This description is accurate for the recommended parameters for SPHINCS$^+$ at category five security; other choices of parameters would require the description to be slightly changed.

is checked by simply comparing the signature value to pk_1. The third digit (3) is checked by iterating the signature value through the hash function 12 times and comparing the result to pk_2. Note that when the digit signed is an f, the verifier does no additional hashing of the value from the signature. Unlike digits 0-e, the verifier's calculation on an f digit does not incorporate the value of the one-time key's ADRS.

The final three hash chains are used to sign a three-hexadecimal-digit checksum value. The checksum value is computed by summing the digits of the 256-bit hash value and then subtracting the result from the maximum possible sum, 960. Including the checksum in the signature prevents an attacker from modifying the signature without performing a preimage attack on the hash function.

The SPHINCS$^+$ submission [2] defines two parameter sets that target category five security: SPHINCS$^+$-256s, which contains eight levels of trees, each with a height of eight; and SPHINCS$^+$-256f, which contains 17 levels of trees, each with a height of four. So, the SPHINCS$^+$-256s parameter set includes a little over 2^{64} WOTS$^+$ keys and the SPHINCS$^+$-256f parameter set includes a little over 2^{68} WOTS$^+$ keys.

3 Building Blocks

3.1 Merkle-Damgård Hash Functions

A Merkle-Damgård hash function is constructed from a fixed-length hash function called a *compression function*. In the case of SHA-256, the compression function takes a chaining value of 256 bits and a message block of 512 bits. In order to process a message, the message is unambiguously padded to an integer multiple of 512 bits (the padding incorporates the length of the unpadded message), broken into a sequence of 512-bit message blocks $M_{0,1,...,L-1}$, and processed sequentially, starting from a constant initial chaining value. Thus, to hash the above sequence of message blocks, we compute (Fig. 3)

$$H_{-1} = \text{initial chaining value}$$
$$H_j = \text{COMPRESS}(H_{j-1}, M_j)$$

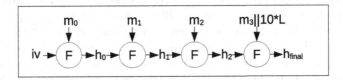

Fig. 3. Merkle-Damgård hashing

After each 512-bit message block, the state of the hash is reduced to a 256-bit chaining value, and this chaining value is the *only information* about the

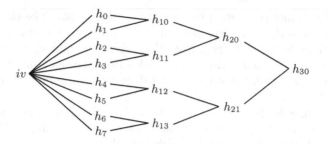

Fig. 4. A diamond structure – constructing eight messages with the same hash

message processed so far that is carried forward into the hash computation. A consequence of this fact is we can choose the beginning of two different messages so that their chaining value h_1 collides, and then we can get a new collision by appending any sequence of message blocks to both messages. As noted in [9], this process can be repeated, constructing many different messages with the same hash value.

Diamond Structures. Applying the techniques from [11], we can extend this attack, finding these internal hash chain collisions in a tree structure. Starting from 2^k different initial message blocks, we find subsequent message blocks that map them all to a single hash chaining value. This structure of collisions is called a *diamond structure*, and is illustrated in Fig. 4. In the figure, lines represent message blocks, labels represent intermediate hash values; each path from iv to h_{30} gives a sequence of four message blocks, and all eight possible sequences of four message blocks yield the same hash value. Constructing the diamond structure requires a sequence of batched collision searches, resulting in a distinct message block for each line in the diagram.

3.2   Multi-target Preimage Attacks and SPHINCS+

Consider an attacker asked to find a preimage – that is, a message that hashes to a single target value, T. If SHA-256 behaves randomly, this should require about 2^{256} trial hashes to accomplish – the attacker can simply hash random messages until one gives the right result. Now consider an attacker asked to find a message that hashes to any one of 2^{64} different hash values, $T_{0,1,\ldots,2^{64}-1}$. Again, if SHA-256 behaves randomly, this should require only about 2^{192} trial hashes – the attacker hashes random messages until one matches *any one* of the values in the target list. Intuitively, the attacker has many targets, so is more likely to hit one. The situation where the attacker tries to find a message that hashes to any one of many targets is called a *multi-target preimage attack*.

Consider the same attacker, given 2^{64} different target hash values, but each target hash value is associated with a different prefix and the preimage is only valid if it starts with the correct prefix. The straightforward multi-target preimage attack no longer works. The attacker must start each message with a particular prefix to get a valid preimage, and if the message hashes to a target associated with a different prefix, it isn't valid.

The SPHINCS$^+$ specification formalizes the above defense against multi-target preimage attacks by (in the "simple" SHA-256 parameter sets) treating the SHA-256 hash of a message, prepended with each prefix, as a separate member in a hash function family. SPHINCS$^+$ also includes "robust" parameter sets, where the hash function members process the input not just by prefixing a constant, but also by XORing the input message with a constant deterministically generated pseudorandom keystream. Our attack applies to both schemes, but for simplicity, we will describe the attack only in terms of the "simple" parameter sets.

Definition 1. PQ-DM-SPR *(definition 8 from [5]). Let* $H : \mathcal{K} \times \{0,1\}^\alpha \to \{0,1\}^n$ *be a keyed hash function. We define the advantage of any adversary* $\mathcal{A} = (\mathcal{A}_1), \mathcal{A}_2$ *against distinct-function, multi-target second-preimage resistance (DM-SPR). This definition is parameterized by the number of targets* p.

$$Succ^{DM\text{-}SPR}(\mathcal{A}) = \Big[\{K_i\}_{i=1}^p \leftarrow \mathcal{A}_1(), \{M_i\}_1^p \leftarrow_R (\{0,1\}^\alpha)^p;$$
$$(j, M') \leftarrow_R \mathcal{A}_2(\{(K_i, M_i)\}_{i-1}^p) : M' \neq M_j$$
$$\wedge H(K_j, M_j) = H(K_j, M') \wedge \boldsymbol{DIST}(\{K_i\}_{i=1}^p)\Big].$$

where we assume that $\mathcal{A}_1$ *and* $\mathcal{A}_2$ *share state and define the predicate* $\boldsymbol{DIST}(\{K_i\}_{i=1}^p) = (\forall i, k \in [1,p], i \neq k) : K_i \neq K_k$.

3.3 Antonov's Attack on DM-SPR

In 2022, Sydney Antonov described an attack against the DM-SPR property of the SHA-256-based keyed hash functions used in SPHINCS$^+$ [1]. The attack takes advantage of SHA-256's Merkle-Damgård construction, using a series of collision attacks against the underlying compression function to transform a distinct-function multi-target second-preimage attack into a single-function multi-target second-preimage attack, using several of the techniques described in Sect. 3.

Figure 5 shows an example of how the attack works.

Suppose there are six target messages, $M_0 \ldots M_5$, each hashed using a different key, $ADRS_0 \ldots ADRS_5$. The attack begins building a diamond structure, as shown in Fig. 4, above. The SHA-256 compression function is applied to the addresses for each of the targets using the SHA-256 initialization vector.[3] This results in a set of intermediate hash values, $H_0^{(1)} \ldots H_5^{(1)}$. Then collision attacks are performed on pairs of intermediate hash values. For example, the attacker searches for random values x_0 and x_1 such that $C(H_0^{(1)}, x_0) = C(H_1^{(1)}, x_1)$. The

---

[3] For simplicity, the example assumes that $ADRS_i$ is exactly 512-bits in length, but this is not a requirement for the attack to work.

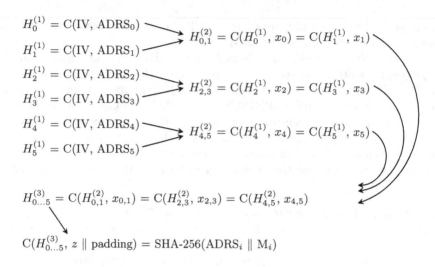

Fig. 5. A multi-target second-preimage attack on a SHA-256-based keyed hash function.

search yields message blocks x_0, x_1 and the intermediate hash, $H_{0,1}^{(2)}$. A second iteration of collision attacks is then performed using the intermediate hash values generated from the first iteration. In this case, there are three intermediate hash values, $H_{0,1}^{(2)}$, $H_{2,3}^{(2)}$, and $H_{4,5}^{(2)}$, and a three-way collision can be found such that $H_{0...5}^{(3)} = C(H_{0,1}^{(2)}, x_{0,1}) = C(H_{2,3}^{(2)}, x_{2,3}) = C(H_{4,5}^{(2)}, x_{4,5})$, for some $H_{0...5}^{(3)}$, $x_{0,1}$, $x_{2,3}$, and $x_{4,5}$. (If there were more targets, then more iterations of collision attacks could be performed until all of the targets had been herded[4] to a single intermediate hash value.)

Next, the attack carries out a multi-target preimage attack, as discussed in Sect. 3. The attacker searches for some message block z such that

$$C(H_{0...5}^{(3)}, z\|\text{padding}) = \text{SHA-256}(\text{ADRS}_i, M_i)$$

for some $i \in \{0, \ldots, 5\}$. If, for example, the final step finds a second preimage for M_3, then $\text{SHA-256}(\text{ADRS}_3\|x_3\|x_{2,3}\|z) = \text{SHA-256}(\text{ADRS}_3\|M_3)$.

Given t target messages, the expected cost for the final step in the attack, finding a preimage, is $2^{256}/t$ calls to the compression function, C. The preceding steps require performing $\tilde{O}(t)$ collision attacks. The expected cost of each collision attack will depend on whether a 2-way, 3-way, 4-way, etc. collision is sought. In general, the expected cost of finding an n-way collision is $\tilde{O}(2^{256(n-1)/n})$ calls to the compression function.

For a generic second-preimage attack, the attack cost is optimized by using $(t-1)$ 2-way collisions to herd t targets down to 1 intermediate hash value.

---

[4] The combination of building a diamond structure and finding a linking message is referred to as a herding attack in [11].

However, when attacking SPHINCS$^+$, messages have fixed lengths, which limits the number of targets that may be used in the attack. Using some 3- and 4-way collisions increases the cost of the collisions-finding step, but increases the number of targets that may be used, which reduces the overall cost of the attack.

4   Creating Forgeries for SPHINCS$^+$ Category Five Parameters

4.1   Turning Antonov's Attack into a Forgery Attack

Suppose the target of Antonov's attack is a set of WOTS$^+$ public keys within the same SPHINCS$^+$ hypertree. After the owner of the key has signed many messages, the attacker has many choices of one-time public key to choose from. Each one-time public key that was used to produce a signature can be computed from the corresponding message and signature, and so is known to the attacker. Further, the attacker can reconstruct the exact hash computation (every 512-bit message block and 256-bit intermediate chaining value) that appeared in the hash computation for each one-time public key used. That hash is computed by hashing some values that are constant for a given SPHINCS$^+$ key, followed by a unique ADRS^C that is guaranteed to be different for every one-time key used, followed by a sequence of 67 hash values. In turn, each of those hash values is the last entry in a hash chain of length 16, and each of the hash computations in that chain is also done with a unique ADRS^C value linked to the ADRS^C of the public key, as shown in Fig. 2.

SPHINCS$^+$ uses a huge number of these one-time public keys – after 2^{64} messages are signed, we expect to be able to find more than 2^{62} such hashes, each a plausible target.[5]

In this case, we can apply Antonov's attack to construct a set of many WOTS$^+$ keys with different ADRS^C values, herd them down to a single chaining value, and then carry out a multi-target preimage attack against the original keys' hashes. The result is a *chimera* – a new one-time public key with the ADRS^C value of one of the target messages, many hash chains at the beginning which the attacker has generated anew, followed by some hash chains at the end from an existing key (Fig. 6).

Original:	PK.seed ADRS^C	$PK_0\ PK_1\ PK_2\ ...\ PK_{62}\ PK_{63}$	$PK_{64}\ PK_{65}\ PK_{66}$
Chimera:	PK.seed ADRS^C	$PK_0^*\ PK_1^*\ PK_2^*\ ...\ PK_{62}^*\ PK_{63}^*$	$PK_{64}\ PK_{65}\ PK_{66}$
	same for both keys	*new values*	*same for both keys*

Fig. 6. Original key and chimera key

---

[5] In this paper we assume that the attacker only chooses target WOTS$^+$ keys from a single SPHINCS$^+$ key. However, an attacker may choose target WOTS$^+$ keys from multiple SPHINCS$^+$ keys, in which case a successful attack would result in the ability to forge messages for one of the targeted SPHINCS$^+$ keys.

$$H^{(1)} = C(\text{IV}_{\text{SHA-256}}, \text{PK.seed} \| \text{toByte}(0, 64 - n))$$
$$H^{(2)} = C(H^{(1)}, \text{ADRS}^c_{i,j} \| pk_{i,j,0} \| pk_{i,j,1}[0 \ldots 9])$$
$$H^{(3)} = C(H^{(2)}, pk_{i,j,1}[10 \ldots 31] \| pk_{i,j,2} \| pk_{i,j,3}[0 \ldots 9])$$
$$H^{(4)} = C(H^{(3)}, pk_{i,j,3}[10 \ldots 31] \| pk_{i,j,4} \| pk_{i,j,5}[0 \ldots 9])$$
$$H^{(5)} = C(H^{(4)}, pk_{i,j,5}[10 \ldots 31] \| pk_{i,j,6} \| pk_{i,j,7}[0 \ldots 9])$$
$$H^{(6)} = C(H^{(5)}, pk_{i,j,7}[10 \ldots 31] \| pk_{i,j,8} \| pk_{i,j,9}[0 \ldots 9])$$
$$\ldots$$
$$H^{(32)} = C(H^{(31)}, pk_{i,j,59}[10 \ldots 31] \| pk_{i,j,60} \| pk_{i,j,61}[0 \ldots 9])$$
$$H^{(33)} = C(H^{(32)}, pk_{i,j,61}[10 \ldots 31] \| pk_{i,j,62} \| pk_{i,j,63}[0 \ldots 9])$$
$$H^{(34)} = C(H^{(33)}, pk_{i,j,63}[10 \ldots 31] \| pk_{i,j,64} \| pk_{i,j,65}[0 \ldots 9])$$
$$H^{(35)} = C(H^{(34)}, pk_{i,j,65}[10 \ldots 31] \| pk_{i,j,66} \| \text{padding})$$
$$\text{SHA-256}(\text{PK.seed}, \text{ADRS}_{i,j}, pk) = H^{(35)}$$

Fig. 7. Computing the SHA-256 hash for a WOTS$^+$ public key.

The chimera key contains the same beginning (PK.seed and ADRS^C) as the original key, and also the same final three hash values. But the rest of the hash values in the key are newly produced by the attacker, and critically, the chimera key has the same SHA-256 hash as the original key. To be more specific, the values of $PK^*_{0 \ldots 62}$, along with the first nine bytes of PK^*_{63}, must be chosen so that the intermediate hash of the chimera key after processing those bytes is identical to that of the original key after processing $PK_{0 \ldots 62}$ and the first nine bytes of PK_{63}. (In Fig. 7, this intermediate hash value is $H^{(33)}$.)

Constructing such a chimera key whose hash matches one of the WOTS$^+$ keys in the SPHINCS$^+$ hypertree is a major part of our attack, but several more steps are needed to get a complete forgery attack. Unfortunately, the chimera key we get from Antonov's attack cannot yet be used to create valid WOTS$^+$ signatures.

The problem is as follows: in order to use the diamond structure, many different starting ADRS^C values might be associated with the same chimera key. We will not know which ADRS^C value should be used until we have found the linking message, that is, found a choice of $\text{ADRS}^C, pk_{0 \ldots 62}, pk_{63}[0 \ldots 9]$ whose intermediate hash is the same as the value of $H^{(33)}$ for one of the target WOTS$^+$ keys. Because the verifier will re-derive $pk_{0 \ldots 66}$ by iterated hashing of the elements of the signature, and will incorporate ADRS^C into those hash computations, the value of ADRS^C is bound to the hash chains. With very high probability, the linking message will be to a different ADRS^C than the one used to compute the hash chains used for the herding step, and so the resulting chimera key won't work.

This leads to a key insight of our attack: Recall that signing a message with WOTS$^+$ starts by writing the hash of the message as a hexadecimal number. Consider the ith digit of the hash. If the digit is any value *except* f, the verifier must use the correct ADRS^C to derive the value of pk_i. The value of pk_i is bound to a single value of ADRS^C in this case. But when the ith digit of the hash is f, the verifier does not have to do any hashing operation the corresponding element of the signature, and so ADRS^C is not incorporated. Thus, when we construct the chimera key, the first X hash chain values can be chosen to allow signing of any digit; the next $62 - X$ chains can be used only to sign the digit f, and the last three chains will encode the checksum. This allows us to construct a chimera key that can be used to sign at least some hashes.

4.2   Summary of Our Attack

The full attack thus happens in multiple phases.

1. **Choose 2^k target keys.** Select a set of WOTS$^+$ keys from the SPHINCS$^+$ hypertree to target in the attack. We do this by examining the set of one-time signature keys that have appeared in at least one SPHINCS$^+$ signature. Each such one-time key will have been used to sign either a Merkle tree root or a FORS public key. We select a set of 2^k target keys whose signatures had acceptably low checksum values, for reasons explained below.

2. **Generate 2^k candidate keys.** Each candidate key starts from the ADRS^C of one of the 2^k target keys; one of these 2^k ADRS^C values will appear in our final chimera key. For each candidate key, we generate X new hash chains using the new key's ADRS^C, ensuring that we can sign any possible hex digit in the first X digits of the hash with this key.

3. **Build a diamond structure mapping all the new one-time keys to the same hash chaining value.** To do this, we start with 2^k distinct chaining values (one for each candidate key), and carry out a set of collision attacks to reduce the number to 2^{k-2}, then 2^{k-4}, and so on until we get down to a single hash chaining value.[6] Each 512-bit message block reduces our number of hash chains by a factor of four. In order to do the herding, we select random values for the ends of the next Y hash chains. Note that we only know the end value of these hash chains, and so when this key is used, the corresponding digits of the hash can only be signed if they are f, but they can be used in this way with *any* ADRS^C. The result of this step is a single hash chaining value (internal to SHA-256) that is reached by all 2^k of our new candidate keys.

4. **Find a linking message.** From that single hash chaining value, select Z random values for the end of hash chains (filling in the values of one 512-bit message block for SHA-256), so that the resulting hash chaining value collides with a hash chaining value at the right position in one of our original target messages. This is a multitarget preimage attack, and requires about 2^{256-k} hash operations. Steps 1–4 are illustrated in Fig. 8. In the diagram, $P1 \dots P8$ are used as shorthand for the PK.seed and ADRS^C of eight different target keys; $t_{0\dots7}$ are the intermediate hash values of the target keys just before the checksum chains.

5. **Construct the chimera key.** We now have a *chimera* key–a WOTS$^+$ key whose first X hash chains are newly generated (and can be used to sign any

---

[6] This assumes we search for 4-collisions at each step; optimizing the attack can vary this–see Sect. 5.

hash digit), while its next $Y + Z$ chains are random (and can be used to sign only an f hash digit), and the last three (used to encode the checksum) are original to the key whose ADRS^C our chimera key has taken. The chimera key has the same ADRS^C and the same hash as that original key. The chimera key produced consists of the following components:

(a) PK.seed
(b) The ADRS^C of the target key – the one that will be replaced by the chimera.
(c) X hash values from newly-generated hash chains with the correct ADRS^C. These will allow us to sign any value in the first X digits of the hash.
(d) $Y + Z$ randomly-generated hash values. These will allow us to sign the next $Y + Z$ digits of the hash only if those digits are all f.
(e) Three hash values from the key that will be replaced by the chimera. These encode the checksum from the signature produced by the original key. Because of the properties of WOTS$^+$, we can *increase* any digit of the checksum and get a valid signature, but we cannot *decrease* any digit of the checksum.

6. **Sign a Merkle tree root or FORS key with the chimera key.** Given the chimera key, we can sign with it. While an ordinary WOTS$^+$ key can sign *any* hash, the chimera key can only sign *a small subset of hashes*–ones with f digits in each of the $Y + Z$ random chains' positions, with the sum of the free digits small enough to yield either the same checksum as the one that appeared in the key's original signature, or a checksum that can be reached by incrementing the original checksum's digits. We must do a large brute-force search to find a Merkle tree root full of one-time keys or a FORS key whose hash this chimera key can sign. However, note that this need only be done once, to allow an arbitrary number of forged messages to be produced.

7. **Forge a signature.** With the chimera key and its signature computed, we now brute-force search for randomized messages until we find one whose hypertree path (determined by the idx value) includes the location of the original key, whose hash is the same as that of our chimera key. (This will take less than 2^{68} work). Once we find such a message, we can use the new one-time key or FORS key we signed with our chimera key to construct a valid SPHINCS$^+$ signature on the message.

Steps 3, 4, and 6 are each computationally very expensive. However, they are done sequentially. The total cost of the attack is the sum of the costs of building the diamond structure (step 3), finding the linking message (step 4), and constructing a Merkle tree root or FORS key whose hash the chimera key can sign (step 6).

Step 6 can only succeed for a very limited set of hash values. In this step, we must create a Merkle tree root or FORS key whose hash value, written as a hexadecimal string, follows the pattern:

xxxxxxxx xxxxxxxx xxxxxxxf ffffffff

ffffffff ffffffff ffffffff ffffffff

where an x may be any digit, but an f must be a hex digit f. Let C be the checksum of the original key that was replaced by the chimera key, and S be the sum of the digits of the hash. Along with following the above pattern, we must find a hash value for which we can sign a valid checksum. Since 41 of the hex digits must be f, the lowest possible value of the checksum is 0x159.

Each digit in the checksum can be increased but not decreased, to reach our goal. If $C > 960 - S$, then the chimera key cannot be used to construct *any* valid signature. For this reason, we choose candidate keys based on the checksum they produced when they signed. In general, we want the lowest checksums possible. The probability of a random WOTS$^+$ signature having an acceptable checksum (for example, 0x140-143) is about 2^{-18}, so with many WOTS$^+$ keys that have been used to create signatures to choose from (around 2^{63} after all possible signatures have been made with a given SPHINCS$^+$ public key), we can always find a large set ($> 2^{40}$) of target messages.

Finding a hash that can be signed by the chimera key is accomplished by a brute force attack–we simply try many inputs to the hash until we get one that can be signed. Depending on the location in the hypertree of the original key that is to be replaced by the chimera key, we will either have to sign a root of a Merkle tree or a FORS key. In either case, we can generate many candidate values relatively efficiently by keeping most of the tree or key fixed and only altering a single leaf in the tree (or leaf in the last tree of the FORS key).

Once we have successfully signed a single Merkle tree or FORS key with the chimera key, we can use the Merkle tree's WOTS$^+$ keys or the FORS key to sign arbitrary messages, as many as we like. Since the chimera key has the same hash as the target WOTS$^+$ key it has replaced, new SPHINCS$^+$ signatures can be constructed, substituting the chimera key and the new Merkle tree or FORS key, but otherwise just like previous signatures with the same key.

4.3 Overview of the Forgery Attack on SPHINCS$^+$-SHA-256 with Category Five Parameters

In this section, we describe the full forgery attack against the SPHINCS$^+$-SHA-256-256f-simple parameter set from [2]. The basic idea behind the attack also applies to the other category five SHA-256-based parameter sets from [2] (including the 'robust' parameter sets), and would also apply to category five SHA-256-based parameter sets that used a Winternitz parameter, w, other than 16. The attacks follow the same basic outline, but some of the details differ.

In [1], Sydney Antonov's goal was simply to find a message of the same length as a WOTS$^+$ public key ($32 \cdot 67 = 2144$ bytes) that would hash to the same value as the WOTS$^+$ public key when using the same prefix (PK.seed and ADRS^C). In order to extend this into an forgery attack against SPHINCS$^+$, we must construct a chimera key which can be used to generate a valid signature for at least some hash values.

In order to do this, our attack takes advantage of a detail of WOTS$^+$ signatures: The one-time public key is computed by hashing together the final value in each of the 67 hash chains used in the signature. The signature contains 67

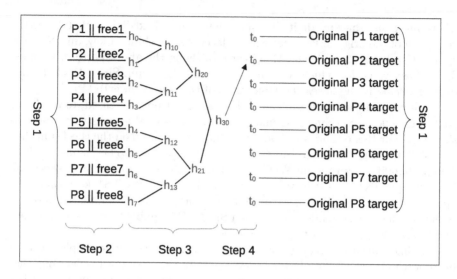

Fig. 8. Steps 1–4 of the attack

elements, each an entry in one of the hash chains, and the verifier must derive the final entry in each hash chain from these.

When a given signature element is signing a hex digit of $0 \ldots e$, computing the final element in that chain requires hashing the signature element, and that hash incorporates the correct value of ADRS. But when the signature element signs a hex digit of f, the verifier simply uses the provided element as the final entry in that chain.

This means that the verifier's processing of that signature element will be identical, regardless of the ADRS.

Step 1 in the attack is to choose a set of $t = 3 \cdot 2^{38} \approx 2^{39.58}$ targets. In order to be able to sign a Merkle tree root, each digit in the checksum for that root must be at least as large as in the original signature. So, targets with small checksums need to be chosen. For this attack, $t = 3 \cdot 2^{38}$ targets are chosen that have a checksum of 319 or less. An attacker that has collected about 2^{58} WOTS+ signatures should have access to $3 \cdot 2^{38}$ signatures with checksums of this form.

Step 2 is to create the starting points for the multi-target second-preimage attack. For each of the t target keys ($0 \le i < 3 \cdot 2^{38}$), we create a new string which starts with the PK.seed and ADRS^C value from the target key, and then construct 22 hash chains using the ADRS^C value and other metadata, so that we will be able to sign arbitrary digits with these hash chains. We compute 22 secret values $(sk_i[0], \ldots, sk_i[21])$, and iterate through the hash chains to compute the corresponding public values $(pk_i[0], \ldots, pk_i[21])$. We then compute the twelfth intermediate hash value, $H_i^{(12)}$.

Step 3 is to herd these $3 \cdot 2^{38}$ targets down to a single intermediate hash chaining value. The process begins by creating 2^{38} 3-way collisions for the thirteenth intermediate hash value, $H^{(13)}$. When creating an input value for the function,

f, values are chosen for $sk[22]$ and the first ten bytes of $pk[23]$. Performing 2^{38} 3-way collision searches would require about 2^{214} calls to the compression function, but this cost can be dramatically reduced (to the approximate equivalent of 2^{196} compression function calls accounting for memory costs) by performing a batched multi-target multi-collision search as described in Sect. 5.4.

The herding process is completed by performing 19 rounds of 4-way collision searches, resulting in all $3 \cdot 2^{38}$ targets having the same value for $H_i^{(32)}$. For each round, the input value for the function, f, is an arbitrary 512-bit value. For the corresponding portions of the WOTS$^+$ key $(pk[23], \dots, pk[61])$ only the public value will be known, and so only a digit with a value of 0xf may be signed. The 19 rounds would require about 2^{230} calls to the compression function, if $2^{36.42}$ separate 4-way collision searches were performed, but the cost may be significantly reduced by performing batched multi-target multi-collision searches. We estimate the complexity of these searches in Eq. 1 in Sect. 5.4. Accounting for memory costs as well as computation, the combined cost is approximately equivalent to $2^{214.8}$ compression function calls.

Step 4 is to find a message block that links with an intermediate chaining value in the right position in one of the target messages. Finding a message block that collides with one of these $3 \cdot 2^{38}$ target vales for $H_i^{(33)}$ should require approximately $2^{256-39.58} = 2^{216.42}$ calls to the compression function.

Step 5 is to construct our chimera key, as discussed above.

Step 6 is to construct a Merkle tree or FORS key that can be signed by the chimera key.

An initial Merkle tree is generated by creating 16 WOTS$^+$ keys and then computing the root of the Merkle tree for those keys. Additional Merkle tree roots may be created by changing just the final public value for one of the 16 WOTS$^+$ keys. Computing the new WOTS$^+$ key and updating the Merkle tree would require 20 calls to the compression function.[7,8] New Merkle tree roots are created until one is generated that has the form

$$\texttt{xxxxxxxx xxxxxxxx xxxxxxxf ffffffff}$$
$$\texttt{ffffffff ffffffff ffffffff ffffffff}$$

and that has a checksum that can be signed using the chimera key. More than $\binom{26+23-1}{26} \approx 2^{44.64}$ Merkle tree roots that have this form, so finding one should require less than $20 \cdot 2^{256-44.64} = 2^{215.68}$ calls to the compression function.

The final step is to create a message whose signature makes use of the forged Merkle tree or FORS key. Since SPHINCS$^+$ uses randomized hashing, any message can be signed by finding a randomizer that results in the forged Merkle tree being used in the signing process. In the worst-case scenario, the forged Merkle tree or FORS key will appear at the bottom the SPHINCS$^+$ hypertree.

---

[7] This can be optimized so that only one call to the compression function is required to generate each additional Merkle tree root.

[8] If the original key was used to sign a FORS key, then new FORS keys could similarly be created at a cost for 17 calls to the compression function for each new key.

As there are 2^{68} WOTS$^+$ keys at the lowest level, approximately 2^{68} randomizers will need to be tried in order to find one that results in the correct path through the hypertree being used. For each randomizer, two hashes will need to be computed. One of the messages to be hashed will be short. The length of the second message to be hashed will correspond to the length of the message to be signed. Note that once the above steps are completed, we can forge arbitrarily many new messages, each one costing about 2^{68} work to create.

5   Optimizations and Attack Cost Calculations

Our attack uses subroutines that find multi-collisions and multi-target preimages in generic functions. Here we review, and where necessary, adapt the best-known techniques for doing this. We discuss how to estimate costs both in models that ignore memory costs and in models that try to take them into account. As this turns out to only make about 2 bits of security difference in the complexity of our attack, we present our results only in terms of a fairly pessimistic 2-dimensional model of classical memory. We also briefly discuss known quantum speedups. While we don't explicitly analyze how to optimize our attack to take advantage of quantum computation, the existence of known quantum speedups for multi-target preimage search, even in models of computation where memory access is expensive, combined with the ability to drastically reduce the cost of herding (e.g., by targeting 2-collisions instead of 4-collisions) likely means that SPHINCS$^+$'s claimed category five parameters using SHA-256, not only fail to meet category five, but category four as well.

5.1   Collision Search and General Framework

All these techniques follow the paradigm of the Van-Oorschot, Wiener parallel collision search [18]. In each case the computation is divided up among p parallel threads that repeatedly compose the function, f, which is being attacked, starting with a seed, and stopping when a "distinguished point" is reached. The distinguished point is defined by an output that meets a rare, easily identifiable condition. For example, if it is desirable that the expected number of iterations to reach a distinguished point is m, the distinguished point may be an output value which is 0 modulo m. If any output value occurring in one chain appears anywhere in a second chain (i.e., a collision occurs in f), then all subsequent values in both chains will be the same, and both chains will reach the same distinguished point. The collision can be recovered by sorting the p distinguished points to find any duplicates. Once a duplicate resulting from a collision has been found, the actual colliding inputs can be recovered for an expected cost of m additional computations of f; assuming a total iteration count and seed value have been saved for each thread, the collision is recovered by recomputing the output values in both chains and comparing each pair of output values with an iteration count offset by the difference in the number of iterations required to reach the shared distinguished point.

If the function f can be modeled as random and has an n bit output size, then it is expected that approximately $\frac{(mp)^2}{2 \cdot 2^n}$ collisions will be found (This approximation holds as long as $p \gg \frac{(mp)^2}{2 \cdot 2^n}$. When $p < \frac{(mp)^2}{2 \cdot 2^n}$ most of the computations of f are duplicated across multiple chains and are therefore less useful).

Depending on the parameters of the attack, (m and p), and assumptions on the relative cost of computation, memory, and memory access, the dominant cost of the attack may be any of the following:

1. Building and maintaining $M = p(n + p + \log_2(m))$ bits of memory.
2. Approximately mp computations of f required to compute the distinguished points.
3. Sorting the list of p distinguished point values.

The last cost depends on assumptions regarding the cost of random access queries to memory. If one, unrealistically, assumes memory access costs are independent of the size of memory, the cost of sorting the distinguished points could be assumed to be as small as $np \log_2(p)$. However, it is perhaps more reasonable to assume the cost of random access to a memory of size M follows a power law where, for a d-dimensional memory architecture, the cost per bit to read a register from a memory of size M would be $C \cdot M^{1/d}$. A popular choice of C and d is given by [4], with $C = 2^{-5}$ bit operation equivalents and $d = 2$. This latter estimate likely overestimates the cost of memory access for very large memories, so we will take it is an upper bound for memory costs in order to demonstrate that our attack does not lose much efficacy when memory costs are taken into consideration. For comparison, we will follow [17] in estimating the cost of the SHA-256 compression function as requiring 2^{18} bit operations.

5.2 Multi-target Preimage Search

The problem of finding a preimage of one of t targets with respect to a function f with an n-bit output is discussed by [3], which considers classical and quantum models of computation, with either $O(1)$ or $O(M^{1/2})$ memory access cost.

Classically, the non-memory cost of multi-target preimage search is $\frac{2^n}{t}$ evaluations of f. Section 1.2 of [3] describes how to modify the techniques of [18] to minimize memory costs without significantly increasing computation costs. By our calculations, with respect to SHA-256, this technique makes memory access costs negligible for $t \ll 2^{106}$, which is the case in all examples we consider.

In the quantum case [3] gives a cost per thread for t-target preimage search, using p-way parallelism of $O(\sqrt{\frac{2^n}{pt}})$ in the $O(1)$ memory access cost case, and $O(\sqrt{\frac{2^n}{pt^{1/2}}})$ in the $O(M^{1/2})$ case (the main result of the paper). If we assume, following the NIST PQC Call For Proposals [17] that the quantum circuit is depth-limited, then these costs represent a cost savings factor compared to single target preimage search of $O(t)$ in the $O(1)$ memory access cost case and $O(t^{1/2})$ in the $O(M^{1/2})$ case.

5.3   Multi-collision Search

The use of parallel collision search techniques for finding k-way collisions is described in [10]. As with 2-way parallel collision search, the computation is divided among p threads, each computing f iteratively on a seed until a distinguished point is reached after an average of m steps. In order for a k-way collision to be found with reasonable probability, the total number of computations of f, mp must satisfy:

$$\frac{(mp)^k}{k! \cdot 2^{n(k-1)}} \geq 1,$$

and to ensure that most of the computations of f act on distinct inputs, p must be set to be comparable to the expected number of 2-way collisions, i.e., so that:

$$p \geq \frac{(mp)^2}{2 \cdot 2^n}.$$

5.4   Batched Multi-target Multi-collision Search

A key step in our attack requires us to herd together t/k groups of k hash inputs where each hash input must have a prefix chosen without repetition from a list of t targets $S_0, ..., S_{t-1}$. We can relate this procedure to finding collisions in a single function f by defining a function $f(x)$ with an n-bit input and output that hashes an input, injectively derived from x with the prefix S_i indexed by $i = x \bmod t$. Then our goal is to find t/k k-collisions in f meeting the constraint that each input x has a different remainder mod t.

While it is possible to compute each k-collision individually, it is generally more efficient to compute the k-collisions in large batches, taking advantage of the fact that we don't care which prefixes collide. This is because finding t/k k-collisions in f only requires $(t/k)^{1/k}$ times as many queries to f as finding one collision. This situation is somewhat complicated by the requirement that each input has a different prefix, but nonetheless we find that efficiency is optimized when k-collisions are computed in batches of size $\alpha(t/k)$, where α is a constant of the same order of magnitude as 1, whose exact value depends on the cost of f, the value of k, and assumptions about memory costs.

We expect a batch of $\alpha(t/k)$ k-collisions to contain approximately $\beta(t/k)$ k-collisions with different prefixes, where β is given by the differential equation $\frac{d\beta}{d\alpha} = (1 - \beta)^k$ and the initial condition $\beta = 0$ when $\alpha = 0$. Once this batch of k-collisions is computed, the search for k-collisions continues recursively with t reduced by a factor of $1 - \beta$.

Optimal values of α and β depend upon whether the complexity of batched collision search is dominated by queries to f or memory access while sorting the list of distinguished points. The number of queries required is proportional to $\alpha^{1/k}$, while the size of the list of distinguished points is proportional to the square of the number of queries, i.e., proportional to $\alpha^{2/k}$. If we assume, according to a 2-dimensional memory model, that the cost of sorting the list scales with the

3/2 power of the list size, then rather than scaling as $\alpha^{1/k}$, the cost of computing a batch of k collisions will scale like $\alpha^{3/k}$.

For $k = 4$ the values of α and β that minimize the cost per k-collision are $\alpha = 3.27$; $\beta = 0.548$ ignoring memory costs and $\alpha = 0.185$; $\beta = 0.137$ assuming costs are dominated by square root memory access costs while sorting the list of distinguished points. Interestingly, the situation relevant to analyzing our attack in a 2-dimensional memory model will turn out to be intermediate between these two cases for reasons we will discuss shortly, so we will use $\alpha = 1$; $\beta = 0.37$. For $k = 3$ the cost of sorting is dominated by the cost of queries for all values of t that are of interest to us, so whether memory is included or not, the optimal values for α and β are $\alpha = 1.89$ $\beta = 0.543$.

We will now go on to give a concrete estimate of the cost of batched 4-collision search for $t > 2^{27}$ assuming the cost to access a bit of memory in a memory of size M is equivalent to $2^{-5} \cdot \sqrt{M}$ bit operations, and the cost of the SHA-256 compression function is equivalent to 2^{18} bit operations.

First we analyze the cost of computing f: Since the function f must retrieve a chaining value corresponding to one of t target prefixes, as well as the address string, computing f will require looking up approximately 2^9 bits in a memory of size $2^9 t$. (We will assume this memory is shared among many threads so as not to inflate the size of the memory in which the distinguished points are stored.) The cost of this memory access is equivalent to $2^{8.5} t^{1/2}$ bit operations, and this is the dominant cost of f for $t > 2^{27}$, even if computing f requires computing a hash chain of length $w - 1 = 15$

The number of queries required by the first batch is $q = 2^{192}(4! \alpha t/4)^{1/4}$, and since the cost of a query is $O(t^{1/2})$, the cost of a batch is $O(t^{3/4})$, which means each subsequent batch is cheaper than the previous batch by a factor of $(1 - \beta)^{3/4}$. If we use the summation for a geometric series to estimate the total cost of computing all batches required to find the full set of $t/4$ 4-collisions, we find that the total cost of queries to f is $\frac{1}{1-(1-\beta)^{3/4}} \cdot \alpha^{1/4} t^{3/4} \cdot 2^{200.8}$.

Now we consider the cost of sorting the list of distinguished points. In order for p to be at least comparable to the number of 2-collisions existing in q queries, we need $p = \frac{q^2}{2 \cdot 2^{256}}$. The cost of sorting distinguished points associated with the first batch is then given by $2^{-5}(2^9 p)^{3/2}$, which is $O(t^{3/4})$. We can therefore use the same rule as before to sum the costs of all the batches. The resulting cost is $\frac{1}{1-(1-\beta)^{3/4}} \cdot \alpha^{3/4} t^{3/4} \cdot 2^{200.9}$.

Summing these costs with $\alpha = 1$ ($\beta = 0.37$) gives a total cost of approximately $2^{203.7} t^{3/4}$ bit operations, or the equivalent of approximately

$$\text{MemoryCost}(k = 4, t > 2^{27}) \approx 2^{185.7} t^{3/4} \tag{1}$$

SHA-256 compression function calls.

If we instead ignore memory costs, then the cost of batched 4-collision search is dominated by approximately $2^{195.5} t^{1/4}$ queries to f. The computational cost of the queries will either be 1 SHA-256 compression function computation (if we can freely choose 256 input bits without needing to know a preimage) or 16 compression functions (if we need to construct a hash chain of length $w-1 = 15$).

We can do similar calculations for $k = 3$. In both the free memory cost model and the square-root memory cost model, the cost is dominated by approximately $2^{173.4} t^{1/3}$ queries to f. In the free memory cost model, the cost of each query is the equivalent of either 1 or 16 compression functions (similar to the 4-collision case). In the square root memory cost model, the total cost of all the queries is the equivalent of $2^{162.8} \cdot t^{5/6}$ compression function computations.

6 Conclusions

In this paper, we have shown how to extend Antonov's attack on the PQ-DM-SPR property in SPHINCS$^+$ into a full signature forgery attack, allowing an attacker to forge signatures on arbitrary messages. This attack requires access to a large number of legitimate signatures formed by the key, and an enormous computation which, while practically infeasible, is substantially below the claimed security strength for the category five parameter sets of SPHINCS$^+$.

We do not believe this attack calls the general soundness of the SPHINCS$^+$ design into question. Combined with the earlier observations on the PQC forum regarding weaknesses in category five security in the message hashing [19], it seems clear that both their attack and ours are made possible by the SPHINCS$^+$ designers' attempt to use a 256-bit Merkle-Damgård hash like SHA-256 to generically get 256 bits of security.[9]

Very recently in [7], Hülsing has described a set of tweaks to SPHINCS$^+$ to address a number of observations and proposed attacks, including Antonov's and ours. The relevant tweak for our attack is to the T_ℓ tweakable hash function–for category three or five security, the function now uses SHA-512 instead of SHA-256. This change means that building the diamond structure and finding the linking message (see Sect. 3) for the hash function requires at least 2^{256} hash function computations, effectively blocking both Antonov's attack and our own.

Our work leaves many questions open. Among them:

1. Are there still places within SPHINCS$^+$ in which the internal properties of SHA-256 can be used to carry out some attack with less than 2^{256} work, despite the tweak? SHA-256 is still used in the definition of F and PRF, even for category five security.
2. Can these or similar techniques be used to attack the category three (192 bit classical security) parameters?
3. Is there a technique to construct inputs to the hash which can be shown to prevent all such attacks, despite using SHA-256 to achieve 256-bit security? This would allow the use of the slightly more efficient SHA-256 instead of SHA-512 for category three or five security.

---

[9] Modeling a Merkle-Damgård hash function as a random oracle can easily give misleading results for more than $2^{n/2}$ queries. Indeed, even modeling the *compression function* as a random oracle may not work, since the SHA-256 compression function is constructed from a large block cipher in Davies-Meyer mode. Note that this means that fixed points for the hash function are easy to find, as exploited in [6,12].

References

1. Antonov, S.: Round 3 official comment: SPHINCS+ (2022). https://groups.google.com/a/list.nist.gov/g/pqc-forum/c/FVItvyRea28/m/mGaRi5iZBwAJ
2. Aumasson, J.P., et al.: SPHINCS$^+$ – submission to the NIST post-quantum project, v. 3 (2020)
3. Banegas, G., Bernstein, D.J.: Low-communication parallel quantum multi-target preimage search. In: Adams, C., Camenisch, J. (eds.) SAC 2017. LNCS, vol. 10719, pp. 325–335. Springer, Cham (2018). https://doi.org/10.1007/978-3-319-72565-9_16
4. Bernstein, D.J., et al.: NTRU Prime: round 3. Submission to the NIST's Post-Quantum Cryptography Standardization Process (2020)
5. Bernstein, D.J., Hülsing, A., Kölbl, S., Niederhagen, R., Rijneveld, J., Schwabe, P.: The SPHINCS$^+$ signature framework. In: Proceedings of the 2019 ACM SIGSAC Conference on Computer and Communications Security, CCS 2019, pp. 2129–2146. Association for Computing Machinery, New York (2019). https://doi.org/10.1145/3319535.3363229
6. Dean, R.D.: Formal aspects of mobile code security. Ph.D. thesis, Princeton University, USA (1999)
7. Hülsing, A.: Round 3 official comment: SPHINCS+ (2022). https://groups.google.com/a/list.nist.gov/g/pqc-forum/c/Ca4zQeyObOY
8. Hülsing, A.: W-OTS+ – shorter signatures for hash-based signature schemes. In: Youssef, A., Nitaj, A., Hassanien, A.E. (eds.) AFRICACRYPT 2013. LNCS, vol. 7918, pp. 173–188. Springer, Heidelberg (2013). https://doi.org/10.1007/978-3-642-38553-7_10
9. Joux, A.: Multicollisions in iterated hash functions. Application to cascaded constructions. In: Franklin, M. (ed.) CRYPTO 2004. LNCS, vol. 3152, pp. 306–316. Springer, Heidelberg (2004). https://doi.org/10.1007/978-3-540-28628-8_19
10. Joux, A., Lucks, S.: Improved generic algorithms for 3-collisions. In: Matsui, M. (ed.) ASIACRYPT 2009. LNCS, vol. 5912, pp. 347–363. Springer, Heidelberg (2009). https://doi.org/10.1007/978-3-642-10366-7_21
11. Kelsey, J., Kohno, T.: Herding hash functions and the Nostradamus attack. In: Vaudenay, S. (ed.) EUROCRYPT 2006. LNCS, vol. 4004, pp. 183–200. Springer, Heidelberg (2006). https://doi.org/10.1007/11761679_12
12. Kelsey, J., Schneier, B.: Second preimages on n-bit hash functions for much less than 2^n work. In: Cramer, R. (ed.) EUROCRYPT 2005. LNCS, vol. 3494, pp. 474–490. Springer, Heidelberg (2005). https://doi.org/10.1007/11426639_28
13. Lamport, L.: Constructing digital signatures from a one way function. Technical report, SRI, October 1979. https://www.microsoft.com/en-us/research/uploads/prod/2016/12/Constructing-Digital-Signatures-from-a-One-Way-Function.pdf
14. Merkle, R.C.: A certified digital signature. In: Brassard, G. (ed.) CRYPTO 1989. LNCS, vol. 435, pp. 218–238. Springer, New York (1990). https://doi.org/10.1007/0-387-34805-0_21
15. Merkle, R.C.: Secrecy, authentication, and public key systems. Ph.D. thesis, Stanford University (1979)
16. National Institute of Standards and Technology: NIST post-quantum cryptography standardization (2016). https://csrc.nist.gov/projects/post-quantum-cryptography/post-quantum-cryptography-standardization

17. National Institute of Standards and Technology: Submission requirements and evaluation criteria for the post-quantum cryptography standardization process (2016). https://csrc.nist.gov/CSRC/media/Projects/Post-Quantum-Cryptography/documents/call-for-proposals-final-dec-2016.pdf
18. van Oorschot, P.C., Wiener, M.J.: Parallel collision search with application to hash functions and discrete logarithms. In: Proceedings of the 2nd ACM Conference on Computer and Communications Security, CCS 1994, pp. 210–218. Association for Computing Machinery, New York (1994). https://doi.org/10.1145/191177.191231
19. Stern, M.: Re: diversity of signature schemes (2021). https://groups.google.com/a/list.nist.gov/g/pqc-forum/c/2LEoSpskELs/m/LkUdQ5mKAwAJ

Author Index

Printed in the United States
by Baker & Taylor Publisher Services